THE LETTERS OF JOHN COLLIER

1731-1746

THE LETTERS OF JOHN COLLIER OF HASTINGS

1731-1746

EDITED BY

RICHARD SAVILLE

SUSSEX RECORD SOCIETY
VOLUME 96

Issued to members of the Society for the years 2013 and 2014

Published 2016 by
Sussex Record Society
Barbican House,
High Street,
Lewes,
East Sussex, BN7 1YE.

ISBN 978 0 85445 078 7

Printed by Hobbs the Printers Ltd., Totton, Hampshire.

VOLUMES ISSUED BY THE SUSSEX RECORD SOCIETY

Vol. 1 *Marriage Licences at Lewes, 1586-1642*
Vol. 2 *Sussex Fines, 1190-1248*
Vol. 3 *Post Mortem Inquisitions, 1558-1583*
Vol. 4 *Ecclesiastical Returns for East Sussex, 1603; Sussex Poll Book, 1705; Sussex MSS in the Harleian MSS; Bishop Praty's Register, 1438-1445.*
Vol. 5 *West Sussex Protestation Returns, 1641-1642*
Vol. 6 *Marriage Licences at Lewes, 1670-1732*
Vol. 7 *Sussex Fines, 1249-1307*
Vol. 8 *Bishop Rede's Register, 1397-1415* (Pt. 1)
Vol. 9 *Marriage Licences at Chichester 1575-1730*
Vol. 10 *Subsidy Rolls, 1296, 1327 and 1332*
Vol. 11 *Bishop Rede's Register, 1397-1415* (Pt. 2)
Vol. 12 *Marriage Licences at Chichester* (peculiars), 1579-1730
Vol. 13 *Cuckfield Parish Register, 1598-1699*
Vol. 14 *Post Mortem Inquisitions, 1485-1649*
Vol. 15 *Bolney Parish Register, 1541-1812*
Vol. 16 *Star Chamber Proceedings, 1500-1558*
Vol. 17 *Ardingly Parish Register, 1558-1812*
* Vol. 18 *Angmering Parish Register, 1562-1687*
Vol. 19 *Sussex Manors and Advowsons, etc., 1509-1833*, A-L
Vol. 20 *Sussex Manors and Advowsons, etc., 1509-1833*, M-Z
Vol. 21 *Horsham Parish Register, 1541-1635*
Vol. 22 *Cowfold Parish Register, 1558-1812*
Vol. 23 *Sussex Fines, 1308-1509*
Vol. 24 *East Grinstead Parish Register, 1558-1661*
Vol. 25 *Marriage Licences at Lewes, 1771-1837*, A-L
Vol. 26 *Marriage Licences at Lewes, 1772-1837*, M-Z
Vol. 27 *Preston Manor Court Rolls, 1562-1702*
Vol. 28 *Sussex Apprentices and Masters, 1710-1752*
Vol. 29 *Abstracts of Documents relating to the Dobell family*, 16th-18th cents.
Vol. 30 *Glynde Parish Register, 1558-1812*
Vol. 31 *Custumals of the Sussex Manors of the Bishop of Chichester, c.1256-1374*
Vol. 32 *Sussex Marriage Licences at Chichester, 1731-1774*
Vol. 33 *Sussex Inquisitions (from Bodleian Library), 1541-1616*
Vol. 34 *The Book of John Rowe, Steward to Lord Bergavenny, 1622*
Vol. 35 *Marriage Licences at Chichester, 1775-1800*, with Index 1731-1800
Vol. 36 *Sussex Chantry Records, 1535-1652*
Vol. 37 *Hastings Rape Records, 1387-1474*
Vol. 38 *Chartulary of Lewes Priory* (Pt. I), 11th-l4th cents.
* Vol. 39 *The Buckhurst Terrier, 1597-1598*
Vol. 40 *Chartulary of Lewes Priory* (Pt. II), l2th-l4th cents.
Vol. 41 *Transcripts of Sussex Wills up to 1560* Vol.1 Albourne - Chichester
Vol. 42 *Transcripts of Sussex Wills up to 1560* Vol.2 Chiddingly - Horsham
Vol. 43 *Transcripts of Sussex Wills up to 1560* Vol.3 Horsted Keynes - Pyecombe
Vol. 44 *Records of the Barony and Honour of the Rape of Lewes, 1265-1466*
Vol. 45 *Transcripts of Sussex Wills up to 1560* Vol.4 Racton - Yapton
Vol. 46 *Chichester Cathedral Chartulary*, l3th-l6th cents.
Vol. 47 *Survey of Robertsbridge Manor, 1567-1570*
* Vol. 48 *The Town Book of Lewes, 1542-1701*

Vol. 49 *Churchwardens' Presentments*, (Pt. I), *Archdeaconry of Chichester, 1621-28, 1664-70*
Vol. 50 *Churchwardens' Presentments*, (Pt. II), *Archdeaconry of Lewes, 1674-1677*
Vol. 51 *Record of Deputations of Gamekeepers, 1781-1928*
Jubilee Volume *Sussex Views from the Burrell Collection*
Vol. 52 *Chapter Acts, Chichester, 1472-1544* (The White Act Book)
Vol. 53 *The Manor of Etchingham cum Salehurst, 1597-1865*
Vol. 54 *Quarter Sessions Order Book, 1642-1649*
Vol. 55 *Ministers' Accounts of the Manor of Petworth, 1347-1353*
Vol. 56 *Lay Subsidy Rolls, 1524-1525*
Vol. 57 *Custumals of Sussex Manors of the Archbishop of Canterbury, 1285-1330*
Vol. 58 *Chapter Acts, Chichester, 1545-1642*
Vol. 59 *Chartulary of Boxgrove Priory*, 12th-14th cents.
Vol. 60 *Custumals of the Manors of Laughton, Willingdon and Goring, 1292-1338*
* Vol. 61 *A Catalogue of Sussex Estate and Tithe Award Maps* (Pt. I), 1606-1884
Vol. 62 *Minutes of the Common Council of the City of Chichester, 1783-1826*
Vol. 63 *The Book of Bartholomew Bolney*, 15th cent.
Vol. 64 *Rye Shipping Records, 1566-1590*
Vol. 65 *Cellarers' Rolls of Battle Abbey, 1275-1513*
Vol. 66 *A Catalogue of Sussex Maps*, (Pt. II) 1597-1958
Vol. 67 *Estate Surveys of the Fitzalan Earls of Arundel*, 14th cent.
Vol. 68 *The Journal of Giles Moore of Horsted Keynes, 1655-1679*
Vol. 69 *The Town Book of Lewes, 1702-1837*
Vol. 70 *The Town Book of Lewes, 1837-1901*
* Vol. 71 *Accounts of the Roberts Family of Boarzell, 1568-1582*
Vol. 72 *Printed Maps of Sussex, 1575-1900*
* Vol. 73 *Correspondence of the Dukes of Richmond and Newcastle, 1724-1750*
Vol. 74 *Sussex Coroners' Inquests, 1485-1558*
* Vol. 75 *The Religious Census of Sussex, 1851*
Vol. 76 *The Fuller Letters, 1728-1755*
Vol. 77 *East Sussex Land Tax, 1785*
* Vol. 78 *Chichester Diocesan Surveys, 1686 and 1724*
* Vol. 79 *Saint Richard of Chichester*
Vol. 80 *The Ashdown Forest Dispute, 1876-1882*
* Vol. 81 *Sussex Schools in the 18th century*
* Vol. 82 *West Sussex Land Tax, 1785*
Vol. 83 *Mid Sussex Poor Law Records, 1601-1835*
* Vol. 84 *Sussex in the First World War*
Vol. 85 *Sussex Depicted: Views and Descriptions 1600-1800*
* Vol. 86 *Sussex Shore to Flanders Fields: E. Heron–Allen's Journal of the Great War*
* Vol. 87 *East Sussex Parliamentary Deposited Plans, 1799-1970*
Vol. 88 *Sussex Cricket in the 18th century*
* Vol. 89 *East Sussex Coroners' Records, 1688-1838*
* Vol. 90 *The Durford Cartulary*
* Vol. 91 *Sussex Clergy Inventories, 1600-1750*
* Vol. 92 *Accounts and Records of the Manor of Mote in Iden, 1461-1551, 1673*
* Vol. 93 *East Sussex Church Monuments, 1530-1830*
* Vol. 94 *Winchelsea Poor Law Records, 1790-1841*
* Vol. 95 *Littlehampton School Logbook, 1871-1911*
* Vol. 96 *Letters of John Collier of Hastings, 1731-1746*

In print volumes marked with an asterisk can be obtained from the Sussex Record Society, Barbican House, Lewes, East Sussex, BN7 1YE or through the Society's website: www.sussexrecordsociety.org

CONTENTS

ILLUSTRATIONS

ACKNOWLEDGEMENTS

The Sussex Record Society and the editor of this volume are deeply grateful to Mrs J. Sayer, Patrick Sayer, and the Sayer family more widely for permission to transcribe and publish the letters and papers which follow, and for access to the Sayer family bible and other materials in their keeping. The survival of the Sayer collection is an extraordinary example of preservation of our history, and we owe our sincere thanks to many generations of the family for the time and effort they have undertaken to maintain the collection.

Numerous librarians and archivists have assisted in the finding of manuscripts and offering guidance on related materials. As the work for this volume has spanned over a decade it is noteworthy to record how valuable has been the association with professionals who care for our national heritage and whose knowledge is a support for the work of historians and genealogists.

I wish to thank the staffs of the National Archives at Kew, London; the British Library for finding a variety of sources, and their Department of Western Manuscripts for access to the Newcastle papers; the librarians of the London Library whose collections provided detailed support for many of the entry notes below; the librarian of the Sussex Archaeological Society, Lewes for her assistance with the Society's collections; the archivists of the Royal Society for access to the Hooker Mss on Wealden weather; the librarians at the Hastings Public Library who found all sorts of materials on the Collier and Milward family and on Hastings, and who arranged for access to the Manwaring Baines manuscripts in their care which form the kernel of the Appendix 9 below. I also wish to acknowledge the contribution made by the following libraries and archive collections: the London Metropolitan archives for insurance records, the London Guildhall library for Parliamentary papers, the Kent History Centre, the West Sussex Record Office, the Institute of Historical Research, the Institute of Advanced Legal Studies, the library of Senate House, the Hastings Museum, Hastings Fishermen's Museum, Rye Castle Museum, the Welcome Library, the Friends Meeting house library, the National Maritime Museum, Royal Bedlam Hospital archives, the Librarian of the Institute of Education library, London, the National Gallery and the National Portrait Gallery; the facilities of several of the public libraries have been consulted and I am grateful to the librarians concerned for their efforts in finding materials: Westminster library; Croydon public library; Edinburgh public library; the Hampstead library; the National Library, Edinburgh; Lewes public library; Eastbourne library; Tonbridge library; Tunbridge Wells library; Dover library.

As custodian of the Collier Letters the County Archivist of East Sussex has permitted and encouraged publication; and my greatest debt goes to the archivists and former archivists of the East Sussex Record Office. The Sayer collection was first calendared by Heather M. Warne (nee Mathews) in her 'The Papers of John Collier of Hastings: a catalogue', (Diploma on Archive Administration, University of London 1966) and all users are indebted to her organisation of this vast archive. Her restoration of the papers to the original divisions in the order laid out by John Collier was a considerable aid to transcription; for advice on these divisions readers are directed to Heather's dissertation and the East Sussex Record Office on-line catalogue. Heather shows huge insight into the thinking of John Collier and William Cranston, and her careful reading of the transcriptions here and advice on the entry notes over several years was most welcome. Elizabeth Hughes the county archivist displayed both patience and understanding about the project for which I am most appreciative. Christopher Whittick and Anna Manthorpe undertook comprehensive checking of the transcription against the originals. In addition, they provided helpful guidance on the variations and idiosyncrasies of the correspondents writing and have provided valuable emendations and corrections throughout. I also received advice on many documents from Jennifer Nash, Andrew Lusted, Philip Bye, Andrew Bennett, and Melissa Williams. Given the scale of the enterprise and the need for repeated access to letters I was grateful for the facilities provided by the search room staff including Isabella Bicsak-Snitter, Drew Boulton and Jennifer Nash.

Others who have provided information used here included: Robin Pearson on finance and insurance; David Padgham of the Hastings Area Archaeological Research Group; Janet Pennington for her work on the Lamb Inn, Eastbourne; Gill Adamson, Gareth Bendon and Maria Woolf of Old Hastings House for advice on John Collier's house; Richard Manwaring Baines for information about his father; David Crossley and Jeremy Hodgkinson for details on the Wealden iron trade; Esme Evans the librarian of the Sussex Archaeological Society; Steve Peak on Hastings fishermen and smugglers; Kent Barker for advice on smuggling and local traders; Jeremy Smith for help with the London illustration. I found discussions about Sussex very helpful over the years with Fiona Marsden, John Farrant, John Bleach, Elizabeth Doff and Pat Combes, and Sue and Pat Berry; Judith and Colin Brent provided assistance on a number of letters. Parts of the background to the volume have been aired before the Sussex Record Society, the Battle and District Historical Society, and the conference on Sussex organised by Sue Berry in 2014. I am grateful for comments from members of the audience.

For kind permission to reproduce the illustrations I gratefully acknowledge the Sayer family, the trustees of Old Hastings House, the Hastings Museum and Art Gallery, Sussex Archaeological Society, the Corporation of London, and the County Archivist of East Sussex. Claire Snoad of the West Sussex Record Office and Mandie Merlin provided generous expertise in the preparation of the images for printing.

When this volume was started Roy Hunnisett was the literary editor of the Society dealing with the work and was unstinting in his advice and assistance on the transcription and the form the words of the documents should take. Janet Stevenson also provided advice on various issues including the use of the computers. Roy sadly died in 2010 and I hope this volume is worthy of his memory. Andrew Foster as literary editor took over Roy's role and has offered considerable assistance across the board in coaxing the volume to completion.

The production process for Society volumes is arduous and time consuming, and it is with respect that I thank Peter Wilkinson, past deputy county archivist for West Sussex, who has undertaken the supervision of the volume. I am grateful also to Wendy Walker, County Archivist of West Sussex for providing facilities at the West Sussex Record Office - and of course for her support as Chairman of the Society, together with her predecessor Roger Davey. David Wise drew up the three indexes of Place, Names and Subject and we are grateful for the work he also carried out on putting the entry notes into a standard form. John Barnes created the dustjacket; and Jack Burton, Marion Woolgar,

Jessica Stoll and Hugh Wilkinson all gave valuable help in the formatting of the pedigrees. Finally, but not least, I wish to thank my wife, Gillian Smith, whose organizational skills and expertise in the drafting of documents proved invaluable throughout.

Richard Saville

February 2016

ABBREVIATIONS

adc	aide-de-camp.
afd	aforesaid.
Bethlem	Bethlem Hospital .
BL	British Library.
Cedb	Clergy of the Church of England database.
CJ	*Journals of the House of Commons 1547-1790* (1803-1813).
CUST	Customs and Excise records, National Archives.
DofN	Duke of Newcastle.
EB 1771	*Encyclopaedia Britannica or a Dictionary of Arts and Sciences, compiled upon a new plan* 1st edn (1771).
EcHR	*Economic History Review.*
EHR	*English Historical Review.*
ER	Renton, A W (ed.) The *English Reports* [legal cases 1220-1866] (1900-1932*)*.
ESRO	East Sussex Record Office.
GM	*Gentleman's Magazine* (1731-1746).
GSJ	*Grub Street Journal* (1730-1737).
HBC	Fryde, E B & Powicke, F M *Handbook of British Chronology* (1986).
HofP	Sedgwick, R (ed.) *History of Parliament, The House of Commons 1715-1754* (1970).
HPL	Hastings Public Library.
HMus	Hastings Museum .
LG	*London Gazette* (1665-).
LMA	London Metropolitan Archives.
LJ	*Journal of the House of Lords* (1485-).
Mortality	*Collection of the weekly bills of Mortality within the London district 1664-1773.*
MIL	Milward archives, East Sussex Record Office.
NRS	Navy Records Society.
ODNB	*Oxford Dictionary of National Biography.*
OED	*Oxford English Dictionary.*
PC	Privy Council.
PGA	*Public General Acts.*
PofW	Prince of Wales.
PS	*The Political State of Great Britain,* ed. Abel Boyer (1711-1740).
SAC	*Sussex Archaeological Collections.*
SAY	Sayer archives, East Sussex Record Office.
SL	*The Statutes at Large* by command of George III (1768-1802).
SNQ	*Sussex Notes and Queries.*
SR	*Statutes of the Realm* Great Britain Record Commission, (1810-1828).
SRS	Sussex Record Society.
TNA	National Archives, formerly Public Record Office.
VCH	*Victoria County History.*
Wel	Welcome Library Archives.
WSRO	West Sussex Record Office.

Portrait of John Collier by Arthur Devis, reproduced by permission of the Sayer family.

INTRODUCTION

Background: The correspondence and papers published in this volume cover the years 1731 to 1746 and offer a fascinating insight into the success of John Collier of Hastings (1685-1760) whose lengthy legal and political career enabled his family to enjoy a rising social standing in the Sussex of George I and II. Collier's business life ranged widely, and the volume here covers his work as an attorney in London and Hastings, his extensive political connections with the Whigs, his involvement with the Customs and connections with smugglers, and the workings of the Hastings Corporation in which he became the dominant figure. Also covered in detail in these letters is the everyday life of his family, many written to and from Mary, his wife, concerning the needs of their children. Numerous letters came from Mary's brother William Cranston, also an attorney, who from 1726 was a partner with John Collier in London.

John Collier's precocious nature was noticed early. In 1706, aged only 20, Hastings Corporation appointed him as town clerk, leading to a succession of posts as diverse as clerk of the militia, joint solicitor for the Cinque Ports, Commissioner for the East Sussex land tax, clerk to the commissions for local sewers, as well as allowing Collier to develop his legal practice based in Hastings and near the law courts in London.

From the years of his first marriage, to Elizabeth Elphick, 1706-14, few papers have survived. However, after her death Collier married Mary Cranston, and they kept in touch whilst he was away with a wide-ranging and regular correspondence. These letters, transcribed in full, include extensive information on family life, and show the love and devotion of the parents through the sometimes precarious years which followed. Reflections on the children's illnesses, with graphic descriptions of their suffering, and the damaging effects of chronic sickness in adulthood are well documented here. The education of both boys and girls is described, especially carefully in the case of the girls who attended Elizabeth Russell's Hampstead girls' school. Letters cover living conditions in London and Hastings, and numerous social matters, for instance the health of the royal family, Sunday sermons and social visiting, and a seemingly endless round buying textiles, clothes and jewellery for dispatch home. Beyond school there are lively descriptions of the periodic residence by the girls in East Sussex country houses, providing an important part of learning the practical side of social life.

1731 marked a new direction in John Collier's life. Since 1706 his ability underpinned a growing influence over Hastings Corporation. This, plus the independent spirit Collier displayed at elections, caught the attention of the Duke of Newcastle and Henry Pelham, and they decided to utilise him for the Whig cause. Early in 1732 Newcastle procured his appointment as the Usher and Cryer of the King's Bench [**15**]. That summer Collier despatched sons John and Jacky to Westminster school, a signal of his rising social position. The excise crisis of 1733 saw Newcastle persuade Sir Robert Walpole that "if he has a mind to have two Whigs chosen att Hasting he must provide handsomely for Collyer" which meant appointment as the Surveyor of the Riding Officers of the Customs in Kent, which produced near £400 a year income and enabled Collier to expand his estate, providing a sound pension and security for their children.

The Collier papers add much to our understanding of how such families lived in the Georgian era. The introduction here raises numerous facets about the lives of the Collier and Cranston families, and is supplemented by additional footnotes for many of the letters.

Early life of John Collier (1685-1760) town clerk and five times Mayor of Hastings. John Collier was born in Eastbourne on the 1 November 1685,[1] the second son of Peter Collier and Sarah, née Cheapman, owners of the Lamb Inn on the High Street.[2] Family papers record four of their children surviving to adulthood, the elder son Peter, and two girls, Mary and Sarah, as well as John.[3] (see Pedigree One) The nearest available parish school was in Eastbourne. Townsfolk nurtured this parish school in the seventeenth century, closely tied to the church vestry, the schoolhouse abutting the north side of the church, with a master required to teach Latin, formally confirmed in 1709, and paid for by the vestry.[4] Whilst a detailed record for John's education is unclear, such general church schooling in the later seventeenth century was usually completed between the ages of 12 and 14, with competence in reading Latin, clear handwriting, prose composition and grammar as essentials, providing a solid grounding for starting an apprenticeship which might lead to a professional or business career. For John Collier this meant a clerkship. His apprenticeship was over by 1706, aged 20, and in June of that year the Mayor and jurats of Hastings appointed Collier as town clerk, replacing Jonas Chambers: 'John Collier took the oath for executing the place accordingly, and also took the oaths of allegiance and supremacy to her Majesty and subscribed the declaration according to law'.[5] The oath of allegiance laid down in 1688/9 was a requirement for a town clerk, as also for all office holders, including the Mayor, jurats, freemen and schoolmasters down to quite minor officials.[6] Officials were also required to take the Test Act, 25 Car II c. 2, which included a need to provide proof of taking the sacraments of the Church of England, delivered in John Collier's case to the Corporation in September 1706.

Payment for the office of Hastings town clerk was under £10 a year for which Collier was to work on behalf of the Mayor and commonalty, acting as clerk to the four Hastings courts, the Quarter Sessions, the Court of Record, the Hundred court and the Assembly of freemen. Moreover, as town clerk he kept a record of appointments to Corporation offices, the granting of ale and corn licences, the administration of oaths, and searched the records of the Corporation when needed. Together with his duties as town clerk and jurat, Collier was a Justice of the Peace, occasional coroner, clerk of the Militia, and worked with the town Chamberlains over supervision of the local fairs and markets.[7] In his capacity of town clerk he was a Commissioner of the land tax for Sussex, appearing on the tax lists from 1707, as well as being joint Solicitor representing the Cinque Ports in outside affairs and clerk of the Hastings militia. Work required frequent travelling beyond the port, for which Collier kept horses suitable for the wetlands and the Weald, and attended the joint meetings of the Cinque Ports, and the Westminster courts as occasion required.[8] The position demanded efforts on behalf of the Corporation tackling legal matters before the Assize courts and infringements of the rights of Cinque Port freemen by citizens elsewhere [**507**]. His office thus dealt with innumerable local town matters requiring details from corporation officers, as well as questions involving towns in the vicinity, some covered by the small fees levied for such paperwork. On 23 October 1708 Collier signed the Hastings corporation records as a jurat for the decision that only two freemen might be created a year; whenever the annual election of town clerk is minuted, Collier is in evidence.

From the time of his appointment Collier gradually acquired agencies for several local estates which included work as a steward of manor courts as well as working for clients on business concerns. Indeed, as early as 1707, he registered as the attorney or solicitor at law employed by Edward Robinson of St Margaret's Westminster to collect rents in Pett, Guestling and Fairlight.[9] In Sussex, as elsewhere, former estuarine marshland had long been drained and turned into 'brookland' and rates raised to maintain the dykes and sluices. Local to Hastings were the Hooe, Barnhorne, Cowding and East levels, and in 1708 the Commissioners of Sewers chose Collier as clerk and collector of charges from landowners and tenants on these levels, paying £12 a year. This could be onerous work, especially when rains and the Channel flooded the levels.[10]

What learning would be expected of John Collier by the time he was town clerk? According to R. Campbell's *The London Tradesman* (1747), a young attorney would need to be well versed in court practices, adeptly handling distinctions between the numerous statutes and court decisions for any case, would require a formidable memory, 'the patience of Job', stamina for detours of cases through various courts, and the 'courage of Hercules'. All the legal advice in the eighteenth century points to subtlety in language as essential: English and Latin conveyed various meanings for similar words, and nuance was all in disputes over the essence of documents. Pleading meant tailoring arguments and illustrations for the judge, as not all would convince in all courts. Collier understood this for the legal cases before Customs and Excise and in the furious disputes over the appointment of freemen in Hastings **[72, 77, 86, 126, 128, 155, 162]**.

Once fully trained the new attorney should be sufficiently adaptable to fill a variety of public and trading posts, as for instance early undertaken by John Collier, and also the position of steward of a manor. This required manorial law, paleography and local custom as well as the ability to interpret and adjudicate on matters relating to land management and disputes over boundaries. Westminster and Assize court procedures required the attorney to comprehend the case, in writing, 'clearly and distinctly' and put forward writs in proper form, ensure that the opponent took notice of it, and follow the action to closure. Should the case go to the Westminster courts, a brief with supporting papers would be prepared for counsel. This does seem rather a lot of complicated legislation and legal practice to absorb for a young man. Indeed, the question has been posed that John Collier may have been acting together with another local attorney, or with several attorneys, sharing part of the late Jonas Chambers' caseload. In a world of disease and early death thoughts of succession were never far from the mind of the middling and upper ranks, and indeed John Collier himself made arrangements for succession long before his serious illness in the autumn of 1746.[11]

At some point in his early life John Collier realised that writing letters and papers and briefs was crucial to the lawyer's existence and as town clerk it was essential to keep a paper record, letters offering the main way to communicate with correspondents in other towns, often using local carriers and pedlars: the use of carriers and coastal shipping occurred virtually every law term [**4**, **29**, **30**, **34**, **56**, **62**, **89**]. When away on business the written word extended to cover family life, with detailed commentaries on the illnesses, the education and the social life of his children, relatives and friends, and on Hastings more widely. Thousands of the Collier family letters and papers, and numerous private account books, together with papers left by the Sayer and Milward families, enable us to explore the workings of this family and Collier's legal business and to see how John Collier raised his income to become the wealthiest person in the town by the time he died in 1760. Samuel Cant, master of Hastings grammar school, 1738-59, and surveyor, drew maps of the town and that of 1750, dedicated to John Collier, shows each field in Collier's Hastings estate which by then covered parts of the East and West hills, stretching to 205 acres.[12] In addition Collier owned farm land in Bexhill, marsh lands at Pevensey and even a farm on the Isle of Oxney, although little on Hastings High Street, and nothing abutting the beach, known as the Stade, where the fishing boats were laid up. The rentals for these and other Collier property and land are listed in financial records which have survived from the later 1720s.[13] Taking a wider view than Collier's family, and using the Sayer papers and the Hastings town archives, we can piece together the workings of the Corporation and look into key issues which moulded the lives of the townsfolk.

In the summer of 1706 John Collier married Elizabeth Elphick, daughter of Edmund Elphick of Willingdon, and, a few months on, in November, Collier purchased the Mansion House for £300 which still stands at the top of the High Street, later renamed Old Hastings House, adding outbuildings and stables, as well as local fields and town properties over the years. The house gave him a residence suitable to his station, with panoramic views of the port from the top of the High Street, with All Saints church and the Old Rectory in view across the road.[14] His sister Sarah later moved into a cottage in the grounds with her husband Samuel Cruttenden. Sadly, Elizabeth died in 1714. Of their eight children only Sarah and Elizabeth are mentioned in subsequent correspondence, Elizabeth most frequently, in part through her marriage in 1727 to George Worge, attorney of Battle, one of the attorneys in the vicinity of Hastings with whom John Collier kept in regular contact. Sarah married Roger Mortimer of Eastbourne.[15] In August 1717 John Collier married Mary Cranston, daughter of Cordelia Delves and the Revd James Cranston the elder, rector of Hastings All Saints parish and Hastings St Clements parish, who owned property including a farm in Bexhill parish. Mary grew up in the Old Rectory next to All Saints church, and she bore eighteen children, of whom only six survived to adulthood: James, the second son, and Cordelia (Dely), Mary, Sarah, Jane (Jenny) and Henrietta (Harriet, Harriot) are referred to extensively in this volume (see Pedigree Two). The eldest son, named after his father, died of smallpox after a term at Westminster School and the harrowing accounts of his last days are included here **[40-45]**.

Marriage provided assistance with his legal work as Mary, who grew up in Hastings, was able to supply all sorts of town information whilst her husband was away. John Collier's legal work took him to London for most law terms and this brought him to the attention of a wide group of Sussex landowners and government officials. For the years 1731 to 1746 we possess a record of these quarterly journeys to and from Hastings. Also, from 1732 to 1742, papers exist in the National Archives covering Collier's annual visitation to the Kent ports on behalf of the Customs for his post as Surveyor of the riding officers of Kent, a survey which took up four to five weeks, and his journeys for both are listed below (see London law terms & Customs journeys). This work was carried on simultaneously with business in Hastings, in the Kent ports and London, part of which involved additional travel in Sussex and Kent. Thus for most of his married life, and all the time covered by the letters here, John Collier was away from home for around five months a year and sometimes longer. This would put a strain on most marriages.

John and Mary Collier addressed this problem through extensive letter writing, which remained their main means of keeping in touch. Sometimes the correspondence dwells on

Old Hastings House, home of John Collier,
reproduced from *Sussex Archaeological Collections* vol. 45 p. 64,
by permission of Sussex Archaeological Society.

local affairs, with John Collier asking Mary to sort out issues in the town: she was eminently suited for such a role having been brought up among the well off in Hastings, and taking an active part in church life. But they also used letters to help to bear the tragedy in their lives, notably, but not only over the deaths of eleven of their children in infancy or when toddlers. We can see the suffering that these deaths caused. In particular, the letters have survived covering the time when John junior died of smallpox in London aged 13, just after the birth of another child in Hastings. Distraction and misery sums up his father's feelings which faded only a little over time. This was the future from whom so much was hoped for: 'I have so many occurrences that revive my losse and bring to my remembrance the dear child, that I can hardly bear it, his name is engraven on my heart in letters of blood, never to be effaced, and really sometimes I can muse upon it. And think I can and ought to bear it with a becomeing resignation, and sometimes it goes through my soul worse than daggers'. [**60**]. Letter writing for the Colliers was not just matter of fact, an indispensable aid to business and politics, this was a way of grappling with the melancholy which beset their lives. Along with his happy marriages and the love for and involvement with his children, this passion for writing was the springboard for the wealth of correspondence that has survived as their legacy and offers us a rare enough vision into the personal world of this Georgian family.

For several years now a new transcription of the Collier correspondence has been favoured, both for the advancement of scholarship on eighteenth century Hastings, and to bring to a modern audience the roles of John Collier, William Cranston and members of their circle in respect of their numerous business, political and social affairs. In the preface to the 1907 edition of the letters Charles Lane Sayer wrote that the extracts then made from the correspondence did not comprise one half of the matter contained in the original letters, and possibly his readers might think 'I have omitted much that was worthy of transcription'. In fact, Sayer's edition proved most helpful both for this transcription and also for his notes, in which Sayer passed on aspects of the oral memory and traditions of the family. As Sayer realised it is more than worthwhile to show how the Collier family, the people they mixed with, and the politics dealt with, connected and interweaved with the important issues of the day, and the problems raised for contemporaries by the conditions of the time. The Georgian age witnessed an enlargement of what political and business life involved, and the letters here also confirm a broadening of social life noticed for this era in the historical literature, in the kinds of conversation which might be undertaken, in addressing the personal issues involved in re-thinking how to cope with illness and bereavement, and for instance, more optimism among those looking at the education of girls from well-off families and their lives in London and Sussex.

Who wrote the letters published here? As implied from the above, John Collier's second wife, Mary, was literate and well-educated in her upbringing. She corresponded widely, taught her children how to compose a letter, and insisted that they wrote regularly and dutifully to their father and others in their circle. Their correspondence underlines the view that the children apply seriously to their studies whilst at school and at University, Latin being encouraged for the boys **[39, 89, 145, 184, 185]**. This was an age which took good handwriting and grammar as necessary accomplishments and both parents expected the children to master a good style and clear handwriting as everyday activities **[12, 26, 37, 140, 141]**.[16] As luck would have it her younger brother, William Cranston, was apprenticed as an attorney, and after finishing his training in 1726 lodged in Johnson's Court, Fleet Street,

Aerial view of All Saints Church and churchyard, the High Street leading to the harbour, All Saints rectory to the immediate left of All Saints church, stables and Sarah and Samuel Cruttenden's cottage to the left of the rectory, Old Hastings House, lower left corner.
Reproduced by permission of Hastings Museum and Art Gallery

thereafter acting as *de facto* partner to John Collier, a position maintained for the rest of Collier's life (see Pedigree Three). As the correspondence and account books attest, this connection was a huge boon for both. Henry Pelham, a key figure in the Whig government from the time of the South Sea bubble who employed Collier as steward for his East Sussex lands, is mentioned frequently in these letters and a few of his own letters and papers have survived [**71, 72, 153, 158**], as have letters from other political and business connections, including Pelham's brother the Duke of Newcastle, other Pelham relatives including Colonel James Pelham and Thomas Pelham (MP Hastings 1728-41) [**77, 123**], from Andrew Stone, Newcastle's secretary and from 1742 MP for Hastings, and the Ashburnham family.

John Collier penned 194 letters and papers transcribed here, written in a form of ordinary clerk's hand, easier to read for the early 1730s than later. William Cranston used a similar script to write 137 of the letters, although under pressure his hand deteriorated. William's prose indicated familiarity with the style of the *Grubb Street Journal*, 1731-37, the *Craftsman* and the *Spectator*. As both John Collier and William Cranston trained for the law, both were registered as country attorneys under the Act of 2 Geo II c.23, which required formal registration for all attorneys and required an appearance before a judge of the Westminster courts to answer to their fitness to act for clients as to legal and statute knowledge, and their ability to read Latin and understand proceedings where Latin was still used and swear loyalty to the Hanoverian succession and the protestant religion.[17] Their signatures on these lists and in correspondence varied over time. In an age before standardised grammar and spelling, Collier, for instance, replaced i with 'y' in some public documents, and as late as the 1740s the Duke of Newcastle wrote Collyer on his correspondence.

Work as attorney for Hastings and the Cinque Ports required office facilities near the Westminster law courts. Chambers in Johnson's Court, Fleet Street, were leased for every law term and by the mid 1720s the offices and living quarters were occupied for the whole year. Further, Collier and Cranston tackled work in the Assize courts on a regular basis, both at East Grinstead and Lewes Assizes and Cranston at Maidstone in Kent and Kingston in Surrey. Both needed servants to manage their chambers, to deal with horses and stables, arrange clean and well tailored clothes, deliver papers and collect goods within London and to post letters at all hours, arrange parcels by coastal vessel and road carrier to and from Hastings and to ports and towns en route.

What was the social composition of Hastings? When Collier married Elizabeth Elphick in 1706 the port of Hastings contained three parishes, St Clements, All Saints, and Castle parish, together home to around 1600 souls, and the historian Thomas Brandon Brett suggested a similar count for the end of the 1720s, with 854 females and 728 males.[18] Most lived on the road across the top of the beach, where the fishing fleet lay up, and around the High Street, All Saints Street and the Tackleway, the three main streets leading up from the Stade. How much information on the town did John Collier receive as town clerk? Auditors and assessors appointed by the Hastings Assembly laid an annual common scot, granted for the maintenance of the town, upon all inhabitants and all houses, lands, tenements, hereditaments, rents, and on profits of foreigners living and trading within the port and the liberties thereof. 251 payments were made for lands etc., in 1742 when the record resumes after a twenty year gap and most ordinary dwellings paid around 1s. Chamberlains' books listed the compositions paid to Hastings by the Cinque Port members of Pevensey, Seaford, Bekesbourne and Grench, and income from past debts, taxes paid by out-dwellers for lands

View of Johnson's Court, Fleet Street, John Collier's London residence, engraved by E F Finden, 1835, reproduced by permission of the Corporation of London.

inside Hastings; the rents of Corporation lands and the charges on tenements and shops listed by trade and owners, plus payments into the port annuity fund. An election paper kept by John Collier records 184 freeholders eligible to vote in the 1734 county election, a list which includes both Hastings and the liberties thereof, the latter being largely agricultural country **[608]**.

The scot upon the 127 tradesmen listed in the Chamberlains' report for 1742 show a similar pattern to other ports of this size, with food and alcohol production, building work, tailor and wig making, shoemaking, smiths, shopkeepers, and several trades specific to boats, chandlery, rope and sailmaking. Hastings even boasted a clocksmith and a bookseller. Additional annual town income came from alehousekeepers; in 1736 eighteen paid the £10 licence fee, with thirty-six cautioners at £5 each. The Chamberlains' accounts listed the charges for fairs and markets, for buying the freedom of the town, the pierwardens' charges on boat owners and fishermen using the port facilities, and undertaking the annual mackerel and herring voyages.[19] The accounts also listed the money paid out for repairs to the capstan, dredging the river Bourne along its descent down to the sea, and payments for repairs to public buildings. Land tax assessments varied according to the annual levy set by Parliament: 4s in the pound would raise £378 6s 0d and at 1s in the pound £94 5s 0d, with All Saints parish, wherein the Colliers lived, paying 19% of the total, St Clements, paid 35%, and Castle parish and the outbounds, including the western side of Hastings, with much agricultural land 46%.[20]

Hastings wealth arose largely from the sea and fishing, and only in part from agriculture, and as the former was vital for the town it helps to explain why Hastings lacked the normal gentry whose money rested on agricultural land. With a population of 1600 some 200 households relied on the sea for much or most of their income and food supplies; several hundred persons crewed the boats, during the mackerel and herring harvests numbers increased, and more folk mended nets and tackle, sorted out the catch for dispatch overland by the rippiers, and packed fish in salt for export. The barrel makers, chandlers, net and twine spinners plus the sail makers helps to explain why fishermen and mariners were a key component of local politics.

For John Collier two fears arose from this reliance on fishing: some years witnessed low catches due to the vagaries of fish movements, and during wartime the press and opponents made fishing difficult. There was also the chance of a change in government policy.[21] Since the Civil war support for fishermen was dispensed primarily through the Navigation system supporting English built ships, crewed predominantly by English mariners, and by a variety of coastal and on-shore work together with subsidies for fish exports. Such exports used salt as preservative, and the key to the level of subsidies was the excise tax on salt. This excise was paid when domestic salt left the salt works, or if foreign salt as landed: when additional salt duties came into force MPs in coastal areas voted for increased subsidies for fish exports which balanced the costs of buying salt. For Hastings the subsidies largely meant herring and mackerel. Packed in barrels and salted with domestic and foreign salt, the export trade provided significant incomes for the town. Corporation records listed the masters responsible for both campaigns and the Chamberlains collected port duties due from each boat. Government subsidies for the fish exports came from revenue officials; thus in the period covered by the correspondence here the drawbacks on the salt duties paid via the allowances on fish exports were payable by the Collector of salt duties and by debentures signed by Customs officials, the paperwork for these was then dispatched to London.[22] The attempt to abolish the salt tax in 1730-1732 was short-lived, with the department reinstated by Walpole before the excise crisis of 1733 [**13**].

Only a few mariners appear to have owned much beyond their houses, boats and equipment, the deezes for smoking and drying fish, and stock in trade. Thomas Brandon Brett listed only eight persons in the town, whom he labelled 'gentlemen of ability' assessed for the scot at above 5s a year.[23] Yet Hastings was also home to 70 freemen and jurats who could vote for the town MPs and 184 registered in the port and liberties thereof as eligible to vote for the county, although many of the latter lived outwith the liberties [**608**]. After the gentlemen of ability and the jurats the boat owners enjoyed the firmest imprint on the port's wealth. Most port tradesmen were of limited means, resting on periodic earnings which rose in the autumn, with agricultural produce coming to market and the sales from the catches: figures collected by Parliament show a fluctuating income from fishing, though rising as the century wore on. Several of the boat owners and families of the coastal traders earned sufficient to raise a comment in correspondence **[13, 89, 143, 144, 151, 583]**, and inventories show fishing tackle and shares in boats which ensured some worth could be passed on. Smuggling and cross Channel shipping also provided valuable trading connections and these are mentioned below.

John Collier would expect to answer the wide ranging requests all attorneys dealt with: to write references for posts in the Customs and Excise, to appeal over mariners remanded in custody accused of smuggling **[493-5, 500, 502]**, occasionally requesting the lodging of folk in Bedlam asylum **[140, 527, 530, 532]** and negotiating with the Navy Board over pay owed to seamen **[622]**, as well as drawing up ownership papers for boats and negotiating with other towns on debts arising from the course of trade. Apart from the fees and income from Hastings and the work in the courts, legal work also provided the avenue for extra income by taking on apprentice attorneys, earning about £20 a year for each apprentice clerk. The details are known due to the statute of 1709 by which Parliament tightened the regulation of all apprenticeships, including those of apprentice attorneys in respect of money paid to a master or mistress for taking on each clerk, apprentice or servant put to learn any trade, profession or employment. From 1 May 1710, a duty of 6d per 20s for every sum of £50 or under, and 1s per 20s for every sum over £50 was to be paid by the master to the local collector appointed by the new supervisory Board. Details of the payment were recorded upon the indenture, and the Board was to stamp all the writings, and keep its own record including the master's name and trade, his place of work, the apprentice's family and origin, and the sum paid to the master.[24] Apart from those put to trade by the public authorities, attorneys charged among the highest fees listed in the Board's records which ranged from a few pence to over £100.

Unfortunately, although Collier's own apprentices were included, his own apprenticeship preceded the statute, and he first appeared in these records on 3 October 1712 as a master: taking on John Thompson of Winchelsea, for five years, at the fee of £100; followed by Anthony Ellesdon of Lydd, 26 September 1714, also for five years at £100; then came Thomas Godley of Chailey, Sussex, 18 January 1717, for five years at £105. Godley took on the town clerkship in 1719 and 1722 whilst Collier was Mayor, and as a Customs employee was killed in a gun and sword fight with smugglers in 1740. Henry Dodson was apprenticed to Collier for seven years on 18 January 1725, at £140, and was appointed town clerk of Winchelsea in 1740, together with Edwin Wardroper.[25] Richard Patrick, already Collier's clerk, was taken on for five years paying only £10 on 23 February 1747. Appointed Hastings town clerk in 1750, Patrick was an executor of Collier's estate from 1760.

Family matters: sickness, mortality and education of the Collier children

Infant death, sickness and disease stalked the Collier family and illness feature in numerous letters below. As mentioned before, his wife Mary bore eighteen children, of whom eleven died in infancy, several whilst John Collier was working in London, from where he recorded remorse at his absence. Five of the girls survived to adulthood, and one boy, James, born 21 May 1721 who died in May 1747, aged 26. It is generally granted within the Sayer family that John junior, born 1720, known as Jacky in this correspondence, was especially liked by his father, who expressed great hopes for his son's future. After the basic schooling at Mrs Thorpe's in Battle **[2, 4, 7, 18]**, both Jacky and James arrived in August 1732 at Westminster school. Well thought of for its teaching of Latin and Greek, the school was a training ground for civic leadership. The boys boarded with the Revd Carleton, a schoolmaster, and the correspondence suggests not all was well with the boys' shoes or the cleanliness of clothing **[27, 33]**; worse still, in the autumn of 1732 a fellow pupil, Talbot Clerk, died of smallpox, and at the end of December William Cranston relayed the news to the Colliers in Hastings that Jacky lay seriously ill, being cared for near the office in Johnson's Court **[40, 41]**.

Eminent physicians examined Jacky and within two days of falling ill, Dr William Barrowby confirmed it was indeed smallpox, and after another night of 'utmost pain' reversed his earlier opinion that this was the favourable sort **[41, 42]**. Dr Richard Mead, whose *De Variolia morbillis* of 1747 was the standard mid-century text on smallpox, agreed this was the worst type. Mead divided the disease into one of limited fever, with small pustules, in which, though showing serious symptoms, death was rare, contrasting with the malignant smallpox evincing a stronger fever with small pustules forming black spots and scabs over the body, with bleeding and eruptions from the eyes, mouth, nose and ears, and from the bowels, with internal organs failing. By the time John Collier arrived in London, Jacky was dead **[44, 45]**.

As Diana Crook explains, smallpox was the great fear of the age, and is frequently mentioned in letters here and elsewhere in the Sayer Mss.[26] A few days on from Jacky's death, his brother James exhibited the early symptoms of the disease, causing no little consternation amongst the doctors and to William Cranston, who wrote urgently to his brother the Revd James Cranston junior, rector of Bexhill, requesting their assistance with Mary Collier, who was unable to travel as she recently gave birth to Thomas, who was already sickly **[42, 47]**.[27] Young James survived to general relief, but his life was henceforth blighted by bouts of headaches and fits, and though he managed at Clare College, Cambridge, and studied law in London, even appointed as Hastings Mayor in 1745, it all proved too much and his life was cut short on 30 May 1747.[28] This afterlife of the afflictions of smallpox appears in several letters here, and elsewhere in the Sayer Mss., with concern over damage to eyesight, over the complexion and texture of the skin, and effect on mental abilities **[309, 397, 403]**.

Understanding of contagion sometimes kept the healthy apart from the afflicted, as in the quarantining of ships with plague on board, and, for fear of the smallpox, at each visit to the ill Collier boys William Cranston changed his clothes. Several acquaintances refused to visit the children. When only eight years old and at Mrs Thorpe's school, Jacky was kept in Battle for the summer and autumn of 1729 while the smallpox raged in Hastings.[29] The girls were despatched to Battle during a later outbreak. Segregation though, was hard in the crowded wynds of Hastings, and to compound the question, inoculation with the live smallpox virus was inadequately understood. According to Thomas Brandon Brett in the 1729 Hastings outbreak 705 persons caught the disease, 91 died, adding in his view 'nearly all of which was caused by the new fangled system of inoculation; when Brett looked at the records of the old parish church in Ore, for just two months in 1729, he found eleven died of smallpox 'in the natural way', and 61 after inoculation, whereon the inhabitants petitioned the parish officers to put a stop to further inoculation.[30] John Collier decided in November 1740 that a recent outbreak in Hastings was caused by the smuggling trade, brought in with goods and smugglers from the continent **[292]**.

As readers of history we are exposed to the lists of infant mortality and the all too common deaths amongst the young, and we may imagine that the parents of Georgian England just accepted it, as being commonplace. Reading these letters shows us how untrue this impression is. Quite apart from the question of John Collier's hopes for Jacky as male heir, his and his wife's humanity and simple love just as parents shine through. Both drew solace from their Anglican beliefs. When Mary informed her husband of the unexpected death of their daughter in December 1718, he searched for comfort in patience and submission to the divine will, the Almighty's pleasure, 'tis this only that can give us solid and substantiall comfort, and tis this as Christians we must resolve to submit when troubles and afflictions happen'.[31] A sense of despair at these events around the death of Jacky has John Collier questioning God's love, as he faced up to the thought that his son would not be replaced **[56, 57, 66]**.[32] These letters demonstrate the philosophy needed for coping in those days, as William Cranston put it to his own father on 9 January 1733, 'A more malancholy Xmas I ne'er know but hope twill be of such service to me as never to sett my heart too much upon anything in this world, since everything is so precarious' **[47]**. John Collier's letter to his wife, 8 February 1733 expresses his fear of loss, and in its own way, of holding on to his wife through a regular correspondence, and his efforts on buying from time to time exactly the clothes Mary and the girls requested **[56]**.

It must have been especially hard to lose James in May 1747 as it was the end of the male line. Letters published by Charles Lane Sayer for this year show the despondency of the parents.[33] In this era it was usual for three months of deep mourning to be followed by three months of slight mourning, although William Cranston was rather firm on 24 December 1747, seven months on from the burial of James in Westminster Abbey, when he stated that six months mourning was enough: 'the mourning a whole year is not customary in your case'. John Collier's depression continued into the following year.[34]

Illness cost money. Medical and burial costs for Jacky came to £46 14s 8d and £31 1s for James.[35] Smallpox was a huge worry in Hastings due to the costs to family incomes and to the town economy with the loss of working folk and lasting physical and mental damage for survivors. Other illnesses and afflictions of the age included gout, a sharp and long-lasting pain derived from the build up of crystal deposits in joints with early signs in the toes, ankles, the ball of the foot, followed by more pain in the lower legs, the elbows and wrists. One of the few diseases of the time understood in the Georgian age, gout was blamed by the Roman and Greek authorities on over-indulgence in rich meat dishes and alcohol, aggravated by lack of exercise. John Collier and William Cranston and many of their acquaintances spent long hours at the desk, poring over judgements, answering correspondence, ploughing through documents and writing up accounts. Advice from their doctors, also relying on the ancients, was to void the system of food, by sweating and vomits, bloodletting, adopting a spartan diet and drinking spa water **[94, 142, 160-165]** as well as abstaining from alcohol, and copying the Romans in bathing, with the addition of exercise by walking and horseback rather than using sedan chairs and hackney carriages.[36] John Collier frequently referred to the common cold which swept London every autumn and winter **[9-10, 27, 59-61, 66, 83-4]**; it immobilised him, virtually every year, and there are references to illness which Charles Lane Sayer suggested was influenza **[399]**.

Fevers and infections from insect bites, with swelling of the skin and blood poisoning were prevalent in the marshes and river localities in Sussex, Kent and Essex.[37] Agues, now known to be caused by the vivax malaria parasite, carried by the *Anopheles atroparvuus* mosquito, aggravated living in and near these low lying areas. Parish records show that life expectancy varied sharply between low lying parishes and those higher up on the Weald and on the south Downs.[38] Wynn Ford's work for the Society on the bishop's visitations for Sussex, 1724, shows the majority of the low lying parishes were run by the curate; few large houses were built in wetland areas, the higher incomes lived at and above the 300 foot contour. As the Colliers traversed low lying areas, including the Romney and Pevensey levels it is not surprising to read of malarial symptoms amongst their children, the agues suffered by Harriet are particularly graphic **[443, 445-7]**. For treatment doctors turned to peruvian bark, quinine, which John Radcliff prescribed 'not only in fevers, but also in all periodical cases, and such as have exacerbations, as epilepsies, convulsions, hysterics and asthma'.[39] Local remedies included the roots of the Essex marsh holly, made up into a paste with honey or sugar, and other calming potions. The treatment prescribed for Jane Collier's fever in January 1735 advised a change of air and the marsh holly to reduce temperature **[117]**.

These letters refer also to gangrene **[41, 161, 182, 184]**, toothache **[66]**, measles **[41, 59, 357, 399]**, scabies and the itch **[65, 162, 163, 288]**, hair lice and fleas **[55, 57, 60]**, insomnia **[161, 162,164]**, lowness of spirits **[66, 69, 70, 93]**, anxiety, including anxiety about falling ill, and skin infections, including eczema, rare among fishermen, for which sea bathing was recommended. Intermittent depression affected Mary Collier, alleviated by conversation with Mrs Thorpe of Battle **[10, 27-8, 30, 114],** and visits to Tunbridge Wells in the summer season, although the suggestion of her social rank being too low to be accepted into the top set clearly rankled **[179-80]**. Visits to London to stay with her brother William at least ensured she met people of her own class, with the legal entourage talking a similar language. Mary disliked the narrow basis for proper society in Hastings, and the absence of her husband in law terms and on his Customs survey periodically upset her.

Cordelia, the Dely of these letters, became a worry to her parents in the later 1730s. Suffering from a mild depressive illness, probably aggravated by the ague, her condition may have preceded her first term at Elizabeth Russell's Hampstead girls' boarding school in Church Row, Hampstead, and was a considerable worry four years later [**117, 209, 211**].[40] Consumption was considered, and that 'ingenious man' Mr Jeake thought riding and a change of air 'absolutely necessary' with a diet free of meat and wine to lower her fever [**208**]. Dr Richard Russell also advised horse-riding as well as sea cures.[41] Russell's work on sea bathing permeated the later Georgian age, and he was consulted over the girls' illnesses including this long-lived condition affecting Cordelia **[117, 209, 211, 360, 397]**. The letters on her condition indicate some divergence of medical opinion **[208-209, 211]**.

How were the girls schooled? These letters give us a vivid picture of the girls' upbringing, and their schooling. Both boys and girls were schooled away from Hastings: all went to Mrs Thorpe's private school in Battle until 11 or 12. The five girls then went to Elizabeth Russell's Hampstead boarding school designed for the education and upbringing of professional and upper class young ladies. London was ringed with towns and expanding suburbs with schools for boarders, often used by families with a father who worked in the City or Westminster.[42] With a modest population of 1800 Hampstead was entirely convenient, being six miles from Holborn, and socially acceptable as to the resident population. The village was famed for its chalybeate springs, and in 1701 a licence was granted for six acres of bowling green, gardens, a lake and a pump room dispensing mineral water, plus an Assembly room known as the Long Room **[134, 313, 316, 360]**, used for music, cards and dances. Weatherall Place was opened in 1734, complete with a ballroom, pump room and long room with restricted access to only suitable folk.

By 1741 Elizabeth Russell's school charged five guineas for entrance, plus a guinea for music, boarding costs extra, and by 1750 the school catered for 29 boarders, each paying £30 a year and 7 guineas entrance if learning music, and £25 a year, with 6 guineas entrance if omitting music; the curriculum on both dates included dancing, French, embroidery, bible study, handwriting, including the Italian hand for older girls, how to compose letters in straight lines, tuition on musical instruments including the spinet, visits to nearby sights and religious instruction. Sunday walks to and from the Anglican church in Hampstead were included, and escorted visits to the theatre for older girls. Parents and guardians were required to supply a chest of drawers, a tea chest, 3 napkins, tea-cup and saucer, teaspoon, knife and fork, and some books and paper.[43] In addition, girls learnt deportment, modes of address, especially how and when to laugh, how to respond to suffering, what to say at table and when to say nothing, and how to recognise the social hierarchy in social events. Servants escorted them from school to meetings with parents in London or Hampstead.[44]

The Collier girls were near the centre of London fashion, and father was expected to supply the demands of changing taste which he duly recorded in his day book, and the correspondence often refers to purchases [such as **60, 64]**. Extensive demands were made on William Cranston and John Collier to learn of and to procure items of fashion, and to provide information for gossip and letters. Elizabeth Russell, picking up from Mrs Thorpe's lessons in Battle, taught embroidery and needlework so the girls could run up their own clothes of fashion, and alter bought clothes, skills especially important for the cottons and silks critical for modern dancing. Fashion and the girls paid no attention to the prohibition of Indian cotton imports **[30]**.[45] For winter wear heavier, woollen outer garments could be bought in drapers shops, and these could be fashionable as well as necessary for riding in inclement weather, and for funeral wear and attendance at the theatre and opera: 43 letters refer to the purchase of gowns, 22 for coats, 17 for gloves and ten for earrings. Mary, Cordelia, Jane, Sarah and Harriet all went to the main playhouses, with the latest fashions and fans in abundance, and there are occasional references to their fellow school pupils being seen with non-relatives. As the girls grew older the London season remained a huge attraction, with its morning soirees, afternoon teas, and evenings watching the latest plays and dancing, with the advantage of dividing those who could afford all this, from the hoi polloi, who would struggle.

This world of fashion also had to be balanced against the reality of adulthood, by living and observing in a similar setting to what the Collier girls might expect on marriage. The letters published here lacking original dates include many which cover many issues such as marriage expectations, how to deal with servants, for instance, how to organise dinners, and who to separate at table, what to ensure was in the larder for the winter, and unless they married much above their rank, how to organise horses, stables and farmyards [**573-82**]. These letters comprise a fine resource on household behaviour in mid eighteenth century Sussex. One has the feeling that such an upbringing could be rather daunting, though to the girls' rescue came the families in the country mansions around Hastings and Battle.[46] Given the transport difficulties invitations went out to stay for a week or more, longer in the case of Cordelia who was popular, though quite ill from time to time, and required emotional support. Dancing partners were rounded up, from the army officers stationed on the south coast, from the church and professionals.

Co-operation between the Cranston and Collier families is central to understanding the correspondence, legal affairs, the organisation of the Collier accounts, and the additional workload borne by John Collier derived from the Duke of Newcastle and Henry Pelham. William Cranston kept books for John Collier's earnings and spending in London, including the fees from the office of Usher and Cryer, the investments in the Bank of England and South Sea company stock, the settlement of Westminster school bills, and accounts for the girls, Cordelia, Jane, Sarah, Harriet and Molly Collier when at Elizabeth Russell's school, and for the Collier purchases in London outside of the legal terms. Cranston lived in London for most of the year, and conversed on business with government and legal officials, keeping his brother in law abreast of events at Westminster and the details of their joint business affairs. Occasionally Cranston visited Hastings, although more often he stayed in East Grinstead, from where Mary Swaysland came, and with his second wife eventually settled in East Court on the north side of the town. Letters refer to work managed by relatives and associates, looking after the Collier girls and Cranston's two sons is a regular theme, and Mary Collier with children at different ages placed reliance on her servants and a few local families [**10, 24, 28, 105, 152**]. Although the Hastings house was not as large as those owned by many local landowners, there was sufficient space for clerical support, with messages and letters to be answered on daily. John Collier relied on Mary's views, and occasionally apologised when he misunderstood her.

These papers record the interesting crisis faced by Elizabeth Hickes. Her estate was left to her by her brother John Dunmoll, and Thomas Hickes, her husband, who died 11 November 1736 aged 63.[47] It was the Dunmoll part of her inheritance that caused her to request help: an ancient family from Wadhurst, the Dunmolls owned lands and houses in Blackheath, Greenwich and Southwark, and some housing on London Bridge. Elizabeth Hickes asked Collier to manage these, she owning the freeholds, and in December 1737 William Cranston rode down to Greenwich, starting with the marshland, and the clay and sand pits bordering the Thames which provided income from the building trades. Here and on the rest of the estate Cranston was tasked with establishing her rights under the freehold, sorting out disputes between the men digging the pits, collecting house rents, and appointing agents. John Dunmoll had difficulties with his partner, Simmonds, and with the workmen who posed typical hurdles for such mineral workings, and the perennial problem of the recovery of ground dug out for sand and clay, for which workmen demanded higher pay [**193-207, 214-5, 224, 227**]. Elizabeth Hickes also relied upon John Collier for the handling of the awkward separation of one of her two daughters from the husband, Mr Boys, for which Dudley Ryder, the Attorney General, suggested creating a trust for part of the Elizabeth Hickes estate which excluded Boys from inheritance [**199, 227, 617**].

By 1727 John Collier's income and expenditure on his London account showed turnover in excess of £500 roughly every four to six months. Monthly accounts were kept by John Collier in Hastings: these were duplicates of his income and expenditure managed by William Cranston, and the record has survived from 1727.[48] Monthly totals doubled in the 1730s, and on occasion reached £500 per month: the London accounts swept up all John Collier's outgoings, including much that was business as well as family spending. His income from lands and houses in the vicinity of Hastings by 1731-35 reached £850 17s gross per year before deductions and costs, with net cash of £652 9s: this came mainly from farms and marsh land and the levels near Hastings.[49] A separate volume for rentals shows figures for 1731 and after, and the accounts show that the estate formed the main investment for his daughters' future. Although the start of his purchases is not listed these London accounts show John Collier's annual net income at several hundred pounds by the time he was 40, with most of his cash balances periodically invested in land, with the residue in stocks.

Conversations between Charles Lane Sayer and his relatives included the long held memory that John Collier acted as a local banker and money-lender, and there is some evidence for this in the correspondence and the town accounts, for instance the funding of mortgages.[50] A few of Collier's clients invested in London based companies or took out fire protection with the Sun Fire office. In 1742-3 the chamberlain's accounts listed £200 of the town reserve lent to John Collier, with one year's interest due 6 October 1743, at 3%, added another £6.[51] Collier loaned money to St Clements church on at least two occasions.[52] Unfortunately, his correspondence also illustrates the sadness and difficulty in the work of a country attorney, dealing with the consequences of death, all too often of the head of a household, the demise of a promising business venture which took up a client's money, and with the results of out of control debts. Thus arose the situation of the Denham family of Hollington: after the death of the Revd Thomas Denham, the vicar of Hollington, his son David failed to find sufficient work despite being a trained clerk. Having lost money in London, he borrowed small sums from both Cranston and Collier and ended up as a debtor in the King's Bench, dying there of smallpox **[486]**. Collier also lent to relatives, including £46 10s to the brother of his first wife Elizabeth, George Elphick, who made and japanned chairs, and who faced gaol for debt in 1723.[53] Some of these payments could be characterised as out relief. Samuel Cruttenden, who married Collier's sister Sarah, received small payments and also food and drink, and pestered John Collier over possible posts in the government service **[62, 74, 83, 106]** and other relations and associates in Hastings behaved likewise. Several letters refer to loans made to the Duke of Newcastle and Henry Pelham usually by paying bills incurred whilst defending the political interests of the government. The Duke spent his working life protecting the Whig interest, battling Tories and Jacobites; his compass was wide and his agents and factors were expected to act in his support. As

John Collier discovered the Duke's interests placed the Duchess of Newcastle foremost when his Grace needed funds, and several expected repayments for sums laid out by Collier were not forthcoming **[192, 204, 221, 248, 250, 252, 266, 267, 268]**.

How did John Collier increase his wealth? Two main avenues were open to Collier when seeking a return above the 5 per cent fixed by the usury Act of 1714. Investments in quoted companies and in business ventures, land and property might grow over time and dividends paid by companies, including the South Sea Company, the Bank of England and the New River were not so restricted. The other legal exemption to the 5 per cent limit was for borrowing by the government which could pay any rate of interest agreed by Parliament and this included tickets in lotteries sanctioned by statute. Lotteries were controversial.[54] In the years covered by the correspondence here nine Acts raised funds which included a lottery. By combining an annuity with the chance of a win on a prize, five Acts paid out a minimum of £6 to £7 10s in prizes for fortunate tickets plus 3% or 4% interest per annum for every ticket. The tickets for the four Acts for raising money for Westminster Bridge paid out nothing for the blanks not drawn for lottery prizes.[55] Little evidence is provided in the correspondence here, or from John Collier's account books that the family did more than break even on lottery tickets **[9, 186, 320]**.

On various occasions Hastings 'gentlemen of ability' considered improving the town water supply. The Bourne stream which ran through the town carried the main supply of water, though the flow fluctuated with the seasons, and sparse rainfall meant the bailiff of the Bourne often penned water at the top of the High Street for release every few days. Indifferent supply from the stream was widely reported **[Appendix 3]** as were conflicts of interest between breweries using the water and townsfolk. Manwaring Baines uncovered a proposal for the use of pipes to carry water within Hastings as early as 1606, although this may have referred to the digging of wells. Thomas Brandon Brett cited the efforts of Henry Carleton in 1723, who offered a plan to lay down elm pipes to carry water from above the town; this important proposal was accepted by the town assembly, though how far this proceeded is unclear.[56]

The inspiration for this proposal, and perhaps for the earlier one, may have come from the example set by Rye, whereat the townsfolk were supplied with spring water from the north-east cliff, and lesser supplies from the north-west. The archives discussed by the town historian William Holloway show 'without pretending to very great exactness' evidence of investment in wood casks and in pipes laid in the town and precincts made from elm and lead, and from 1597, conduits built from outside to convey the water to town reservoirs.[57] Serious efforts to improve the water supply through more pipes and conduits were carried out thereafter and in 1734 inquiries were made as to whether houseowners would pay a scot for extra pipes, and though this scheme was laid aside, investment in mains pipes and conduits continued. Henry Carleton jun., was one of the Rye officials at this time, and this effort follows on from his second attempt to improve the water supply at Hastings, in the previous year, this time in association with John Collier with the agreement of landowners across whose lands the pipework would be laid **[Appendix 3]**. Plans were endorsed by the town assembly and jurats in 1733, with capital costs to be paid by Carleton, Collier and friends. The theory was clear, to supply the town with enough water through elm pipes to meet demand would require less water than used to flush the Bourne. Robert Rosam, an engineer and landowner from Herstmonceux, supplied the elm pipes and workmen, and William Harrison the ironfounder who took over Robertsbridge furnace in 1734, cast the ironwork.[58] A reservoir was dug above the town and as waterworks required a permanent oversight to repair burst mains and stopcocks, users would pay a water rate to cover such costs and also to repay the capital. Several costings for Robert Rosam's works have survived in the Sayer archives **[590-2]**.

Although the waterworks were a technical success in that water was conveyed via taps and stopcocks to a few households, the number subscribing was insufficient to pay even the ongoing costs without further payments from Carleton and Collier **[125-6]**. At least two brewery owners took out legal cases alleging that the flow of water coming down the Bourne was reduced by the new works,[59] and opposition came from ordinary townsfolk complaining about charges for water previously free **[82, 108, 595]**. Thomas Brandon Brett summed up the failure, the objectors 'being mostly poor people were so numerous, and the well-to-do persons so few and far between, that as a looked for remunerative scheme, it fell to the ground' confirming that the prospective income was not 'sufficiently encouraging to justify the expense of construction and maintenance'.[60] Efforts were made to maintain the works until 1740 and then the record closes.

The discussion of John Collier's business career offers key facets about his life and income: the need to be in London in law terms, often overstaying to deal with Customs and Cinque Port business, on horseback as Surveyor General of the riding officers of Kent which paid well but kept him away from Hastings a month every year; the two or three days to ride the forty-six miles from Hastings to Southwark, the cost of inns at Stonebridge, Battle, Tunbridge Wells and Tonbridge recorded in his London journal.[61] Travelling on manorial affairs and on the levels and journeys as political agent for Newcastle and Pelham required traversing some of the worst conditions in southern England. Indeed, little correspondence about Sussex is complete without reference to the difficult travel over the Weald, and across the levels and marshes of the coastal fringes. The letters here point to mud and water, the dire conditions south of Tonbridge and Tunbridge Wells **[27, 56, 122, 169, 170, 216]** and the annoyance of his daughters at having to squelch through the tracks and across causeways. Improving roads was a project which the daughters referred to, with their experience of the superior roads and turnpikes of London, including the road to Hampstead. Eventually, John Collier and local landlords contributed to the initial capital for the Battle to Hastings turnpike begun in the later 1740s, although road conditions over the Weald remained dire for many years.[62]

Politics and Political Circles

What was the importance of politics for the Collier family? Although opportunities to improve on local earnings proved limited in the reign of George I and the early years of George II, John Collier's legal reputation and his skill in managing the Hastings corporation eventually provided opportunities. At the start of George II's reign 28 MPs were elected from Sussex, with the Duke of Newcastle and his brother Henry Pelham having a clear interest in the results.[63] Two MPs were elected for Sussex county by the 40 shilling freeholders, and two apiece from the towns of Arundel, Bramber, Chichester, East Grinstead, Horsham, Lewes, Midhurst, New Shoreham and Steyning, and two each from the Cinque Ports of Hastings, Rye, Seaford and Winchelsea. Other Sussex towns, including Battle, Eastbourne and Brighthelmstone were only represented through the county vote. The most favoured electors thus held four votes. In Hastings it was only the freemen, numbering around seventy, who possessed a vote for the town MPs, and if they also owned property with a rental value of 40s, they received an extra two votes for the county election. The list of electors eligible to vote in the county election of 1734 shows Hastings and liberties with 184 county voters, who, by virtue of meeting the 40 shilling freehold qualification could vote for the two members to represent Sussex [Appendix 5]: if also freemen of Hastings they enjoyed two more votes each for the Hastings MPs.

Hastings freeholders remained obstinately independent in elections, with a town group taking advantage of the short-lived Tory revival in the 1710 election to elect Sir Joseph Martin alongside the local Whig landowner Sir William Ashburnham: both were returned again in 1713. The arrival of George I led to a reversal of fortunes, the Tories lost Sussex county in 1715, and in Hastings the support of Newcastle and Pelham saw Archibald Hutcheson, the Duke of Ormond's lawyer and accountant, returned alongside Ashburnham.[64] Hutcheson proved popular with his constituents for his generous benefactions,[65] cemented by his vociferous opposition to the Septennial Act in 1716, which Act lengthened the life of each Parliament from five to seven years, thus decreasing the opportunity of electors to receive gifts from candidates.[66] Hutcheson proved an independent minded MP, and when the Whigs decided to ingraft £31 million of government debt onto the stock of the South Sea Company, the Hastings MP denounced the resulting rise in the share price as unwarranted, and the company's prospects as lacklustre, with difficulties besetting trade in goods and slaves in the south Americas, not the least of which was conflict with Spain and Spanish merchants. His warnings on the potential for financial crisis were well publicised, as was his vote against the conversion in Parliament. When the crisis broke in August 1720 Archibald Hutcheson was appointed by the Commons to the Committee for Secrecy to investigate the saga, and his *Collections* on finance and money sold widely, with a set accepted by the Hastings Corporation.[67] Newcastle and Pelham now regarded Hutcheson as an opponent, only too likely to strengthen the Tories, and so decided to replace him with John Pulteney, a Commissioner of Customs. The general election of 1722 took place in the full glare of the popular fury over the South Sea crisis, Hutcheson standing as an 'old and loyal Whig and a modern Tory'.[68]

Whilst Sir William Ashburnham topped the 1722 Hastings poll with 56 votes, otherwise this election proved a rebuff for the Newcastle and Pelham interest; Edward Milward and John Collier, three jurats and 28 freemen voted for Hutcheson, against six jurats and 26 freemen for Pulteney, of whom eleven were Customs and Excise employees, and seven their relatives.[69] Thus was the picture clear: a discredited majority in Parliament which engineered the Septennial Act, the local magnates Thomas Pelham and the Duke of Newcastle in favour of conversion and reams of damaging evidence to the Committee of Secrecy. From this committee came the proof of the widespread misuse of public funds for speculation, and gaol for the Chancellor of the Exchequer, several MPs and revenue collectors, plus seizures of landed estates and the flight abroad of the Secretary of the South Sea company: even accusations against George I, governor of the South Sea company, and his two mistresses were current.

How did the aftermath of the 1722 election affect John Collier? Aside from some financial papers no correspondence for John Collier has been recovered among the Sayer

Mss from 16 February 1719/20 to 11 February 1723/4; while only 15 letters survive down to 23 November 1728, four of which cover the inauguration of George II and Caroline in 1727, at which John Collier was one of the canopy bearers for the new Queen.[70] In stabilising the country's financial affairs the political wind blew for the new king and Sir Robert Walpole, in alliance with Newcastle and Pelham. As Hutcheson was out of contention due to illness, in the election of 1727 Hastings leant towards the government candidates, Sir William Ashburnham and Thomas Townshend, the Duke's nephew, who were returned unopposed. The latter was later replaced by Thomas Pelham junior.[71] Yet the Duke of Newcastle and Henry Pelham were never complacent about voting intentions, and the 1722 polling lists suggested that the town's freemen could not be relied on at elections unless the Mayor and jurats united behind the Treasury candidate.[72]

Ever alert to the need to manage elections years in advance, and with sharp reminders of the volatile nature of the Hastings fishermen, Newcastle offered John Collier the reversion of the post of Newcastle estate manager and election agent in the rape of Hastings.[73] By 24 February 1731-32 Collier also accepted the position of Usher and Cryer of the court of King's Bench, a place whose staff could be managed by William Cranston located in Johnson's Court **[15, 87]**. Income from bails and judgements, clear of staff wages and other costs, rose from £108 17s in 1733 to an annual average of £123 8s 1737-39.

Work as election agent was to absorb much of John Collier's time from the abandonment of Sir Robert Walpole's general excise bill in April 1733 until the Hastings election a year on and the Sussex county poll of May 1734. Continued antagonism to the excise bill unnerved the government: rumours circulated about what might now happen with onerous taxes on pork and beef and with tradesmen forced to act as unpaid excisemen, and rumours of new powers to enter houses and farms to be conferred on officials.[74] Worse, the Tories seized on the disquiet. In Sussex they were led by John Fuller, the former Sussex county MP, Wealden ironmaster and Jamaica plantation owner, together with the landowner Sir Cecil Bishop, and local landowners and gentry including Sir Thomas Dyke, Sir Charles Eversfield of Grove and the Webster family of Battle Abbey. Months of campaigning were to irritate Newcastle and occupy John Collier's time. Together with Thomas Godley Collier canvassed the 40 shilling freeholders living in and near Hastings and in the liberties thereof, and whilst a majority supported Henry Pelham and James Butler for the county, twenty to thirty refused to say, and more declined to engage so long before the vote **[72-3]**.[75] This canvas was awkward, and in August 1733 Newcastle thought Rye and liberties, with a larger vote than for the Hastings MPs might veer toward Fuller and Bishop **[71]**; with the Weald liable to vote against Pelham and Butler the question loomed: could the Tories also win in the county?

At this juncture Henry Pelham decided to appoint John Collier as his steward for manors and lordships in Sussex, a useful station bringing in manorial fees and legal settlements, and useful for Pelham to have an energetic attorney working for his interest **[601]**. Collier was certainly energetic, and prepared to pay out for election expenses, such as £119 0s 9d food and alcohol for prospective voters in the rape of Hastings on the 20 and 30th October 1733 and on later occasions **[73, 86]**.[76] To make quite sure of this assistance the Duke of Newcastle explained to Sir Robert Walpole, about this time, that Collier would benefit from a seriously lucrative post: the exact wording in the letter suggests something might be amiss among Hastings voters: 'As to Collyer you can't do too much, for if I can judge that town absolutely depends upon him, and perhaps if he were cool, would leave you. I desire therefore, you will from me tell Sir Robert Walpole, if he has a mind to have two Whigs chosen att Hasting he must provide handsomely for Collyer'.[77] This resulted in John Collier being granted the post of Surveyor General of the Riding Officers in Kent, salary £250 a year, plus a staffed office in Hastings shared with Major William Battine, the Surveyor General for Sussex, election agent partly responsible for the Whig position in West Sussex **[76]**.[78]

There were wide roots in policy for these appointments. From the election of 1727 Walpole, Newcastle and Pelham agreed the Treasury should take responsibility for appointments in revenue collecting departments, including the Customs and the Salt department. This was initially about control of local appointments, and was completed before the 1734 election, though within two years was extended to Commissioners posts.[79] In practice neither of Collier's new posts was a sinecure. As the Customs Commissioners impressed on Surveyors it was not just that Customs revenues were vital if the land tax was to be held down, but keeping a watch on port officials was essential. So Collier faced a month long annual tour of all ports in Kent, and several inland centres, including Canterbury and the part of East Grinstead which lay in Kent. Progression was along the Kent coast by horse, riding inland as required, including to the Isle of Thanet. On return his report was read by the Commissioners, orders were given to Kent officers and requests made for co-operation with the Excise and the armed forces. Furthermore, the threat to tax collection from the smugglers was a political test for the government as some smugglers were freemen of the Cinque Ports or related to freemen, and from Collier and William Battine the Duke of Newcastle received careful and well worded advice as to the mood of the freemen, and how dealing with the smugglers might affect voting.[80]

How did the Tories campaign in Hastings? Given the influence of the Ashburnham family Sir William was unlikely to lose, although the Tories thought it possible to unseat the second member, the unpopular Thomas Pelham.[81] The Tories focused on extending the local franchise to dilute the votes from officials in the Customs and Excise. The custom of creating freemen could be understood in differing ways, as the papers and correspondence here show **[583-4]**, and increasing the number of freemen might work to the disadvantage of Newcastle and Pelham. Thus the efforts of the Webster family, led by Sir Thomas Webster, and John Fuller ironmaster and past county MP had to be thwarted, not just for Hastings, but for the potential impact on registration in other Cinque Ports by a dilution of pro-government votes from officials and their relatives.

The Whig position was to hold the line against the creation of new freemen in Cinque Ports, especially where there were several routes to being free. Rye, Seaford, Sandwich and Dover, as well as Hastings, were of particular interest to the government. In Rye's case, the Custumal seemed to indicate the right to freedom by the eldest surviving son of a freeman, with other rights for strangers; in Sandwich marriage to a free woman by a stranger secured freedom. John Manwaring Baines concluded that the right of entry to the freedom of one of the Cinque Ports 'meant admission to the freedom of them all'.[82]

The move by Sir Thomas Webster is fundamental to understanding the legal side of Cinque Port politics in the mid-1730s. Webster decided the claims at Hastings should be tested in the King's Bench and the evidence was to come from the ancient Hastings Custumal, which, it was assumed, provided written proof of a right established by the custom of centuries that the elder son and indeed, younger sons, could claim the right to be elected a freeman on reaching 21. Older townsfolk who could testify to these claims were to be called upon **[122]**: various grounds were thought possible although the right of the elder son was the central one, and was used in drumming up support amongst non-freemen descended from ancient port folk. The correspondence in this volume relates to several efforts by the Tories applying to the Westminster courts, and encouragement given to younger townsmen to petition the Mayor and jurats directly.[83]

Sir Thomas decided to fund cases in the King's Bench with the object of establishing the right of the elder son, and, interestingly, the right of a husband who was not the son of a freeman, but who married the daughter of one, as allowed in Sandwich, to be sworn as a freeman. The first of Webster's legal challenges covered in the correspondence resulted from the refusal by Hastings corporation to admit John Sargent, eldest son of a deceased freeman, whose request for a mandamus was heard before Lord Hardwicke in the King's Bench in January 1734 **[78, 583]**. Hardwicke ruled that John Sargent baptised 18 November 1712, born after the admission of his father, should 'immediately after the receipt of this writ' be admitted by the Corporation to the freedom, according to custom. At the same hearing John Shorter requested admission on the grounds of marriage to Mary Meadow, daughter of Benjamin Meadow, freeman, she having been born within the precincts of Hastings after her father had been sworn. Hardwicke dispatched this case with similar intent **[584]**.

Neither the Duke of Newcastle nor Sir William Ashburnham were prepared to let this pass: Newcastle called in Thomas Pelham and told him to ask Hardwicke how the King's Bench understood the case, and was also instructed to write to John Collier requesting that 'effectual steps' be taken 'for preventing the admission of any freeman by virtue of such mandamus' as already served on the Corporation in favour of Sargent and Shorter **[77]**. Meanwhile William Cranston worked on a challenge to the court orders, his advice being to deny everything put forward by Sargent and Shorter, demanding proof that the Custom was as alleged, for the 'proving all this without the Custom will be of no manner of service to them' **[79, 80]**. Henry Pelham spent some time in the late spring and early summer of 1734 dealing with the legal arguments: in the Trinity term 1734 John Collier records a mandamus against the Mayor and jurats, against which 'a return made that Henry Moore is not entitled to his freedom' and later in the Michaelmas term 1734 Collier and Cranston were occupied with the 'mandamus against the Mayor and jurats' although additional detail was not listed in Collier's day book.[84]

Parallel to Webster's legal challenges, John Collier found himself and Henry Carleton facing writs from the Sargent family and Benjamin Meadow over the Hastings waterworks, alleging the new pond erected above the town caused restrictions on the flow of the Bourne. The case was inconvenient owing to its timing, although Collier secured deferral until after the elections, and it was settled in August 1734 by modest fines imposed on John Collier and Henry Carleton. As so often with legal disputes, the correspondence here contains useful local information, in this case how the town's water supply worked, and how the new waterworks were understood by the different factions in the town **[593-5]**.[85]

Also in April 1734 thirteen sons of Hastings freemen petitioned the Corporation for their freedom and encouraged by Revd Thomas Broadway, who supported the Webster family, a total of twenty-two aspiring freemen went to hear Whistler Webster, the Tory candidate for Hastings and John Fuller the ironmaster, standing again for the county alongside Sir Cecil

Bishop **[86]**.[86] At the Hastings Court of Record for 1734 the claims for freedom from these townsmen were rejected, and none of the three new freemen created that year were sons of freemen, present or past, and John Sargent was kept waiting for another two years. In the Hastings election, 29 April 1734, both Sir William Ashburnham and Thomas Pelham jun., gained 50 votes, and Whistler Webster, 29, in the county election of 9 May 1734, 45 from Hastings and liberties voted for Bishop and Fuller, 123 for Pelham and 122 for Butler: 5 out of 6 from the Serjeant family voted for Fuller, and both the Shorter family and Benjamin Meadow as well. The Duke of Newcastle need not have worried about Rye and liberties: 79 voted for Pelham, 9 for Fuller, 78 for Butler and 8 for Bishop.[87]

The correspondence here records Sir Thomas Webster trying again in May and June 1735, this time for a mandamus from the King's Bench in support of Henry Moore's request to be elected a freeman. This also involved the arguments about the right of the elder son, supported by testimony from older townsfolk, and John Collier named four such witnesses who were to appear for Webster; for the Corporation side six jurats surrendered their places and privileges as freemen to support the opposition in court. William Cranston set to work on all the 'necessary dispositions for a defence', including briefs for counsel retained by Henry Pelham and the Corporation.[88] But Sir Thomas withdrew the application on 27 June 1735, the day before the proposed hearing, leaving the Corporation's costs unpaid **[119, 122]**.[89]

A similar, and this time, decisive, legal contest ensued a year later. Again this revolved around the request by Henry Moore to be sworn a freeman and was included in Howell's *State Trials* with the pleadings and the lengthy testimony of witnesses **[155]**: the summaries of Sir John Strange and Hardwicke's reports are also noticed in *English Reports*.[90] As before, the case for the Webster interest depended on the interpretation of centuries of custom, whether the eldest son of a freeman should be automatically elected a freeman and the Mayor and jurats 'stubornly defended the case'.[91] William Cranston duly prepared papers, briefed the witnesses, the ancient Hastings Custumal was called as evidence and lodged with the court; six jurats resigned as freemen etc., and left for London.[92] After a lengthy discussion the jury accepted the arguments put by Sir Thomas Abney and ruled for Henry Moore's admission, i.e., upholding the right of the eldest son was upheld.[93]

Hastings jurats and a majority of the Assembly were unimpressed, and a discussion ensued as to how far this decision of the King's Bench could be thwarted. Whereas Henry Pelham and John Collier thought the Corporation should now accept this ruling rather than risk an appeal enlarging the decision, the jurats and the Assembly refused. Hardwicke and other judges rejected their appeal.[94] The Corporation then refused to convene a special Assembly, and at the next Court of Record, 16 April 1737, whereat a freeman was created, Moore was ignored. A month on, at the next business session, 14 May 1737 only after normal business was finished, did the Assembly agree to his admittance as a freeman and he kissed the deputy Mayor's cheek **[162]**.[95] Anticipating this, John Collier left the town the previous day.

So what happened to the Hastings Custumal? According to Manwaring Baines, the original vanished after the Attorney General read out sections to the King's Bench. This venerable manuscript, which contained so many details of the town's customs, precedents and history provided evidence for the Corporation's case, and yet the skill of Sir Thomas Abney used the custumal to prove the right of the eldest son. As T H B Oldfield pointed out in 1817, the same evidence by which Henry Moore availed himself, established the 'right of every other son of a freeman to his freedom', so underpinned Sir Thomas Webster's case for an increase in the number of freemen. Worrying for Newcastle and Henry Pelham was the thought that this verdict might be cited for the situation of freedom for other Cinque Ports. Indeed, during subsequent legal challenges in King's Bench in respect of Seaford, requests were made for the lost Hastings Custumal.[96] Fortunately, other versions of old Hastings Custumals have survived: William Durrant Cooper and Thomas Ross transcribed a copy from Norman French found in the Rye archives and published in *SAC* in 1862; Manwaring Baines augmented this in *Historic Hastings* using a 'tattered copy' in Elizabethan handwriting found in the muniments room of Hastings museum; R F Dell described the collection of customs and precedents in *Records of Rye Corporation* which included folios of Hastings customs written in 'a late 15th-century hand'; and a set of Hastings customs and precedents is with the Newcastle Mss in the British Library.[97]

Smuggling

Why was smuggling a permanent problem? By the early years of Georgian Sussex smuggling was a growing threat to the collection of the Customs and Excise duties. 'I find' wrote John Collier to his wife in 1737 that 'the smuggling trade goes on at a high rate and soe there is accounts from all parts, but more particularly Sussex and Kent' **[168]**. For four years since his appointment as Surveyor of the riding officers for Kent John Collier gained a closer understanding of smuggling than available from his horizon as Hastings town clerk, engaged as he now was on the capture and prosecution of offenders from all over Kent. As mentioned above from 1733 for around a month his tour as Surveyor took him to all the ports of Kent, looking into the work of the riding officers, and much else. Apart from his base in the Hastings office shared with William Battine, Collier worked in the London custom house: he was highly regarded by officials, especially so for his insight on how to make prosecutions effective. The correspondence collected in the Sayer Mss constitute one of the more important collections on Sussex and Kent smuggling, and books and papers penned by John Collier in the National Archives describe the detail of numerous prosecutions he undertook.

Smuggling was encouraged by protectionist legislation and rising tariffs: from 1660 to 1745 no fewer than 23 anti-smuggling statutes passed through Parliament, and Sussex and Kent ports were adversely affected both by warfare in the Channel, and the refusal by Parliament in 1713 to ratify the economic clauses of the Treaty of Utrecht. Local farmers and fishermen supplied the horses and carts and provided the warehouses that smugglers needed **[121, 129]**. The evidence printed in this volume suggests numerous fishing boats and trading vessels in the illegal trades had little difficulty in recruiting crews. The ordinary labourers on land, used to wages set by the Lewes Assize courts at around 8d a day out of harvest, could earn 2s and more a shift from exporters of raw wool, an illegal trade, and likewise from importers of illegal goods from the continent, unloading vessels close to beaches, or directly through ports. Organising this smuggling activity by British subjects and foreign merchants was quite legal on the continent, and thus beyond the reach of the British customs officers. It should be noticed that the sheer number of references to smuggling operations in the public records for decades since the early seventeenth century betokens the development of a traditional acceptance by many in the coastal areas and further afield towards carrying and distributing smuggled goods. To what extent such a tradition might have existed beyond the lure of ready money is unknown, though these papers suggest smuggling operations were growing in scale and impudence in the years covered by this correspondence and were not just the agitated response of officials hoping for more income and staff.

How did politics affect smuggling prosecutions? John Collier's work was more complicated than prosecutions for smuggling, infringements of customs rates, and alterations to the work of Kent riding officers. The Customs Commissioners used every possible legal route to interfere with smugglers: alongside regular alterations to statute law, Customs officers tried to block licences for premises used by smugglers **[241]**, information was sought from local folk, confiscation of horses and carts and boats was a regular topic discussed between officers and the courts.[98] Indeed, being close to the central office in the London Customs house gave John Collier and William Cranston an excellent overview of how the officials saw their legal duties, and how cases might proceed. But any case relating to the Cinque Ports had political ramifications, especially so if the accused were freemen, or related to freemen. Such a case emerged whilst John Collier was canvassing in August 1733. Over sixty freeholders signed a petition begging for leniency from the Duke of Newcastle in the case of the smuggler Thomas Black of Hastings. Collier suggested that Black's brother ask all to sign a letter asking the Duke for compassion confirming that 'they shall esteem it a great favour and will entirely join in his Grace's interest at the next election'.[99]

Such cases are interesting not just because of the audacity of the accused in their dealings with authority or even the apparent widespread support amongst freeholders and local worthies for smuggling: it was the voting implications which the Duke took seriously. Even the convicted appear to assume their position was as much a political matter as well as a legal one, an interesting concept which fits a pattern applicable to other cases recorded in the Collier papers in the National Archives.[100] Smugglers and their legal and business advisors and financiers evolved legal defences against revenue officers which would stand up in court, even launching their own prosecutions against officers and soldiers, prosecuting for wrongful arrest, for false accusations, for illegal woundings and gaoling of smugglers, and for seizure of smugglers' vessels. Literalist defences were built around the precise meanings of the English used in statutes, of the starting date for new offences and of legal moves to defer cases until a later court thereby making it more difficult to gather witnesses, and resulting in time and expense keeping officers away from work.

As part of their concern for the scale of illegal activity, by 1735 the legal authorities and the Customs and Excise Commissioners decided on a form of legal amnesty, designed for the smuggler known to have committed serious crimes although now claiming to be a reformed character and who might be granted immunity for past crimes. Such a generous approach would absolve many smugglers in this era of Anglo-French peace when they could obtain legal fishing, seafaring and haulage work. So it came to pass that by an Act of 9 Geo. II c. 35 anyone who before 27 April 1736 transgressed the Customs and Excise laws, and any person who 'beat, abused, obstructed, or hindered any officer in execution of their duty', or who gave or offered bribes to any officer, should [now] be acquitted, indemnified, released and discharged, providing that they had ceased any illegal activity, and where applicable 'any receiving the benefit of this amnesty [will] have stopped any prosecution of Customs and Excise officers'.[101] This Act tightened up loopholes, and did not extend to murder, although the central feature was an amnesty offering smugglers a return to normal trade and work without fear of arrest.

The correspondence here highlights difficult Customs cases regarding the amnesty where the timing of exemption from prosecution was part of the plea for the defence and raises questions as to whether the wording of the section 1 amnesty clause in 9 Geo. II c. 35 clashed with wording elsewhere in the Act. To be on more certain legal grounds some Hastings ex-smugglers asked the town Mayor for guidance, and, after reassurance about the legal powers of Hastings courts, at the Hastings General Quarter Sessions, on 10 January 1737 twenty-eight acknowledged smugglers requested immunity from prosecution under the terms of this Act, and were severally discharged by proclamation under the Mayor's hand.[102] This meant that they were indeed free to resume ordinary trade without fear of arrest for past misdeeds. But there arose a question: were the twenty-eight right to assume the Hastings General Quarter Sessions could extend the amnesty beyond section 1 of the Act, from 27 April 1736 to 10 January 1737, and did the Hastings ruling cover all other sections of the Act? On 13 March 1738, four of these repentant smugglers, John Grayling, John Taught, John Bird and Nicholas Harman were arraigned before the East Grinstead Assizes charged under 9 Geo. II c. 35, sections 28 & 29, together with Thomas Holman and William Harman. These sub-sections provided for 7 years transportation for the wounding of Customs officers on board a vessel within the limits of any port of the kingdom, on or after 24 June 1736. The accused on 24 June and 11 August 1736, all armed, confronted James Lever am, a mariner on the *Amelia* sloop, under Captain Nathaniel Epigram and 'wound and beat him'. The upshot was that John Grayling, as well as John Bird, William Harman, John Taught, and Thomas Holman received 7 years transportation to the colonies or plantations in north America. The deportations were carried out.[103] Fifteen months later on 12 December 1738 John Collier informed the Customs Commissioners that these convicted smugglers had escaped and now lurked in or near Hastings operating as smugglers.[104] For five years they evaded justice and later evidence suggests they lived in France at various times.

By 9 Geo. II c. 35, s. 28, should any such offenders returning to Britain or Ireland before the expiration of their seven year sentence, 'shall suffer as felons' and be hanged. However, with the outbreak of war with Spain a shortfall in crewing warships emerged and in May 1741 a proclamation was issued pardoning smugglers who joined the navy **[313]**. The declaration of war against France, 29 March 1743, aggravated the labour problem.[105] So, to ease the manpower problem of the navy on 9 May 1744 the privy council issued another proclamation 'for pardoning persons guilty of clandestine importation' who joined the naval service, so offering pardon to such recruits.[106] Grayling and the other smugglers, who had not completed their seven years of transportation, in June 1744 sailed across to Sussex and requested clarification from the Duke of Newcastle of the terms of this second amnesty, issued as a proclamation **[452, 455, 457]**. The Duke's office passed the question to the Attorney General, but before a decision was reached the smugglers decided to flee to France being informed by William Cranston that the decision might be unfavourable. Captured by a privateer they ended up in Newgate, where William Cranston and John Collier informed them the proclamation probably did not cover their case.

The Mayor and jurats of Hastings argued the case for the smugglers, alongside John Collier and William Cranston and whilst this was ongoing Parliament passed an 'Act to indemnify persons who have been guilty of the unlawful importing, landing or running or prohibited, uncustomed or other goods or merchandise'.[107] Widely heralded by officials it was assumed in Hastings that this Act would be similar to that of 1736, and bring the amnesty dates forward to 1745. **[493-5, 500, 502]**. But it was clear to William Cranston that the Act omitted mention of assault on Customs and Excise officers, and he passed this worry to Collier on 9 May 1745 [**500**]. The new line of defence was written up in a petition to the Duke of Newcastle, arguing that if the indemnity Act did not include these men, 'it was by an inadvertence only, and that their case was a hard one, and one in which a pardon might well be granted'. The Duke of Richmond, a senior military commander, in frequent contact with the Duke of Newcastle, was not sympathetic, and showed evident delight in discovering that neither the Act nor proclamation covered the smugglers misdeeds. Quite how this was going to be resolved shows us much about the political position of the Cinque Ports in swaying legal affairs. William Cranston was certainly prepared to push leniency as far as possible, even offending the Duke of Newcastle at one meeting. It may perhaps be inferred, as Charles Lane Sayer reasoned from a letter to Mr Pelham **[519]** that Collier thought 'a greater degree of lenity would have produced a better effect.'[108] Eventually the Admiralty Commissioners solved this awkwardness by recruiting Grayling and the other miscreants directly into the navy.[109]

John Collier was now accused of aiding the enemy. In command of the Channel naval forces from the summer of 1744 was Admiral Edward Vernon, a popular MP and hero of the combined army-navy assault with 30 ships of the line on Cartagena, Cuba and Panama in 1741-2. Whilst this military operation cost the lives of most of the British land forces, it enhanced Vernon's reputation and ensured his leading place in the effort to stop Marshall Saxe from invading the south east of England. Vernon knew that the Cinque Ports were home to smugglers who plied the Channel, and intelligence from the Dutch and foreign based agents confirmed these smugglers acted as pilots and guides for the French in planning the invasion, and in passing information on army positions in Kent, Essex and Sussex. In his letters to the Admiralty, Treasury and the Duke of Newcastle reference is made to the economic damage of smuggling, although, with the invasion looming, greater weight is placed on such 'traitorous correspondence with his Majesty's enemies', the passing of information on English fleet positions, and recruitment of smugglers to support the enemy's supply chain.[110]

Admiral Vernon demanded quartering of more dragoons and soldiers in the Channel ports along John Collier's tour of Kent to intercept the export of labour, break up the spy rings, and enforce a tougher press on the able bodied layabouts in the Cinque Ports who 'have no visible way of getting a living but by the infamous trade of smuggling'. Such action would address the tragedy that 'smuggling has converted those employed in it, from honest, industrious fishermen, to lazy, drunken and profligate smugglers, and now to dangerous spies on all our proceedings for the enemy's daily information' adding 'I should think it criminal in me not to inform their lordships of it. I can't but think it a national reproach upon us to have let their villainy and treachery run to such extensive lengths'. He blamed lack of action at all levels of civil authority in the ports opposite France and the Low countries.[111] The shortage of sailors ought to be addressed by pressing those in the Cinque Ports 'now thought to be principally employed in the ruin of their country, by the smuggling trade, as daily spies to give the enemy intelligence of all our proceedings'. In Deal no fewer than 200 young men and seafaring people lived by smuggling, at Dover there might be 400, and at Ramsgate and Folkestone 300 each, with regular sailings to Boulogne.[112]

On 8 December 1745, with the invasion threat at its height, Captain Scott of the *Badger* seized two Hastings fishing boats belonging to George Harrison and Zebelton Morphett, the latter being one who forswore smuggling by oath under the first amnesty, in front of the Mayor and jurats in 1736, though arrested since, and Harrison being from a family of known smugglers. This was even more serious as Captain Scott found not only evidence of tea smuggling, but of gun running for the Jacobites.[113] 'Whatever calamities are like to befall us' wrote Vernon, 'I am persuaded their treachery has in a great measure contributed' adding that Morphett, the traitor, was being protected by John Collier.[114] The letters on his time in the Channel Command were published in the new year, accusing the Admiralty of curtailing the provision of ships, of sailing first rates in the late autumn and winter instead of smaller vessels, the Customs for failing to fight the smugglers effectively, the MPs for the Cinque Port towns who spent their time worrying about the voters, and, by implication, the Duke of Newcastle and his circle for failing to ensure the proper defence of the realm. However, when Vernon's case was put finally to the Commons the Treasury bench was buzzing with the nearness of victory over the Jacobites, and brushed the complaints aside.

John Collier's answer to the accusations was limited. Perhaps he thought a public argument with Vernon would be mistaken, and the Secretary of the Customs told him to stay quiet. For the record, Collier posted a lengthy defence to Henry Pelham around the 29 May 1746: after dismissing the newspaper alarms about smuggling gangs in and around Hastings, and declining to refute them for fear of encouraging further comments, and 'apprehending I should be esteemed as an encourager of [smuggling] practices, especially as it was so insinuated in one of the pamphlets of Mr Vernon. I gave the latter an account of ships appearing, and sent off boats express to him thereof, for which I had his thanks, but when he thought proper to print his *Seasonable Advice* he takes notice of one letter I sent him, with a sort of an insinuation of my being an encourager of smugling, but ungenerously leaves out that point that I think should clear me from such an imputation' adding that a copy of that letter **[538]** was posted to Andrew Stone 'and to several other gentlemen in town'.[115] The Duke of Newcastle and Henry Pelham understood the considerable efforts by Collier on behalf of the defence of the east Sussex and Kent coasts, and his success in thwarting the Jacobite correspondence with France: the capture of James Bishop before his escape to France is discussed here **[549, 550, 551, 556, 558, 560]**. As for George Harrison and Zebelton Morphett they eventually escaped execution, the former was absorbed into the navy and Morphett likewise was in service by 26 November 1745, through careful work by William Cranston and town worthies.

Later years.

Towards the end of his life John Collier simplified his paperwork, reducing the number of out of date accounts, including most financial paperwork from before the later 1720s. Accounts survive for Hastings property, farms and marshlands from September 1731 to July 1746. From these papers his estate showed an average gross rental of £850 17s each year from 1731 to 1735, with net cash of £652 9s; overall higher land and sewer taxes for marshland, and lower deductions for Hastings houses[116]. By 1743 gross rentals had risen to

£1077 3s, net £718 5s[117]. As Manwaring Baines noticed, yearly deductions from estates varied, with the land tax down to one shilling in the pound in 1731 though the later years of war, and costs of fencing, brickwork plus damage to farms and buildings, could see net cash income decline, occasionally sharply. Net house rentals tended to be stable over time, although the larger incomes came from farms and marshland. Thinking of his family, in particular the future of his five girls from his second marriage, who also survived infancy encouraged John Collier to spend the rise in his legal and government earnings on more land, and to diversify his holdings, which eventually included 54 acres 2 rod on the Isle of Oxney[118]. At Michaelmas 1758 a list of the rental of the Collier estate showed a gross income of £1459 2s 10d, with arrears of £1858 4s 6d.

How high was Collier's social standing? Collier occasionally attended extravagant evening dinners run by the leading Whigs, including at least one organised by the Duke of Richmond **[176]**, although it was more in a professional and political capacity that he was invited to dinner; even so, he wrote to, and spoke often, with Henry Pelham, the Duke of Newcastle, Sir William Ashburnham, the Attorney and Solicitor General, various counsel and London lawyers, and fellow Sussex lawyers and landowners. By 1742 Collier decided he not only needed a coat of arms, but a robust carriage to put them on [**495-497**]. Heather Warne has noticed that in all the letters he wrote Collier does not mention the Duke of Norfolk and his associates, indeed, the only reference to Catholics were as nurses or servants, including Mrs Nouns, a reputed Jacobite **[191, 218, 219, 273, 308, 312, 352]**. Tradesmen and the more modest ranks are mentioned, though only a few, such as James Bossom, the seafarer, seem to have been on equal terms, and Collier may have genuinely disliked some of the earthier conversation among the lower ranks.

Until his mid-sixties John Collier managed his places and income as usher and crier of the King's Bench and Surveyor General of the Riding Officers of Kent, his work on behalf of the Duke of Newcastle in local politics and for the estates of Sir William Ashburnham, Edward Caryll and Henry Pelham. As gout and ailments crept over him occasional concern was expressed at the pressures of business, and the threats from the smugglers, and he confided in the Customs Solicitor **[471]** that he would prefer to do fewer prosecutions. Collier suffered a paralytic fit in late 1746, aged 60, followed by serious physical pain. Visits to Tunbridge Wells and Bath provided sufficient relief to allow resumption of short-lived energetic responses during the worst of the smuggling gang upsurge in 1747 and 1748. John Collier was ailing though and much of his legal and corporation work in Hastings was conducted by his surviving son, and after James's death in 1747, by his wife and daughters and Richard Patrick, now his main assistant, and soon by Edward Milward who married Collier's daughter Mary. This volume carries the correspondence of his most successful years in local politics and business and the upbringing of his children, when he was at the height of his powers. The Sussex Record Society is deeply grateful to the Sayer family for the opportunity to bring these papers to a wider audience.

John Collier's papers:

The transcripts in this volume come primarily from correspondence and papers in the Sayer Manuscripts in the East Sussex Record Office, a collection which includes over 6000 documents. The archive is named after the family into which Sarah Collier married and which were preserved in Old Hastings House and then in Suffolk until their eventual loan to the East Sussex record office, lodged at the Keep, near Brighton. These relate primarily to the affairs of John Collier, Mary his second wife, and her brother William Cranston: there are also materials relevant to the Hastings corporation and the life and times of several other relatives and associates. Most of the archive dates from the early years of the 1730s: unfortunately, much earlier business correspondence, as well as some legal records and account books, were destroyed as John Collier neared death, believing that the removal of out of date material would 'make the task of my executors easier'. Several letters in the Newcastle papers held in the British Library penned by John Collier are included here in respect of the election of 1734, and other manuscripts consulted are referred to as appropriate in the entry notes.

On Collier's death in 1760 his executors and family sorted over the thousands of personal letters, household papers, legal documents, account books, title deeds, Customs and Excise memoranda, and materials relating to events in Hastings and other of the Cinque Ports. John Collier and his wife also collected a library of historical, literary and religious books as well as sermons, statutes and miscellaneous papers in Old Hastings House. A list of these has survived.[119] The larger group of manuscripts, including most of the correspondence, were preserved by his daughter Mary, who married Edward Milward of Hastings in 1754, and by their daughter Sarah, who married Henry Sayer of Lincoln's Inn in 1763. A group of account books and papers were collected by John Manwaring Baines, curator of the Hastings Museum, bundles of advices on prosecutions written by John Collier survived in the Customs House library before their removal to the Public Record Office, now the National Archives, Kew Gardens, and the Hastings Corporation archives cover Collier's record as a public servant of the town, as do additional papers in the British Library. The volumes written by Thomas Brandon Brett (1816-1906) contain material from the Collier archive, and include reference to papers since dispersed.[120] In 1902 the *Sussex Archaeological Collections* published W V Crake 'The Correspondence of John Collier, five times Mayor of Hastings, and his connection with the Pelham family'[121] which article prints part or all of fifty-seven letters plus portraits of John Collier, Edward Milward, senior and junior, and a genealogy of the family. John Manwaring Baines published material from the Collier correspondence in *Historic Hastings* (1986). Charles Lane Sayer, *Correspondence of John Collier (Deceased) 1716-1760* (1907) published two volumes of letters including a number which have not been found. Several of the books and articles cited in the bibliography below include extracts from the Collier archive and refer to records lodged in the British Library and the East Sussex Record Office. Included in this volume are more portraits of the family, painted by Arthur Devis (1712-1787), and the Society is most grateful to the Sayer family and the Trustees of the Magdalen and Lasher charity who own Old Hastings House for permission to publish these. We also wish to thank Hannah Miles, the Archivist of the Hastings Museum, for her assistance in locating additional papers, photographs and drawings of Hastings, several of which are published here, and the staff of the Hastings Fisheries Museum for their assistance on drawings and photographs. The Collier archive was first calendared by Heather M Warne (nee Mathews) in her *The Papers of John Collier of Hastings: a Catalogue*, Diploma on Archive Administration, University of London (September, 1966)[122] and all users are indebted to her organisation of this vast archive. Her restoration of the papers to the original Georgian divisions in the order laid out by John Collier was a considerable aid to transcription: for work on the collection members are directed to Heather Warne's catalogue.

NOTES

[1] Charles Lane Sayer gives his date of birth as 12 November 1685 (Sayer vol. 2, 230).

[2] Both Peter Collier and his eldest son, also Peter, were listed under Eastbourne for the 1705 poll for the Sussex county, voting for Henry Lumley and Sir George Parker, alongside the other 40 shilling freeholders resident in the town. John Collier was not recorded. Peter Collier's will, proved in 1717, indicates income sufficient to provide for his wife Sarah and the children at his death, although as John Collier was then 32, and established as an attorney since 1706, it is likely that his own income was sufficient for his children's learning. John Collier and Sarah his mother were the joint executors for his father's will. Sarah died in 1734 **[84, 85]**.

[3] SAY 3539; Sarah Collier married Samuel Cruttenden of Hastings and they lived in a cottage next to her brother John.

[4] See Caffyn 104-5; other schools followed in Georgian Eastbourne (*ibid.*, 105-8; J E Wadey *Schools and Schooling in Sussex* (2) *1579-1686 SNQ* 14 (1954-57) 270-7); if this was not John Collier's first school it is likely he would have had to travel and board away from home.

[5] Oaths were repeated each year, 'John Collier, jurat, produced a certificate of his having received the sacrament of the Lord's supper according to the usage of the Church of England and took and subscribed the oaths of allegiance, supremacy and abjuration and likewise made and subscribed the declaration against trans-substantiation as the law directs' (ESRO HAS CAA/4, 476, 31 August 1728).

[6] The basis for the oath was laid out in 1688/9 by 1 Wm & Mary c. 1 and c.8 with subsequent amendments; *EB* (1771) vol. 2 404 defines an oath sworn on the Bible as 'a solemn affirmation, in which the persons sworn invoke the Almighty to witness that their testimony is true, removing all claim to his mercy, and calling for his vengeance, if it be false'; oaths were required to be overseen and witnessed by town magistrates; R F Dell *The Records of Rye Corporation: A Catalogue* (Lewes, 1962) 10-12, lists the collection of registers and papers relating to these oaths for Rye; C Condren *Argument and Authority in Early Modern England: the presupposition of oaths and offices* (2006) discusses some relevant developments.

[7] Dell describes these roles and lists the Customs, Precedents and Custumals at Rye; for the administration of the Cinque Ports see K M E Murray *The Constitutional History of the Cinque Ports* (1935).

[8] Baines 377 lists the dates of Collier's office as town clerk as 1706-1718, 1720-21, 1723-29, 1731-36, 1738-40, and 1742-49, where is listed the fees and payments for town clerks and notes on his children. All Hastings jurats were included in the Parliamentary list of Commissioners for the annual land tax.

[9] SAY 1332.

[10] William Dugdale *The History of Imbanking and Drayning* (1662) discusses the complexity of management of the levels.

[11] Both Sue Berry and Peter Wilkinson have raised this question of succession in the Georgian age.

[12] Caffyn 287; for detail of 1750 map showing John Collier's residence, see SAY 1415 f. 289; Hastings Public Library also has one of the maps drawn by Cant; S Peak *Fishermen of Hastings: 200 years of the Hastings fishing community* (1985) reprints the Hastings map of 1769 which shows the main streets, the strand, and the roads above the town.

[13] ESRO MIL 7/23.

[14] John Manwaring Baines, appendix to the booklet in the Hastings Public Library on the Old Hastings House, then styled the Mansion House. It is unclear where the funds for the purchase came from, or how credit might have been organised.

[15] Dunkin 1907

[16] See Caffyn 379 for a facsimile of letter from John Collier, 14 June 1729 SAY 1529 to eldest son, John, at Mrs Thorpe's school in Battle.

[17] The Act required all to swear an oath of allegiance to the Hanoverian succession, including a refutation of the claims of James VIII and his successors: continued by 12 Geo. II c. 39. Collier and Cranston again appeared before a judge and signed the lists, as did other Sussex and Middlesex

attorneys who appear in this correspondence. Both Collier and Cranston were indeed fluent in written Latin, necessary for attorneys as Latin was used for numerous legal documents, and Latin was required for work in the Westminster courts before 25 March 1733, when 4 Geo II c. 26 required legal documents and proceedings henceforth to be in English. For the signatures and required oaths see TNA KB 24/3; an explanation is given in Edmund B V Christian *A Short History of Solicitors* (London: 1896) 112-6.

[18] Brett vol. 3, 6.

[19] For church tithes and pierwardens' accounts see Baines 226; the Church of England took a tithe of these catches.

[20] Window taxes for 1742 totalled £55 4s 0d: St Clements paid 67%: All Saints 27% and Castle parish and outbounds, with few houses, just 5%.

[21] For the detail of salt and fish policy see E Hughes *Studies in Administration and Finance 1558-1825 with special reference to the history of salt taxation in England* (1934).

[22] For the years covered by this volume government fish policy was laid out in Acts of 1705, 1718, 1723 and 1733 and was designed to support the workings of the Salt department, established in 1702 and which by 1730 employed 438 officers. The MPs with an interest in salt and fish policies formed an effective economic interest in Parliament; in wartime MPs also protected the fishermen against the press, and negotiated temporary and often unsuccessful arrangements with the French designed to allow the fishermen of either country free access to Channel and North Sea fishing grounds.

[23] The assessments of 5s came from St Clements parish, Edward Dyne, Edward Milward, Edward Welsh, Henry Carleton, Richard Chambers, Thomas Godley, Thomas Gyles and John Collier, Brett vol. 3, 1-5.

[24] See Garraway Rice *Sussex Apprentices and Masters 1710-1752* (1924); those put out to trade by public charge were exempt from payment, and thus a stamp was not required, though the apprenticeship was recorded by the Board.

[25] Pratt 249.

[26] Diana Crook *Defying the Demon, Smallpox in Sussex* (2006)

[27] Thomas Collier, born 10 December 1732, died 2 August 1733.

[28] James Collier died at Johnson's Court; letters in the Sayer Mss refer to James' fits (Sayer vol. 1, 344, 371).

[29] Sayer vol. 1, 40-44.

[30] Brett vol. 3, 12, 27.

[31] Sayer vol. 1, 18-20, 2 December 1718, John Collier to Mary.

[32] In his London day book Collier penned a short elegy to Jacky:

> ah my poor son, ah my tender child
> my unblown flower, new appearing sweets
> If yet your gentle soul flys in the air
> and is not fixt in doom perpetual
> hover about me with your airy wings
> and hear your father's lamentations
> (SAY 1418 f. 79b).

[33] Sayer vol. 1, 379, 22 August, 31 October 1747.

[34] *Ibid.*, 389, 24 December 1747.

[35] SAY 681 gives the itemised bill for Jacky's treatment, SAY 687 likewise the bill for James' treatment.

[36] Advice summed up in *EB* 1771 vol. 3, 125-8.

[37] Dobson, M J *Contours of Death and Disease in Early Modern England* (1997).

[38] *Ibid.*, Dobson's work contains numerous charts and analyses for such comparisons.

[39] Radcliff 31.

[40] Sayer vol.1, 144 implies the illness Cordelia suffered when sixteen was different from four years earlier.

[41] I am indebted to Sue Berry for information on Dr Richard Russell.
[42] Elizabeth M D Morris *The Education of Girls in England from 1600-1800* (Kings College, M.A, 1926, ch. 4) on boarding schools in Hackney and Chelsea; texts which discuss the social attraction of Hampstead include the *VCH* Middlesex, vol. 9, A Maxwell *Hampstead: Its Historic Houses, its Literary and Artistic Associations* (1912) and T J Barratt *The Annals of Hampstead* (1912).
[43] ESRO SAY 2019, 2072.
[44] Jonathan and Anne Russell, owners of the boarding school for educating and bringing up of young ladies at Hampstead in Middlesex, were involved in a legal dispute over inheritance with the trustees for Elizabeth Hoskins, aged 12, over a will drawn up 6 July 1724 which made Anne Russell the executor of Elizabeth Hoskins' estate. Hoskins died of alcohol related poisoning five days after, on 11 July 1724 (TNA PROB 18/39/28, PROB 18/39/94).
[45] Imports of plain, stained and printed cottons from India rose fast in the later seventeenth century; preferred for feel, ease of washing and superior colours for clothing, and a wide range of printed patterns for curtains, chairs, cushions, bed and table linen. Such imports of printed cottons were forbidden after pressure from woollen interests 11 & 12 Wm III c.10, though difficult to enforce, as legal disputes following seizures created uncertainty over the Act's intent. The complicated sequel, 7 Geo I. 1, c.7, 'An Act to preserve and encourage the woollen and silk manufactures of this kingdom', confirmed Pierre Mantoux's verdict that 'rarely does law triumph over fashion', a view illustrated by the letters from John Collier, and his day book. Amongst other complexities the Act omitted certain cottons from prohibition, and manufactured printed goods were not clearly excluded; also, although a ban on buying and selling of named calicoes was incorporated, dealing for exports was allowed as was domestic British manufacture designed for export. Smugglers proved adept at supplying demand, as recognised by 9 Geo II c.4, which, among several clauses, specifically excluded from prohibition printed linen and cotton goods made in Britain (Mantoux 207; B Krishna, *Commercial Relations between India and England 1601 to 1757* (1924) 326).
[46] Ashburnham Place, Chiddingly Place, Brickwall, Battle Abbey, and other East Sussex residences visited by the Collier girls all needed reliable servants; and here personal recommendation was everything, as with the upper ranks at all times there was little care about formal training: house and kitchen servants should be personable, discreet, clean, tidy and good at their work.
[47] Elizabeth Dunmoll, of East Grinstead, married Thomas Hickes of Mountfield, gent, 22 July 1707 (Dunkin 1907; Llewellyn plate 15, 235 for Thomas Hickes).
[48] These accounts are available in the East Sussex Record Office (SAY 677 to SAY 706), and cover several years before this volume begins, and continue to 1746: they record both debit and credit and the resulting balance, and were originally kept by William Cranston in London, with a regular correspondence and a month-by-month balance sent to John Collier in Hastings, or given to him when he was in London. These accounts are similar to those of many partnerships and associations at this time, and enabled both sides of the partnership to see how financial affairs progressed over the years.
[49] This gross income was reduced by the charges for the land tax, for repairs to farm buildings, for fences and for digging out the drains on the levels; the making of bricks and roof tiles is discussed in M Beswick *Brickmaking in Sussex: A History and Gazetteer* 2nd edn., (2001).
[50] Charles Lane Sayer cites correspondence over a loan of £400 made by John Collier to an official of the London Customs house in 1746, not repaid by 1760 (Sayer vol. 1, 320-1).
[51] A complicated boundary dispute between the Corporation and Sir Charles Eversfield, an outdweller, for which John Collier represented the Corporation, left John Collier owing only £61 1s 2d for this debt.
[52] On 10 August 1723 Collier lent £100 at 3% to pay off debts due for building work for the church; as the building costs overran by another £200, Collier also advanced the remaining debt and charges amounting to £213 (ESRO PAR 367/12/1).
[53] On 19 June 1733 John Collier wrote to Mary that having supported Elphick 'long enough' the time was nigh when this should end, but would probably continue if she thought fit **[67]** (ESRO SAY 1339-1342).

[54] Ewen 108, 125, 176.
[55] *Ibid.*, 163 table.
[56] J M Baines, *The Bailiff of the Bourne and his office* (Hastings Museum pamphlet no. 20 5-6) gives the date as 1609, and Baines 164, cites a scot of £100 to be levied to buy and place lead pipes to convey water from higher up the town. The state of knowledge available is reviewed by R J Forbes 'Hydraulic Engineering and Sanitation' and B Gille 'Machines' in C Singer, E J Holmyard and T I Williams (eds) *A History of Technology*: vol. 2, *Mediterranean Civilization and the Middle Ages c. 700-1500* (1956); B Rudden *The New River: A Legal History* (1985) 99ff. discusses the technical challenge presented by wooden pipes.
[57] William Holloway, *The History and Antiquities of the Ancient Town and Port of Rye in the County of Sussex* (1847) 333-6; the town papers for these waterworks are listed by Dell 85-88.
[58] Hodgkinson 2009a 82-3; Cleere and Crossley 200, 203-4.
[59] These cases were brought during the election disputes of 1734 by opponents of John Collier and the Whig interest.
[60] Brett vol. 3, 15.
[61] ESRO SAY 1418.
[62] Charles Lane Sayer, vol. 2, 173-5, transcribes a letter from William Cranston to John Collier, 1 November 1755 which gives a clear account of winter road conditions from Battle over the Weald to Croydon; J A Chartres 'Road carrying in the seventeenth century: myth and reality' *EcHR* 2nd series 30 (1977) explains the gradual improvement of English roads.
[63] S B Nulle *Thomas Pelham Holles, Duke of Newcastle, His Early Political Career 1693-1724* (1931) explains the importance of the Pelham family and the early work of the Duke of Newcastle; for the Pelham family genealogy see Coxe 1829 vol. 1, Genealogy of the Pelham family, tables B, C and Williams 1966 15-18; before 1727 the usual fee for election as a Hastings freeman was 13s 4d, and 6s 8d for sons of existing freemen or those holding the post of Chamberlain; when the young Newcastle was created a freeman of the port, he paid £388 18s 7d for the entertainment of the Mayor, corporation and freemen (*SNQ* 7 232-3; Baines 41; BL Add Ms 33064 f.38 17 January 1714); after 1727 the ordinary fee rose to 40s and 20s (Baines 36); figures for the number of MPs varied slightly between elections; for 1702 see A Browning (ed.) *English Historical Documents* vol. 8, *1660-1714* (London, 1953), 217-222.
[64] *HofP 1690 to 1715* vol. 2, 594-98, 759-63; on 26 January 1715 Hastings returned Henry Pelham with 66 votes, Archibald Hutcheson on 55 votes; the defeated Sir Joseph Martin received 23 votes (*HofP 1715-1754*. vol. 1, 365-6).
[65] Baines included in the list of Hutcheson's benefactions the record from a chancel tablet in St Clement's: £100 for church repairs, £125 in paving with marble, wainscoting, painting the chancel, making iron rails for the altar piece, gifts of communion plate, velvet for the communion table; plus £300 for the building and re-building of ships registered with the Corporation, and for the benefit of the poor, £100 as the fount of a perpetual zero interest fund for poor working fishermen, and funding for the free school organised by the SPCK. The zero interest fund chimed well with Hutcheson's indictment of the damage to the poor caused by compound interest charges (Baines 48-9).
[66] Among the accusations levelled against Hutcheson from this time were crypto-Jacobitism and other pro-Tory leanings (*HofP 1690-1715* vol. 2, 163-4; vol. 4, 451).
[67] Archibald Hutcheson, *A Collection of Treatises Relating to the National Debt and Funds* (1717-19); *A Collection of Treatises Relating to the South Sea Stock and Scheme* (1721); Coxe 1798 vol. 3, 73; *Political State* vol, 33, 308-10; BL Add Ms. 33064 f.38.
[68] Archibald Hutcheson, *A Collection of Advertisements, Letters and Papers, and some other facts relating to the last election at Westminster and Hastings* (1722) viii.
[69] When the campaign opened in the autumn of 1721 John Collier was town clerk, with Edward Milward, also an attorney, as Mayor: the Jurats and freemen were split. On the 25 November John Pulteney announced his candidature, with Newcastle 'strenuously' opposed to Hutcheson's re-election. His Grace even canvassed freemen and jurats in person, and Captain James Pelham, the Duke's cousin, accompanied Sir William Ashburnham on a house to house canvass in support of Pulteney. His Grace

later wrote to the Duchess that two freemen turned down £500 apiece to switch from Hutcheson, blaming John Collier for persuading them otherwise adding that Collier even asked for a place as a tide-waiter, with an enhanced salary of £100 as the price of his vote (Archibald Hutcheson, *Copies of some letters and papers relating to the election at Hasting, in Sussex*, which includes the poll list; BL Add Ms 33073 f. 13; *HofP 1715-1754* vol. 1, 365-6).

[70] Representing Hastings the canopy bearers for the King were Sir William Ashburnham, Thomas Pelham of Stanmer, Edward Dyne, Mayor elect; for the Queen, John Collier, solicitor of the Cinque Ports and deputy Mayor, Thomas Townshend, nephew of the Duke of Newcastle, and James Pelham of Crowhurst.

[71] *HofP 1715-1754*, vol. 2, 333-4, 474.

[72] Basil Williams made a similar point in respect of the difference between Hastings and the three other Cinque Ports in Sussex, (Williams 1897 459).

[73] John Collier to Duke of Newcastle 4 September 1733 (BL Add Ms 32688 f.251).

[74] Although the land tax declined as a proportion of total direct and indirect taxes from the 1690s to the 1720s, landowners felt that the cash paid out of rentals was a burden and should be redistributed more widely, and this question was raised in Parliament every year. Walpole made efforts to hold the tax down, thus for 1722-26 it fell to 2s in the £ of every land valuation, but with fears of war in 1727 it rose to 4s, the usual wartime level, and for the next two years land tax stayed at 3s. In fact the principles underlying foreign policy worked to maintain peace with France and Spain, and so the opportunity arose to reduce this level and shift the tax burden towards indirect taxes. In 1730 Walpole reduced the land tax to 2s, and in 1731 to 1s. As this fall to 1s required a modest rise in indirect taxation, Sir Robert agreed to resurrect the salt tax. As Rapin paraphrased Walpole's summary, 'no tax could be more general as that in salt, scarcely felt by individuals, be they ever so poor'. On 9/10 February 1732, the Commons carried the motion for the re-raising of the salt tax for three years by 225 to 187; as a result the land tax continued at 1s in 1732, and from 1733 to 1738 the charge was 2s in the £ (Dowell 2nd edn., vol. 3, 85-6; Ward 71-2; Rapin vol. 20, 113-6; Cobbett vol.8, 943, 9 February 1732; A E Bland, P A Brown, R H Tawney *English Economic History* (1914) 6, speech by Sir Robert Walpole). The concern over possible new Excise proposals is discussed in Williams 1897.

[75] BL Add. Ms. 32,688 f.123, f.139.

[76] Basil Williams concluded that Newcastle paid all the bills forwarded by his agents at this election (Williams 1897).

[77] Henry Pelham to Duke of Newcastle BL Add. Ms. 32688 f.307; the relevance of this letter was noticed by Williams 1897, 477, and by Heather Warne in her catalogue of the papers of John Collier.

[78] John Collier was sworn as Surveyor General on 20 November 1733 [**83**]; Guy Miege in listing the senior Customs appointments, noticed Collier as the 'Surveyor General of the Riding Officers appointed for the guard of Kent, at £250 a year, and Major William Batten, £250 a year for Sussex, for a clerk between them'.

[79] Hughes (1934) 311-13.

[80] In the general surveys, the Surveyor General was to comment on the attitude to work and the general conduct of the Customs officers, the difficulties of their station, how they kept their ledgers and journal books, whether they were full or part-time, and what type of outside work they undertook, if any. Their horses were to be inspected, how they kept in touch with neighbouring officers and how often, whether suitable arrangements were made for warehousing seized goods: were they, for instance kept in separate buildings under proper locks, or merely in locked rooms in public houses or corporation offices. The co-operation with the Customs cutters was of particular concern, and where relevant, how the joint patrols with the dragoons were conducted. Where officers patrolled roads from the coasts, the efficacy of stop and search was inquired after. Reports listed the method for keeping the wool registers (required by statute), whether officers should be moved and if their stations reduced in length the exact end-points to be noticed. In addition, Collier and Battine were to watch for indications of any Jacobite sympathies, and to notice the mood of the local population. Hoon 182-3 refers to Instructions to be

observed by Supervisors, 1734, and those to be observed by the Riding Officers, also 1734. Parliamentary debates and committees regularly referred to the workings of the Customs.

[81] Sir Thomas Webster also undertook a door to door canvas of the 40 shilling freeholders in Hastings, bringing along John Fuller, and offering free beer.

[82] Baines 33.

[83] Dell 43-58 gives a detailed listing of the creation of freemen from surviving Custumals and Precedents for Rye, which cover customs from other Cinque Ports.

[84] SAY 1418 f. 22v-23, and f. 26v-27.

[85] Legal cases on the waterworks were recorded by John Collier for the autumn of 1734 (ESRO SAY 1418 Michaelmas term 1734 f. 26v-27).

[86] BL Add Ms. 32689 f. 200.

[87] In the county election Henry Pelham gained 2271, James Butler 2053, Sir Cecil Bishop 1704, and John Fuller 1581 (Crossley & Saville xiv-xv).

[88] KB 1/4/5, Crown side, Affidavits, Michaelmas, 9 Geo II no 1, 24 October 1735.

[89] There was a political gain for John Collier. Countermand of the trial came at '10 at night' and the notification only reached William Coppard, Mayor of Hastings, the following morning 28th June. As Hastings Assembly was to deliberate that day on support for the Corporation's defence, Coppard sat on the letter; nineteen freemen refused their support for the defence, with sixteen signing the book, and who was who is carefully recorded in the Collier papers **[128]**. An accusation was also made that the Corporation books were tampered with **[124]**: folios 8r to 9 are missing from the Assembly book sent up to London, which pages cover the relevant dates.

[90] Howell vol. 17, 1726-1743.

[91] Baines 37.

[92] Sir Thomas Abney, for the plaintiff, referred to the Custumal's entries, in Latin, for 1573, whereof, article 34, among 59 articles, supported the right of the eldest son, as one method acceptable for election. A group of elderly Hastings residents were called: John Cousens, 60, who lived all his life in Hastings, declared that 'several ancient people say the eldest son of a freeman had a right by his father's charter; Joan White 62, Anne Sargent 63, and Thomas Colebrand 80, supported this view. Others were not so clear cut: Robert Evernden 65, born at Robertsbridge, and fifty years in Hastings, agreed that a freeman must have been born in his father's freedom, but 'never heard anybody say that they had such a right.' John Boykett, a Quaker 'over 60', who was refused his freedom by Thomas Lovell in the 1690s, stated that he understood from the town officers, 'that if my father had been free, I should have had a freedom'.

[93] *ER* vol. 95, 228-9; Moore and the Mayor etc., of Hastings; proof of payment of a certain fine is sufficient proof of a custom to pay a reasonable fine (T H B Oldfield, *The Representative history of Great Britain and Ireland, being a history of the House of Commons, and of the Counties, Cities and Boroughs of the United Kingdom* (1817) vol. 5, 380-1).

[94] *ER* vol. 95, 234-5.

[95] ESRO HAS CAA/5, 25r, Court of Record 14 May 1737.

[96] T H B Oldfield reiterated a tradition, which may have been hearsay, 'through fear that some future claimant of a freedom should attempt to accomplish and perfect what Moore left undone, it was thought expedient to commit this highly important and venerable record to the flames' in order to protect the Pelham and Newcastle interest, adding that the relevant part of the Custumal reiterating the rights of the elder son of a freeman and thus the right to vote in the Cinque Ports was preserved by the Moore case (Oldfield vol. 5, 386).

[97] William Durrant Cooper & Thomas Ross 'Notices of Hastings and its municipal rights' *SAC* 14 (1862) 65-118; Baines ch. 3, 37; Dell 43-56. BL Add Ms 28,530 includes a Custumal for Hasting; Custumal records in the ESRO are at HAS BJ 1-2; much useful information on the old Cinque Ports will be found in K M E Murray *The Constitutional History of the Cinque Ports* (1935).

[98] Hoon ch. 8 has much on the powers of search and seizure.

[99] Basil Williams, who cited this case, noticed a similar plea from freeholders living on the coast between Chichester and Arundel on behalf of Thomas Newman, a smuggler lodged in Horsham gaol,

which drew support from both Pelham and Butler, sufficient to secure his release (BL Add. Ms. 32688 f.158, Williams 1897 471). Newman's release came with strict conditions, including a bond for £500.

[100] TNA CUST 148/11, 12.

[101] 9 Geo. II c.35, *An Act for indemnifying persons who have been guilty of offences against the laws made for securing the revenues of Customs and Excise and for enforcing these laws for the future* s.1 stated that anyone who before 26 April 1736 incurred any penalty or forfeiture, by or for the clandestine running or receiving any prohibited goods, or any foreign goods liable to payment of Customs and Excise, and who are or may be subject to any information or other prosecution whatsoever for the duties ... or for making of any false report or entry of the loading of any ship, or in a wrong name, or for not reporting any such ship, or for breaking bulk before reporting, landing without an officer present ... and any persons who have beat, abused, obstructed or hindered any officer in execution of their duty, or who have given or offered a bribe to any officer and all persons aiding, assisting and abetting any of the offences, shall be acquitted, indemnified, released and discharged, against the king, heirs and successors and against all other persons, bodies corporate and any officer of Customs and Excise ... provided that any receiving the benefit of this amnesty have stopped any prosecution of Customs and Excise officers, or any assisting them (*SL* vol. 6 237-46); the Act tightened up numerous aspects of the law, and imposed strict penalties on transgressors who claimed the benefit from the Act but continued with smuggling activity. Hughes (1934) explains the Salt Acts.

[102] Answering on their own recognizances to be bound over 'on the late Act of Parliament entitled an Act for indemnifying persons who have been guilty of offences against the laws made for securing the revenues of customs and excise' were: John Dighton, Thomas Cobby, John Taught, Thomas Winter, William Gurr, William Swane, William Miles, Benjamin Harrison, Mark Caruther, William Peirce, Robert Gurr, Thomas Barry, Francis Adams, John Grayling, John Bird, Robert Henson, Nicholas Harman, James Taught, William Harrison, Zebelton Morphet, George Fellowes, Joseph Turner, Thomas Chadderton, William Langford, Richard Burgess, Esau Frith, Robert Phillip, John Earl (ESRO HAS CAA/5 10 January 1737).

[103] TNA ASSI 94/625; CUST 148/12 139, 211; ASSI 31/1 f.92.

[104] TNA CUST 148/12 273.

[105] Sayer vol. 1, 252-3; this point was also mentioned in Richmond vol. 3.

[106] For pardoning persons guilty of clandestine importation who join His Majesty's service (Bibliotheca Lindesiana vol. 8, 60 9 May 1744).

[107] 18 George II c. 28 SL vol. 6, 628-9.

[108] Sayer vol. 1, 253; Sayer was at pains to add, 'it would be unjust to assume from Mr Collier's having interested himself on behalf of these men that he had any sympathy with smugglers, as such'.

[109] See SAY 827 26 November 1745 for Zebelton Morphett and others entered into the Navy.

[110] Admiral Vernon, *Some Seasonable Advice from an Honest Sailor* (1746) reprints letters from August to December 1745; the reference to traitorous correspondence was penned on 25 August 1745, *ibid.,* 18*;* part of this collection is reprinted in B McL Ranft (ed.), *The Vernon Papers* Navy Records Society vol. 99 (1958).

[111] Ranft *The Vernon Papers* 519-20, 13 November 1745; Vernon *Some Seasonable Advice* 16 September 1745, 41.

[112] Vernon *Some Seasonable Advice* 13 November 1745, 108-10.

[113] *Ibid*., 14 December 1745, 149-50.

[114] *Ibid*., 18 December 1745, 158.

[115] Sayer vol. 1, 329-331, 29 May 1746, John Collier to Henry Pelham.

[116] ESRO MIL M7/23 John Collier rental book.

[117] ESRO MIL M7/23 loose leaf papers.

[118] Thus in September 1737 his farm in Bexhill, later Sivier's, worth £500, was conveyed to James Cranston in exchange for land in Ewhurst, plus £100 in cash. In January 1738, Collier purchased from

Ralph Norton and wife, nine acres of upland and twenty acres 2 rods of marshland in Hooe 'plus deeds'; later came farms in Wittersham from Francis Weller, in Castle parish from Mr Worge, one from Samuel Cruttenden, from John Bendon an estate in Udimore and Brede for £1400; on 25/26 May 1743 John Gibbon conveyed his estate in Stone parish, Isle of Oxney, for £800, and from Mr Couchman John Collier bought farms and lands in Icklesham for £600 ESRO MIL 7/23.

[119] John Collier's library dates from c. 1760 (SAY 2707); the library held many religious books bought for his wife or inherited from her father, and included Rapin' *History of England* in 10 volumes, 11 volumes of House of Commons debates, plus the legal decisions from the reigns of William and Mary, Anne, and the first two Georges, and much else of use for his varied business and political activities. Much care was bestowed on this library which was placed in its own room in Old Hastings House.

[120] Thomas Brandon Brett (1816-1906) writer, historian of Hastings and area, newspaper publisher; his monument is in Hastings cemetery and his volumes of local history are preserved in the Hastings public library.

[121] W V Crake 'The Correspondence of John Collier, five times Mayor of Hastings and his connection with the Pelham family'*SAC* 45 (1902) 62-109.

[122] Since Heather Warne's dissertation the East Sussex Record Office has acquired Collier and Milward family account books from the Hastings Museum, catalogued under MIL, and records of the Hastings Corporation listed under HAS.

BIBLIOGRAPHY

Printed Sources

Acton, J E D, *The Cambridge Modern History planned by Lord Acton* vol. 6 *The Eighteenth Century* (1909)

Adams, W H, *England at War* (1886)

Anderson, A, *An Historical and Chronological Deduction of the Origin of Commerce* (1801)

Arbuthnot, J, *An Essay concerning the nature of aliments, and the choice of them, according to different constitutions of human bodies* (1731)

Arthur, G, *The Story of the Household Cavalry* (London, 1909)

Ashton, T S, *Economic Fluctuations* (1959)

Baines, J Manwaring, *Historic Hastings* (1955)

Baker, J H, *The Order of Serjeants at Law A chronology of creations, with related texts and a historical introduction* Selden Society (1984)

Barker, K, *The Smuggling Life of Gabriel Tomkins, the extraordinary life of an 18th century rogue* (2011)

Barratt, T J, *The Annals of Hampstead* (1912)

Berry, S 'Pleasure Gardens in Georgian and Regency Seaside resorts: Brighton 1750-1840', *Garden History* vol. 28, 2, (2000) 222-30

Berry, S, *Georgian Brighton* (2005)

Berry, W, *County Genealogies, Pedigrees of the families of the County of Sussex* (1830)

Beswick, M *Brickmaking in Sussex: A History and Gazetteer* 2nd edn., (2001)

Bibliotheca Lindesiana, *Handlist of Proclamations issued by Royal and other constitutional authorities 1714-1910* vol. 8, (1913)

Blackstone, W, *Commentaries on the Laws of England* vol. 1 ch. 6 (1773)

Blaikie, W B, *Itinerary of Prince Charles Edward Stewart from his landing in Scotland July 1745 to his departure in September 1746* Scottish History Society vol. 23 (1897)

Bland, D S, *A Bibliography of the Inns of Court and Chancery* vol. 3, Selden Society (1965)

Boyer, A (ed.), *The Political State of Great Britain (1711-1740)*

Brent, C E (et al.), *Sussex in the Sixteenth and Seventeenth Centuries: A Bibliography* 2nd edn., (1980)

Brent, C E, *Georgian Lewes 1714-1830, the heyday of a country town* (1993)

Browning, R, *The Duke of Newcastle* (1975)

Burchall, M J, *A Catalogue of Sussex quarter session settlement orders and cases 1730-1749* (1982)

Burney, C, *A General History of Music From the Earliest Ages to the Present Period* 2nd edn (1789)

Caffyn, J, *Sussex Schools in the 18th Century,* SRS vol. 81 (1998)

Caldecott, J B, 'Sussex Seventeenth century tokens', *British Numismatic Journal* vol. 23, (1938-1941), 301-320

Chamberlayne, J, *Magnae Britanniae Notitia or the Present State of Great Britain* (1735, 1736, 1737, 1741, 1743, 1745)

Charnock, J, *Biographia Navalis or impartial memoir of the lives and characters of officers of the Navy* (1796)

Cheney, C R, *Handbook of Dates for Students of English History,* Royal Historical Society, no 4 (2000)

Chester, L, *The Marriage, Baptismal, and Burial Registers of the Collegiate Church & Abbey of St Peter Westminster* (1876)

Cleere, H & Crossley, D, *The Iron Industry of the Weald* (1985)

Comber, J, *Sussex Genealogies* 3 vols (1931-1933)

Cobbett, W, *William Cobbett's Parliamentary History of England,* (1811)

Collection of the weekly bills of Mortality within the London district published by the Company of parish clerks 20 December 1664 - 21 December 1773

Court, W H B, *The Rise of the Midland Industries 1600-1838* (1938)

Coxe, W, *Memoirs of the Life and Administration of Sir Robert Walpole* (1798)

Coxe, W, *Memoirs of the Administration of the Rt Hon. Henry Pelham* (1829)

Crake, W V, 'The Correspondence of John Collier, five times Mayor of Hastings, and his connection with the Pelham family', *SAC* 45 (1902) 62-109

Crook, D, *Defying the Demon, Smallpox in Sussex* (2006)

Crossley, D & Saville, R, *The Fuller Letters, Guns, Slaves and Finance 1728-1755,* SRS vol. 76 (1991)

Cunningham, W, *The Growth of English Industry and Commerce in Modern Times* 6th edn *The Mercantile System* (1919)

Dalporto, J, *Women in service in early modern England* (2008)

Davey, R, *East Sussex Land Tax 1785* SRS vol. 77 (1991)

Dawson, C, *Castle and Collegiate Church* (1909)

Deutsch, R, *Handel, A Documentary Biography* (1955)

Dell, R, *The Records of Rye Corporation: A Catalogue* (East Sussex County Council 1962)

Dickenson, H T & Logue K, 'The Porteous Riot A Study of the Breakdown of Law and Order in Edinburgh 1736-37' *Journal of the Scottish Labour History Society* vol. 10 (1976) 21-40

Dickson, P G M, *The Financial Revolution in England A Study in the Development of Public Credit 1688-1756* (1967)

Dobson, M J, *Contours of death and disease in early modern England* (1997)

Doyle, J E, *The Official Baronage of England* (1886)

Dowell, S, *A History of Taxation and Taxes in England from the Earliest Times to the year 1885* 2nd edn (1888)

Downing, S J, *The English Pleasure Garden 1660-1860* (2009)

Dugdale, W, *The History of Embanking and Draining of Divers Fens and Marshes, both in foreign parts and in this kingdom and of the improvements thereby* 2nd edn (1772)

Dunkin E H W, *Sussex Marriage Licences...for the archdeaconry of Lewes 1670 to 1729...for the deanery of South Malling 1620 to 1732* SRS vol. 6 (1907).

Dunkin, E H W, *Sussex Manors, Advowsons, etc., recorded in the Feet of Fines Henry VIII to William IV* (1509-1833) SRS vols 19, 20 (1914-15)

Eachard, L, *The History of England from the first entrance of Julius Caesar* (1707) vol.3, *to the convention Parliament 1689* (1718)

Eden, P, *Dictionary of Land Surveyors and Local Cartographers of Great Britain and Ireland 1550-1850* (1975-6)

Egmont, P, *Manuscripts of the Earl of Egmont* 3: *Diary of the First Earl of Egmont (Viscount Percival)* vols 2, 3, Historical Manuscripts Commission (1923)
Encyclopaedia Britannica, or a Dictionary of Arts and Sciences, compiled upon a new plan 1st edn (1771)
Evelyn, J, *Sylva, or a Discourse of Forest Trees* (1664)
Ellis, H, 'Commissions of Sewers for the Lewes levels' *SAC* 10, (1858) 95-9
Ewen, C L E, *Lotteries and Sweepstakes: An Historical, Legal and Ethical Survey of their Introduction, Suppression and Re-establishment in the British Isles* (1932)
Farrant, J, *Sussex in the Eighteenth and Nineteenth Centuries: A bibliography* 4th edn (1982)
Farrant, J, 'The Making of Francis Grose's Antiquities, Evidence from Sussex' *SAC* 131 (1993) 152-8
Farrant, J, (et al.) *Sussex Depicted, Views and Descriptions 1600-1800* SRS vol. 85 (2001)
Ford, W K, *Chichester Diocesan Surveys 1686 and 1724* SRS vol. 78 (1992)
Fortescue, J W, *A History of the British Army* (1899-1920)
Fryde, E B & Powicke, F M, *Handbook of British Chronology* (1986)
Garraway Rice, R, *Sussex Apprentices and Masters 1710 to 1752* SRS vol. 28 (1924)
Gentleman's Magazine (1731-1746)
Gilboy, E W, *Wages in Eighteenth Century England* (1934)
Giles, J, *The Compleat Court-Keeper or Land-Steward's Assistant* 2nd edn (1715)
Grove, *The New Grove Dictionary of Music and Musicians* (ed. S Sadie) vol. 24 (2001)
Grub Street Journal (1730-1737)
Hasted, E, *The History and Topographical Survey of the County of Kent* (1797)
Hay, D (et al.), *Albion's Fatal Tree* (1976)
Hervey, J, *Some Materials towards Memoirs of the Reign of King George II* by John, Lord Hervey (ed. Romney Sedgwick 3 vols 1931)
Highfill, P H (et al), *A Biographical Dictionary of Actors, Actresses, Musicians, Dancers, Managers & other stage personnel in London 1660-1800* (1984)
Hinderwell, T, *The history and antiquities of Scarborough* 3rd edn (1832)
Hodgkinson, J, *The Wealden Iron Industry* (2009a)
Hodgkinson, J, 'The Legas Remnant Letters' *Wealden Iron* (second series) no. 29 (2009b)
Holdsworth, W S, *A History of English Law* 3rd edn., vol. 1 (1903) vol. 2 (1909)
Hoon, E E, *The Organization of the English Customs System 1696-1786* (1968)
Horn, D B & Ransome, M, *English Historical Documents* vol. 10 *1714-1783* (1957)
Hoskins, W G, 'Harvest Fluctuations and English Economic History 1620-1759' *Agricultural History Review* 16 (1968) 15-31
House of Lords, *Public General Acts* (1701-)
Howell, T B, *A Complete Collection of State Trials and Proceedings for high treason and other crimes and misdemeanours from the earliest period to the present time* vol. 17 1726-43 (1816)
Hughes, A, *Sussex Clergy Inventories 1600-1750* SRS vol. 91 (2007)
Hughes, E, *Studies in Administration and Finance 1558-1825; with special reference to the history of Salt Taxation in England* (1934).
Hunnisett, R F, *East Sussex Coroners' Records 1688-1838* SRS vol. 89 (2005)
Jeake, S, *Charters of the Cinque Ports, Two Ancient Towns and their Members* Translated into English with annotations, historical and critical thereupon (London, 1728)
Journals of the House of Commons1547-1790 by command of George III (1803-1813)

Kelch, R A, *Newcastle: A Duke without Money: Thomas Pelham-Holles 1693-1768* (1974)
Lang, A, *A History of Scotland from the Roman Occupation,* vol. 4 *1689-1746* (1907)
Le Neve, J, *Fasti Ecclesiae Anglicanae 1541-1857* Part 7, *Ely, Norwich, Westminster & Worcester Dioceses*, compiled by J M Horn (1992)
Lecky, W E H, *A History of England in the Eighteenth Century* (1883-92)
Lewis, P, *Building Cycles and Britain's Growth* (1965)
Lewis, W S, *The Yale Edition of Horace Walpole's Correspondence* (1937-83)
Lillywhite, B, *London Coffee Houses: A Reference Book of Coffee houses of the Seventeenth, Eighteenth and Nineteenth Centuries* (1963)
Lipson, E L, *The History of the Woollen and Worsted Industries* (1921)
Lipson, E L, *The Economic History of England* vol. 3 *The Age of Mercantilism* 4th edn (1947)
Llewellyn, N (et al.), *East Sussex Church Monuments 1530-1830* SRS vol. 93 (2011)
London Gazette, (1665-)
Lysons, D, *The Environs of London being an historical account of the towns, villages and hamlets within 12 miles of that capital* vol. 1, *County of Surrey* (1792)
Mahon, Lord, *History of England from the peace of Utrecht to the peace of Versailles 1713-1783* vols 2, 3 (1853)
Mantoux, P, *The Industrial Revolution in the Eighteenth Century* (1961 edn)
Mawer, A & Stenton, F H, *The Place Names of Sussex* (1929-30)
Maxwell, A, *Hampstead: Its Historic Houses, its Literary and Artistic Associations* (1912)
McCann, T J, *The Correspondence of the Dukes of Richmond and Newcastle 1724-1747* SRS vol. 73 (1984)
Mead, R, *The Medical Works of Dr Richard Mead* (1765)
Miege, G, *Magnae Britanniae Notitia, or, The Present State of Great Britain and Ireland* 8th edn (1738)
Montague, H, *Poll taken by Henry Montague (Sheriff of the County of Sussex) at the City of Chichester, Thursday & Friday, 9 & 10 May 1734* (1734)
Moss, W G, *The History and Antiquities of the Town and Port of Hastings* (1824)
Murray, K M E, *The Constitutional History of the Cinque Ports* (1935)
Muskett, P, 'Gabriel Tomkin Smuggler, Customs Officer, Sheriff's bailiff and highwayman' *Sussex History* vols 2, 3 (1981-2)
Nadel, G H, 'The Sussex election of 1741' *SAC* 91 (1953) 84-124
Neal, L, *I am not the master of events: the speculations of John Law and Lord Londonderry* (2012)
Nenadic, S, *Lairds and Luxury The Highland Gentry in Eighteenth Century Scotland* (2007)
Nicoll, A, *A History of Early Eighteenth Century Drama 1700-1750* (1925)
Oldfield, T H B, *The Representative History of Great Britain and Ireland: being a history of the House of Commons and of the Counties, Cities and Boroughs* (1816)
Ollard, S L (et al.), *A Dictionary of English Church History* 3rd edn. (1948)
Ogilby, J, *Britannia Depicted or Ogilby Improved* (London, 1720); this map collection was published in several editions and includes the main roads from the south coast to London
Owen, J B, *The Rise of the Pelhams* (1957)
Oxford English Dictionary (1888-)
Parry, C, *The Consolidated Treaty Series* (1969-81)

Peak, S, *Fishermen of Hastings: 200 years of the Hastings fishing community* (1985)
Phelps-Brown, E H & Hopkins, S, 'Seven Centuries of the Prices of Consumables, Compared with Builders wage rates' in E.M Carus-Wilson *Essays in Economic History* vol. 2 (1962) 179-96
Pinkerton, J, *A general collection of the best and most interesting voyages and travels in all parts of the world* (1808-14)
Plomer, H R (et al.), *A Dictionary of the Printers and Booksellers who were at work in England, Scotland and Ireland from 1726 to 1775* (1932)
Pomet, P, *Complete History of Drugs* (1737)
Pratt, M, *Winchelsea: the tale of a Medieval Town principally telling the story of the ancient town from the earliest times until 1800* (2005)
Prior, M, *Women in English Society 1500-1800* (1985)
Probert, R, *Marriage Law and Practice in the Long Eighteenth Century* (2009)
Pyle, E, *Memoirs of a Royal Chaplain 1729-1763: The Correspondence of Edward Pyle DD, Chaplain in Ordinary to George II, with Samuel Kerrick DD vicar of Dersingham* (1905)
Radcliff, J, *Pharmacopaedia Radcliffeana or Dr Radcliff's prescriptions* (1716)
Rapin, P, Tindall, N, *The Continuation of Mr Rapin's History of England* vol. 20 (1769)
Razzell, P E, 'Population Change in Eighteenth Century England: A Re-interpretation' *EcHR* 2nd series vol. 18 (1965) 312-32
Renton, A W (ed.), *The English Reports* [legal cases 1220-1866] (1900-1932)
Richmond, H W, *The Navy in the war of 1739-48* (1920)
Rogers, A G L, *A History of Agriculture and Prices in England 1259-1793* vol. 7 *From the year after the Oxford Parliament to the Commencement of the Continental War* Part 2 *1703-1793* (1902)
Russell, R, *Dissertation on the use of seawater in the diseases of the glands* 4th edn (1760)
Sainty, J C, *Treasury Officials 1660-1870* (1972)
Sainty, J C, *Admiralty Officials 1660-1870* (1975)
Sainty, J C, *A list of English Law officers, King's Counsel and holders of patents of precedence* Selden Society, Supplementary series vol. 7 (1986)
Sainty, J C, *The judges of England 1272-1990* Selden Society, supplementary series vol. 10 (1993)
Sayer, C L, *The Correspondence of Mr John Collier (Deceased) And His Family 1716-1780* (1907)
Scouten, A H, *The London Stage 1660 -1800* Part 3 1729-1747 vol. 1, 1729-36, vol. 2, 1736-47 (1961)
Sedgwick, R (ed.), *History of Parliament The House of Commons 1715-1754* (1970)
Shaw, J S, *The Political History of Eighteenth Century Scotland* (1999)
Shaw, W A, *The Knights of England, A Complete record from the earliest time to the present day of the Knights of all the Orders of Chivalry in England, Scotland and Ireland and of Knights Bachelors* vol. 1 (1906)
Sheridan, R B, *Sugar and Slavery: An Economic History of the British West Indies 1623-1775* (1974)
Singer, C (et al.), *A History of Technology* vol. 2 *The Mediterranean civilization and the Middle Ages, c. 700 BC to AD 1500* (1956) vol. 3 *From the Renaissance to the Industrial Revolution* (1957)

Shrine, F H, *Fontenoy and Great Britain's share in the War of the Austrian Succession* (1906)
Sykes, N, *Edward Gibson, Bishop of London 1669-1748* (1926)
Statutes at Large, by command of George III (1768-1802)
Statutes of the Realm, Record Commission, (1810-1828)
Steer, F W, *The Ashburnham Archives: A catalogue* (1958)
Strutt, J, *The Sports and Pastimes of the People of England* (1967)
Swift, J, *Gulliver's Travels* (1726)
Tawney, R H (et al.), *English Economic History Select Documents* (1914)
Taylor, S & Jones, C, *Tory and Whig: The Parliamentary Papers of Edward Harley 3rd Earl of Oxford and William Hay MP for Seaford 1716-1753* (1998)
Temperley, H W V, 'The Causes of the War of Jenkins's Ear' *Transactions of the Royal Historical Society* (1909) 197-236
Thomas, K, *Man and the Natural World: Changing Attitudes in England 1500-1800* (1984)
Timmins, S, *The Resources, Products and Industrial history of Birmingham and the Midland hardware district* (1866)
Thompson, E, *Whigs and Hunters* (1967)
Underdown, D, *Start of Play: Cricket and Culture in Eighteenth Century England* (2000)
Vaucher, P, *La Crise du ministere Walpole en 1733-34* (1924)
Venn, J & J A, *Alumni Cantabrigienses. A biographical list of all known students, graduates and holders of office at the University of Cambridge from the earliest times to 1900* Part 1 *to 1751* (1922-27)
Vidler, L A, 'The Murder of Allen Grebell' *SNQ* 11 (1946) 49-51
Walker, P, *Croydon and its Pubs* 1 (1999)
Ward, W R, *The English Land Tax in the Eighteenth Century* (1953)
Weatherill, L, *Consumer Behaviour and Material Culture in Britain 1660-1760* (1988)
Webb, S & B, *English Local Government from the Revolution to the Municipal Corporations Act* vol. 1 *Parish and County* (1906)
Webb, S & B, *English Local Government from the Revolution to the Municipal Corporations Act* vol. 4 *Statutory Authorities for Special Purposes* (1922)
Whatley, S, *England's Gazetteer or an accurate description of all the Cities, Towns and villages of the Kingdom* (1751)
Willan, T S, *The English Coasting Trade 1600-1750* (1938)
Williams, B, 'The Duke of Newcastle and the Election of 1734' *EHR* vol. 12 (1897) 448-88
Williams, B, *The Whig Supremacy 1714-1760* (1945)
Williams, B, *Carteret and Newcastle* (1966)
Williamson, G C, 'Trade Tokens of Surrey issued in the Seventeenth Century' *Surrey Archaeological Society* vol. 10, (1891) 79-95
Winslow, C, 'Sussex Smugglers' in D. Hay (et al.) *Albion's Fatal Tree* (1975)
Woolrych, H W, *Lives of Eminent Serjeants at Law* (1869)
Wroth, W, *The London Pleasure Gardens of the Eighteenth Century* (1896)

Unpublished and Digital Sources

Baines, M, History of Hastings families, Mss in Hastings Public Library
Brett, T B, Historico Biography: History of Hastings families; volumes in Hastings Public Library

British Library: Newcastle MSS (Add Mss 32679-32992) the volumes of manuscripts in this collection contain letters on politics in Hastings written between the Duke of Newcastle and John Collier and several are reprinted here to amplify materials in the Sayer Mss

CCed, Clergy of the Church of England database (http://theclergydatabase.org.uk/)

Davey, R, East Sussex Window and House Tax Assessments 1747 (http://www.sussexrecordsociety.org/olb/wtax/)

East Sussex Record Office: Sayer MSS the thousands of letters and papers in this collection are the primary sources used here for the years 1731 to 1746, the years when John Collier was at the height of his powers; this is the collection first catalogued by Heather Warne in her 1966 Archive Diploma Dissertation, *The Papers of John Collier of Hastings*; there is also an internet catalogue available via the ESRO website

Hooker, John, Mss in the library of the Royal Society

James, T M, 'The Inns of Croydon 1640-1830' MA Leicester (1969)

Muskett, P, 'English Smuggling in the Eighteenth Century' PhD Open University (1996)

National Archives: Customs and Excise records contain several volumes of bound papers originally written by John Collier as part of his work for the Customs Commissioners; a number of John Collier's papers and letters relating to the Customs are dispersed amongst the Treasury and State papers

ODNB Oxford Dictionary of National Biography (http://www.oxforddnb.com/)

Old Bailey Online (http://www.oldbaileyonline.org/forms/formMain.jsp)

Saville, R, 'Some Aspects of the role of Government in the industrial development of England 1686-1720' Ph.D Sheffield (1978)

Warne, H, *The Papers of John Collier of Hastings*, Archive Diploma Dissertation (1966)

PEDIGREE 1: THE CHILDREN OF PETER COLLIER AND OF JOHN AND ELIZABETH COLLIER

Peter Collier m. Sarah Cheapman
1653-1717 | 1663-1734

Peter

John Collier m. Elizabeth Elphick
1685-1760 1706 d. 1714

Sarah Collier m. Samuel Cruttenden
b.1693 (they lived in a cottage next to Old Hastings House)

Mary m. Thomas Smith

Children of John Collier and Elizabeth Elphick:

Elizabeth m. George Worge
b. 1707 of Battle

Mary
b. 1709

Mary
b. & d.1710

Sarah
b. 1711
m Roger Mortimer

[daughter name unknown]
b. 1713

John
b. & d. 1714

Main sources for all pedigrees:
Manwaring Baines Mss in Hastings Public Library
Warne, H, Catalogue of the papers of John Collier (ESRO 1962)
Sayer family Bible
St.Clement's Hastings parish registers
Crake, W V, 'The Correspondence of John Collier, five times Mayor of Hastings, and his connection with the Pelham family', *SAC* 45 (1902) 62-109
ESRO SAY 3539.

PEDIGREE 2: THE CHILDREN OF JOHN AND MARY COLLIER

John Collier 1685-1760 m. 1717 Mary Cranston 1696-1768 Daughter of Rev. James Cranston

John	James	Cordelia (Dely)	Mary	Jane	Sarah	Henrietta (Harriet)
1720-32	1721-47	1722- 1779	1725-83	(Jenny; Miss Fidget)	b. 1740	b. 1741
		m. 1748	m. 1754	b. 1727	m. Henry Sayer	m. Henry Jackson
		General James Murray	Edward Milward	m. William Green		

Eleven died in infancy:
Cordelia d. 1718
John d. 1719
Jane 1723-25
Mary d. 1724
William d. 1726
William b. & d. 1729
Margaret d. 1730
William d. 1731
Thomas 1732-33
Thomas b. 1734
William b. & d. 1738

PEDIGREE 3: THE CHILDREN OF JAMES AND CORDELIA CRANSTON.

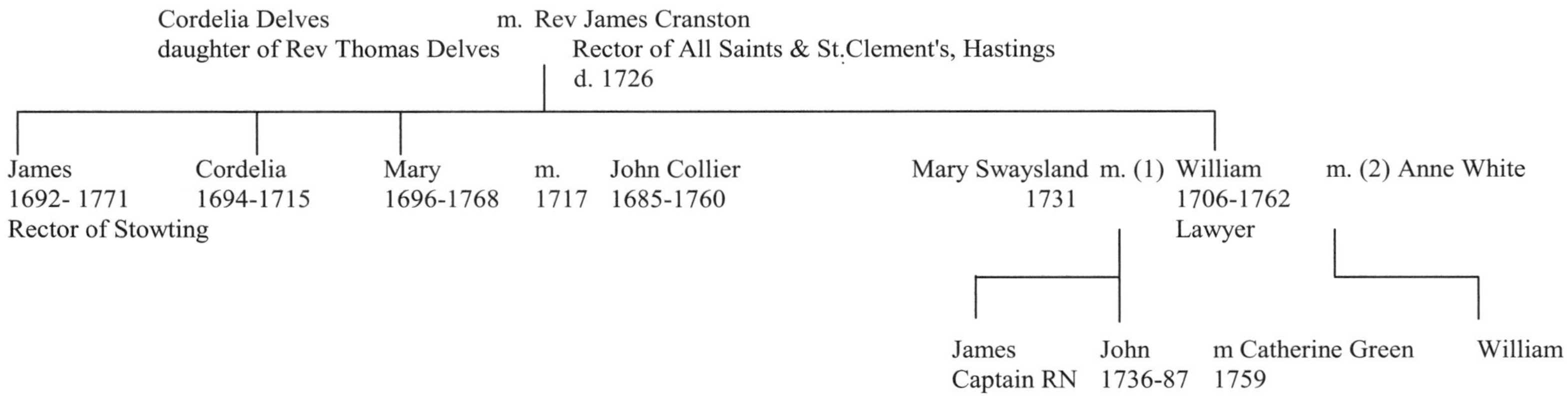

EDITORIAL CONVENTIONS

The letters and papers printed in this volume are from the Sayer Manuscripts in the East Sussex Record Office or the Newcastle papers at the British Library: they are printed exactly as originally written. Thus, the original spelling of all words and their order in each letter is retained for all the letters and papers here. Where words are duplicated in the original, whether as the deliberate intent of the writer, or by inadvertence, these remain in the printed text as written. Several letters are written in a form of Sussex dialect and are likewise transcribed exactly from the originals. In accordance with the Society's house-style the word 'ye' is rendered as 'the', the ampersand is extended to 'and', and for some words the use of an apostrophe in the original is replaced by the most appropriate letter, usually 'e' or 'l'. Additions to punctuation are also made where the original is unclear, and where alterations may assist the reader. Capitals follow modern usage. Payments and receipts covered in the letters are standardised as, for instance, £8 13s 6½d and £0 03s 0d, and this procedure is also employed for the waterworks accounts and the estate rentals. Letters printed in previous collections, notably by Charles Lane Sayer in his *Correspondence of Mr John Collier (Deceased) and his family 1716-1780* (1907) and W V Crake 'The Correspondence of John Collier, five times Mayor of Hastings, and his connection with the Pelham family' *SAC* 45 (1902), have all been compared with the transcriptions here.

The original documents use the Old Style of the Julian calendar where the year began on 25 March, and this calendar continued in use in England until 1752, and thus all dates given here are eleven days behind the Gregorian calendar used on the continent. For this volume the documents are arranged by date order from 1731 to 1746, with the start of the year given as 1 January, and the month and the days within each letter follow the originals written on the documents; where the dates are missing the editorial insertions follow the Old Style Julian calendar.

Above each letter the line in bold is given in the following format:

2 To John [Jacky] Collier, [Mrs Thorpe's school] Battle, from John Collier, 15 May 1731 [SAY 1570]

It provides in sequence: the chronological number of the manuscript (1 to 622): the intended recipient and the address to which the letter is sent; the person signing the letter and the place written; if known the date as written, or where missing the post mark if readable; if neither are available the date is given from evidence within the SAY manuscripts, from the handwriting of the writer compared with other letters, and otherwise from documentary or printed sources. The line ends with the ESRO SAY or British Library reference.

As these titles are editorial additions, the names are those commonly used in the letters, using the writer's signature as a guide to spelling, and places take their modern usage. For undated letters estimated dates are supplied in square brackets; the convention 1735 - 1737 is used for letters which are not earlier than the first year or later than the second. Conventional salutations and valedictions at the beginning or end of letters have normally been omitted. John Collier used a variety of personal endings for his letters to Mary, and several are included here (e.g. **[35]**, **[57]**, **[60-62]**, **[69]**. Their children were taught always to end their letters with dutiful enquiries or remembrances to others (e.g. **[12]**, **[16]**, **[32]**, **[36]**, **[259]**, **[265]**, **[299]**.

The editorial notes at the close of each letter are of two sorts. References to the spelling, and to words and discrepancies in the text are given an entry note number hanging from the relevant text, and the detail in the entry note is preceded by 'MS': for instance, where a word is crossed out it is placed in an entry note after 'MS'. Where the text is damaged, or unreadable, this is signified by three dots ... inserted into the relevant place in the text. The second type of entry note contains information relating to the text, drawn from documents and archives and published works. Citations to sources are of two types: where a printed work is cited more than once a short title reference will be given in the entry note, and the full reference will be found in the bibliography. In cases where the work is cited only once, the full title and author is given in the entry note, and this is not copied to the bibliography. Where, in the Introduction, notes and elsewhere, reference is made to a letter, its number is given in bold type within square brackets (e.g. **[139]**)

It is unclear whether some of the correspondence and depositions in the SAY manuscripts are 'as sent'. It may be assumed that many of the letters and depositions where words are struck through are drafts. In several cases words are overwritten in the text, and from these an entry note is hung and in the entry note after 'MS', the omitted words are placed followed by *struck through*.

As this volume is not intended as an expansive 'Life and Times of John Collier and his friends' the editorial annotations closely follow the correspondence and papers, meaning that the entry notes for London and national affairs are confined to matters relevant to Collier and Cranston and their daily life, and likewise for Hastings. Similar topics which emerge from the Hastings Corporation records in respect of the port may also be found in the records of other Cinque ports; such topics as the creation of freemen, the roll of electors, preparations for the elections to Parliament, the recruitment of the militia and supply of arms are raised by all Cinque ports, whether in Kent or Sussex. Furthermore, the economic concerns of the ports over the fish trade, the coastal trade, protection from the press in wartime, the award of government contracts for local shipping, and local co-operation between landowners and the ports on causeways, the marshes and the sewers are also annotated. Smuggling and seafaring go together, and the TNA Customs papers range over all ports in coastal areas. In the case of the Hastings waterworks referred to below, the waterworks in Rye which originated in the time of Queen Elizabeth is referred to, as this is of material interest to the events in Hastings. Readers interested in these wider aspects of relations between the Cinque Ports, landowners and the government are referred to K M E Murray *The Constitutional History of the Cinque Ports* and to the various studies and catalogues listed in the bibliography and entry notes.

Arrangement of the Text

The correspondence in numbers 1-572 is divided into 16 sections, one for every year from 1731 to 1736. The remaining papers are divided up into eight appendices:

Appendix 1: Undated Letters [573-582] lists 10 letters for which only approximate dates have been found.

Appendix 2: Hastings town business [583-588] contains papers which relate to the appointment of freemen in 1734, the provision of arms for the Hastings forts in 1742, the loyal address of October 1745, and the instructions in December 1745 from Admiral Edward Vernon to the Church Wardens from South Foreland to Beachy Head.

Appendix 3: Hastings water supply [589-600] contain information on general conditions in the port apart from the details of the water supply and the waterworks.

Appendix 4: Pelham estates [601-607] covers John Collier's work for the estates owned by Henry Pelham and Thomas Pelham of Stanmer, and lists their tenants.

Appendix 5: List of residents of Hastings and environs eligible to vote in the 1734 county election, re-used in 1741 [608].

Appendix 6: Smuggling affidavits and depositions [609-616].

Appendix 7: Elizabeth Hickes estate and the case of her daughter Martha Boys [617-618].

Appendix 8: Miscellaneous Collier family business, including work for the Earl of Ashburnham [619-622].

THE COLLIER LETTERS

1 To Mary Collier from William Cranston [1728 - 1731][1] [SAY 1569]

After having inwardly bid your house and Mrs Wimble's goodbye,[2] I reach't Battle at 10. Jacky not being in the way, went to Mr Worge's [3] and sent for him, borrowed of George a pair of jack boots,[4] and sett out at 11 exactly. About 10 minutes after, in Watlington Lane, my horse fell down, I with him, in the dirt. Got up, thankt God I had received no hurt, viewed myself in the figure I then cutt, mounted again and arrived at Stonecrouch ½ an hour past one. Eat a mutton chop, staid till 3, my horse tired at Tunbridge and myself soon after, but with much bodily labour my horse and I, or rather I and my horse, arrived under a triple discharge of cannon and ringing of bells, at Sennock at 7 precisely, greatly fatigued.

Went to bed supperless at 9, rose at 10 next morning very well, but was all day very formall. Staid at home till 5, went afterward down town, staid till 12, went then home and soon after to bed supperless again. Rose at 9, to church at 11, home at 12 edifyed but a little, otherwise not at all. Memorandum, at thirty five minutes and an half past eleven Mrs Roffe was safely delivered of a female child.[5] Dined at 8, great coated and horse out at 3 but the wind turning and rain falling I went into the parlour, took my leave of the gossips, pulled off my great coat and resolved at 4 to a moment to stay all night. Went upstairs at 6, wished Mrs Roffe joy and kist something they told me was the child, but whether twas its face or a – e thas[6] what, as Dele says, I don't know. Sat very gravely with her 2 hours then went down to my supper and afterwards with 2 young girls had a game of romps.

Waited, like a gay fellow, upon one of em home, staid longer than ordinary, Mrs Rosse sent her two maids after me, a type of matrimony, went home and to bed at 2, rose at 7, waited again on the lady, breakfasted together, I drank no tea, chatted some time after and at 11 I took horse and arrived safe in London about 3 and found all things as I left em. And now as I am got to the end of my journey, so likewise am I to that of my letter, excepting to that necessary part of it, love and service which I would have distributed in manner and form following, that is to say, accept of some part of the former yourself, other part to my brother Cranston, other to my cosin Betty,[7] other to my cosin Tarpe alias Thor-pe alias Thorpe and the remainder to the children share and share alike as to service. After having given a good lump of it to Mr Collier, I leave it to you to portion out what's left and to give to whom you please provided it be not given to more than 100 people.

I've inclosed you some patterns of calamanco.[8] I received Mr Collier's letter last post and before I had seen the taylor.

1 Sayer offered 1730 or 1731 for this letter, 'but I must leave this to some future time, or to future commentators' (Sayer vol. 1, 54). The parish registers for Sevenoaks suggest November 1728.

2 The usual route followed by William Cranston from Hastings to London was via Battle, Stonecrouch, Tonbridge and Sevenoaks, and the route is shown on the road maps published in Ogilby.

3 George Worge, attorney at Battle, who married John Collier's daughter, Elizabeth. For their house at Starrs Green see Farrant 2001 156 view 14.

4 Jackboots: leather riding boots with square block toes and wide heels, bucket tops to fit over knees and a starfish design for the rowels.

5 Mrs Roffe, wife of William Roffe. Sevenoaks parish registers record two daughters, Isabella Terisia, baptised 12 October 1722, and Sackfield, baptised 1 November 1728: next and last offspring recorded,

Richard, baptised 28 March 1730, died 2 April 1730. No further christenings recorded for the Roffe family in the 1730s, (Sevenoaks PL.)

6 MS damaged: thas or thats.

7 Unclear which cousin Betty is referred to.

8 Woollen cloth, resembling satin.

2 To John [Jacky] Collier, [Mrs Thorpe's school] Battle, from John Collier, 15 May 1731 [SAY 1570]

Your mother received your letter and I had the books which I have put to the other, and we are very sorry to hear your master is soe ill. I don't intend to buy any lock for your box till you come home again at Whitsuntide.[1] Your mamma would have her gloves washed white. You must tell Jemmy that I take it very ill that he did not come near me at the market and he may be sure I shan't be satisfyed with such impudent behaviour for the future.[2] You must take care this hot weather and not sweat too much and drink when you are hot.[3] We are all very well and send service to Mrs Thorpe and her daughter and blessing to you and Jemmy.

1 Whitsunday, Sunday, 13 May 1731.

2 Battle market, Thursdays from 1566; cattle market second Tuesday every month from 1670; Hastings fairs, Whitsuntide Monday and Tuesday; the Rock fair, 26/27 July, autumn fair, 23 November.

3 Contemporary medical advice veered towards avoidance of exertion and sweating in hot weather; for reference to sickness caused by heat and fevers and the damage therefrom see Mead vol. 1, 141-2, vol. 2, 132; allieviated by reduction in temperature (Arbuthnot 250; *EB* 1771 vol. 3; Radcliff 101).

3 To Mary Collier, Hastings, from Ann Collier, Portsmouth, 20 August 1731 [SAY 1571]

I return you humble thanks for receaving my daughter and I hope you will excuse her bringing one with her, but indeed, I could not till how to let her go by water alone. But I wish I had since Mis Ann makes so many reflictions for coming home by herself. She made it nine days before she came home. She came to Bread Hampson by 3 a clock in afternoon that day she came from Hasting.[1] She have made me very uneasey by telling me Sal is so very ill, and so bad she can't go three steps and looks like death. But I hope she is noe so bad as she says because Sal do not wrigh to me.

I don't desire to deny her the pleasure of enjoying her frinds nor I do not want her to come home presently, madam, and if she is agreeable enough for you to except of her company she is at your service as long as you pleas and when you think fit send her home.[2] With me she have a dul living for I keep no company but am allways alone, but her being a littel while you she will have a good oppertunity of improving herselfe, and I shall take it as a very great favour if you will be so kind as to instruct her. I resign her over to you so long as you think proper and I hope she will take care to intrueduce herself into your favour with good manners, and then she need not doubt her uncle's favour. Madam, I hope you will be so kind as to let me hear from you whether she be so bad as I am told and if she is ill to make her what I shall set down, this with my humble service to my brother and hope you will except the same.

A handfull or two of rusty hobnayls boyled in white wine vineger halfe a pint, boyle it a quarter of an hour, strain it of, when cold, put the vineger into a bottle of stal bear, but ad a penyworth of powder of steel, let her drink a glass morning and a four a clock in the afternoon, shaking the bottle, and walk a little.[3]

1 Bedhampton parish, ten miles west of Chichester, and close to navigable water.
2 MS sentence end unclear.
3 Powders and sweats of iron and steel in vinegar and milk were a common remedy for weakness and chronic fatigue and a specific treatment for female disorders and passions.

4 To John Collier, Hastings, from John [Jacky] Collier, Battle, 8 October 1731

[SAY 1572]

This is to let you know that I am in good health and I hope you are well. I got very safe here, and tell Jo I desire him to send us some shoes which he promised to do by my Dame Palmer.[1] Give the inclosed letter to my uncle James.[2] I hope you will be here at the markett, and also my uncle Will[3] or I believe he want go not till then, but if he does I hope he will call upon me for I shall be very glad to see him. I hope my mamma will come quickly for she has been a coming a long time. I give my duty to you and my mamma and my love to my sisters. Tell Mary Edbourough I have had her gloves to be washed; and give my service to Mrs Thorpe.

1 Dame Palmer, road carrier between Battle and Hastings; cartage services and prices on London to Sussex routes regulated by Lewes quarter sessions, ESRO QR/E/411, which series also records the regulation of the wages of servants and labourers; for the work of the quarter sessions see Lipson 1947 260-4.
2 Revd James Cranston junior.
3 MS damaged.

5 To Mary Collier, Hastings, from Ann Collier, Portsmouth 22 October 1731

[SAY 1573]

This is to let you know that my daughter came home the first of this mounth, but so very bad that nobody that saw her could belive she would have lived a week. She could not go acros the room, going upstairs to bed she dropt down that I thought she would never have come to herself againe. But I thank God now she is very well and can go anywhere and looks very well and a coullar. I made a bottle of what I desired you to make for her and in three days drinking of it she found herself much better. She have dank at most to bottles and I belive one more will be enough. I belive it was out of kindness to her that you went to a docter for her, not supposing so slender a thing as that could do the good that it doe. You have the receit and you may do a great deal of good to poor people and indeed I think the rich may prise it, for it is present cure for the virgin's fever,[1] but if ever you make it you have powder of steel prepared with sulpher.[2] Madam, I return you humble thanks for all your favours to my daughter. Pray be so kind as to let her aunt Critenton know how well she is.[3] She gives her humble duty to her uncle and yourselfe with her humble service to all her cousins is all from your sister. I wish you had made it that you might have seen the effect of it, but you need never question the truth of it.

1 Virgins fever: hysterical disorders and state of intense, nervous, excitability; seldom required bleeding; purges to be used with caution; during fits medicine to replace loss of spirits, such as pills comprising gum ammoniac, Russian castor and salt of amber (*EB* 1771 vol. 3, 112, 148): Richard Mead stated that he never found it difficult to cure such fits by a cold bath (Mead vol. 1, 208-9).
2 A common ingredient in ointment for skin diseases and fungal infections; also effective for mange in cattle, horses, foxes, squirrels, and for sheep rot.
3 MS lower case aut or aunt. This is Sarah Cruttenden.

6 To Mary Collier, [Hastings], from John Collier, [Johnson's Court], 18 November 1731 [SAY 1574]

This informes you of my safe arrivall in London last night. I dined at Hailsham and lay at Uckfield a Tuesday evening, and came from thence yesterday, being 42 miles. There is prodigious robbing on most of the roads about London and severall of my acqaintance have had their boxes and portmanteaus riffled.[1] I found my brother very well and Johnson's Court just in the same way, vizt noe alteration in the house and noe manner of notice has been taken to me of the match. There is noe servant in the room of Nicholas soe that Mrs Alice and her helper are all in all.

It is whispered about town that the king of F is soe much dissordered in his senses as to be confined and that there is a great struggle between the queen and the princes of the blood who shall be regent during the d…s minority.[2] The cardinall hangs fast by the petticoats, noe doubt following the example of Spain, not to mention any other country. I am just goeing to the play,[3] if I can get in, with Page, to see the Duke of Lorrain, though it is something inconvenient, but I am sure you would laugh at me if I did not see his serene highnesse. I am with humble service to Mrs Thorpe.[4]

1 Highway robbery was felony punishable by hanging, dealt with in succession of statutes (4 & 5 Wm & Mary c. 8, 6 Geo. I c. 23, 7 Geo II c. 21, *SL* vols. 3, 4, 5).

2 France, dauphin; the cardinal was Andre-Hercule de Fleury, chief minister to Louis XV from 1726 to death in 1742, favoured peace with England and expansion of trade.

3 18 November 1731, Lincolns Inn Fields, *The Amorous Widow, or, The Wanton Wife*, by Thomas Betterton, also *Perseus and Andromeda, or, the Cheats of Harlequin*, for the entertainment of several foreign persons of distinction; the king, queen, prince, duke and princesses present (Scouten pt 3, vol.1, 1729-36, 170).

4 The Duke of Lorrain, after touring the Low countries and holding political and trade discussions at the Hague and Ostend, sailed from Rotterdam with a retinue of diplomats and military officers arriving in London 14 October 1731 (Rapin vol. 20, 104-5; McCann xviii-xxv).

7 To Mary Collier, Hastings, from John [Jacky] Collier, Battle, 19 November 1731 [SAY 1575]

This is to let you know that I am in good health and hope you are well. My uncle James was here at the fair,[1] and told me he had not received his letter and names of the churches. But I hope you have given them him now and tell him I hope he will not forget to send me a letter. I desire you to send me a fairing at the fair and also Jemmy. I shall send a letter to my pappa tomorrow. Tell Mrs Thorpe that Mrs Philcox's child was christned yesterday and Mr Weller, Mr Birch, Molly Phillcox stood for it. I desire you to send me a letter, I give my duty to you and love to my sisters.

1 Revd James Cranston junior.

8 To Mary Collier, Hastings, from John Collier, Johnson's Court, 20 November 1731 [SAY 1576]

I received your agreeable letter that all with you are well and shall speed the directions about the bed and buy the cloake you mention. I think it was silly for Abby at this time of the year to ask or desire the girle to goe, and if I had been at home should possitively have deny'd it, for part of the road is very bad, and on a causeway, and I think dangerous, as she cannot ride behind.[1] Yesterday I dined at home with my brother, and the match came on the carpet, and we had it throughly over. I find it goes forward, and Mrs Swaysland is to be in town next week to settle the affairs, but I beleive noe time is as yet fixed for the marriage, nor nothing done to the house, etc., which really wants.

I think by the last post I wrote you word of goeing to the play to see the Duke of Lorrain. We were in by 5 minnetts after 4, and if wee had been 5 minnetts later could not have got a place. The king, queen, duke and 5 princesses were there, and a numerous audience, and it was past eleaven before the play and entertainment was over, soe that I was heartily tired, and got a little cold. The Duke of Lorrain is a young, good looking man, dressed very plain, and not at all like the modern butterflys. I have given Mrs Elcock your credentialls and she promises me the things next week. We have had very good weather soe that I hope the workmen have continued on. Pray tell the girles I have bespoke their cloggs and to be all alike for the ages of 12, 10 and 5. My humble service to Mrs Thorpe and all freinds. If there are any letters you will mention from whom and what about, that's enough. I intend to write to the boyes this post.

1 For road conditions see Crossley & Saville xi. The rains essential for filling the furnace ponds clogged the roads with mud.

9 To Mary Collier, [Hastings], from John Collier, [Johnson's Court], 23 November 1731 [SAY 1577]

I received your letter by yesterday's post with pleasure to hear a continuance of your health, and as this has been a fine day, don't doubt but the fair produced a grand appearance. The lottery[1] will be finished a Thursday and as all the great prizes are drawn the shew is almost over, but such is the extravagance of people that this morning they gave £17 a ticket for those undrawn. I had one of my 5 in this morning but don't know what has hapned to it, but there is 9 to one whether itt's a prize of £20. A Fryday morning 3 of my tickets were undrawn and they then sold for 18 guineas appeece but that day all the great prizes were drawn and one of mine a blank. A Saturday I had a £20 prize which brings me to near equall that I can't loose above 50s.

William's mistresse came to town this evening, soe I don't expect to see anything more of him this night. Mr Hill's preferment, he was sent to town for, I find comes to nothing for the dean and chapter of Windsor require residence, tho the late incumbent enjoyed it without, soe he must wait till something else happens.[2] I heard today that Mr Halsted affronted Mr Lardner at the court, and that out of the 33 parishes' churchwardens that appeared but 3 parishes dined at the Swan and the rest at Barnes's.

I desire you will get Halsted up and let him examine if the pipe of wine wants filling up, as likely it may on being brought home and standing, never soe little empty, receives prejudice, soe let him have a bottle if it wants to fill it full. My cold continues and I have an inflammation in my eyes that is a little troublesom but it don't increase and I much fear there will be noe decrease till I can leave London. I hear Lord Ashburnham, with whom I dined a Sunday, this day was to kisse the king's hand, for the place soe long talked of.[3] I am with due respects to all friends,

1 The lottery authorised by 4 Geo. II c.9, Act for raising £1.2 million by annuities and £800,000 by a lottery; s.13, on blank tickets, i.e., those not drawn for a specific prize to receive a yearly payment of £3 per cent. Drawing of all tickets due for completion, 18 November 1731 (*SL* vol. 6, 45-54; Ewen ch. 5 no. 17, table 163). John Collier was correct on the price of tickets which 'rose soon after the drawing began to about 16 gns each' (*PS* vol. 42, October 1731, 424). See Introduction for explanation of lotteries at this time.

2 Edward Hill, rector, Hastings St Clement, 6 November 1731 to 5 May 1742; he was also vicar of Fletching from 28 November 1732 to 1742.

3 The Earl of Ashburnham was appointed Captain of the Yeoman of the Guard on 23 November 1731. (J.E. Doyle *The Official Baronage of England* (1886) vol. 1, 89-90; F W Steer described the Ashburnham family and estate in *The Ashburnham Archives* (1958)).

10 To Mary Collier, Hastings, from John Collier, [Johnson's Court], 25 November 1731 [SAY 1578]

I received your letter by this post and am obliged to you for the length of it, tho I am much concerned that you have been indisposed, but I hope itt's entirely over. You may be sure, my dearest, that I have not any the least objection to Mrs Thorpe's being at Hasting, but on the contrary much approve of it, and desire if she must goe home for some time after my return you will engage her return soon again. You will excuse what I wrote about Dely's journey, but I really think it a wrong time of the year. I considered after I had wrote it that you would receive my letter before she set out, which I did not think of when I wrote it. I have forgot whither I mentioned in my last that I had seen Mr and Mrs Carleton and the family, which are all well, and I find they much expected the boyes and seem to presse for them at Christmas, as saying it will be an advantage at that time in their schooling, etc.

I received the hare and am obliged to Mr Godley and Mr Cruttenden for it but wish more had come with it, but hope for better luck next week. My other lottery ticket came up a blank a Tuesday and the lottery ended this morning. My cold continues and I have noe hopes of getting rid of it till my return and I am as yet very uncertain when I can get out of the town. There was a splendid ball at Newcastle House,[1] which lasted all night. If I had convenient time, and been rid of a cold, I had been there, haveing an intimation for that purpose from Colonell Pelham. I had a letter from Jacky and Mr Worge who came hither yesterday and it is a very handsom one. Pray let me hear every post but I cannot as yet ascertain my return.

1 Newcastle House, Lincoln's Inn Fields, northwest corner, nos. 66 and 67, the centre of Newcastle's business and social life whilst resident in London.

11 To Mary Collier, [Hastings], from John Collier, [Johnson's Court], 27 November 1731 [SAY 1579]

I was in great hopes and satisfaction of haveing a letter from you by this post and the more soe because your last mentioned your being somewhat ill. But I hope that tis not a continuance or increase of your indisposition that has prevented it, and I the rather flatter myselfe to the contrary because my brother Cranston or somebody else would have wrote. Thursday night, after I had wrote my letter to you, I saw your brother's mistresse. I shan't entertain you with a description of her, but save that till my return. She lodges in Fleet Street. We have noe particular newes but you may tell the girles I have got their cloggs home. I saw Mrs Milner today.[1] She really looks very well and sends you her humble service and is much concerned she did not see you when in London. I am very sorry I can't inform you of my being able to fix a day for returning to Hasting, much fearing I must tarry this next week.

1 Mrs Milner, 5 Gloster Street, near Red Lion Square, London dressmaker and draper, who supplied the Collier family in the later 1720s and the 1730s (SAY 1418).

12 To John Collier, [Hastings], from John [Jacky] Collier, Battle, 28 January 1732 [SAY 1580]

This is to let you know that I am in good health, and hope you are well. My brother Worge told me he had some tops and books for me, but I have not received them yet, he being not at home when I have been up there. I heard that Dele would come tomorrow, which I hope shell doe, for I love she should be here. I hope you will call upon me when you goe to London, and send me a letter to let me know when you'll goe. I desire you to send [1] us some pens and paper for we have none to write our exercise, but we have a great deal of letter paper such as this, so you need not send us none of that. I send my duty to you and my mamma, love to my brother and sisters, and service to Mrs Thorpe. Give my love to my Master Wicking and all their family.

1 MS *me* struck through

13 To Mary Collier, Hastings, from John Collier, [Johnson's Court], 10 February 1732 [SAY 1581]

I received your agreeable letter, and hope for a continuance of your health and that the vapours will vanish. I shall observe your commands about spaw water.[1] I am sorry poor little Welly is judged to be out of order to be sure it is right to have Dr Carleton. I think Jones a sorry mortall not to have been with you according to his promise. I fully intended to have left Mr Weller's will with you thinking of it the morning I left Hasting when I rose. I am sent to for it this post and have wrote down the heads, which is all can be had till my return. Mr Worge is come to town this afternoon and brought me a letter from Jacky. I saw Mr Carleton today at Colonell Pelham's, he and the family are well and he enquired after the boyes comeing up.

I got into the House of Commons today to hear the debates, which lasted about four hours, and very warm.[2] It is carried for 1s in the pound, and the duty on salt to be revived.[3] The Torys to a man voted for 2s in the pound along[4] with the discontented clan, purely on the sake of party, which I really think monstrous. The speeches were prodigiously warm on both sides, and I am heartily tyred and fatigued. Pray let me know when Salmon's vessell is expected to come up again.[5] I am sorry I can't guesse at a time for my return.

1 Spa and mineral waters; the letters here mention Bath, Tunbridge Wells, Streatham and Scarborough waters, most available in bottles. Immersion in water advised for allieviation of disease, including what was later understood as lead poisoning; for bathing in sea water see Russell; for chalybeate waters as part of a diet (Arbuthnot 245; *OED*); spa and mineral water for medicinal use (Mead vol. 1, 156, 210); although Radcliff 56, 57 states that 'chalybeates are very disagreeable to persons troubled with catarrahs, coughs and stiflings in the lungs' due to the astringent particles in the water.

2 For the background to the Land tax, see Introduction.

3 Opposition to the Land tax at 1/-, and to the re-raising of the Salt tax, comprised disaffected Hanoverian Whigs, supporters of the exiles in France, and a variety of Tories. Amongst the speakers against the Government were William Pulteney, Sir William Wyndham and Lord Dundas (Williams 1945 194-5; Vaucher 62-5); Sayer relied on Mahon vol. 2, 239-49; for William Pulteney's position *ODNB* which also discusses his break with Walpole and Queen Caroline.

4 Thomas Salmon, master, merchant vessel, Hastings to and from ports to London; for the coastal trade see Willan 150, appendix 7, 220-2 and BL. Add Ms. 11,255 for numbers of ships belonging to Hastings, divided into foreign trading ships, coastal shipping, and fishing vessels; the Hastings Chamberlains' books list Hastings ship masters in the herring and mackerel trades; TNA Exch. KR. Port Books E. 190 series lists information for taxed imports and for exports due bounty payments.

14 To Mary Collier, Hastings, from John Collier, [Johnson's Court], 19 February 1732 [SAY 1582]

I received your letter per this post and tis with a great deal of concern and regret I am obliged to inform you that I cannot come out of town a Munday morning in the coach for Tunbridge, soe must loose my earnest.[1] However, I desire Nick may set out a Munday morning with the horses, and lye at Sen'nocke, and soe come to London Tuesday forenoon, set up the horses at Mrs Heberden's, and come over to my brother's and wait there till I come in. For I hope to get out before Fryday, and there is noe coach day before, and as I have the horses, can set out the moment I have done my businesse. I am sadly shagreened on the dissappointment, being very heartily weary of the town, and longing to see you and yours. I beleive you must furnish Nicholas with money, but I should be glad if he has enough to bring him up of his own. My brother goes out tomorrow and Mr Frewen a Munday by the coach, soe that I am almost left alone. Pray tell Nicholas he must call at Tunbridge and bring up with him my bootes and saddle left there in comeing up.

1 London to Tonbridge coach service, Monday, Wednesday and Friday in winter; also coaches every weekday from London to Sennocke, a common name for Sevenoaks.

15 To Mary Collier, Hastings, from John Collier, Johnson's Court, 24 February 1732 [SAY 1583]

This day I have finished Mrs Brewer's affair, which has deteyned me in town, soe farr as to have her consent to leave London, but last night I had orders from the D of N to tarry three or four dayes. Though, perhaps, it may and will be only a wildgoose chase, there is a little place dropped in the law that I would gladly accept of, and did make some application for at my first comeing to town, but now gave it over.[1] He told me last night, he thinks I shall have it. The place is to be executed by a clerk, and easy and creditable, and I beleive about £80 a year, a serjeant at law[2] had it before, vizt Generall Webb's brother.[3] soe I now determine to tarry and see the event, though I shall be confoundedly vexed if I misse it, but will take no manner of notice to anybody till determined. My brother Cranston is not returned to town, I mean was not at 6, and since I have not been at home I am heartily tired, and shall grow more impatient every day. I begg, my dear, you will write a letter a Saturday night that I may a Munday have the satisfaction to hear of your being very well. I cannot say but I have businesse to emply me but none in such a condition but I could leave to my agent's[4] conduct. Pray give my humble respects to all friends and beleive me as I am with invariable resolutions. I have sent my boxes this week. In the long one is only a new coat and breeches and a gown for me. The 2 boyes gownes and cloathes for Nicholas and your camlet which if you'l want you'l open it.

1 John Collier appointed Usher and Cryer, King's Bench, in the life of himself and son James, and survivor; after James' death, the lives of John Cranston, the second son of William Cranston by marriage to Mary Swaysland, and Michael Rowe, were inserted.

2 Serjeant at Law, a rank granted to the most knowledgeable and experienced in the work of the Westminster courts; although serjeants could plead in any Westminster court, the Common Pleas was reserved to serjeants only. Judges appointed only from this rank see J H Baker *The Order of Serjeants at Law: A Chronology of creations, with related texts and a historical introduction* (1984) 42; and also (*EB* 1771 vol. 3, 579).

3 General John Richmond Webb, Tory, dismissed from command in 1715 on orders of George I. MP Ludgershall died1724 (*HofP 1715-1754* vol. 2, 526-7)

4 MS has no apostrophe.

16 To Mary Collier, Hastings, from John [Jacky] Collier, Battle, 26 February 1732 [SAY 1584]

This is to let you know that I am in good health and hope you are likewise. I desire you to send me a letter to let me know whether my pappa is come home for he has not called here, and if he is, I desire him to send me the 4th and fifth volume of the Arabian Tales.[1] I desire you to send me my greatcoat and boots, both which I want very much. We have had very ill fortune at our cocks,[2] and we had'nt had any money, had not Mis Nelly lent us some. I and Jemmy and two or three more were at Mrs Botting's, where we were handsomely treated. I give my [3] duty to you and my pappa and love to my brother and sisters.

1 The first English edition of the *Arabian Nights entertainments, one thousand and one stories* trans. from Antoine Galland's 1704 French edition was published in 1708, more editions followed: John Collier's library in Old Hastings House contained a 6 volume edition.
2 Cockfighting, see J Strutt *The Sports and Pastimes of the People of England* (1967) 394-5.
3 *Pap* struck through.

17 To John [Jacky] Collier, Battle, from John Collier, Johnson's Court, 18 March 1732 [SAY 1585]

I received your letter but not goeing home to dinner cannot send you any paper, but as you have but a week to tarry would have you buy some to supply that want. I hope God Almighty will give you grace to perform your promise of not gameing again at soe high a rate, and to abstain from all sin and wickednesse; for the contrary will loose you all my favours, and incur God's displeasure, and you must be miserable in this world and the next. My blessing to both of you. All are well here except your little brother who is much out of order, your affectionate and indulgent father.

18 To John [Jacky] Collier, Battle, from Mary Collier, Hastings, 1732[1] [SAY 1586]

I received your letter and am very glad to hear you are well but sorry to find the smallpox is in your town.[2] I desire you would always goe to the side of the way when you goe to school and never play near the house. I hear your pappa will not be at home till next week which I am very sorry for. Your aunt Cruttenden has had her sore throat but is now pretty well again. Give my service to Mrs Thorpe and daughters and tell Miss Molly she must change the air for her cold and I should be very glad to see her here.[3] I hope you be a good boy. I pray God bless you and make you soe and pray be carefull and avoid Mr Brewer's house. I am your affectionate mother, mother M.C.

1 MS no date given, and this letter is placed as in Sayer vol. 1, 61; Both John and Jacky are on the original.
2 For smallpox in Sussex at this time see Crook ch. 2; also P E Razzell 'Population Change in Eighteenth Century England: A Re-interpretation' *EcHR* 2nd series vol. 18 (1965).
3 Change of air was recommended to alleviate coughs and chest infections with a preference for outdoor air in the country; the venting of foul air long regarded as necessary in coal and mineral mines, and in naval and merchant ships; hot air blamed for breathing difficulties in smallpox, and thought to check urine and increase number of pustules inside the body; (Mead vol. 1, 'Venomous exhalations from the earth, poisonous airs and water' 141-2; in respect of fevers *EB* 1771, vol. 3, 69-70). Air from marshes and drains and putrid air from decomposition were blamed as a cause of illness. Advocates of visits to Hampstead, Tunbridge Wells, Bath and Scarborough emphasised their air quality.

19 To Mary Collier, Hastings, from John Collier, [Johnson's Court], 17 June 1732
[SAY 1587]

I have the pleasure and satisfaction of writing to you an account of my arriveing here yesterday about one or two a clock. G. Worge came with me and as we got to Seavenoak Thursday before 8. Sent to know if my sister Cranston was at home, she was not, but in halfe an hour had a message, and went to her, where I introduced her nephew Worge, he having not seen her before. We had bespoke a couple of ducks for supper, and I invited her to goe with us, but she excused it much, and did not, though I told her, as it was in a brother and nephew's company, it would take of any objections. We tarried till a message of suppers being ready, and when we came to the inn found Sir William Ashburnham and Mr Frewen,[1] with whom we joyned company, and soe continued till we came to town.

I find the workmen have almost finished and I think great alterations for the best. My brother is gone this evening to Seavenoake to return a Tuesday, being to sell of all goods and clear the house, and she to come to town for good the latter end of this next week. I invited her to Hasting this summer, and find she intends to come. Sir William intends to goe out of town again a Munday, comeing only to advise with a new doctor and to buy a table. I find he intends to see none of his friends or acquaintance, not even Dick Tilden. I have heard noe newes since I came to town worth imparting. The ridotto at Spring Gardens is a little talked of, but I find did not extreamly take.[2] There were 10 men to a woman, and thought none of the last but prostitutes; the P of Wales was there, but went away in 2 hours. There is to be another next week, but it is not thought that any good company will be increased.

The P of W, the moment he heard that Vanella[4] was ill drove away in his coach and 6, and seems highly delighted with the produce of his intrigue. I quite forgot to put up my gown for which I am at a very great losse but shall not buy another. Pray speak to Mr Mead when he alters the windowes in the little parlour and other rooms in that front, that he takes all the care he can to prevent the rains breaking through in the winter. I have nothing more in particular to write but wishing health and happinesse to you and ours, and that health may continue till my return to you and that I alwayes am with inviolable attachment.

1 Thomas Frewen, Brickwall House, Northiam.

2 The new ridotto, at Vauxhall gardens, on the south side of the Thames, 12 acres, at the site of the old Spring gardens. Re-opening night Wednesday 7 June 1732, advertised with ridotto al fresco in a quadrangle with orchestra, 5 or 6 p.m., to 9 p.m., pavilion with outdoor dining in boxes lined with country and arcadian paintings, elm lined walks lit by oil lamps. Company of soldiers to keep order, attended by Frederick, Prince of Wales (Downing 19-24 for picture and map; W Wroth *The London Pleasure Gardens of the Eighteenth Century* (1896) 286, 290-2).

3 Miss Anne Vane, sister of Lord Darlington, maid of honour to Queen Caroline, mistress of Frederick, Prince of Wales who provided her house in Soho Square (Hervey vol. 1, xxix-xli).

20 To Mary Collier, Hastings, from John Collier, [Johnson's Court], 27 June 1732
[SAY 1588]

I received your letter with the account of Mr Broadway's notice.[1] I find he was very exact to give it on the very quarter day, which looks as if he had consulted the learned in the law, but he is therein egregiously mistaken if I would insist upon it but that will passe over. I am really quite weary of tarrying in town and uneasy that I cannot fix a time for my return. G. Worge went out of town yesterday afternoon about 5 a clock, but I did not hear one word of the designed meeting, whither itt's wit or great management to keep such triffles secret, I am not a judge. I hope you are got rid of the carpenters and that a little while on my return will compleat our room to be rid of them. I have bought all the things you directed me and shall remember the bason to send down the first vessell.

I never knew the town more barren of newes than at present. There are great preparations makeing for the instalment of the Knights of the Bath.[2] But I don't intend giveing myselfe any trouble about that affair, but compleat my businesse as soon as possible to have the pleasure of returning home to you, my dearest, in whom centers all my happinesse and satisfaction. I have really been in a continuall hurry ever since I came to town and see noe end to it as yet. I have generally dined at home ever since our sister came up except Munday last and the Saturday before. They are not as yet free from workmen. I find my brother James had a pair of stockings at 7 oake according to custom but they were black as indeed most suitable. H. Dodson has been in town 3 or 4 dayes but I think is gone out.[3] I took noe manner of notice of him. I wonder there is not by this time something come forth.

1 Thomas Broadway rented a house from John Collier in Hastings, late Gurrs, at £6 year, reduced to £5 year, see the rental book for John Collier's estate (ESRO M7/23 f.33); Broadway voted for Fuller in 1734.

2 Order of the Bath, created by letters patent, George I, 18 May 1725, statutes of the order issued at Hanover, 16 November 1725 OS; order not just to resuscitate and maintain 'honours of knighthood in its former lustre and dignity, but to erect the same into a regular military order'. George I was at the apex, just below came a royal prince, followed by the master and thirty-five companions; the initiation ritual explained (Shaw vol.1, xvi-xix).

3 Henry Dodson, attorney, apprentice to John Collier, town clerk Winchelsea 1740-47 shared with Edwin Wardroper (Pratt 249).

21 To Mary Collier, Hastings, from John Collier, [Johnson's Court], 1 July 1732

[SAY 1589]

I received your letter and doe assure you that itt's impossible for you to desire my return home more than I doe myselfe, and I am come to a resolution of leaving the town as next Wednesday soe as to be at home a Thursday, if nothing very extraordinary happens; if it should I shall write next post and not otherwise, for I am determined noe little matter shall keep me here. Notwithstanding I did not design to be at the instalment yesterday, I was there and saw the whole ceremony and dined in the painted chamber with the esquires of the Knights of the Bath and very elegantly.[1] I am sorry you are without company but I hope to bee soe happy as to reach Hasting at the above time.

1 30 June 1732, four companions initiated, Henry Brydges, Marquis of Carnarvon, later 2nd Duke of Chandos; William Bateman, 1st Viscount Bateman; Sir Charles Downing, Charles Gunter Nicoll (Shaw vol.1, 168-9).

22 To John [Jacky] Collier, [London],[1] from Mary Collier, Hastings, [?August 1732]

[SAY 1590]

I hope this will find you and Jemmy in good health which I shall be very glad to have an account of often. Your uncle and aunt came here last Saturday and send their love to you. Pray tell Jemmy I insist upon his writeing a letter next week and wonder he does not enquire after his poultrey, which he left behind. Tell him I want him sadly to call them together, for the white hen has not sett at home since, and am afraid we shall loose her. His great ship has been demolished to make spits to roast wheat ears, it being too bigg to give it house-room, but hope he'll be a better engineer when he comes home again. I hope, my dear, you both like London which I shall be always pleased to hear. Dely and Molly are to enclose each of them a letter in this, and you must answer one, and Jemmy tother, tho I am afraid you will not be able to send either. Mr John Hall has beat his wife and Skimington was rode,[2] which woud have pleasd you to see, though you see much finer things every day. I take it very kind of Mr Page to take soe much notice of you and especially as your other freinds are out of town.[3] I find your uncle intends to take you home for a week at Chrismas, which will be pleasant for you. Give my service to Mr and Miss Carleton and tell her Miss Nanny is very well, I have sent for her severall times and shall take particular notice of her upon their account, but still more as you are under her care.

1 Then at Westminster School.

2 Skimington, punishment of the violent behaviour by a wife towards her husband and vice versa, by procession of neighbours and townsfolk (Underdown 25; E P Thompson 'Rough Music: Le Charivari Anglais' in *Annales, Histoire, Sciences Sociales* 27, no 2, (1972) 294-5). John Hall rented a house in Hastings from John Collier at £10 year, 1731-35 (ESRO M7/23 f.25).

3 William Page, attorney who worked with John Collier and William Cranston.

23 To John [Jacky] Collier, George[1] Carleton's, Great Dean's Yard, Westminster, from Mary Collier, Hastings, 12 August 1732 [SAY 1591]

I received both your letters and am glad to hear you are both well. That afternoon you went in the morning we went to Mr Luxford's and stayed three nights, and called upon your old maid Abby who was mightily concerned att your goeing to London without seeing you, and don't know whether she won't take a journey on purpose to make you a vissett. I am glad, my dear, to hear you like London and hope I shall always hear a continueance of it, and of your health which will be great satisfaction to me. I think you had a little too much courage to venture soe farr as your uncle's[2] with little George. I woud have you be very careful upon all accounts.

Tell Jemmy his dirty hen has brought forth five chicken, two half bantum, but the true bantum egg had the misfortune to be broke in peices just as it was coming out of the shell. Dely is as carefull of your sqiriell as she can, but tis almost too much for her, for it gets loose and runs all under the ceilling.[3] Nedd Miller is come from Battle again and I fancy will follow Jemmy to London. Betty Wickens is gone to the races which are now att the height but they are nothing to what is to be seen every day in London.[4] I hope God will bless you both and make you good boys, for which reason you must not omitt your prayers to him morning and night, which which will not fail to procure blessings for you. I find by your letter you soon break up, at time I desire you woud not run too much about, which woud be dangerous. Mis Thorpe sende her service to you both, mine to Mr Carlton and lady;[5] you must send a new song somtimes.

1 MS has Henry, although the boarding house was in the care of his son George Carleton.

2 MS *uncles*.

3 By the seventeenth century it was common for the well-off to keep animals as domestic pets, including monkeys, tortoises, rabbits and red squirrels, as well as cats and dogs, farmyard animals, oxen and horses K Thomas *Man and the Natural World: Changing attitudes in England 1500-1800* (1984) 110-11.

4 Parliament legislated on the dangers from gambling and idleness among the lower ranks, 13 Geo II c. 19 (1740), 'An Act to restrain and prevent the excessive increase of horse races, and for amending an Act made in the last session of Parliament intitled, an Act for the more effectual preventing of excessive and deceitful gaming' (*SL* vol. 6, 396-7).

5 Revd Mr George Carleton MA, chanter of the Abbey, subdean of the Chapel Royal and king's chaplain, August 1732, annual salary £91 5s 0d, plus annual £73 for the six months of each year waiting to give a sermon, January, March, May, July, September and November.

24 To John [Jacky] and James [Jemmy] Collier, at Revd Mr George Carleton's, Dean's Yard, Westminster, from John Collier, Hastings, 17 August 1732

[SAY 1592]

I have been very much from home since you went to London, or should sooner have wrote to you, but as I have seen your letters to your mamma, and saw your uncle at the assizes, and, by him and letters from Mr Page, and Mr Steevens, hear you are both well and like London, it is very agreeable to me. I shall expect to have a letter from you, where you are placed in the school, and how long your recesse is at Bartholomewtide,[1] and what tasks you have for the time, and anything more you have to write. Your mamma, sisters and Mrs Thorpe, are very well, as are all friends here. I hope you will both take care not to doe anything to dissoblige Mr or Mrs Carleton, but carry yourselves very civilly in the house, and not goe anywhere without leave, nor be drawn into any ill practices by other boyes, but serve God, mind your books, and be of a handsom behaviour and everybody will love and respect you, and you shall in such case have all encouragement and everything that is reasonable.

Wee see by the newespapers that Mr Carleton is appointed subdean of the king's chappell, and as Colonel Pelham told me a week since that he thought Mr Carleton would have it. I hope itt's true and your mamma joynes with me in humble service to him and Mrs Carleton, which, with our blessing to you both, and chargeing you to be good and kind to one another.

1 Bartholomewtide, annual festival and fair 24 August, West Smithfield 1133 to 1855; gambling, entertainment, sales of miscellaneous items and household goods.

25 To John [Jacky] and James [Jemmy] Collier, at Revd George Carleton's, Dean's Yard, Westminster, from John Collier, Hastings, 7 October 1732 [SAY 1593][1]

Your mamma and I have been in great expectation of hearing from you, for these last two or three posts, but hope this will find you both very well, and good boyes, and that we shall have such an account by next post. We are all here in good health, and your aunt Denham has been here about a week, and sends her kind love to you, as indeed everybody with us. Your uncle and aunt Cranston, talk of goeing away the latter end of next week, and as soon as they come to London will send to you, and you will have a place to visit at any leisure time. I beleive I shall be in London myselfe about a month hence and shall think it a great satisfaction, to find you well and to hear you are diligent in your books, and behave in a handsom manner. If you want anything Mr Carleton will please to supply you; Misse Nanny Carleton is very well and brisk, we have a company of players in town that act at the court hall and she was there last night.[2] Your squirrell, last night, unfortunately hung himselfe by his table, but he was grown mischeiveous, soe that I beleive you will think it noe great losse. We expect Dr Carleton's return very soon, by whom we are satisfyed to hear from you, your sister Worge has been here a week and had gone home today but it has been very terrible weather, pray give our humble service to Dr Carleton, if with you, and to his two sons and Mrs Carleton, the same to Misse Ford if in London.

1 MS both Jacky and Jemmy are on the original.

2 Court hall, Hastings; old court hall, replaced 1700 by the new court hall, High Street; funded by town MPs John Pulteney and Peter Gott, ironmaster; (*VCH Sussex* vol. 9, 5; Cleere & Crossley 194-5; Saville 1978 vol.3, Table 12:4); Gott and son received payments for ordnance from 1697, and during the war of the Spanish Succession (Hodgkinson 2009a 80-2; Baines 56).

26 To John [Jacky] and James [Jemmy] Collier, at Revd George Carleton's, Dean's Yard, Westminster, from John Collier, Hastings, 24 October 1732 [SAY 1594a][1]

Your mamma and I received Jacky's letter of the 10th instant, informing us of your being both well, but as we expected to hear again from you, on your uncle's arrivall in town, deferred writing. We both very much wonder that Jemmy has not once wrote, and think him very naughty in not doeing it, and shall not excuse him without his writeing next Saturday, and as I have enclosed a frank, you may both write and put both letters in it.[2] I shall not be in London soe soon as I intended, and beleive it will be towards the middle of November before I come. Your uncle Cranston from Bexhill was here today, and is very well, and sends his love and joynes with us in humble service to Mr Carleton and his wife.

We have noe manner of newes here to send you, but that our Yarmouth herring fishery has made out very well and got a great deal of money.[3] Pray continue to be very good boyes and let your behaviour in all respects answer that character, if you expect any countenance and encouragement from us. Misse Nanny Carleton is very well and was up here yesterday; our humble service to Misse Foord.

1 SAY 1594 is the envelope; both Jacky and Jemmy are on the original.

2 Franks, official signature for letters and parcels sent by MPs, Lords on government service and the armed forces, attached to envelope or cover; recognised by postmasters as not liable for postal charges (Pyle 105).

3 Sussex proverb, 'By June, mackerel is in tune,' (F Sawyer 'Sussex Folk-lore and Customs connected with the Seasons', *SAC* 33). The Rock Fair marked the close of the mackerel fishing by the end of July. The Yarmouth herring fishery commenced early September and lasted for just over two months declining to early December; herring was a staple of the economy of Sussex ports.

27 To Mary Collier, [Hastings], from John Collier, [London] 16 November 1732 [SAY 1595]

I have the satisfaction to inform you of my save arrivall in London but found the roads intollerable bad. My brother and sister Cranston are pretty well and send their humble service; though the latter has the remaines of a cold of ten dayes standing in which she has not been out of doors. I heard by them of the boyes' welfare. But we expected them every moment till 3, when they jumped in very brisk and lively, and I think both grown, but I was amazed to see them without a shooe to their feet, especially Jacky. I sent for a shooemaker and equipped them each a new pair. They had their best cloaths on, but Jemmy's in a sad condition with grease. They had what they called clean shirts on, but I think looked but bad. Jemmy looked very thin, and I had him took measure of for some other cloathes.[1] They seem very brisk, and to like the school and their master. Mrs Carleton is not brought a bed but daily expected, and I think my sister begins to look bigg. I intend to goe tomorrow to Mr Carleton's. I think it is odd they would let them bee without shooes for itt's enough to catch their deaths. They are to come to me a Saturday and tarry all night. I hope Mrs Thorpe is, by the time this reaches you, come safe to keep you company, to whom and all friends I desire my service.

1 Payments by John Collier for clothes and household goods in November 1732 (SAY 1418 f. 4-5v)

28 To Mary Collier, [Hastings], from John [Jacky] Collier, [Johnson's Court], 18 November 1732 [SAY 1596]

Being with my pappa, and he writing a letter to you, directed me to do the same. Though I have no news to acquaint[1] you off, but that Mrs Carleton was brought to bed last night of a girl and is as well as can be expected. My pappa will goe to see my master before he goes out of town, and I hope we have behaved to his satisfaction. We are to lie at my uncle's tonight. My pappa says Mrs Thorpe was to come to our house yesterday to whom I desire my humble service.

1 MS *a qu^t* extended here.

29 To Mary Collier, [Hastings], from John Collier, [Johnson's Court], 18 November 1732 [SAY 1597]

I received your letter wrote a Thursday and hope you had mine of the same date. I am sorry to hear that the children have got the chicken pox neer you but hope they may not enter our house. I dined at Mr Carleton's yesterday and paid him what is due from the boyes which is a high amount but upon enquiry I am determined to have somethings regulated for them. They came to me this evening and are both very well and brisk and hope in God they will continue soe. As Jacky's letter mentions Mrs Carleton's being brought abed I doe not repeat it. I beleive the house is under hopefull management, I have not paid their schooling, intending to doe it in person and wait on Mr Nicolls for that purpose.[1]

I desire you will send the letter accompanying this to Mr Mead a Munday morning, and if he sends up a paper let Nick carry it to Battell a Munday to be brought by the carrier. My sister Cranston promises to buy your coat the beginning of the week, and I have bought the bibles and shall send them. Jemmy's cloathes is to be made against Tuesday morning. Pray let me hear from you every post and I shall see the boyes as often as possible whilst I tarry in town. I can't perceive but that they learn exceedingly well and will goe through the school with honour. Mr Carleton took noe manner of notice to me of George's[2] disgrace but softened the matter by saying he wrote bad and soe put him to learn better. He don't as yet goe to Westminster school but I beleive is to goe again soon. Misse Foord sends her service but as Mrs Carleton was a little ill and had her midwife I did not see her.

1 John Nicoll, undermaster, Westminster school, 1714-1733.
2 George Carleton, junior, contemporary with John (Jacky) Collier.

30 To Mary Collier, Hastings, from John Collier, [Johnson's Court], 21 November 1732 [SAY 1598]

I received your letter by last post and had your little boyes along with me who are very well and this day Jemmy has his new warm cloaths. I was yesterday at Mr Carleton's, intending to talk over some regulations, but had not an opportunity of doeing it throughly, there being company, but am determined of having it set to rights. However, I have had their breakfasts and about the fire setled. Next Fryday I design to wait on Mr Nicholls, and as he has been exceedingly kind to them, think it best to give him handsomly for their schooling. I beleive I shall send your red rugg and bibles and chocolate tomorrow by the carrier.[1] I saw Mrs Carleton yesterday who is mighty well, but as they are such a parcell of people shall keep the hoggs pudding for the boyes at my brother's, for they come three dayes in a week.

A Sunday they wore 2 of the new shirts and fit them very well, being but a little matter to bigg for Jemmy. The other two are left at my brother's for I beleive itt's the last time they will be soe clean again. Itt's a great pleasure that the dear boyes goe through their hardship with courage and cheerfulnesse, and seem very well pleased with the school. I shall see after the portmanteau at Mr Carleton's. I hope, my dear, you continue in perfect health, and I shall have the pleasure to find you soe on my return, and am sorry I cannot ascertain any time for it. Mr Carleton told me that, on any complaint of the servants' ill behaviour, it shall bee rectifyed and they say he is very kind to them. I told the boyes about their shirts airing and Jacky sayes they alwayes air them but doe it themselves. My humble service to all friends; I am glad Mrs Thorpe is with you for company. The covering of the stools is a flowered cotton[2] and some stiff paper under them to prevent dust and keeping them from tarnishing. The paper must be sometimes taken out and dryed but not put on hot. I hope they will come down safe for their cost £2 7s 0d.

1 SAY 1418 f.4v.

2 For reference to the import of India cottons, see Introduction.

31 To Mary Collier, [Hastings], from John Collier, Johnson's Court, 23 November 1732 [SAY 1599]

I am to assure you that I received your letter this post with a great deal of satisfaction. And I am to inform you that the writeing from Mr Mead and the hoggs puddings[1] came very safe yesterday, and this afternoon the boyes were with me and eat part, and the rest are kept for them at Johnson's Court. Our sister eat some of them and much liked it. The boyes are vastly desirous of seeing a play and entertainment and, as they have a holyday tomorrow afternoon, I have promised to carry them. There was a sad misfortune hapned today at Mr Carleton's: Mary, one of their maids, was taken suddenly ill about ten this morning with convulsions and dyed immediately. I have sent Mr Nicolls, the boyes' master, a hare and 2 wild ducks and intended to goe tomorrow but cannot, but shall certainly see him before I leave London and Mr Carleton fully to regulate everything for I shall fully insist on it. I have just sent the boyes home in a coach[2] and with them a couple of wild ducks for Mr Carleton. Jemmy has got his new cloathes and is as also Jacky very brisk and well. I hope in God they will escape the smallpox but if they are taken with it shall leave the conduct to Mr Page, etc., for really Mrs Carleton is hardly to be depended on. I am as yet very uncertain when I shall come out of town, but hope it will be the latter end of next week. I observe by your letter that there is a report of an invitation to Bishopston[3] as next Munday, but I fancy it is without foundation for the duke doth not goe out for that place, as I hear, till next Wednesday.

1 Hog's pudding: stomach and entrails of a pig or boar, stuffed with oatmeal, suet, or flour and tripe, with raisins, currants, salt and spices for flavour.

2 Georgian London saw a growing demand for hackney coaches and sedan chairs; by 9 Anne c. 23 commissioners were appointed to regulate the trade in the City, Westminster, and the parishes covered by the Mortality statistics; by 10 Anne c. 19 s. 158 (1710), the maximum number of hackney 'sedan' chairs was fixed at 300 and widows of hackney chairmen could inherit the licence. By 1 Geo. 1. c. 57, from 24 June 1715, the number of hackney coaches was limited to 800, each to pay 5/- per week for their licence; by 12 Geo. 1 c. 12 maximum number of sedan chairs was raised to 400; (*SL* vol. 4, 489, 560; vol. 5, 97, 577).

3 Duke of Newcastle's Bishopstone estate near Seaford, used for hunting and entertaining (McCann xxvi).

32 To Mary Collier, [Hastings], from Jacky Collier, London, 25 November 1732 [SAY 1600]

Being come to my uncle's with Jemmy, to tarry all night, my pappa directed us both to write to you, to let you know we are well, as well here as at home. Jemmy has given you account of the play last night,[1] so I have only to say we were highly delighted with it, and my pappa sent us home in a coach, and Harry went with us. My pappa and me and uncle and aunt are all to dine at Mr Greene's tomorrow. My pappa says you will come to town against Easter, which I should think a great happiness and pleasure, and shall wait for it with a great deal of impatience. The post being now just ten of the clock I have only time to add that I am, honoured madam, your most dutiful son.[2]

1 Three performances, Friday 24 November: (i), Drury Lane Theatre, *The Double Gallant, or, The Sick Lady's Cure*, by Colley Cibber, also *The Country Revels*, the royal family present: (ii), Lincoln's Inn Fields, *Duke or no Duke*, by Nahum Tate, also *Perseus and Andromeda, or The Cheats of Harlequin*: (iii), Goodman's Fields, *The Spanish Fryer*, by John Dryden (Scouten pt 3, vol. 1, 1729-36 250).

2 MS y^r. most Du: son.

33 To Mary Collier, Hastings, from John Collier, [Johnson's Court], 28 November 1732 [SAY 1601]

I received your letter by last post which was very agreeable to me and I have given directions for buying your present to Mrs Thorpe, which I think is very well judged, but it will cost 25s. It is with a very great concern that I must send you word that I am not certain when I shall come out of town but hope the latter end of this week. Our boyes are perfectly well and brisk, and I hope I have regulated a great many things at Mr Carleton's that were, from their supine negligence, barbarously omitted. I have bought Jacky a watch, and as Jemmy was displeased at it, think I have made him satisfactory promises. They are to come to me tomorrow night and lye at my brother's, and I have given them strict charge about the water and ice,[1] and everything that I think will bring them into any danger. I hope by next post to acquaint you when I shall return to Hasting and have the pleasure of enjoying your company.

1 John Hooker, the meteorologist who owned Tonbridge castle, cited the onset of this winter as marked by coughs, pleurisy, peripneumonia and throat inflamations (Royal Society, Hooker Mss).

34 To Mary Collier, Hastings, from John Collier, [Johnson's Court], 30 November 1732 [SAY 1602]

I called at the coffee house[1] today between 12 and one for my letters and finding noe letter from you made me not a little uneasy. But when I went home to dinner at 2 a clock found Jemmy had a letter which, I think, my dear, was vastly agreeable. For the poor boyes haveing a vigill yesterday and a holyday for St Andrew,[2] I directed them to come last night, and they lay with me both in the same bed, and I sent them home this evening in a coach with Harry. Mr Subdean made me a present of 2 tickets for a concert of musick, and I this night carried my sister. I really think she is very kind and civill to the boyes, and upon that account I would shew her any civillity.

I am heartily sorry that I am obliged to tell you that I cannot possibly leave the town till next Munday when I think nothing shall prevent my comeing out of town, and being at home a Tuesday night be assured, my dearest soul, that I am heartily concerned at being dissappointed in comeing home soe soon as I intended. I have bought the hood you desired but sent nothing per the carrier this week, for I was in the city the whole day and could not put them up in the evening. Mr Worge came to town this day and with Mr Page and Mr Cranston, now with me, and drinking to our Sussex friends, and my dear, to yours in particular.

1 Sussex coffee house, 17-18 Bouverie Street, Fleet Street (Lillywhite 560 no. 1304). 132 coffee houses were sited on the east side of the Strand from Drury Lane to the Fleet ditch and 551 overall sited within the parishes covered by the collection of the bills of mortality statistics.

2 MS *holyday* St Andrew's day, 30 November 1732.

35 To Mary Collier, Hastings, from John Collier, [Johnson's Court], December 1732 [SAY 1603]

I received your letter this evening with a vast deal of surprize and concern as bringing an account of Mr Gyles's death,[1] tho am exceedingly pleased with a continuance of your health. I doe assure you that noe emergency shall make a greater delay of my setting out for Hasting beyond Munday, soe as to get home Tuesday night or Wednesday noon, tho I would tarry willingly 3 or 4 dayes on this unexpected alteration. Till tomorrow 2 a clock I am not certain whither I can get out Munday morning or afternoon, but one of it am determined upon. Our good boyes came this afternoon and tarry tonight, and as I have not got them one holyday, intend to keep them tomorrow night likewise, and send a letter to the school. I am obliged to buy Jemmy a watch likewise, I find noe promises will doe, and I really think he must not be discouraged. I am with all esteem and affection; Mr Gyles' death embarasses me much.

1 Thomas Gyles burial, Hastings St Clement's 4 December 1732.

36 To John Collier, from John [Jacky] Collier, Dean's Yard, Westminster, 9 December 1732 [SAY 1604]

Honoured pappa, we were at my uncle's this day, who told me he had had a letter from you, and that you were well, which we were very glad of. Tuesday morning we went to school and Mr Nichols asks us were we was, and we told him, so he said twas very well. Thursday last I had a silver threepence gave me, and this day a silver twopence. Mr Carlton and Mrs and Mis Ford give their humble service to you and my mamma and all other friends. Our watches make out very well, but I have not got a string yet, but my uncle says he will get me one. I believe we break up about next Thursday, when I hope to be at my uncle's for Christmas. Georgey desires you would not forget to tell his pappa about a watch. We was to go to the king's scholars' play last night,[1] only Tommy Green is ill, pray give my duty to yourselfe and my mamma and love to my sisters.

1 Westminster school, *Eunuchus* by Terence, performed in Latin by Westminster scholars in their dormitory 13 November 1732 (Scouten pt 3, vol. 1, 1729-36 254); performed again by Westminster scholars, 6 February 1733 (Scouten pt 3, vol. 1, 1729-36 270); epilogue in (*GSJ* 15 February 1733).

37 To John Collier, Hastings, from John [Jacky] Collier, [London], 19 December 1732 [SAY 1605]

Honoured sir, I hope you will pardon my false writing in my last letter, and to be sure, I will take care for the future not to write any false concords, as, - (we was) or to spell anything [1] wrong. I am glad to hear [2] of the birth of a new brother, and that my mamma and the child are both well.[3] We came to my uncle's last Friday for the Christmas holidays, which end with us, next Monday fortnight. I have for my task 24 verses to make upon the 45th psalm,[4] and a chapter of the heathen gods to turn into Latin, and 120 lines to get by heart in the twelfth book of Ovid's Meta: viz Ajax's speech. And Jemmy has for his, the 103d psalm to turn into Latin, the same to get by heart, and some of Aesop's fables to translate into English. We have done all our writing, and I can say most part of my Ovid, and Jemmy has nothing but the psalm to get, so that very little remains for either of us to do.

The frosts being broke up, the streets are very dirty, which makes it very indifferent travelling abroad, but live in hopes it will soon return again, when, my uncle's has promised to shew us a great many places. Amongst the rest we are to go to Putney to stay one night with Mr Tilden.[5] We had some intimation today of Mr Carleton's design to part with us, of which my uncle this post, will give a more particular account. The gentleman who [6] informed us of it, and who seems to be recommended by Mr Carleton as a proper person for us to board with, I know very well, and if, upon enquiry, his house should be thought equal with any other for that purpose, I hope we should all be put to him. For he is a very good natured man, and has, in many instances already been very [7] civil to us, and we should think ourselves very happy to be put under his care. Notwithstanding Jemmy has referred to my letter for news, yet I don't know of any worth sending, so shall follow his example and conclude with duty to my mamma, and love to my brother and sisters, and service to all friends, and with subscribing myself, your most dutifull son.

1 MS *false* struck through.
2 MS *my* struck through.
3 This was Thomas, who died in infancy.
4 45th Psalm, 17 verses; it was common in grammer school for pupils to translate commentaries and verses from the bible into Latin. John Collier's library contained many theological books, including Sternhold & Hopkins *Whole Book of Psalms*.
5 George Tilden of Putney died in 1744. For the Tilden family records, see ESRO Raper & Fovargue papers.
6 MS *was* struck through.
7 MS useful struck through.

38 To John Collier, [Hastings] from James [Jemmy] Collier, Johnston's Court, 19 December 1732 [SAY 1606]

I am very sorry that in my last letter I made so many mistakes in my spelling, but promise to be more carefull for the future. I am glad to hear my mamma is safely brought to bed and wish you and her much joy of my new brother, who I should be very glad to see at Westminster School. Though I beleive he has not much occasion for it for he is already so great a scholar that he, I don't doubt, as fluently talks Latin, Greek and Hebrew as

English. News at present is so scarce that there is not enough to fill up two letters. Therefore, I leave that article to my brother and shall conclude with my duty to my mamma, and love to my sisters, and service to all friends, wishing you all as merry a Christmas, as, honoured sir, your most dutifull and obedient son.

39 To John [Jacky] Collier jun. from Elizabeth Denham, Hollington, before end December 1732 [SAY 2183]

Sir, I take it as a great favour that you have honoured me with the first spring of your endeavours which by its early bloom promises a fruitfull harvest and that you will no way degenerate from father or mother to whome pray give my humble service. I hope your cosin Betty and you are very great and that you divert her often with your company which I am sure is gratefull to her as was your letter to your loveing aunt, my and marie's service attends Mrs Bea and all our yong cosins,

40 To John Collier, [Hastings], from William Cranston, [Johnson's Court], 26 December 1732 [SAY 1607]

I received yours on Saturday but for 2 days before and to this minute have been within doors, much out of order, but thank God, am now in a good way and hope to gett out tomorrow or Thursday. I am sorry likewise to tell you that Jacky was yesterday, about noon, taken with a violent pain in his head which continuing till night I sent for Dr Tilden. And upon inquiry finding that Jacky and Jemmy were tumbling over one another's heads in the morning, upon the carpet in the parlour, thought it might proceed from thence. So nothing was done save giving him some white wine way, and hartshorn in it, to drink warm in bed, which put him into a breathing sweat all night.[1] He did not sleep much but in the morning was free from the headack, but had a pain cross his stomach. Often very sick has eat nothing, but not the least feaver. This evening by the doctor's order he took a gentle vomit[2] which workt with him very well and he brought away vast quantities of filth but notwithstanding that still continues very sick and restless; he's just now going to bed and takes a draught by the doctor's directions. I have one to sett up with him and Jemmy is to lye tonight with Harry that Jacky may be by himself. I hope a good night's rest will sett all to rights; he is very cheery at intervals and has good spirits. By next post you shall know how he goes on but by that hope in God I shall give you an account of his perfect recovery.

1 Hartshorn, hart's antler, acqueous solution of ammonia, derived from burnt hartshorn or shavings, with white wine or sack whey, brings out the cold from the body; for rheumatism, shavings of hartshorn with anodyne waters or citrus fruit juice, also dilute in smelling salts (*EB* 1771 vol.3, Medicine 63; *OED*).

2 Vomit, aim to empty contents of stomach, in cases of smallpox to clear system of phlegm, bile and food; vomit comprised salt of vitriol powder, solution of tobacco, plus oxymel of squills made from ground ivy, maidenhair (Mead vol. 2, 120; *EB* 1771 vol. 3, Medicine 154).

41 To John Collier, [Hastings], from William Cranston, [Johnson's Court], 28 December 1732 [SAY 1608]

In my last I ended my account of Jacky with his going to bed after taking his vomit, and was in hopes should have had no occasion to have said any more upon that head. But since it is otherwise I shall give you a very exact account of both his and my proceeding.

Tuesday night he slept very little being mighty restless; between 7 and 8 the nurse called me up at his desire. I found him much out of order and he complained of a great pain cross his bowells. I imediately sent for Mr Tilden with an account of his complaint. He came about 9 and brought a medicine proper for it, gave it him and he then was very easy.[1]

About 10 the pain came again much more violent than before and twas to such a degree I thought he could not long hold it. Upon that I imediately left him and with Jemmy took coach to Mr Tilden. Met with him at home, went together to Dr Barrowby, and after some time found him, and he soon [2] came after us hither. He viewed Jacky and [3] made inquiries as to what he had eat, drank, etc., and viewing him with a candle narrowly, he thought he saw something over his left eye like the small pox; and by being told of his headack the Monday, his sickness a Tuesday, and by what he then saw as to his pains, he was verily perswaded twas it.[4] Upon being told in such case he must be moved, my wife not having had it, he advised it to be imediately done, for till then he must take nothing. He wrote a prescription:[5] as soon as twas possible I got a place and all things ready, and about 6 he was carried in a [6] hackney chair with all the blanketts and sheets about him thither. During all this time he was in the utmost pain.

As soon as he came to his lodging, a glister[7] was given him, which worked very well. He brought away a great deal of excrement and most of it so hard twas like sheep's turds; half an hour afterwards he took a bolus[8] with some pearl inlep[9] and was very easy and going to rest. About 9 I left him in that hopefull way, but just as I sat down to supper I was sent for again. I imediately went and found him in a worse condition than ever. I sent instantly to Mr Tilden and he came, went to the doctor, but nothing further could be done, but both agreed that the bolus, etc., had not been in him long enough to operate, but did not doubt but that it would have its desired effect but must wait with patience. Accordingly, thank God, it had; for about 11 the pain left him and he went imediately to sleep. I left him at 12 but during the last time the doctor was there the symptoms of the smallpox were much more visible and almost out of doubt.

I was with him at 8 this morning, having when I came home left word to be called if his pain returned, but it did not. He lay very still, and this morning was very free from all pain, and very chearfull and merry. About 11 Dr Barrowby came again, looked upon him and then was very certain as to the smallpox and [10] gave me his authority to write that twas his opinion twood[11] be of a favourable sort and that the vomit was the happiest thing that he could have taken preceeding such a distemper. He advised as proper that his hair should be cut off which I accordingly had done imediately. Between 5 and 6 he was pretty feaverish but I am just now come from him and left him in very good case. In all my life I never saw anybody so patient, takes everything is given him with the greatest willingness, and is very high in spirits, being very hearty and has laughed severall times this afternoon, seems glad he has got the smalpox and is not in the least disheartened, and in my own opinion think him in a very good way. For that he has it is now out of dispute with me, a great many being already come out in his breast, hands and face.

I don't doubt but twill be as agreable to know where he is, as tis almost to know how he is. We had not a great deal of time to consider upon that head. We at first went to a woman who takes in persons in such circumstances as well as all other, had a room there, everything ready and terms agreed upon.[12] Afterwards I did not like it; first twas the lower end of Fleet street, very noisy and the thoughts of such a sort of house did not relish well with me, but then I thought no private house that lets lodging would take him in. However, I was resolved to try and to my great satisfaction succeeded. I went to Mrs Canan's in the square part of Johnson's Court where I once took lodgings for Mr and Mrs Roffe. She knowing of me did consent to it; accordingly there he is, two pair stairs, a very warm wainscotted roome. I have hired a nurse to attend him, who is to eat and drink with the woman of the house: all necessary things for him which I had I have sent to him, what I had not, that I bought, and at this time nurse can't think of any one thing she wants. All that has hitherto been in my power I have done, and all that will be hereafter shall not be wanting. Have often reflected how happy twas he was at my house and that I was able to scour about in it for had it been last week I don't know what I could have done being then myself in a bad way.

As to Dr Barrowby, upon talking to him this morning I find he knows Dr Carleton. Pray inquire of him as to his caracter; he is looked upon here to be a first rate man and to me seems to be a very humane, good natured, man and not at all voracious. I gave him a fee yesterday but would take none today. I spoke to him to call every day, which he promised to do till he could tell me we should have no farther occasion for him. All in my power shall be done for if he was my own son I could not have a bigger regard or more concern at his welfare. Assure yourself at present he's in a hopefull way. I repeat it because I am told it and firmly beleive it; everything that happens between this and next post, shall, God willing, be sent you.

As to the kitchen physick[13] Dr Barrowby gave me directions in which I took in writing from him: a pint of milk, a pint of water well boiled, then a gill and half a gill of sack or mountain white wine put in it and just to boil one gull up; - another, half a chick with the skin and fatt pulled off, boiled in two quarts of water till the goodness is out. These he is to drink alternately, blood warm, and the more the better, and accordingly he has already drank the whole chick boiled and a quart of sack, and you may depend upon his being constantly plyed. His physick tonight seems to me to be only some Gascoign's powder[14] mixt in pearl inlep, he is to take a paper every six hours. He took likewise a draft at 9 but what that was I know not. You'll excuse any answer as to business, having had no time for anything of that sort.

1 To allieviate pain, a paregoric draught, of black cherry water, compound peony water, sugar, extract of Egyptian opium, take at bedtime to ease pain (Radcliff 24); for violent pains, an anodyne draught, alexierial milk water, compound peony water, syrup of white poppies, and opium 'somewhat strong'; needs to be taken with care, because it fixed humours, and in old people might cause gangrene (Radcliff 88; Mead vol. 2, 120, 132). Where smallpox not suspected, Mead suggests electuarys to aid rest, such as a cordial electuary, comprising wormwood, rosemary flowers, crabs' claws and eyes, syrup of orack and made up to the size of a nutmeg with ¾ spoonfull of a julap; corrects acid winds and revives sufferer (Radcliff 10; Pomet 216-8), opium to allay fermenting humours, procure sleep, to relieve pain, to stop diarhroea and vomiting, calms excitability.

2 MS *after* struck through

3 MS *many* struck through

4 Richard Mead, who advised on the treatment for Jacky Collier divided smallpox into distinct or confluent, identified by size, number and manner of eruptions. Distinct or simple smallpox had a modest fever of short duration and fewer, small, pustules, and though many symptoms are dangerous, disease is 'almost void of all danger' to life. Confluent, malignant smallpox began with a stronger fever, pustules struggle to mature, ending in little crusts, black spots over the body, bleeding and eruptions from mouth, nose, eyes and bowels. Death was usual, for pain relief, *ibid* n.1, (Mead vol. 2, 113-5), Richard Mead's text on smallpox *De Variolise morbillis* 1747.

5 MS this letter was written in haste, whether o or e is unclear in third letter.

6 MS *chair* struck through
7 Glister, or clyster, a liquid injected into anus, designed to empty the intestines and thus clear the system of ill humours; (Radcliff, 111; *EB* 1771 vol.2, 213).
8 Bolus, a purgative to tackle ill humours, by mouth, size of a nutmeg (Radcliff 34): Bolus leniens, rheubarb, wormwood, syrup of clove-gilly flower, given with chalybeate water, a julep or fruit juice.
9 Julep.
10 MS *did* struck through.
11 MS two[d].
12 For the duties of a nurse, see Thomas Fuller *Exanthematologia, or an attempt to give a rational account of eruptive fevers*, especially of the measles and smallpox (London, 1730); discussed in L.R. Seymer *A General History of Nursing* (1954) 63.
13 Kitchen physic, remedies from herbal collections, gardens, woods, often written into commonplace books; able to be made up at home, includes nourishment for convalescence. The library in Old Hastings House included editions of Thomas Fuller, *Pharmacopoeia domestica or the family dispensatory* (1739); John Quincy, *Pharmacopoeia officinalis et extemporanea or a compleat English Dispensory* (1722); and *The family companion for health* (1729)
14 Gascoigne's powder, noticed by (Mead vol. 2, 132). Various powders were advertised in newspapers.

42 To Dr Henry Carleton, at Hastings, from William Cranston, [Johnson's Court], 30 December 1732 [SAY 1609]

By the [1] last post I gave Mr Collier an account of Jacky's having the smallpox and after writing every minute circumstance attending it, I concluded with the doctor's (Dr Barrowby's) opinion, that twould be a good sort and had great hopes of his recovery. In that fine way he continued all day yesterday but this morning about six he was taken delirious, the pock went in, he pissed and spitt nothing but blood; the purples appeared in his breast and eyelids. I got Dr Barrowby and Dr Mead together to him this afternoon and after their consultation together had the malancholy sentence pronounced that twas their opinion he would not outlive this night.

This news is too shocking to come to my sister's ears too sudenly as I was afraid it would be the case had I directed this letter imediately to Mr Collier, for I imagine he will be set out for this place before this reaches Hasting. Therefore inclose a letter to him in this and intreat the favour of you to wait upon him yourself, if he's at Hasting, or to my sister in his absence, and break this sad account to them in such a manner as you shall think proper. But beg it may be imediately done because either of them will be much supprized to find no letter when they will wait for one, no doubt, with the greatest impatience. I hope you'll excuse my troubling you in this affair, but of that I make no doubt since it has always been your character to assist the unfortunate with the greatest alacrity and a more unhappy story than this can't befall that family to whom it belongs, I am with wishes of a happy new year and many.

1 MS *two* struck through

43 To John Collier, from William Cranston, [Johnson's Court], 30 December 1732 [SAY 1610][1]

I ended my last letter with the happy scituation of Jacky at that time. I saw him again yesterday morning; he had had a good night, was then very easy, the pock out much fuller than the night before, and with a better head. Dr Barrowby came to him at noon and was pleased to find him in so good a way. In the same manner he continued and I left him in it, about nine. But this morning I was called up at 7 and was told that from 2 to that time he was very ill and restless, and that just before 7 he had made water, which I looking up on found to be terribly bad,[2] just like blood, and looking upon him found, to my thinking, the pock much gone in. It supprized me vastly. I imediately went to Dr Barrowby. He came and thought he never saw so sudden an alteration and such an unhappy case, he was not the least apprehensive off.

I lost no [3] time but telling Dr Barrowby my intentions. I went to Dr Mead and about 12 I found him and fixt him to come at 4, and went and acquainted the other doctor of it. They both met at that time and were with the poor child above half an hour, and at their coming from him I had the most unhappy sentence pronounced that ere yet peirced my ears, that they were both of opinion that he would not survive this night. They prescribed some medicines part of which he has taken. I don't find him worse now than then, but I think much in the same way: at intervals he is sensible, but much the greater part of the time the contrary.

I'll say no more. I have wrote as long as I can and but too much for you to read. If words can't express my concern, I am sure they can much less yours and my sister's for whom I'm in the utmost fear, considering her spirits in her present scituation can much less support themselves than at another time. I pray God give you both courage to go through this most terrible tryall, and hope you'll be able some way or another to give me directions of what I am to do for the future, for nothing but the last offices can be wanting. The doctors, if not forbid by message from me, will be here again tomorrow.

1 This may be the letter included with **[42]** SAY 1609, the time on which is past 9, and the time on SAY 1610 is past 10.

2 MS At this time Cranston's t and h are similar.

3 MS *thought* struck through

44 To Dr Henry Carleton, Hastings, from William Cranston, [London], 2 January 1733 [SAY 1611]

After what you received from me last post, little hopes could remain of Jacky's living. And accordingly, as the doctors but too truely foretold, he died Sunday morning at six. Mr Collier came at ten and my grief was then but too fresh to be able to conceal the unhappy news a moment. The suddeness had just the effect I dreaded, but, thank God, with all proper care being taken of him he is now very well and only stays to see him decently interred which will be on Thursday, and then he proposes to to sett out a Fryday of which an account will be sent by that post. He joins with me in service and, if my brother Jemmy is at Hasting, begs upon receipt of this you'll send for him and both consult together how to inform my sister of this last fatall account which I hope she'll get over for nothing else could be expected. The same goodness will excuse this which did the last and herein you'll not only much oblige Mr Collier, but sir, your most noble servant; thank God Jemmy continues very well, which pray also mention to my sister.

[*Cover*] Mr Halsted, pray send this letter as directed imediately upon receipt of it. W.C.

45 To Revd Mr Cranston, Hastings, from William Cranston, [Johnson's Court], 4 January 1733 [SAY 1612]

The receipt of yours today was highly agreable to us all, for we were under the same, terrible, apprehensions of the effect the malancholy news would have upon my sister which you were it would have upon Mr Collier. But thank God he is pure well and intends to sett out tomorrow morning provided the weather will admitt for at present tis very bad. I intend to see him to his first night's stage, which is intended to be at Tunbridge, and would throughout [1] was my wife in a condition to be left so long a widow, but as it is tis impossible. I mentioned something in my last as to the burying of the poor child but that has since been otherwise resolved upon and nothing to be done in it till my sister has been consulted. We have got him in a leaden coffin, so no harm can come if he's kept above ground a month longer. With some difficulty Mr Collier was perswaded not to see him; poor man was in a sad way Sunday and Monday, but has ever since continued mending and really is now very well. Had I been sure of your being at Hasting the two letters wrote to the doctor would have been sent to you, but in this case there was no trusting to chance. Mr Collier sends his love and blessing to my sister and children and hopes she'll excuse his not writing, he being still too full to say anything upon this malancholy account. My best respects also attends her with wishes to you both of a happy new year and many, and hope none may end, in our time, as the last did.

1 MS *were* struck through

46 To John Collier, Hastings, from William Cranston, [Johnson's Court], 9[1] January 1733 [SAY 1613]

I was glad to hear of your safe arrivall at Hasting by a letter from my brother yesterday. I got to Sennocke about noon, lay there that night intending to sett out from thence soon enough the next day to get to town by night. But a letter that morning from my wife brought me to town some hours sooner than I intended. The contents of it were that Jemmy had been ill ever since I had been gone and with symptoms like the smallpox.

Upon my coming to town and enquiring, I found that Fryday morning about an hour after we left him he drank some coffee for breakfast, soon after complained a little of the headack, and eat only some mutton broth for dinner. In the afternoon Mr Tilden accidentally came and upon Jemmy's telling him of the chocolates making him sick, and he then having no headack or feaver, he concluded a night's rest would entirely carry it off. He lay with Harry in the best bed, my wife made him some wey which he drank and slept very well all night. Saturday he drank tea for breakfast but soon afterwards brought it up, eat two eggs for dinner which staid with him and drank some sages tea, which staid also, but he being thirsty and a little to warm my wife sent for Mr Tilden who gave him a vomit which he took very readily, and afterwards was very well and wrote a letter to you.

That night Harry lay with him again with a candle in the roome and he slept all that night without waking. Sunday, Mr Tilden came, found some pock appearing advised him to be moved and I came about noon. I went to 3 or 4 places but nobody would take him in; at last the woman were poor Jacky was consented that the bed she lay in the garrett should be brought down into the parlour, a handsome warm, quiet roome. Accordingly, it was imediately done and about 5 Harry and I carryed him in our arms, ropt up exceeding warm, to his lodgings. During all this time he was as well as ever anybody was in the like circumstances; no pain in the back or head, no sickness in the stomach and but a very slight feaver. He slept well all night, was just in the same condition in the morning as the evening before.

Dr Barrowby came, liked him mightily; he continued very well all day and complained that twas very hard he could have nothing to eat, being very hungry, but I easily satisfyed him and was contented with liquids. He talked as distinctly as ever and was quite brisk that he had cheated [2] his master of some more holydays. Last night he did not sleep much, but was very easy and lay quiet, was exceeding jolly, as he called it.[3] This morning the doctor came, liked him better still and said the pock were all out and were a very favourable sort. He has a pretty many in his face, but upon his breast [4] they stand an inch apart, as they do also upon his hands and arms. I asked him whether he might not eat a buttered toast and drink some bohea tea[5] but he refused it and desired he might live only on spoon meat, and drink as much beer as he woulds. He has drank but little of that sort, not having been at all thirsty. When I left him this evening he was in wonderfull good order, asked me whether I had wrote to you and desired me to send his duty to you and mamma, and was very glad to hear you got home safe, and I assure you he hoped you would not put yourself to the fatigue of coming up to him.

I always dreaded if he should fall down we should have some difficulty to make him take things but he does it to admiration, refuses nothing but, on the contrary, takes everything most willingly. I talked to the doctor a good while and asked him what he thought of an assistant. He told me that if I was for it, he [6] would not be against it, but that it was in his opinion entirely unnecessary, for there was the greatest probability of his recovering without ever being in the least danger and that it would be a 7 day pock. You shan't fail of accounts, God willing, every post; he does not know where he is.

1 MS *past 10.*
2 MS *the* struck through.

3 MS *in* struck through.
4 MS *that* struck through.
5 Bohea tea, the finest black tea being the first pick from the tea plant; this tea was used as nourishment during convalescence.
6 MS *was* struck through.

47 To Revd Mr Cranston, Hastings, from William Cranston, Johnson's Court, 9 January 1733 [SAY 1614]

The reason for my not answering yours of the 4th by Saturday's post was being at that time out with Mr Collier, of whose safe arrival I was glad to hear of by yours of yesterday. As one misfortune seldom comes alone, so neither has it in our case, for I received a letter from my wife Sunday morning, at Sennocke,with an account of Jemmy's having the Fryday and Saturday before some symptoms like the forerunner of the smallpox. You may be sure this hastened me from thence imediately. I lost no time in rideing for I got from the Crown at Sennocke to my inn in Southwarke in 2 hours and 40 minutes.[1] I hasted home and found it too true. I shan't give you any farther particulars, referring them to Mr Collier's letter, only I can't help telling you that the symptoms at coming and the condition he has ever since, and now at this moment is in, are the most favourable imaginable, and ever since I come to town he has been no more out of order than I am in at present, which, thank God, is pretty well.

I sincerely take him to be in an extraordinary good way, though [2] after the late unhappy accident I would not be too certain, but he's is a quite different pock and am assured tis a seven day one. I don't doubt but my brother and sister will be vastly uneasy at this news, but should it please God to spare this, as to all human appearance he will, twill then be an unspeakable pleasure. It's some uneasiness to me to know what Mr Collier will do about coming up or staying at home. I think, nay am sure, he can't take more care of him than I shall, together with Mr Page who is exceeding good on this occasion, though unfortunately happened to be out of town at first. I am satisfyed Mr Collier cannot have recovered his last journey and in the condition he must be in I think he should be perswaded not to undertake a second, but this affair I leave to your better judgment to manage for I shall say nothing of it in this.

As to the question in yours my sister may be assured I should most willingly satisfy her in though Mr Collier, in most particulars, may have done it already and as the funeralls is not yet performed that part of it cannot be answered. Till I received yours I had made no enquiry as to what he was put in and, being in a great confusion when I gave orders for a coffin, I did not think anything of it and therefore find he is in woolen. I, at first, gave directions for a leaden coffin, into which he was put the day he died, that is put into an oak one, and that is covered with black cloth very decently, nailed with white nails, a plate upon it of his name, age and the day he died and above it and below are to figures of angells.

As to the nurse she was recommended by the apothecary and seemed to me, for I carefully examined her motions, to be a person of judgement and humanity and very diligent in attending upon him. During the 3 first days, that is Wednesday, Thursday and Fryday, of his illness he often talked of his father coming up and wanted much to see him, though did not seem to be uneasy that he did not when I told him. He could not have my account of his being ill till Fryday night, and that he would be in town a Sunday, at which he was very easy. Saturday, when he was so bad, he often called upon his father and when he seemed to be sensible he could not be perswaded but that his papa was there the Fryday. He likewise often spoke of you and said you had often promised to come to see him whenever he had the smalpox.

I don't remember his mentioning anybody else. When his head acked on the Monday, I think I wrote word that we imagined it to be occasioned by his and Jemmy's rolling over one another's heads that morning in the parlor, upon the carpet, which Mr Collier I beleive often saw em do last terme. Tuesday, the headack being gone and no pain in his back, but a little sick and a pain in his belly, I [3] nor any of us had any notion of the smallpox, and when Mr Tilden came about 4 he then concluded to give him a purge[4] the next day. But he staying to drink tea and the boy in the interim vomiting, he changed his resolution from a purge to a vomit which he sent him that evening and he took it not a word mentioned among us of the smalpox he having no pain in his head or back.

However, he continued ill and still complained of his belly though but little Wednesday morning when his belly was exceeding bad; I had not the least notion of the smallpox till the phisycian came and apprehended it to be it. But it is my opinion that though the smalpox did come out, yet that that violent pain in his belly proceeded from some hidden cause, and was the imediate occasion of his death, for he complained of a pain there just as he made the bloody water Saturday at 6 in the morning. Mr Carleton, Mr Chelsum and Mr Page were the only persons visited him. I spoke of it to nobody for twas the doctors desire he should see as few persons as possible.

The misfortune in my own family today, though inconsiderable to any of the above, yet I can't help mentioning it, that my wife's watch was stole from her side this morning in Fleet Street. I perswaded her to go out for a little air and that was the consequence. Thank God she continues pretty well, though the fright she was in a Saturday about Jemmy and my being out of town, was like to have brought a young one to town. Nothing could have happened more unfortunately to her than what has done, and the same power that has hitherto caried her through I hope will still continue his further assistance. A more malancholy Xmas I ne'er know but hope twill be of such service to me as never to sett my heart too much upon anything in this world, since everything is so precarious; I am with my hearty wishes of welfare to my brother and sister.

1 Crown Inn, Sevenoaks to Southwark, 23 miles by *Ogilby's* map, so 2 hours and 40 minutes at 8.64 mph.
2 MS *since* struck through.
3 MS *had* struck through.
4 Gentle purge to empty bowels, used also for dull headaches, comas, lethargy, vertigo, convulsions, nightmares, epilepsy, asthmas, pleurisy, coughs and rickets; a decoction of senna, manna, cream of tartar, and compound peony water. Aim to clear ill humours hindering recovery and in malignant smallpox to lessen the secondary fever (Radcliff 67).

48 To John Collier, Hastings, from William Cranston, [Johnson's Court], 11 January 1733 [SAY 1615]

I ended my last with a good account of Jemmy, and, thank God, have the pleasure by this to continue it. Tuesday night he slept exceeding well for I found him as fast as a church yesterday at 9. About 12 the doctor came and declared he liked him still better than the day before. He continued brisk all day, but slept severall times, and when I saw him in the afternoon he told me he had had a bushell of sleep. The pock was much fuller than the day before; he had no manner of complaint but that his throat was a little sore. The doctor ordered him some gargarism[1] to wash it often with which has now cured it. He slept well last night and I found him asleep again this morning. About the old hour the doctor came, Jemmy complained of being hungry and desired he might have some buttered toast, or anything else the doctor should think proper. The doctor told him he might have some toast in ale but that he had much rather he would eat nothing, for, says he, nothing but some such tricks could possibly make him miscarry. So Jemmy was contented to submitt to his former way of living. The doctor thought he had a little more feaver than yesterday but that was owing to the pock being nigher the height which he was satisfyed would be a Saturday and he thought he never saw a person in a better way that had a pretty many.

I [2] and Mr Page were with him about 8 this evening but found him asleep but staid till he waked when the poor rogue could not open his eyes which I was glad to hear for this eyes looked very watery today, and was afraid, if he was not blind, might be of bad consequence, but that is now not to be feared. His feaver is very inconsiderable and he's very cheery but begins to grow almost tired of doctor's stuff but with a little perswasion he is pretty tractable. I make no doubt, under God, of sending you the same good news per next as this and that I shall continue it till he's good abroad. I received yours and my brother's today and shall take care of the contents of both. My wife, who has been pure well these two days, joins in respects to you and all friends.

1 Cough mixture, liquid, including herbs, marshmallows, linseed oil, almond oil, sugar candy; mixture lubricates the throat, obstructs acrimonious humours, eases pain and contributes to well-being (Radcliff 61).

2 MS *was* struck through.

49 To John Collier, Hastings, from William Cranston, [Johnson's Court], 13 January 1733 [SAY 1616]

Yesterday morn I found that Jemmy had slept well the night before, and was then in pretty good order, though as I imagined when the doctor came he told me his feaver still kept encreasing, though but gradually, and no danger need be feared from it. But he thought it proper by way of prevention to order a mild blister for the evening which was according put on his back.[1] We would have cheated Jemmy about it but he was too cunning for he knew what it was. However, it did not much disturb his rest for he slept well enough, though not quite so well as he had done the nights before, neither could it be expected. I saw it dressed this morning, but it did not run a vast deal, but it certainly did good for his feaver today has be very low and he very hearty, but the pock and the blister being both sore he is pretty peivish as he well may. The doctor came about 11 but he could not discern any turn but by his water; he did beleive it was at the height and that it would certainly be visible by tomorrow morning. Page and I called about 4 and could not see that twas turned, but this evening bet 8 and 9 I was there again, and I thought the head of the pock were flatter than before and seemed to be drier, and Jemmy told me he thought his nose was much less than in the morning.

The nurse beleives also tis at the height and does not doubt but by the morning twill be out of dispute. Nobody upon earth can be better in the condition than he, and the doctor told me he might safely gett up for an hour or two by Wednesday. Jemmy does not talk so much as he did but he's mighty quiet and still. But I don't take it to proceed for want of spirits but from a notion that much talk will be prejudiciall, for when he's asked any question and does speak at all tis very hearty and spiritous. Sack whey he drinks but very little of, not liking it, but he's drink is barly gruel, small beer, water gruell and thin milk porrage, these he takes very often.

He's feaver's so small that I'm in no fear of convulsions, neither has he had any the least symptoms of it. The composeing draught he has had every night and are still continued, and as to quantities of physick my sister need be under no fears upon that head for nothing is given but was is prescribed and that but very little. He has left off taking powders and has only every six hours a draught and that's all the physick he takes, and has never once taken any physick but every six hours, except his sleeping draught at 7 over and above. I can't help calling upon him 3 times a day, morning, noon and night, but my wife knows nothing of it. I keep a coat, waistcoat and cap there, which I put on when I go into his roomes, and pull off again when I come out, and afterwards take a turn for half an hour. With this precaution, and her knowing nothing of the matter, I don't apprehend tis possible any infection can be brought home, but none of my family, or anybody else save Mr Page, know of it, neither would I have it.[2]

1 Round plaster patch of Cantharides, Spanish flies, used to raise a blister containing fluid, removes ill humours in smallpox, blisters placed between shoulders and on arms and legs (Mead vol. 2, 126).

2 As illustrated by William Cranston's behaviour, an understanding that particles from glands of the body and mouth of an infected person being drawn into the lungs and pores of another, may replicate infection as understood for outbreaks of plague, and thus behind the enforcement of quarantine (Mead vol. 1, 152).

50 To John Collier, Hastings, from William Page, Lincoln's Inn, 13 January 1733

[SAY 1617]

I don't doubt but that Mr Stanwig will consent to another commission for which I shall apply to him. I have drawn the interrogatories and if you think propper it may be executed in term time. I really was in the greatest concern and surprize at my poor little friend's being taken so soon ill after you left him, and have not been a day without seeing him since. I really think him in a very fine way and the doctor seems not to have the least doubt of his doing well. It was thought to be the 7th day pock, but I question if they turn before Monday which is the 9th. They have all along appeared plump and full without ever falling as I am informed sometimes happens in this unlucky distemper.

Yesterday the doctor thought his fever a little higher than usuall, and therefore ordered him a moderate blister last night to prevent any disorder happening in his head. This as had a very good effect, and I beleive it was done more out of caution than necessity. He's pretty full in the face, especially about the nose and mouth, but his throat seems clear and voice holds without any alteration. He's not very thirsty but often takes little warm suppings which does him service. He has slept pretty much till this day which he has been more wakefull in than any of the former, but that I take may be occasioned by the blister and the increase of the pock. His spiritts hold exceeding good and I assure you performs to admiration, taking a good deal of care of himselfe and observes directions.

The nurse seems a good, understandig, carefull woman and I verily beleive indulgent and kind to him. I hope God Almighty will preserve him to you and Mrs Collier and depend of my utmost services for him, though my friend Cranston is so good as to be often with him, unknown to Mrs Cranston, who I hope will not suffer in the least. I shall be glad of all opportunitys to give you an account of him and with the greatest pleasure of his perfect recovery. My humble service waits on Mr Collier. I sent the cheeses by Wednesday's carryer. I hope they'll prove as good though different from the other.

51 To John Collier, [Hastings], from William Cranston, [Johnson's Court], 8/15[1] January 1733 [SAY 1618]

Our kinsman Thomas arrived her yesterday morning just as I rose, vizt about 9. I went soon afterwards to Jemmy and found him pretty well after having had but little sleep the night before. I could then plainly see the pock had sunk and many in his face were quite changed black which plainly shewed that, that which was but guessed at the night before was then actually come to pass, and when the doctor came he said the height was over and he out of danger. He continued well all day though was very uneasy for want of sleep,[2] he not having had a stole lately, the doctor ordered him a glyster, but he had not been gone a quarter of an hour before he had a fine one in the naturall way. This upon a consultation between the nurse, Mr Page and myself we thought very happy and concluded to send to forbid the glyster which I accordingly did. I left him about 8 and, calling this morning about the same hour, I found he had slept the whole night exceeding well. I forgot one circumstance of Sunday morning, vizt that he could then just see and he found out my sword, and the pock were in his face entirely changed.

I desired our cousin to be sure to be with me by 11, that he might be present when the doctor came in order to tell you what he heard, as well as for me to write. He came in time and saw both the doctors, and had it from Barrowby's own mouth that the child was as well as any one then present in the roome and should not have prescribed, only Jemmy made a slight complain of his water hurting him in coming from him; this the doctor said was only occasioned by a little heat remaining in the blood which what he directed would certainly take off, and that he should give him nothing else till he took physick besides a paragorrick every evening. The boy is entirely free from any pain whatever and was highly delighted at the doctor's declaration as to the condition he thought him in and upon the doctor's telling him if he did not pick his face he would be as handsome as ever. He promised not to meddle with it. He can now see almost as well as ever, and I had the doctor's approbation as to our putting a stop to the glyster yesterday. At present much company is not very proper but as soon as he getts up I'll take care he sha'nt want.

1 Sayer vol. 1, 77 has 14 or 15 January, also 8 January is written in on the original.
2 MS *I left him about 8 and call* struck through.

52 To John Collier, Hastings, from William Cranston, [Johnson's Court], 16 January 1733 [SAY 1619]

I make no doubt but T. Holman,[1] before my writeing this, has reached Hasting with my letter and his own agreable account. He continued in the same good way in which T. left him; all day, slept well last night and was better today than yesterday, that is has more strength and consequently better. The doctor came about 3 and said he should come no more there being no occasion for him, but that he would call the end of the week. But Jemmy told him he did not desire to see him again; said he might eat fish tomorrow, fowl a Thursday and so alternately, should take physick a Saturday, but ordered nothing bet this and then, unless a paragorick, which he would have nurse keep by her to use in case he did not sleep but did not much question but he would do without it, for getting up would tire him and make him sleep without it. He got up this afternoon and had his bed made and soon went into it again, not so much at his own desire as my request. About 12 he complained bitterly of hunger and nurse boiled half a fowl and would have eat it all but as I fed him I also stinted him and confined him to a wing and the breast; he eat with a vast appetite. I ventured this without the doctor's directions, but when he came he approved very well of it. Nothing remains, thank God, but care that he takes no cold which shan't be wanting. I've enclosed you a halfpenny ballad which is not ill wrote. I must mention that Jemmy has always liked his physician and what he said to him was out of joke, which made the doctor laugh, but told him he would call whether he liked it or no. The nurse he also likes very well and really she is a very good sort of a woman, and has taken a great deal of care of him; she's the same as at first.

1 Thomas Holman, cousin of William Cranston and Mary Collier, may be the Thomas referred to in [**51**].

53 To Revd James Cranston, from William Cranston, Johnson's Court, London, 18 January 1733 [SAY 1620]

I was in too much a hurry last post to be able to give you an account of the solemnity of poor Jacky's funerall which was performed Monday night.[1] I was in expectation of [2] particular directions upon that head, but yours was without any, and between the willingness of showing a proper respect, and the unwillingness of making it too expensive, I was greatly divided but at last concluded upon it in the following manner which I thought would be sheering between. But I almost think tis needless to tell you I advised my friend Page in it. Jemmy being in the same house with the other, I thought it convenient to move him from thence because Jemmy might know nothing when it was for fear it would sink his spirits.

Accordingly he was carried Tuesday sennight to one Mr Legg's, an undertakers in Bloomsbury, he and T. Green being in this way partners. I ordered to be sumoned to attend Mr Carleton, Mr Chelsum, Mr Page, Mr Green, Mr Isted, and here also I'll mention myself. We all met, save Chelsum, who the day before was taken ill; at 9 drank a glass or two of white and red wine, had each of us a pair of black shammy gloves, a black silk hatband, and to Mr Carleton I also ordered a scarf which he had. About 10 we set out in two coaches and pair. Mr Carleton and I went next the hearse in one coach, Page, Green and Isted in the other. The hearse was drawn by a pair also, with 13 plumes of white feathers upon that and the two horses, and the two horses and hearse were covered with black velvet. 10 men with branch lights attended, with 2 men in black and white scarves preceeding the hearse. The coach and hearemen had white gloves and favours, as had also the 2 men last mentioned.

We gott to the Abby before 11. Mr Carleton[3] put on his surplice – the corpse was taken out of the hearse – a lid of white feathers was put on it, and in that manner it went to the grave, which was very near Sir Talbot Clerck's,[4] and in the same part of the cloysters. Mr Carleton performed the service, which, when done, we went home. The grave I beleive was 5 foot deep at least. I thought proper to direct that a pair of white gloves should be given the next day to the following persons: vizt Mrs Carleton, Miss Ford, Geory Carleton, Miss Betty Carleton, Mrs Green, Tommy Green, Mrs Isted, Mrs Canan, her two women prentices, the nurse and maid, my wife, Miss Russell, Mr Wall, my 2 maids, man, and nurse Davis who sat up with him when here. I gave to Mrs Canaan's people because all, as well to the poor deceased as to Jemmy, they have upon all occasions been very handy and willing to assist the nurse. And really Mrs Canan's civility in both these circumstances has been beyond what I could expect from one who I only just know by name and sight as a neighbour, and were to have put either of em if she had not taken em, I did not then, nor now can't tell, for before I thought of her I was denied by severall in the neighbourhood. I think I have omitted nothing relateing to the above account, except a velvet palls being over the coffin, from the hearse to the grave. I have not been farther than Jemmy's lodging since, so can send no news, for I don't know so much of publick affairs as yourself, not having seen a paper since Saturday. You'll present my love and respects were due and accept of the same yourself.[5]

1 John Collier, d. 31 December 1732, age 13, bur. north cloister, Westminster Abbey, 15 January 1733. (Chester 337).
2 MS *generall* struck through
3 Revd Mr George Carleton MA, Chanter of the Abbey.
4 Sir Talbot Clerck (also sp. Clerke), 5th bar., also at Westminster School, buried north cloister, 25 November 1732, only son of Sir Talbot Clerke, 4th bar., of Laude Abbey, co. Leicester, by Barbara, daughter and coheir of Thomas Gladin, Durrent Hall, Chesterfield, Derbyshire; John Collier warned of the danger from smallpox, [**31**] 23 November 1732 (Chester 336).
5 John Collier's payments for the medical and burial costs are listed in SAY 681 and are noted in the Introduction.

54 To Revd James Cranston [Bexhill], from William Cranston, [Johnson's Court], 25 January 1733 [SAY 1621]

Dear Brother, I am sorry you make so many excuses for asking the questions contained in yours of the 23rd instant, because anything that I can at any time do, which will be either a service or satisfaction to my friends, I look upon rather as a duty than an obligation. You may be sure I am pleased to find my endeavours as to poor Jacky's funerall are in a great measure approved of already, and hoped what still remains in suspence will meet with the same turn. I am sure I acted as I then, and still do, think was the best and for which, God knows, I have the testimony of a good conscience. The reason given in my last [1] for moving the corps, as you mention, was upon Jemmy's account. I then thought that was enough to mention but as tis desired I'll tell what to me then was much stronger, vizt the apprehension I was under of Mr Collier's coming to town again;[2] this was the principal reason; for what could have been a more malancholy thought than to have one child dead and another in a doubtful condition in the same house?

Would it have been possible to have kept him from the sight of the coffin (for the corps he could not have seen) and would not such a sight have put him in the utmost disorder? Had he staid in town a month during that time twould have been impossible to have buried him from the same house where he himself would always have been and which, as the child was at another house, might have been done without Mr Collier's knowledge. These were the reasons and he was moved so early that Mr Collier might not possibly come to town before twas done. It was about 7 clock in the evening and was carryed in a herse; nobody attended, nor there never was an instance were ever anybody did. It was put into a back parlour.

It is a very usual thing to move corp in such a manner and almost as many persons are buried from the undertakers as from their own houses; nay, 10 to 1 buried from thence that are lodgers. Mr Page but last spring had an aunt of his moved to and buried from the same house, and as to the person I have known him personally these 7 years. He's a mighty crony of Page's and Tom Green's and I dare say a throught, honest man; he is brother to Mr Legg who was rector but now is curate of Pulborough.[3] He was not watched with there,neither would he have been so long at Mrs Carnan's as he was but that she requested it, for I was going to turn the nurse away while Mr Collier was in town. But Mrs Carnan desired me to continue her so long as the corpse remained at her house; for, without somebody's being in the roome at nights, her children, she and her servants would be afraid to go by it. For this reason I continued her, and not upon account of the poor dear child, for when he was soddered up in lead, and his wooden coffin screwed down, he was as safe from any accident as if he had been 5 foot underground. I think I am answered yours, and the clock now shrieking 11, I can say no farther than that.

1 MS *was* struck through
2 MS *upon* struck through
3 John Legg, curate of Pulborough, King's College, Cambridge, inst. 26 March 1719, Deanery of Storrington, 1724 (Ford 84).

55 To John Collier, Hastings, from James [Jemmy] Collier, London, 27 January 1733 [SAY 1622]

I received the favour of yours last Monday, and was glad to hear by it that you, mamma, uncle, sisters and and all friends were well. Ever since I wrote mine I have, thank God, continued mending, and am now strong enough to get out of doors were it convenient. But as I sha'nt make an end of purging before tomorrow, so till after that I must not stirr. My hands are quite clear off the pock and but a few are remaining in my face, and them I am in daily expectation of falling off. I am almost tired of staying within, though one body or another are mostly with me and divert me with a game at highest, lowest, Jack and the smallpox. I wish it had been farther in the terme that I might have had one spat with you, for I make no doubt but I should beat you, having reigned conqueror almost with everybody that has encountered me.

My hair will be preserved without much much[1] trouble to me, and the gentry in it are but few, and those so lean that they are half starved. Dr Barrowby has invited me and my uncle to come to see him which I promised to do as soon as I get abroad. I have a whole budget of new trick and stories to shew and tell my sisters when I see them. I hope you'll write me another letter before you come up, to lett me know how you all do, for I love to hear, and if there is anny, pray put in a scrap of news.

1 MS *much* is repeated in the original.

56 To Mary Collier, Hastings, from John Collier, Sevenoaks, 8 February 1733 [SAY 1623]

Being all alone this long evening and in a very pensive mood on the losse of our dear child, and the necessity I was under of comeing from you, and as the post will convey this to you tomorrow evening, I could not devote the time better than in writing to you; and tho I have nothing in particular to say, itt's a pleasing satisfaction to me, and I hope not dissagreeable to you. To lament our losse in too great a measure, I am satisfyed ought not to be done, but I have all the tendernesse of a parent in thinking of him, and the memory of it is not without a tear. I never went from home with soe great reluctancy, and the thoughts of it all the way were very anxious and affecting. As there is nothing can better alleviate it than a punctual correspondence, I am sure it shall not bee wanting in me.

The roads are extream badd, and though we had a great deal of rain I was much surprized to see the waters up to a great degree. That at Robertsbridge I could not ride over; soe got a man to lead my horse, and the clappers and the ends of the cloak baggs were wet by the height of the water as it lay on the boyes horse. Helden water was also much up, and very long, but not soe high as Robertsbridge. I got safe here just as it was dark and not a little fatigued. I rode about an hour in the rain which is come on very smart. I shall long to hear of you a Munday, and am with all affection and faithfulnesse. As Mr Godley and Mr Cruttenden are absent from the port, I can expect noe hares or other game, and therefore desire the inclosed note may be sent to Thomas Crunden[1] at Broomham. If you seal and send it to Mr Geery's I fancy they can send it a Saturday morning and let Jo goe over to him a Munday; and if there is any let him carry them to the carrier directed for me at my brother Cranston's. The clock is certainly halfe-an-hour to slow.

1 Thomas Crunden, steward, Broomham Park, Guestling, the seat of Sir William Ashburnham MP.

57 To Mary Collier, [Hastings], from John Collier, [Johnson's Court], 10 February 1733 [SAY 1625]

I got to town yesterday between one and two a clock, but had a very uncomfortable journey by rain and wind that not a little fatigued me, and I had a great pain in my head which lasted the afternoon but the night's rest and lying a bed till nine a clock this morning has quite taken it of, and I have noe more cold than I had when I came from Hasting.

I found dear Jemmy at my brother's where he has come for above a week, tho he lyes at his lodgings and the nurse is still with him. I find he generally dines here and today breakfasted, and I beleive for the future will doe soe unlesse anything particular happens to prevent it. My brother sayes by last post he informed you of the increase of his family, and the wife and son continue very well. I have not as yet seen her but design it tomorrow and if a fine day to take Jemmy out into the country. I find my sister's nurse is terribly afraid of the smallpox and keeps close upstairs. Mr Pryor has not been near me today, I suppose got in his old condition; but I was this morning prodigiously surprized at what Mr Wall, my brother's clerke, told me that when Pryor came last night and saw Jemmy, he seemed under a great surprize and declared he never had the smallpox. I am confident there is noe danger from the child but I am very certain that before I took him he told me he had had the smallpox, and my brother, Cranston sayes the same. That I want much to see him to know how the matter stands.

Jemmy is houskeeper, and Mrs Canham where he is provides for him what he will eat or drink, and Jemmy sayes they are all very kind to him. I went today to the house and saw the old nurse who is just such a peice as one would imagine but I beleive very carefull and humours him very much. I did not see the woman of the house who I find is a roman catholick, but very good sort of a woman, and is a mantua maker[1] and has some women lodgers; and they are all mighty kind to him and keep him now company when he is there and much divert him. I thanked them all for their civility to him and shall often call there and see Mrs Canham who was out of doors. Mr Green's sons is to goe to board at Mr

Chelsum's, and Jemmy and he are to be bedfellows, but I find he has not as yet gone to school since the breaking up.

Mr Chelsum has called very often to see Jemmy, and Mr Carleton I hear has sent often to know how he did but has not called. I have not, as yet, heard a word about the child's christening, but intend to tell my brother that I am at their service, and I really beleive the family have been very kind to the poor boy; he is very brisk and I play with him at cards 2 or 3 times a day.

What you would have bought I desire you will send me directions and I will take all imaginable care of it. With the greatest sincerity I wish and long for your dear company, and cannot avoid haveing some heavy anxious thoughts of our great inestimable losse; but I know it is our duty humbly to submit to the dispensations of God, and strive at it with all manner of resolution, yet cannot as yet be conquerour, but hope and pray for patience and resignation. Jemmy's hair is vastly knitty and I don't what to make of it. The lice are very few but there are multitudes of the former. It is combed every day and I have ordered the nurse to get the finest combs to try to eradicate them, but if ineffectuall it must come off.

1 Mantua, loose gown or coat without stays for women, numerous designs, encouraged by imports and improved printing techniques for silk and cottons. John Collier records numerous payments to dressmakers, tailors and drapers including the payment of £1 3s 0d for Mrs Hammond, mantua maker and dressmaker, on 29 November 1731 (SAY 1418 f.5v); see [**62**] for orders for a mantua maker referred to Mrs Hammond; also [**164**] [**166**] c. 22 February 1737 for Mrs Hammond's bill for dressmaking and drapery.

58 To Mary Collier, [Hastings], from James Collier, [Johnson's Court], 10 February 1733

[SAY 1624]

I was very glad yesterday to see my pappa come to my uncle's and to hear you was pretty well. The weather has been soe bad that my uncle has not sent me into the country, but my pappa sayes if tis a fine day tomorrow we shall goe out in a coach and dine in the country, and that I am to treat, which I am afraid will reduce my pocket, but I will entertain handsomly. My uncle has sent you word of my aunt having a little boy. I don't goe up to see her, but run away if anybody comes that has not had the smallpox, though they say there is noe danger. I desire you will present my service to Mrs Thorpe and my sisters and little brother Tommy.

59 To Mary Collier, Hastings, from John Collier, [Johnson's Court], 11 February 1733[1]

[SAY 1626]

Being a very fine day I thought it very proper to take Jemmy into the park and have the benefit of the air. And from thence I went with him to Mr Chelsum's, and wanting to speak with Sir Thomas Hales I went to the Parliament house to enquire for him, and had an opportunity of shewing the child the house and the speaker in the chair etc.[2] And being pretty well tyred with his walk I took him back in a coach when I found your letter, and though it gave me an account of your dissorders continueing it was a great deal of satisfaction and hope they will by degrees wear of.

I have been at Mrs Elcocks and bespoke your things and hope to send them per next Wednesday. She imagined that you intended handkercheifs and ruffles with the nightcloaths but as it was not mentioned in your letter I did not direct it. I find my brother writes to his this post about standing godfather, and that the child is to bee christened next week, and that he intends my brother James and I godfathers, and the old Seavenoake grandmother is to be godmother, and I fancy a private christening which will certainly be right. I saw D. Denham[3] yesterday at the coffee house and he talked of setting out for Hasting this day. I thought him a little in the old way.

Mrs Chelsum told me today that Sir William[4] was yesterday in a most terrible dissorder, that he was sure he could not live six hours, and would send to Mr Carleton to give him the sacraments. But in an hour's time he dressed himselfe and went out pretty brisk. I am glad you approve of postponeing Jemmy's goeing out to Chelsea. I hope there will be noe occasion for he continues very brisk and well. I went home last night and played at cards and read with him from 7 to 10. My brother being obliged to be out, I am very sorry I cannot guesse at a time of setting out, but I have an affair that will certainly oblige me to tarry till Thursday, if not longer. You'l see by the Evening Post that the burialls last week are decreased between five and six hundred and now brought down to about the usuall number, and I hope thus fair weather will continue and put an end to this epidemicall distemper.[5]

I will tomorrow see about your gown and enquire and consult what will be most proper. I have not been at Mr Carleton's as yet. I intend it though it will be with reluctancy etc., to talk over anything relating to our dear deceased child. As I hear nothing to the contrary, I hope your family enjoy health and intirely free from these colds.

1 Date from Sayer vol.1, 81.
2 Hales, Sir Thomas, (1666-1748) MP Canterbury 1715-34, 1735-41, 1746-7; the Speaker was Sir Arthur Onslow, who sat from 1728 to 1761 (*HofP 1715-1754*).
3 David Denham.
4 Sir William Ashburnham.
5 The bills of mortality show total deaths for 1731 at 25262, deaths rose from the autumn of 1732, seeing a total of 29,233 for 1733, falling to 26,062 in 1734. The main cause of increased mortality in 1733 came in the categories of: old age, 2207 against 1781 for 1732; 896 for asthmatic disease against 573; 4601 for consumption against 3719; 9336 for convulsions against 7428; 3831 for fever, malignant fever, scarlett and spotted fevers against 2939; 605 for measles against 30; and 1623 deaths from diseases associated with teeth against 1361 (*Mortality*).

60 To Mary Collier, Hastings, from John Collier, [Johnson's Court], 13 February 1733 [SAY 1627]

I received your kind letter by last post and hope to hear often that there is a continuance of your health. I am sorry your letter did not intimate what things you would have bought that I might give directions for them accordingly. Since my last, vizt Sunday, Mr Chelsum called here, and as it was a blastring[1] day it defeated my intentions of goeing out with Jemmy into the country. Soe we dined at home and have come to a resolution not to put him out at all, but every fine day to walk with him in the park and other places near the town. And that night he having put on all clean and fresh things he lay with me and soe is to continue, and he is to goe to Mr Chelsum's the latter end of next week. Yesterday I was there and find Sir William Ashburnham and Misse Dyne[2] both in the house, and I dined with them. I told Mr Chelsum that upon Misse Dyne's account it would not be proper for him to come soe soon. But it is fixed upon, and he very desirous, and said he should be glad it would drive her, for he took her only to oblige Mrs Carleton;

but I find Misse is not at all afraid and really she looks very well. I saw the room he is to lye in and Mr Green's son is to be his bedfellow who goes there tomorrow, I beleive th ...[3] are very good sort of people, and fully know Mrs Carleton's management.

I was goeing down the park from Mrs Brewer's yesterday, and met Mrs Carleton. I was soe struck at her sight, that I could hardly conteyn myselfe, and did not tarry a minnet to talk to her, and could scarce look up, and though Misse Dyne was with her, and the only person, I never saw her. Poor Jemmy has about 200 pock in his face and looks a little red. We went to the park in a coach a Sunday and walked up the Mall and tho Jemmy had his great coat he could hardly bear it, soe we come directly back and did not goe out that evening, and I went up and saw my sister and the child who both continue very well. I have been today with the gentleman that promised to carry me to the new master of Westminster school, and we have fixed the beginning of next week.

I have soe many occurrences that revive my losse and bring to my remembrance the dear child, that I can hardly bear it, his name is engraven on my heart in letters of blood, never to be effaced, and really sometimes I can muse upon it. And think I can and ought to bear it with a becomeing resignation, and sometimes it goes through my soul worse than daggers. Writeing this in a museing posture, I have let my thoughts run too far, but I verily beleive myselfe that I have fixed greater resolutions on the unhappy affair, and hope to keep them.

I am sorry I must tell you that there is a necessity for Jemmy's hair to be cut of, for it growes exeeding thin and therefore a wigg is now bespoke against next Sunday. I find my brother's child is to be put to nurse to Chelsey, tho I never heard them say anything of it. I have had all this day a little cold and running of the nose but have noe feaver or pain in the head which are the usuall attendants as I hear on the distemper. Dearest Creature, I think of you with great tendernesse and respect, and have your image impressed on my soul, and I am with all faithfulnesse.

1 MS *blastring* the a not completely closed.
2 Mary Fletcher Dyne, daughter of Edward Dyne, coronation canopy bearer, 1726.
3 MS damaged.

61 To Mary Collier, [Hastings], from John Collier, [Johnson's Court], 17 February 1733 [SAY 1628]

I received your letter this post, which I impatiently longed for, and read with pleasure as comeing from you, and am exceedingly concerned at your ilnesse; and wish to God it was possible for me to contribute anything to your releife more than a hearty and tender concern not to be expressed. My value and true respect, if possible, rises every thought, and you are the only refuge and sheet anchor I can depend upon when anxious killing gloomy thoughts attack me. As your gown was not bought before your letter came your orders as to the colour are obeyed and it was bought this afternoon. Itt's a dark colour, but I think the same you intended, and besides that is upon enquiry the proper colour. Dear Jemmy's hair was cut of this afternoon. It was not at all practicable to be preserved for I have combed it two or three dayes and it came of in a prodigious manner. I find the christening is fixed for Tuesday, and suppose my brother Jemmy by this post gives an answer to the letter sent him on that occasion. I am glad I can acquaint my dearest that I have not increased my cold and hope that will be the case till my return.

I have neither read nor heard any newes worthy your acceptance, and indeed have not any great inclination for an enquiry. There is a new play[1] that seems to run much by the account one hears, but that is what it is not possible I can have any relish for. I will, if possible, get out of town the latter end of next week, longing for it, and have often thought and wished to have done with London journeys and plague of businesse, and entirely to enjoy your company till it pleases God to send us to meet and enjoy poor dear Jacky. He knowes we love and lament him, and don't doubt but we have now his assistance, for to be sure he was the best of children.

I really have a great comfort in Jemmy, and take all possible paines to represent to him everything that is laudable and praiseworthy, and give him instructions in writeing, and have all the reason to think he will be good and doe well. I begg my dear heart will cheer up, and be satisfyed with what is really a comfort to me, that we have a dear pledge and saint at the throne of heaven making an intercession for us.

1 Covent Garden Theatre, *Achilles* by John Gay, 1st performance Saturday 10 February 1733, 17 performances in February and March (Scouten Pt 3, vol. 1, 1729-36, 270).

62 To Mary Collier, [Hastings], from John Collier, [Johnson's Court], 20 February 1733 [SAY 1629]

I hope to send your things by tomorrow's carrier, being faithfully promised them, but there was like to be a sad blunder about your gown, for by mistake, notwithstanding I sent to Mrs Hammond to know the quantity, it was carried to my sister's mantua maker and with it a strict charge to be brought home as tonight and noe other directions but to be for her. The mistake was not discovered till yesterday morning, 10 a clock, when it was more than an equall bet that it was cut out; however it hapned otherwise. I bespoke your apron and ruffles[1] and am promised them with the other things. I received your letter with a great deal of pleasure and am glad you have got more company.

I am not at all surprized at our good brother Cruttenden's being in the condition you mention, and hope it will keep him from Hasting, for I cannot be hardly civill to him. I had a opera ticket[2] given me this day but I have noe heart to use it, soe gave it my brother to doe what he would with it. Two go by it into the gallery or one into pit or boxes. I fully intended that Jemmy should goe tomorrow to Mr Chelsum's and a Thursday morning to school. But this day Lord Ashburnham invited me to dinner and with a strict charge to bring him with me, and as I fully intend to get out Saturday or Sunday, will now keep him with me, and he shall not goe to school till Munday. I hope in God we shall have comfort from him, for he doth not want parts. I find Colonell Pelham and his nephew set out tomorrow for Sussex and intend to treat their Hasting friends next Tuesday afternoon.

The poor woman that kept our Sussex coffee house dyed last Sunday morning, and has left 4 young children in a miserable condition, everything being seized. It has been a little talked of to make a collection for to put out one of them, which I shall readily come into. Harry Fowle, that was apprentice to Samuel Edwards, is in Newgate for robbing the master he now lives with of very considerable goods, and tis discovered he kept a bitch and has had severall children by her. He will, I beleive, be tryed at the Old Bayley this week. He ought richly to be hanged, but I pitty his friends that are by this brought to soe much sorrow.[3]

The christening that was to be this evening is put of till toomorrow. Mr Worge dined at my brother's today and I find he has got a little cold. He talks of leaving London a Thursday. I have bought 3 straw hatts for the girles and that is to be Jemmy's present;[4] they will cost about a guinea. My dear soul, I long much to be with you, and doe assure you that businesse setts very heavy upon me. I begg you will be assured you have a faithfull friend in a truly affectionate and compassionate husband for ever. I shall not expect an answer to this, hopeing to get out a Saturday.

1 Ruffles, strips of lace, cotton, silk, gathered on one edge, tied as a frill on wrists, necks and front, and on some of the new fashioned men's jackets and shirts and army uniforms of the time.

2 Three operas on this date; (i),Covent Garden Theatre, *Achilles* [**61**]; (ii), King's Theatre, *Orlando*, set by Handel, king, queen and three eldest princesses present 20 February, 1st performance, 23 January, singers and dancers included Montagnana, Senesimo, Signora Celeste, Strad and Bertolli, originally by Braccioli, 1713, Venice. (iii), Haymarket Theatre, *Tamerlaine*, by Handel (Scouten Pt 3, vol. 1, 1729-36; 272, 273). For Handel's impact on music and opera, see Burney vol. 4, ch. 6. John Collier arrived in London after the triumph of the Italian style on stage in opera; the extensive development of dance and music interludes in plays was common at this time.

3 After completion of apprenticeship to Samuel Edwards, draper, Harry Fowl started business as a supplier of printed textiles, also listed as a servant to Nathaniel Adams, mercer; on conviction of theft of textiles from Adams he was ordered to be transported; (Old Bailey online 21 February 1733, ref: 17330221-21).

4 Straw hat manufacture, widespread, stalks of wheat, barley, oats, marsh reeds, also used for thatch, fodder, bedding, padding in sofas, divans, chairs, woven into carrier bags and beehives as well as hats.

63 To Mary Collier, Hastings, from John Collier, Johnson's Court, 22 February 1733 [SAY 1630]

I received your letter, and am very much concerned for dear Tommy and hope in God that the humour he has will be carried of without being soe fatall as it was to the last poor baby.[1] I am sorry I cannot inform you that my businesse is compleated, but neverthelesse, as I cannot bear London any longer, will set out sometime a Saturday, soe as to get home Sunday before itt's dark, and at present think nothing shall prevent me, for I long to be with you and hope it will alleviate my concern, which I think growes upon me. The christening was last night. I shall not write any particulars about it, but deferr it to be told on my return. Jemmy dined with me today at Lord Ashburnham's, and he gave him a guinea.

1 Thomas Collier, born 10 December 1732, died 2 August 1733.

64 To Mary Collier, Hastings, from John Collier, Johnson's Court, Saturday, 21 May 1733 [SAY 1631]

I am just returned to the coffee house from celebrating Jemmy's birthday, where there were Green senior and junior, Jeake, Coles and my brother, and your health was not forgot. I am obliged to go into Holborn for half an hour by appointment this morning, so have not time to write a long letter as I intended, but hope to do it next post. The intended ear rings are put in motion.[1]

1 Among purchases made by John Collier during the summer term 1733 were a cap, fringe and gloves for Mary Collier and Molly's earrings listed at £1 14s 0d (SAY 1418 f. 13).

65 To Mary Collier, Hastings, from John Collier, Johnson's Court, 12 June 1733
[SAY 1632]

I received your letter by last post and am glad you took care of the hay. I am pleased I mentioned it to you knowing Webb was a dreaming fellow and might delay it. I am really sorry for poor Molly's[1] illnesse, but hope it will goe of without any long continuance or bad attendants. I shall settle your hat or cap affair but beleive it will be the latter and will remember 6d sugar. Yesterday the child was brought from Kensington, or where it is at nurse. I never saw a child of his age halfe soe bigg. I think the face as bigg as mine and itt's limbs vastly large and has a voice would drown a watermill and really beleive it of the brobdingnag kind.[2] It seems never to have been ill and that is the account given if it.

Yesterday an anodyne necklace[3] was bought for it; I beleive abundance of faith is requisite in that matter. As your letters have not mentioned poor Tommy I hope he is well, at least not worse then when I came from home. This has been a very hot day here and sadly troublesom in bustling about. I am very much concerned about Jemmy for fear he is growing of one side. On examineing him his right shoulder sticks out a good deal more than his left tho I never minded it till my brother told it me. Noe more did not he, or his wife, till old Mrs Stileman when he was at Seavenoake took notice of it. Parry the Taylor took measure of him yesterday and did not mind it and as he is grown very tall since I see him hope it will not have any very bad consequences. However, as I design to dine at Mr Chelsum's a Thursday, I intend to have a danceing master and take all the precautions that may be.[4]

Pray give my service to Mrs Thorpe and tell her I have met Botting's lawyer about her mother's affair twise to discourse it over, but we come to noe resolution. I have taken an opportunity to inform Lord Ashburnham of itt's situation and Mr Botting's behaviour. I am sure my lord is at noe expence on the affair but it came out as imagined in good measure.

1 Mary Collier, the eldest daughter.
2 'The nurse came in with a child of a year old in her arms, who immediately spyed me, and began a squall that you might have heard from London Bridge to Chelsea.' (Jonathan Swift 'A voyage to Brobdingnag' in *Gulliver's Travels* (1726) 1st edn); John Collier purchased John Boyle Earl of Orrery *Remarks on the Life and Writings of Dr Jonathan Swift*, as well as *Gulliver's Travels*, listed in his *Library*, editions unclear.
3 Anodyne necklace, for soothing the pain of teething; also anodyne creams available for sores, mouth ulcers, fungal and scabies infections (*Notes & Queries* 6th series, ix 85, 132; x 377, 7th series iv 394); for itch or scabies, caused by insects easily passed by sheets, towels, handkerchiefs, gloves, cured by corrosive medicines penetrating the skin, such as ointments of salts, sulphur, vitriol, and solutions of mercury, with frequent bathing see Mead vol. 1, 243; Pomet (bk. 8, 212) has tar from resinous trees, as a cure for scabies, the itch, ringworm, telfans and coughs.
4 Dancing instruction widely advised by schoolmasters, as necessary for improving deportment and for training young gentlemen and ladies in social skills, although not always approved of (Crossley & Saville 534, John Fuller to the Revd Bear, 18 April 1744).

66 To Mary Collier, Hastings, from John Collier, [Johnson's Court], 14 June 1733
[SAY 1633]

I received your letter this day on my comeing home from Mr Chelsum's where my brother Cranston and I dined, and I took the opportunity of seeing Mr Bone,[1] the master, under whom he will goe in about three weeks time. We think it absolutely necessary that he should forthwith goe to danceing which he is accordingly to doe, but I could not meet with the master.

I am very sorry to hear that your lownesse of spiritts continues and that you have got the toothack.[2] I thank God I am pretty well, though have had a little cough and cold, but it is better. Some dayes I have terrible conflicts with dear remembrances of -[3] that cut me worse than swords and severall times hope and think I have resolutions to repell them, but wofully find the contrary. I am sorry I cannot inform you when I shall be at home for at present I can fix noe time which makes me uneasy and under great dissatisfaction, being weary of the bustle of the town, fatigued with running after businesse, and have noe tast of agreeablenesse in any one thing here.

1 Vincent Bourne, 1694-1747, poet, educated at Westminster and Cambridge, returned as master to Westminster, his *Poemata* was published in 1734.
2 Within the bills of mortality, 1731-39, 13,744 died of tooth related illness, 5.8% of all recorded deaths in these years (*Mortality*).
3 MS one inch straight line.

67 To Mary Collier, Hastings, from John Collier, Johnson's Court, 19 June 1733
[SAY 1634]

Your letter by yesterday's post gave me very great satisfaction as signifying that dear Tommy's feaver had left him and he was recovered. I was really under a very great concern and fear of hearing worse newes. I am very much afraid that I shall not be able to leave London till next Munday, but then I am determined to doe it at all events. I really think I have supported my brother Elphick[1] long enough; however, on my return home will, if you think proper, further consider him something. I have bought the gloves, but know not how they will fit, and it is pitty I had not an old glove; indeed, my sister bought them for me, her size in the hand and a little bigger in the arm. I would have Morris work on upon the hay till itt's done but as we had yesterday and this afternoon abundance of rain here, imagine it was a generall one and will make it but poor haying weather. Poor Jemmy is now with me and keeps his place as captain of the second form and the remoove is expected next week; he sayes Mrs Carleton goes out of town tomorrow and master George comes this night to Mrs Chelsum's. I am full weary of London and much want to be with you, pray let me hear from you by Thursday's post.

1 George Elphick, brother to John Collier's first wife Elizabeth Elphick, daughter of Edmund Elphick of Willingdon; a tradesman making and japaning chairs, some for export to Spain in 1722, borrowed from John Collier £46 10s 1721-2; faced gaol autumn 1723 (SAY 1339-1342).

68 To Mary Collier, Hastings, from John Collier, [Johnson's Court], 20 June 1733[1]
[SAY 1635]

I was very much concerned at the receipt of your letter by this post, in bringing an account of the ilnesse of the poor child; and am much more soe as itt's not in my power to come immediately out of town being concerned in an affair for my Lord Ashburnham that is in a scituation not to be left, but hope 3 or 4 dayes will make it feazable for me to come out of town and you may be certain I will not tarry a moment longer then absolutely necessary. I hope in God as the feaver is gone of it is only the breeding of teeth, but I shall be much uneasy till after hearing next post. Jemmy come this afternoon and has wrote a letter, but

I was not with him, but beleive my sister helped him tho she sayes but very little. He learns his book very well, but I cannot bring him of from his ratling way that makes me something, at sometimes, displeased with him but I hope we may have comfort from him. An humble submisśion must be to the divine will who knowes what is best for us; and it pleased him not to permit us the enjoyment of our other dear child; I have sad conflicts on the occasion. I begg his protection and blessing on us and ours.

1 Sayer vol. 1, 87, gives this as [?] 20 June 1733.

69 To Mary Collier, Hastings, from John Collier, Johnson's Court, 21 June 1733
[SAY 1636]

I think you was very obligeing in writing last post, and it gave me some satisfaction in hearing from you, tho it brought me at the same time an account of your lownesse of spiritts, but hope it will wear of again. I am still at an uncertainty of getting out of town. My businesse being still delayed and doe not see I can get out till Wednesday, soe as to be at home sometime a Thursday, but am determined not to exceed that time. Hearing a Saturday of poor Tommy's ilnesse gave me a very great uneasenesse, and I was quite overwhelmed that I hardly know what I wrote, but if I expressed myself in any harsh termes of Jemmy tis what I did not design, nor doe I think he deserves it, for I hope and beleive if it pleases God to spare his life we shall have great comfort in him. I solemnly assure you I long to be at home to converse with you and enjoy your company. Adieu my dear creature and I subscribe myself your ever faithful husband.

70 Mary Collier, Hastings, from John Collier, Johnson's Court, 23 June 1733
[SAY 1637]

Though I have tarried soe long in town in prospect of finishing an affair before the court of Chancery, I almost dispair compleating it soe as to get out of town a Wednesday. Yet neverthelesse, have determined the latter done or not done, for I will tarry noe longer and hope to be at home with you sometime a Thursday for I am heartily tired of the town. I received your letter this day and am very sorry to hear your lownesse of spiritts continues. I heartily pity and simpathize with you well knowing the direfull train attendant on that reall distemper. Jemmy is come this afternoon and very brisk. If I have time will make him write to you. I beleive he will be removed into the third form a Tuesday.

71 To Duke of Newcastle, from John Collier, Hastings, 16 August 1733
[BL Add Ms 32,688 f.123]

I had the honor to receive your grace's commands of the 14th and have in obedience thereto made out and inclosed a list and present situation of this town, and have noe reason to doubt but that I have given the opponents all their votes and the five mentioned as dubious think shall not fayle of three or four of them, and more especially Fellowes firmly fixed, if he is appointed mate of Rye Customs sloop, which I have been in hopes to hear was finished.[1] Your grace may depend that though there is such a majority, I shall not be too sanguine, but behave to all as if the numbers were a greater equalling. Sir Thomas Webster is not come to Battle; our bells have rang twice for his arrival there, but they have been false alarms. The party give out mighty things to bee done on his comeing down, but a good look out shall be kept and I am not apprehensive of his breaking in upon the interest.

The mayor and I went round the whole ton last Munday and find about 160 freeholders, of which a list is taken. We applyed to every one of them for Mr Pelham and Mr Butler for the county election and, though Mr Eversfield, Mr Broadway and Capt Milward had been very diligent, we met with very good successe and don't doubt but a good account will be given of this place. There were between 20 and 30 that refused us, and not more. Had an actuall promise and engagement from a majority, and from the rest noe cross answers, but declined engageing soe long beforehand and this was what Mr Broadway etc., insinuated to all when they could not get an engagement. The freeholders are promised an entertainment when Sir T. Webster comes down, soe before the herring fishery begins we think to drink your grace's and the two candidates' healths.

I hope in three or four dayes to complete the list of freeholders in Hastings rape and send Mr Pelham pursuant to his command, but before we went round the town, as the opposites were busy and some letters came from Mr Fuller, I was obliged to give some attendance which retarded its completion. The country hereabout stands very well. There is some discourse that Rye will bee much against your grace's interest, but I have not as yet been there. Capt Markwith's apostacy is not a little surprizeing, but beleive he will not be able to make much of it. I can't help sending your grace the copy of a circular letter, sent by Sir W. Parker to the freeholders of his neighbouring parishes. I humbly return your grace thanks for your kind remembrance of me and am with all attachment. I will soon send your grace a list of our freeholders and how it's beleived they will stand.

1 John Collier wrote to Robert Burnett, agent for the Duke of Newcastle, to recommend George Fellowes as mate of the Rye Customs sloop (TNA SP 36/30); in the event Thomas Giles was replaced by Nathaniel Pilgram junior (TNA CUST 18/178-182).

72 To Duke of Newcastle, from John Collier, Hastings, 18 August 1733

[BL Add Ms 32.688 f.139]

I have herewith inclosed a list of the freeholders in this town[1] and have marked those that have actually promised, being 96, and don't doubt of a great many more and severall of the others are very antient and will not goe. I had an absolute denyall from about 20 and several others that I have reason to think will goe in your grace's interest gave civill answers but would not promise so long before hand. Mr Boyse, one of our juratts, ded yesterday and I forgot in my last to mention to your grace the deaths of John Crouch senior and poor Jeffery Glyde, two of our freemen. I have this post sent Mr Pelham a list of the freeholders in Hastings rape. I have been at Rye and find it much better than what was given out as to the freeholders there.

1 Appendix 5 **[608]** SAY 10, this list was compiled for the 1734 election and was re-used in the 1741 election.

73 To Duke of Newcastle, from John Collier, Hastings, 10 November 1733

[BL Add Ms 32,689 f.17]

Pursuant to your grace's commands I have been at the houses where your friends met on the 20th and 30th of October, and notwithstanding the strict and possitive cautions and directions given, the expence amounts to an extravagant sume. I assure your grace that I have, in the strictest manner, examined into every particular without releife unlesse breaking of intirely with them, soe have paid the same.

20th of October	£36 4s 0d
30th including the 20 guineas then usually given to the corporation	£82 16s 9d
[*Total*]	£119 0s 9d

Last Wednesday an invitation was given to the wives of the mayor, juratts and freemen to breakfast at Mr Broadway's and proceed in a body to dine with Lady Webster that day at Farleight. There were but 16 went. Thursday last there was an entertainment to the freeholders of some neighbouring parishes at a little alehouse on Farleight Down. Mr Webster, Nairn, Willes, Puckle and more under managers were there. Tarried till about 3 or 4 o'clock in the morning, but I don't hear or believe a convert was made. I have the honour of being with all respect and gratitude. The 30th of October we had the neighbouring parishes which increased the expense.

74 To Mary Collier, Hastings, from John Collier, Tunbridge c. November 1733 [SAY 2153]

My Dearest life, According to my promise I write to you from this place informing you that I got hither last night at 7 a clock but had a very bad journey and goeing round by Cranbrook a very long one but I thank God noe accident. Rideing a pretty way with a wet great coat has made my shoulders very stiffe and a little matter increased my cold but I thank God I slept very well goeing to bed at ten and did not hear the town clock till he struck five. I hope you will cheer up and if fine weather get out of doors for I beleive the air will give you a good assistance. Pray send T. Holman the inclosed a Saturday morning. I am with the greatest tenderness and affection. I did intend to have took out and examined the beer that is left of Mr Mead's in the vault and cleaned the bottle for there is but little of it. If Samuel Cruttenden visits you often I desire he may have the second bin to regale with which is the brown beer for I am sure if he could get at it would drink all the other up, my dear, your most faithfull and affectionate husband.

75 To Mary Collier, Hastings, from John Collier, [Johnson's Court], 15 November 1733 SAY 1638]

I hope you got as safe home to Hasting a Wednesday evening as I arrived here at one a clock today. I found all in Johnson's Court very well and there heard Jemmy was well a Sunday. My brother seeing him a Sunday and went with him to Chelsey. It seems he dined at Mr Green's and now the dayes are soe short and their exercise pretty long that there is not time for his comeing soe often as before; I expected him this afternoon, or had sent, but have been in a very great hurry.

I was prodigiously surprized to see John Ellames come to my brother's about 2 hours after I arrived there and was sadly afraid of some accident in our family; but on receiving the letter find it was an account of the death of poor Mr Geery, which I am heartily concerned for and think there's a great family left in a poor scituation.[1] I reckon we shall have plague enough about the post office, but if I can have my will for sometime, it should be to the family, but I shall see how it goes on. Halsted sent the messenger and to have the place but I see noe reason. I need not caution you not to take any notice what I write about Halsted. I have not seen any of the Newcastle family, but shall tomorrow, but I have sent a letter to postpone any disposal of it.

I imagine you was much dissappointed a Wednesday night in not having an account of the marriage.[2] The Prince is still very ill and noe time is fixed for the marriage. I find his person is not extraordinary but all, even Will Cranston and Page, say he is a person of great abilities. I hope Mrs Franckwell is with you to whom I send my humble service. Misse Steevens is in Johnston's Court to whom I gave your complements and had a return of the same.

1 John Geery.

2 Anne, princess royal, aged 24 in 1733, fluent in Latin, marriage arranged with William, Prince of Orange, who arrived at Greenwich aboard the *Fubbs* yacht, 7 November; he contracted pneumonia, then ill at Bath for month after 27 January 1734 with fatigue so the wedding was postponed. Much sympathy expressed for the prince and princess, although little from the royal family. The wedding was finally held at the chapel royal, St James, 14 March 1734. The Princess royal and Prince of Orange sailed back to Holland on the *Fubbs* yacht, 24 April 1724; (*PS* April 1734, 321-326, Egmont vol. 2, 43, 46-8, Hervey vol. 1, 232, Rapin vol. 20, 235-6).

76 To Mary Collier, Hastings, from John Collier, Johnson's Court, 20 November 1733 [SAY 1639]

With a great deal of pleasure I received your letter yesterday as it brought an account of your welfare, tho I am very sorry Mrs Anne Franckwell is not come to your aid. As Jemmy is with me I make him write a letter accompanying this. Upon enquiry I find he learns his book, and behaves exceedingly well in school and has a good character from the masters.[1] He is got captain of the lower remoove of the third form and has been soe for above a fortnight, tho he never sent word of it or so much as let my brother Cranston know it for fear, as he sayes, he should loose it again, but he still maintains his post, and thinks he shall continue it. His stockings are a little too short for him.

My affairs promised are almost handsomly compleated. I was sworn this day surveyor general of Kent and have my commission and the patent place that you see to dear Jemmy and myselfe is passing the great seal, and hope to have it compleated this week.[2] I have bespoke yours and the girles' things and am promised them a Fryday.

The Duke of Newcastle goes out of town a Thursday or Fryday for Bishopston, and I have promised to be there a Sunday night, from whence I design to be at home a Tuesday or Wednesday. I desire you will send Nicholas out a Thursday after dinner upon Trumble's horse, soe as he may come to town a Fryday evening, for I propose to get out a Saturday afternoon. If he has noe money give him to bear his expense on the road; let him bring only the portmanteau and my slippers. The Prince of Wales is still ill though his feaver is interrmitted and ceased on taking the bark. Everybody are getting out of town till the marriage which is gone of without any time appointed, and really every body pities him in his condition and scituation.

I beleive Mr Mayor will meet me at Bishopston. I think it will be proper Mrs Geery should speak to him about the place, because I would not take it upon myselfe wholly but I don't think it proper that she should know that the mayor is to goe to Bishopston soe soon unlesse he tells her. I assure you Jemmy's intelligence about the Prince of Orange is noe more than what is told every day in town.

1 Discussion as to whether children should be taught Latin from grammar or literature (Crossley & Saville 534); the Collier library contained several grammars including a constitution of the Latin grammar and an introduction to Latin syntax.

2 John Collier's appointments referred to were the Surveyor General of the riding officers of Kent, and the usher and cryer of the court of King's Bench.

77 To John Collier, Hastings, from Thomas Pelham, 29 January 1734 [SAY 81]

In answer to the letter which my uncle received from you yesterday, my lord duke desires me to acquaint you that his grace hopes you will take the effectual methods for preventing the admission of any freemen by virtue of such mandamus's, as you mention, are already served on the mayor and jurats in favour of John Sargent and John Shorter. Mr Strange[1] was retained some time ago for any affairs we might have depending in the law courts here relating to Hastings and Lewes before the next election, but if you can likewise have the Attorney and Sollicitor General for this particular business my lord duke has no sort of objection to it. You may tell William Bourne that he is appointed boatman in the father's room who is superannuated,[2] and I will gett Mr Forbes to take the warrants accordingly from the Treasury.

1 Sir John Strange.
2 William Bourne, Customs boatman; superannuation payments for Customs officers were by dormant warrants and local payments: as these were often erratic, in 1713 the Customs board authorised the Controller and Receiver of the superannuation fund to collect for officers 'worn out by age after long and faithful service', disabled in action, and deficient in means of support, although only certain officers qualified and the means test continued for the 18th century (Hoon 105-6).

78 To Sir William Ashburnham, Broomham, from William Cranston, [Johnson's Court], 29 January 1734 [SAY 723]

Imediately upon rect of yours I went to Mr Masterman, who, as you imagined, is concerned on the other side. But I told him yours and dare say shall have his best endeavours, as if only on ours. Upon asking some questions I found that a writt of mandamus[1] is a writt of common right and every person entitled to it that asks for it, and without any previous affidavits whatever. He doubts whether the court will give any time to make a return in, if they do twould not be above 3 or 4 days upon the return. If the opposite party except to it tis formally argued, and if tis adjudged to be a return good in law, they may then traverse the custom and come to tryall whether the custom alledged in the writt is a custom, or not, and which he says they may bring to tryall at next assizes.

I went also last night to the Attorney and Solicitor[2] and saw both of em, the first would not take a retainer as not knowing whether he could attend but promised I not to ...[3] a ret on the other side but that he would serve us if he could. I took an oppurtunity to tell him in whose interest he was to be in, till which he would hear nothing of it; so I don't doubt but on a properer application he may be got there, if occasion. As to the other, he would upon no terms attend, and indeed, as he has been very little conversant with the court of King's Bench I don't apprehend he could do you much good. Abney, Strange and Marsh are retained by the opponents and as this matter may come to the assizes I thought proper to retain Darnell.[4]

Masterman tells me Sir T.[5] is very hot and beleives he will push it to the utmost. Masterman has drawn me a sketch of the returns and as there is not time to send you a copy and have your directions upon it, and after that to consult consill and to transmit to you in order to return it in due time, I thought it adviseable, and the best way that I could apprehend, that I go tomorrow to Fazakerly. And before I give him his fees to get a promise that will peruse and settle em so as that I may depend upon having em to send you per next post. If I can't have such a promise from him I shall go to Masterman and take his recommendation; I would have gone tonight but tis now just eleven and he but sent the returns to me this moment. I'll take all the care possible in it.

[*Reverse, Signed*] William Page. Sir, The crumbles[6] came on the stage this day and after four hours debate reteyn the bill for a twelve month, in the meantime bring an ejectment special jury and view. Bean and Denman, we have taxed the costs and hope to present you with the report against you runne up.

1 Writ of mandamus; presumption by judges in the Westminster courts that every corporation affecting and involving the public was erected for a public purpose, even where endowed with privileges exclusive to members of the said corporation. Any person, however affected, could petition the King's Bench for a writ to enforce compliance with any part of the corporation's remit including compliance with rules for elections and appointments to the corporation. In addition to records of statutes and parliament, the library of John Collier contained works on Westminster courts, including Thomas Blount *A Law Dictionary and Glossary* (1717); W Stubbs & G Talmash, *The Crown Circuit Companion, containing the practice of the assizes on the crown side; with the courts of the general and general quarter session* (1738), which includes laws on execution and administration and reports of legal cases.

2 Sir John Willes, Attorney General and Sir Dudley Ryder, Solicitor General.

3 MS damaged.

4 Lawyers listed were Thomas Abney, Sir John Strange, John Marsh, Sir John Darnall, Nicholas Fazakerley, and Henry Masterman.

5 Sir Thomas Webster.

6 The key meanings relate to crookedness or crooked, and also to the division of legal and political discussion into small crumbs and fragments (*OED*).

79 To John Collier, Hastings, from William Cranston, [Johnson's Court], 31 January 1734 [SAY 724]

Pursuant to what I wrote in my last I yesterday morning went to Mr Fazakerly with the returns, etc, but he was too busy to look em over. I then went to Masterman who recommended me to the person I should have gone to, had I not asked him, vizt Mr Draper, a very considerable man and particularly skilfull in these affairs. He perused em and made some though not a great many alterations and fixed em in the manner they are here sent to you. The denying everything alledged in the writt, he said, would do you neither harm nor good but tis chiefly…[1] done , as tis almost so in all such cases, to put the plaintiffs to all the trouble and expence possible. For the denying it here obliges them to prove it and the proving all this without the custom will be of no manner of service to em. As you or I may fixt the mayor's hand to the return which is all the hands necessary and even that not absolutely, and as I suppose you will be in town by the return of em, or if within a day or 2 after, will be soon enough. I fancy you had better defer the doing em till we meet here. For between this and then tis not impossible but that something may be determined in the court of King's Bench which may be of some service to us …[1] being a thing now depending there apropos to this:

Foster v Harman: Inclosd you receive this warrant or Fieri Facias: Adams v Pollard:[2] I've sent an alias and copy this post to Cole. I received a letter from Butler in it yesterday with a long story about his endeavours to get the former served etc. Reynolds v George:[3] Wellard having given Mr Butler an account of our attendance in this, and what then passed, had a letter since from him to desire that he would put of the attendance as last Monday and in the interim go to Baynes and take his opinion upon it and give him his answer, and that if Baynes could give him no hopes, he would have us the trouble and charge of an attendance on the baron. To this letter Wellard has sent a answer and expects every post to have orders to consent that the record be delivered to us; though this has put of a little, yet I think it makes it sure and I would not be overfond of an argument, for things, though sometimes very clear, take a wrong turn.

I am furbishing up old cloths in order to make T. Denham's boy a new suit. I have an old coat in a closet in the brewhouse chamber which would help towards it so that if you have a spare corner in your box should be obliged to you for bringing it up.

1 MS damaged.

2 Mary Adams, Marden, Kent. Linen worker and widow of Richard Adams. Richard Adams v Richard Pollard: intervention of poor law officers on the side of Mary Adams after distraint against her by Pollard who seized her linen manufacturing equipment, which reduced her and children to penury (TNA C11/110/9; bill and answer, 5 May 1735, 8 Geo. II; C11/235/32, 23 January 1736 9 Geo II, country commission, 31 January 1736, C11/1264/14; this case is listed in SAY 1418 f. 26v).

3 Lewes assizes, 7 Geo. II, 28 July 1733, Reynolds v George: before Sir John Comyns, Richard Michell, John Darvill, serjeant-at-law, cause no. 3, case awarded for plaintiff, damages £15, no attorney listed (TNA ASSI 34/5). The case is listed in SAY 1418 f. 26v.

80 To John Collier, Hastings, from William Cranston, [Johnson's Court], 2 February 1734 [SAY 725]

I was of the opinion as you as to the method of obtaining mandamus's till I saw Masterman in this; but since yours of today have enquired farther and find tis even as he says. I went this afternoon to Mr Strange and saw the retainer you speak of entered in his book, though tis not quite in so particular manner as you mention. I offered him one de novo in this particular case but he declined accepting of it, or saying whether he would be with us or not, but sent me to Masterman to know in what manner he, Masterman, apprehended he, Strange, was retained against us and I had from Masterman that he gave Strange a guinea to move that mandamas at serjeant's suit which Masterman looked upon as a retainer. This I afterwards told Strange who seemed to think it could be no retainer because the intent of giving it him was for a particular purpose, vizt a motion which he had done, therefore the consideration of that guinea was over. On the other hand, he seemed to think that by the wording of Mr Pelham's retainer, twas given him as one to be for him in case this election was brought into the House of Commons, and, if the words implied so much and nothing else, he thought he ought to stay the refusal of the opposite side before he took mine. Upon the whole he took a memorandum of it and designs to speak to Masterman a Monday about it and in the evening will give me my answer.

It appears by the words, the answer of the mayor, etc., which is to be indorsed on the back of the writt, that the return is to be on a parchment to be annexed to the writt and which is to be without stamp. But as you'll be up a Wednesday I apprehend upon receipt of mine last night you'll deferr the return till you come yourself. Jemmy is now here and gives his duty etc. Tom Frewen is just now arrived. Fuller comes to morrow so nobody remains but you to compleat the sett.

[*Reverse*] This came last night. Hythe, 31 January 1733. Sir, I ask pardon for forgetting to acquaint you that Mr John Gates,[1] a riding officer at Dimchurch, wants instructions; he being the last officer made, he slipt my memory. I am with all due respects to you, Thomas Clare or Clan or Claw,[2] I don't know which.

1 John Gates, Customs riding officer, Dymchurch (TNA CUST 18/190).

2 Thomas Clare, Customs supervisor of the riding officers from Camber Point to Hythe (CUST 148/11),

81 To Mary Collier, Hastings, from John Collier, [Johnson's Court], 7 February 1734 [SAY 1640]

I am to inform you of my getting to town yesterday noon, very well and found Johnston's Court soe, and an account that Jemmy was here the night before, very brisk. I this day went to Westminster and met him in the hall; looks very healthy and much like a schoolboy, haveing outgrown his cloaths not a little. He is to come a Saturday afternoon, and is then to answer Dely's letter. I find he goes on at school with courage and successe which I am sure will be as agreeable to you, as it is to my satisfaction and comfort. I have not as yet seen Sir William Ashburnham but hear he is well, though he sayes otherwise, and gives constant attendance at the house. Your gown was this day sent to the dyers and I ordered it a deep green. I have not heard any particular newes of any kind, soe nothing of the Prince of Orange but various accounts of the day appointed for the princesse royall's happy nuptialls; itt's generally thought the first of March will be the day, tho some think sooner. I have promised Jemmy to give him a play before I come out of town, it being what I find he has much reckoned upon.

Sir Thomas Webster has given himselfe very great airs about the mandamus's in Westminster Hall, but I beleive there will be a dissappointment to him and his party in that matter.[1] I hope, my dear, if you have anything particularly to be bought I shall receive your orders and beleive you are well satisfyed, it will be with great pleasure.[2] I can tell you and Mrs Thorpe and likewise my daughter Worge if she is with you, a parcell of --- ,[3] that affairs goe swimmingly on, all opposition falls to the ground and Sir R.W. and the ministry daily get ground of their opponents and abundance of halfe faced creatures either out of remorse of conscience, or something else, which I mean the imminent danger of their king and country, has made them very steady. This last peice of newes I would not have goe further than our own house, though itt's fact that the court gain ground.[4]

1 The mandamus' refers to the financial support from Sir Thomas Webster to applications to King's Bench in the cases of John Serjeant and John Shorter. Lord Hardwicke was testing the writ, 23 January 1734 (Appendix 2; Hastings Town business; SAY 82; SAY 83).

2 Items bought in early 1734 by John Collier included 40' of matting, a new carpet 6' wide, soft wax, stockings, slippers, shoes, bottles, ink, land collector's warrants, pistol charges, powder flask, stove blacking, barley sugar and sugar candy, cheese, clothes from Mrs Elcock and Mr Parry the tailor, a ring for Dely, a doll for Molly, for Jenny a fan, and caps for all the girls (SAY 1418 f. 19-22).

3 MS one inch line.

4 John Collier has several references about the influence in court circles of Queen Caroline; for her position in support of Walpole see Sykes 131-3; Williams 1945 193.

82 To Mary Collier, [Hastings], from John Collier, [Johnson's Court], 9 February 1734 [SAY 1641]

I received your letter by this post with those accompanying it, and have a great deal of satisfaction by not hearing anything to the contrary of yours and the children's welfare. Jemmy is come and writes a letter to the girles which I hope will be delightfull to them but he has not begun it, as yet he really looks very well, but a right ragged schoolboy. I beleive his hair will be fit to wear against Easter, for now he makes but an odd figure between both he seems to goe on very well with his learning and hope in God we shall have comfort in him. Tomorrow morning the taylor is to come and fix upon cloathes for him. I beleive I forgot in my last to tell you that a quarter of an hour after I arrived in

Johnson's Court a Wednesday, our cosens Masons came thither and tarried dinner; he was almost drunk and ratled just as he did 20 years agoe. She desired her service and was much concerned for poor Mr Wicking. I have sent your gown and bespoke your gloves and ordered an alteration in Molly's cap, and as you don't like the chocolate will find out a new chap. I am surprized at the behaviour of Mrs Geery, tho I think it exactly like her. Pray tell Mrs Thorpe I have been with old Eyres and he gives some hopes of finishing the affair. He went to Croyden today and is to return a Wednesday or Thursday when I am to know for a certainty.

I dined yesterday at Coll. Pelham's with Sir William Ashburnham etc; he is, and looks, very well but complains much as usuall. Poor Lord Ashburnham is very ill and don't see company. There is noe manner of newes stirring. Itt's expected to be a short sessions of Parliament. Sir Thomas Webster much blusters about the mandamus's but I beleive they will come to nothing in the end. The doctor's newes about the water suites being at an end is a very great mistake for itt's pushed on very warmly and will be try'd at next assizes,[1] as I beleive. I hope every post will bring me the satisfaction of your welfare and that of the family. All here send respects. Misse Steevens goes down with Mr Frewen about a week hence. You may tell Thomas Holman that as Mr Worge has wrote to him about Gunter he need not goe to serve the writ.

1 The subsequent assizes, East Grinstead, Monday 18 March 1734, 7 Geo. II, has no record of such actions, although two actions over water rights were brought against John Collier and Henry Carleton by Hastings freemen, Taught v Collier, for trespass, and Meadow v Collier and Carleton, at Horsham assizes, causes 3 and 4, Monday 12 August 1734, 8 Geo. II, before Sir Robert Eyre, Chief Justice of the Common Pleas, and Sir Edmund Probyn (TNA ASSI 34/5; [**108**] Appendix 3: Hastings Water Supply SAY 23).

83 To Mary Collier, [Hastings], from John Collier, [Johnson's Court], 12 February 1734 [SAY 1642]

I am to thank you for your kind letter by last post and am glad to find nothing contradictory to your welfare. I shall think Sam Cruttenden's coming to live in town, considering as matters are situated something very extraordinary, and am at a losse to think what his expectations are from it, and by whose advice. But I fancy he may be dissappointed in his projects, if he has any for me to be concerned in, for it will goe down very hard to be forced into any measures contrary to my own sentiments. Jemmy went home a Sunday evening but I have seen him to day. We fixed upon some cloaths for him a Sunday. I have had a great cold these two dayes and my throat has been a little sore and sadly troubled with a tickling cough as you had. I hope it will wear of. If not I beleive I shall be blooded.[1] Mr Coppard wrote me word that Mr Broadway and Mr Milward had been round the town with a petition about the poll relating to future elections of knights of the shire, but did not tell me their successe.

1 Bloodletting by leeches, for the alleviation of symptoms in various ailments, and in recovery from smallpox (Mead vol. 2, 120, 131). On occasion this treatment had adverse consequences; Edmund Pyle refers to Miss Greenwood who, in early 1733, was 'lamed with bleeding and her arm is quite withered now' (Pyle 45).

84 To Mary Collier, Hastings, from John Collier, [Johnson's Court], 14 February 1734 [SAY 1643]

I received your letter with an account of my poor mother's ilnesse.[1] I am very much concerned for it, though I can't say greatly surprized considering her age and the attendant infirmities. I take it exceedingly kind that you went over to see her, and am sure you will neglect nothing that may contribute to her recovery, ease or satisfaction. I cannot possibly come out of town at present and cannot fix a time, soe must ardently and with some impatience wait for the accounts the post will give. My cold continues very much though I thank God don't increase.

1 Sarah Collier, widow of Peter Collier.

85 To Mary Collier, Hastings, from John Collier, Johnson's Court, 16 February 1734 [SAY 1644]

I cannot say that your letter I received today was much to my surprize because I could not, considering the former account, expect to hear or imagine that my poor mother could get over such a shock at her age, and a long train of distempers and infirmities. When I came to my brother's, I found a letter from my brother Cruttenden, that she dyed a Thursday night. It all happens very unfortunately, for I cannot possibly come out of town, without being obliged to return in 5 or 6 dayes at furthest, which will be a great fatigue. I thank God my cold is not worse, but something better, though still hoarse. Yesterday and today it has been very uncomfortable weather haveing rained very much. Jemmy came this afternoon and is very well.

As to my mother's funerall, I desire it may bee just in the manner she has directed or desired, if any such thing is known. If not then to be interred in a private, handsom, decent manner. I beleive it was her intentions to be buried at Borne.[1] Mr Worge went out of town this morning soe will be at home and hope he and my brother Cranston will assist in giving directions about it. I did design to get out next [2] Thursday, soe as to be at home a Fryday night, but yesterday was put of by a particular affair that will hold me that very day, and I can't propose getting out soe soon, but will embrace the first moment I can, much longing to be at home. As it is bad rideing, etc, I desire you would not have the fatigue of goeing even to Hollington, for it cannot be desired, nor thought unhandsom, and I am sure I acquit you from it. I cannot think of any particular directions in the affair.

1 Sarah Collier, buried 20 February 1734, St Clement's Hastings (Sayer vol. 1, 95 n).
2 MS *Tuesday* struck through.

86 To Duke of Newcastle, from John Collier, Hastings, 18 April 1734 [BL Add Ms 32689 f.200]

I had the honour of receiving your grace's commands of the 13th and 16th and shall take all possible care relating to the elections, and make it my business to be at Halland the 24th or 25th at furthest; and in the meantime endeavour to settle the method of conveying our friends to Chichester. But I beleive some must goe by sea, and they assure me that by keeping close by the shore they shall run noe hazard of being there in time, but can tide it up and if a strong wind is against them they will by waggons or horses get on.

I have informed Sir William Ashburnham, Sir Nicholas Pelham and Mr Hay of the absolute necessity there is of their being at Lewes sessions and they will all be there, and I hope to wait on Sir William to Halland the night before. The barrel has been much sunk this 2 or 3 days but I hope itt's over, and tomorrow I design for Broomham about regulating the neighbouring parishes for the journey. I was this day at Bexhill and settled with Mr Cramp for that parish.

Munday last in the afternoon 13 freemen's sons came to the mayor, when I was with him, to demand their freedom on the pretended usage. In an hour after, a person went round to the mayor, juratts etc., and all the freemen with an invitation to meet Mr Webster at Chambers's the next day about 3 a clock, on which we gave a counter invitation to the juratts and freemen in our interest and those that hang between both and I believe there is noe reason to think the opposites made any converts. Mr Eversfield came with Mr Webster to town; they came down last Saturday together from London by posthorses, and Jack Fuller came hither a little after them. The two former came to the Swan, sent out for the mayor, drank a bottle of wine and expostulated but they lost time by it. That night there was 22 freemen's sons summoned togeather by Mr Broadway, and Mr Webster and Mr Fuller were with them and they are next Saturday, one court day, to come in a body to demand their freedom and Mr Fuller pressed those that are freeholders for their votes, but I can't think we shall loose 5 by this artifice.[1]

Today Mr Eversfield invited several from this town to his house, but I don't hear there is any gone but 6 or 7 stauch freemen against us. John Hide that we presumed to recommend to your grace's favour is the son of a freeman of Dover and by the custom of that town is entituled to take up his freedom.[2] I hear that election will be the 24th; if your grace would have him goe down, he will readily doe it. I have got two to send from hence for Papillon and Revell. I this post write to Mr Forbes to send down our 5 freemen in London, Gillart, White, Thatcher, Wales, and Daw that they may not be forgot.

1 Claim to freedom supported by Thomas Broadway, Sir Thomas Webster and John Fuller (Appendix 2: Hastings Town Business; **[583]** SAY 82; **[584]** SAY 83.)
2 John Hyde, Customs boatman, Hastings (TNA CUST 18/178, 190).

87 To John Collier, Hastings, from William Cranston, [Johnson's Court], 30 April 1734 [SAY 726]

I received yours of Saturday last and am glad to hear of your success at Lewes,[1] and make no doubt but that all went well yesterday at the port. My thoughts as to the certioriaris[2] in the first place is that they were only delivered in terrorem and that as the purpose for which they were delivered is over so there is an end of them. But I have taken care as to time to return em in, though tis presently done, the originall order being to be ingrossed on a peice of parchment, without stamp, and signed by the justice himself, and as to the indorsing the writt, that I can do here. As to the mandamus, the course of the court requires a speedier answer to it than to the certiorari's and I don't at present apprehend that any other answer can be given to it than non suit electus, but as I shall have more particulars per next I shall then wait upon Masterman about the whole and will be able to give you a full account at our meeting at Chichester, for I begin to dispair of seeing Hasting. I have had Lott with his chap, as also another about your usher's place but have put all off till I see C. Frewen,[3] who comes to town tonight. I find Bagshaw is dead.

1 Lewes election 27 April 1734, returned Thomas Pelham of Stanmer with 84 votes, and Thomas Pelham of Lewes 83, the sitting MPs, who defeated Nathaniel Garland 75, and Thomas Sergison 70. For allegations that Thomas Freind and James Reeves, high constables and returning officers, exercised their power in favour of the Pelhams see Brent 1993 175-6; *HofP 1715-1754* vol. 1, 335-6; Taylor & Jones lxxxiv-v.
2 Writ from a higher court calling for the records of a case at a lower court heard, or due to be heard, upon the complaint of a party that the lower court has not dispensed justice, or that an impartial trial has not been, or will not be, held.
3 Charles Frewen.

88 To John Collier, Hastings, from William Cranston, [Johnson's Court], 21 May 1734 [SAY 727]

Since I last saw you I have had two or three meetings with[1] Mr Lot and his chap, Mr Thomas Chamberlin, and Mr Philip Castill, never having seen inter alia and each of em seperately and am sure, at least from me, neither one knows of the other's application. And yet they all exactly agree as to the price, having all of em had their information from the same person, vizt one Daniel who was formerly one of the cryers, and since my memory and the best of em that I ever do remember, Chamberlin and Castill come to 150 guineas and no more, and Lott's chap £[2]156 and no more, and also insist that he be at liberty to resign in a year's time if he thinks proper, without giving any gratuity to you for it. Castill I by no means like the countenance of. Chamberlin is pretty well but Lott's chap is by much the best, his name is Cary Cree of the parish of St George's, Hanover Square, oilman.

I have undertaken, seperately, to give all of em their answer by Monday evening next. For my part I cannot get to any certainty as to the value of it, though by what inquiry I have made, tis generally agreed tis not worth more than is offered. I am told the Common Pleas chaps don't give more than £200 and am sure their places are much better, and am apt to think that as Bagshaw intended,[2] if he had lived, to have sold his place, he gave out that it cost him more than it really did, in order to gett more for it. You'll do just as you please in it and perhaps if you let it alone till you come to town, you may chap better yourself, or if you are content with the above you'll please to let me know which, that I may give answers accordingly. I suppose you took a copy of one of the deputations and took notice also what stamp twas wrote on, if so and you should approve of any of the above, you might ret one to me and then an end will be put to it at once.

1 MS *with* removed in MS to wax seal.
2 MS damaged.

89 To John Collier,[1] [Hastings], from William Cranston, [Johnson's Court], 30 May 1734 [SAY 728]

I ingrossed the return to Mr Lund's mandamus and delivered in that together with the returns to the certioraris to Mr Masterman for him to file. I think Mr Pelham has employed a great many hands in the mandamus but perhaps he may be of Soloman's opinion that in a multitude of lawyers there is safety. I hope by this time your indisposition, which prevented you coming hither is [2] intirely removed and shall be in expectation of seeing you here soon enough to make your appearance the first day of terme.

The wine came safe to hand Monday morning and for which I am extreamly obliged to you and return you 10,000 thanks. I sent the two dozen of spaw water on board Sargent a Monday. A letter came to you here from Clare at Hythe informing you that he intended to set out in a week or ten days for London, and that he should be glad to be favoured with a line of leave from you. Your packett of yesterday came time enough just to send back your box, but not the linnen, for though you wrote upon it to be sent to me as soon as the carrier came in, yet it did not come till between six and seven, before which time I was gone out for the evening. But not then being very well I returned about 9 so was soon enough for the box, though not the other and twas 10 to 1 that the box went. I did not go from home till past 6; you shall have the linnen etc, next carrier.

A letter was left for you at the coffee house from Captain Pigram, in which he desired you would reimburse Mr Edward Wyatt what money he paid for councill's fees etc, and that he would wait on you and make up the account. I met with Mr Whitehead this evening and shewed him your affidavit and the receipt, and acquainted with your request that he would forbear any proceedings till you came to town when you would certainly make an end of it. He seemed to be a little angry that this affair had been so long upon the anvill and that without producing Mr Wroth's receipt he could not give you credit for the 34 5s 8d mentioned in your affidavit because Wroth's widow would not refund the money without actually seeing her husband's receipt, and that upon seeing it she would. But upon the whole matter she insisted on the imediate payment of the arrears since those in dispute, and that in such a case he would stay till you come to town in order to settle the other.

I did not then tell him that I had any authority to pay a farthing because while we were talking of it, it came into my head that I once had Wroth's receipt and some other papers in my custody. But I could not then recollect whether I had em now or had delivered em to you. So that I got time till Thursday next in order to have your answer as to the paying him any money down now, intending during that time to rumage over all my old papers in search of these. But upon my returning home I looked into one place only and their to my great satisfaction I actually found Wroth's receipt with which I imediately run back again to Whitehead, but he was gone from the office but by giving him this receipt in order for his getting the money of Mrs Worth I make no doubt but he will stay for the remainder till you come to town. And tomorrow I shall accordingly tell him that I did not write tonight but staid to have his answer upon my finding this receipt and what he does sayupon it. I'll lett you know per next. He told me that he wrote you a letter last post but I told him that you was gone to Dover, and that he should not expect an answer before next Thursday, so that you may omitt writing to him till you receive his farther answer in my letter which I shall send you. I was greatly pleased in finding the receipt and dare say you had quite forgot that ever you gave it me.

Lott and I have set upon your Latin deputation and upon turning it literally into English it run very bald and concise, upon which we made some aditions to it and I here send it as we fixed it. I don't apprehend there's anything in it that can be any ways prejudiciall to you. The article in respect to his fees Lott as been more particular in that was in the other, but I could not see how I could make any objections to it since tis no more than I what I should have incerted had I been in his place. I've also sent a bit of parchment and etc., to ingross it upon and have appointed em both Tuesday and Fryday morning next to ends all that, in case you had not time so as to remitt it to me per next post, it might be done that following one. I'll settle with Masterman these holydays how we are to proceed in the certiorai measures and if anything necessary farther to be done in the country will lett you know, as I don't know who to get I will be bail myself for Dighton and Page.

1 While the recipient is omitted on the envelope, notes in John Collier's handwriting appear on the letter.
2 MS *by this time* struck through.

90 To Mary Collier, [Hastings] from Thomas Denham, [Hollington] 16 June 1734[1]
[SAY 2184]

Madam, pray let Mr Mead make a frame for the picture at Mrs Wimble's, and send somebody home with it next Monday, there's much work in it that I can do better at home. We shall have it up in little time. If you will give me a little oyle and 2 or 3 cucumbers it will be an obligation to your cousin and most humble servant, I don't mean that Mead shoud send the frame to Hollington. I must do one from yours for Mr Carleton, all things are set out. I have a perfect notion of it and you'l see it next time much more beautifull.

1 Or earlier year, Thomas Denham, rector, Hollington, buried 21 September 1734; valuation of his goods at £38 3s 6d with administration granted to Elizabeth Denham, widow, 13 March 1735 (Hughes 105-6).

91 To Mary Collier, [Hastings], from John Collier, [Johnson's Court], 2 July 1734
[SAY 1645]

I yesterday received your kind letter with a great deal of satisfaction, and hope you will continue to write every post a continuance of your health. All here are pretty well. I walk as little as I can for my feet are but very little or at all mended. I called at Robertsbridge about your stayes; Jones was not at home but I saw his wife. She promised not to forget sending him over and if he is not come tell Nich to let the post boy call and remind him. My brother Cranston I find was down at the Kentish election and returned immediately to London but never mentioned it being ashamed of the successe. I hear Sir Henry Farmer's will was made about 4 years since, condemned by everybody, and abundance of people that had expectations are dissappointed as well as our Sir Charles, who about that time unfortunately had a difference with the houskeeper who brought in this boy upon him, etc.[1]

Misse Steevens and her sister, who is exceedingly like one of the Miss Eversfield's, only her teeth don't stick out and is her namesake, breakfasted here yesterday morning and Misse Steevens sends her humble service. My sister has got the old thimble she brought up for your size, soe that affair will be easily managed. Jemmy's cloaths came home a Saturday, but it rained a Sunday and was not worn and indeed his stockings, shooes and hat were not of a peece, but I intend to equip him against Sunday. I think the town but scanty of newes as well as company. Jemmy has paid a visit to the Indian king and queen, but don't find he is enamoured.[2] I have hitherto lived perfectly regular not haveing been once at the tavern or in any company, out one evening and hope to have resolution enough to continue it. Pray let Dr Thorpe have the letter accompanying this. I don't know how the post affair will come out but I have this day, as being the only time of seeing the duke or any of the family, mentioned it as much as I can, consistent with other things, in his favour.

1 Sir Henry Fermor (Caffyn 223-5).

2 Tomachihi, or Tomakeeky, chief of the Yamacree Indians, a branch of the Crick Indians, lived near Savannah Town, Georgia. This chief was brought over by the Georgia Society to confirm a treaty of peace made with his nation and eight other Indian tribes in 1733. Lodged at the Georgia offices, the chief wished to learn English and study the Christian religion, and agreed to move his tribe to lands reserved for their use. Yamacree Indians then fielded only fifty warriors, their number depleted by smallpox. For a report of their embarkation to Savannah, 4 November 1734, see Egmont vol. 2 112-5, 157.

92 To Mary Collier, Hastings, from John Collier, [Johnson's Court], 6 July 1734

[SAY 1646]

I congratulate you on the marriage of Mr Mayor and his, now, wife[1] as it is something very extraordinary, notwithstanding the evill behaviour of the relations. I make noe doubt but you will visit her on the occasion because it will, of course, on her usual polite behaviour, be taken well for my part. I think his worship has the wrong end of the staffe. I will purchase the medicine my cosen Denham desires, and send it as desired, but I have noe faith in any quack medicines with that distemper.[2] I assure you I much wish to have a little Hasting air and am perfectly weary of the town, though I cannot foresee any certainty of quitting it. I have enquired about ruffles and find there is noe alteration, but that they make them narrow and broader wristbands. Dr Carleton and his two sons called in Johnson's Court yesterday about 4 and I was just gone out, but they have fixed to dine there next Wednesday and I am this evening obliged to be at Lord Wilmington's that day soe unless altered shall not meet them. Jemmy being now come I am goeing home and will make him write a letter to accompany this. You will observe by the printed papers that the Princesse of Orange is with child, soe it's needless to mention that, but I may add the pleasing prospect of security there is of the consequence as being a prospect of security to the protestant interest, beleive me. I had about 4 yeers since a letter about Honeychurch to the same effect, soe will discourse him on it. I need not desire you will keep it a secret.

[*Reverse*] From James Collier, London.

Hon'd madam, my papa is very well and though he had wrote a letter to you obliges me to do the same to let you know that I am very well and intend to be a beau tomorrow if it's fine weather, and shall long to be at Hasting to shew my fine cloaths. Bob Page is not recovered of his ilness, and it is beleived that he must return into the country, the town not agreeing with him. As I am a near neighbour to the Indian king and his queen, prince and cheifs I shall often visit them, but hardly learn their language, or go over to see their country. I hope all my friends are well at Hasting and desire my love and service and tell my sisters I will, if I have time, write them a long letter and shall expect an answer. I am, Madam, your most dutiful and obedient son.[2]

[*End of letter*] Your humble servant Mrs Thorpe.

1 Anne Gyles married Thomas Carswell, Hastings Mayor, 3 July 1734.
2 John Collier arrived in London 29 June and returned from the 17 July (SAY 1418 f. 24).

93 To Mary Collier, Hastings, from John Collier, [Johnson's Court], 9 July 1734

[SAY 1647]

My dearest joy, I am very sorry that it's not in my power to fix a time for my leaving London, for I am weary of it, but cannot see any prospect of getting out till next week, and you may be sure I shall not tarry a day longer than my business obliges me. Your letter was a great deal of pleasure and satisfaction and am very glad you are got out of doors again and hope it will divert your lowness of spiritts. S. Wicking dined at my brother's a Sunday, when I informed him of Mrs Gyles marriage, and found by him that his sister Betty is to come up to London with Nanny Geery, but that it was not to be till August. I was at St Pauls with Jemmy, forenoon and afternoon, a Sunday and afterwards went to Mr Carleton's and saw them all. The house is very pleasant backwards but I fancy will be very cold in the winter. There came in 4 or 5 or 6 ladyes and the doctor, 2 sons, grandson and 2 nephews, Steevens and Jemmy and I and Chelsum and another young spark. I drank tea there but it was all in confusion as usual. Mrs Carleton looks very bigg, I think more soe than our sister who holds it up very well.

I hear our county poll is actually a printing and will be out very soon.[1] Upon my desk there is a paper of Sir William Ashburnham's handwriting which is instructions for a recognizance which he will want against the Lewes sessions. I therefore desire you will send it me inclosed by next post that I may prepare it here and send him down. Dr Carleton don't talk of comeing out of town till the latter end of next week soe imagine it will be the week following first. The doctor and sons are to dine in Johnston's Court tomorrow by appointment, and I have now recieved a message to dine at Chiswick with my Lord Wilmington and am afraid I can't avoid it which vexes me not a little. I think to make Jemmy's old cloaths serve till he getts down, though itt's bad enough and beleive must bring down some of his shirts. Poor Bob Page is farr from having a good share of health and I beleive itt's determined to carry him again into the country. I shall not be able to send anything this week by the carrier. The Princess of Orange, they say, looks thin with her breeding.

1 See **[71]** and **[72]** for the printing of the poll list, and Appendix 5 1734 Election **[608]** for the list of names.

94 To Mary Collier, Hastings, from John Collier, [Johnson's Court], 11 July 1734

[SAY 1648]

I received your letter and am very glad to find you have been abroad and hope you will continue pretty well and that I may be soe happy as to make a perfect cure. How you'l manage with your aunt Denham I cannot tell, but think a speaking trumpet would be very necessary. I yesterday sent the desired specifick for my cosen Denham's gout[1] and hope it will come safe and be of service to him, but I find people much differ in their sentiments about it. I am really sorry I cannot fix a time for leaving London and am afraid it will be the middle of next week before I can think of getting out. I was obliged to dine at Lord Wilmington's yesterday to my mortification as missing the doctor and his sons, etc. I find they went away in very good time, vizt 5 a clock. I have not seen Jemmy since Sunday; he was here a Tuesday but I was engaged at the Custom house all day.[2] I am afraid I must goe to Mr Pelham's a Saturday and not return to town till Munday; however, shall write you by Saturday's post if I doe goe.

[*Reverse*] Pray tell Mrs Thorpe that I have often seen Mr Eyres since I have been in town about her mother's house, and he has given promises and hopes of haveing it compleated, but nothing is done. I saw him today and now he puts me of till Tuesday morning soe I imagine nothing will be done.

1 Gout, disease of the joints and muscles, widely referred to; the pain derived from a build up of crystal deposits in joints; described by ancient Greek, Roman and Arab physicians, a disease caused by over indulgence in rich and meat dishes, wine and port, and aggravated by over weight and lack of exercise. Advice in the early 18th century was to use vomits to rid system of food and drink, abstain from rich food and alcohol, take medicines to induce sweating, cold baths, plus horseriding in country air and bloodletting (*EB 1771* vol. 3, 125-8).

2 John Collier was required at the Custom house for preparatory work in prosecutions of smugglers and for his duties as Surveyor General of the riding officers of Kent.

95 To John Collier, from William Coppard, Hastings, 20 July 1734[1] [SAY 338]

This morning John Hide came and informed me that last night, in the evening about 8 o'clock, he spied a sail as he lay at anchor off this town which he took for a smugler; and there being but little wind, left his cutter in the road and rowed after him in his small boat, and about 10 o'clock came up with him off of Kentsway, which is about 2 miles to the east of this town and he beleives about the same distance from the shore,[2] as soon as Hide's boat came near the smugler. They haled from whence and who was master, was answered John Hide of Hasting, on which the smuglers bid them keep off pouring out a whole volley of oaths threatning to murder every man. But Hide and his people not regarding their threats rowed up alongside, and going to leap on board, had a blunderbuss fired into their boat, which wounded one of Mr Hide's men in the hand and slightly wounded Hide himself on the right temple. One of Hide's men fired a musket and as they rowed off they heard the smuglers say that one of their men was shot. The smuglers having so much the advantage, they being in the cutter,[3] and Hide in his small boat did not think it prudence to make a second attempt to board him. Hide don't know the vessell nor any of the men, he heard them say they were strangers and would not be taken. The smuglers are got to such a height of insolence both by land and sea that it is not to be expressed.

1 William Coppard's letter was sent to Major William Battine, Surveyor General of the officers appointed to guard the coast of Sussex, who forwarded it to the Customs Commissioners (Appendix 6: Smuggling **[612]** SAY 337). John Collier and Major William Battine shared an office and staff in Hastings; John Collier left London on 17th July and was back in Hastings on the 19th July (SAY 1418).

2 Customs boatman John Hide's attempt to board the *Prince George* of Flushing, and if necessary, seize the vessel, was a lawful proceeding under 6 Geo. I c. 21, 1719, s. xxxi: 'any vessel at anchor or hovering within two leagues of the shore, 50 tons or under, laden in part with brandy, may be ordered into port'. For rules on the measurement of tonnage see (*ibid* s. xxxiii). Smugglers were reluctant to cooperate as by 5 Geo. I c.11 (1718), s. 1, vessels under 15 tons, found to be used for running brandy, etc., were forfeit to the Customs. By 8 Geo. I c. 18 s. 1, confiscation extended to 40 tons, which clause covered most cross Channel vessels and coasters capable of sailing between beaches.

3 The smuggler's vessel was a cutter or sloop, not a cutt, a flat-bottomed rowing boat commonly with sails, used in the Channel to move horses, oxen, donkeys, to navigate shallow water, and also referred to in Customs papers in respect of smuggling operations (Appendix 6: Smuggling; SAY 271). .

96 To Mary Collier, Hastings, from Cordelia Collier, Johnson's Court, 29 July 1734 [SAY 1649]

Hon'd madam, since I received yours have been so busy in making new aprons and handkechifs, etc., that I could not spair time to write before, so hope you'll pardon this neglect, and I will write again in a shorte time. I came to my uncle's last Satterday to take my leave of them for the summer, to my no small mortification, and goe to school again tomorrow. Sunday we dineed at Mr Green's, and Mrs Green has promiseed my aunt to fetch me herself from Hamsted the first week after St Bartholomew day to stay with her one hole week. Miss Stevens set out for Sussex last Thursday senight, wich is a great loss to me, she being my very good friend, but hope her stay ... not[1] be so long as my uncle and aunt's. Pray tell my sisters that I am glad they have such fine wether to go to Rock fair as we have to walk in the fine gardens abought town. My duty to my papa and love to my sisters, from your dutifull daughter.

William Cranston[2] Thomas v Best, Thomas v Chaddock, notice of tryall in these 2 causes are countermanded.[3]

1 MS damaged
2 In the margin.
3 This may be Thomas v West (SAY 1418 f. 24v).

97 To Mary Collier, [Hastings], from William Cranston, [Johnson's Court], 24 September 1734 [SAY 1650]

You ask me by Jemmy whether I knew of Mercy Wicking and Nanny Geery's being in town. My answer is yes, for upon coming home one evening, my wife told me they had both called here, but that she herself was so ill that she sent em word she could not then see em but should be glad of their company another time. My reply was twas very well and that tomorrow I would go to see em and fix a time for their coming here, but then you'll say why did you not? My answer to that indeed is a pretty one, odd, but tis not less most solemnly true, that from that moment to the day they went out of town, it never once entered my head or thought the least of em. Why, you'll say, how came I to think of em the day they went out of town? I'll tell you; I was that evening at our coffee house in company with Charles Smith, Mrs Willard's brother, and amongst other discourse he said the Hasting beauty had been in town but went out again that day.

It imediately occurred to me what a monstruous neglect I had been guilty off, and do assure you it has given me a great deal of uneasiness ever since. I can't say but that twas a little stiff in the young ladies not to call again, after such a message to em, because if they stood upon the pink of curtesy, to be first waited upon themselves before they came again, the pink I say would have been for my wife to have gone, since their visit must be presumed to her and if so, she did not go out of doors till a pretty while … left town but such triffling ceremonies as these [1] are rediculous … that I can say so it is, that the whole happened through forgetfullness of our side and … little too much upon the punctilio on theirs but I should think Stephen Wicking ... have brought em a second time imagining that something of that sort[2] … did for I am sure since he has been in town I have ... him thereby testifying my regard I always had and ...nobody can imagine that I would pay it to one and not ... don't know through the course of my reign that I can change my ... of shewing a due respect to anybody that I ever esteemed ... and those anyways related to them - I desire you would give ... to Mrs Wicking and assure her of the truth of what I now write ... much concerned if she does not beleive it, as to the other I am ... designe but in regard to Mrs Wicking… and don't much care whether she takes the omission to be as I … designe but in respect to Mrs Wicking tis quite otherwise for I would have her be assured that I would do everything in my power to her, and hers, for her own and poor Mr Wicking's account. I received a letter from Mr Collier dated a Saturday from Deal and I wrote him last night and directed to him at Canterbury where he designs to be this evening.

I should be much obliged to you if you'd speak to Mrs Hart about our butter and to quicken her in sending it up, and you'll also be so good as to settle what it all comes to, and I have already begged of Mr Collier to pay it for me, which I shall reimburse when we next meet. My wife went last week to East Grinsted so that I am at home as well as in town quite alone and everything about me mighty melancholy, insomuch that I have a months mind even now, to take a trip port ways. I reckon Master Cranston is pretty much within the Mr Collier's absence. I owe him a letter but I don't know how it is, I find materials of that sort very scarce. I had once a mind to give him the butter comission as a good ingredient towards it and which would yearly serve me, as Mr Ott's money half-yearly does him but for this time I trouble you with it and may perhaps the next time him. You sent Jemmy up a fresh as a rose and plump as a partridge; his honour and I dined together at Mr Green's last Sunday, when he presented Dely's love and service to Tommy. Jemmy told me, his master said, he was sure his staying a week past his time was the mother's fault.

1 MS *is what* struck through.
2 MS damaged for 15 lines.

98 To Mary Collier, [Hastings], from John Collier, Canterbury, 25 September 1734
[SAY 1651]

I received your letter on my arrival here last night and am exceedingly pleased that it brought nothing to the contrary but you and yours are very well. I heartily wish myselfe at home with you being quite weary of my journey and travelling in the manner I am obliged to doe. Last night and all this day here has been abundance of rain and the wind very high, that I have not been able to stirr out of doors. I wrote to my brother Cranston from Deal, and received a letter from him in answer last night by which I find that Jemmy is very well and that my sister Cranston is gone to Eastgrinsted.

I am very sorry for my poor cosen Denham's family, and also for Mr Cooper who I beleive was a very honest man. I hope by this day sennight at furthest to get home and lye by for some time to recover my journey etc. The weather is soe very bad that I have seen nothing of this city soe cannot write you any particular account of it. I am very fortunate in getting out of the Isle of Thanet just as the rain come. Itt's a fine delightful, fruitful place but a cold, cleer air, hardly a tree in the whole island unless at a gentleman's where I dined yesterday. I shall now close my letter but not without assuring you that I never more wanted to return home to you, and without your company nothing is perfectly agreeable, nothing pleasant.

99 To Mary Collier, [Hastings], from John Collier, Dover, 19[1] September 1734
[SAY 1652]

I arrived at this place last night being very glad to have Romney marsh at my back as soon as I possibly could, and shall be obliged to tarry here two or three dayes. I am quite fatigued to death with complements, respect and ceremonies that are quite surfeiting and troublesom. The weather hitherto has been exceedingly fine and would have contributed much to the pleasure of the journey, but that I am alwayes surrounded with a groupe of officers, and are obliged to hear all their complaints and magnifying of services never performed, that I am heartily tired of their company and wish it was in my power to travell alone. I hope my dear, that you and all the family are and will continue in good health till my return. Notwithstanding I told you to write to this place, where your letter will not arrive till Sunday night, I hope to leave it a Saturday and proceed to Deal but shall direct the officers to bring me your letter and any others that may come. If the weather continues favourable and noe new orders of business come from the Commissioners I hope next week to have finished the greatest part of my survey.

The smallpox is still pretty much here. I have given Pryor a strict charge to keep close in and he has faithfully promised it. Here is no particular newes to send you, nor noe packet boats lately arrived from France. Wheat is nine pound a load and they are now shipping some of in this harbour.[2] I am going to dine at Mr Henshaw's, a merchant here, and the post goes out at 3 a clock soe write this before dinner. I was last night in company with a gentleman who is an acquaintance of Captain Story's and he tells me that his rich uncle did not leave him a shilling nor mention him in his will, that he has £3000 or £3500, but that is given him by the person to whom all the estate is disposed of by will. If it is soe, the old gentleman could not have any manner of regard to him, but he must have forfeited his good opinion. I would not have this publickly mentioned till more is heard of it, because it is not much to the reputation of the captain. My humble service to Mrs Thorpe, my brother Cranston and all friends.

1 MS 29 overwritten by 19. According to the Customs record John Collier left Hastings on 16 September, riding first through Rye and on to Lydd, New Romney, Dymchurch and Romney Marsh and through Hythe, Folkestone and on to Dover (TNA CUST 148/11).

2 1734 suffered from a 'bad' harvest by W G Hoskins' definition; wheat prices at Lammas 1734 St John's Cambridge 28/8 qr., Michaelmas 33/4 qr., London 6 September 26/-, 31/-, on 18 September 28/-, 31/- to 33/-, by autumn 1735 London wheat prices were 28/-, 30/-, 34/-, 36/-.

100 To John Collier, Surveyor General of Kent, Custom House, Rochester, from Sir Robert Baylis, Sir Charles Peers, Henry Hall, Customs Commissioners, London, 3 October 1734 [SAY 268]

Having received a letter from Mr Grey, secretary to the Commissioners of Excise, concerning the notorious practices carried on by a large gang of smuglers to the number of 200 particularly at Lydd, inclosed we send you copy of the said letter, and you are to excite the several officers on the coast to be very diligent in their respective districts and enquire where the goods are generally landed and propose what is necessary to be further done to prevent these frauds; whether the Dover or Rye sloops may not be of service to cruise in the bay where the goods are generally landed, and what number of troops will be necessary to assist the officers on shore, and where to be stationed, and whether more will be wanted than are proposed in your letter of the 23rd ultimo, to be quartered at Hyth, Dimchurch, New Romsey and Lyd for which we have already applyed to the Secretary at War.

[*Cover*] Commissioners' letter sent to Rochester, date 3 October 1734, inclosing a copy of a letter[1] from the secretary of the Commissioners of the Excise about gangs of smugglers in Romney marsh; and my answer the 10th wherein I take notice of reprimanding Mr Parnell and send an account of his acquitting Thomas Darby, a smuggler.

1 See [**101**] SAY 269 below.

101 To [Customs Commissioners][1] from Samuel Grey, Excise Office, London, 1 October 1734 [SAY 269]

The Commissioners of Excise have received a letter from Mr Dodd, their officer at Romney in Kent, giving an account that, since an additional number of officers for the Customs have been sent to Dymchurch, the cheif place now for running of goods is at Lydd, through which the smuglers pass and repass to and from the seaside, forty and fifty in a gang in the daytime loaded with tea, brandy and dry goods; that above two hundred smuglers mounted where seen one night upon the sea beach there, waiting for the loading of six boats and above. One hundred were seen to go off all loaded with goods. That they march in a body from the beach about four miles into the country and there seperate into small parties; and that on the 19th past, twenty one horses loaded passed from Lydd as little from New Romney between twelve and one o'clock in the daytime and the smuglers who were armed with blunderbusses,[2] etc., baited above half an hour an the warren house, in sight of the hole town, and declared they would be opposed by nobody. You are therefore desired to lay this before the Commissioners of the Customs for their informations.

1 MS to whom not stated.
2 By 8 Geo. I c.18 s.6 'from 25 March 1722, every person passing with foreign goods without due entry and payment of customs duties, through the coasts, or within 20 miles of the coast, more than five persons, carrying any arms or weapons, or wear any vizard, mask or other disguise, to be transported as in 4 Geo. I c. 23, and 4 Geo. I c.11, as a felon'.

102 To Mary Collier, [Hastings], from Cordelia Collier, [Hampstead],[1] 4 October 1734 [SAY 1653]

Dear Mama, having a frank sent me by my papa whose letter I recivd on Thursday last and am not willing to lose that opertunity of writing to you my papa sent me word of my sister's present, which I am very glad of; I beg you will give my duty to him. I have done half a side of my handkerchief and hope to finish it by Christmas for I can mark any letter. Pray give my love to my sister Jenny and tell her I except a long letter from her, and a littel news, and desire to know what worke she is about. Pray make my service acceptable to all my acquaintance. I have no more to say at present but that I am, your dutyfull daughter, pray give my love to Jenny and tell her I wish her much joy and shall not forget to drink her health tomorrow.

1 Pencil lines drawn on the page to guide Cordelia's handwriting.

103 To John Collier, Surveyor General of Kent, Hastings, from Charles Carkasse, Secretary, Customs Board, London, 12 October 1734 [SAY 270]

The Commissioners have received your letter relating to Mr Parnell, mayor of Winchelsea and supervisor of the riding officers, discharging a smugler who had been committed for assaulting the officers of the Customs in the execution of their duty. You are desired to make a more perticular enquiry into the behaviour of the said Parnell as to the discharging the smugler, and report your observations and opinion on the whole without loss of time, which I am commanded to signifie to you.

104 To Mary Collier, [Hastings], from John Collier, Deal October 1734[1]
[SAY 2154]

My Dear, I am just now arrived here from Dover and as the post is going out have only time to acquaint you that I am in the land of the liveing but am throughly surfeited with my officers' company and attendances and find there's noe avoiding it. The weather has hitherto moved very favourable and I hope for itt's continuance notwithstanding I am come from Dover I expect your letter's arrival there to morrow night and have ordered the officers to escort it along to me forthwith for I much long to hear from you. Grandeur sitt's very heavy upon me and I would sooner live in a cottage 10000 times over then have it in this way. I shall tarry here till to morrow evening and then proceed to Sandwich and hope to meet your letter at Canterbury. The Collector here is a very well behaved gentleman and I find I am this afternoon to have Capt Baker one of the members of Parliament for Hythe.[2] My Dearest, your most faithful husband,

1 [*Reverse*] MS Sayer, in pencil, dates this letter 'about 1734'.
2 James Carr, Collector, Deal (TNA CUST 18/178); Hercules Baker, 1683-1744, MP Hythe 1722-1744, devoted Whig, naval officer, appointed treasurer of Greenwich hospital 1736 to death; inherited East Langdon, Kent, from uncle Admiral John Baker who died in 1716 (*HofP 1715-54*).

105 To Mary Collier, [Hastings], from John Collier, [Johnson's Court], 31 October 1734 **[SAY 1654]**

I got safe to town yesterday about one a clock getting to Seavenoake the evening before, though part of the way from Bivelham, where I kept a court that day, was exceedingly bad. The weather proved very agreeable, which took of some part of the fatigue of a journey at this time of the year. On my coming to Johnson's Court I found Jemmy very free from his feaver, but really looks very pale and thin, but has a good stomach and perfectly brisk and cheery and my brother and sister inform me that he is prodigiously mended since he came hither. I have not been at Westminster and not seen Mr Chelsum, who I shall talk too a little smartly for not having that due regard and care of him as he promised, for I find he come about ten dayes before taken ill of a Sunday to Johnson's Court, without hardly any sole to one of his shooes and, to be sure, took cold and might hasten on his feaver which was a pretty high one. The doctor thought it a good deal occasioned by immoderate eating of fruit, and he is hardly to be prevayled on to leave it of, but he eats very heartily at dinner and has but one sleep in the night. I intend to keep him here 4 or 5 days longer and have bespoke 3 pair of strong shooes to come home tomorrow, and made on purpose, and shall take all the possible care to prevent a relapse.

My brother has not as yet got a man, but find he is soon to have one, and indeed, as the child is come home, which is still very stout, don't see how they can manage without. Sir Thomas Wilson's son is come here as a clerk,[1] and I find Mrs Betty goes away the 10th of November, thinking the work too hard. Misse Green is with my sister, who has been returned from Eastgrinsted, and brought her hither about a fortnight hence. I have sent to Mrs Hammond about your gown, and find there is to be 14 yards of shagreen.[2] My sister is to buy it but I am to see the silk and have told her of the diamond figure. I have also spoke for your shooes and gloves. I have not heard anything particular about the company or cloathes yesterday at court, or who shewed away most on the occasion. I spent the evening at home last night and intend the same this. Jemmy shall answer Dely's letter by next post but, indeed, this afternoon I have been in a little hurry and had not time.

Brother and sister send you their service and respects and the same to Mrs Thorpe and my brother Cranston.

The town now begins to fill every day but has been very melancholly. I presume you observed by the Wednesday night's papers an account of the earthquake from Portsmouth.[3] I enquired of it on my journey to London, but to [4] noe purpose, meeting with noebody that knew anything of the matter, and if a testimony is required from Hasting don't find but you and I are the only evidence. Adieu, my dear soul, and am with all respect and gratitude, entirely and most faithfully yours.

1 William Cranston was paid £157 7s 0d by Sir Thomas Wilson as a consideration for taking his son Edward Wilson as a clerk for four years, and the son was to go to Cranston at the beginning of the Michaelmas term or a little before, noted John Collier on 2 July 1734 (SAY 1418 f. 73v).

2 Shagreen, a white silk fabric, with a slight rough surface, suitable for lining trousers, jackets etc; a cloth with a velvet nap, usually silk, one side unshorn, as with blankets (*OED*).

3 Earthquake felt at Portsmouth, Havant and Chichester and elsewhere on the coastal parts of Hampshire and Sussex, (McCann xxxiv, noting BL Sloane Ms. 4025 ff. 224-238).

4 MS *little or* struck through.

106 To Mary Collier, [Hastings], from John Collier, [Johnson's Court], 2 November 1734 [SAY 1655]

I received your letter this day about noon with perfect pleasure as hearing you was well and nothing to the contrary here. Your gown was bought this morning before your letter came. There was but one yard over the sufficient quantity, and that was bought in a provident way. It is not the little specks, but I beleive, the exact pattern you wanted and I beleive will be very handsom. I know noe news in particular worthy to send you. I know you are noe politician, and shan't trouble you that way. The Revd. Mr Goole's case being revived by Grub is much talked of, and there has exactly the same or in some circumstances worse, hapned to another reverend, Mr Baker of the king's chappell, who was preceptor to the Princess of Orange, and the next two eldest princesses, and what he is prodigiously laughed at for, the disparity of the yeers a little exceeding the other.[1]

I took upon me to treat last night, but at home, and soe sent in a few fish, and 2 chickens and 4 bottles of wine. There were Mr Green and his wife and son, and Mr Coppinger, but I only knew of the 2 men. We played at quadrille, a penny a fish, and did not drink all our liquor.[2]

The Duke of Newcastle set out yesterday afternoon for Sir R. Walpole's and Mr Pelham goes for the same place tomorrow at 5 in the morning. I bought Jemmy this afternoon two pair of stockings, not having a pair fit to wear, the most he has too short and too little. Those he has now new are very indifferent, and I am sure one pair knit in Sussex will wear out 6. I wish you would have some made there full bigg and long. I have given Mrs Elcock your lace and she says t'will make a handsom double handkercheife. I had this day a haunch of venison sent me, and we eat it tomorrow for dinner, being determined not to make an invitation to any one person but eat it at home. I am not all surprized at my brother Cruttenden's silly impudence about a place. I thank God I am very well and hope for a continuance thereof till I have the pleasing satisfaction of returning to your, who are all in all to my dearest joy, your faithful husband, 2 November 1734, in my 50th year.

My humble service to Mrs Thorpe and all friends. Jemmy's letter to Dely accompanys this. If Rowe directs any more letters let it be as on the other side, 'To John Collier, esquire, Surveyor General at the Custom house, London'. Let him send a letter by next post if he has received any and what money for me, and of whom, and if anybody has been about business, and tell him that Mr Slade's debt from Winton is £2 14s 0d.

1 The attempt by the Revd John Goole to have a verbal promise of marriage by one party confirmed as a valid contract of marriage, even when repudiated by the party concerned, was rejected by the Court of Arches in 1732 (R Probert *Marriage Law and Practice in the Long Eighteenth Century* (2009) 31-2). Goole explained his views in *The Contract Violated, or the Hasty Marriage* (1733).

2 Quadrille, four person card game, with complicated rules, forty cards, 8s 9s 10s of pack discarded; the game gradually displaced ombre, and was in turn replaced by whist (*OED*).

107 To Mary Collier, Hastings, from John Collier, Johnson's Court, 5 November 1734 [SAY 1656]

I received your agreeable letter by yesterday's post and I beleive you think it was a great satisfaction to me not to hear a contradiction of you and the children's being in good health. Jemmy has continued on his recovery, and every day mended, that he really looks and is very well and this afternoon gone to Mr Chelsum's in order for school tomorrow. He has promised to keep in and not use any violent exercise and in return I have promised him a day or two for holydayes before I leave London. Had he not been perfectly well to be sure he should not have gone.

The Scarborough water is arrived, and will come down by the vessell. If you drink any this cold weather, you must, before the cork is drawn put the bottle in a paile of blood warm water, and a pint will be sufficient for you in a day or morning. I have bought a set of cupps and sawcers and 2 dozen of plates, but the last I think vastly dear, and could not meet with any chocolate cups of an agreeable size.[1] These will also come down by the vessel. You'l observe by the newspapers that an earthquake was felt in other parts of the kingdom the Munday after the shock at Hasting. Mr Stone that came into our house last Sunday sennight after dinner, the mayor's brother in law, is named as one of the three persons for high sherriffe this next year.[2]

The Prince of Orange has fought a duell in Germany with the Prince of Baden Dourlach and actually dissarmed him, soe you may perceive what a hero he will be in time.[3] The account of the misunderstanding between them fully justifyes the Prince of Orange's conduct therein. The queen has been very ill, 3 times let blood, but now much better.

1 1 November John Collier spent £3 1s 0d on china, glasses and plates (SAY 1418 f. 28v).

2 John Collier relayed to Robert Burnet, agent to the Duke of Newcastle, that Andrew Stone wished to be excused the office of sheriff for Kent for the coming year, (SP 36/73 fol. 125, 7 December 1734). William Stone was appointed as sheriff of Sussex for 8 Geo. II, (Berry 1830 x-xi).

3 Whilst hunting in Germany the Prince of Orange's horse bolted, and ran into the Prince of Baden's horse. Baden later 'purposely' rode against Orange and 'almost unhorsed him'. Orange was slightly wounded in the resulting duel, and Baden was wounded in the sword arm and disarmed, (Egmont vol. 2, 133).

108 To Mary Collier, Hastings, from John Collier, [Johnson's Court], 8 November 1734 [SAY 1657]

The post coming in is a great pleasure to me and by hearing that you are well. We have very foggy weather in town except for about 3 hours, the sun breaking through about 11 or 12 to three. I have hitherto escaped a cold, though most people have them, but I must tell you I have been very good and have been at a tavern but once, and that was Munday evening, and then on business. I have ordered Jemmy to have something warm every morning before he goes out to school, and told Mr Chelsum that I will allow him chocolate before he goes out 2 or 3 times a week, as not thinking it proper that he should drink it oftner.[1]

I received Mr Cruttenden's present of game, which I think very handsom, and desire you will let him know it with my humble service and that we drank his health more than once on the occasion. I am at present on a daily attendance on the Commissioners of the Customs from about 11 to 3, and it will hold 3 or 4 dayes longer. I think Mr Battine's stay at Rye a long time; had he the solid true affection for home as I have, and always wish for to enjoy, I should imagine he might shorten his time. I cannot at present fix any time or guesse at any for my returning home, but I doe assure you that as soon as itt's possible will be the moment for my setting out. The queen continues still indisposed,[2] but not any way dangerous, and I don't here any particular publick newes. Pray tell Molly I shall execute her commission by buying the book she desires, and I have told Jemmy to buy each of his sisters a thimble for a present. Since writing the within, Georgy Carleton came to me, powdered out, and a clean shirt on, I having told Jemmy to send him that I had something from his grandfather for him. I beleive he was attired out on purpose, but I had noe message or invitation by him. I think to write to the doctor if I have time about our water affair.[3]

1 Few inventories in England record hot drink utensils before 1695, when 8% listed at the Orphan's Court, City of London, rising to 48% in 1705, 78% in 1715 and 96% by 1725, (Weatherill Table 2:1).

2 Queen Caroline ill, 6, 26 November 1734, (Egmont vol. 2, 132, 134).

3 Water suit cases, Sussex Assizes, Horsham, Monday 12 August 1734, referred from the King's Bench, damages against Dr Carleton, 5/-, details received by the King's Bench 28 October 1734; Sussex Assizes, East Grinstead, Monday 17 March 1735, cause 7, Sargent v Collier, damages 1/-, cause 8, Taught v Collier, damages 1/-, and cause 9, Guy v Collier, damages 1/-, details received by the King's Bench for the three cases, 29 April 1735 (TNA ASSI 34/5; Appendix 3: Hastings Water Supply **[595]** SAY 23).

109 To Mary Collier, [Hastings], from John Collier, [Johnson's Court], 9 November 1734 [SAY 1658]

I received your letter this post with Dely's to her brother, and I have deferred writing an answer till I saw him. Itt's now past 7 and he is just come hither but my brother's man went for him. I think he continues mighty well and is indulged by the master not to goe to school till 8 of the clock. We have had this day cold, a little wet and comfortlesse, that it has been very indifferent weather abroad. As Jemmy is but just arrived an answer can't be expected this post. I begin to be weary of London not a little, but really can't propose any time for setting out with my face towards the south; having nothing in particular to write of newes makes me conclude this epistle. I have sent you King Stanislaus' account of his escape from Dantzick, which is a very extraordinary account.

110 To Mary Collier, [Hastings], from John Collier, [Johnson's Court], 12 November 1734 [SAY 1659]

I am very much concerned that itt's not in my power to fix on any time for returning to you. The absence already is very uneasy and my business is in such a situation as not allowing me even to guesse at an end, or at a time to leave the town. I have been very good hitherto in keeping good hours, and not being at the tavern, and really beleive it has in great measure kept me from a cold, though I have today a little cough. Jemmy came this afternoon and I gave him Molly's letter, which he now answers. The weather is very sharp but farr exceeding that of last Saturday. I hope I have executed all your commands excepting that of buying a muffe, and which I shall not fayle doing. I have bought a little quadrille table and some fish and counters, thinking we have not enough.[1] Your handkercheife came home this afternoon, and gown sometime since, but I shall not send anything this week. If a box comes it will be only the stationary ware allowed me by the Commissioners of the Customs.

Newes I have none in particular to impart to you, there being none worth sending. Operas, plays and concerts goe on as usual but I have been at neither being resolved first to finish my businesse as well as I can. To...[2] Smith came to London a Sunday, with a letter to my brother about business from Mr Willard, and returned yesterday noon.[3] I imagined when I first saw him that it was with a dun about a place. I thank almighty God Jemmy continues very well.

1 7 November John Collier paid 5s for fish counters and pool fish (SAY 1418 f. 28v).

2 MS damaged.

3 7 November John Collier paid money received via Mr Smith from Mrs Martin to buy £150 worth of South Sea annuities (SAY 1418 f. 28v).

111 To Mary Collier, Hastings, from John Collier, Johnson's Court, 14 November 1734 [SAY 1660]

I have your letter by this post and am sorry I am yet in a state of uncertainty about my return home, for I cannot as yet make any calculation of the time. Abundance of people have coughs and colds and it is very uncomfortable weather, but I thank God I have hitherto escaped pretty well; though I have got a little cough but it does not as yet increase. I am much obliged to Mr Godley for his hares. I have pretty well deserved them too, having got his post affair regulated. I write to Captain Story this post who I presume is still at Hasting and hope he makes up one at the coffee house. I have not seen Mr Carleton, nor have I been as yet at Mr Chelsum's, having been obliged daily to attend from 10 to 3 which may be justly reckoned all the day we have here, except about an hour for dining.

There is a report that the Princesse of Orange is in such a scituation that she must miscarry, and has had a fall at Harwich which contributes towards it, but I don't observe it in any of the publick papers.[1] Betty is gone and a new maid come but I have not as yet seen her face; she comes, they say, well recommended. The man I find has got master Pryor's failing and I fancy will not be long lived. When I came up Mr Worge intended to be here this day, as he told me, and his wife would goe to Hasting. But he is not come and my brother had a letter from him today mentioning nothing of comeing to town.

1 Anne, princess royal, Princess of Orange, m. 14 March 1734, sailed to Holland from Gravesend escorted by two naval ships, 24 April, moved to Leeuwarden Palace with Prince of Orange; Anne returned in June to Kensington Palace, ordered back by George II,and after delays, including news of the duel between Orange and Baden, sailed again from Harwich (J Van der Kiste *The Georgian Princesses* (2000) 68-9). For the official version of her return to Holland see *PS* 5 November 1734, 445.

112 To Mary Collier, [Hastings], from John Collier, [Johnson's Court], 16 November 1734 [SAY 1661]

I can now inform you that I have a much better prospect of getting out of town then I had yesterday morning, having put my affairs a good deal forwarder, but have an affair that is fixed in the court of Exchequer for next Friday, soe that it will be wholly impracticable to get out till sometime the week after, and you may be sure I shall leave the town as soon as I can. We have had black, dark, excessive cold weather which makes it very comfortless being out of doors.

It being soe cold weather I sent for Jemmy home yesterday, and as I had 3 of my capons from master Cheesman sent one to Mr Chelsum by my brother's man and he was to bring a shirt etc. The fellow went out at 11 a clock but not coming home to dinner, and being drunk the day before, soe that he was turned out from waiting at table, we imagined he was got at it again, tho he had a reprimand. And I sent Mr Pryor at 5 a clock, and Jemmy come with him but the fellow had never been there, nor is not as yet returned, nor I beleive will not for he will be denyed admission, though I hear today, sending Pryor to Westminster, that he came to Mr Chelsum's last night about 8 or 9 a clock with the fowle and a letter I sent for Mr Chelsum to send Jemmy, and to goe to Mr Johnson, to excuse his absence on my account.

I promised to give Jemmy a play,[1] but itt's soe cold that it is deferred. I desire you will look in the upper great draw of my escritore in my study and take out the fine red box that has my patent in it as cryer and usher of the King's Bench and send it by Nich to the carryer a Munday, for I want it. Send all the papers in the box with it and put in officers' journals that lye in the corner next the fire place to fill the box quite full, or the seal will be in danger of breaking. Then wrap him up in two or three sheets of brown paper and I will send a Wednesday to the carrier for it. I am not a little uneasy at my continuing here soe long but it can't be avoided in any tollerable shape.

1 Plays and opera for Saturday 16 November 1734; (i), Drury Lane Theatre, *The Double Gallant*, by Colley Cibber, also, *The Intriguing Chambermaid*, by Henry Fielding; (ii), Covent Garden Theatre, *Terpsicore*, an entertainment by Handel, and *Pastor Fido* an opera composed by Handel; (iii), Goodman's Fields, *The Fond Husband*, by Thomas D'Urfey, also, *The Necromancer, or Harlequin Doctor Faustus*, by John Thurmond, King's Theatre, *Artaxerxes*, the opera by Pietro Metastasio, with music by J.A.Hasse and R. Broschi (Scouten Pt 3, vol.1, 1729-36, 426, 432 and [**116**]).

113 To Mary Collier, Hastings, from John Collier, Johnson's Court, 19 November 1734 [SAY 1662]

I received your letter and assure you that I am heartily weary of London, and am very uneasy that I have not been able to despatch my affairs soe as to leave it and return home. But as I wrote last post it will be utterly impracticable till sometime next week. The cold and comfortless weather still continues, and we are here perfect strangers to the sun, not having blessed us with his benign influences or shewed us his face a great many dayes. I am now on an attendance at the Custom house and write this on a book there. I have got over the report of my survey through Kent and hope to have the orders thereon signed in 2 or 3 dayes.[1] I thank God I have hitherto escaped a cold and got only a little cough which doth not increase upon me and hope it will not. Next Saturday's proceedure in the court of Chancery in an affair of Mrs Brewer's, will I hope, make me able to fix a time for my return to Hasting.

1 John Collier to the Commissioners of Customs, survey of the riding officers of Kent, 16 September to October 1734 (TNA CUST 148/11).

114 To Mary Collier, Hastings, from John Collier, [Johnson's Court], 21 November 1734 [SAY 1663]

I am very much surprized by your letter that Mrs Thorpe has left you. Tis much she did not tarry till my return. I really liked her very well and soe indeed I shall anybody that is agreeable to you, and unless she intends soon to return again hope you will think of somebody else, for I would not have you without a companion. Mr Worge came to town yesterday about noon very well. I am very sorry that my stay in London is soe long and precarious, for I really cannot as yet fix on any time for leaving it. I shall desire to hear from you a Saturday and hope that will be the last time you will have occasion to write this time. Remember me to your guesse.

115 To Mary Collier, [Hastings], from John Collier, [Johnson's Court], 23 November 1734 [SAY 1664]

I received your letter and am heartily concerned to hear of your present situation and hope it will all goe happily on, and as I desired by my last letter you would write once more, soe I shall much want to hear that your reasons are vanished. I am sorry I must tell you that I began to have a cold a Thursday night, which increased yesterday, and have a cough pretty much but noe sore throat or at all feaverish. This has been a terrible day of rain that I have not stirred out of doors, but at 3 a clock for 2 hours. I pity the poor children about the fair for we have had here noe intermission and it seems to be a general rain.[1] I was last night at Mr Coppinger's where were also my brother, sister and Mr Worge and we supped and played at quadrille.[2] I was very much against going, but as I had promised went taking my great coat and don't think my cold was increased thereby.

All the discourse is about the poor Princess of Orange; she has undergone already a vast fatigue and has a great deal more to follow in her condition. The queen, they say, is exceedingly concerned about her, and did not know she was with child till she came into England; and as she was, people condemn her coming for that if possible she must not goe into the bed of straw in England. Tis not impossible that she concealed it for fear she should not come over if known. I cannot really fix a certainty of setting out, much desiring to settle all my favours in such a manner as not to come up next term unless you can come with me. I pray to God for your safety and protection. Jemmy is come this evening and very well, but has not time to right.

1 Hastings autumn fair, 23 November.
2 John Coppinger, attorney.

116 To Mary Collier, Hastings, from John Collier, [Johnson's Court], 26 November 1734 [SAY 1665]

I received your letter by yesterday's post and as I was heartily glad to hear of your continuing well, soe I am vexed with myselfe for writing in my letter of Thursday last that I should not expect any more letters from you, but only an answer to that because I am not certain when I shall be able to get out of town, and shall have a longing desire to hear how you are. My cold continues very troublesom, but I hope to have noe bad consequences from it. I was, by promise, to dine this day at Colonel Pelham's and goe from thence to the opera to hear the famous Farinelli, that charms and surprizes every body, and return thence to supper.[1] But in regard of my cold I withstood the temptation and sent word I could not possibly come. Mr Worge designs to get out of town Thursday or Friday, but I beleive I shall be obliged to come by Rochester, which is not above 12 or 14 miles about, and if I don't, must goe up there before Christmas. By next post I verily think I shall reduce my leaving London to a certainty. Jemmy was here this afternoon very well.

1 King's *Theatre*, Haymarket, the opera, *Artaxerxes*, by Pietro Metastasio, music by J A Hasse & R Broschi; on the 29 October, prolonged applause for Carlo Broschi Farinelli, singer and musician, attended by the royal family. Farinelli left London in the summer of 1737 and after performances in Paris was resident at the court of Philip V of Spain for nearly 25 years, (Scouten Pt 3, vol. 1, 1729-36, xx, lxxi, c, 426, 435. [**112**]).

117 To John Collier, Hastings, from Dr. Richard Russell, 13 January 1735 [SAY 1666]

I apprehend Miss Collier's case to be worms, and sour slimes on her stomach and bowells. I beleive her hectic that proceeds from this will be subdued by the use of the following medcines and asse's milk or candiied eryngo[1] and pearl barley water, drank with cow's milk warme, after each dose. When the child's pulse drop and she is a little recovered, this method may be laid aside for a fortnight, and 15 or 20 drops of elixer proprietatis[2] may be given night and morning for a weeke in a glass of spring water, and then, if occasion, the same method may be repeated.

I think she will find benefit by change of air in the spring; children are sensibly advantaged by it most times and as she is not above seven you should be carefull how she is heated, by diet, or regimen, least she get into a consumptive state. I beg my most humble service to your lady, Dr Carleton, and all friends.

For Miss Collier, R. Ethiop: mineral. Occul.lanc

Zoj syr. balsam q.s.f elect: de quo cap quant nuc mosch mane et vesper superbibendo huust last asinine vel in ejus defectu last eryngiat. RR.

Pray let me hear after a weeke's takeing this medcine.

1 Candied eryngo or Colchester candy, a sweet syrup from the roots of Essex marsh holly, combined with sugar and water, used for agues (Dobson 263).
2 Essence or spirit for recuperation and convalescence, containing myrrh, aloes and saffron. For reference to a variety of recipes and cures common to kitchen physic see H Dingwall & P Worling 'A box of chymical medicines: an Italian medicine chest presented to Sir John Clerk of Penicuik in 1698', *Journal of the Royal College of Physicians Edinburgh* vol. 42, 364 (2012).

118 To William Cranston, Johnson's Court, Fleet Street, from John Collier, Hastings, 11 February 1735 [SAY 729]

I received yours of the 8th with an account that the matter of the deputy ushers and cryers and court keeper is to be heard before my Lord Hardwicke and the other judges of the King's Bench at his lordship's chambers next Fryday evening …[1] I happen not to be in town to attend it, neither can I with any conveniency be up by that time, and therefore desire the favour of you to attend and hear their lordships' determination. I am much concerned that their quarrels and disputes amongst themselves should occasion any trouble to the court and have done all I possibly could to prevent it, and for that purpose have had frequent meetings to reconcile the differences; and as I am the patent officer, apprehend it to be my duty and business to see the offices are duly performed; and, as the 5 persons are only my deputys, look upon myself to have an authority over them and to check and controul them on any occasion not contrary to the commands of the judges.

I must say I think Swindon much to blame, and has been sawcy and impertinent to me; and am of opinion that I can displace him, appointing another proper person, and hope on this occasion his constitution will be produced and read before the judges. Since I have had the office I have made the best enquiry I can relating thereto and about the deputys, and on the best information I can get have reason to think till of late yeers the court keeper had not a distinct constitution, but was subordinate to the deputys and accountable to them, and what power I have vested in me consistent with my duty to the court, and in obedience to their orders and commands, I shall exert towards Swindon. I shall not at present give you any ... [1] trouble but desire you will let me know the determination on this attendance. As you have the patent it may be proper to take it with you to my lord's chambers.

1 MS damaged

119 To John Collier, Hastings, from William Cranston, Johnson's Court, 5 June 1735 [SAY 730]

Henry Masterman. [to William Cranston] This is to acquaint you that my client, Sir Thomas Webster, is determined to try all the mandamus causes in Hastings the sittings after this next terme, of which it would not be amiss if you advised your clients.[1] If you write to my friend Mr Collier, I beg you will make my compliments to him.

[Fees due to John Collier] Easter term 1735. 1219 bayls at 4d each is £20 6s 4d; 767 judgements at 4d each is £12 15s 8d; [Sub-total] £33 2s 0d; deduct my fee £2 7s 0d;

[Total] £30 15s 0d.[2]

The letter of which the above is a copy I received yesterday, and this day being at the King's Bench office, Master Clarke paid me your fees as above, inclosed is your fieri facias.

1 Affidavit sworn at Serjeants Inn, signed by William Cranston countersigned by Lord Hardwicke, in the case of Henry Moore against the mayor, jurats and commonalty of Hastings: 'William Cranston, of Johnson's Court, Fleet Street, agent for the defendants in this cause maketh oath that he received on 6 June 1735, from Henry Masterman a notice of trial, upon which William Cranston made all necessary dispositions for a defence by drawing briefs, giving the same to council, and other proceedings, by which the defendants were put to considerable expence. On Friday 27 June around 10 o'clock in the night, and not before, William Cranston received from Henry Masterman a countermand of the said notice of trial. Affidavit to move for costs for not going to trial pursuant to notice' (TNA KB 1/4/5 Crown side affidavits, Michaelmas 9 Geo. II 24 October 1735).

2 The total net sum earned by John Collier for bayls and judgements, by law term, 1733-40 (SAY 1418 f. 70v). For the yearly figures see ESRO MIL 23/25, SAY 2699. Among John Collier's law books were texts on the Exchequer and on fees levied by the law courts.

120 To Mary Collier, [Hastings], from Cordelia Collier, Elizabeth Russell's school[1], Church Row, Hampstead, 7 June 1735 [SAY 1667]

I send this to inquire after your health and my pappa's, hopeing this will find him safe at Hasting, and to let you know I like school very well and will endeavour to improve myself as much as possible. Pray give my love to my sister, and tell her I thought I should heard from her before now, but expect a long letter from her very soon to make amends. Miss Stevens are very obliging to me; they joun in service to you and my papa. This, with my duty to him and yourself and love to my sisters, is all from your dutifull daughter.

1 For details of Elizabeth Russell's girls' boarding school for the education and upbringing of middle and upper class young ladies, from around the age of 12 see Introduction.

121 To John Collier, Surveyor General of the riding officers of the Customs, Hastings, from Hartfleet Sprat[1], Sandwich, 11 June 1735 [SAY 274]

On examining the journals that belong to Mr John Jordan and Mr Thomas Jordan, doe find thirteen hundred weight of tea and coffee seized by them without any of the horses. I told them I thought it impossible to make such a seizure without taking some of the horses,[2] and that if they had but taken halfe the quantity as might happen, and halfe the horses with it, would be off much more service to his majesty. For it is a common practice for one of them that belong to the boat to hire men and horses and to goe along with them to carry off the goods, which if those hired horses was taken with the goods, it would be a much greater disopointment, by reason they must pay the owners of the horses att an extravegant rate, notwithstanding the loss of the goods. After I told Mr John Jordan of this he told me he had ordered a dragoon to take care of four of the horses which are not now in custody, and one Radcock, a noted smuggler, who was lately sworne against, was in this gang and taken by a dragoon, but I don't know what Mr Jordan has reported to the honourable commissioners about it. These men was all of Folkstone. Sir, I thought it proper to informe you with this affair that the Jordans have before this ordered the smugglers to cutt away which …[2] their horses. I think it … [2]favour to …[2] smuglers …[2].

1 Hartfleet Sprat, Customs supervisor of the riding officers at Dover covering the Customs mid-division which included Sandwich.

2 Seizures of horses, oxen and equipage customary by common law, although reiterated and tightened up by statute; thus 9 Geo. II c. 35 s. xiv, in reference to the seizures from smugglers by Customs and Excise officers, 'all the goods, wares and merchandizes, and all weapons and arms, as well offensive as defensive, found upon or with such person or persons as aforesaid, and all the furniture of their and every of their horse and horses, and other cattle and carriages, and the chests, boxes, bags, casks and other package of all goods, shall be forfeited and lost' (Hoon 284).

3 MS torn and damaged where the seal was.

122 To Mary Collier, [Hastings], from John Collier, [Johnson's Court], 17 June 1735 [SAY 1668A]

I received your letter with great pleasure and am much concerned that I am obliged to tarry so long in London. I fully expect my Lord Wilmington's cause will be over tomorrow,[1] but as Sir Thomas Webster goes on with one of his mandamus's, beleive I can't come home without the greatest hurry and fatigue till that is over. I find by your letter that it is the subject of conversation at Hasting and that his creatures have stamped success on the trial before itt's over. I will not take upon me to be soe possitive but don't at present see any reason to despond, and it is one comfort that it cannot be determined by the swearing of Boyket, Wood and Bevile, and the rest of that wretched crew.[2] I think you did perfectly right about Samuel Cruttenden and desire no manner of notice may be taken of him. I doe assure you the road to Battell was but very indifferent when I came and not fit for you to venture, and I am sure is farr from being better soe can't think it prudent for you to venture on that expedition.

Jemmy came here a Saturday afternoon. The next morning we all went to St Bride's and after dinner my brother, Jemmy and I set out for Hampsted and came there before they came from church. Dely is very well and really improved in her looks and behaviour. We drank tea and walked two hours on the heath, and though we went up in one of the stage coaches, were obliged to walk home.[3] I told Mrs Russell that she should have everything there was occasion for, and I assure you I gave Dely all encouragement I possibly could, and she is to come hither next Friday and I intend she shall tarry till Munday, and will not have her doe anything but what shall be a pleasure and agreeable to her. Jemmy came hither this afternoon and is very well. We have sad, rainy, dismal weather, and abundance of hay spoyled. I beleive it will be the best way not to have our field cut till itt's better setled. Pray give Mr Rowe the inclosed as soon as the post comes in. Keep the franks for they are scarce.

1 Spencer Compton, Earl of Wilmington v Nathaniel Garland, Duchy of Lancaster Court, before the Duke of Rutland, Chancellor of the Court, assisted by Rt. Hon. Lord Hardwicke and Mr Baron Thompson, on the boundaries of Stonebeach manor and other lands in Sussex, 800 acres in all, the issue to be tried at common law, before a special jury at next Lent assizes in Sussex. Six of the jury to examine the writings of both sides, and to take a view of the lands [**143**], (*ER* Duchy of Lancaster Court, *GM* June 1735, 330-1).

2 For the evidence given by witnesses in the case of Henry Moore, plaintiff, against the Mayor, jurats and commonalty of the town and port of Hastings see Howell vol. xvii, columns 876-887 for Robert Evernden, John Couzens, Drew Shengleton, John Boykett, Joan White, Anne Sargent, Susannah Medhurst, Thomas Colebrand.

3 Stage coaches plied the four miles from Hampstead to west of the City, among which: from The Black Swan, Holborn; The Blue Posts, Tottenham Court Road via Oxford Street; and from James Street, Covent Garden, (T J Barratt *The Annals of Hampstead* 3 vols (1912) vol. 1, 193).

123 To John Collier, at William Cranston's, Johnson's Court, from Colonel James Pelham, Kensington, 18 June 1735 [SAY 1668B]

I am much obliged to you for the trouble you have taken to fix a meeting with Mr Porter. I like Friday next very well, and if you will bespeak a diner at any tavern about the Temple, I will be sure to meet you and Mr Porter, and his freind Graves, at three a clock. You must let me know where to find you. I shall lye in town tomorrow night.

124 To Mary Collier, Hastings, from John Collier, [Johnson's Court], 19 June 1735 [SAY 1669]

Yesterday and this day took up the hearing of my Lord Wilmington's cause and his lordship gains everything thereby that was expected and thought of.[1] I am but just returned home, and have the pleasure of your letter, which I have only to acknowledge, being past 10. Dely comes tomorrow morning and by next post we will all write to you fully. I find by a letter from the mayor that he is served with a rule of court about the books of which there is no occasion, for we are not afraid of their pretensions, but find there is a rascally insinuation as if we had altered these books, but I despise the assertion.[2]

1 Wilmington v Garland [**122**].

2 The Hastings Assembly court of record volume (HAS CAA/5, formerly Hastings Museum reference C/A (a) 5), covers 1734-1749; in this volume pages 8v to 9, covering the date of 19 June 1735 have been removed, and the record restarts from 28 June 1735.

125 To Mary Collier, Hastings, from John Collier, [Johnson's Court], 24 June 1735 [SAY 1670]

After I had sent my letter to the post a Saturday evening, Jemmy came soe we spent the remainder and Sunday togeather. The morning was very indifferent soe tarried at home but went all to St Bride's in the afternoon and heard Dr. Middleton.[1] Dely continued with us till this afternoon and is gone home in high spirits. She has a new silk gown bought that cost £1 11s 6d at the mercers, and is made up by Mrs Hammond. She looks, and is, very well. Her governaunt send word that she must have a book to read at leisure times, as all the other boarders have, soe I bought her *The Christian Pattern*.[2] I forgot whither I have before mentioned that Jemmy's shirts fit him very well. We are all taken up with our great cause though tis uncertain when it will come on; but I beleive that Dr Carleton, Mr Bayley, Mr Bartholomew, Mr Carswell, and two or three more, must come up as witnesses. I hope the pipes are finished and that you have a supply of water to your satisfaction, notwithstanding the villanous usage we have met with about the pipes. By your account about the grasse it must be in a melancholly condition, but hope you will now have better weather. I hope, my dear, that this will find you chearful and the girles very well. I long to be with you.

1 Revd Dr Middleton, Lecturer at St Bride's and rector of St Peter's Cornhill.

2 George Stanhope, Dean of Canterbury d. 1728. His *The Christian's Pattern, or A Treatise of the Imitation of Jesus Christ* contained much information on behaviour and devotion.

126 To Mary Collier, Hastings, from John Collier, [Johnson's Court], 26 June 1735 [SAY 1671]

I received your letter this day's post and presume before this reaches you Mr John Daw, who is dispatched as a special messenger to the mayor with orders to hold an assembly etc.,[1] will have called to let you know; he saw me about 2 a clock. I had a letter by the post from the mayor by which I find that the persons set out for London against us are Thomas Hide, John Phillip, Totteigh and Mark Sargent. I have wrote to the mayor for Dr Carleton, Mr Bartholomew, Mr Bayley and Mr Carswell, and also for William Bourne, junior, and Mark Bayley, junior, to bee disfranchised and come up, and likewise Mr Rowe must come. I beleive the cause will come on Tuesday, or Wednesday, but there is as yet no certainty.

I am very sorry to hear you are not better and assure you that I am heartily weary of the town and uneasy that I cannot leave it. I am pleased you like the water and think they may easily stop the force of it with any manner of management. I this post write to Sir William Ashburnham to send up Parnell of Winchelsea about the tryall relating to the method of making freemen there.[2] I hope you will have fine weather for making the hay, and as to the mixing the hay in the croft with this, I desire you will ask the opinion of Mr Mead. I hope by next post to give directions for my horses to come up and for that purpose would have Nich take up the mare out of the marsh directly and keep her in 2 or 3 days with little or noe meal to empty her.

1 Assembly called by William Coppard, mayor, 28 June 1735; thirty five freemen attended in addition to four jurats, Edward Hall, Thomas Godley, Nathaniell Cruttenden, William Thorpe. The defence counsel for the corporation asked for suitable persons to give evidence in the King's Bench and Henry Carleton, Robert Batholemew, Thomas Carswell, Mark Bayley, William Bourne, Mark Bayley the younger, surrendered to the mayor, jurats and freemen of Hastings their places, relinquishing all privileges, interests, liberties, franchises and offices as freemen of the port. On 12 July 1735 at the court of record before William Coppard, mayor, these six were re-admitted and were remitted the 20/- fine on admittance to the freedom of Hastings (ESRO HAS CAA/5 17v).

2 John Parnell, of Winchelsea, Mayor on 19 occasions 1710-1752 (Pratt; Appendix 2).

127 To Mary Collier, Hastings, from John Collier, [Johnson's Court], 28 June 1735 [SAY 1672]

I received your letter by the post but hope before that reached me you had heard that Sir Thomas Webster's heart fayled him; for after striking the special jury at 6 last night, and waiting on Lord Hardwicke who had appointed next Tuesday morning to try the cause, at eleaven a clock at night notice of tryall was countermanded.[1] My brother and I got a coach and drove to the post office to send an express and stop our witnesses if possible. If they had given notice 2 hours before, 30 guineas had been saved to councell.

In short, his proceedings are very odd to carry it soe farr and then fayle, but I am glad it was soe conducted, and it casts not a little reflection upon him, besides giving us more cause of triumph. I find Thomas Hide, Mark Sargent and John Phillip were up to be evidence; they lay at a little alehouse at Battell Bridge and pretended they were swore against for smuggling. I remember the first of them was a spy in the queen's time, at which your father and I used to laugh heartily.

I desire you will send Nich with the horses a Munday, soe as to be in town a Tuesday. He may bring my mare and ride the black horse and let him come on very softly. Tell Mr Rowe that he should goe to the Sluice houses a Munday and carry the decree book, and I have wrote to Mr Worge that he may save that journey. I hope to get out of town a Wednesday or Thursday at farthest, longing to be with you. I think to goe a Munday and see Dely.

1 [**119**]

128 To John Collier, at William Cranston's, 4 Johnson's Court, Fleet Street, from William Coppard, Hastings, 28 June 1735 [SAY 32]

Last night, about half an hour before the post came in, I received your letter with instructions and the assembly book by Mr Daw. I find by yours that you think Daw might have been with me soon enough to have the assembly yesterday afternoon, but it being so late could not have it before this morning 9 a clock, when Dr Carleton, Mr Bartholomew, Mr Bayly, Mr Carswell, William Bourn and Mark Bayly delivered in their resignations. The freemen imagined, that is our opposites, that it could not be done but by a majority of votes. Mr Mead, Captain Moore, Henry Sergent and Ben Meadow declared that they would not come into it. We adjourned till 2 in the afternoon, and while we was at the Swan Mr Godley received your express, but determined to keep that as a secret till our going again to court that we might then know by there signing or refusing who were our friends and who not.[1] I don't mention the names of those that did or did not sign it, but refer to the book which you will see on your return home.

I went this morning to Broomham to get the chariot,[2] for I can't think Mr Bartholomew could come any other way unless he had more notice, and Dr Carleton is much out of order, and if the tryal had not been countermanded my lady told me she would send it over this afternoon in order to get part of the way today. We are all very heartily glad that the tryal is countermanded and the gentleman join with me in humble service to you. Although I mentioned on the other side that I should not give the names of those who signed and those that refused, my mind is altered and have here inclosed a copy of them, that you may inform his grace or any of our other friends in town. Those whose names are under mine signed the book, those on the other side refused, and our friend Captain Moore in a great passion in court stretcht out his arm at full length and declared that he would have his hand cut off rather then he would sign it.

1 Those 'who were our friends' and signed the book are listed in column one, and those who refused and 'did not sign it' are listed on column two in the following list.

2 Chariot, four wheeled carriage designed for speed, attention paid to the suspension, with only back seats and a coach box; the main purpose was to convey two or three persons and luggage (*OED*).

List enclosed with 128[1] **28 June 1735** [SAY 33]

William Coppard Esq., mayor C.

[*Those who signed the book*]	[*Those who refused*][1]
jurats:	Benjamin Meadow F
Edward Hale	John Broadbridge P
Thomas Godley	Robert Gourlay
Nathaniell Cruttenden	Robert Hussey F
William Thorpe	Henry Sargent P+F
	Thomas Moore P
[*others*]	Roger Harrison F
John Phillip C+P	Robert Thatcher F
Robert Taught C	George Fellows
John Crouch	John Bossom P
John Hall C	John Olliver
William Sansum C	William Shorter F
Charles Steevens	Philip Stevenson
Richard Halsted Post	Richard Geery F
William Markwick P	Thomas Webb
William Gawen	Benjamin Carswell F
Robert Meadow	John Mead
Edward Lintot	Thomas Sweetlove P
	Robert Lucas

1 The 1734 election results show that of those who refused to sign 8 voted for Fuller (F) and 5 for Pelham (P); permanent Customs staff listed as (C), and Richard Halsted was the postmaster.

129 To John Collier, Surveyor General of Kent, Hastings, from Commissioners of Customs, Sir John Evelyn, Sir Charles Peers, Brian Fairfax, Sir Robert Corbet, Custom house, London, 8 July 1735 [SAY 275]

Having transmitted to the Commissioners of Excise copy of your memorial of the 31st March last, relating to the dragoons quartered at Romney and Lydd frequently making seizures of brandy and horses and delivering them again to the smuglers for one guinea each horse, and the brandy to an officer of Excise from whom they received two shillings for each half anchor; they have in their secretary's letter of the 2nd instant transmitted us copy of a letter from Mr Brookes, supervisor at Ashford, copy whereof is inclosed, whereby it appears that the dragoons quartered at Folkstone frequently made seizures without any officer and carryed them to Thomas Jordan, officer there, who always gave them half a crown for each half anchor of brandy and twenty shillings for every bag of tea. We direct you to charge Jordan herewith and demand his answer thereto in writing, which you are to transmit to us with your observations and opinion pursuing the rules of the 18 July 1717.

130 To John Collier, Custom house, London, from John Vavasor, riding officer Hythe, James Hills, riding officer Dymchurch, Joshua Coates, riding officer New Romney, 9 August 1735 [SAY 276]

We, John Vavazor and Joshua Coates, went out on duty, and two dragoons with us, on the 3rd instant, and meeting with some smuglers, we had a suspicion of a smugling boat lying of at sea. We called on Mr Hills, riding officer at Dimchurch, and Mr Otbie, tide surveyor there, in order for the latter to launch his boat, but he could not, the water being so far falln.[1] But we proceeded together as far as Mr Coalman's boathouse where we stayed upon the sands untill we had sight of the boat. We kept sight of her till shee came on shore, and it being ebb tide the boat could not git off againe.

Then Mr Otbie and his men and one of the soldiers wadeing into the water, the smuglers bid them keep off or otherwise they would fire at them, and accordingly they did fire at the officers, and then the officers fired at the smuglers and wounded one of them, namly John Swift, disableing him in his thumb. Then Mr Otbie and his people and the soldier, advanced nearer the boat and bid the smuglers, in the king's name, deliver their goods, which they denyed and swore they should not have any of them. But at last the officers took all the half anchors they had on board, vizt 124 half anchor of brandy, and also seized the boat and one brass blunderbus which was charged with twenty bulletts. Mr Otbie hath the blunderbus in his possession, and he sent the boat to Dover by three of this own men; and two or three smuglers who were unknown to the officers carried off and made their escape with three brass musquitoons. The brandy we brought to his Majesty's warehouse in New Romney.

1 At this time, Edward Bridges, James Hills and John Gates were stationed at Dymchurch as riding officers; William Otbie, tide surveyor and commander of the Customs' sloop and six men, her station from the South Foreland to Dungeness; Otbie and his men were required to guard Dymchurch wall when not at sea. John Collier noted in his survey 8-30 September 1735 that Otbie was negligent in command of his men, two of whom were mostly absent, another refused orders and even threatened to assault Otbie. John Gates kept the Dymchurch wool register. Stationed at New Romney were three riding officers, John Vavasour, John Dray and Joshua Coates; Dray kept the New Romney wool register; at Hythe were stationed five riding officers, James Bath, John Vavasor, Richard Lawrence, Thomas Rogers, Soloman Sparks junior (TNA CUST 18/186 f. 19); John Collier, survey of the riding officers of Kent, report on the survey (TNA CUST 148/11).

131 To John Collier, Hastings, from Sir Charles Peers, Brian Fairfax, Sir Robert Corbet, John Hill, Custom House, London, 6 September 1735 [SAY 278]

The Commissioners of Excise have, by their secretary's letter of the 1st instant, transmitted us copys of some letters they have received from their officers at Folkstone[1] complaining of the behaviour of John Jordan, riding officer there, who, it is alledged, screens the smugglers and is guilty of other irregularitys. Inclosed we send you copy thereof, and, having desired the Commissioners of Excise to direct their collector to meet you and examine into these complaints; you are in conjunction with him to examine strictly into the several allegations contained in the said letters, calling all partys before you, face to face, and report to us a state of the case with your opinion.[2]

(i) To Commissioners of Customs, from Samuel Grey, Excise office, London, 12 September 1735.

The Commissioners of Excise, having received a letter from Charles Pepper, their officer at Folkstone, dated the 18 August last, complaining of the behaviour of John Jordan, riding officer of the Customs, and one of the warehouse keepers there, deferred sending a copy thereof to the Commissioners of the Customs, as it came only from one officer, till the facts mentioned therein were enquired into and reported by their collector and supervisor, which reports being now come to hand, I am directed to send you a copy of them and the said officer's letter which you are desired to lay before the board.

(ii) To Board of Excise, from Charles Pepper, Folkestone, 18 August 1735.

In humble obedience to your order by my collector, I pray leave to represent to your honours the proceedings of Mr John Jordan, riding officer of the Customs, and one of the warehouse keepers at Folkstone. There are two, but they are brothers and partners. When I came to this division, Mr John Jordan told me, as the Excise officer was ordered to keep a book at the warehouse, they had made him one of the appraizors; the justice's clerk being allowed 10s 6d and the appraizors 5s each; but the Commissioners allowed of no charges at condemnations; the justice's clerk and appraisors spent half their money to treat the justices. I told the warehouse keepers if it was so I was willing to comply with it as my predecessor had done; according I signed their account for 5s and received but 2s 6d and this went on for a considerable time till at a condemnation the receiving was £1 19s 0d and all paid by Mr Michael Baily, the then tyde surveyor, though the warehouse keeper's brother had much more goods condemned than Mr Baily …[3] he paid nothing and our money stopt as usuall I could not …[3] notice of this management haveing great reason to beleive …[3] rest of the money was sunk and in a little time the warehouse keeper turned me out from being appraizor and put in his apprentice.

I humbly pray leave to take notice to your honours, notwithstanding the law expressly says that all goods seized shall be condemned in the county where the seizure was made,[4] yet these officers condemn it all at Folkstone, where I never say any custom officers sworn or offer to prove his seizure. I humbly pray leave to acquaint your honours with the proceedings of these officers with their smugglers. These officers were born in town, and never employed out of it, and as I am well informed are related to several of the great smugglers, and the only reason I can give for smuggling being brought to such a height in this place is these officers screening the smugglers. They very seldom take goods from any other but their neighbours and never have prosecuted any one since I have been in town. I have asked them why they did not prosecute the smuglers … [3] as well as the officers of Excise; they gave me for …[3] that their Commissioners always ordered them to prosecute at their own cost, therefore they never would discover any persons, always reflecting on me for prosecuting the smugglers.

On July 16th last past at ... 10, I went to the waterside where the said Mr John Jordan was, and without any provocation he begun in a very insulting manner to ask me if my supervisor, Mr Brooks, with the assistance of the dragoons, had arrested any man the day before; I told him not that I knew of. On the 14th of the said month, by your honours' orders, was heard before the justices of Folkstone an information against several smugglers for selling brandy, without notice or entry, and they were fined. Which proceedings the said Mr Jordan took upon him to villify very much, saying it was a rascally villanous prosecution, I told him I should acquaint the honourable Commissioners of Excise with his proceedings; he told me I was a villain and a rascal and that he valued the Commissioners of Excise no more than he did me, and threatned to take me by the nose. I have since assisted Mr Stott, by your honours' orders, in arresting two smugglers, which has highly affronted the said Mr John Jordan; in so much that about three days after he begun to insult me in the street, but I did not stay to hear any more of it. There were many smuglers present, who, hearing these insults from a Custom house officer and cheife magistrate, have since threatned my life. The truth of this representation I am ready on oath to attest.

(iii) William Pennington, Thomas Brooks. Pursuant to your honours' order we have examined into the truth of the inclosed letter. Pepper and Jordan, face to face, and Mr Jordan said but very little to the articles against him and indeed nothing to lessen the charge other than that he had been an officer elsewhere. But we beleive he looke upon our enquiry as insignificant, he not belonging to the Excise and was pleased to express himself it was little petty stuff and we find his greatest clamour to proceed from the prosecuting one Deverson, who is porter of Sandgate castle, near Folkstone, of which castle the said Jordan is lieutenant. We offered Mr Jordan a copy of Mr Pepper's letter for his answer, but he declined to accept it. These are the particulars we have to offer to your honours.

(iv) [5] This is a true copy of all the papers relateing to the complaint against Mr John Jordan from the Commissioners of the Excise to the Custom house about screening the smugglers etc., and abusing the officer of the Excise there etc., to be examined into by me and the collector of the Excise, September …[3] from Sandwich wrote to Mr Pennington and asked to meet me at Folkstone, Tuesday the 23th, at …[3] a clock, [6], at noon in order to examine into the matter of complaint referred to us by the Board. Quere: this is in Dr Sprat's district, whether not to send it by him?

1 Michaelmas 1735, three Customs riding officers were stationed at Folkestone, John Jordan jun., his brother Thomas Jordan, and John Redsole (TNA CUST 18/186).
2 Copies of three papers i, ii, iii, from John Collier follow here.
3 MS damaged
4 For the law on seizures see **[121] [147]**.
5 iv. John Collier, his comments on the three papers.
6 MS *in the forenoon* struck through.

132 To John Collier, Hastings, from William Pennington, Folkestone, 12 September 1735 [SAY 277]

I have received a letter which informs me that the Commissioners of the Customs have ordered you to examine into the complaints which Mr Pepper,[1] officer of Excise, has against Mr Jordan, riding officer of the Customs; and wherein I am ordered to meet you on this occasion and to bring Mr Pepper with me, of which I presume you have notice. I should be glad to know your time and place where to meet, but am now on my collection which I shall finish the 26th instant; your answer to this will oblige. Please to direct to me at Goudhurst where I shall be the 19th.

1 Charles Pepper.

133 To Mary Collier, Hastings, from John Collier, Dover,[1] 22 September 1735 [SAY 1673]

I came hither from Deal yesterday in the afternoon, and shall tarry here till tomorrow morning, and then proceed to Folkstone. I have had very good weather ever since I left Canterbury and hope for a continuance of it. Unless I receive any new affairs from the Commissioners I hope to dispatch soe as to be at home a Thursday, being heartily sick of the journey by having no recess nor retirement. I dined yesterday with the collector of Deal very elegantly and the day before with the collector of Sandwich, where there was great profusion and excuses for the dinner, etc., and these are the only places I have dined at since I have been out, determining not to dine with any of the officers, but were overperswaded. I this post write a letter to Dely.

1 John Collier, survey of the riding officers of Kent, 8-30 September 1735 (TNA CUST 148/11).

134 To John Collier, from Cordelia Collier, Elizabeth Russell's girls' school, Hampstead, 14 October 1735 [SAY 1674]

I received your affect letter, and am sorry my dear mama has been so bad with a cold, and I hope this will find her much better. I am glad to here my sister has had so good a present as a wacth and equipage and think it was very kind of her to send Molly one of them, so suppose they are both very fine; it is a great sattisfaction to me that I shall see my uncle and aunt so soon. I wish I had any news worth your hearing; the long room shut up yesterday which hast sent all the company away.[1] My govrerness is very well and sends her complyments. Pray give my duty to my Mama and except of the same yourself.

1 The advantages of being at school in Hampstead are noted in the Introduction.

135 To John Collier, Hastings, from Brian Fairfax, Sir Robert Corbet, Sir Charles Peers, Custom house, London, 8 November 1735 [SAY 279]

An affidavit having been laid before us in relation to an opposition given to Robert Serjeant and other officers of the Customs at Hastings by some smuglers in April 1733, we have sent copy thereof to the collector and comptroler of Rye and directed them to order Serjeant immediately to attend you with the said affidavit; and you are to take the said Serjeant's information as to this opposition, in which he must set forth the whole transaction, as far as he knows, in order to confirm the evidence already given, taking care to be as particular as possible as to time, place, persons' names and all other circumstances, and transmit the said affidavit to us.[1]

[*On cover*] and my answer thereto, 13 November.

1 See Appendix 6: Smuggling **[615]** SAY 283.

136 To John Collier, Hastings, from Joseph Tucker, Collector, Henry Carleton, comptroller, Custom house, Rye,[1] 12 November 1735 [SAY 281]

In obedience to their honours' commands of 8th instant, we have sent over Thomas Sargent, riding officer, William Horsfeild, surveyor, and Moses Peadle and Joseph

Cooper, boatmen, they being the persons opposed in the execution of their duty by some smuglers near Stonecrouch in April 1733.

1 Rye Customs establishment lists for 1735: Samuel Jeake as collector, replaced by Joseph Tucker in 1738, the deputy controller Henry Carleton, William Horsefield the surveyor, and the tidesmen and boatmen Moses Peadle, Joseph Cooper junior, John Weight, Thomas Kennett (TNA CUST 18/190).

137 To Mary Collier, Hastings, from John Collier, [Johnson's Court], 18 November 1735[1] [SAY 1675]

I presume before this reaches you Nich will be returned home, by whom you will be informed of my getting safe to town yesterday about one a clock;[2] though I had an ugly water to goe through at Riverhead occasioned by the great rain that fell on Sunday and that evening. Sunday was a very uncomfortable day for riding, but I got to Sennock without being wet through. I found Jemmy at my brother's, it being a holyday as queen Elizabeth's birthday,[1] who was founder of their school. And he is very brisk and well, but don't perceive he is any way altered as to gentility, but I find he learns very well and is uppermost of the fourth form. He informed me that Mrs Carleton was delivered of a daughter a Saturday night, and this day my sister sent to her and she is very well in her condition. Dely was well a Saturday and this day I send her a letter to come to town a Thursday, and that somebody shall meet her about 3 in Holborn. James Bossom is gone home and told my brother he should come up again as soon as he could. I desire you will send up by him half a hundred of the best and largest red herrings[3] for my brother. I have not said anything of the hoggs puddings, but I beleive they will be an agreeable present.

I can with pleasure tell you that the mandamus cause cannot be tryed this term for they are now too late to give notice. I attended last night at the Temple about the affair I come up about, and finished my examination thereon, but the report on my survey will take up some time at the Custom house. I would make a present of 2 or 3 dozen of the white wine to my brother, but don't know how we can manage about a permit for it, soe beleive must deferr it till my return home. The town has noe particular newes. The Prince of Modena is returned home. My brother did not see him but my sister did at a play. I don't find much about him as to his person or dress, but that he is a black, thin, man and has a forreign look. Little Jemmy is very brisk and well. My humble service to Mrs Thorpe and all friends.

1 Queen Elizabeth's birthday 7 September 1533, her accession day 17 November 1558.
2 John Collier arrived in London from Sevenoaks 17 November, and returned to Hastings 17-19 December 1735 (SAY 1418 f. 37v).
3 Government policy supported the herring fishery by direct purchasing and statutes granting allowances on exports in barrels, as with 5 Geo.I c.18, 1718. Those involved in the mackerel and herring trades at Hastings are listed in HAS DA/4/1 and in other of the Chamberlain's accounts.

138 To Mary Collier, Hastings, from John Collier, [Johnson's Court], 20 November 1735 [SAY 1676]

This afternoon just as I received your letter and before I had done reading it Dely came in from Hampsted, looks mighty well and is very much grown. I wrote to her for bringing Mrs Russell's account in order to itt's being discharged, and I herewith send it you for your perusal, having just taken the heads of it. She has this evening played a tune upon the spinnet[1] and I beleive we are to have a song by and by, being but just come home, and have a pretty many letters to write but this is my first address. Jemmy was here yesterday afternoon and I hope to have them both togeather a Saturday, for I design she shall tarry till Munday and will direct her to write next post. G. Worge came hither about a quarter of an hour after her and is to supp here, soe we shall have some chat. I saw S. Wicking last night at the coffee house who looks very well and beleive my sister and Dely will goe tomorrow afternoon to visit him and his wife and my brother and I are to fall in about half an hour after, if it suites. I find Miss Steevens is at last got to Hampsted and that it is agreeable to Dely. I have noe news to tell you, the weather is too warm and most people have got colds.[2] I met Dr Nicholls yesterday at Newcastle House who is headmaster of Westminster School[3] and had a very good account of Jemmy and talked an hour with the doctor who seems a very good sort of a man. I presume you take my letters and peruse what they are before sent and seal them up if occasion.

1 Spinet, a musical instrument with keyboard. (Grove vol. 24, 183-7).
2 Edmund Pyle held similar views on the colds and sickness attending visits to London, 74, 4 April 1742.
3 Dr John Nicoll, headmaster 1733-1753, previously undermaster 1714-1733 (G F R Barker & A H Stenning *The Record of Old Westminster, a biographical list of all those who are known to have been educated at Westminster school from the earliest times to 1927* vol. 2, 1082).

139 To Mary Collier, Hastings, from Cordelia Collier, Hampstead, 22 November 1735 [SAY 1677]

I received a letter from my papa last Tuesday for to come to my uncle's a Thursday which I according did and had the pleasure of seeing him well and hearing that you and my sisters were well. As my papa gave me leave to tarry here till Munday morning we went to see Mr and Mrs Wicking yesterday afternoon, and it was his birthday. I will not pretend to describe the lady but suppose my papa will give you an account for he and my uncle and aunt were all there. My hoop being so short my aunt has bought me a new one and the other is to be for Molly. I have a cap and pinner making new with my edging that was upon my short mob at Mrs Elcock's and it is called frokee, being the newest fashion.[1]

1 Hoop, made from flexible material, such as whalebone or thin steel, worn under a petticoat; a wool tuft in the hat (*OED*).
2 Short mob, a cap, the ordinary morning headress for ladies, cotton with lace edging widely copied by the lower ranks (*OED*).

140 To Mary Collier, Hastings, from John Collier, [Johnson's Court], 22 November 1735 [SAY 1678]

Dear Polly, I hope you will not be surprized at the above expression, or take it amiss, since I am well satisfyed itt's the mode, because S. Wicking makes use of it to his spouse. I am pleased, my dearest, with the receipt of your letter, and think you behaved perfectly right not to concern yourself about D. Denham's affair.[1] He had by a scandalous neglect and behaviour worn out my patience, and therefore determined to have my money, and am not at all sorry that he obliged me to it. Jemmy and Dely are now with me, and I spend the evening at home with them much to my satisfaction and expect Mr Worge will come. We are to have saps and cheese for supper and I have bought three easterlings to help make out.

In short, S. Wicking's wife is like noebody I ever saw; her mouth not bigger than the breadth of my thumb, but dressed out handsom enough, but stiffe, and I beleive good humoured; but a monstrous place to live in, being exactly the cobler's description of his mansion house in all respects. But this is a secret, and soe to be, for I would not have anything said as to come from us. Dely could hardly forbear a description, but I made her decline it. I am glad you have ventured on brewing and think it very impudent of Foord.

The Sargents' behaviour to James Bossom is all of a peice with the treatment other people meet with from them. Robert Sargent has behaved in a very prodigal silly manner about poor Hadden, in taking him out of Bedlam, and had the impudence to huff Mr Mannooth; but I write to the mayor tonight and mention this affair.[2] I am sorry Mrs Thorpe continues lame, and think my brother not sufficiently complaisant in deserting you during this black month. Dely had a sad pen and ink and was all alone when wrote, though I told her what, and she has been but a day in the italian hand.[3] Just at conclusion of this Mr Ott[4] come in; has not been as yet down to Peterborough, but intends it soon. I have asked him for a dispensation that his curate may come to Hasting sometimes.

1 David Denham, by this time already in debt.

2 Mark Haddon was admitted on 14 April 1733 to Bethlem hospital and discharged on 7 November 1735 (Bethlem Hospital Admission Books); John Collier paid Mr Mannoosh £3 13s 0d on 19 November and £4 18s 0d on 11 December 1735 (SAY 1418 f. 37v).

3 Cordelia Collier altered her handwriting whilst at Elizabeth Russell's school, and again in the early 1740s.

4 Revd John Henry Ott, Bexhill, listed in the 1724 Survey, (Ford 96-7).

141 To Mary Collier, Hastings, from John Collier, [Johnson's Court], 27 November 1735 [SAY 1679]

I received your letter with great pleasure, and hope to hear from you every post during my continuing here. I think my brother Cranston is not neighbourly to be soe long absent from you but hope this will find him at Hasting, and that he will make up the absence in point of time. I am really concerned for poor Mrs Thorpe about her legg, for it may be of dangerous consequence. The hogs puddings came yesterday and are exceeding well liked. I have a collar of brawn come from Canterbury as a letter informes me, tho it is not as yet arrived in Johnston's Court.[1] We have had exceeding bad weather, with abundance of rain, and last night a violent storm of wind, and this day rain without ceasing. I am sorry I can't propose any time for returning home. I have paid Mrs Elcock and will send to Mrs Hammond. If you would have anything bought besides tea and coffee, candles, vinegar, basket, salt and corks, let me have your commands. Mr Worge goes out of town a Saturday next, as he says. I am glad Molly has not forgot her writing. I really hear no news, have not been at, or thought of, a play or opera. Mr Chelsum says that Mr Carleton is often troubled with the gravell.[2]

1 Brawn, flesh of pig or boar, boiled, then pickled with salt or potted (*OED*). The book trade published information for servants and household supervisors, including instructions on how to preserve food. J Dalporto *Women in Service in Early Modern England* (2008) reprints text by John Shirley from 1687 on household supervision and kitchen physic.

2 Gravel, the accumulation of urinary crystals, indicated by pain or partial blockage in passing urine.

142 To Mary Collier, Hastings, from John Collier, [Johnson's Court], 29 November 1735 [SAY 1680]

This acknowledges the receipt of your letter by the post. My sister had a letter from Miss Steevens this afternoon that Dely is very well and brisk, and desires I would not come to Hampsted, there being such great robbing in the coaches. Jemmy is now here and very well. I intended he should write you a letter, but itt's past 8 a clock, and I am but just come in, soe it must be excused. My brother Will says he has been very sincere and impartiall in his search, and is surprised that the dispute is not surrendered up at discretion, and in short the opposition is here universally exploded.

I am not at all surprized at Mr Mead's purge; it fully demonstrates their misery with such an affluence of fortune. I shall buy the things you mention and have some brawn to send down.[1] I this day saw Mrs Milner who is in statu quo and sends her humble service to you and my brother. The account of little Milward's accident is very shocking and plainly shews the dangers and hazards run by all children.

By Thursday's post I had a letter from D. Denham, by the style wrote when he was half d---k, though couched in civill terms, and he desired I would answer it to Mr Dodson, which I accordingly did by last post, and agreed to his request of ceasing further prosecution. G. Worge left London this morning and I am concerned I cannot fix a time for following him. I have for about a week had something of a cold, and have been much apprehensive of itt's increase, but it has not to a great degree, and I have been alarmed with the gout, but I hope both will goe of well.

1 John Collier bought Scarborough water, half a pound of tea at 12s, half a pound of canister tea at 9s, one pound of coffee 5s 6d, a map and table of trade, mustard, plus the brawn [**144**] (SAY 1418 f. 37v).

143 To Mary Collier, Hastings, from John Collier, [Johnson's Court], 2 December 1735 [SAY 1681]

Your letter wrote last Saturday I yesterday received with much pleasure and satisfaction and am sorry I must tell you that Saturday night, after I had wrote you an account that I hoped I should escape a severe cold, it came on very strong, soe that I did not put on my shoes all day a Sunday, nor yesterday till 4, when I was obliged to goe out and though I wrapped up very warm beleive I increased my malady having a very indifferent night and have kept within all this day and hope to get it of. Jemmy came hither to dinner and brought the song accompanying this but as the days are very short there is really not time for him to write, but I sent him to Mrs Elcock's to have 6 new necks made most of his being worn out, and indeed he wants more shirts having outgrown severall of his old ones.

I wrote Dely a penny post letter yesterday for amusement and expect an answer to it this week. This confinement putts it more out of my power to guess at any time for leaving London, which I much long for; but hope now I am here to compleat my business soe as not to come to town again in hast, unless on some great emergency. Your not mentioning Mrs Thorpe's lameness makes me hope that she is better. Mr Forbes came to see me today and he says my lord Duke has some thoughts of going for Bishopston next Saturday.[1] I shall not be ill pleased with it because I shall then hope to escape that journey. Lord Wilmington's cause with Mr Garland is in a fair way of being fully concluded, which I am heartily pleased with, for I could not avoid going through with it which would have been long and tedious.[2]

Salmon called here this morning and says he shall sayle for Hasting, soe I shall send by him candles, cheese, sugar, vinegar, a barrell of Queenbro oysters and the brawn. I do assure you that the brawn comes very dear; I cut of about six pound for my brother and about that quantity I would have you send Mr Worge, and the remainder will be full enough for us. The whole at first weighing 22 pounds, soe by waying the peece that comes you will better guess at about 6 pound. I beleive in my last I forgot to take notice of your brewing again for strong beer. I think it was perfectly right. I have sent you Mrs Elcock's two bills, which I have paid her, and shall not forget Mrs Hammond's. My brother and his clerk, Wilson, had a quarrell this morning and he went out and was not at home at dinner, but returned in the afternoon. I beleive he is one of the family, and a poor silly creature, and not a little proud of being a baronet's son. The words of this song are made by Mr Bourne.

1 Peter Forbes, steward for the Duke of Newcastle's estate, and in the 1734 election chief agent for the Duke.
2 Earl of Wilmington v Nathaniel Garland 17 June 1735 [**122**].

144 To Mary Collier, Hastings, from John Collier, [Johnson's Court], 4 December 1735 [SAY 1682]

I shall take care to speak to my sister for the worsted[1] you mention, and discharge Mary's debt to Alice. I am not able as yet to guess at any time for my return to Hasting, though I much long for and wish it. Salmon sending only two boys for my things, I omitted sending my box of books and the brawn, but the latter I have sent by the carrier. You must have it tyed fast round with broad tape and immediately make a pickle to keep it in, which must be of two handfulls of bran and two handfulls of whole malt, or more in proportion, with sufficient salt to season it and boyled togeather and then strained of.

I was at the Custom house today and find that John Hall will be removed to Bexhill, but as I have no manner of hand in the affair would not have any notice taken of it till itt's done. Colds are very much here and mine has been exceedingly troublesom but I hope and beleive the worst is past though itt's now very bad,[2] but I thank God I have noe feaver. As soon as possible I shall leave London and have the pleasure of giving you an account of the time.

1 Worsted yarn, long staple wool, closely twisted together; weaving combined shades and colours, suitable for jackets, suits, and waistcoats (*OED*).
2 MS *become so troublesome* struck through and obscured.

145 To Mary Collier, Hastings, from John Collier, [Johnson's Court], 6 December 1735 [SAY 1683]

I received your letter by this post though by what you wrote the last was not in any great expectation of it. We have very bad uncomfortable weather that I am not got rid of my cold and intend to take your remedy this night. I had all last night and today a great pain in my head, which I wholly attribute to my cold and have not the least feaver, but am a little hoarse. Last night there was a latin play acted by the king's scholars at Westminster,[1] and as I had a ticket, could not refrain going. There was a great appearance of gentlemen and it was well performed. I took my roquelaur,[2] and, going and coming in a coach hope I did not increase my cold. I send you a letter I this day received from Dely and Jemmy is now here.

The duke and his brother set out this morning for Bishopston. There went with them only Mr Spence and Mr Stone, what company are to follow I know not. I this post write to Mr Cruttenden and Mr Godley signifying the same at his grace's request, and desiring their company with such Hasting people as Mr Cruttenden will carry, for I write to Mr Godley at Chailey. I have also mentioned it in a letter to the mayor. I begin to be impatient but will endeavour to get my affairs dispatched and put in such a method as not to return soon to London if it can be avoided. I have no more to add but respects from all here. Duty from Jemmy and that I am and ever shall be with all regard and faithfulness. I shall buy what you desire.

1 Westminster school, King's Scholars, *Andria*, by Terence, acted before 'at least' 200 spectators, 5 December 1735 (Scouten Pt 3, vol. 1, 1729-36, 533).
2 Roquelaure, after Duke of Roquelaure, 1656-1738, cloak reaching down to the knees, with collar fitting round the shoulders, similar to French University gowns, though more robust.

146 To Mary Collier, Hastings, from John Collier, [Johnson's Court], 9 December 1735 [SAY 1684]

I received your letter last night and I think you very obliging and kind in continuing a correspondence. I was this forenoon as much uncertain of fixing a time for to leave the town as I was when I first came hither; but I have now a prospect of being able to get out next Monday or Tuesday, tho itt's not reduced to a certainty. However, am determined to take the first moment of returning and for that purpose, unless by next post you hear to the contrary, let Nich set out with the horses a Sunday morning and he may get to Seavenoak and come in with ease next day soe that I may get out a Tuesday if nothing extraordinary happens, but on second thoughts find Monday will be impracticable. I thank God my cold is almost over, but have a very troublesom cough and had a good mind to be blooded this morning, but would avoid it if I can. I beleive Dely breaks up this next Saturday, but Jemmy not till Saturday sen'night. He was here today, and I equipped him with 6 necks and two pair of stockings, and he has a new pair of breeches. I shall not write more at present but would have you eat some of the brawn.

147 To Thomas Brian, Solicitor for Bonds and Criminal Prosecustions, Customs Board, from John Collier, Hastings, 9 February 1736 [SAY 339]

The collector and comptroller of Rye[1] came to me [2] this day with a letter from the Board of the 7th instant.[3] in answer to one they sent of the 5th [4] whereby they had informed their honors that Gabriel Tomkins having arrested Thomas Moore on a capras at Rye and taken bayl for his appearance the said Tomkins was afterwards attacked by the said Moore, Richard Lesly, Thomas Young, Joseph Swift and Susan his wife and forcibly carried on board a cutter where he was abused and his papers taken from him and that the mayor of Rye have [5] granted his warrant for apprehending the said persons.

They are all fled except Susan Swift who was committed to gaol. The Commissioners letter directed [6] the collector and comptroller to apply to me to take care to prosecute the said Swift for the assault and imprisonment of the sheriff's officer. I shall readily obey their honours commands, but there must be examinations and affidavits of the fact from Tomkins and [7] as his assistant as well as what can be got at Rye, and they must personally [8] appear when any prosecution is carrying on and I am informed they are gone for London where to be sure they have complained of the abuse.[9]

I [10] happened to be the same day sitting on a comission of sewers at Rye; the usage to Tomkin was violent and barbarous and he was very much abused, and did not hear but that the mayor [11] readily gave his [12] assistance and Captain Pigram and his mates and marriners of the sloop on searching the ships and boats in the harbour found where Tomkins was kept imprisoned and prevented the smugglers [13] carrying him out of the harbour after Moore was arrested.[14] I saw Tomkins and his warrant [15] found it was from the sheriff of Sussex and [16] as Moore was taken in the [17] Cinque ports [18] the warrant should have been from the constable of Dover Castle.

I privately told Tomkins [19] it was not regular but he saying [20] two persons had proposed being Moore's bayle [21] I told him to take it and [22] say [23] nothing [24] about the warrant and a bayl bond was accordingly executed as I was informed [25] 2 or 3 hours before the [26] assault [27] no person in Rye [28] but Captain Pigram who I mentioned it to, knew any thing about the warrants not being regular, but I hear [29] [30] the rioters took from Tomkins his book warrant and bayl bond [31] and all his papers. I will take care to get what [32] information and [33] proofe I can at Rye and [34] and prosecute, Tomkins and the other person [35] will give their information and affidavits at London.[36] I thought proper to send you this account.[37]

1 At this time the Customs Collector for Rye port was Samuel Jeake, the Deputy Comptroller was Henry Carleton, the Surveyor was William Horsefield, the tidesmen and boatmen were Moses Peadle, Joseph Cooper jun., John Weight and Thomas Kennett (TNA CUST 18/190).

2 MS *yesterday and produced* struck through.

3 MS *whereby it appeared that they were directing them to apply to me to prosecute* stuck through.

4 MS *instant* struck through.

5 MS *having* struck through.

6 MS *them* struck through.

7 MS *his assistant the person that was with him* struck through.

8 MS *from Rye* struck through.

9 MS *It was a violent unjustifyable behaviour and Tomkins was much exceedingly abused as it was report and by force put on board a vessel in order as was given out to be carried to France or Flushing*. struck through.

10 MS *was at Rye that day sitting* struck through.

11 MS *and magistrates as soon as they heard of the assault* struck through.

12 MS *their* struck through.
13 MS *Moore was arrested and in custody and gave bayl but I am* struck through.
14 MS *When he was in custody* struck through.
15 MS *which I* struck through.
16 MS *he taking* struck through.
17 MS *liberty of the* struck through.
18 MS *it ought to* struck through.
19 MS *him that I did not think* struck through.
20 MS *as he said told me* struck through.
21 MS *told him he should* struck through.
22 MS *not make any* struck through.
23 MS *any* struck through
24 MS *of the mistake and the same* struck through
25 MS *was sone* struck through
26 MS *smugglers they* struck through
27 MS *and imprisoned Tomkins* struck through
28 MS *knew anything of the mistake* struck through
29 MS *that they took away* struck through
30 MS *these people* struck through
31 MS *from him* struck through
32 MS *all the* struck through
33 MS *affidavits* struck through
34 MS *but to be sure* struck through
35 MS *assistant* struck through
36 MS *be the most material and on a prosecution they must be personally present* struck through.
37 For the career of Gabriel Tomkin(s) see P Muskett 'Gabriel Tomkin Smuggler, Customs Officer, Sheriff's bailiff and highwayman', *Sussex History* vols 2, 3 (1981-2); K Barker *The Smuggling Life of Gabriel Tomkins, the extraordinary life of an 18th century rogue* (2011).

148 To Commissioners of Customs, from John Collier, 19 February 1736

[SAY 285]

May it please your honours, pursuant to your commands of the 12th instant I have been with the person taken notice of in my letter to Mr Brian, your solicitor,[1] of the 10th, relateing to the smugglers and goods they had when one of them was shot at Hollington in October last and I have procured his examination and affidavit relating to that affair, and other frauds relating to the revenue, which I inclose to your honours. He seems yet very averse to appear at the assizes, but beleive that will be got over; he is but in mean circumstances and I have supplyed him with 25s and am humbly of opinion that, if your honours please to allow him subsistence, it will be a great encouragement and of service in the affairs and if so to be paid by the deputy collector of this port that the person may not be further know till the assiszes.

Mentioned in the enclosed affidavit are reputed persons of substance: Thorpe Diamond,[2] William Wood,[2] Thomas Blackman.[2] I do not know William Weston,[2] William Woodger, Richard Vidler[3].

1 The affidavit from Thomas Pettit of Battle; Pettit rented a farm from John Collier at £11 3s 0d a year (ESRO MIL 7/23 f.23).
2 Listed as a farmer (TNA CUST 148/12).
3 Labourer, from Battle.

149 To John Collier, Hastings from Thomas Pettett, 22 February 1736 [SAY 286]

I have conset heard about going for a witnes about the Houllington mattear, and I don't care mouch for going for a witnes, for I dont know but what it may cost me my life, for them Holkhourst genge ear bloudthoursty fellows. But becouse I am the only witnes that can be found of, and will do you all the good I can in the mattear, so if you do intend for me to appear for a witnes, this is to let you know that it mourst be consrued for me to have som money, for to by me clouse fitten to apeare for a witnes; for I have no more clouse then that on my beack so I houp you will conset hear of it; and if you please, you may let Mr Casuell know my mine, for he I sopose was at Houllington, cornear, when the man was shoot. So gentelmen I whould have you please yourselves about it, for if I han't money to by me clouse I will not go for a witnes, so I thought fit to lett you know my mine. Sir, if you please you may send me a few lines of what you intend to do in it by the nixt post, for if you don't want me I shall go in to Kent for about 8 or 9 wicks, your searvant to command. For if I haden't though it ould be for my prophet I should not have reveled souch a secret to you.

150 To John Collier, from Elizabeth Pickering, Dover,[1] 11 March 1736 [SAY 340]

I beg pardon for takeing this freedom with you who am an intire stranger, and could have no assurance for excuse but this. At the time you visited Dover it unfortunately happened that my spouse and Captain Lambe had a quarrell, which a lady that then was a visitor did in part relate to you. Captain Lambe's challenge as not been forgot by Mr Pickering, by reason he would not except the offers of reconciliation sent to him by Mr Pickering, vizt that as a gentleman he could put up with nothing less then that Captain Lambe should acknowledge himself to be the agressor, or see him according to the challange given by him, although he had rather chuse friendship provided his honour was not to suffer, and without one or the other was complyed with. Mr Pickering said it should not be forgott by him.

Captain Lambe not excepting either of these and not meeting an the other, Custom house excepted, but at a distance untill about a month agoe when Mr Pickering met Captain Lambe, in company with three or four more, coming round a corner took Captain Lambe by the nose branding him with cowardice in challanging him, and not fight him and on Monday last Captain Lambe served Mr Pickering with a King's Bench writ,[2] and says he will prosecute it as far as any law will give it. Mr Pickering on the other hand as employed a lawyer determining to see the end.

Now the favour, sir, I would crave of you is your good offices in the affair, as I humbly conceive you a verry propper person to reconcile this unhappy difference, as they being both officers under your inspection, which I judge them both to bee, that a stop by youre interposing between these two great spirits, who will not submit to another, may soon have a period without the law decideing of it which good offices I do not question will redound to your honour, but am assured to the thankfulness of.

1 John Collier was in Dover c. 21 September 1735, his Customs survey ran from 9 to 30 September 1735 (TNA CUST 148/11). The Lamb family of Dover were brandy and geneva merchants. At this time James Lamb was the Customs Surveyor for Dover and Stephen Lamb the tide surveyor; John Lambe was mayor of Dover in 1726.

2 11 March 1736 fell between the Hilary and Easter law term.

151 To Mary Collier, from John Collier, [Hastings], 22 June 1736[1] [SAY 1685]

I had Jemmy's and my brother's letters a Sunday night which were very agreeable, as not contradicting your welfare. We have been this whole day a botling out the wine; and as John Sargent's vessell goes this night for London it happens very luckily, and I have put on board for my brother 11 dozen of quarts and 4 dozen of pint bottles, thinking that the last may be sometimes convenient and agreeable.

Saturday night after writing my letters I sallied to the end of the walk, all forlorn, and the doctor's house, window shutters all up close, his maid and Misse Nanny being at Battell. I saw Mr Sansum at his door, and went along and sent cross for Mr Cant,[2] and took them home to supper, and we set till 12 a'clock, in which time Cant was wondrous wise. Sunday Mr Mayor and Mr Hill invited the jurats in, though few went. I there saw Mr Hill's sister and invited her and Mrs Wicking to come up yesterday afternoon and drink tea. Molly desired me to send for her aunt Cruttenden to be here when they come, and Mr Mayor and Hill came with them, and presently after our cozen D. Denham and I found they had been soulding[3] togeather, they tarried supper, which was two little chicken, prawns, and pease, an elegant supper, and went away a little after ten.

I have seen nothing of my brother Cranston[4] till this day; he came over and dined, and returned at six. Molly was down at her aunt's to breakfast, and was there invited to Mr Hill's to dinner, and my sister Cruttenden[5] and she went accordingly; and as there is a puppet show in town, fancy she tarrys to goe thither, not being returned. Yesterday Jack Denham was bound apprentice to Bolds of Battell, and I paid down the money; it took me up two or three hours, and was not a little vexed with the man's nicety, though I believe he will be a good master.[6] I was almost in a passion once or twice, but refrained; his uncle promised to be here in the morning but never came near.

I hear Dr Carleton comes down a Thursday, and his granddaughter Betsy, a perfect whim, I imagine, of Mrs Carleton's, when he will be obliged to goe up again soe soon. I am yet uncertain about my return to London, and much fear I shan't cleverly manage soe as to set out from the Watercourt at Borne, which is midsummer day. We drank all your good healths today at dinner and my brother sends all this best respects, in which I joyn. Just as I was putting up my letters Mr Cant, his wife and son came in to hire Mr Mead's house and are to enter upon it at Michalmas.

1 Sayer vol. 1, 114, suggested that as the ink was faded for the date it might be 1730, though went on to note that in June 1730 John Collier was in London, Mary Collier in Hastings, that John Collier was mayor in 1730, and William Thorpe mayor in 1736.

2 Edward Milward probably encouraged Samuel Cant (schoolmaster, surveyor and mapmaker) to reside in Hastings from 1731. Between 1746-48 Cant drew maps of Hastings showing the forts located at both ends of the town wall facing the sea (Baines 278).

3 Souling in pairs or as a group, a form of begging for money or food (*OED*).

4 Revd James Cranston junior, Bexhill.

5 Sarah Cruttenden, John Collier's sister, who married Samuel Cruttenden.

6 Bolds of Battle took on Jack Denham as an apprentice 21 June 1736.

152 To Mary Collier, Hastings, from M. Thorpe, Battle 25 June 1736. [SAY 1686]

I ask pardon for my neglecting to acquaint you how we manage. I designed letting you know Miss's ears were bored, and to desire your orders for rings. We took her whilst in the mind, all that knew of it thought she would have but one done. Mr Collier sent word I should buye a paire. She should like just such as Miss Markwick's. Her ears are very well, and Sunday wore her cap, which we have given the name of Mary, Queen of Scots; her face swelled towards night, though had been dressed severall days before, she was restless all night, but so well next day we went to Mrs Worge's, and no more uneaseyness then fear of her mouths never recovering its proper place.

You'll be surprised when you see her, for this warm sun, which she is all day in, has made her a nutt brown maid.[1] She gives her duty and love, on condition you send her such a hoop as Miss Molly's, to go with me some morning to Catsfield. Miss has given me leave, at Mrs Hill's request to make her a visit for two or three days. My brother is to fetch me in a chaire today, she sees Hasting to a vast disadvantage. I wanted some perswasion to go for fear Mr Hill, and I shoud agree as usal, but my brother insisted on it. I don't hear any have viseted her but Mrs Meadhurst, and that was by voilence, Nany Geery keeps at a distance, the only favour they boast of is supping with Miss Collier. Mrs Worge and sister is gon a ramble to Westham; poor Molly Philcocks has been dying this week,[2] I never heard of anybody in so sad a condition hold it so long, exceped her sister. Pray my service to Miss and Mrs Cranstone, etc. My mother and sister desire their service to yourselfe and all friends.

1 A pale and white complexion indicated absence of outside manual labour, though such preference never dominant, horse-riding was recommended for ailments, and sea bathing and exercise grew in favour as the century wore on.
2 Mary, daughter of Thomas Philcox, buried Battle 28 June 1736.

153 To John Collier, [London] from Henry Pelham, Esher,[1] 30 June 1736

[SAY 389]

I received your letter here this morning, and have accordingly sent you up my book,[2] that the account may be transcribed att your leisure. I am not certain that I shall be in town either this week or the next. If you can therefore come down here any day this or the next, except Satturday, we can in a very short time pass the whole account. If you come early in the morning, you may go back the same day or go on your journey to Sussex as is most convenient to you;[3] but if you can spare time, you will be very welcome to a bed here, and I shall be very glad of your company, that it may not be said all our friends att Hastings only look upon Esher and know nothing of the master of the house. I desire your answer by the first oppertunity and shall trouble you no further now but to wish you good success against Sir Thomas, and desire you would come as early next week as you can, and if you can spare an evening first, you will much oblige, your very good friend and servant.

1 Esher Place, acquired by Henry Pelham in 1729
2 An efficient method of settling accounts, providing original chits were retained by the sender and delivery of books effected; this was a common practice within estates and between lawyers and factors.
3 John Collier was at Johnson's Court from 2 June to 28 July 1736. It is not clear from his books when he made the journey to Esher (SAY 1418 f. 41).

154 To Mary Collier [Hastings] from John Collier, Stonecrouch c. 1736[1]

[SAY 2155]

I forgot to tell Mr Rowe that I would have him send me up Harry Moore's writ by the post a Sunday morning directed to the Custom house and if there's any letters of any signification come by to morrow's post give them him to send likewise with it. The chariot was just setting out from Battell as I came through, I but did not stay there a moment. I see Thatcher the cooper along with the chariot so Mr Broadway knew of his, guesse tho it was kept a secret. My horse has come along extraordinary well. There has been a great deal of rain. Mrs Lauder cannot tell me the gentlewoman's names but says they have a country house at Wandsworth.

1 [*Reverse*] MS Sayer, in pencil, dates this letter 'about the time of Moore's case 1736'.

155 To John Collier, at William Cranston's, Johnson's Court, from William Thorpe, mayor of Hastings, 15 July 1736 [SAY 34]

I fear I have made a mistake in what I wrote concerning Will Boorne, for he has since been repeating the method in which he was made free and it is as follows. He went three court days runing and desired to be made free; the two first was refused, the third Mr Stevens and one or two more spoke in his behalf and said the freedom would be more seviceable to him then to the rest, who were four landmen, and he having then a ship ready to be launched. After several arguments, but no mention that it was his right, the mayor ordered him to be sworn, and none objected to it. He was born since his father was made a freeman. He has talked with his father who declares he never knew a freeman made by demanding it as his right. I have heard since my last that Boyket[1] sayes he was once designed to be made free himselfe, but the jurats objected against him, and the town clerk, Mr Waller, asked him if he was the eldest son of a freeman. He said no. Then gentlemen, says Mr Waller, it's in your breast whether you'll make him a freeman or no.

I hear Colbrun is ill and can't attend. Mrs Milward is set out in the waggon this afternoon for town, as she sayes, but I hear as an evidence, but to what purpose I know not. There's with her Shingleton, Joy, Evenden, Sargant, White; they have sent to Appeldore after Couseens. Mrs Meadow is gone in a chair and Boyket to attend her. John Hussey is expected in the road every hour. I have detained the subpoena least the coach should be gone e'er he comes, and shall send it by the post a Sunday if not before. Mr Carswell will take care to defray all expences on the road. The coach is safely arrived. Dr Carleton set out yesterday. We are making preparations to receive the Duke of Richmond next Saturday, at breakfast, in the most repectfull manner we are able; but fear we shall miss of Sir W's company,[2] he being in the old way.

The town rings with our being all disfranchised.[3] Captain Milward is to be mayor and eldest jurat, Broadway a bishop, no less can be a recompense for the pains he has taken. Captain Moor I find has been employed to pump Mr Carswell and Will Boorne, but could not gain his ends. Mr Carswell has shewed me a copy of a resolution of the brotherhood in 1668[4] which he brings with him.

1 John Boyket, the Quaker [**122**].
2 Sir William Ashburnham.
3 For disenfranchisement see [**128**]. In preparation for the legal case before King's Bench on the creation of freemen, the Hastings assembly accepted the resignation of Henry Carleton, Robert Bartholemew, Thomas Carswell, and Mark Bailey as jurats, and from William Bourne as a freeman (ESRO HAS CAA/5). On 21 August 1736 all five were re-admitted as freemen, and in accordance with the town by-law of 6 April 1725 the entry fines were remitted, and all but Bourne readmitted as jurats and JPs, 'all five shall have the same rank and precedency in the corporation in every respect and be incerted in the roll of the jurat and freemen in the same place as they respectively stood before the 28th May last'.

4 Resolutions and grievances, general brotherhood and guestling, New Romney 21 July 1668 (Felix Hull (ed.) *A Calendar of the White and Black Books of the Cinque Ports 1432-1955* (1966) 521-527).

156 To John Collier, at William Cranston's, Johnson's Court, from William Thorpe, mayor, Hastings, 17 July 1736 [SAY 35]

I have this afternoon sent Barry by the carrier and given him directions to the same inn with the rest. He was very ready to come and sayes he'll do us all the service lyes in his power. His grace of Richmond breakfasted here this morning; we met him at the priory[1] where Captain Robertson had pitched his tents, and gave him a salute, and as we approached the town with flags before, as usual, the guns fired, bells rung and all demonstrations of joy appeared, but no Sir William appeared; they proceeded for Rye about one a clock. His grace seemed well pleased, and so did all the town with the honour done us. Miss Molly is much better and begins to have a good appetite. I am very glad to hear of your recovery from your late indisposition.

1 Augustinian priory of the Holy Trinity, Cambridge Road, Hastings; for reference to the move of the old priory to Warbleton, 1413, see: *Baines* ch. 15; Revd Edward Turner, 'The College and Priory of Hastings and the Priory of Warbleton' *SAC* 13 (1861); *VCH Sussex* vol. 2.

157 To John Collier, Hastings, from John, Lord Ashburnham,[1] 24 October 1736 [SAY 594]

If you have the rough draught of those articles you drew between Mr Hussee etc., and me for takeing the furnace and woods,[2] I wish you would bring them over here, any day, you will before Thursday next. I want to discourse you upon that affair.

1 John Collier was steward of the manors of Ashburnham, Catsfield, Broomham Parkgate, Broomham Allfreys, Penhurst and Hasleden. For accounts of these manors see SAY 593 and also SAY, 592 & 593.
2 Ashburnham Furnace (Cleere & Crossley 310-11, map 197). Thomas Hussey, born 1680, Bayton, Worcs., died 1735 Burwash, worked in the Sussex iron trade before 1709, in partnerships from 1725 with John Legas, William Harrison, Maximilian Gott and William Jukes; Legas was co-executor with Hussey's sister-in-law of the estate (Hodgkinson 2009b 15-24; Hodgkinson 2009a 82).

158 To John Collier, from Henry Pelham, Esher, 26 October 1736 [SAY 390]

I received both your letters with the enclosed abstract of the last audit. I am glad to find the tennants came in so well, and am of your opinion that I should be very cautious how I hearken to any application about the fines. I did not approve of myself when I yeilded to Tom Butler's impertunity, and for the future I shall refer them all to you. When Buckle wrote to you I thought to have been in Sussex in a short time. But my brother has been obliged to put off his journey for three weeks, which alters my motions. I shall go to Norfolk next Munday sennight, and return in about a fortnight. A week or ten days after that I may possibly come down to Bishopstone, if my brother is there. I desire therefore you will by the return of the post let me know, which will be most convennient to you, my bringing the book down with me, or delivering it, sealed up, to any person you shall appoint in London.

I wonder Burfeild should be in doubt what to do in relation to his mortgage; what I proposed, I meant for his good, if he don't think so, I shall be very well satisfied, and better pleased with having my money any other way. I hope you will have an oppertunity of talking more att large to Mr Legas before I see you, for as the lease will be out in two years,[1] it will be necessary for me to consider what to do soon, that I mayn't be att their mercy when the time is expired. I have a duplicate of that lease, as well as some others, which I think it will be proper for you to have; when you come to town, therefore, I desire you will remind me to give em you. We hear there has been a wedding in your neighbourhood lately, if so, I conclude the ladys are in good humour, and the knight, by this time, sorry that he has put his estate out of his power. The colonel is so true an electioner that he is even gone to country a voluntier to serve the Duke of Grafton.[2] His absence makes us here not thoroughly informed of what passes att Broomham. My service to all friends.

1 John Legas, leased from the Pelham family Crowham and Waldron furnaces, where Legas cast shot and pig iron, and Westfield, Bibleham and Brightling forges, (Cleere & Crossley 363 365; Hodgkinson 2009b). Legas made a deposition in Roberts v Hood [**372**] [**379**].

2 The Duke of Grafton was in fact George Fitzroy, Lord Euston, son of the 2nd Duke of Grafton, and the by-election was at Coventry, 15 February 1737. Fitzroy lost though was returned 12 April 1737 when the original election was declared void; Colonel James Pelham was the volunteer.

159 To John Collier, Hastings, from John, Lord Ashburnham,[1] 27 November 1736

[SAY 595]

I received your letter and inclosed Mr Bridger's letter to you and your answer to him, considering how I was used by the old man, on the account of his herriots they ought not to thinke anything hard, besides doing of favours out of one's estate. And makeing a president, sure is not a method for any reasonnable man to do, many others are much more expedient, when it's propper. Mr Maynard and John Breale are very good people, but I doe not know why there judgement is to determine my fines. I am sure I would not do a hardship to any man, and much less begin to Mr Fuller, though I thinke they use me ill. I return you Mr Bridger's letter.

1 John 1st Earl of Ashburnham died 10 March 1737.

160 To Mary Collier, Hastings, from John Collier, [Johnson's Court], 10 February 1737 [SAY 1687]

I received your letter by Mr Rowe who came here about 3 a clock. Mrs Selby was then here, and I read your instructions about your satten, and find it will center in a gown which they now make very full, and call it. She was come about Dely's gown which they went to market for yesterday. They brought home one of the pale coloured sprigged, which was handsom enough, but it seems Dely had fixed her eyes and thoughts on a brocade;[1] so would not let her be dissappointed tho it's 2 guineas more in the gown, being 14 yards of white ground brocade at 8s 6d. a yard. On your letter, they went out again this afternoon and bought another gown, which is a brown changeable colour, spotted, at 3s a yard; both togeather at the mercer's cost nine pounds.

Mrs Selby thinks it much bettter than to have made her blew into a gown and that as there was a yard of that left when made up she says it will by being turned look very fresh and new. Dely has bespoke a pair of shooes, and stockings are bought and that is all I at present hear of. After I had wrote my letter a Tuesday night she sat down to play on the spinnet and is vastly improved in it.

I was yesterday at the Westminster scholars' play,[2] and called before and drank tea at Mrs Chelsum's. Jemmy is to take something of physick next …[3] a day of his own appointing for he has broke out very much …[3] his head and Mrs Chelsum would have perswaded him to it before, but he was very averse. He is very well and grows much. I forgot whether I mentioned in my last that your godson was a nurse at Putney. I was taken a little lame this morning and have been soe all the day, very troublesom to walk, but not in great pain, but just such a weakness as after a fit of the gout. My pain is increased tonight but not to any great degree which makes me afraid of it's coming on to a fit of the gout, but I have kept in as much as possibly I could.

1 Brocade, origin India, Syria, Persia, at this time silk, or satin with taffeta, woven pattern of flowers, animals or people, etc., proud of the basic textile, garnished with gold and silver thread, often used as a shoulder throw, or for chairs.

2 Westminster school, *Eunuchus*, by Terence, 9 February 1737, played by the King's Scholars. Scouten Pt 3, vol. 2, 1736-47, 620 cites performance of the play on 3 December.1736.

3 MS damaged.

161 To Mary Collier, Hastings, from John Collier, [Hampstead],[1] 15 February 1737 [SAY 1688]

I was very much surprized with your letter by yesterday's post, to find you did not receive mine of the 10th, and am sorry to hear you had a cold, but hope it's gone of easily. It has been the epidemical distemper of the town and greatest part of the kingdom, and has generally been attended with lowness of spirits.[2]

Dely went away between 11 and 12 a clock very well, and about an hour after Jemmy came who I intended should have wrote to you this post, but as he had a pretty deal of exercise, did not press him so he went away before 4 a clock. I am sorry I must give you the following account of my gout. Saturday night I was in extremity of pain with my left foot, and had not a moments sleep till 6 in the morning. At 8 I felt it coming in my left foot and increased the whole day, so that Sunday night was just the same which made me almost impatient and wish for anything to give ease without thinking of consequences. I did not rise till about 4 either of the days. Last night I hoped to have got some sleep and sat up till 10, but could get none till past 2 till 4. The continual pain had ceased but frequent and violent plunges continued. I slept about 2 hours this morning, lying easy and comfortable, and got up at one a clock but cannot stand or goe or put a foot to the ground. I thank God I have had no feaver but never was so severely handled with it.

I remember you mentioned something about a habit for Dely, soe must know what you would have it of. I really think she seems very indifferent about coming home unless she was to come again, ... [3] in my opinion it's time, for she is a great girle and I told her she must depend on coming as Easter. As to coming again I could at present say nothing to it. She looks very well and is very brisk and I find there's another boarder from Norfolk, of her size, and they are very great and battail it for Sir Robert and the Duke of Newcastle against all the rest, being great politicians. My sister is a very good nurse, too good, for I could very well spare some of the time, but am now obliged to take all.

I at present see no prospect when to get out of doors, so can form no judgement of returning home having done very little of my business, or hardly seen anybody. It's not a little troublesom to write being under a necessity of sitting high with my leggs which is painful and fatiguing. The gout come at a very unhappy crisis; a week more would have in all probability have brought my affairs into some method to have left London, as soon as able, but now cannot see any prospect. I have seen no newspapers since Saturday, the death of the Lord Chancellor is very much surprizing, being so sudden, well in court a Wednesday, and dead a Munday morning. As he was a very able man, is lamented by all, and must be a great losse to the present ministry. It's thought he dyed in mortification in the pleura.[4]

1 MS cover, from Hampstead.
2 Bills of mortality, 1737. Deaths by fever: 4586. Yearly average 1731-36: 3336 (*Mortality*).
3 MS damaged.
4 Lord Chancellor Charles Talbot, died 14 February 1737 of gangrene of the pleura, the membranes lining the thorax and lungs - an intensely painful condition (Hervey vol. 3, 659).

162 To Mary Collier, Hastings, from John Collier, [Johnson's Court], 17 February 1737 [SAY 1689]

I am sorry I must acquaint you that your letter by this post found me as the former did: sitting in a chair with my leggs laid up in another and incapable of moving. I have had a pair of large shoos made, which came home last night, but I am unable to get any one of them on. I have much repented sending Dely to Hampsted, and was not I in hopes of being soon better would send for her again, for I have more company generally than I care for, or else am all forlorn, and am plagued with visits and messages that I often wish I could transport myself to some place wholly unknown. Today and yesterday have proved very bad weather, and that, or my ilness and confinement, or both togeather, have sadly sunk me, that I know not how to bear up, but live in hopes.

I have had for 2 or 3 days my armes from the wrist to the elbow and my hipps and leggs very much come out as it did when I was in London in the summer; but I have not been sick with it but beleive it will be proper to take rheubarb or something else when I am got a little better.[1] It itches very much before it comes out. I will remember your combs and pomatum.[2] Dely has shooes, 2 pair, but made at Turnstile, Holborn. I sent yesterday to Holladay's about your shooes, but he has left of trade and retired and it's now a sort of millener's shop there is no way but your sending up a shooe that is just fit and then I will bespeak them.

There can't be anything in Sir T. Webster's coming down with Moore to demand his freedom, for they cannot have a peremptory mandamus to oblige his admission before next, though they have attempted gaining it before. Mandamus's have been moved for making the underwritten freemen.[3] Some of them are very clever chaps. Mr Worge came to town yesterday but I have seen nothing of him today. I received yesterday by the carrier a present of 7 woodcocks from Mr Cruttenden, some of which I sent to Mrs Chelsum.

Henry Sargent, Richard Hart, Henry Sargent, John Hussey, Thomas Hide, John Curtis, Robert Thatcher, Thomas Grayling, Thomas Winter, John Meadow.

Mr Luxford came to see me today, from whom I had some account how the world goes at the court end of the town, and he was very communicative. Poor Lord Ashburnham is quite emaciated and sunk, though he has been something better for 2 or 3 days, as Mr Luxford tells me, and soe did Flower yesterday, who brought me a writing and message from his lordship. Your cloathes is gone today to Mrs Selby, my sister having sent it to be cleaned, and I think it looks well. I have just now tryed and got a shoo on my right foot but don't attempt the other. I goe to bed at 10, but for 3 nights running can't get to sleep till after 2, and then very little till about 6 and then am sleepy and easy till 9; but the first part of the night my feet are troublesom. I just write the mayor the names of the persons for whom mandamus's are granted.

1 Ground rheubarb root used in purges and as an astringent (Radcliff 35). It was originally imported from the Ottoman empire and India.

2 Pomatum and pomade, a skin and hair cream with a base of pig grease, lemon juice, apple pulp, rose water, usually fragrant. Dried ingredients used as a powder (*OED*).

3 Henry Moore, son of Captain Samuel Moore. The following law term was Easter, 27 April to 23 May; at the Hastings Assembly on 14 May 1737 before the jurats and mayor, 'Henry Moore produced a peremptory mandamus issued out of the King's Bench directed to the mayor and jurats and commonalty of Hastings,' for his admittance to the freedom of the town, and, 'in obedience thereto Henry Moore admitted freeman,' and kissed the deputy mayor's cheek. John Collier did not attend, having left Hastings the previous day, 13 May 1737. Of the list here, John Meadow was admitted freeman 1737, and Thomas Hide in 1740. For the records of the assembly see ESRO HAS CAA/5.

163 To Mary Collier, Hastings, from John Collier, [Johnson's Court], 19 February 1737 [SAY 1690]

I received your letter, and write this being in statu quo. I yesterday got one shooe upon my right foot, but can't, as yet, bear the other, though it's exceeding soft and almost as bigg again as those I usually wear. My breaking out much continuing, I thought it necessary something should be done, as taking some little physick, but on account of the gout would not doe it on my own head, soe this morning had an apothecary. He says abundance of persons have now such eruptions, and severall as mine without being sick or having a fever, and that the usual method is bleeding and purging and a little matter to sweeten the blood; but did not think the former at all proper in my situation and I am to take rheubarb tonight which he says is no way prejudicial, but good in the gout, and that I must take some two or three times and take care of cold. I find no help but must use patience. I had a letter from Dely today which I send you. I design to have her again before I come out of town or goe to Hampstead.

I beleive it will be best to have the old cherry trees in the long walk quite taken away, for they have bore but little a great many years.[1] I should be glad to know how spring comes on, and whether the pease are come up, and if the birds wake you in the morning with their chearfulness, for I must be contented to have it at second hand. Mr J. Steevens called here this afternoon from whom I had a description of Mr Carleton's house and find she is with child again. My sister informs me she has bought of Mrs Bolton new lace and accoutrements for Mrs Worge for a head ruffles, etc., and that Mr Worge …[2] her new cloaths and told her he would bring the patterns and shew her but none are yet come. I suppose they must be from cosen Johnson. I met French with his horses as I came to London just by Sevenoak, so suppose he has visited you before this time.

I hope Morris takes care to have everything proper for the season of the year planted and set in the gardens. I shall send him some matts, and if he wants anything else you must write word. I have a great deal of pleasure and satisfaction by your letters in hearing you and all with you are well. The contrary would be to me the utmost uneasiness and concern and that alone keeps up my spirits more than anything else possibly can at this distance from you. Jenny is just come in and he shall write a letter to Molly and Jenny instead of writing to you this post. I was in less pain and slept better last night, though I heard the clock every hour but 2, for I waked very often and my breaking out was very troublesom, itching extreamly. The conversation in Grubb is looked upon to be well done and a perfect description of the talk of such creatures as are there represented.[3]

1 John Collier's library held several works on gardening including Richard Bradley *A General Treatise on Husbandry and Gardening* (1724) vol. 1, and John Evelyn's *Sylva, or a Discourse of Forest Trees* 4 Folios.

2 MS damaged.

3 Grub Street Journal, 7 February 1737 the article *A modern polite conversation between Miss Courtly, Miss Fidget, Mr Spritely, Miss Trifle, Miss Edging and Miss Weldon* was a careful rendering of the talk amongst the young and well-off on the London social circuit and mentions dress sense, fashion, the opera with Farinelli and 'that dear Adagio', quadrille and whist, the latest dances, horses, boat rides from Portsmouth to Gosport and variegated gossip on their acquaintances, which included disparaging comment dressed up as praise.

164 To Mary Collier, Hastings, from John Collier, [Johnson's Court], 22 February 1737. [SAY 1691]

I am obliged to write this from my old apartment, not being able to get out of my chamber; but have this day got on both my shoes and am to take some more rheubarb tonight and hope in a day or two to get abroad, but we have had very indifferent weather. I have taken something this 2 nights and mornings. I fancy neither to doe hurt or good but the apothecary says it's a sweetner of the blood. My breaking out is not quite over and is very troublesom. I wrote to Dely yesterday but did not send for her, being unwilling she should loose much of her time. Yesterday Mrs Hammond sent me her bill. Seeing it was a pretty deal, I would not pay it without first sending to you and have your approbation. I quite forgot the firkin of herrings and think they should not be spoyled and as I have not otherwise disposed of them let them be sent to my brother Smith, for they are great lovers. I suppose you have begun ours and if we don't make of with them give some away.

I had a sad evening last night; my brother Cranston came in at 4 and said he had promised to goe to the play with Frewen and Worge, soe I had the whole time with my sister, but wrote and read till I was quite weary.[1] She went of at 10, and I set up an hour, for I cannot sleep, though I thank God am not now in pain. I waked last night before 1 and did not goe to sleep till past 7 this morning. As I can see no prospect of leaving London and having not farther for Mr Rowe, intend he shall set out a Thursday morning for Hasting. I have heard nothing more about Mrs Worge's cloathes nor shall ask no questions about it. He talks of leaving London a Thursday. I think it was very right to brew, and for strong and small beer, and as I best remember there is another large stand to set under the water spout. I hope Pain will be very careful about the trees and that this cutting will bring them to rights so that we may expect some fruit.

If my brother is with you, he must make use of good glasses and he will see a comet.[2] I think they say Venus is some directions about it, but I don't know whither it's going to or from the sun, but it's the same as appeared in Julius Caesar's time, as calculated by Sir Isaac Newton. Lord Hardwicke had the great seal yesterday delivered to him. Everybody agrees he was the most proper person for it, but the court of King's Bench will have, I am afraid, a great losse. He has gone through all stations in the law with the greatest reputation, and is now arrived on the summit at an age when most people first begin to be taken notice of for any superiour abilitys. A glory to the county of Kent, being a native of Dover.

This day there is great expectation of a motion in the House of Commons in behalf of the Prince of Wales, relating to his having a certain settlement. It has made a mighty noise about town and a great hurly burly, as it's said, at court. The motion is, they say, to be made by Mr Pulteney and the modern patriots. I think it's very odd that this was not set to rights without all this noise. Jemmy is come this evening to stay till Thursday.

1736 [3]

28 March:	for making a red gown	£0 5s 0d;	for body lineing	0 2s 0d
	for 3 yards of white stuff	£0 3s 9d		
22 April	for pleating a gown	£0 4s 0d;	for silk	£0 1s 0d
30 April	for making a blew gown	£0 10s 0d;	for canvas	£0 1s 6d
	for ribbon buttons and loops	£0 3s 0d;	for making a striped gown	£0 5s 0d
	for canvas	£0 1s 0d;	for pleating a linnen gown	£0 4s 0d
	for Scots cloth	£0 1s 6d ;	for altering a blew coat	£0 1s 0d
	for blew Persian	£0 1s 6d		

1 Monday 21 February 1737, (i), Drury Lane Theatre, *Timon of Athens*, adapted from Shakespeare by Thomas Shadwell, also *The King and the Millar of Mansfield*, by Robert Dodsley, report of riotous behaviour by footmen at this performance; (ii), Covent Garden Theatre, *Cymbeline*, adapted from Shakespeare by Thomas D'Urfey, also *The Royal Chace*, by Edward Phillips; (iii), Lincoln's Inn Fields, *A tutor for the Beaus; or love in a labyrinth*, by John Hewitt, 1st performance, also *Hymen's Triumph, or, Trick upon Trick* (Scouten Pt 3, vol. 2, 1736-1747, 640).

2 Comet, close to Venus, observed by Rose Fuller in Jamaica, January to March 1737, who communicated the details to the Royal Society. The same was also observed by James Bradley, Savilian Professor of Astronomy, Oxford.

3 This is Mrs Hammond's bill, referred to in [**166**] SAY 1693.

165 To Mary Collier, Hastings, from John Collier, [Johnson's Court], 24 February 1737 [SAY 1692]

I received your letter by this post and am sorry I can't acquaint you of my being downstairs today, as I fully intended last night, but about 2 this morning I was seized with a great pain at the bottom of my best foot which lasted all night and this forenoon and much put me out of heart. The pain is much abated but it's very tender. The weather continues very windy and blustering, and I really beleive it has some effect on my distemper. The affair of the Prince of Whales came on a Tuesday about 4 in the House of Commons, moved by Mr Pulteney, and held till 12 a clock; and on a division was carried against the motion by 30 only, vizt 234 against 204.[1] Soe it was a very full house. It much distressed a great many members how to vote, and I am sure must in particular Colonel Pelham, but I have not heard how he behaved. It engrosses, as I hear, all the conversation of the town. The king a Munday sent a committee of the Privy Councell with the new Lord Chancellor at the head of them, with a message to the Prince of Wales, conteyning, as is said, some reasons why the settlement had been deferred, and a promise of making a handsome settlement; and also a dowry for the Princess of Wales, but this did not occasion its being stopped or postponed.

Mr Worge is gone out of town today about noon and Mr Rowe with him; if he wants any paper you will give him some out of my study. D. Denham, I understand, came up a Munday or Tuesday and hear he is gone out with Mr Worge. I saw nothing of him and was glad of it; he was to come with G. Worge as I find, but delayed it, and hear there was not time to advise on his affairs. I beleive him to be in so bad a condition as nothing can be of any real service. I last night saw Mrs Worge's head cloaths and handkercheife which is Brussells lace; the former 19s a yard, the latter 28s, and cost, with making up, sixteen pound.[2] I don't understand that her cloaths is bought, that cosen Johnson told him the fashion of silks, etc., was not yet perfectly setled. Tom Frewen I hear goes out of town tomorrow morning in the coach soe I shall be left almost forlorn. Jemmy came hither a Tuesday and is gone home this evening. His great coat grows too scanty and it is come into my head that he shall have one made out of my dark coloured, little great coat, that I beleive hangs in the little hall; and for that purpose desire you will send it by the carrier a Saturday, and fancy it may be made up in a little bundle without a box. Till I can get out of doors I cannot so much as guess when I shall be able to get out of town, but hope in a fortnight's time for I begin to grow a little impatient at my long absence from home. I have expected to hear that James Bossum was again come to London but suppose he will come to me when he arrives. I wish you all health and imaginable happiness, and long to be at home with you which I am sure is more solid satisfaction and agreeableness than can be had anywhere, or in any state or condition.

One of the daily papers of yesterday said Lord Ashburnham was very dangerously ill and his life not expected, but I have heard nothing of it today, but by all accounts he is not expected to hold out long. Send down to the mayor and borrow the vote of Tuesday, and you will therein see the motion for the address, and the king's message and prince's answer. The votes are sold for a shilling or 18d appeece, and but just now come out.

1 Before the Prince of Wales ascended the throne his allowance was £100,000 a year; on accession as George II he granted his son only £50,000 a year. Relations between the prince and the king and Caroline, already poor, deteriorated when the prince was refused permission to marry into the Prussian royal house, marrying instead, Augusta of Saxe-Gotha. When George II left for Hanover 24 May 1736, the prince was refused a

part in the regency. In February 1737 William Pulteney and Sir John Barnard moved that the king be asked to increase the prince's allowance to £100,000 a year, a move which allowed members to display their knowledge of precedence and the rights of the heir. Sir Robert Walpole, Henry Pelham, supported by the Master of the Rolls, the Solicitor General, and the Secretary at War, contributed to the defeat of the motion, 234 to 204 (Hervey vol. 3, 661-705; *PS* February 1737; Lecky (1892 ed.) vol. 1, 447-8; Taylor & Jones 24-6; Egmont vol. 1, 10 April 1730, vol. 2, 21 Sept. 1737).

2 John Collier set out for London on 4 February 1737, and soon after reaching Johnson's Court noted in his day book his affliction with gout; among the drapery and supplies purchased for Dely, for his wife and his daughter Elizabeth were gloves, 2 pairs of stuff damask, shoes with straps, combs of different degrees of fineness, pomatum, patterns of Dely's clothes, a pair of fustian pockets drawn and fine cruells, 100 needles, head clothes and a habit, light blue or green, a black cap, livery stockings; among other goods John Collier bought 2 dozen bottles of spaw water, powder for Elizabeth 'of the best sort', mustard seeds, tea, chocolate, glasses and hams (SAY 1418 f. 47v).

166 To Mary Collier, Hastings from John Collier, [Johnson's Court], [after 22] February 1737 [SAY 1693]

I received your letter by this post and hope there will be no occasion for your caution about Mr Rowe, tho to be sure it's well to have a little previous consideration of such an event. I don't know of any proper place, all houses at a little distance being inhabited, and can't think of any but Morris's and, as his family is small for him, to remove to his friend John Baker's, and for which I would allow, etc.[1] I will give my sister Mrs Hammond's bill and endeavour to have it setled as well as I can, but to be sure itt's rude and scandalous and a very great imposition. I have no objection, if you think proper, to buy Molly Smith such a gown as you mention. As to the herrings, it's perfectly equal to me to which you dispose of them. I thought of my sister Cruttenden, but as I beleive we shall not eat half ours she might have the residuum, but doe just as you think proper.

I got downstairs yesterday to dinner, and in the afternoon went out in a coach for about an hour and a half which agreed very well, and I really slept, as I believe, the better for it. My feet are still very tender and weak, that I was helped up into the coach but I have no pain remaining. Your gown is come home and I think looks very well and intend to send it next week. They don't wear any aprons or girdles with them, but tyed round the wast with a twitcher, which is a little cord and small tassells; yours is blew and silver. S. Wicking called here yesteday, but I had a gentleman with me so did not see him. He told my brother that he expected his mother in town in a little time; also that Sir William Ashburnham dined with him a Thursday, with his Dr Cliffe who is come from the infirmary and I beleive lives on Sir William; and that Sir William and his led doctor were to goe as this day to Dr Tilden's at Leatherhead for a week. I think the barronet, as he was soe near, might have called or sent to ask how I did.

The affair of the P. of W. came on yesterday in the House of Lords, where it was very strenuously debated for a great many hours, and on the division 103 against 79, as I heard today. So the proposed address went also there in the negative. I hear that there were a great many, on both sides, that changed over in their votes, but all the Pelham's went togeather, and that the colonel went a Munday night to the prince and told him soe, and that he was ready to resign.[2] This I had from a gentleman of knowledge, but have seen none of the family since.

The Duke of Dorset was a half faced christian, one son of one side the question and Lord John for the address.[3] The affair engages all company and discourse, and various are people's sentiments. The king, they say, looks very thin, and is not recovered, and some of the speeches regarded his late going abroad not a little. The dialogue in Grub street last week is again reprinted in that paper of last Thursday and is much admired for being in a great measure the usual converstation of the beaus and belles, and which reduced into writing demonstrates what a ridiculous peece of jargon reigns amongst the young ladys, etc.[4] I hope to be able a Munday to get out soe as to call on people about business and get it dispatched as soon as possible, and leave the town. I have been out a little while in the garden etc., for a little air. I wish you a continuance of health and all imaginable pleasure and happiness. I wrote a letter yesterday to Dely and expect an answer Munday or Tuesday, and if I can't goe to Hampsted, she shall come here next Saturday. From my arms, hipps and leggs where I came out very thick all the skin peels of; now it's well.

1 John Baker, tenant of John Collier, Hastings (ESRO MIL 7/23 f.35).
2 Although secretary to the Prince of Wales, Colonel Pelham voted for the Government and thus offered his resignation, but remained in post until the prince was evicted from St James in 1738.
3 Sackville, Lionel Cranfield, 1st Duke of Dorset, devoted Whig, his elder son Charles Sackville Earl of Middlesex, MP East Grinstead 1734-1742, voted for Pulteney's motion; Lord John Philip Sackville MP Tamworth 1734-47, 2nd son, voted for the Government
4 Grub Street Journal, for which see **[163]**.

167 To Mary Collier, Hastings, from John Collier, [Johnson's Court], 1 March 1737 [SAY 1694]

On receiving your letter about Dely's coming down, and thinking it rightly judged, I have sent her a letter signifying the same and that she should bring all her cloathes with her a Saturday, for that whither she is to return or not you would be willing to see in what condition it is. I desire you'l now consider what she will more want and send me an account by next post, that they may be got in time. I design to get out next Fryday sen'night, or the Munday following at farthest, and can't see any prospect before those times, neither do I think I should be able to ride sooner.

I went out a Sunday afternoon in a coach to the park with Jemmy for a little air, and yesterday about 11 went to Colonel Pelham's, and from thence to Lord Ashburnham, who is a most shocking sight, especially to one that has the gout. I can't think it possible he can live, neither can I give any description of him, for he is quite emaciated, his spirits sunk and his speech much altered. He is carried out for about 2 hours in the middle of the day to see if the air can contribute any releif. He asked me and pressed to dine there, which I did, and only Mr Ashburnham and our friend Luxford. He went out with my lord in the vehicle, and whilst they were gone I paid a visit to Mr Carleton, found him at home and she dressing her head. She looks very bigg, tho is well and brisk, but all the bloom gone. There was Master G. Carleton attending her, fetching and carrying her glass, combs, water, etc., so he is a regular groom of the chamber. I think he is something grown. I asked Mr Carleton when he went to the university, but he gave me no answer, but I understood by Mr Chelsum that he is not at all fitting for it. I really think the house very well and much better than I expected. I beleive they have no boarders nor indeed room for any.

Mr Pelham's eldest daughter was married a Shrove Tuesday to Dean Cresset by Mr Ashburnham;[1] and there was that night to be an entertainment at her father's for all the family; but that hapned the long day in the House about the P. of W, so that at 11 Mr

Pelham sent word they could not come. So it was put of till the next day, Ash Wednesday, very proper for a dignifyed priest. Whilst I was at Colonel Pelham's the dean came in. He looks to be more than forty, well sized, a pretty thin red face and white eyebrows, and I found they were to be carried to court that day and introduced to the royal family.

I was wrong informed of the numbers in the House of Lords on the debate, for there was 103 against 40, vizt lords present 79, proxies 24; lords present 28, proxies 12. James Bossom was here yesterday and brought your shooe and orders are gone for 2 pair to be made. It has been a fine day for the grand shew of fine cloaths at the court, but I have heard nothing in particular, only that the Princess of Wales was expected to be very fine. The wind is very sharp and makes but indifferently …[2] my gout last night I had a great pain in one of insteps but tis better today. I am sorry Mrs Thorpe goes away before my return and leaving you, to whom I desire my humble service if she departs. Jemmy come hither this afternoon. I heard that the queen desired all the court ladys not to buy new cloathes for the day and to appear in a plain dress. They say the king is far from being well.

1 Dean Edward Cresset, Canon and Dean of Hereford Cathedral, 1736-49; married by Sir William Ashburnham's nephew who was ordained 1733, Dean of Chichester, 1742, Bishop of Chichester 1754, succeeded as 4th baronet Ashburnham in 1762 (G Aylmer & J Tiller (eds) *Hereford Cathedral A History* (2000).

2 MS damaged.

168 To Mary Collier, Hastings, from John Collier, [Johnson's Court], 3 March 1737 [SAY 1695]

I have sent a box this week by the carrier in which is your gown, but I beleive not all the peeces that are left for I think my sister said she had more. There's only a great coat of mine and my intended servant's cloaths and your gloves and the girles' stockings besides two or three other little things to fill up, but at the top there is a small parcell for Mr Worge, from Mr Isted which I beleive are wiggs he left. By a letter from him this post he intends to be at Hasting a Saturday and wants a writing made by John Moor's widow to his father. Unless it is in a bundle or two of parchments that lye in the window to the street near my writing desk, which I desire you'l carry out to him to look over, I don't know anything where it is.

We have had very fine weather but it has been excessive cold till this day. My feet recover strength very slowly and I am not able to walk 40 rodd without a great deal of pain. I have not seen any person to have an account anything in particular of the queen's birthday, but in general it's said the court was vastly numerous and the cloaths very rich. I shall expect by next post your directions about Dely, from whom I had a letter yesterday, and she is to come a Saturday with pack and package. Tell Mr Worge of the mistake in the Lords' division, for I wrote him a letter the same post I did your first about business and mentioned at the bottom as I did to you. I send this post a letter to Grover of Bexhill; desire you'l tell Mr Rowe to take care it's sent as early as may be a Saturday if he is not in town, because I want an answer by that post. I find the smuggling trade goes on at a high rate and soe there is accounts come from all parts, but more particularly Sussex and Kent.

D. Denham is still about town in a strange, forlorn, condition, not a penny in his pocket; he came to me a Tuesday for 2 guineas, but I refused him, but tonight on his earnest request I let him have a guinea and I found he got another from my brother Cranston. My feet are extreamly tender and the least walking which it is impossible to prevent though I take coach as much as I can, quite founders me. I shall keep in as long as possible I can. Tell Mr Worge I will pay the surplusage of the money to my brother for him, but he need not send it up by the carrier.

169 To Mary Collier, Hastings, from John Collier, [Johnson's Court], 5 March 1737 [SAY 1696]

I received your letter and was all this day in expectation of Dely, directing her to come in the forenoon and had the man waiting for her a great many hours, but this day afternoon, after 5, she came and Mrs Russell with her whom I have paid of. It has been a terrible day, and I have very much felt its effects in my feet, having been hardly able to stirr and have kept close in. I will give directions about Dely's linnen a Munday and what else she wants. I am at present of opinion that I shall be obliged to be at the assizes which are next Munday sen'night, at Eastgrinsted.[1] If soe at present think to have my horses through to London, and Dely come down the Tuesday in the coach thither, but this will be reduced to a greater certainty by next post when I shall give directions accordingly. Jemmy is also here; he took some physick a Thursday, and I beleive when he come down it will be proper for him to drink some diet drink, having pretty much broke out in his head.

Not having been out of doors I can send you no manner of newes. The Bexhill skirmish is in the newes, but that makes the officers heroes, instead of running away on the smugglers attacking them. I sent to Mr Sheels about a spinnet; he called here yesterday and told me he had seen one that was good and new, but the lowest price was 8 guineas. I will endeavour to buy a second hand one, if I can, and may save half the money, but if I can't get a good one will have this: in for a hundred, in for a thousand. If I am obliged to come by Eastgrinsted, I am afraid it will be too far in a day to Hasting, the roads being bad, but we must get to Mr Burnett's if she can't reach to Battell.

Dely has come full fraught with newes; in the first place she has seen the comet, and by her description beleive she did.[2] That it appeared the night the debate was in the Parliament; that the king was the death of the Lord Chancellor, by giving him a great blow that threw him into a fever; and that the prince would never goe to court as long as the king lived and that my Lord Wilmington would give the prince all his money. She is strong for Sir R. W. and the D. of N. but yet is against the king; but it's such a medley of politicks as is very mysterious, with abundance more of the like stuffe. I would have you discourse John Ellams about a horse that he may be ready and have a good, easy, sure footed one.

1 East Grinstead assizes, Monday 14 March 1737, 10 Geo II 1736-7 (TNA ASSI 34/5).
2 For this comet [**164**].

170 To Mary Collier, Hastings, from John Collier, [Johnson's Court], 8 March 1737 [SAY 1697]

I am sorry to find by your letter that you are so low spirited, especially as Mrs Thorpe has left you, but hope Miss Fidget may in some measure divert you.[1] I find it is impracticable for me to get out of town this week, but if I could, as I must be at the assizes which begin next Munday, I should not attempt it. I had thoughts of having my horses through a Saturday or Sunday, to have set out a Munday morning for Eastgrinsted and Dely to come down thither in the stage coach a Tuesday, but it being uncertain what company she might have, and I beleive would not like it to travail alone.

I have altered my resolution and resolve to hire a chariot, or 4 wheel chaise, and pair of horses and carry her down with me a Munday morning and she may lye with Miss Green with whom she is acquainted. This being the resolution, I would have you send out the horses early a Tuesday morning so as to reach Grinsted in the afternoon; and I hope we shall set out for Hasting a Wednesday morning; but as I beleive it will be too far for Dely to ride through in a day beleive I shall lye at Mr Burnet's. I write to Mr Worge this afternoon and have desired him to send to the man I am to have, to come to Hasting a Saturday for to stay, and then he may come with John Ellams upon the gray horse and lead my mare, for I suppose pony is well for Mr Rowe to come to the assizes a Munday morning upon. The man must bring my bridle and saddle and straps to his own to tye on the portmanteau.

John Ellams well knows the road, but it is come into my head that all the bad way may be missed, about which I would have you talk to him; that is, as he comes to goe into the ground at Netherfield Down, just before he goes down Darvell Hill on the right hand, and so cross the ground to Mr Burnet's, and from thence there is a road through the land, and otherwise to the Three Cupps, which misses all the worst way. The man must come with the horses to me at the Crown, but I suppose Ellams will goe to the widow Beeching's; let him come in his own cloathes, not the livery.

Dely has a habit bought but she desired to have it a brown colour, and she has cut out an old shift to make a sham and ruffles to wear with it. My sister and she seem to be of opinion she don't want any headcloaths. Your shoos are come home, but I verily beleive they are not bigg enough. My sister and I almost huffed about them, for I give her very often directions about them, to be sure to be larger, but they don't seem so to me. If they don't doe they must be returned. I shall remember tea and coffee etc. Dely's bureau is not come from Hampsted. G. Luxford called on me last night and says Lord Ashburnham is extreamly bad and I can't think it possible he can live but a very little time, I am heartily sorry on all accounts. I don't doubt but that you'l order the man's bed to be aired, tho I just menton it.

1 Miss Fidget, Jane Collier, born 1727; Sayer suggested Jane's nickname may have come from contemporary drama; William Wycherley *The Country Wife* (1675) features Lady Fidget and her daughter Dainty Fidget.

171 To Mary Collier, Hastings, from John Collier, [Johnson's Court], 12 March 1737 [SAY 1698]

I received your short epistle; I really expected a little reprimand for mentioning the man's bed, but willingly submit to it. No alteration happens about my leaving the town with

Portrait of Cordelia Collier (1722-79), wife of General James Murray, by Arthur Devis, reproduced by permission of the Sayer family.

Portrait of Jane Collier (born 1727), wife of William Green, by Arthur Devis, reproduced by permission of the Sayer family.

Dely a Munday in the manner I mentioned. I would have you give Ellams a strict charge about the horse. In the box that came a Saturday there is, in one of the shirts, a bottle of paradise water. Lord Ashburnham is to be carried out of town for Ashburnham next Munday morning in a very private manner. I long, my dear soul, to be with you and hope to have the happiness, at furthest next Thursday.

172 To Mary Collier, [Johnson's Court], from John Collier, Hastings [? 1737][1]

[SAY 1699]

As I was dissappointed in my expectations of receiving a letter from you by last post, I did not design to write this, however, have altered my resolutions so far as to let you know, I hope we are all pretty well. My cousen Denham came here this afternoon with her daughter Betty, but our company were all gone to Dr Thorpe's; she says the child is well. The fierce east wind puts of all thoughts of Dely's riding out, she is cheerful but I can't say she looks better. They are very merry all day long, and think Mrs Worge a very good companion for her. She is a little sick, or inclinable to a stomach ach, or pain on one side of her head, but in the main I think much one, and eats pretty well. As you wrote to me no news, I am silent, but indeed have nothing worth while to communicate. Give my brother the other side [*no longer attached*].

1 This date is suggested by Sayer vol. 1, 131.

173 To John Collier, Hastings, from Mr Robert Burnett, Halland, 22 March 1737

[SAY 391]

I was very aprehensive that you would have a very bad journy yesterday, not only from the watters being out but from the badness of the weather. I sent last night to Mr Burfeild's to see how you did anyhter your journiy, but you wass not come. I am glad to hear you arived safe, as you have so little time for so much buisness. I am shoore it would be very unreasonable to desire you to come to Haland, though we should have all bin made very hapy by it. It's always a great pleasour to me to waite on Mr Collier att any time or place, nither can it be a mortification to me, lett the dinner be what it would, if I have the pleasour of your company; besides your dinnors are always very good, or att least what I have seen of them. But Dr Russell and Mr Stonestreet have putt me under a corse that it may not be so proper for me to waite on you att that time so hope you will please to exkews it, but should be glad to waite one you either morning or any anyhter noon which you would be most att leasuour; and I could leve what bills you care to exsept and send my man for money in the evning. I aske pardon for interupting you whilst you read so long a letter.

174 To John Collier, Hastings, from Nathaniel Lamb,[1] Lincoln's Inn, 31 March 1737

[SAY 597]

I find upon the death of Lord Ashburnham, to whom I am an executor and one of the guardians of the present earl, that there are severall herriots demanded; and not knowing whether there are so many payable, I have here sent you a particular of what are demanded, and desire you would lett me know if you can tell what are payable. I should be glad to know if you had any concerns with the late lord, and if you know of anything in the country that is proper wee, that are the executors, should be acquainted with.

Herriots demanded: Mr Fuller, 1 herriot capt, a breeding mare valued at 8 pounds by him not worth half the money; Sir Walter Parker, £5, 2 yearlings £13 15s 0d, - 10 guineas; Mr Nicholls, £1, a barren - he valued at £5, worth £3; Bishop of Chichester, £3, 3 milch cowes, 3 guineas each worth £4 each; Mr Collins, £1, a scotch cow value £3; Morehall manor £1, a little mare, 4 guineas, Mr Flower to make an end; Sir Thomas Webster £5, 5 coach horses, £55, he returns £27 10s 0d; Mr Pelham's, 2; Lord Wilmington, 1, an old horse, £5 the top; Mr Mackwith 1, 3 guineas, a horse worth £4.

1 Called to the bar 25 April 1733, later a KC.

175 To Mary Collier, Hastings, from John Collier, [Johnson's Court], 14 May 1737 [SAY 1700]

I presume George has informed you I got to town a little after one yesterday, and had a safe and pleasant journey, it being neither hot nor cold. Near London, it began to be a little dusty, but about 5 or 6 a clock here was a very smart shower. I ordered George to be sure to get back to Bromley last night, and get out of town at 6. It did rain smartly about that time, but I shall be angry if he stayed all night. I found my brother and little Jemmy well; my sister was gone to Hammersmith with some cosen Russell, who is a servant at the Duke of Dorset's, but is expected tonight or tomorrow morning. I understand my brother Cruttenden called yesterday forenoon at my brothers, and he gave him the magazine, and sessions paper for you. I have seen Mrs Elcock and spoke to her about your things.[1] Mrs Wicking and her son, and James Bossum and his wife, dined with my brother a Thursday; he says Mrs Wicking looked sadly, and was not well, perhaps being confined to her son's close apartment, and I find she and Dame Bossum lye togeather there. I would have my old mare turned out to grass, which I forgot to tell George. It rained this morning for about an hour or two, and I looked out of the window and read: here is old cole, charcole charme and smal cole dust etc.

The buggs have been very strong in my sister's bedchamber, so that they have layn in my room this month, but yesterday Mr Steevens was putting up their bed de novo. I enquired of him after Mr Carleton's family; he told me he believed she laid in, but could not tell anything of certainty, nor what she had got. He said that their fine footman is going away for being saucy, and that he heard they did not design to take another. I have heard no manner of news nor seen any persons to enquire after any. I wrote a letter today from the custom house to Mr Rowe with a writ inclosed to send Lewis Gillart to Rye.

I enquired today at the Custom house about the Bexhill officers, and don't find they are restored, nor their charges and answers as yet read; so there's at present no prospect, but I admire that no application has been made for it, since I think you told me you heard that Lady Ashburnham had wrote in Walsh's behalfe. Parnell is also under suspension and it's not as yet taken of, and notwithstanding his good interest it will give great trouble to him and friends. I think Pigram has been too warm in the affair.

Mr Godley went out of town unmarried this day sennight. The widow went out the same day in the Grinsted coach. I find there is some demurr about setling her fortune relating to her present children, made by her brother Sergison; but the bottom of it is his own sordid temper, for he thinks the money sinks to him if those children dye and she has no more; they say she is a bouncing bona roba. Mr Godley was very ill in town with chollicky pains and the jaundice and the widow visited him three times at his lodgings during his ilness. I am told he seemed resolved against the match, if the terms were not complyed with that had been actually given underhand, which Sergison now shuffles about. I think I have at present no more newes to inform you of, and therefore bid you adieu. My sister is come home since writing the above. Jemmy, I hear, is very well. I expected him this afternoon for that they were to break up today.

1 12 May 1737 John Collier left Hastings for London via Stonecrouch and Tunbridge; he bought a Paris cap or mobb to be dressed to come forward, 4 yards of Brussels edging about two fingers broad, a fan 'a peece' and silk shoes for the girles, and patterns of brown and changeable shagreen (SAY 1418 f. 50).

176 To Mary Collier, Hastings, from John Collier, [Johnson's Court], 19 May 1737 [SAY 1701]

I received your letter of this post and am sorry I was obliged to write so very short a Tuesday night, but I had no time to be longer. I find that my continuance in town will be something beyond what I expected, for I was in hopes of getting out the beginning of next week. Master Bossum intends to sayl next Sunday, and my brother says he has invited Mrs Wicking to dine here a Saturday. She will return to Hasting full fraught with all the wonders she has seen.

I dined yesterday at the Duke of Richmond's where there were 27 Sussex gentlemen, amongst the rest, the Duke of Newcastle, Earl of Wilmington, Lord Abergaveny, Lord Ossulston, who is the Earl of Tankerville's son.[1] The entertainment vastly splendid, and served all in plate, dishes and all, and a fine desert. There were 24 footmen waiting at table, and as he is master of the horse to the king, 16 of them in the king's livery and the rest in his own, which is very handsom. In short, the dinner, side board, desert and grandeur, surpassed almost everything I ever saw, and the house vastly rich finished. We tarried till 12 a clock dining at half an hour after 4. Jemmy came here this morning for to stay, the election of the school being over. I have got your patterns of shagreen but not the things from Mrs Elcock. The Parliament continue sitting but how long is something uncertain. I find they have done everything, except the Scotch bill about Captain Porteous's affair.[2]

1 London residence of the Duke of Richmond, Vanbrugh Castle, Greenwich, rented 1730s (McCann xxviii).

2 Captain John Porteous, Edinburgh town guard, found guilty by the Court of Justiciary of ordering his soldiers to fire on a mob opposing the execution of a smuggler, September 1736. Six of the mob killed and several wounded. Porteous held in Edinburgh tolbooth awaiting outcome of his appeal; Queen Caroline, as regent, granted a stay of execution, but the mob stormed the tolbooth and killed Porteous at the site of the original shooting, 7 September 1736. In response, Parliament passed two Acts, 10 Geo. II c. 35 'An Act for the more effectual bringing in to justice any persons concerned in the barbarous murder of Captain John Porteous, and punishing such as shall knowingly conceal any of the said offenders', and c. 34 'An Act to disable the Provost of Edinburgh from holding office again' (Shaw 1999 69-70; W Ferguson *Scotland 1689 to the Present* 144-6; H T Dickenson & K Logue 'The Porteous Riot: A Study of the Breakdown of Law and Order in Edinburgh 1736-37' *Journal of the Scottish Labour History Society* vol. 10 (1976) 21-40; Rapin vol. 20, 336-43; *Gentleman's Magazine* 1736, reprints the trial of Porteous before Lords of Justiciary, 514-22, 549-550; *SL* vol. 6, 1737, 289).

177 To Mary Collier, Hastings, from John Collier, [Johnson's Court], 24 May 1737 [SAY 1702]

I had Dely's letter yesterday, and thereby the satisfaction of hearing you was well, and designed going to Battell, and as it mentioned nothing of Morris hope he is on recovery, for I was really much concerned for him. I am very uncertain about coming out of town and cannot tell anything more of it till tomorrow, however, would have George come with the horses to Tunbridge a Fryday and wait there till I come; for as my sister is going down to Sevenoake I have made her a complement of carrying her in a chaise, and as Jemmy Collier is here for the holydayes with his uncle, could doe no less; besides any coming out of town is so very uncertain that I can't take earnest for the coach, and George not having the smallpox is very inconvenient.

Jemmy had new cloaths against his birthday, and at his own desire has a paduswoy wastcoat with silver lace.[1] I have been at Vauxhall, where there is great improvements of the musick. The Prince of Wales was there with a party that night, but not the princess. It was last Saturday night after my letter, being a sudden motion; Mr Fuller, Coppinger, brother Cranston, self and Jemmy. My sister not a little affronted, I beleive, about it with my brother at her not going, though she had complained the whole day, and I don't know whether she yet knows the prince was there. We accidentally went with them on the water from about Westminster, and there was a musick boat with trumpets and french horns that made it very agreeable. I hope if you went to Battell you had Barnes's horse, and that you did not let Dely ride pony, for I think he is by no means a proper horse. Poor Mrs Green is very ill with the stone, but they have a gallery at the play tonight and are to come, and I beleive we are all to goe.[2] It is exceeding hot weather that I heartily wish for a return home. I shall send your headcloaths tomorrow and the girls' caps, etc.

1 Padusway waistcoat with silver lace, from Padua where centuries of silk manufacture developed a corded or cross hatch silk fabric, of various colours, popular for waistcoats, coats, breeches (*OED*).
2 24 May 1737, Drury Lane, *The Miser,* by Henry Fielding, also *The What D'ye call it,* by John Gay; King's Theatre, *Demofoonte,* an opera by Egidio Duni, (Scouten Pt 3, vol. 2, 1736-47, 674).

178 To John Collier, Hastings, from John Flower, 8 July 1737 [SAY 598]

Mr Shedwell was with me yesterday, and he cannot be att Battle marcket for he his ableaged to be with Sir Walter Parker's a Friday, and he desiers that you will send the money for the herets to Asburnham, and the money for quit rents, if you please. I tould him that for the quit rent I thought he must stay tell Mr Brien coms, if you can send the money to Ashburnham; if not, if you pleas I will pay him the ten gineys for the herets and you pay me when you see me again. If you please to lett me no by Sunday's post I will do as you pleas. I have sent Mr Shadwell's noat.

179 To Mary Collier, [Tunbridge Wells], from John Collier, [Hastings], after 17 July 1737 [SAY 2159]

My Dearest, I received your letter and am very glad you are well but much concerned that there is nobody at the Wells that you are acquainted with and to be sure it must make it very dissagreeable but hope your drinking the waters regularly will be of service to you. I think Colonel Pelham's behaviour farr from being complaisant. As to the ball I did not express my meaning for I only intended the country dances which were begun by my Lord

Howard.[1] There was trawl fish yesterday, but an hour too late for the post, and there was no rippier bought for the Wells which I was sorry for. All opportunitys of sending any shall be taken.

I hope nothing will prevent my getting back from Dover a Thursday, and then I will not fayle being with you a Fryday. We had some fish yesterday and I had two jucken killed and had some thoughts of having my sister and Mr Mead and his wife and Mrs Mason and Mr Cant and his wife in the afternoon and supper but the girles went to their aunt and she was busy a washing and could not come so the whole laid aside. Benjamin Carswell's wife is dead.[1] I heard this afternoon that Mr Worge intended to set out today after dinner for the Wells which I was pleased with. I shall expect to hear from you to Hasting next post though I shall not be at home to write to you. You must write on the back of your letter only 'post paid to Stonecrouch' and giving two pence with it. Twill come safe. My respects to all with you concludes this epistle from him that is with all possible truth my dear your most affectionate husband, my Dear, your most affectionate husband,

1. If this Lord Howard is in the Dukes of Norfolk line rather than Howard de Walden it could only be Charles of the Deepdene in Surrey and Cumberland, who became Duke, (10th) in 1777. They were immersed in country life and history. For further details of the Dukes of Norfolk, see J M Robinson, *The Dukes of Norfolk: A Quincentennial History* (1982) ch. 11. However, it is likely this was Lord Howard the son of the 1st Earl of Effingham, who is referred to in [**180**] (SAY 2160).
2. Anne Carswell, buried 17 July 1737, St Clements.

180 To Mary Collier, [Tunbridge Wells], from John Collier, [Hastings] after 17 July 1737 [SAY 2160]

My Dearest, I received your letter of Sunday noon which convinced me that you was in a sad melancholly situation and I am hearily vexed it's not in my power to make you a visit and which is utterly impracticable till the latter end of next week.[1] I am sorry I have not been able to send you some fish I have expected it every day and the white sattin and some of the small rolled tobacco lyes ready to accompany it and I hope a day or two will enable me to send it. I hope drinking the waters will be of service to you and my daughter Worge but did not think your time was to be spent as perfect invalids but along with the waters partake of the diversions and wish that some lucky incident has introduced you in some measure into company. If not as you happen to have money in your pockets you must be contented. I hope Mr Worge's business will permit him to visit you before I can but I will not delay a moment. The Earl of Effingham and his son Lord Howard and Colonel Pelham was at Battell market today.[2] The Colonel told me he saw you at chappel a Sunday. Lord Howard was he that first took out a partner in the country dances at the ball.

On my coming home tonight at 8 I found Molly at home at which I was much surprized knowing nothing of it but it's now come out that word was sent a Saturday by Lawrence the glover that she was to be sent for today, he told Morris and Morris George, and nobody else, and these 2 blockheads never took any notice to any person till today at noon. So master Ellams happening to be at home I find he and George went and she is come safe and likes Rye prodigiously. I shall school Morris tomorrow and have given the other fool his lesson. Miss Jenny Worge is at Battell with Nelly Thorpe and they came a Saturday. Mr Lushington and Brother Smith came to Battell yesterday and returned this afternoon. There was an assembly but I did not goe I heard that Mrs Rochester and the 2

Miss Eversfields were there, Mrs Hay etc. I drank tea at Mrs Thorpe's, the doctor was not at the market but Mr Hill was as I heard them two with Mr Cruttenden and Mr Frewen were to goe a tour to Rochester, with Lords etc., next Munday. I bolted it out at the tea table and found they knew nothing of the affair. Not a word about Betty Eldridge and I am sure I would not give the least distant hint but Sir Charles Eversfield was at our Sunday club and attacked Thorpe prodigious strong and swore she was the homeliest creature he ever saw and did not at all admire his tast but promised to be godfather, after my kindest respects to you and also to your two daughters, I am my dear, your faithfull friend.

1 For the season at Tunbridge Wells see L Melville *Society at Royal Tunbridge Wells in the Eighteenth Century and after* (1912) which discusses the social hierarchy under Beau Nash.
2 1st Earl of Effingham, Francis Howard, 1683-1743, his son Thomas Howard, the 2nd Earl, 1714-1763.

181 To John Collier, Hastings, from Daniel Brien, Ashburnham, 30 August 1737

[SAY 599]

Mr Lamb is now here looking over books and peapers that relate to the Earl of Ashburnham's estate; and as you have been concernd for the late lord in keeping courts and receiveing quitt rents and heirrotts for his lordship, Mr Lamb desires the favour of your company here anyday this week that is most convenient for you; and bring what accounts and peapers with you as may sattisfie him what hath been done, and what is further to be done for the advantage of the present lord.

182 To Mary Collier, Hastings, from John Collier, [Johnson's Court], 17 November 1737

[SAY 1703]

I presume George got last night to Hasting, by whom you had an account of our journey to Sen'oak, and I now acquaint you that we arrived safe here yesterday about 3 a clock. The box did not come till 6, and when I went to open it was not a little vexed about the key, and was obliged to have the hinges taken of, but as you design to send the key by Bossum have not broke the lock. I observe the pipe of wine came safe, but am sorry to hear Morris's account of the turf. I hope it was only occasioned by the rain and that it will now roll again, or it will be a very unfortunate stop to the work and I don't know where any is to be had. I found my brother, sister, etc., very well and Miss Green is here, but a poor creature.

The account about the queen is so various and contradictory that puts all things in the greatest suspence.[1] Tuesday noon I heard at Tunbridge that she dyed the night before, and that a messenger had brought a letter with an account of it.[2] When I came to Sen'oak it was contradicted. On my coming to London the reports were perfectly contradictory, but the greatest number was that she was dead. This was declared a mistake in the evening, but that she was in a very dangerous condition. Early this morning an account was brought of her death, but soon contradicted, so that people are all at a stand. Upon the whole, it's beleived she is in the utmost danger and that there is only the old saying, whilst there is life there are hopes. This I had today at noon, from a gentleman that had been at St James' the whole morning. It puts a perfect damp on all publick proceedings, and the trade of mercers, woollen drapers, taylors etc, for there is no close bought, and all black cloath etc, very much advanced, particularly black silks are risen 4s a yard. I have postponed Jemmy's cloathes and likewise Dely's gown till it's reduced to a greater certainty.

There is not a distemper incident to human kind but it has been said the queen is afflected with, but the best account is that she had a rupture and they were obliged to make her undergoe an operation of her belly being cut open, and the guts put in their right place, and the danger is whither there is a mortification of the intestines. If there is she must dye with it; if not, she may recover and the melancholly symtoms are that nothing has passed through her by stool. The princesses Emelia and Carolina have been exceedingly ill with the fatigue, and the first has a sore throat with a violent inflammation, and the other has been thought so low, as to be in very great danger of her life. There are various accounts likewise of the queen's being taken; but they generally say that she had walked too much a Wednesday morning, after going out of a very warm room, and drank some ice water. It's also said that it was not discovered that she had a rupture till they were puting blisters upon her thighs for her fever, and that she was so modest as not to discover it till it was observed by the doctors, etc. I hope per next post to give you a more agreeable account.

Postscript half an hour after 9. Delayed sealing my letter in expectation of more news about the queen but hear none in particular.

1 For Queen Caroline's illness see Hervey vol. 2, 9 November 1737; Egmont vol. 2, 442-3.

2 John Collier passed through Stonecrouch and reached Tunbridge on the 15 November, and Sevenoaks on the 16th (SAY 1418 f. 53v).

183 To Mary Collier, Hastings, from John Collier, [Johnson's Court], 19 November 1737 [SAY 1704]

I received your letter by this day's post; I have no manner of objection to what you have done with with the evergreens that were in the parlour garden, nor displeased with anything you direct in our present works. I am sorry poor Molly is so ill, but I hope the lengthening of the days and spring will contribute to a recovery. My brother Jemmy and I did not forget an observation on the conjunction of Jupiter and the moon and it happened to be a fine evening for the purpose.[1] Jemmy is gone to write you a letter; what it will contain I don't know. Today has been a very raw, cold, wet and uncomfortable day, and sadly unpleasant to be out of doors. I had this post a handsom letter from Davis that married Mrs Evers, which I this post answer.[2]

The town is still in great suspense about her Majesty; it puts an entire stop to all manner of cloaths, and I have not ordered any for Jemmy, nor Dely's gown to be made up. It's generally thought she is still in a very dangerous condition.[3] Her behaviour has been vastly extolled, behaving with some chearfulness and an entire resignation. The king has shewed all the concern that was possible for a man to doe, and indeed the whole family. The 11th she took leave of all her daughters and the duke in a very particular manner. I have not seen the Duke of Newcastle or any of that family, for he lives and lyes at the palace and is constantly with the king. I shall not at present enlarge my epistle but only with giving my humble service to all friends. I have ordered 6 sugar loaves of a sort, and a hundred of raisins of the sun, the new ones being come in, and on the best enquiry I can make they are best for wine. Smyrna raisins are esteemed good, but there will be none this year. Gave Mr Rowe the note on the other side, the inclosed note is for my brother to sign and return, [*no longer attached*] but only with giving my humble service to all friends, and assuring you that I am my dearest, your faithful husband.

1 The connection between emotional well-being and recovery deriving from the conjunction of Jupiter and the moon was long established in astrology.
2 Theodosia Evans of Hastings married Richard Davis of Ewhurst, 26 August 1737.
3 The *GSJ* 17 November 1737 reported that Caroline was attended by the doctors and surgeons Ranby, Dickens, Amyard, Shipton and Bussiere, adding that her Majesty also saw the Prince of Wales.

184 To Mary Collier, Hastings, from John Collier, [Johnson's Court], 22 November 1737. [SAY 1705]

I presume before this reaches your hands you will have heard a certainty of the queen's death, which happened Sunday night about ten or eleven of the clock.[1] She was thought to be dead about 3 in the morning, having no pulse, or hardly discerned to breathe, but she then revived, but without a possibility of recovery. She was sensible all the morning, and took speechless about 2 in the afternoon. There is a very great concern shewn by all ranks of people, and I have not heard one indecent or reproachful word on the occasion. The king has during her whole ilness shewn the greatest regard and tenderness, in a manner, as they say, not to be expressed. The Prince of Wales did not see her; he sent a message to the king, who thereupon advised with all the physicians, and they gave their opinion that considering her weak and dangerous condition, they were afraid of the consequences of such an interview, so that the king returned a civil answer to the prince, and gave that for a reason and as the opinion of all the physicians.

There are various discourses about her infirmity, and some of the surgeons say, if she had at first made a discovery of it, in good probability she might have done well. It's also said that the king insisted upon her telling it to the surgeons, otherwise it had been not been known so soon. The king and the two eldest princesses are very much indisposed, particularly the princess Caroline, and the young duke is confined to his bed and has a fever. When the physicians and surgeons were of opinion that it was absolutely necessary for her Majesty to undergoe an operation, the king addressed himself to the surgeons and begged they would use her tenderly. Mr Bussiere answered that though they had all the respect possible to her Majesty, in her situation they must act as they would to any other woman, to which the king said he could only repeat his request and begg it as far as possible.[2]

The order of mourning is not come out that people are uncertain, but it is not thought so material for persons in the country, the order being only confined to the court. But as it is thought that unwatered tabies will be generally wore for night gowns for those that don't buy dressed suits, and multitudes are bought, and that the best will be soon gone,[3] I have this afternoon ordered enough for a gown for you, and let Dely's alone till I have your orders. And as to linnen, it is at present suspended for you and Dely.

I went yesterday to Greenwich in a coach about business and took Jemmy with me. It was a delightful day. I just called upon Mrs Dansay, the captain not being at home she is very brisk but looks sadly, the bloom being all over. I am sorry for poor Sansum. I will do anything I reasonably can for Geery; but as to my brother Cruttenden, though I wish he was provided for, it's impossible I can now do anything for him, and he well knows my interest is engaged for my brother Smith, though I don't know how it will come out. I can't see the Duke of Newcastle and all are in a hurry. I was this day with his brother 2 hours and could hardly get away. Great part of the discourse was on the melancholly occasion, but I don't find there is any the least doubt but that affairs will continue in the same hands in all respects.

I hope that the people will be able to goe on with the work and that they can be supplyed with turf, and think you did right to bottle of the remainder of the strong beer. I expected Jemmy would have wrote to his [4] uncle last post or this, but I find it is to be a Latin epistle and not finished. I desire, my dear, you will let me have your directions about mourning, but I thought best to buy the gown. I am a little hoarse but have no great cough, and Jemmy is very well and with me for I have not had time to goe to Dr Nicholls. Inclosed is a Grub street elergy for Molly and Jenny. Keep the frank.

1 Queen Caroline died at 11p.m., Sunday 20 November 1737, (Egmont vol. 2, 445; Hervey vol. 2, chs. 38-40). The details of her demise were reported on 24 November by *GSJ* which added a short biography, and the issue for 1 December 1737 states that 500 gns was granted to each doctor, and 300 gns to each surgeon; *PS* January 1738 published the cause of death as a 'mortification of the bowels', which issue also printed the eulogy on her death, the official account of the funeral which took place on 17 December 1737 in King Henry VIII's chapel, Westminster Abbey, the words of the Anthem by Handel, performed with 80 vocalists and 100 instruments, as well as 'a moral essay on the death of her Majesty', and see Deutsch 442-4.

2 Paul Bussiere, Huguenot doctor, favoured by members of the royal family and aristocracy.

3 Tabi, Japanese cotton stocking, usually white, with separate toes; for mourning dress the ladies to wear black silk, plain muslin or long lawn, crape hoods, black glazed gloves, black silk shoes and to carry black paper fans, stockings black or dark grey unwatered tabies.

4 MS *brother* struck through.

185 To Mary Collier, Hastings, from John Collier, [Johnson's Court], 24 November 1737[1] [SAY 1706]

I had your letter by the post, and Jemmy writes a Latin epistle to his uncle that accompanys this. As I have been obliged to be almost every day at the Custom house I really have not seen Westminster, nor consequently Dr Nicholls so Jemmy remains with me. The regulating of mourning is in all the newspapers where you will of course see it, and therefore forbear taking any notice thereof. I shall expect by next post your directions on the affair. I find my sister bought a mantua silk for herself. The princess Caroline continues very ill. The queen's death and the necessary discourse thereon and of mourning engages all conversation, and by the talk and behaviour of all people there is shewn a very great concern, and appears in a decent handsom manner. If you send up anything on the occasion presume it will come by next carrier. I write this in hast.

1 This date is suggested by Sayer vol. 1, 137.

186 To Mary Collier, Hastings, from John Collier, [Johnson's Court], London, 26 November 1737 [SAY 1707]

I received your letter by this post, and think it very surprizing that you did not hear of the queen's death before my letter came, especially as it was your fair day. I shall give my sister directions about your's and Dely's cloaths in the manner you desire and speak to Mrs Elcock, but I don't find shammy gloves are worn by anybody but a full dress.[1] The mourning was at first appointed as tomorrow, but is postponed till the Sunday following. I cannot at present form to myself anytime of returning home, but if you want any money

Mr Rowe has received some for me, from whence you'l take as you please. I think Sir Charles Eversfield hath had very good fortune in the lottery,[2] but I have heard nothing of it in town. I beleive Jemmy will goe to school the beginning of next week, for I have been with Dr Nicholls, who gives him a very good and handsom character.

The queen is the subject of all publick conversation; when she received the sacrament the archbishop of Canterbury told her she must not be offended at asking her a question, which was, whether she had forgiven the Prince of Wales, which she said, she did with all her soul.[3] The princess Caroline is in a very ill state of health, and as she was amongst the rest attending on her Majesty, and shewing a great concern, the queen said, poor Caroline, you will not be long after me.

The queen sent a message to the king by one of the ladyes in waiting, for form sake, to desire his Majesty's pleasure, whether he gave her leave to make a will, though they say she had a right to doe it. He answered, by all means, deny her nothing, and after her death, when the councell and her attendants were summoned, the king commanded it to be read, but before it was a quarter gone through he quitted the room, directing they should keep on. The day she dyed she asked one of the doctors how long he thought she might live: he told her Majesty, but a little time. She answered with a perfect resignation, she was prepared and death would be welcom to her. Thus I give you little accounts of the talk of the world, but I have it not from bad hands, nor from any persons extreamly attached to the family in a near relation, or dependance. I begin to be weary of the town and desire to return but am afraid it will be sometime first. Bossum is not yet arrived, at least I have not seen or heard from him. I think it is more handsom for you to ask Rowe for money on my account, than to give any directions therein.

1 Shammy gloves, soft, pliable, leather.

2 10 Geo II c. 16, 1737, the 'old' Westminster Bridge lottery Act, authorised collection of £700,000; after payment of the prize tickets residue to be applied to build Westminster Bridge. Should sufficient not be raised, George II could incorporate the trustees after 29 September 1737: they were not allowed to discount bills of exchange, or take up lending under six months, though when trustees converted to Commissioners they might borrow on the credit of the Act. Work on the bridge began 13 September 1738 and completed November 1750.

3 Queen Caroline, deathbed views on, and refusal to see the Prince of Wales whilst he 'conversed with the king's enemies' (Egmont vol. 2 443-4; Hervey vol. 2, 519). Dr John Potter, archbishop of Canterbury, previously the bishop of Oxford, pro-government, 'pious and eminently learned' (Egmont vol. 2 323).

187 To Mary Collier, Hastings, from John Collier, [Johnson's Court], 29 November 1737 [SAY 1708]

Jemmy went to Mr Chelsum's a Sunday evening in order for school a Munday, I having been with Dr Nicholls a Fryday. I have much repented, from his averseness of going, his staying at home so long, for it was never talked of but he was a very mope; and it really gave me concern, though I never gave him one harsh word about it. But a Sunday morning talked it a little over and let him know I saw his unwillingness, but at the same time and always assured him that he should not be abridged anything. I told him to come this evening which he has not as yet done.

I am sorry you think Hasting so desolate a place, and your so often repeating it makes me imagine you are unfortunate in being there. For my part I should with satisfaction spend the remainder of my days there without seeing any other, and I can't at all agree with you in the politeness of our two neighbouring towns. I have seen nothing of Bossom or about Dely's shooe. Her cloaths was bought yesterday and inclosed is the bill, as also of the china and I shall buy my brother's milk pot. If you don't think proper to ask Rowe about money, as I best remember in the lowest books in my study, in the middle partition, there is a book with white leaves, and wrote upon the leaves Co: Litt.,[1] behind him is some money, and you will take what you please.

1 It is unclear which edition of Edward Coke's works was in John Collier's library: Coke's, *The First Part of the Institutes of the Lawes of England, or a Commentarie upon Littleton* (1629) ran to twelve editions by 1738; *Synopsis and an exact abridgement of the Lord Coke's commentaries upon Littleton* (1652) ran to several editions; early in Collier's legal career came William Hawkins edition of the abridgement (1711).

188 To Mary Collier, Hastings, from John Collier, [Johnson's Court], 3 December 1737. [SAY 1709]

I this post received your two letters, that which should have come a Thursday as well as today, and as the postmark is the same imagine there may have been some neglect at Hasting in carrying it to the post or putting into the bagge. I remember I mentioned something about your complaint of Hasting, but did not imagine it could have occasioned any uneasiness, much less be construed as a reprimand, not being any way in the least so intended. As to Jemmy, I own his behaviour and silent unwillingness to goe to school was then very recent in my memory, and I assure you cost me some tears, but I hope my last letter cleared up that affair to you. I forbear giving any answer to that part of your letter where you intimate that you have of late had the misfortune not to please, and only say I know no instances.

I think it odd that Mr Rowe should say he had but little money in his hands, for at last Battell market I paid the mayor's fee farm rents and gave him to collect it, which is near £25. All my tickets are come up, and amongst them a twenty pound prize, so that I shall loose or pay towards building the bridge about eleven shillings. I am not as yet certain how Mr Sansum's place will be disposed of, but am satisfyed Captain Moore will not have it.[1] I have insisted on my promise for Tom Smith and the same has been strongly seconded by Lord Wilmington, but there is a powerful opposition from Mr Butler etc., also founded on a promise, but mine is years before his. My brother Smith sent his son on purpose last Tuesday, ten days after Sansum had been dead, which ruffled me much as not signifying anything, and, to crown all, sent a silly letter to my Lord Wilmington which he was very angry with and indeed has great reason as well as the behaviour of the son, though I still beleive he will stand strong.

Tomorrow all this world appear in mourning. Several mantua makers have more than a hundred women employed, and work night and day, sleeping every 3 hours by turns. I hope I shall send yours and Dely's cloaths per next carrier. Miss Green went home this morning in Grinsted stage coach by her father's orders, for he was sent to about mourning and would not allow her any the most cheap that could be bought.

I do assure you that it's impossible any person can have a greater love or inviolable respect for another than I have for you, and am not conscious to myself of any actions that have not demonstrated it. I will not pretend to account for every word or expression of my life; but hurry, dissappointments, heat, or I don't know what, may ruffle me, and I don't know a mortal totally exempt. I begin to be impatient in tarrying in town and yet can't at present propose any time of returning. I know my respect is perfect and sincere and have always had the pleasure of thinking it reciprocal, and that is all it's possible for me to wish. Most sad, rainy, and black, dismal weather of late, except today.

1 William Sansom, freeman 1730, Customs riding officer, Bexhill, buried St Clement's 22 November 1737; replaced 1738 by Thomas Smith a cousin of John Collier (TNA CUST 18/190 f. 20).

189 To Mary Collier, Hastings, from John Collier, [Johnson's Court], 6 December 1737

[SAY 1710]

I am still in suspence as to the time I shall be able to get out of London, but at present hope it will be sometime next week; and that by next post or Saturday I shall send an account for my horses, but am satisfyed, at all events, it will be the latter end of next week before I can propose to be at home. I hope I shall be able to send your cloaths by tomorrow's carrier, but though all faithfully promised to be at home tonight nothing is yet come, being 8 a clock, except your gown which came last week, but I shall send to all tomorrow and endeavour at fending them. Last Sunday all the pulpits had funeral sermons. Dr Bundy's a very good one on the text, let me dye the death of the righteous, etc., but did not say anything particular, but left the application to the audience.[1] I shall buy you some powder as you desire, and will send down by James Bossum 3 quarters of pale malt, some flower potts etc. I am very glad you think Molly is better.

1 Dr Richard Bundy, Canon of Westminster, pubd. 24 August 1732, Prebendary of Westminster, died 27 January, 1739, succeeded by Thomas Hayter (Richard Bundy, *Sermons on Several Occasions, with a course of lectures on the Church Catechism* 2 vols (1740))

190 To Mary Collier, Hastings, from John Collier, [Johnson's Court], 8 December 1737

[SAY 1711]

With a great deal of plague and attendance I got your things to the carrier yesterday afternoon, though I was not a little provoked at the things not coming in according to promise. I think the shoos looked very clumsily made, and are black callemanco, but that is my sister's direction. Dely's lipsalve is in the box and some writings that you'll take care of. I am not certain when I shall return, but at present desire, if my next letter don't contradict it, that George sets out next Wednesday morning, very early, and reaches Sen'nock that night, and stays there till I come to him. Let him ride the grey horse and bring the old mare for me.

I received your letter and am very sorry for Mrs Geery, and to be sure, her situation is very dangerous. Jemmy was here a Tuesday but I did not see him being out all day at the Custom house. I have no particular newes to write you and much want to leave London. The head cloaths I brought up is not given to Mrs Elcock, and I desire by next post you'l let me know whither I am to give it her, or not, and whether you want anything else to be bought, because I hope I shall not stay in town long enough to receive from you but one letter more. Dr Hammond with Mr Wicking was at the coffee house this evening. I told him I would drink a glass of wine any other night but this. He says he was in company with Miss Cotterell, one of Dely's school mates, and asked much after her when she heard he had been at Hasting. Mr Wicking brought me the musick books tonight in which he says is charming cloe, but too late to send per the carrier.[1] The queen's funeral obsequies are fixed for Saturday sen'night. The marble urn is made large enough for two, the king commanding it, to be interred in the same. It's impossible a greater respect can be paid to a person's memory, as they say, than he does, he held her by the hand when she dyed, and she spoke almost to the last breath.

1 Thomas Gladwin, music, Mr Jersey, words, *Charming Cloe* appeared in Ms. London, 1730, published in *Calliope or English harmony: A Collection of English and Scottish songs* (London) 1739-40.

191 To Mary Collier, Hastings, from John Collier, [Johnson's Court], 10 December 1737 SAY 1712]

I received Dely's letter and think it handsom and well wrote. I hope the box came safe with your cloaths. I have not the least objection to your brewing with sweetlove's malt for Bossum's may be used hereafter. I have sent some currants, jarr raisins and spices by Bossum, also a peice of a collar of brawn and two rands of sturgeon.[1] There is also a box with paper, knives and forks, and some flower pots and walking sticks, and colours and oyle.

I am quite weary of absence from you and hate the place I am confined to, and though I cannot ascertain the day I can get out, desire the horses may be sent a Wednesday to Sen'nock pursuant to my last letter. I find Jemmy has a strong inclination to walk in the procession of the queen's funeral in a surplice as a king's schollar, and I believe I shall consent. We have sad inclement weather in town. Sansum's place remains in suspence; I hope I may have it, but let it be otherwise have taken true paines.

Since writing the within letter I came home and found Mrs Nouns with my sister, and though I shewed her Dely's letter, she had forgot to give her service, so I did it myself, and she expressed herself very handsomly. We had a little run of politicks, but I told her I would leave it till Dely and she met. Mary Edborough I find was here a Thursday to desire I would get her husband a place, hearing I had some to dispose of at Whitehall. So I am afraid it is poorish. Jemmy is come tonight very well. I send Dely a song you desired, in return for her letter; there is no *Craftsman*, the whole impression being seized last night.[2] The papers are universally condemned for the reflections on the queen or any the least appearance thereof.

1 Rand, a strip or slice, often with reference to fish, about an ell in length *(OED*).

2 *Craftsman* magazine founded and edited by Nicholas Amhurst, financial support from William Pulteney, Lord Bolingbroke and their circle, caused difficulties for government during the Excise bill, opposed the foreign policy of Walpole and Pelham; circulation of 10-12,000. In July 1737 Amhurst was gaoled by the government for publishing a letter claimed to be written by Colley Cibber, the poet laureate, suggesting that the Acts for licensing plays, 10 Geo II c. 19, and 10 Geo II c. 28, by which the Lord Chamberlain could prohibit any new play, should be extended to old plays as well, adding that a good deal in Shakespeare could be seen as seditious, and suggesting that Colley Cibber should be the licenser and corrector of old plays. Amhurst died in poverty, abandoned by Pulteney when the opposition circle moved closer to Walpole; (*ODNB*; Williams 1945 397).

192 To John Collier, Hastings, from Robert Burnett, Dallington, 18 December 1737. [SAY 392]

I wass yesterday favoured with yours of the14th and am much obleagd to you for it but am very sorry for the disapointment you mett with aughter all the pains you have taken for us. I wass very much in hopes, by what Mr Forbes wrote me word, of that you would have brought it to some conklewsion, which I feind you wass not able to accomplish. But be that as it will, I am shoore for my own part I am very thenkefull for the pains you have taken; and I doubt not but the rest of us who are concernd in it must be the same, and I dare say will joyne with me in earnastly requesting of you to continew your good offices till it can be brought to a hapy conklewsion. I have wrote to Mr Johnson today to inform him of the purport of your letter which I am shoore will be a great disapointment to him as well as my selfe.

I have just received an express that Mr Pelham of Stamer is dead.[1] I gues he died this morning. I sett out early tomorrow for Lewes where I sopose we must live in a burgising way till the Parliament meets. I fear whilst you wass in town nobody thought of mentioning to you my lord duke's presant to the poore of your corporation att Christmas; that time is drawing near.[2] I hope Mr Palmer will send the wheat according to custom, and I beg you will dispose of the money for my lord duke as usuall. I shall write to Mr Palmer to send the wheat. I hope this will feind you safely arived in the country and in perfect health, that you may long continew so are the sincear wishes of. Your taking no notice about the lease for the severall parcles of land which I am tennant for to the honourable Mr Pelham makes me fear it has slipt your memory or Mr Pelham has not signd it.

1 Thomas Pelham of Stanmer. For his accounts see Appendix 4: Pelham estate **[607]** SAY 372.
2 Duke of Newcastle, presented grain and money to the people of Hastings at Christmas; paid for by John Collier, followed by a lengthy and tedious recovery from the duke.

193 To John Collier, Hastings, from William Cranston, [Johnson's Court], 29 December 1737. [SAY 731]

Fuller v Wood. I shall tomorrow lodge an eligit as well in Sussex as the port, which will affect the goods as well as the land, though the first only from the time of the delivery, and the latter from the day judgement was signed, which was the 23 October.

I went with Jemmy Tuesday morning to Greenwich and took your advice about a coach.[1] I got there about ten, went to the Greyhound and laid a foundation and ordered dinner at 4. From thence went to Whiter's and with him and Messrs Simmons and Clarke; went first to Blackheath and viewed the estate there, which, though so lately built, seems to be but in a miserable condition and repairs wanting already; a little of which absolutely necessary to be forthwith done I then ordered. Two of those three houses are tenanted, the other empty; the peice of ground adjoining to it is about 4 acres, but a miserable soil and the rent 30s is really as much as tis worth; here I received £1. From thence I went to the sandpitt, surveyed that and the peice of ground in dispute, and unless the opposite side have a title under [2] the same person from whom Dunmoll claims it cannot belong to them for the ground now confesedly his and that in dispute, was most certainly all one formerly.

I then surveyed Swinburn and Wilby's houses. The first is a tolerably good one from the beginning; the other was at first but indifferent, but has since been altered and is now convenient excepting as to dismall smoaking chimneys and which was principally occasioned by the late amendments to it. And as I was an eye witness to their truth of their complaint, I took upon me to order an amendment by raising them higher which I beleive will answer the end. I then viewed the meadow ground which consist of two peices and is called 6a, but think there can't be so much. I afterwards had the horses appraised which was done at £33 6s 0d, then the carts and harness which came to £8 8s 0d, total £41 14s for these were appraised before with the things in the garden, so consequently no knowing what anything in particular was worth.

After this we two adjourned for an hour to the Greyhound and soon after dinner the chaps followed us. Swinburn I partly agreed with for his 10 acres of garden and house at £31 10s for when twas let at £40 the marsh was into it; and forbid the partnership from that day, and ordered an appraisement to be made of the goods and tackle in trade, and of the woods etc., in the ground, distinguishing what was there at Michaelmas day and what since, which I am to have next Monday when Swinburn is to be here and settle his accounts. And the whole money due upon that as well as the stock, etc., is forthwith to be paid down, and he commence tenant from Xmas.

Simmons was my next chap, who much wants the whole, but am glad that neither you, nor Mrs Hickes comes into it, for upon a more strict inquiry I am satisfyed he is good for nothing. So he stands as he did before, only the half of the sandpitt at 6d per load, and I shall draw up a proper agreement forthwith. He seemed much disgusted at the preference given to Whiter and talked of parting with his lease of half the wharfe upon a consideration. I told him that if that was his inclination and he would make proposalls, I would recommend em to Mrs Hickes, for am satisfyed twould be best for the estate that he had nothing to do with it. But when I saw him next morning he seemed to be off that part of it his story.

Whiter came next, to whom I agreed to lett the other halfe of the sandpitt upon the same terms with Simmons, and to sell him the horses etc., for which he was to pay ready money as also what was due from him upon his account to this time, which were are also to settle next Monday. He is also to hire the marsh land for which I ask 50s per acre, but he seems to think that too much however beleive he will give it. He also proposes to take the house he now lives in and the stables, but does not care to continue it an alehouse for my part I don't see any advantage a little dirty alehouse is to the estate, but I would undertake as to that without Mrs Hickes consent. I don't doubt but in a little time things may be put in a good method and the estate bring in some money, for which purpose I would do all in my power.

Farrin was not in the way but left a letter for him and as he often comes to town shall soon expect to see him. Clarke was serviceable, and as the cole was not upon him and he seemed to want it much I advanced 5 peices upon the strength of his bill of £6 odd delivered to you. Soe lay at the Greyhound all night, sat up with the gentry till near 12. Our reckoning next morning ran high, but when these present affairs are setled there will be no occasion to treat any, but things will be reduced. I fancy we must still employ …[3] to look after Simmons and Whiter as to the sand, notwithstanding their oaths, but I shan't say anything of it without your orders and this will do it in the most moderate way. Turkeys and geese came safe, thanks, a lamb came last night which I hope will so well this frosty weather.

1 This is the estate of Elizabeth Hickes, Robertsbridge, and is discussed in the following group of letters.
2 MS *Dunmoll* struck through.
3 MS word obscured by seal.

194 To John Collier, from William Cranston, [Johnson's Court], 3 January 1738
[SAY 732]

Our Greenwich account for the conveniency of all parties was put off from yesterday till tomorrow morning. Wood v Fuller. I suppose GW poped the same questions to you as to me, for I have had a reasonable modicum. You herewith receive warrants fieri facias both in Sussex and port, though before you execute em I would consider whether the land is not sufficient to pay your debt and all the mortgages; for as yours is the first judgement, you are consequently next to mortgages; for put the case the defendant should confess other judgements, yet nothing that he or any other person can do, can defeat, your judgement for the assigning over his lands in trust for creditors is nothing at all to your client. If therefore the land is sufficient, I should think it might be as well to let the goods alone, for possibly his executing the bill of sales before you are in possession may divest him of the property and put it in the trustees, but as you know the affair much better than I do you'll act as you think proper and will excuse my mentioning it. I received of Master Clarke today clear money £40 15s 8d as per a note of particulars also inclosed. [*no longer attached*]

195 To John Collier, from William Cranston, [Johnson's Court], 7 January 1738
[SAY 733]

Yours with the advertizement I received on Thursday, and which I beleive you'll see in this evening's papers, and have ordered it in also this day sennight. I made a little alteration, for in your hurry you had seemed to lodge the nobility and gentry in the stable. I wrote to Ginger about his £50 note, within a post or two after you left town, but have received no answer.

The ejectment received today I shall take care of; I had before looked over the papers in the former and I beleive for the sake of delay and to gett us time to look about us, it may not be amiss to go on in the same steps. I shall take the first oppurtunity of seeing Southwarke and the bridge. Whiter, Swinburne, Clarke and myself spent yesterday poreing over accounts, are to be together again Monday at 9 and as I'll dedicate the whole day, beleive shall get through. I have agreed to lett the marsh to Whiter at £12 per annum, which upon inquiry I find to be as much as tis worth. For the half of the wharf he is to give £3, for the house he lives in £10, and for the stables £5 per annum. The horses, etc., valued at £41 14s 0d I have sold also to Whiter for £50. The garden affairs are appraised at £47 odd, the half of which Swinborn is to pay down, and to give £31 10 per annum for his garden and house.

Whiter and his brother, etc., are to meet me next Fryday when I shall finally agree with him as above and lett him into possession of the whole, unless by Thursday's post you should disapprove of any part of our agreement. The £50 is then to be paid down as well as the ballance of his account, but this will be triffling, for though there will be something due from him at Michaelmas day last, yet his expences since have exceeded his receipts so that by what I can at present see, Mrs Hickes will loose all her sand from that time and be out of pockett into the bargain; for though Whiter has made it one account to this time yet we must certainly seperate it, for the carrying the trade since Dunmoll's death must certainly be to Mrs Hickes seperate account whether profitt or loss.

Swinburn's account is pretty misterious and he's a cunning, sharp, fellow more knave than fool; however, for the future we may manage him well enough when we have nothing to do with him but to receive his rent. The ballance from him according to the account given you comes to £18 odd, in opposition to which he has brought in a discharge amounting to just the same summe, or within a few shillings; £3 of which is for looking after the sandpitt for six weeks whilst Dunmoll and Simmons where partners in it, about 50s more is for letters; and 1s each errand he did for Dunmoll in town; and £11 17s 2d is for damages and cost he paid in an action brought against him by Simmons. As to the first item, I think he ought to be allowed it and as to the second, he shewed me abundance of nonsensicall letters from Dunmoll, with directions to go to Scrase, Rooch and twenty other people and therefore think 1s a time not unreasonable, but the main difficulty is the last summe, that affair stands there.

Simmonds and Dunmoll were originally partnerrs in the garden, but Dunmoll being tired of Simmonds in August 1735, he put Swinburn into his share of it and who was and did take the whole michaelmas following, but before that came Swinburn cut up some carrotts sown by Simmons upon which he brings an action. Dunmoll indorsed the writt, which I have seen to Rooch and promised to pay the charges, judgement was obtained by default a writt of inquiry executed and execution for £11 17s 2d which Swinburn paid. This Swinburn says Dunmoll always promised to allow him. There is a letter or two of Dunmoll's, which seems to intimate as if the suit was carryed on at his instance and at that time Swinburn was only a servant to Dunmoll in the garden. So that upon the whole I think he ought to be allowed it, but that you may judge of the affair yourself. I have inclosed what few papers relate to it, which you'll please to return me again by the return of the post with your thoughts what to do in it, for I shall deferr closing his account till I receive your orders, for which purpose I shall adjourn him from Monday to Fryday to conclude, for all but that may be done next Monday.

I wrote to Henman to know about what time Hodsell died and received a letter but yesterday, so intend to begin search in two or 3 days. I'll receive the 50 guineas draft on North. I delivered Action's note to Wagg this evening, but first took his receipt for it. I paid Ott and setled S.S. for bro before the holydays but as this letter has already run to a decent length, he'll excuse my particularizing till my next.

196 To John Collier, from William Cranston, [Johnson's Court],[1] 17 January 1738 [SAY 734]

Madam Hailstone has been with me as you may perceive by the inclosed, a smart woman! as her mother is satisfyed Holliday has no demands upon her, she does not desire a release. Bossom versus Sargent.[2] I thought that I had before acquainted you that these cost were setled at £19 and which I have received. I shall observe your directions about the Hasting affair, and do as well as I can in it, and also shall take care to pay your drafts on me.

Swinburn's accounts are drawn up and ballanced and setled, that is by me only, but he makes such objections as are very unreasonable, and can by no means come into, having allowed everything that he had the least shew of pretence to, and in order to bring him to reason Master Clarke has an ejectment to deliver to him, which I beleive is done by this time,and fancy that will make him come to. He was debitor to Dunmoll on the 30 Sep.

£24 6s 9d and Mrs Hickes was debitor to him on 24 December £1 13s so he is to pay £22 13s 9d.

Whiter's account is also fixt,vizt Dunmoll on the 30 Sep. 1737 was debitor to him £18 12s 10d, and Whiter is indebted to Mrs Hickes from that time to 14 January £40 19s 11d, so he is to pay £22 7s 1d.[3] I have received the £50 for the horses and am to have the ballance this week. He commenced yesterday morning upon his own bottom and consequently Mrs Hicks left off. The particulars of these accounts are very long, in the distinguishing them, all the bills which were owing at Dunmoll's death, though paid since are put to his account and that makes Dunmoll debiter to Whiter at Michaelmas not that he really was so, but the paying a great deal since, which was due before, makes it to be so. I've had a deal of plague about it and am glad tis so farr over, and have settled it entirely to my own satisfaction, and hope twill be so also to yours and Mrs Hickes when you come to peruse it.

1 [*Reverse*] William Cranston's account of Mrs Hickes affairs at Greenwich 17 January 1737.

2 Bossom v Serjeant, Kingston, Surrey Assizes, plaintiff's damages 1d, costs 40/-, Attorney, William Cranston (TNA ASSI 34/5 Surrey Assizes). Reference to receipt in King's Bench 3 November 1737 from Bodysher Sparrow, assistant to William Cranston.

3 John Dunmoll, of Tunbridge Wells, was Elizabeth Hickes' brother, so for purposes of these accounts they are the same party.

197 To John Collier, [Hastings], from William Cranston, [Johnson's Court], 26 January 1738 [SAY 735]

Your bills came safe to hand which I shall receive the first oppurtunity. I shall take care to get your returns to the elegitts fixed and entered upon the roll regularly, and then nothing remains but to bring an ejectment to recover the possession; and if any prior mortgages should be sett up, then to a court of equity to pay off, etc., Jeake gave me a long detail of last Fryday's proceedings which was very agreable. I intend to wait on Lord Westmorland tomorrow with some exceptions to defendant's answer, and also to know what he intends to do in the petition about upper levells commissicon, for Frewen is to be here next Tuesday, and if anything is to be done it should be set about forthwith.

I should have some account of the value of Dunmoll's house and furniture for I have a little chap that plagues me daily about it. I had drawn a bill against Ginger but he came Saturday evening, sets up a counter demand and did promise to let me have it as yesterday but failed; so if don't hear from him by Saturday evening shall go to work with my bill Monday morning. He seems to be a slippery chap I've really not had time to search after Hadsoll's will, for Wilson was all day last Wednesday seeing Carr hanged; got such a cold, etc., by it has not been out of bed since.[1] A nurse, phisician and apothecary attends him, and I doubt will pay his life for his curiosity tis a sad disappointment to me. Expect Tod Green up tomorrow to assist, for whom I wrote last Saturday, seeing then no hopes of Wilson this terme.

I have sent twice after North for his 50 guineas, tis a day's journey, once was not at home, a second time was, was just going to dinner; insisted upon Sparrow's staying till twas over, words arose, ill mannerly jeers upon you and me, Sparrow afronted! Came away without. Q. shall I go again and is it any affair upon which he may be served with a writt, for he is a most saucy, impertinent fellow, and twould be no small pleasure to make him bring it to me as well as to pay for his rudeness. I've paid Bayly £100 as appears by the inclosed. I charge 6s 8d Collett lives in Well Close Square at least 3 miles from hence, and sent twice; you know by what channell the inclosed warrant come.

1 Robbery of William Quarrington of a gold ring set with diamonds and money, 9 September 1737; Quarrington withdrew £100 from the Bank of England, and was killed in the course of a robbery in the Angel and Crown tavern, Temple Bar, by six assailants led by Thomas Car, gent., an attorney who had served out his clerkship, and kept chambers in Elm Court, Temple; Car's girlfriend Elizabeth Adams was among the gang. Trial 12 October 1737, all assailants sentenced to death. Car buried in Covent Garden, Adams in St Andrew Holborn. (Old Bailey online t1737 1012-3, OA 1738 0118).

198 To John Collier, Hastings, from William Cranston, [Johnson's Court], 28 January 1738. [SAY 736]

I was with Lord Westmorland yesterday. He thinks as Tom Frewen is coming to town and the upper levells commission intended soon to be taken out, that no time ought to be lost in sending up the petition which was agreed upon at the last sessions of sewers;[1] and by this post by his direction have wrote to the cardinalls to the same purpose.

There's a strong quarrell at Greenwich come to me fresh this afternoon. Simmons has locked up the wharf and won't let Whiter come in with his cart, etc. I have look over the lease etc, and find the moiety still belongs to us, upon which I have given Whiter an authority under my hand, in the name of Mrs Hickes, to breck open, etc., and so from time to time as he shall be obstructed, and for so doing have promised to stand by him. And in order to chastise Simmons for his insolency have given him warning under hand that if he presumes to go upon the sandpitt and get any more sand I'll sue both him and his servants. I am sure he has not the least pretence to go there without leave and am also certain that we can upon the wharf as we please. I don't know whether it may not be a good oppurtunity to get entirely ridd of him as to the sand, for I never liked him, and in the next vacation there will be an oppurtunity fully to look into his affairs and to make sum lid of em. The new sherriffe of S was sworn in this day, so return me the warrant with Carsingham.[2]

1 For Commission of sewers see Dugdale; S & B Webb *English Local Government from the Revolution to the Municipal Corporations Act* vol. 4, *Statutory Authorities for Special Purposes* (1922) 33ff; for Romney Marsh see H Ellis 'Commissions of Sewers for the Lewes levels' *SAC* 10, 1858.

2 John Payne, 12 January 1738 sworn into office as sheriff of Sussex for the regnal year 12 Geo. 2; sheriffs regulated as to fees and passing accounts, 3 Geo I c 15., and 3 Geo I c. 16. Sussex sheriffs to receive £90 5s a year, and sheriffs not required to pay the costs of passing their accounts (*SL* vol. 5, 148-63). For Sussex sheriffs by regnal year see Berry 1830 x-xi.

199 To John Collier, Hastings, from William Cranston, Johnson's Court, 2 February 1738 [SAY 737]

In answer to Dunmoll's affair, I have found out Hodsoll's will, a copy of which I shall have from the commons tomorrow.[1] I have Scrase and have told him of it, who upon sight of it will confess himself satisfyed, and the money will then be forthwith paid. Ginger gave me the slip. I wrote him last post that if the account was not setled, and ballance paid by Saturday night, I would Monday morning file the bill against him. Farrin I received a letter from his day who has appointed Tuesday morning next peremptoly to settle and pay the ballance.

The affairs at Greenwich are all subsided. Simmons has been here and submitted and cryed peccavi, his affair may be looked into at more leisure for am satisfyed we may turn clear and therefore will settle with him what is due, which may be paid as is convenient. The other dower of Pope, who is in possession, I think is very doubtfull. I have looked over the pleadings in Chancery and really think Dunmoll has made a good case for equity, and shall advise Mrs Hicks at least to take an opinion whether tis proper to revive, to be sure Dunmoll could not help failing at common law, and the matter of the dissolving the injunction, which let her into actuall possession, appears to be more a slip of the solicitor and default in pushing on the cause than from the meritts of it. The estate was bought in Mr Hickes name in trust for Dunmoll; Hickes two daughters, Boys and Mercer, and their husbands joined in a conveyance to Dunmoll with a fine.[2] The caption is in the deed, consequently the fine never passed, sure it should be done, for the title is not clear without it. I'll see the bridge houses in a day or two.

I 'll send Lord Westmoreland in a day or two, I know as little of his thoughts about the petition as you do, and had his directions to express myself just as I did. If Captain Thompson's ticketts come up a Monday, they'll be soon enough to accompany yours, etc. Is there anybody and who and where to be found to shew Dunmoll's house at the Wells?

Bossum v Sargent, entering cause, £0 12s 0d; to councill with brief, £4 4s 0d; to their mes, £0 3s 6d; court fees, £1 13s 0d; and if not too much; attend at the assizes, £2 2s 0d.

Michaelmas 1727, rule on postea, 2s returning and entering £0 5s 0d; drawing judgement, etc., 7s: entring 3s: doggett $^{1}/_{8}$, £0 1s 08d; affidavit of extra expence, £0 4s 0d; tax cost and attend 7s 4d, capiatur fine 6s 8d, £0 14s 0d, clerks' fees, £0 1s 8d. [*sum*] £10 10s 10d

1 College of Civilians, known as Doctors Commons, courts under jurisdiction of civil law, high court of Admiralty, court of Delegates, Arches court of Canterbury, Prerogative court of Canterbury; the College held a large archive for civil concerns (*EB 1771* vol. 2, 221)

2 Dudley Ryder, Attorney General. For his opinion on the case of Mrs Martha Boys, daughter of Mrs Elizabeth Hickes, 29 Sept 1738 see Appendix 7: Hickes estate **[617]** SAY 1354.

200 To John Collier, Hastings, from William Cranston, [Johnson's Court], 18 February 1738 [SAY 738]

Walsh v Gibbon, this defendant is arrested and has given bail and I yesterday paid 10s 6d for it. Wood v Wells ex dismiss Butler, these tenants in possession have appeared, I shall make up the issue and give notice of tryall but proceed no farther. Grover v Thorpe, I send you a copy of this issue with notice of tryall and also your warrant v Carsingham.

I was this week in Southwarke at Dunmoll's houses there, and also upon the bridge. This last is occupied by a milliner, Mrs Gatliff, is £16 per annum. She has paid to ladyday last, and refuses to pay any more at present, having been forbid so to do by one Mrs Todd, and upon looking upon her receipts given by Dunmoll, he confirms her having some right, for they run for Mrs Todd and self, tis a sad house, and appears to want more repairing than tis worth, but before anything can be done in this, Mrs Todd's title and Dunmoll's should be cleared up.

The other three houses I found to be in the possession of Jane Woods, Joseph Merry and Isaac Brooks, the two first appear to be good tenants, and the houses in good order, their rents each are £6 per annum. They have both paid to lady day. Brook's house is £5 per annum, the worst I ever saw habited in all my life, and did not venture myself in for fear of its falling on my head. He has paid to Christmas 1736; he appears to me as poor as his house having seven small children, however promises fair, though I shall think I wrong my conscience to take above 2s 6d per annum. I have left with all of them my name and place of abode, that they may make me known to em again I call for money, which will be soon.

Mr Hodgson had drawn a case about the 2 £10 notes. I have looked into it as well as the Act of Parliament and, as they are each under £20, I doubt they need not have been protested, and if so it may be some question whether they might not have been recovered of Dunmoll.[1] But I have been considering that we are disputing about nothing, for as they are both accepted, the acceptor is liable at all events, and as I personally know him, and have made inquiry of those who intimately know him, and his origin, I am by them as well as my own notion satisfyed he is very able to answer em and wants only forcing to it. He at this time living in a good house, and in creditt, by Covent Garden, so that really to avoid more trouble on this head as well as the risk of being demolished if we proceed, I would advise to payment of both to Hodgson, and take the recovering them again of Morris, the acceptor, upon ourselves and am satisfyed we shall be no sufferers by it. I should be glad of your answer by the return for Hodgson is my daily orator and beleive wants the cole.

Scrase has promised me ... [2] the £500 next week without fail. I thought Swinburne after Greenwich would have been able, for he seemed to make no question of it, to have paid for our moiety of the garden affairs and have got in it clear, but the cash is wanting and none likely to come. I mention formerly my having served him with an ejectment though at that time not the least suspecting his ability, however, as this last has since appeared, I moved it the last day of terme, and will proceed to judgement and have given Clarke orders privately to get some other chap, which when got, I can then turn him out.

Simmons and Whiter go on calmly in the sand affair. I have two of their accounts in ending last Monday each containing a fortnight, the first they then paid me, being £3 2s each, and shall insist and so they promise, to pay one under another. Upon more mature deliberation I have thought it best not to entangle ourselves with any written agreement with them, but to keep the power in our own hands to put a full stop either to one or the other or both at a minute's warning whenever we think proper which I think will keep them to their mettle better than any other way. I doubt Ginger and Farrin are both slippery chaps neither of them keeping their words, hope shall bring them to, by fair means, otherwise currat lex the first day of next terme and nothing to prevent.

1 Small bills of exchange Act, 5 & 6 Wm & Mary c. 20; also 9 & 10 Wm III c. 17; 3 Geo II c. 26 on coal notes; 3 & 4 Anne c.8, 7 Anne c.25 s. 3. By 9 & 10 Wm III c. 17, all bills of exchange for £5 and upwards may be protested, but not for under £5 (*SL* vols. 3, 5). Significant case law developed on this question.

2 MS damaged.

201 To John Collier, Hastings, from William Cranston, [Johnson's Court], 21 February 1738 [SAY 739]

Inclosed send you a copy of the issue in Butler's ejectment and Grub which somehow escaped me per last post. I think I gave you a history of Dunmoll's affairs in part per last post and will now finish it. I appeared to the ejectment served on Mrs Hickes and prepared a bill which I filed for injunction, and upon an affidavit that the defendant was abroad I got an order to served the attorney with a spax[1] which was accordingly done before the last day of terme. So by next seal shall have an injunction to stay execution but not tryall, which will at least keep us two or 3 years longer in possession of the way; and I hope they won't go to tryall this assizes, for have heard nothing from em since.

As to Johnston's claim of his wife's mother's dower, upon considering more of that matter I make a doubt whether the suit can be revived, or whether he can recover against us at law. I think there's something in my objection; have therefore drawn a case which I sent a week ago for Clive to peruse, and we agreed upon the Solicitor General.[2] Tis not yet returned so as long the fault lies at their door; they must be quiet, if I don't hear in a little time will carry it ex parte. As to the other dower though am of the same opinion as in one of my former upon that head; yet upon farther search I beleive we must submitt, for it appears upon the pleadings that the person in whom we would have the legall estate to be from 1699, became a bankrupt in 1717, and we purchase under his son in 1733 and the person under whom she claims and made the deed of 1699 died in 1726, so that, if the estate was the son's and not the father's in 1717, we by proving all we can shall bring the creditors of the son upon our backs, so that of the two evills, I fancy the dower will be the least. I shall attend Mrs Gibbins. Sparrow and I have parted. I was necessitated to it; there's a mortall peice of work between the father and mother about it, and I am slaved finely by madam, but meet with quite different treatment from him.

1 Subpoena.
2 Solicitor General, Sir John Strange.

202 To John Collier, from William Cranston, [Johnson's Court], 25 February 1738 [SAY 740]

Very happily for me, I never heard from Lord Westmorland or Mr Hall since the gout has attacked me, but if I continue to mend as I have done since yesterday morning, I shall be able to get out by Monday. Tucker lost his cause yesterday, but so much against the sense of the court and everybody present that the verdict shocked all bystanders, and as we have actions against the assignees for ten times as much money as theirs against us and laid in rent we shall at the ensuing assizes try the sense of our countrymen.

Simmons was with me tother day and informed me of what you now writ, but the affair of parting with the wharf is entirely bad, for our sandpitt will not then be worth one penny. I am throughly satisfyed he's not worth 6d, was a great crony of the famous Mr Carr's, and a through rascally fellow; and was the estate my own and he would give me £500 a year for it, he should by no means have it upon that or any other terms whatever; as to tears, he has em at command and has ten times cried like a child before me. Though Whiter is poor yet I beleive him honest, and as to payments I'll make him keep touch, and that one is much better looked upon by the world than tother is manifest; for that Simmons has not one quarter the demand for sand that Whiter has and that must soon end in selling his carts and horses and giving up his part of it; and as then Whiter will have the whole, for that I would advise, I am satisfyed more sand will then be drawen per week than ever has been, as is already clear by the two fortnights' account I have now by me. I much want the old commission for Wittersham. My brother's jobb shall be done, so as to send the receipt per next post.

I can't think of going to Greenwich till after the assizes and Wittersham petition is over and then will, and then will spend time enough fully to settle those affairs. I think twill be entirely right to sell Blackheath houses, and the old houses in partnership with Simmons, but these latter I would rather advise Mrs Hickes to take and to sell to pull down and to lett a building lease of, but not to Simmons for he should be totally routed, which will then make then a good street and would be very advantageous to the new houses already there but this is only my present thoughts, which a regular survey, when we have our engineers there, may either confirm or refute.

203 To John Collier, Hastings, from John Curteis, 4 March 1738 [SAY 741]

I don't design to take my money out of Mrs Hickes' hands, but think to continue it on the terms you mention. I shall be at Rothersbridge in a short time and will discourse her on that head.

204 To John Collier, Hastings, from Henry Pelham, Esher, 1 April 1738 [SAY 393]

I received both your letters and am very well satisfied with the money you have returned from the audit. I am only sorry my brother's rent does not come in. I think you must return him in arrear for both quarters, unless you receive the money from Mr Waller before I pass your account,[1] which by what he says you may possibly do. I doubt Burfeild carn't last long; one way or other, I am afraid, he must go off. I hope you enquired a little as to what is to be done att Mrs Thomas's, for though I trust to my servant Buckles very much, yet I would always have you know what is going on in the farms in Sussex.

We have had close sitting in Parliament upon the merchants affair,[2] but now I think it is over, I hope to their satisfaction, though I am told not; they are such unreasonable people, nothing can please em. Undoubtedly the Spaniards have behaved most abominably, and you will see by our resolutions in the votes that the Parliament thinks so. We Englishmen are very stout upon our own dunghill, but when this nation is engaged in a war, which the merchants are driving att, the country must pay for't, and then who is bear the blame.

1 James Waller, Duke of Newcastle's agent for Sussex, accountant and paymaster for the Newcastle trusts; Waller appointed to support Peter Forbes in the role of steward in 1738 when Forbes was unwell (Browning 125; Kelch 21-2, 84-7).

2 4th session of Parliament, 28 March 1738, petition to the House of Commons from the West India merchants complaining of Spanish assaults in the Caribbean; William Pulteney placed a resolution citing the Anglo-Spanish trading agreements which guaranteed the rights of the traders of each country, listing the transgressions by the Spanish garda costas, and demanding restitution. Sir Robert Walpole preferred a diplomatic approach, and the government motion passed 256 to 209; the opposition motion for a further sitting on the question was defeated 224 to 163 (Taylor & Jones 34, 52-3).

205 To John Collier, [Hastings], from William Cranston, [Johnson's Court], 6 April 1738 [SAY 742]

Your Monday's letter found me at Greenwich, to which place I set out that morning with Chrochley, and did not return till today at noon. I picked up from the severall tenants about £45, though parted with the greatest part of it in discharging debts contracted, as well before, as since Mr Dunmoll's. We surveyed during that time all the houses as well the 16 new houses which lye together, as Willby's, Swinburn's and the Blackheath gentry. As to the first parcell, they are agreed to be exceedingly badly built. But as Dunmoll in his lifetime setled that account with Simmons, and took from him an absolute reconveyance of em, as appears by a counterpart of it executed by Dunmoll, in Simmons keeping, though where the originall is does not appear to me, the intent of looking on them, was to see what was wanting to make em tenantable and the people easy inhabiting them. For which purpose I gave orders to the severall workmen to do what was judged absolutely necessary to keep the tenants in, who appear to be very good ones and pay well, and when things are fully setled and Simmons got ridd of, the whole estate in generall will turn out a very pretty thing.

I took from all the tenants attornments in form,[1] which they readily came into, and which I think is right, it giving us a clear justification in case of a distress, and is a compleat evidence upon an action for rent. As to the survey made of the other houses, that the surveyors keep to themselves till the beginning of next week, and then they are to deliver in their valuation, and in the meantime have appointed Simmons next Monday morning, to begin to go through his account which I will finish out of hand, and then I think affairs will be reduced to a certainty in that corner and the rents etc may be then gott in at a much easier expence for the future than at present.

For what with the surveyors, workmen, tenants, extravagancy of Easter Monday and Tuesday at Greenwich, our bills came to a good deal of money. I have inclosed you an exact rentall of the estate and as to the yearly produce of the sand it may be guesed at by the neat money I have received for what hath been drawn from the 16 January, the time Mrs Hicks left off, to the 11 March inclusive, which is £24 9s 6d. I had a chap with me about buying the Blackheath houses and field, he bids £180, beleive will give £200 if so would advise the taking it, for that is the worst part of the estate and can only be tenanted by perhaps one tolerable good ale draper but the other two must be thieves. As to Chossam and St Albans, that must be referred to another oppurtunity having already spent more time abroad that I can afford and though we were there four days, yet I declare, I was every morning up before 7 and did not spend two hours of daylight idly. I saw the attorney's answer to lawyer Hawer's case, which is exactly agreable to what I always entertained of it, and Skinner then told me that he would deduct the £40 interest out of the £200, as to the £8, I wont be a week longer without it.

As to Dely's hoop, I don't often take notice of such things, but did of that when it came home, and found the same fault my sister now does of it, but was assured by her and Miss Selby that it was only a hoop *a la mode* and not an inch to bigg for my neice, and have since been convinced of the truth of it, for the ladies take up so much roome, that they have fairly jockyed us the wrong sides of the post, for there's no walking within em.

I've sent to Miss Selby about another hoop. Since I wrote the other side Mrs Gatliffe, who I saw last week, has been with me with her brother in law the famous Forrest. They say Todd still continues to threaten, and therefore have scruples to pay to either of us, I can't say but that Dunmoll's receipts do give a strong suspicion to people unacquainted with the affair, of Mrs Todd's right to something, and therefore in such a case do think a tenant should have occular conviction, and that only is to be done by black and Whiter, and think tis but reasonable to gratifie her in it. For which purpose if the writings of the estate, which I understand is only a lease from the bridge's house, and the papers in the cause in chancery were sent up, the affair might then probably be sett in a clear light.

1 Attornment, an assignment; a transfer of homage and service to a new feudal lord; although the need for an attornment abolished by 4 Anne 16, it was kept in this case for the reasons given by William Cranston.

206 To John Collier, [Hastings], from William Cranston, [Johnson's Court], 11 April 1738 [SAY 743]

Clarke and myself spent the whole day yesterday in looking over Simmons demand upon us, and preparing a counter one on him. Today Simmons came, we soon was at a full stand and in conclusion, as I know nothing of my own knowledge and therefore he can out talk me in that respect, I concluded to have a hearing of Swinburn, Clarke, Whiter, Farrin etc. And when I have heard both sides, I'll endeavour to judge as equitable as I can, and as I should be glad to have this troublesome affair over and know of no other time to spare, I have appointed to be at Greenwich, Saturday evening, in order to take the whole of next day before me, for I think it better to go upon the spott where the whole business was transacted where if we should want farther evidence people will be at hand. But I despair of making an end of it at one bout, for tis most confused story, and Simmons as well as Dunmoll's papers all in sad disorder, and concessions must be made on both sides, otherwise nothing but a 10 years suit in chancery can end it.

Ginger I shall attack first day of terme; Morris the two drafts ditto. I'll advertise St Thomas out of hand, the tenant at the old house tells me there is but two years to come of his lease as he heard Dunmoll say just before he died. Tunbridge Wells shall be in Saturday's Evening Post. I am sorry for Sharp, I don't suppose his widow will keep on and anything that you shall think proper I'll come into.

207 To John Collier, [Hastings], from William Cranston, [Johnson's Court], 18 April 1738 [SAY 744]

I have at last got the Attorney General's opinion upon the Hasting case which you herewith receive. Serjeant Eyre this day assured me, that I should not fail of his, per next post.[1] I advertised the houses in St Thomas's yesterday, and today have had a chap. I have appointed him tomorrow sennight to treat farther, by which time I hope you'll either bring yourself or send the lease of em.

After a deal of to do both Sunday and yesterday, for I cam not back till this morning, I have gone through Simmon's account excepting two queries to him and three queries to our account, and which may easily be fixed. We did not together but I have since just run through it to see how we stand, and allowing him his two queried articles, and disallowing our three, he is in our debt £86 14s 05d; in answer to which he will then have an equall share in the Blackheath houses, which at £200 will be £100. But then he is to disallow us out of that purchase as much as the fee is worth, which being valued at about £15 or £20 will much about bring us even, so that I really beleive that instead of £150, he won't have above £5 coming to him; and in order to bring matters as farr as they are am sure I have allowed 20 or £30 more than I think he is strictly intitled to. As your coming to town is so nigh, I sharn't finish this affair till you arrive, for it may not be amiss to get his lease up, at least of the old houses leaving him half the wharf, and the leaving this open may induce him to terms.

1 Giles Eyre, appointed King's Serjeant, 26 January 1736, died 25 February 1740.

208 To Mary Collier, Hastings, from John Collier, Johnson's Court, Fleet Street 2 May 1738 [SAY 1713]

This informs you of my arrival in town today about noon, after a melancholly anxious journey on considering how I left you and Dely. I hope in God I shall have some comfort in a letter by the post, for I am now under the greatest uneasiness in being obliged to leave you at this time. My sister Cranston came from Eastgrinsted but last night. I shall send you some tea, coffee, chocolate and spaw water tomorrow by the carrier.

I have found out Mr Jeake, who I beleive an ingenious man, and told him in the best manner I could Dely's case and situation. He says it's a very favourable part of the year and thinks riding and change of air absolutely necessary, but is of opinion that a very low diet and not eating any meat is the best way to put an end to her fever and seems not to think spaw water or any steely mineral waters good for her and that the more she drinks any small liquor the better, but to avoid heating her or increasing the fever by any meat or wine. I thought proper just to mention this and think it reasonable. I hope this fine weather will contribute to her getting abroad and frequent riding and being at Bexhill, Battell, etc.

I must begg and insist on your keeping up your spirits as much as possible and I shall not stay any longer then I am absolutely obliged, but if I hear she still continues so ill shall break through everything to be with you. I am with all cordial affection and esteem. If my sister Cranston's horse is too brisk she had better ride pony.

209 To Mary Collier, Hastings, from John Collier,[Johnson's Court], 4 May 1738. [SAY 1714]

I received your letter, which I waited for with the greatest impatience and anxiety, and really can't express my uneasiness since I have been in London. I am very glad to find that Dely is not worse and that you was in hopes her fever was not so much. By my last letter I wrote Mr Jeak's opinion as to her regimen and for my own part think the fever much more dangerous than the cough, for the former must tear her soon all to peices.

I was much advised today to goe to Dr Hulse, for that he has done great cures in such cases with vitral drops.[1] I fully intended it, because I think I could tell her case, but then considered I had not the prescriptions given her by Dr Russell and a change might be attended with fatal consequences. I have been in a very uncertain situation, and hardly attempted any business but a particular affair I was obliged to come up about, being determined, if my daughter had been worse and thought dangerous, to have returned home at all events. But now hope her medecins may have been taken long enough to have some good effect and that I shall receive agreeable accounts thereof every post.

I have been told abundance of remedys in consumptive cases where extraordinary cures have been made, but those cases may be very different from dear Dely's. One is cow dung steeped in milk overnight and drawn of next morning upon a cold still, and drink as much as the patient pleases to satisfy thirst. Another, balsam of sulphur and oyle of turpentine, but of this could not be informed what quantity, nor how to be mixed and taken, only that it was to be taken three days, and then miss three. But as Dr Russell has prescribed, under God we must trust to his judgement unless it's thought otherwise. I presume Dr Thorpe has, if occasion, wrote to Mr Russell how she goes on and whether the medicines have any and what effect. I hope, my dearest, you make yourself as easy as possible under this affliction, for your own sake as well as that of him who values you beyond all this world, and is your most faithful husband.

1 Dr Edward Hulse; vitral or vitriol drops, composed of sulphates of metals and used as medicine (*OED*).

210 To Mary Collier, Hastings, from John Collier, Johnson's Court, 6 May 1738

[SAY 1715]

I had your letter by post, which I waited for with the utmost impatience. It's so far pleasing, that there was no particular account came to you of her being worse, which I judge would certainly have been if my brother had any suspicion of that kind. I have enquired of every person I thought proper, and all agree change of air, and riding out, absolutely necessary. I kept John because if I received any account of an alteration for the worse I would immediately return, so shall keep him on, and quit London as soon as I can, but as I am at present here if no necessity, shall stay and do some more business. I hope you will cheer up as much as possible. I beleive Bossum is gone, if not, will send some cheese. I have sent on board him a carpet and some glass cans and glasses.

Colonel Pelham comes to Crowhurst a Fryday next I beleive. T. Pelham is to be married next week; his father has behaved in a mad, strange manner, and I beleive is confined. I have heard of no news, nor enquired after any, and I beleive in my last letter I sent you the above about Mr Pelham, for I am in so much uneasiness about dear Dely that I hardly know what I do. Adieu my dearest, and beleive me most faithfully.

[*Reverse*] Tell Mr Rowe I received his letter but would not have him do anything as to arresting Puckle, for if he don't keep his word he can expect no favour hereafter. The charges are £1 16s 0d which tell him of.

211 To Mary Collier, Hastings, from John Collier, [Johnson's Court], 9 May 1738

[SAY 1716]

I received your letter by yesterday's post and have been ever since very uneasy about Dely, not finding you think her any better and her fever continuing. I received also a letter from Mr Thorpe with Dr Russell's two prescriptions, and have been this day with Dr Hulse and told him her case as well as I could and shewed him the two prescriptions. He asked me a great many questions, to which I gave him the best answers I could. Inclosed is his prescription, which he explained to me: it's 3 gentle vomits to be taken for 3 days togeather, and the other some medicine to be taken with Stretham purging water; his intention thereby is only to cool her and keep her body just open, and if half a pint of it is not enough she may take more.[1] 6 bottles of the water you will receive by Quoife a Saturday. The doctor desired that Mr Thorpe will give him an account what effect the medicines have and he will further consider, if occasion, but hopes this regimen may be of service.

Though he saw Dr Russell's prescriptions I must leave it to you whether it will not be proper to have Dr Russell, or Dr Carleton, or both, consulted before put in practice, but if it is must be done forthwith and you'l also hear what Mr Thorpe says to it. I will get out of town as soon as possible, I hope a Fryday, but would not have you wait for my coming. I hope it will please God to direct us for the best, for if every shilling I have in the world could contribute to her recovery I should not repine. I begg you will bear up and encourage her as much as possible. The plague and hurry of the town, and Dely's illness, is heavy on me, for I have no peace or can think of any enjoyment here. I hope to be down time enough for Mr Thorpe's writing to Dr Hulse.

1 Water from medicinal springs at Streatham, Surrey, four miles north of Croydon, described by Dr Richard Russell in his *Dissertation on the use of seawater in the diseases of the glands* as a purgative water containing salt, partly marine and partly nitreous, with a little sulphur and a greater proportion of absorbent earths, used as treatment for a range of illnesses including disorders of the eyes (Russell, 264-65).

212 To Mary Collier, Hastings, from John Collier, [Johnson's Court], 11 May 1738 [SAY 1717]

Though I had not the pleasure of receiving a letter from you this post, I had the satisfaction of two from Jemmy and Mr Worge, that our dear girle was better, in all appearance, which was vastly agreeable. I hope to get out tomorrow, but, if not, shan't be so anxious and impatient as I should have otherwise been. I hope your health and spirits have kept up. News or fashions, etc., I cannot acquaint you with, hating to goe by Mrs Elcock's shop, and always turn my face another way. I dined with Mr Coppinger today after the letters came in; she is very bigg.

[*Foot of letter*] Give Rowe the underwritten [*torn off*]

213 To John Collier, Hastings, from Browne Willis,[1] Whaddon Hall, nr Fenny Stratford, 16 May 1738 [SAY 97]

I have abundance of thanks to return you for your most excellent and accurate accounts of Hastings and Winchelsea, which are so instructive and particular that, could I meet with more such exact and kind freinds to give me information, I should with the uttmost pleasure goe on with what I began about Parliamentary boroughs. I was very much to seek about those 2 towns, otherwise, as they stand so low in my method I needed not have so soon in the course of my collections wanted them. I think I have a pretty good account of Rye and Seaford. If it tis in your way to say somewhat of Shoreham, Steyning, Bramber, Arundel, sir, I should be thortful[1] As just such these notices as these follows, viz query, 2 about how many houses in each, some description of their churches and publick buildings, town halls, castles etc., and if corporations as I think none are but Arundel of them, and that all the corporations in Sussex are only these following:

Chichester: which has a mayor, high steward, recorder, bayliff and an certain number of aldermen because all such as have been mayors are reputed aldermen ever after, and all the whole body as mayor, etc.,[2] are chosen out of 38 persons who are common councill men.

Arundel: A mayor, steward and 12 burgesses; q. how many common councill or what other members: Hastings a mayor, recorder and 12 jurats: Rye a mayor and 12 jurats:

Winchelsea a mayor and 3 jurats: Seaford a bailiff and 4 jurats: I think Pevensey has a titular bailiff, as has Midhurst, and Grinsted and Horsham 2 bayliffs, but none of those, nor is Lewes, corporations.

What more I should have enquired after was who were lords of the towns and mannors of Hasting and Winchelsea and who they purchased these of in memory of man. I would also have been glad to have known as there was a collegiate church at Hastings, consisting of a dean and 4 prebendarys, and whether it was in the castle of Hastings, or if St Clement's, the parish church, was not the collegiate one.[3] I can sir and will gladly, if of curiosity to you, send you a list of the members of Parliament for Hastings and Winchelsea and some names of the deans of Hastings college which my collections furnish.

The draughts of Hastings is a quear curiosity and gives a perfect idea of the place; it is pity that of Winchelsea was not got and preserved especially as the town is gone. There is in Leland some account of it taken 200 years agoe; the tombs in Winchelsea church was, as he seems to tell us, of the Alards, one of them, and I think another, of the Finches. As I have been curious in picking up traders' coins as they made them in all market towns from 1649 to 1673 their own farthings, and halfpence, so I prayed Mr Fairfax to mention how glad I should be to I get one of Hastings. I have of Chichester, Steyning, Haylsham, Rye and feign would I get of Hastings and Lewes. I was shewed one of Seaford by one Mr Gouldham, but he having an estate there keeps it as a rarity. I would gladly purchase any of these having a collection of above 310 different market towns.[4]

Have you in your town hall no chamberlayns account of paying the members their wages at Hastings. The returns were all destroyed in the publick office in London from 17 Edw 4 to 33 Henry 8; so that we cannot recover them anywhere in our boroughs but from town books. I have got some of these which perfect them as Norwich, Wells City, Stamford, Northampton, etc., towns. At Canterbury and Rochester I am quit but meet with little satisfaction at York only 2 or 3 ... at Winchelsea was standing 1534 St Giles' church and possibly some of the ruins remain. In 1291, there were churches in Hastings of St Leonard, St Margaret and St Nicholas, St Peter, neither of which are mentioned in your excellent account. These are in the Valor Ecclesiastica Angliae, or Pope Nicholas's taxation made tempore[5] Edw I. Q. if some of these churches were not within the rape.

1 MS part obscured by seal.
2 MS unclear
3 Hastings churches (*VCH Sussex* vol. 9, 15-19; C Dawson *Castle and Collegiate Church* (1909); Baines ch. 16).
4 Farthings and halfpenny tokens suppressed by royal proclamation in 1672. For the Sussex seventeenth century tokens and a list of 183 coins see J B Caldecott 'Sussex Seventeenth Century Tokens', *British Numismatic Journal* (1938-41) vol. 23, 301-320.
5 Record Commission publications, Valor Ecclesiasticus; Taxatio Ecclesiastica Angliae et Walliae anctoritate Pope Nicholas 1V, circa A.D. 1291

214 To John Collier, Hastings, from William Cranston, [Johnson's Court], 18 May 1738 [SAY 745]

I have just now received intelligence from Greenwich that our chap Simmons was yesterday arrested, but, geting bail, moved off in the night all his goods, carts, horses, etc., and that this morning an execution, at his wine marchant's suit, came but found the nest and all the birds flown. He's £10 or £11 in our debt for sand, which I doubt we shall loose. Tis all in confusion at the pitt, so doubt must take a trip down Monday morning, perhaps Saturday evening, and put matters to rights and see about another chap, or let Whiter work two, for one cart won't serve the customers. I am greatly concerned at my neice's still continuing ill, and by sending for Jemmy's shirts doubt your design of being in town by the end of next week is laid aside.

215 To John Collier, [Hastings], from William Cranston, [Johnson's Court], 25 May 1738 [SAY 746]

I returned from Greenwich Tuesday evening, where I found the sand pitt in a sad sictuation almost choaked up, partly through carelessness, and partly by quarrells between Simmons, Whiter and the people who incally[1] for em, who complain they don't allow them sufficient to live, and do the work and lay the ground and mould as it ought to be done. They allowing em but 4½d per load, when it should be 6d, which would enable em so to work, as not to lose one load of sand, and also to lay the cally and mould upon that so as to make the ground ever the better after the sand is gone than it ever was before.[2]

On the other hand Whiter says that he can't allow so much and live; and therefore in order that Whiter or Simmons may not be hurt, and that the three half pence may be made up to the men and another halfpenny, which I think will serve Clark for his whole stewardship, I proposed the raising the customers here 2d per load, which I am convinced may be done, and will and must be come into. This will answer the whole compleatly. Whether the scheme will succeed I am not certain, but think it will and Whiter and Clark are to go to em all tomorrow, so that in a post or two I shall be able to lett you know. If it does, twill be a good jobb for then Mrs Hicks will have her 6d clerum clarum, and her land better when the sand is all gone than now.

As Simmons sent to me to tell me he hoped to make up all his affairs in a week or ten days and desired I would not absolutely preclude him. As yet I consented to his coming again, upon paying all arrears, and setling and passing all his accounts, etc; so that Whiter has hired another cart and horses, pro tempore, that the affair may not stand still. I doubt I must put off my Chossum journey till after next terme, for I don't see how I can get out for so long time next week, for amongst other things our consultation upon Hasting must be had Wednesday or Thursday. I send you your warrant v Foster. You will have your dedimus's Tuesday post next.[3] If you execute Poadle's deeds before, they must bear date before last terme, for the fine must be of that terme otherwise the recovery cannot be compleated next.

1 Replacing the callow, the stratum of vegetable and humus soil lying above the subsoil or top bed of a quarry

2 The figures here, and those from building sites around London, suggest wage rates rose above the rates recorded by the assize courts. Lewis 1965 14-16, pointed to a trough in the building trades, 1727, a gentle rise to 1736, and then a decline, in part due to fears of war to reach another trough in 1744. For prices and wage rates see Phelps-Brown & Hopkins 1962 186. E W Gilboy *Wages in Eighteenth Century England* (1934) has a useful discussion of the various trades.

3 A writ of dedimus potestatem, allowed the legal process to be carried on outside the Westminster courts by a country attorney.

216 To Mary Collier, Hastings, from John Collier, [Johnson's Court], 17 June 1738 [SAY 1718]

I have the pleasure to acquaint you that we arrived in town today between 12 and one a clock, but wet through, having a continual rain from six in the morning when we set out from Tunbridge. We dined at Mr Worge's according to my intention, and set out before two, and got to Tunbridge in good time, though the roads are exceeding bad,[1] and I think very hazardous even to men in travailing, and I never rode in a more heavy rain than today. I hope we have not got any great cold though I am very stiff for we changed all our cloaths immediately.

I much fear these great rains will make the roads bad between Battell and Hasting,[2] and make it bad for Dely to get home; or else should think it much better for her, for I don't at all think she is regular enough in going to bed, etc., with Miss Worge; for I found by discourse that they were a Thursday night frightned by the dogs coming up stairs, and both were out of bed in their shifts, which can't be at all proper for her in the present situation. I took her other headcloaths and a little parcell of hair in order for locks and her cloaths are to be a gown and tayle; there was a little discourse about earrings, and I don't know but I may buy her some; and by Mr Worge's discourse beleive he has some intention that way. I have not been out of doors so can only tell you I hear of no news in particular.

I have had the taylor, shoomaker, etc., for Jemmy, in order for his equipment with everything we can think proper for Cambridge, and hope by next post to send you word when we shall set out. Tell Morris I would have him fetch my brother Cranston's other horse from Sampson's, for we have now grass enough to keep him in my fields. My brother and sister and little Jemmy, and also the other little one, as they say, are very well. I hope my dear your breasts are better and that I shall hear by next post that you and all yours are well.

1 Heavy rains between Battle and Hastings, also recorded at Tonbridge, 8-14 June; on 10 June, storms with thunder and lightening, 1.417in of rain (Hooker Mss). On 12 June John Fuller explained that Heathfield furnace was ready to blow out, the 'wayes are yet so bad it is impossible to get anything to the seaside, those that have attempted it being laid fast' Crossley & Saville 275; and to Samuel Remnant, his London agent, 30 June 'we have had nothing but rain and wett weather all this summer, so that it is impossible to stirr anything in our wayes as yett', adding 'I hope the weather is now changed into summer, which if it continue, we shall soon gett them to the seaside' (*ibid* 276).

2 John Collier, George Worge, and associates, formed the Hastings-Battle turnpike trust in 1753; (17 May 1753, Sarah Collier to Mary Collier SAY 2072).

217 To Mary Collier, Hastings, from John Collier, Johnson's Court, 27 June 1738 [SAY 1719]

I returned from Cambridge this day,[1] where I left Jemmy very well, and I beleive extreamly well satisfyed with his new habitation, and am sure he ought to be soe, for it's not only a delightful situation, but I have not been niggardly in setling him as well as any gentleman in England can be as to reputation, and an improvement in his studys. I am not a little fatigued with the journey; tho it was really a pleasant agreeable one, and we met with a handsom genteel reception, and civilitys there, in particular from my Lord Lincoln, who is about a year older than Jemmy, and has the applause of the whole university for his sobriety, studys, and the behaviour of a gentleman. I hope it will be attended with the desired success to our son, and he will make the proper use of what I have at a great expense put into his power.

On my return I found your letter, and also Mr Rowe's, of last Thursday. I opened yours first, which if I had not, should have been afraid, and concluded the child had been dead. Your letter was a pleasure, not only to hear it was better, but that you and Dely were well. I hope it will be possible for you to get a proper nurse and that you will not, in your situation, think of giveing it suck. I have not seen my sister a minute hardly, so can tell no news, only that Dely's cloaths is bought and will in all probability be sent tomorrow sen'night with Mrs Elcock's preparation. I have seen Price about the earrings, but don't know how that will at present come out, Jemmy's expences being very large. I hope, my dear soul, you and yours are, and will continue very well till my return, of which I can at present say nothing to. We went to see Mrs Philcox and her son who is in a very weak, poor, condition and I heartily pity here situation. G. Carleton is very brisk and well. I invited him to supper and he came yesterday in the stage coach to London in order for Sussex in about a week, I am, with humble service to Mrs Thorpe and all friends.

1 James Collier entered Clare Hall College on 23 June 1738 as a fellow commoner (Venn Pt 1, vol. 1). The Duke of Newcastle attended Clare, a college founded by an ancestor on his mother's side (Browning 2).

218 To Mary Collier, Hastings, from John Collier, [Johnson's Court], 29 June 1738 [SAY 1720]

I received Dely's letter by this post with the satisfaction of hearing you was well and a continuance of health to little Willy. I have spoke to my sister about Dely's shoos and gloves but she seems puzzled about having them made a proper size. She must have the mortification of not having her cloaths against the visitation, which I hear is this day sen'night, for they are not done, nor indeed her things from Mrs Elcock, but hope they will be all compleat and goe by next carrier. The weather is now very hot in town and I begin to be heartily weary of it, but am afraid I shan't be at home till the latter end of next week. Mrs Nouns dined today here and wants to see Dely very much to talk over the court affairs, but she is still a strong j-e.[1]

I hope the hay is pretty well got in under the conduct of Mr Morris. I beleive Mr Worge goes out of town tomorrow, but I have seen nothing of him today. I wish the girles a good journey to Bexhill fair.[2] I forgot whither I mentioned in my last that little Jemmy was gone to E. Gransted. It's at present setled that my sister's maid is to goe down with Master Bossom the next time he comes up.

1 Jacobite.
2 Bexhill fair, end of June 1738.

219 To Mary Collier, Hastings, from John Collier, [Johnson's Court], 1 July 1738 [SAY 1721]

I received your letter by today's post and much wonder there has been no Hasting visitants to Crowhurst. I have no objection to what you write about Mrs Thorpe and will speak to Mrs Elcock accordingly, and if Master Bossom is not sayled send you soap and the glasses you mention. I think it's much that you cannot meet with a proper nurse for your little boy. I can't say that I am sorry your milk is gone for I should have been unwilling that you should have attempted giving him suck.

There's a most shocking scene of Mr Malling and family who made so great a figure at the Wells. He dyed lately, as was in the news, under a salivation for the pox; his wife has been under one on the same account and last week it was thought she would have dyed under it, but now beleived she will recover. His circumstances come out but indifferent, notwithstanding the great figure he made there and indeed everywhere. She it seems was deep in with the distemper when at the Wells but did not know what her dissorder was. In short, he is condemned as a sad fellow and it's said was one that frequented all common brothells. I hope to get home by this day sen'night at furthest but can fix on no certain time. I was last night at Vauxhall with my brother and sister and Mrs Nouns. There were abundance of people, but not many of the tiptop company.

220 To Mary Collier, Hastings, from John Collier, [Johnson's Court], 20 July 1738 [SAY 1722]

I had a letter from Rowe by last post about some business, and as he mentioned nothing relating to you or the little boy, presumed you are pretty well. Mr Worge had a letter from Battell by last post and says Dely is very brisk. I hope she will by some contrivance be got home, but think it very impracticable unless she rides double. Jemmy is very well, and I think I have got everything ready for him and hope to get out for Cambridge a Thursday afternoon. I shan't think much of anything as to the expence provided he turns out well, and indeed I have no doubt upon me at present on that head. George Worge told me today that he should write home and acquaint Dely about the k – g's mistress, as they call her, Madam Volmont.[1] We have had very bad, dismal weather that makes it very uncomfortable. I have bespoke Dely's and Molly's things that were desired. I desire that my mare may not be rode, unless Morris to attend Dely when she rides out. I have been in a great hurry this evening and but just time to write upon this slovenly peece of paper. I hope, my dearest, you are very well and will so continue, my service to all friends.

1 The Bishop of Gloucester lamented the king's decision to bring his mistress from Hanover to the court (Egmont vol. 2, 482, 27 August 1738).

221 To John Collier, Surveyor General of the riding officers of Kent, Canterbury, from William Cranston, 29 July 1738 [SAY 747]

I took my Chessam journey in company with our stationer where I found the estate rather better than worse as to condition than I imagined, but I think very indifferently tenanted and all of em a great while in arrear. Notwithstanding which I neither did nor could receive a farthing, but they faithfully promised payment of some to our deputy there and I was to have had an account of it by yesterday's post, but none came so I conclude no coal could be got.

I went from thence to St Albans where I not only inquired of but carefully viewed the waterworks there; the sictuation is very feasable and I don't know a more probable scheme to succeed than this. But I find the management is got into two or three hands, others not regarding it, who make the benefitt of it to themselves only. I met with severall that had some shares, which added to our 54, but 600 in all, will make a tolerable good figure, and we concluded to stay till November and then advertize a meeting and try whether it cannot be taken out of the present chap's hands, for I am sure with good honest management the shares would turn to a good account.

I set out from St Albans by a bye road, and in a place called Coney Street met with that terrible tempest of hail as mentioned in the news; it was extreamly shocking and frightfull, so dark that you could not see to write within doors, and the lightning the most gastly that I ever beheld, and the hail carryed ever thing before it. The corn was all levelled, toops of oakes and elms, for three mile together, all cut off as with a knife, not a pane of glass left in that part of the houses which faced it, ducks and geese killed on the commons by hundreds, and no wonder for many of the hail stones were six and seven inches in circumference; in short, nothing in nature could be more horrible, and nobody that saw it could help imagining to himself the day of judgment being at hand.

Mr Forbes[1] called here today and informed me that Waller was paying off money and desired I would take the notes in my hand and make a push. I accordingly went, saw him, told him a story of the necessity you was under of paying a large summe away instantly and that I did not know the consequence of a disappointment; but all to no purpose. He said, he wondered you should send when he, Burnett, nay, Mr Pelham told you that you could have none till toward Xmas, that your accounts were not yet setled, that these £1000 notes, though given, yet twas upon a presumption that the accounts were right, and as they were not yet setled gave me to understand none would be paid till they were. I made my bow, told Forbes the conference, who waited at a coffee house for my return, at which he seemed really angry and thought Waller behaved himself very oddly in the affair. I think of setting out for the base Monday evening or Tuesday morning, so that unless you make haste in your survey I shall reach the port before you.

1 John Waller assisted Peter Forbes in the role of steward to the Duke of Newcastle from 1738 [**204**]. A serious situation emerged in the Newcastle finances from the early 1730s as revenues and rentals declined; in 1738 the duke turned to Hoare's Bank for a settlement, and whilst with a new trust it was hoped to curtail the duke's extravagance, the estate balance sheet continued to weaken (Browning 124-8, 190-1; Kelch 123-4). Although some control was imposed upon the Newcastle estates by this new trust established in 1738, both old and new debts imposed a burden on current income. The duchess's lavish expenditure, and her suffering a variety of illnesses and attempted cures, aggravated the problem. Both Browning and Kelch examine the diverse financial problems facing the estate: the insufficient controls, the attitude of the duke who regarded politics before money; thus, those appointed to places should support the duke's political and estate needs from their own pocket. For reference to these difficulties, see Sayer vol. 1 142: John Collier remained unpaid for part of his debts whilst alive, though his executors later received some monies from the duke's estate [**248**].

222 To John Collier, Hastings, from Henry Pelham, Esher, 22 September 1738. [SAY 394]

I this day received your letter, and remember I did say to Mr Legas that I would write to you upon the subject of the woods and iron works, but when he told me that he should be in the country with Mr Harrison, I understood that he would then talk to you.[1] And upon what you should discourse together, Mr Harrison would propose something to me in London, where I expected to see him last week. What Legas said to me was much to the same purpose with what they both said to you. And I told him, in general, that I had no inclination to change tennants, that I should be unwilling to fall in the price of my woods, especially as Lord Ashburnham's were now let att that price. I agreed with him, that it would be for both our advantages not to cutt much these next seven years, but he, nor I, never talked of abatement in the price for the small quantity that might be proper to fell.

I do beleive that such a house as you speak of would be for the benefit of the furnace, but upon what part of the estate it is proper, or convenient, to build one, I don't know. I wish you would make some enquiry about that.[2] If it comes to any considerable sum there ought to be an addition in the rent of it, as to cleaning of the pond, you may be assured I am willing to do that, when the season is proper. I am apt to think the great decrease in the growth of my woods, doth not proceed only from the cutting of em too soon, but also, if not cheifly, from the want of care of em when they are young. I should be glad therefore, if you would turn it in your thoughts how to put that upon a better foot.

What has occured to me is this, that Harry Walker should have the care and inspection of all the Jerent woods, and such as are properly in his neighbourhood; these I beleive were formerly under the direction of old Austen, and the Waldron, Chiddingly and Hellingly woods to be under the same inspection of such person as I shall appoint to succeed Burfeild. Mr Hicks, my tennant att Chiddingly, has desired that, and I think, since Harry Walker does not care to remove from Burwash, he is the properest person that has been mentioned to me. The audit may be kept att his house, there is very little difference to any of the tennants, and none at all to you. But in this scheme of mine, I hope there will be some abatement of the allowance which I now give to Burfeild; not for the service he does me, but out of charity and reguard to his family as old servants. It is impossible for me to make any regular proposal to the iron masters, you see by the first part of this letter what I think about it. I would not oblige them to take more wood than is convenient for them, or properly fitt to cutt, but I don't care to abate in the price. As to the other particulars they can have no difficulty in making a proposal for they know much better what to offer, than I can do what to take.

I shall be in town next Thursday, and if Mr Harrison has anything to say to me, I conclude, I shall see him on Friday morning. I expect to hear soon, when you appoint the audit, I doubt it will be the last that will be held att poor Burfeild's, but I think it will be best to have this there, if his wife can take care to have the tennants summoned according to your order. I conclude I shall see you in London, or att Bishopstone, time enough to settle what to do for the future. I hear his grace has made you all very merry, as I find by him your town, in particular, have made him happy. Pray my service to the mayor, Dr Carleton and all friends.

1 John Legas and George Harrison, Conster-Beckley ironworks (Cleere & Crossley 284, 313). Wood prices rose during the war of the Austrian succession.

2 For the increase in demand for cannon and shot at this time see Hodgkinson 2009a 82-4.

223 To John Collier, Hastings, from Robert Burnett, Halland, 1 October 1738
[SAY 395]

Att the earnest request of poor Mr Burfeild and his wife as well as Mrs Thomas, I give you the trouble of this. I feind they have some of them bin so indiscreet as to tell him you have either apointed your audett att some other place, or do intend to do it; which I wonder att theire troubling him with, for in all liklyhood he can hardly live to the time which you wass mentioning of. But I feind both by Dr Hargraves and the neighbours he is the most uneasy creatur that can be under his misfortunes. Att the thoughts of the audett not being held att his house and under his present sircomstances, I could not refuse troubling you one the ocaison, which I beg you will please to exkews. I feind he fanceys he shall not give you the least interruption or be of any ill convenacy to you, but that I thinke imposable; if in nothing eles, I am shoore it will afect your compasionate temper to those in distress.

I beg therefore what I have sayd hear may not alter any resolution which you may have taken about it, and indeed had not Dr Hargrave, who has taken a good deal of pains to convince them all that if you should alter the place for the audett that it is designd purly for theire ease, desired me to aprise you of it. I should not have venturd to take this liberty, which I hope you will please to pardon from. Many theinkes for the last very great honnor you did me which made me very hapy. Mr Waller came hear last night, but we have not yett tucht one anything, only he inquired very kindly after you.

224 To John Collier, Hastings, from William Cranston, [Johnson's Court], 28 November 1738. [SAY 748]

I yesterday entirely ended the long affair between Mr Dunmoll and Mr Simmons, upon the ballance of which account there was due to Simmons £12 17s 11½d, which I paid him. We also setled accounts between him and Mrs Hickes since Mr Dunmoll's death, upon which there was due to her £2 0s 8½d which he paid me. The next affair was the surrender of his lease, about which I had not time to consult you, but upon considering how we might be hampered with him or his assignee, I ventured to give him 20 guineas. Upon which I drew up a regular surrender on the back, stampt, which he executed, so that now we are intirely got ridd of him and he has nothing upon earth to do with the estate. I assure you it was very satisfactory to me and hope twill be so to you and Mrs Hickes. We had many meetings about it before we could finally finish but I did not think it worth while to trouble you with any of them, till the whole was compleated. I shall now see about the finishing the sale of the Blackheath houses, Simmons joining therein not being now necessary, the £200 being to be all Mrs Hickes'. The cinque port tol is to be next Thursday against which time I have prepared myself.[1] Rowe arrived here yesterday. I will take an oppurtunity before he leave me of discoursing him.

[*Reverse*][2] wrote her the 30, made an end of for between 40 and 50 pounds, writings and all, thought it would be double the money.

1 Cinque Ports were required to present accounts annually to the Pipe office in the Exchequer, on which a fee or toll was payable.
2 This last sentence written by John Collier.

225 To John Collier, Hastings, from Henry Pelham, Esher, 27 December 1738 [SAY 396]

By a letter which I received from Thomas Freind of Lewes, I find Mr Chilley of Chichester, son to old Anthony Chilley of Hellingly, wants to borrow two thousand pounds upon his estates att Hellingly and Heathfield; which he proposes to give four per cent interest for this; Thomas beleiving I am a moneyed man has proposed to me, which, though I don't deserve that character, I beleive I can muster up if you find it is a good title, and that there are no engagements which shall weaken the security. The estate lies where I should not be sorry to become a purchaser, and that makes me more willing to strain a point than I should otherwise do. Thomas Freind will send you this by some messenger, and give you what further information he can; I desire you would tell Mr Chilley that the person is a client of yours, who has entrusted you with this sum to lay out on a mortgage, that you will pay him the money and the writings may be drawn in your name, which will make it the easier for you to receive the interest from time to time.

I conclude a declaration of trust from you will be sufficent security for me, but that we can settle when I see you in town. The money shall be ready for you, when other things are settled. I have referd you to Thomas Friend but desire you will let me know how this matter goes on. I understand the writings are in the hands of Mr Shadwell of Burwash[1] I don't doubt but you will take all proper care of me in this affair, and shall therefore entirely rely on your prudence and conduct.

I received your letter of the 19, and very much approve of what you have done with Harry Walker and John Vine; I hope my woods and other affairs will now be better managed than they were in poor Burfeild's time. As to the fine upon admission you will take care of that, for I suppose Mr Burnet and you will settle that account together. I wondered I have heard nothing from Legas or his partners, but conclude I shall sometime this winter. William Shoesmith has been here and told me what has passed between you. He begs hard not to be turned out of the tythes, seems unwilling to raise above ten pounds rent, but att last proposed he and Saxby should go halfs att the present rent. This I ordered to be wrote to Saxby who seems to me, by his answer, to like that better than an abatement of ten pounds per annum only. I think therefore to close with that; if Shoesmith is impertinent or gives any further trouble, he must go out, otherwise I shall be glad to please em both, for all I desire is to be no looser amongst em. I beleive you will heer from Mr Waller soon after the holydays, he is gone to his own house in the country during the recess of business, but he told me everything would be ready upon his return. I would not have anything mentioned about this mortgage. I conclude there is no occasion, and therefore it is better not, I shall expect a letter from you upon these affairs as soon as it is convenient.

1 William Shadwell, gent, Burwash, attorney; voted for John Fuller 1734 (Crossley & Saville 187).

226 To John Collier[1] from John Curteis, Tenterden, 12 December 1738 [SAY 749]

I return you many thanks for the care you have taken in the affair with Mrs Hicks.[2] I shall alwaies think it a pleasure whenever it lyes in my power to serve you.

1 MS may have been posted to William Cranston, then forwarded to John Collier.

2 The nearest legal reference is from the Kent assizes, Rochester, Tuesday 13 March 1739, 12 Geo II 1738/9; Elizabeth Hicks, late of the parish of East Grinstead, for unlawfully laying two cart loads of sand, dirt, and other filth in the common footway leading from the north end of Queen Street in the parish of East Greenwich, to the parochial church, and permitting the same to remain there (TNA ASSI 31/1 f. 56 no 17).

227 To John Collier, Hastings, from Elizabeth Hickes, Mountfield, 5 January 1739

[SAY 750]

If it is not to much trouble, I should be glad to know your thoughts about the affair I am going to mension, which is that if my daughter Boys should in time come to my house, with an intention to goe to London without her hussband's consent to get better advice for her health, how fer I may assist her in it, without being liable to any damage from her hussband; whether I may send or hir a man and horse to cary her, and whether I may send her cloths from my house by my servant to the carriers, and in case she dus not come back again, whether Mr Boys can have action against me on these accounts; pray let me have your thoughts by the next post.[2] As you mention goeing to London this term, I should be glad to see you before that time, but if that is ill conveint then I hop you will call as you goe I should be glad to hear that you ar now perfectly free of the gout, and I heartly wish yourself and family many happy years.

1 Elizabeth Hickes intended to divide her estate between her two daughters, Martha and the elder daughter Elizabeth who married Samuel Boys [**199**]. For Sir Dudley Ryder's legal opinion see Appendix 7: Hickes estate **[617]** SAY 1354.

228 To John Collier, Hastings, from Henry Pelham, Esher, 22 January 1739

[SAY 397]

I find by your letter of the 11 that you have done everything in relation to Mr Chilley's mortgage as I could wish. I should have answered yours sooner, but I have been in some hurry, and thought it could be of no consequence as you had acted entirely agreable to my instructions. I conclude, when you draw upon me for the money, your bill will not be payable but in two or three days notice, least I should happen not to be in town, when he comes to my house. Though from Wednesday next, I beleive I shall not leave London, but of a Satturday for sometime. I don't in the least doubt, but you have well examined the security, and think a declaration of trust from you will be sufficient, as to the mortgage being in your name, and a collateral security by bond, safe against the annuitants.

I am glad to hear you are likely to be in town soon, for besides this affair, I have several things to talk to you upon. I have heard from Saxby, that William Shoosmith is satisfied with my last proposal, which was that they should go halfs in the tythes att the present rent; if so, you will take care to alter the rentall accordingly. Pray let Sir William Ashburnham know that the Parliament sitts on Thursday sennight to proceed to business, by which time his friends expect him in London.[1] I hope he will excuse my not troubling him with a letter, having a great many to write, and knowing his zeal for the publick, and the service of his friends, is sufficient to bring him to Parliament.

1 This was the fifth session of the Parliament elected in 1734, 1 February 1739 to 14 June 1739 (*HBC* 578).

229 To Mary Collier, Hastings, from Mrs Mary Markwick,[1] 6 February 1739

[SAY 1723]

In your obligieing letter, you mentioned a want of servants as well as myself; my head maid I can recommend as a neat workwoman, good-natured and willing to do anything she is bid. She is but 19 years of age and never was out before I took her. I have a pretty large family and want one at the head, in some degree to manage the rest, and likewise to understand a kitchen, which are the reasons I part with her; but if you should think her fit for you I'll endeavour to send her to talk with you. Miss Collier is very well, as is Miss Nolly, both just come from Battle; but instead of being dispirrited by the worst walk that any poor souls ever had, they are so noisy that I must only subscribe myself, as I realy am, madam, your most obliged humble servant. Miss Collier desires you'l accept and dispose her duty to her papa with Nolly, and my service to Mr Collier and Miss Thorpe and Miss Colliers.

1 Mrs Mary Markwick lived at Catsfield Place, then called the Church House. She was Sir Charles Eversfield's sister, and married James Markwick of Catsfield in 1735. The Markwick family later adopted the surname Eversfield.

230 To Mary Collier, Hastings, from John Collier, [Johnson's Court], 10 February 1739 [SAY 1724]

I presume John will be at home this evening, by whom you have been informed of my getting to Bromley, where I hired a chaise, and sent him back, having no want of him here, and some fear on account of the small pox. But I understand by my sister that her maids were much dissappointed by John's not coming, which they were in great hopes of, for it seems when I was here last, they had very good game with him. Thomas went away about ten days agoe, and they don't know where he lives, being very private; he gave warning without any quarrel or misunderstanding on any account, and went away persuant to it. I find they are all certain there was an amour between Alce and him, strongly carried on at Hasting, and say that he has had several letters that they beleive came from her; his privacy going of makes them think he has a mind to drop her, and she shan't know where to find him, or it may be to settle somewhere. Perhaps her London intentions may be with regard to his affair. I think I have wrote more than the subject deserves. A new servant also named Thomas is come today. I have given my sister the memorandum relating to Miss Nanny Carleton's stays and orders to the man to send them Dr Carleton when made in order for tryal etc., but find they will not goe till next Wednesday sen'night.

According to custom, I left the key of my box at home, imagine it is hanging on one of the tacks in my study. Let Patrick, if there's any letters, send it with them directed to the Custom house. Miss Nanny Green is here, but returns a Tuesday. I met Mr Green of Sackville Street accidentally today, he really looks well, and says his wife is very well, which I think amazing. I have seen nobody to hear newes or anything as to fashions etc., to communicate. My service to all friends ends this epistle with an assurance of being, my dear, your affectionate husband.

231 To Mary Collier, Hastings, from Cordelia Collier, Catsfield Place, 13 February 1739 [SAY 1725]

Mrs Marquick received your letter a Sunday night, and his very sorry that the maid wont do, for she can't recommend any of her others. She desires her service to you and hopes you will no send for me yet, for the whether has been so very bad that we have not been anywere yet. Miss Nolly and I are to goe to Battel tomorrow to make an asemble, and we are to lye at Mrs Telden, and I shall not fail of waiting upon Mrs Thorpe. Miss Sofy is gone to London and Mrs Marquick, who will return this week. I must bespeak a pair of pumps[1] at Battel for I am quite out of shoose and have none at home but my best, which will be of no service here. If you please to give my service to Miss Thorpe and tell her Mr Webbster drank tea here a Sunday and we was very merry. Mrs Markquick and Miss Nolly desire there complyments to you and if you please to give my love to my sisters and accept of my duty. I hope you have heard my papa got safe to town.

1 Pumps, a light shoe, comprising textiles often of bright colours, kept on the foot by a close fit without fastening; slippers for indoor use; also, a low heel shoe for dancers.

232 To Mary Collier, Hastings, from John Collier, [Johnson's Court], London, 17 February 1739 [SAY 1726]

I am to acknowledge the receipt of your by this post and acquaint you that though my cold is not of, it's much better and don't confine me within doors. I had a letter yesterday from Jemmy who is very well and hope that you have had, or will soon, receive a letter from him. The king, duke and princesses have been at the play twice since I have been in town and the Prince and Princess of Wales the like number but I have not gone to see any of them.[1]

I don't hear whether Sir William Ashburnham is come to town or not. My brother was yesterday taken with the gout and confined all this day. The little boy came home from nurse today. I am no judge of likeness but think he is one of the plainest children I ever saw. We have a poor heavy fellow for a footman and he is to goe away. I beleive Alce's intrigue quite drove Thomas away to the great regret of my brother, etc. I have seen nothing of Mr Carleton, nor indeed been hardly anywhere, so send no news, fashions, etc.

1 Drury Lane Theatre, *Mustapha, a Tragedy*, by David Mallet; five performances from 13 February to 17 February; 16 February by command of the Prince and Princess of Wales (Scouten Pt 3, vol. 2, 1736-47 760). Plays attended by members of the royal family, Covent Garden Theatre, 11 January, *King Henry V*, by Shakespeare, the first occasion George II visited the theatre since Caroline's death; Drury Lane Theatre, 10 February, *King Henry VIII*, by Shakespeare; King's Theatre, *Saul*, by Handel, king, duke and princesses; Covent Garden Theatre, 14 February, *Emperor of the Moon* by Aphra Behn, by command George II, with *The Necromancer,or, Harlequin Doctor Faustus*, by John Thurmond (Scouten Pt 3, vol. 2, 1736-47, 753 759 760).

233 To Mary Collier, Hastings, from John Collier, [Johnson's Court], 20 February 1739 [SAY 1727]

I heartily compassionate you on the dissorder you complain of and am very sensible of it by experience, for tongue or pen can't describe the anxiety and disquietude attending it. An unalterable regard to each other, without any mixture of the bitter draught, will, I beleive, be the greatest comfort or relievance. I will not say I am blameless, but think I have not sometimes such allowances made as I ought, and often set on fire by reflections and contradictions that may, and ought, by you to be spared. When your box arrives I will give orders about the things you mention and buy the compound briony water.[1] I had a letter by yesterday's post from Dely and you'l think me complaisant when I tell you I now answer it. I think it's time she comes home. She wrote that they heard there was a great dissagreement between Lady Ashburnham and her neice and that their parting is for good.

Mr Northey's will and his lady's conduct is much talked of, and she abominably censured and to be sure a sad creature.[2] The poor man absolutely dyed of what they call a broken heart for she had many intrigues of gallantry on her hands. I was yesterday at Mr Carleton's but did not see him. Mrs Carleton looks very well, but Miss Betsy such a thing as I can't describe and could hardly bear to see. She is learning Italian, and her master hapned to be there, but with all this exquisite breeding think she has lost all her manners, if ever she had any, for she did not get of from her seat when I came into the room, etc.

I did not see Mr Thomas Steevens till yesterday when I gave him orders about the window curtains, etc. I understand by him that his brother Sam came to town a Saturday night but he had not seen him. I find he writes him as scurrilous letters as he does to Charles. Mrs Carleton said Mr Carleton had been with Sir William Ashburnham, but when he came to town I don't know. She said he was to sup there last night and desired my company but I had enough with my short visit. I think you was exceedingly well of in not seeing the man tyger, and should have laughed heartily. It is the filthiest, beastly lascivious creature that can be seen.[3] There is a new tragedy called Mustapha in acting, which has a great run, but I have not seen it nor been at the playhouse.[4]

I send by old James Bossom's vessel a box in which is only a saddle and bridle and filled up with writings. I also sent some sugar loves, corks and cheese, and will buy a little parcel of 6d to send by James. I think they say sugars are fallen.[5] There's no hams yet come in, at least very few. I could hardly forbear telling Mrs Carleton that Miss Nanny had a pair of stays making in Moorfields, but I was afraid it would have been such a shock that she would have fainted away. My sister for these last two or three days has not been very well, and has put on her grievous looks. Their new man went away early a Sunday morning without saying anything to anybody, but as he carried of only himself the loss was not great. There was more stuff in Alce's letter, for she pressed for an answer that she might have some comfort in this world, and that she was a miserable, distracted, creature and I don't know what.

1 Compound briony water; Bryonia, south of England climbing plant, juice extracted from the roots mixed with honey or oil was a cure for deafness.

2 William Northey of Compton Bassett (1690-1738) attorney, appointed to Chancery 1712, MP Calne for 1713-15 and 1715-22 for Wootton Bassett, defeated 1722 and 1727; married 19 Sept. 1721 Abigail, daughter of Sir Thomas Webster.

3 The man tyger, brought from Angola in the *Portfield*, East Indiaman, Captain Dalbiac (Sayer vol. 1, 154).

4 Drury Lane Theatre, *Mustapha* [**232**] additional performances, 19, 20, 21, 24, 27, 28 February (Scouten Pt 3, vol. 2, 1736-47 760).

5 Average price of a cwt of muscovado sugar shipped to London in 1738, 21/7¾d; rising to 25/8¼d 1739, and 32/0½d 1740. Losses in shipments and insurance costs due to the war caused this rise, although prices dipped, briefly, to 27/3½d in 1743, by 1745 and in 1746 a cwt was above 39/5d, with a high of 42/9½d in 1747 (Sheridan 496-7). For the effect of sugar prices on the income of the Fuller family of Heathfield see Crossley & Saville xxv-xxvi; R Saville 'Gentry Wealth on the Weald in the Eighteenth Century: the Fullers of Brightling Park' *SAC* 121 139-40.

234 To Mary Collier, Hastings, from John Collier, Johnson's Court, 1 March 1739 [SAY 1728]

I am much concerned at the contents of your letter and at the smallpox breaking out so much; sure there must have been a great remissness in care for to have it spread in so extraordinary manner.[1] I am surprized at the death of poor Mrs Grayling because the representation was so very favourable when I came from home.[2] I think Mary's going to

Broomham full as much surprizing, and look upon it to be a little out of the way, to say no worse of it. Her pretence of going to Newcastle is base, and as I think you have been very kind to her impudent, and it being such a secret and never any notice taken from Broomham very extraordinary, sure old madam must have had a hand in the conduct. Your letter determines me to return home as soon as possible and to leave London a Saturday, and hope to doe it so as to get home, barring any accident or bad weather, by Sunday noon, if not in the evening at furthest.

1 In late 1738 and 1739 the justices adjourned the Hastings quarter sessions on several occasions; the receipts for Hastings markets and fairs fell by nearly half in the two years to 28 May 1739 (ESRO HAS CAA/5). The annual burials in St Clement's in 1731-38 averaged 22, and for 1738-40 fell to 16.

2 Mary Grayling, died 27 February 1739, wife of Edward Grayling.

235 To Mary Collier, Hastings, from Lady Margaret Ashburnham, Broomham, 7 March 1739

[SAY 1729]

I am mighty sorry to find by Mary Wimble you dislike some blunder made between Lucy Steveens and me, about a servant in your family, which makes me give you this trouble to repeat what has passed upon this occasion. Lucy knowing I wanted a cook, sent me word there was a servant going from you, and another from Mrs Cruttenden at Ladyday;[1] that yours was a good cook and could do a great deal of work, but she was going to Newcastle from whence she came. I knew somthing of the other and desired she would inquire of Mrs Cruttenden if she parted with her; but I had much rather have had the maid that went from you, thinking it most likely she would have been fitter for my place. A few days afterwards she wrote to me again that she had now seen your maid, who was willing to come to me if I could stay till she came back from Newcastle, and that you told here she was to leave your service at Ladyday. I think it was the begining of last week, she desired Lucy would let me know I must not depend upon her, for she could not come to me, which was some disappointment.

But I soon bargained with another, and last Friday she sent me word if I would stay till midsummer, she would not fail to come back from Newcastle and be at my service. I heard you was so kind to design us a visit when it was good walking, and I thought that would be time enough to inquire after her character, but if you propose her staying with you I have nothing more to say to her, or else I have no dislike to her performing quarentine at Newcastle, and at her return shall depend upon her coming as she has bargained to do. I am extreamly sorry the smallpox is at Hastings, but now Mr Collier is come home I hope you will be under no apprehension of your young people being in any danger and wee shall soon have the pleasure of seeing you here. I must leave the bearer to make an excuse for my long letter. All here send their compliments. I would not write such another letter for the best cook in Europ.

1 For notes on servants' contracts, January 1761 to March 1765 see Mary Collier ESRO MIL 7/5.

236 To John Collier, from Duke of Newcastle, Whitehall, 16 June 1739

[BL Add Ms 32,692 f.83]

Having received from the Lords Commissioners of the Admiralty two orders, the one for impressing seamen within the vice admiralty of the county of Sussex and the other directing me to cause a general embargo to be forthwith laid on all ships and vessels whatsoever within the said vice admiralty, except such as are employed by the officers of the navy, ordnance, victualling and customs which are not cleared at Gravesend, and to continue the same till further order;[1] I take the first opportunity to transmit to you copies of the said orders, and I am to desire that you would forthwith take effectual care, that the same may be punctually complied with; and you will from time to time send me particular accounts of what shall be done in consequence of the said orders. If there should be any thing further which may be proper to be done by me on this occasion, you will be so good as to let me know it.

1 Britain declared war on Spain, 19 October 1739 (Crossley & Saville 285 287); for anticipation of the war and complaints of the press on the crew of vessel due to ferry Fuller's guns to Woolwich see *ibid*, 297, 298.

237 To John Collier, from Duke of Newcastle, Whitehall, 28 June 1739.
[BL Add Ms 32,692 f. 93]

I send you enclosed a copy of a letter, which I have received from the Lords Commissioners of the Admiralty, containing directions that such men as shall be impressed for the service of the navy within the vice admiralty of Sussex, should be sent to Rye, Hastings and Shoreham; at which places one of his Majesty's ships will frequently call for and receive them and that the officers within the said vice admiralty should be strictly charged not to take up or entertain any persons who are not seamen, seafaring men or able bodied land men capable of doing service in the fleet. And I am to desire that you would give immediate notice thereof in all proper places. And you will send me an account of what you shall do in consequence hereof, as also of what number of men have been impressed within the vice admiralty of Sussex in persuance of the order transmitted to you in my letter of the 16th instant.

238 To John Collier, from Duke of Newcastle, Whitehall, 3 July 1739
[BL Add Ms 32,692 f. 102]

Having received another order from the Lords Commissioners of the Admiralty directing that the embargo should be taken off within the vice admiralty of the county of Sussex from all coasting vessels, which go from port to port, and likewise from all fishing smacks and other small craft which ply on the rivers, bays and creeks within the said vice admiralty, I send you herewith inclosed a copy of the said order and am to desire that you would forthwith cause the same to be punctually executed.

239 To John Collier, from George Bernard Ellis,[1] Frindsbury, near Rochester, 12 July 1739; with draft of reply
[SAY 341]

In regard to the esteem you have always been pleased to shew me, I should accuse myself of want of gratitude if I neglected informing you of a base underhand design against you. On Monday last I saw Mr Tomkins who told me he had seen Forster,[2] who showed him an order to survey in your stead, and that Forster said your report should be set aside relating to the great seizure of tea made by the Lidd officers and that Tomkins should have his part thereof according to his pretentions. Many disrespectful words were spoke of you, which I shall forbear mentioning in a letter, but find Forster's your hateful enemy and endeavours all he can to lessen your conduct. Please to keep this secret, as the hints may put you on your guard and give you an opportunity of disconcerting the idle schemes of this upstart, illiterate fellow, and as they flow from a warmth sincerely attached to your interest I hope you'l accept of my hearty wishes for your health and prosperity.

[*Reverse*] July 1739. I received your letter of the 12th, for which I return you my thanks. I am under no concern at the behaviour and expressions of such reptiles and know it's not in their power to doe me any real prejudice. If ever it was to [3] happen that [4] their misrepresentations [5] can have weight enough to give me any uneasiness in the proper enjoyment of my office I shall throw it up with contempt, but I am under the same obligation to you for the hint as if it could be attended with any ill consequences[6].

1 George Bernard Ellis, riding officer, Dartford (TNA CUST 18/202).
2 Gabriel Tomkins, surveyor of the riding officers on the Kent side of the Thames, from the buoy of the Nore to Gravesend (TNA CUST 148/11). William Forster, inspector of journal books (TNA CUST 148/11).
3 MS *come to* struck through.
4 MS *such creatures* struck through.
5 MS *should* struck through.
6 MS *to me* struck through.

240 To John Collier, Hastings, from Henry Pelham, Esher, 13 July 1739

[SAY 398]

I had the favor of both your letters. As to the first, I think the division you propose of Mr Plummer's land seems pretty reasonable, though I am afraid when we come to lett it, I shan't have great interest for my money. As things are likely to go, if we have a war, as I doubt is now unavoidable, the interest of money will encrease and of consequence the price of land should fall.[1] However, as all partys have been very civil, I wont go off from any bargain you think adviseable, and especialy when Saxby speaks so well of the land. I can't but observe one thing, that as it is now agreed, I am to pay all the money; Sir Thomas's share depends upon contingencys and will be a better bargain if the interest of money rises, for I think all the charges are fixed att four per cent.

John Turner was with me; I told him I would talk to you before I came to any resolution, but gave him no hopes att all. It was but two or three years agoe that he was just to throw up the Great Lulham,[2] his circumstances were then thought very bad, and what was worse, his head was reckoned a little disordered. I can't perceive much recovery in the lattter, and I don't see how it can be expected that the other can be much improved. I think it right to let the three parcels together, which will make one very good farm, and as I am informed a very good house upon it, much better than he has ever lived in, or can expect to keep up in the manner such a house should be kept. I have heard nothing yet of Bishop, you or John Vine should know what he says. In my own mind, young Mr Durrant of Framfield was the person I thought of, but, if he has agreed with Sir Thomas Dyke, that is over. I wish you would give yourself the trouble to enquire after some proper tennants which by the time you come to Ifeild, you may probably have an opportunity of being well informed of. Buckle shall meet you att Ifeild on Wednesday the first of August, and if you can spare time, I should be glad, if you would return with him hither; that I may settle those affairs thoroughly with you.

As to any exchange of lands with Sir Thomas Dyke, when they suit both our conveniences, I can have no objection; Saxby will be the best man, I can think of, to consult about that. If we agree, the money shall be ready on my part, of Michaelmas day.

I think I have now answered most of the points in your letter, excepting that of Mr Plummer's proposal to be a tennant, I should be glad if you could put him off from it; he is by no means a proper person and yet I should be sorry to refuse him. If you can come to Esher, it may not be amiss for you to order John Vine to meet you here.

1 Henry Pelham was correct; in the 18th century the price of land always moved inversely with interest rates. The rate of interest on loans to the government, in anticipation of land, malt and salt taxes, moved from 3 per cent 1736-9, to 3½ per cent in 1740, and 4 per cent in1741; thereafter rates fell.

2 Great Lulhams (Appendix 4: Pelham Estate **[606]** SAY 373).

241 To John Collier, from George Herbert, Southborough, 23 August 1739, attaching letter from George Bernard Ellis, riding officer, Rochester, to Charles Carkasse, Secretary, Customs Board, 23 August 1739.[1] [SAY 342]

By order of Mr Carkess, I have here inclosed sent a coppy of a letter sent him by George Ellis of Darford.

Good sir, I am well informed that on Wensday morning, allso about break of day, a gang of smuglers of 21 horses heavy laden and about 14 or 15 men, openly armed with pistolls and blunderbusses (particularly one of them had a great brass blunderbuss slung over his shoulder), passed thro a village called Ogham,[2] neer Town Malling, in the road to London.[3] And on Saturday last eleaven of them same horses, with 3 men and a boy, repassed the same place on their road toward the sea coast, as is supposed to fetch more goods. I think proper to give you notice hereof, and if this will be of any service you may if you please communicate the same to the board that measures may be taken to discover these daring fellows, who in so formidable body are not to be opposed but by a strong military force.

1 George Herbert and George Ellis were Excise officers.

2 Offham.

3 The Commissioners of Customs considered the use of public houses by smugglers, and in September 1739 directed the collectors at outports, where proof was available of this practice and when the owners 'know them to be such, to wait on the justices at their special sessions on the day appointed for renewing licences' and to request a refusal from the justices for 'the licences of any persons keeping such disorderly houses' (TNA CUST 148/12 327, 19 September 1739, Charles Carkasse, secretary of the Board of Customs, to John Collier).

242 To John Collier, Surveyor General, Custom house, London, from George Adams, Yalding, 6 September, 1739 [SAY 399]

The day after I saw you at Coxheath I heard of the death of Richard Stevens, holder of the mannor of Widehurst.[1] I went and seized a horse of about six pound value; the executors of the deceased dispute it whether it be heriotable and that they never paid any heriot before, it being charged at 12d per yeare quit rent. The executor was with me yesterday to debate with me about it and I told him that I woud have three pound fifteen shillings, charges included, for the heriot or otherwise I would take the horse. Mr Strother, the minister of Brenchley, being of your acquaintance, designs to write to you in favour of the executor who desired me to stay a fortnight longer till they heard from you. I am well assured that I have made a moderate composition for the heriot and desire you'd send your pleasure and whether it be heritable or not, for if they do not come within the time appointed I will send for the horse and dispose of him for the most I can git for him. Pray sir, give me a line or two the first opportunity.

1 The lady of the manor was Jane Brewer, lands at Marden, five miles from Yalding, four miles from Brenchley (Halsted vols. 5, 7). On the death of Richard Stevens, Joshua Strother, vicar, Brenchley, under whose care came Stevens' son, objected to the heriot unless proof was offered that such was paid in the recent past; Strother was appointed as vicar of Brading, Isle of Wight, 17 April 1703 to 1725, though office in the care of others from before 4 May 1709 when Strother appointed as vicar of Brenchley, where he remained until d. 28 April 1744 (Cedb).

243 To John Collier, Hastings, from Joshua Strother, Brenchley, 19 September 1739 [SAY 400]

I am obliged to you for your immediate and civil answer to my letter. But one thing you have not answered and that is the main point in question: you have not told me that you have proof from any of your books of entry that ever any heriot was actually paid for this piece of land. Without such proof you know the claim can't be defended. My friend Mr Courthop was newly put upon this proof for a heriot he demanded on the death of Mr Halsey of Hertfordshire, and he has proved it; and Sir Walter Roberts told me very lately that he himself, for want of such proof, was forced to depart from the claim of some heriots to the value of £15 which the rolls, rentals, etc., of his manor of Glassenbury told him were his right. If therefore you will be so kind once again by a line to assure me that you have such proof, either anno 1654 or in any other year I will neither doubt your veracity nor dispute your right; but if not, you will not expect that I should either advise or allow my ward to comply with the demand.

244 To Mary Collier, Hastings, from John Collier, Canterbury, 28 September 1739 [SAY 1730]

I was much dissappointed yesterday in not receiving a letter from Hasting, and almost made me resolve not to write from this place. Colonel Pelham came hither last night in his way to London, and we are just a going to dine with the dean, so that I shall not set out for the Isle of Thanet till tomorrow morning.[1] There was as great a shower of rain this day about ten as I ever remember; it was very short of duration but almost flowed the great street. I can't help being a little angry that neither you or Jemmy wrote one line. It makes the old proverb good, out of sight, out of mind, but it's not so with your faithful and affectionate husband.

1 Dr John Lynch, Dean of Canterbury, 1734-1760; John Collier was on his survey of the riding officers of Kent from 17 September 1739.

245 To Mary Collier, Hastings, from John Collier, Sandwich, 1 October 1739 [SAY 1731]

I received yesterday, at Margate, Jemmy's letter directed to that place, and last night on my coming hither had the pleasure of yours directed to Canterbury. How it was that I did not receive it there I know not, for the post mark is right upon the cover, but as it did not come I could not help complaining. I think I wrote you from thence that I was just going to dine at the dean's with Colonel Pelham. I really was surprized and charmed at the grandeur of the house and the magnificence of the entertainment. I have heard he lived very handsomly, but it far surpassed my imagination. There were two neighbouring gentlemen and their ladys also dined there, one of which stayed the evening, as we also did. Played at cards as soon as evening came till 9, then a very handsom supper, all entirely new, and we stayed till 12.

I set out from thence Saturday morning for the Isle of Thanet and found a very sensible alteration in the air, and yesterday there was a strong north easterly wind that was very sharp and peircing at the northforeland, and today it's cold, cloudy, ugly weather. I intend to set out for Deal this afternoon. As Jemmy's letter is dated a Thursday and no mention made of the cricket match, I presume there has been none played. I hope to manage so as to be at home a Saturday or Sunday but shall, I beleive, be more capable of judging by Tuesday's post when I think to be at Dover and shall have the pleasure of writing to you from that place. I saw Colonel Armstrong, the engineer, at Canterbury, and find he has been here viewing their fort, and it's said he is to inspect all the ports along this part of the coast.[1] If so, I hope Hasting is in his list and that he will put us into a condition to frighten a least a Spaniard, or even a Frenchman, if they are sawcy. I am my dear soul with the trust, sincerity and affection.

1 Brigadier-General John Armstrong, military engineer, cousin of Colonel John Armstrong who surveyed the forts at Portsmouth in 1738, and left for Minorca the same year; he later published *History of the Island of Minorca* (London, 1756).

246 To John Collier, Custom house, Deal, from George Adams, Yalding, 2 October 1739 [SAY 401]

I received yours dated the 15 September last, wherein I find you have searched the rentalls of Widehurst manor and that a heriot is due to the lady of the mannor upon the death of Richard Stevens. Whereupon I sent my son to the executor to know what he designed to do upon the affair and whether Mr Strother had received any answer from you, but gave him no notice that I had wrote to you nor of my answer. He sent me word that he had, and that he would come over soon. Michaelmas day last he came over to me with an open letter in his hand directed to me from Mr Strother, the contents whereof are as underwritten.

To Mr George Adams of Yalding, from J. Strother, Brenchley, 26 September 1739.

"I have received 2 letters from Mr Collier about this heriot, but as he has not yet made appear that Mrs Brewer has any right to it, I look upon the demand as nothing less than a design to robb an orphan who is under my care. Therefore, be it at your own peril if you offer to touch any beast of his; if you do, I shall know what course to take with you, and I belive I shall treat you in the same manner as I would do any man that I should find attempting to steal or carry away my own horse.

You may acquaint Mr Collier, if you please, that these lands at Marden were lands of ancient free soccage, long before the year 1654, and never were holden in military tenure, and that, I think is a better indication that they are not heritable than any he has given me to the contrary.[1] If you have anything further to say upon this subject pray come to me, but don't go about to terrify a young lad that is scarce entered into the world, though I can tell you, he is as hopefull a one as most of his years. I am, yours as you use me"

Upon the perusal herof I was not a little surprised at shuch threatinng expressions, which I was shure I had noways deserved either from him or his friend. After breathing a little I cast my eye upon the conclusive. "I am, yours as you use me", thought to myself I could not well use him with more scurrility, either by word of mouth or letter, than I found he had done me, being a stranger to him, and undeservedly. Told the executor, plainly, that I would neither wait on him nor answer his, and that I would present the parson's favour, both to you and the lady of the mannor, and if there was no heriot we must desist. I told him plainly I had received answer that there was one due, and that he could not expect the same favour as I offered. Desire, therefore, if you please, answer soon, whether I may be safe and indemnified, for I told him he should here from me in a fortnight's time.

If there should be any room, I no ways dispute the veracity of the cloth of what he has declared. I am ready to execute my office at all times, but are not willing to except of a felon's reward, being first a stone dublet and then a rope. Tis true, I am ordered to seize heriots upon the death of all tenants, but am not certain whether all be heritable, therefore do expect to be indemnifyed both by the lady and you, as well from all charges and trouble as from rope and transportation, or otherwise I will quit my post.

This is the 3rd hieriot I have been like to lose after seized, which is occationed by the errors following, viz the heriots as by order when seized are left in the hands of the heirs of the deceased, to deliberate upon the composition, and often some distance from me, and if I give them a month to consider, they will take two, and often more, till forced to go or send. And in such space of time they apply to one friend, and then to another, for advice to know how others have been used in that case, and some tells them I paid but so much, and another so much, and another persuaides them at last that none is due to the lord or lady. And this last advice sounds best in their ears, and here they stand, so that the lord must, to give content, either compound very low or go without anything.

Therefore, as I have often heard the musick and seen the error, for preventing the like for the future is immediatly to take away the beast when seized, which they will soon follow, and without doubt more readily comply to the composition that shall be offered. Good Sir, I ask pardon for troubling you with this long epistle, but thought it needfull, and beg you'd send me answer soon, for if the horse comes to my hand, I will make no compounding for him, but will make the most of him for such indirect usuage. I have received since I saw you about £4 quit rents in arrere.

1 By 12 Car. II c. 24 Parliament intended a consistent basis for the rights and obligations of the lord of the manor; the organisation of tenure in relation to the manor is discussed in all the law books of the time. W Blackstone *Commentaries on the Laws of England* vol. 1, ch. 6 has a commentary on free and common socage and on the requirement that fines were reasonable. Kent forms of tenure were generally different from those in Sussex.

247 To Mary Collier, Hastings, from John Collier, Dover, 3 October 1739

[SAY 1732]

I dispatched my business at Sandwich before the post came in several hours and did not stay to receive the letter. I told Jemmy to send to that place, nor the same hath not as yet been sent after me, but I hope you and all the family enjoy perfect health. The wind continues to blow very hard at east and makes a very great sea all along this coast and very cold by the seaside. I propose getting out tomorrow for Folkstone and if nothing extraordinary happens, hope for the satisfaction of seeing you a Saturday evening, and am heartily tired with the fatigue of the journey and company and teased to death with some of the officers' impertinence. I dined yesterday with the collector of Deal in a very elegant manner.[1] Adieu, my dear creature and I am, most affectionately, your faithful husband.

1 James Carr, Customs collector at Deal, 1734, 1736 (TNA CUST 18/178/182).

248 To Duke of Newcastle, from John Collier, Hastings, 13 October 1739
[BL Add Ms 32,692 f. 372]

I humbly hope your grace will pardon my presumption in giving you this trouble relating to the bill of £318 17s 2d due to me for the charges in this corporation causes in the court of King's Bench.[1] As your grace was pleased to take us under your protection and to defend the attack made on the corporation, by your commands, I supplyed the whole money for the councel, and all other incident charge, and was from time to time to be repaid by Mr Paxton but never could get sixpence and since Mr Weller has been concerned I have time after time frequently waited on him, and sent from one to the other of them fruitlessly.

I humbly begg your grace will please to consider the time I have been out of the money and the disappointments it has made me, and please to order an immediate payment. By the usage I have had I am constrained to apply to your grace in this affair, though with the greatest reluctance and humbly hope for your forgivenesse. I humbly wait for your grace's orders to the trustees about the three notes for £1000 which I advanced on the account of Trumble's executorship on my own credit, or leaving your grace's drafts on Mr Hoar, that I may be paid the same by degrees as the money comes in.[2] I am with all possible gratitude and respect. Mr Paxton assured me it was far from his fault that I had not the £318 17s 2d.

1 Claim for payment of charges in Henry Moore v Mayor, etc., of Hastings ([**122**] [**155**] [**162**] and *ER* vol. 95,228-9 234-5; Howell vol. 17, columns 876 ff), tried on the 20 July 1736 before the Lord Chief Justice on a mandamus for admitting the plaintiff to be a freeman of Hastings.

2 Duke of Newcastle owed Anthony Trumble, solicitor, £1000. John Collier agreed a settlement with the creditors of Trumble's executors, and paid over the £1000, borrowed at interest, on being given drafts from Newcastle on Hoare & Co, bankers, in 1735/6. This debt remained unpaid for some years and at least a part was outstanding on John Collier's death.

249 To John Collier, Hastings, from Duke of Newcastle, Whitehall, 23 October 1739
[BL Add Ms 32,692 f. 415]

I send you inclosed a copy of an order which I have received from the Lords Commissioners of the Admiralty dated the 20th instant,[1] by which I am required to cause to be forthwith seized and secured, in all the ports within the limits of the vice admiralty of the county of Sussex, all ships and vessels appertaining to the subjects of the king of Spain, or having goods or effects belonging to them on board, together with all such goods on board and all mariners, wheresover they shall be found within the limits of the said vice admiralty, being subjects of the said king. And I am to desire that you would take effectual care and give the proper notice and directions for putting the inclosed order into immediate execution and you will transmit to me constant and particular accounts of what shall be done in consequence of the said order.[2]

1 By the Commissioners for executing the office of Lord High Admiral of Great Britain and Ireland etc, to his grace the Duke of Newcastle, vice admiral of the county of Sussex; signed, Sir Charles Wager, H Powlett, J Campbell, 20 October 1739, *Warrant to the Duke of Newcastle to seize and secure Spanish ships, goods and mariners and to inform the Admiralty of proceedings therein* (BL Add Ms 32, 692, f. 417).

2 Britain declared war against the King of Spain on 19 October 1739.

250 To John Collier, Hastings, from Duke of Newcastle, Newcastle House, 25 October 1739 [SAY 98]

I hope you will excuse my not having sooner returned an answer to your letter. I am very much obliged to you for the trouble you have taken in our corporation affair and for the money you have advanced on that account. Mr Paxton did promise me that he would furnish the money for the last hearing, which I thought he had done, but beleive he had no money for that purpose, so my obligation to you for doing it was the greater. I shall take it as a favour if you can stay some little time longer, and the better to enable you to do it I will speak to the trustees to lett you have some money on the notes and to put them all in a course of payment. I wish you would lett me know in what proportion and att what times you are willing to receive the money on the notes, and how long you can stay for the 300 pounds due on the corporation account, all which I find has been expended since February 1737-8, and when I know how long you can stay with conveneincy to yourself. I will endeavour to make you easy as soon and as punctualey as is possible.

251 To Duke of Newcastle, from John Collier, Hastings, 27 October 1739 [BL Add Ms 32,692, f. 431]

I have the honour of your grace's letter of the 23rd with a copy of an order to your grace as vice admiral of the county of Sussex from the Lords Commissioners of the Admiralty, dated the 20th of this month, for the seizing and securing all ships and vessels appertaining to the subjects of the king of Spain and all goods and effects on board, all mariners being subjects of the said king. In humble obedience to your grace's commands I gave directions for putting the said order into immediate execution and shall make it my business to transmit your grace constant and particular accounts of what shall be done in consequence of the said order.

252 To Duke of Newcastle, from John Collier, Hastings, 30 October 1739 [SAY 99][1]

I have the honour of your grace's letter of the 25th relating to the £318 17s 2d due to me for money advanced on the proceedings in the court of King's Bench against this corporation, and as your grace is pleased to mention my staying some little time longer for the same I hope you'l please to order the payment thereof the 1st of May next. I am humbly thankful for your grace's intentions of speaking to the trustees that I may be paid the £1000 in the trust, being money I took up at interest to discharge Mr Trumble's creditors on having your grace's drafts for the same on Messrs Hoar & Co, vizt March the 12th 1735, one draft for £300, another for £400; September the 2nd 1736, a draft for £300.

I humbly hope to be repaid the interest, and beg your grace will please to direct that I may receive £400 of the debt before Christmas and the remainder at 2 following ½ yearly payments. For the honour and happiness I have had of your grace's friendship, if I may presume to make use of the word, and the obligations I am under for the many favours your grace hath conferred upon me, I shall never cease to be with the greatest gratitude and respect. My Lord, your grace's most obliged and most faithful, obedient and humble servant.

1 Sayer vol. 1, 163-4, has this letter as a draft of this date; see [**266**] SAY 99r, for reverse of this document. There is a draft for a subsequent appeal to his grace, which Sayer allocates to April 1740 (*ibid* 168).

253 To John Collier, Custom house, London, from George Adams, 5 November 1739. [SAY 402]

Received yours dated the 11th [1],October last, and on the next day I went to Brenchley for the horse; but was informed by a friend that the horse was not in the way, did not goe to them to enquire after him. Two or three days after I sent my son with a witness with him, and a note of my hand to be left according to your former orders, and when they came to the young man the executor, and demanded the horse, he told them plainly that they, nor I, should not have him; and that Mr Strother had given him orders not to part with him, but desired them to goe to Mr Strother's with him. And when they came the old parson fell into a passion with him, and used him with his tongue in like manner as he did me by letter, and declared possitively that if they took him they should not have him away, and that the lady of the mannor should not have the horse till you have given him better reasons, than you had done, that there was a heriot due. I was informed that the horse was to come to Maidstone last week for seed wheat. I waited on the road for him, but was disapointed, or otherwise I had wrote to you before. Sir, desire you'd give me further advice, for if the beast be under lock and key, I cannot immagine how I shall recover him without proper orders to search for him.

1 MS *September* struck through

254 To John Collier, Hastings, from William Cranston, [Johnson's Court], 8 November 1739 [SAY 751]

Your £300 bill came to hand, which I shall go after in a day or two, for doubt Hoar's people don't much traffick that end of the town. A box went yesterday and in it, rolled up in a pair of gloves, is my sister's watch, but I am a very unhappy prince, forgetting to put up the chain with it. I wish my brother had let me known his mind one post sooner about stocks, for I yesterday agreed to tell em and was just going to finish when I unluckily left my warrant account behind me, so could not compleat then; but agreed with my chap to meet him tomorrow at 12 at Wednesday's price be it tomorrow, more or less, so can't possibly gett off. Holland and Thorpe, this cost is setled at £5 13s 4d.

Since writing the above I find poor Mar Spillett is dead, and have had Bardmore, and one Lloyd, the present Lord Chancellor's train bearer, with me. I took it for granted that Bardmore came on his own behalf, but it seems it was on Lloyd's, who has a mind to purchase it. Lloyd, I remember, spoke to me about such an affair when trained bearer to Lord Hardwicke when Chief Justice. He was originally his footman, as I well remember, when he was Attorney Generall. He is a person of an exceeding good character and he has all his life time been a retainer to the law in one shape or another, I really think he is exceedingly well qualifyed. He's a good natured, civill, sensible, fellow and well respected by the barr and say, if tis necessary he doubts not but to be recommended by the Chancellor as well as his grace of Newcastle from whom he says he has often the honour of a shake by the hands.

He desires only to have the favour of the refusall, and is willing to give as much for it as anybody. I beleive at first he would execute it by deputy which should be approved of by you. I told him that I would write to you about it, that I could not take upon me to give him any answer, but beleft I might hear something by the return of the post. I find the reason, why Bardmore and Creed join with Lloyd, is from a beleif that he may be of some service to their office with my Lord Chancellor in the progress of the Commissioners in respect to their fees, which it seems is now coming upon the carpett before them. And in case they can't make an interest there, but it should go as the jury have left it, they'll be extreamly lowered. This I beleive is true, but whether this scheme can be of any service I know not, though tis certain Lloyd has his lordship's ear, and probably something might come of it, you'll be so good as to give me a line in answer and about which sume I am to ask this chap, or any other.

[*Note at end*] he died but this morning.

255 To John Collier, Custom house, London, from George Adams, Yalding, 9 November 1739 [SAY 403]

Received yours dated the 10th instant and find you censure me of failure in duty, which I do assure you I no ways deserve, nor am in the least fearfull of the threats of any person, but have done to my utmost to recover the horse seized, but cannot obtain my ends. The very day I received yours I was informed the horse was at work in the ground. The next morning I sent my son with a note to be left, and a witness, who was down there before light. In the morning the servants went into the stable where the horse was. My son pushed for the dore, but was discovered by them before he could enter and they immediately lockt him up, and could by no means persuaid them to let him have the horse.

This is the fourth time I have been and sent early and come home late in a cursed durty and wet country, being at least eight miles from me, and cannot be rode and all in vain. And on the 26th instant I was informed of the horse, and on the 27th in the morning I sent as before, who was there by 7 in the morning, and just as he came into the yard he espyed the stable open and pushed in in with the witness and seizd the horse. The master came in before he could get him out and called a workman and servant to his assistance and took him from them by violence and immediately lockt him up. This is the usuage I meet with, and, if allowed of, must expect the same of others. In short, there will be no ways to regain him without a warrant and an officer to execute the same, as they have declared, or some other way by law or justice as you know best.

I should think if there be any law for lords of mannors to seiz heriots as their own right, sure either by law or some other course may be taken with those persons that assault the seizer and by violence wrest the same out of his hands after seized. Sir, pray consider what is to be done in such a case as this, and also the consequence. I am fully determined to be with them again soon and, if it be possible, to recover him. Mr William Fleet, East Peckham, and holder of the mannor, dyed the week before last. I have seizd two heriots, a horse and a heaffer, both about the value of £6. Desire you'd send your pleasure of what composition; they seem to dispute the two heriots and say they never paid but one; I produced my rentall and showed them there was two, and two I seized. Sir, I desire you'd answer me soon.

256 To John Collier, Hastings, from William Cranston, [London], 15 November 1739. [SAY 752]

Mr Lloyd and self have been together at the Mitre over the way, from 7 till now, talking over the cryer's place, and have at last come to the following agreement for it, vizt he is to pay down £250 and to give his bond to pay £50 more that day four year his appointment bears date, if he be then living; or he is to pay down now £300 and you to give a bond to pay his widow £50 in case he dies within four year from his appointment; so that you'll please to determine which of the two you'll accept of. I can't say but that Colonel Pelham's chap bid £300 down, on the nail, without any conditions, but as you have empowered me to act for you, as I would for myself, I really think there is that and more difference in the men and have accordingly struck the above bargain and hope twill be agreable to you, for I think I have done the best. I quite forgott to ask his christian name, otherwise you might have sent up his deputation by the return of the post, for tis to bear date as today that he may come into part of the fees of this terme, but you shall have it per next post. You'll have your dedimus per next post. The bureau has been bespoke long since and only waits Bossom's arrivall to go down.

257 To John Collier, [Hastings], from William Cranston, [Johnson's Court], 17 November 1739 [SAY 753]

Inclosed is your dedimus, Elliott v Elliott. I am afraid twon't be safe to venture to go into possession of defendant's goods. I have not, indeed, had time to inquire among my brethren as to this cause but will both Monday and Tuesday next, and if I meet with any encouragement will send a warrant. But it must first be made plain that we shall incurr no breach, for I know you have good reason to beleive that his lordship would lay it on thick, if in his power. I have sent the Latitat v Mrs Hammond to Fisher, though as he is such a sad dog I doubt whether he'll do it as working for a dead horse. Two brace of woodcocks came safe for which thanks are due. Lloyd's name is Richard, Spillett was a cryer; I take it for granted you have a copy of Creed's deputation and suppose twill be only altering usher to cryer. I hope your box came safe by this day sennight carrier and your chair in Cole's parcell this day.

258 To John Collier, [Hastings], from William Cranston, Johnson's Court, 22 November 1739 [SAY 754]

In Mrs Hickes' account passed in Sussex last vad I find an item as follows: 23 February 1738, to a year's insurance of goods etc., at Tunbridge Wells. This I take to be what you inquire after in your last. I send you inclosed your dedimus. I am sure I intended to pay £83 12s 0d to Mr Ott and verily beleive I did, notwithstanding the receipt does not mention it. This I should have thought had and I had no other authority for it but recollection, but as it happens I gave Mr Gardes a draft for the whole on Messrs Hoare, and upon going over thither just now I find my draft for and that he actually received £83 12s 0d.

Lloyd has appointed to pay his cole Monday evening next when the whole affair may be compleated; for by that time you may return the bond the condition of which I take it may be after the inclosed sketch; and whilst I was writing of which it shott in my head that I must have omitted, by youre answers, one part of our agreement, which was that you was either to pay or receive interest for the £50 at four per cent, as you either took his or gave your bond. I'll look into Smith and Philcox and let you know per next how it stands.

259 To Mary Collier, Hastings, from Cordelia Collier, Battle [December 1739][1]

[SAY 1733]

I supose my papa told you of Miss Webster's peticion for my spending my Christmas here, and my lady bid me write to you to let you know that she will not let me come till the hollerdays are over, for we are to have a ball the first week. I hope you will send me my gown and petticoat and hed, and if Jenny will lend me her tipet[2] should be very glad, for mine is durty and not so hansome neither. We had no play a Friday the wheather being so very bad. I called upon Miss Thorpe a Thusday and they are all well. I should be glad when my cloths comes of a clean pair of pockets for these are black enought. My lady often wishes for some fish, and if they catch any, belive a dish whould be liket prodigiously, for here is none calls. Mr Webster come home today with my brother Worge; we drank tea there yesterday and my sister goes to Burwash tomorrow to stand for her cousin Hickes' child Mrs Hay is a diecing, I beg my duty to my papa and love to my sisters; from all here desire there compliments.

1 Sayer vol. 1, 167-8, places this letter in December 1739.
2 Tippet, a long, narrow cloth, on the hanging part of the outer dress, and attached to the hood or head dress.

260 To John Collier, Hastings, from Sir Thomas Dyke, Lullington,[1] 26 December 1739

[SAY 404]

I this moment received the draught of the conveyance, for which I thank you, and will look over it and send you my opinion on it as soon as the hollidays will give me leave. I think you judge well in not troubling Mr Pelham at present about this affair; for my part I think it would greive me even to see him.[2] It would suit me best to pay my mony as follows: to the widow Lulham, 250; to Molly Plummer now married in this neighbourhood, 150; allowed for Mrs Plummer's annuity of 30 pd per annum, 400; remainder to Mr Plummer, Josias Smith or wherever else you please: if I mistake in any of the sums excuse me and also haste in.

1 Lullington castle, near Eynsford, Kent, seat of Sir Thomas Dyke (Hasted vol. 2).
2 In November 1739 Henry Pelham lost both his sons, Thomas and Henry, possibly due to diptheria (Sayer vol. 1, 167; Pelham family table, Coxe 1829 vol. 1, pedigree B). The deaths affected the new trust for the Newcastle estates, and led to eventual agreement that the entail would be broken (Browning 124-5).

261 To John Collier, Hastings, from Sir Thomas Dyke, Ormond Street, 4 March 1740 [SAY 405]

I have looked over the writings you sent of Mr Plummer's estate by Mr Cranston, and shall be glad, farther, to see an exact copy of the will of Mr Thomas Plumer,[1] also his pedigree from his ancester, James, who purchased of Mr Evelyn; and desire to know whether his ancestors made any wills, and desire to see them if they did. I want also to be reminded how the agreement now stands between John Plummer and his mother, and you had need be well satisfied before we proceed that she will be satisfied with my part of the estate for her security. Favour me with an answer to this queeres the first post and then I will let you know my opinion concerning the method of proceeding, and tis certain that way that is best for me will be best for Mr Pelham. I shall see him next Thursday at Mr Monson's in Spring Garden, his late great misfortunes having made his own house insupportable to him.[2]

1 Such inquiries were a common undertaking to ascertain incumbrances on land.
2 Robert Burnett noted the 'repeated misfortunes which has attended my Lord Duke and Mr Pelham's family' in ESRO DUN 51/30 14 March 1740 [**260**].

262 To Mary Collier, from Miss Mary Thorpe, Battle, 13 March [1740][1] [SAY 2201]

Dear Madam, I had heard somthing of Miss Jenny's coming to Mr Worge's which made me the less pressing for her company pray give my service to her and tell 'tis only my love for her that makes me resign my pretentions, having the first promise, but as it's her desire I wont resent her coming there, but cant promise I wont if she dont come often to see us. I have your family often in my thoughts and very much pity your confinment. Mrs Denham and Bett was here one afternoon, I was mighty glad to see them, being the only people I have meet with that had seen you, she told us of your walk. I can't reconcile theire and my brother's account, of Mrs Medhurst, he says she blames Mr Hill, that he disliked her going to Mrs Denham's for fear he should be at some expence, and they that fowls etc., were not to be had. We had a woman removed in a cart a Wednesday for the small pox, it had been out four days or more, the doctors were both doubtfull but we hear to day 'tis not it. The maid is at the George, she come to ask my pardon and give the true reason for her behaviour, I dont know how 'twill hold at present, Mrs Slater likes her very much. She had just bargined when I saw her and was scarce reconciled to a publick house. Please to tell Miss Collier I looked as long as I could after the Captain without any hopes of his coming next Christmas, I fancy she's not so scornfull now as when I see her. Sir Charles had disappointed her that she could not bear the name of him or Mr Stevens. My mother and sister desire theire humble services, your most obedient, I received a letter from Mrs W the third and answersd it the fifth, as I dont think myselfe a match for her anyway, espesaly writing, I proposed an interview and so it rests.

1 MS Sayer, in pencil, writes 'thereabouts 1740'.

263 To John Collier, Hastings, from William Cranston, Johnson's Court, 20 March 1740 [SAY 755]

I thought I was right in my notions of Mr Cruttenden's being bond with you for Mr Godley, and that your speaking to him about it must naturally make him recollect and be assured, but as his memory is so very short I must tell him upon verbum sacerdotis, if a lawyer's won't do, that he is the man having this afternoon seen his fist upon that occasion at Mr Robinson's. The 9 bank notes for £50 each with the other papers came safe to hand, and the former I shall tomorrow make £700 and pay as you direct. I'm sorry for my brother Jemmy, and hope he'll take your advice and post to Lewes, unless he has an inclination to come hither for the same purpose where I think he need not be told he'll meet with a hearty welcome.

I have just now seen Sir Thomas Dyke, who cursorily run over the draft of the consequence as tis now setled, but he referred me to Mr Toke to peruse for him, which I shall do imediately upon his coming from the Kentish assizes.[1] I mentioned to him the affair of the £240 mortgage, when he told me that he was to sett out for Horeham tomorrow, when he would send to the mortgagee who he did not doubt but would take his money at any time at his request, but that, if he would not, he would allow him the interest. I think this mortgage should at all events be now paid off, otherwise, if Sir Thomas should die in the meantime, there might be strange confusion between the mortgagee, the children under age, and the widow and the children must then have recourse to Mr Pelham's part, for the other would by no means be sufficient and twill be loaded enough with the annuity and the £700, and that Mr Pelham may be as safe as he can. I have created a terme for the raising that summe, besides a covenant from Sir Thomas to indempnifye him and his part of the estate, from that money, for I think both are proper; and don't know of any compliements to be made upon any person's abilitys upon those occasions, where the thing must be a work of time and life uncertain, and probably infants in the case if he should drop in the meantime. As the two mortgages are to be seperately assigned, Sir Thomas has named Mr Toke for trustee and [2] shall lett Dr Hargrave stand for Mr Pelham and have made the proper alteration in that part of the draft.

I don't beleive I shall have any occasion to consult Mr Ward unless Mr Toke should cutt and flash too much. When the draft is compleated I am under doubt whether Master Hall should engross em or not, he writing an exceeding good hand of that sort, and so send em per next carrier if possible, or whether I should send you the draft and Master Patrick dig at it, for there must be 3 parts of the release, 1 for Mr P, 1 for Sir Thomas and one for the widow, and 2 parts of the lease for a year, but will consider of it again my getting it from Mr Toke which perhaps may not be till I can have your answer upon this head by Monday's post. I have sent William with the tea etc., after Bossum, but as he is not yet returned can't tell whether he is sailed or not for this is about his time as he said when he called here last Saturday. [*Reverse*] William was in time, Bossom not sailing till Saturday.

1 John Toke of Godinton, Kent, MP East Grinstead 1702-8, died 1746, trustee for Sir Thomas Dyke.
2 MS *I'll think* struck through.

264 To John Collier, Hastings, from William Cranston, [Johnson's Court], 25 March 1740 [SAY 756]

I have just now, past 8, the draft sent me from Mr Toke in which many alterations are made, but upon a cursory view of em, I think not very materiall from what I made it, though shall consider of em more fully tomorrow. I perceive he still insist on trustees and has put Mr Bramston in for Sir Thomas,[1] and I shall wait upon Mr Pelham tomorrow or next day to know his; and as this is the case [2] these new chaps must be put into the dedimus instead of Mr P and Sir Thomas and which you'll return me for that purpose per next post for I am just now told that this gift seal will be either Saturday or Tuesday next. The first Q. made is whether any of the daurs are married if so their husbands must be parties.

The 2d is whether it is the intention of Mr Plumer's agreement with his mother about her jointure, that the full of the krs tax should be deducted, or only in proportion as the estate is taxed.[3] This by the agreement I think is clear vizt that if the krs tax is 4s in ye pound, she is to deduct for her £30 to the full vizt £3 and not according as the land is taxed, however let us have your opinion. The 3d how the Athrell's mortgage is vested in the Lulham, and how Matthew's, in Pilbeam. I havn't been able as yet to see Robinson he being out of town but expected tonight or tomorrow, I have fixed Greenwich journey to Monday next.

1 Thomas Bramston, steward of the manor of Berwick.
2 MS *your* struck through.
3 The land tax for 1740 was settled at 4s in the pound sterling.

265 To Mary Collier, [Hastings] from Cordelia Collier, Johnson's Court, 17 April 1740/1743[1] [SAY 2169]

Honoured Madam, I am very glad to find by my papa's letter that he was better, and hope will continever so. I am sorry to here Sally's couf dose not mend, Jacky has one coming and his very ill but dose not houp yet, I should have wrote a Thursday, but did not come from the reharsall till tow aclock, and then was very tired, being oblige to stand the greatest part of the time, there were tow very fine anthems, one by Doctor Green, and the other by Handle, and the colection was too hundred and threescore pounds, which his a great deal more, than ever was gathered before.[2] I have bought my head, and it is a ground Brussells, it being quite the mode, the lappets and caul was just ten guinys, and the ruffels and tucker come to preaty nere as much, my close is a last year's silk, upon a pink ground, but have seen a great many of them worn, and could not get anything tolarable under half a ginney a yard, and this year's silks are thirteen and fourteen shillings, I have not bought my night gown yet, for exceeding the price in my other did not know wheara you whould have me buy one or no, though think I shall want on, ore must whare my other common, which I think will be pitty, my tabe comes home today,[3] and then shall bespeak my sisters, which will be done to send down next week.

Miss Green is come to town and dined here yesterday, and the evening mall not being yet began, we shall be there tomorrow morning just at a aelven, and walk till the qualaty goe home, Monday I am to goe in form to Sir Thomas Webbster's I have bespoke the hoops at Paulins, and they weare them very larg, and she said that mine must be four yards at least but have ordered it but three and half ell thinking that preaty well for me, if you please to tell Mrs Cruttenden there no new fasion mops but what is chiefly worn in a dres is belinder ones which I am shure have been a long while, if you please to give my duty to my papa and love to my sisters, from, honoured madam, your obedient and dutifull daughter, my uncle and aunt desire their compliments.

1 The most likely dates are in 1740 and 1743. On the 24 and 29 April 1742 Dely was in Hastings, and in 1744 Mary Collier was at Johnson's Court in April. On Friday 11 April 1740 two anthems by Handel were performed at Thomas Hickford's Music Rooms (Scouten Pt 3, vol. 2). Handel was at Covent Garden 23 March 1743; in April 1741 and 1742 he was in Dublin.
2 Maurice Greene, organist at St Paul's 1718-55, worked closely with Handel; from 1735 Greene was composer of music at the Chapel Royal working with Revd George Carleton.
3 Tabe, an ornament of dress.

266 To Duke of Newcastle, from John Collier, April 1740 [SAY 99r][1]

I had the honour of your grace's letter of the 25th of October last, relating to the £318 17s 2d [2] due to me about the corporation [3] suite and which I advanced on Mr Paxton's failure to supplying the money according to promise; and in humble obedience to your grace's commands [4] wrote an answer to your letter and begged [5] to have the [6] money paid the first of May, and, as the time is near, most humbly [7] take liberty to remind the same and that I may have an order for the same to be paid accordingly. I take the liberty of mentioning that your grace [8] took notice in the same letter that you would speak to the trustees [9] for my being paid part of the £1000 notes and to put them all in a course of payment,[10] but I have heard nothing on that subject. Charles Steevens is our mayor,[11] an honest, sober person and to be entirely depended on. I have the honour to subscribe myself with the greatest gratitude and most perfect attachment.

1 Written on the reverse of **[252]** (SAY 99, 30 October 1739).
2 MS *I had adv* struck through.
3 MS *affair* struck through.
4 MS *gave* struck through.
5 MS *for me* struck through.
6 MS *same* struck through.
7 MS *intreat your grace* struck through.
8 MS *was pleased in the letter to take notice* struck through.
9 MS *that I should be* struck through.
10 MS *and the* struck through.
11 MS *very good* struck through.

267 To James Waller, from John Collier, [before] 3 May 1740[1] [SAY 101]

The 10th of January last I gave you the trouble of a letter [2] relating to the money due to me from my lord Duke of Newcastle, hoping then to receive the same; but as I had the favour of an answer from you the 15th of the [3] month that it was [4] very inconvenient and that the [5] money or indeed any part could not [6] be then paid, I acquiesced therein. But as [7] the money has been long due and the last sum all money out of my pocket, I must now begg and insist on having the same [8] .I hope you'l please [9] to order it accordingly [10] and [11] save me the writing to his grace thereon which [12] I shall suffer the greatest uneasiness and anxiety, but am determined to be paid for I am now [13] more in disburse.

1 Written before 3 May 1740.
2 MS *from* struck through.
3 MS *same* struck through.

4 MS *would then be extream* struck through.
5 MS *same* struck through.
6 MS *with any conveniency* struck through.
7 MS *it has* struck through.
8 MS *paid* struck through.
9 MS *comply without* struck through.
10 MS *that* struck through.
11 MS *prevent the* struck through.
12 MS *will to me will be with* struck through.
13 MS *some* struck through.

268 To John Collier, Hastings, from James Waller, London, 3 May 1740

[SAY 102]

My lord Duke of Newcastle has commanded me to acquaint you that you may draw upon me for one hundred and sixty eight pounds 17s, part of the £318 17s, the amount of your bill about the corporation suit. At the same time I cannot help telling you that the making this payment is very inconvenient to his grace's affairs and I wish you would let it be deferred; but if you insist upon it I shall not fail to answer your draft for the said £168 17s, or any less sum that you will be content with at present. Last night I spoke to the trustees about the three notes for £1000 and as it is impossible for them to pay it of some time I proposed to them to settle it so as you may have interest for it, which they sayed they would take into consideration. We shall have another meeting next week and I shall be sure to press them again about it.

269 To John Collier, Hastings, from William Cranston, [Johnson's Court], 8 May 1740

[SAY 757]

I yesterday sent all the trapps in Mr Pelham's affair with Plumer to the carrier vizt two parts of the lease for a year, three parts of the release, 7 skins each, and the assignment of the two mortgages, two skins each, totall 27 skins, together also with the dedimus and the caption of the fine and likewise the copys of the two mortgages, all which I hope will come safe. In the mortgage of Stuckles, the land is there said to be 14 acres, and in the conveyance to be 44 acres; the parcells in both do not indeed exactly agree but the boundaries do, so that I am apt to think there is a mistake in that copy you sent me.

As I suppose you will make two of the releases originalls I have wrote receipts on both and put seals for all parties on all; but I presume it will be sufficient for Mrs Plumer to have hers only executed by Sir Thomas Dyke; therefore have indorsed no receipt on that part intended for her, neither need I, I believe, have sent it to you, nor need all the seals been on it, but that was done before I was aware of it, though it can do no harme. Having from Mr Read an account of Athrell's executor but last Saturday, I did not till since then draw and ingross that assignment and upon doing which I really apprehend the terme is at an end by the payment of the money and as tis not in being that it cannot be kept on foot; for tis not like a common mortgage, wherein a day stated is appointed for the payment of the money and if not paid then the term to be absolute, but in this case the condition is to pay the interest to Athrell for life, and afterwards the principall to his grandchildren, and which is now done. So consequently, as I conceive, the terme at an end and if I had observed it soon enough would have incerted this part of the affair into the body of the release. But, however, in case my notion of this matter should be right and the terme at an end and cannot be kept on foot, yet this assignment executed by the parties will at all events amount to an release and discharge of that part of the estate to Sir Thomas Dyke, which is all that is or can be wanting.

Smythe v Philcox.[1] I have given notice of tryall in this cause for the sittings after terme in London, which are the 21st instant. I hope by next post to be able to send you the sollicitor's opinion upon it. I shall wait on Mr Waller for the cole as soon as the money is due, though by that time hope to see you in town, having told everybody inquiring after you that I expect it by next Thursday or Fryday at farthest, imagining you won't go back back from Horsebridge but keep directly northward from thence.

I think my sister's thoughts of tyeing Jemmy to some part of the vessell will be right and hope twill be put in execution, for twill be terribly malancholy for him to sit all the while in the cabbin as well as very unsafe to be loose on deck. Therefore, this middle way will be right to steer, and he must be told that upon these terms and no other he may see the open air, of which you'll be so good as to acquaint Master Bossom and I hope he'll observe em. Mr Cant and the rest of Jemmy's creditors you'll give yourself the trouble to discharge.

1 Smith v Philcox, Trinity term 1740 (SAY 1418 f. 66v).

270 To Mary Collier, Hastings, from Miss Mary Thorpe, Battle, 13 May [1740] [SAY 2202]

Dear Madam, I have endevoured my utmost for roasmery flowers but very unsuccessfully. I sent where I heard they had bushes and in all got about a spoonfull you might think I had forgot it, not hearing from me, but I expected Miss and you at the market if the good weather had continued. Mr Collier drank tea with us or we had neither company nor business to engage us. There was no coffe house, as was intended, the Crowhurst ladys not coming. A Thursday the new coach was sent for Mrs Weller in a new night gown and Mrs Tilden in her habit and he in boots, theire own horses and servants went to fetch them home at night. I cant get my gown made, I have shown it Mrs W, and in return seen all hers, 'tis very handsome but I cant describe it. The ladys, Tilden and Hammond dislike the new fashion, and think fitt only for such as cant afford dress gowns, my sister has made her red and I my blew to be first. I hear Miss Rachel has done me an ill office with Mr Nairn or put it in good hands that wont let it lose, 'tho it had gained it was so fare true, I could not clear myselfe of saying her gown was yd wide, etc. She takes no notice but by a strangness which others dont mind 'tis so common, and perhaps I should not if I had not been told. I was of two or three minds whether I should mention it to you or not, I have not to Mrs Worge, nor any here, but I hope you'll excuse it. I belive Mrs Bro has ridiculed her more than I possibly could but I will take no other reveng then to forgive it.

Mr Judge made one viset a month agoe, but how the match goes on cant hear, I fancy Mr Worge has set both off. I hope you dont think commiting such stuffe to writing more criminal then a littel gossiping at a tea table, I think it both inocent or should not take this freedom with you, without it I could not furnish a letter in a month, what art they have that can three a week constantly I know not, for the present I shall only add the humble service of my mother, sister and selfe to you and all your good family, your most oblidged servant, last night I come in the rain near two miles over my shooes in dirt, that I can scarce move my hands today.

271 To Mary Collier, Hastings, from Elizabeth Denham, [Hollington] 19 May [1740] [SAY 2181]

Madam, I dont know whether you are dead or alive but I send this to see I should be glad to here how thing goe and where my yong cosins are. I did by chance here you and two of them were gone to London. I should be willing to know what becomes of poor Tom's family but you know I canot by any wais excuce you be so kind as to let me here it, I wish them well but must make no great enquirie I have writ to my cosin James by Mr Jones by whom I send this I should liked to have spent my time I have been in this place in the old house for this is a place I cant by no means like it is attended with so many inconveniencs I should be glad to see you my sight is all most gone and can onely asure you that I am, your humble servant and loveing aunt, it's a great trouble to me to writ and can onely give my service to all your family.

272 To Mary Collier, Hastings, from John Collier, Stonecrouch, June 1740 [SAY 1734]

Though I think I take all precaution to put up everything I want when I go for London, yet very often leave some papers etc., I want; now I have left a memorandum paper of business and things to buy and a book with green vellum cover which I have in London to write down everything in.[1] They are togeather in one of the partitions over the place I write upon. The paper I desire may be sent Fryday's post. If you have nothing else to send that may be made up in a letter and directed to me, if any letters or anything more to send, then in one of the franks. The book to be tyed up in paper and sent me by the carrier a Saturday. I thought of this just as I got to Bredsell Green,[2] when too late to send back.

1 Several of John Collier's surviving green vellum account books are at ESRO MIL 7/1-5. The one referred to here is SAY 1418.
2 Bredsell Green, between Stonecrouch and Battle.

273 To Mary Collier, Hastings, from John Collier, [Johnson's Court], 19 June 1740 [SAY 1735]

As Mr Green of Grinsted and his wife went out of town this morning I am now got into my old lodgings. Yesterday I desired Mrs Nouns to buy the things you want for the little girl, etc. The Duke of Leeds was to have been married today to Lady Mary Godolphin, but it's put of till next Tuesday. The newspaper mention it is to be at Claremont, but it's not so, and the ceremony is to be performed at the Earl of Godolphin's, and they set out soon after for Yorkshire, and the Dutchess of Newcastle goes with them.[1] There's great talk about town of the Duke of Beaufort and his lady having parted and some say she was taken in bed with a certain young lord. She was only child to the lord Viscount Scudamore, a prodigious fortune, and there's a great many of these peeces of gallantry about town.

Roffe is quite demolished, 3 or 4 executions in the house, and it's thought he is 2 or 3000 worse than nothing. I find some blame him and others her, but I beleive both have strongly contributed and there's a great number of children unprovided for. This afternoon we had an account that poor Mrs Greene was tapped a Tuesday but without any or the least relief, and afterwards her leggs much scarifyed but without having the desired success.[2] Two or three physicians were present and Mr Chesilden and it's said they agreed she could have but a very little time. I have sent to Mr Holmes about Jenny's stays. Molly's trappings rise very high to £12 12s 6d.[3] Inclosed are two of the bills and Belson's is just five guineas, but it seems it's calculated hereafter that it will make her a suit of cloaths. I have paid my sister the other bill, £1 13s 6d.

1 Lady Mary Godolphin (1723-1764) married Thomas Osborne 4th Duke of Leeds.
2 Procedure involved piercing the skin, to drain a cavity of fluid, mucus and blood (*OED*).
3 Decorations for clothes and horse riding equipment.

274 To Mary Collier, Hastings, from John Collier, [Johnson's Court], 21 June 1740 [SAY 1736]

I received your letter per the post and am glad you are all pretty well. I did not know anything it was intended to send little Sally's things by James, or he might have carried them. I wish you had mentioned who the letter from the Custom house came from, and the contents, for there are so great a number of offices, and all hurry in business, that it may happen proper I should see it not having met anybody that told me of sending so lately.

Poor Mrs Greene dyed about 5 this morning. I had a letter yesterday from Jemmy and he will not be in town till Tuesday. I gave James leave to goe to Borne next week for two nights if you don't want him, but not to stay any longer on any account. My brother desires I would remind him of letting his horse be sent by the carrier next week, he spoke to him in town, he says, but would not have it forgot. If he did not send him today, he must goe with him to Battell a Munday.

My brother and Mr Frewen set out tomorrow morning with their sons to school to a place called Wormley, about 14 or 15 miles distant, in Cambridge Road. Jemmy seems very easy, and indifferent where he goes, but says, whether out of cunning or reallity, he wishes he was at Hasting.[1] The town is very barren of newes, and not a great many people of fashion, and dayly growing more thin. I hear Mr Carleton and family all out of town and now without any excuse unless the ilness of one of the children. It used to be his being obliged to attend the court there, and he is now obliged to come daily to town. I find he is in a most sad way as to money, and drove to the most desperate expensive shifts, and they have hardly a pair of sheets, tablecloath, or [2] wearing linnen fit to be used, and this encampment will demolish the sub brigadier by being obliged to have a tent and keep a horse and look after him himself or hire, for he has hitherto only hired a horse when obliged to be on duty.[3] It has been fine weather in the daytime, but very cold mornings and evenings.

I really forgot in a hurry last post whether I put in a note for Patrick to the effect of this now sent for just on sealing my letter I had the notice of the affair.

1. James Cranston, son of William Cranston.
2 MS *lace* struck through.
3 Militia duty. George II did not visit the militia encampments in 1740 and 1741 (Owen 9). For obligations on officers undertaking militia duty see J R Western *The English militia in the Eightenth Century: the story of a political issue 1660-1802* (1965).

275 To Mary Collier, Hastings, from John Collier, [Johnson's Court], 24 June 1740 [SAY 1737]

I was with Mr Parsons today about your stockings and gloves. He had none of the first that was good but promises to get two pair in two or three days. The spectacles I have bespoke and will send for the pomatum. I expected Jemmy in town today but had a letter that he don't come till tomorrow. There has been a great deal of rain today and going along near Temple Barr George Luxford called to me out of a stocking shop and I was surprized to see him. I find he came up with Dr Russell and his wife and son who is entred at Eaton School and they all return to Sussex tomorrow, staying but two days in London. There's no manner of news or scandall stirring worth puting into a letter. Jemmy Cranston marched of Sunday morning with the usual unconcern, but my brother says he thought he looked a little down at his coming away from him.

276 To Mary Collier, Hastings, from John Collier, [Johnson's Court], 26 June 1740 [SAY 1738]

Jemmy came to town yesterday about 3 in the afternoon but his cloathes did not come till this afternoon. I beleive it's in a tattered condition on seeing him sorting it out though I did not look very near. Mrs Greene was to be buried this afternoon at Keston in Kent. My brother and I were invited to accompany her out of town, by 6 this morning, but it hapned at such a time that none of us could goe without the greatest inconveniency. I am uncertain about getting out of town, but hope it will be the [1] middle of next week and unless you hear to the contrary by next post, let James set out a Monday with the 2 mares I come up with, and the other we call Jemmy's.

Master Bossom designs to sail tomorrow. I hope he will bring down some pipes for the water. To be sure there can be nothing amiss to borrow some coals from Mrs Broadway, but I am against buying any. There's a box of china and glasses, a small box of candles, two close stools, and a few other things aboard Bossom. Abundance of people go every night to Vauxhall, but I have not as yet been there, or seen any diversions. There was a great deal of rain here a Tuesday morning, but I don't find it reached far out of town anyway. Jemmy sends his duty and respects and I intend he shall write by next post.

1 MS *beginn* struck through.

277 To Mary Collier, Hastings, from John Collier, [Johnson's Court], 1 July 1740 [SAY 1739]

I received your letter by yesterday's post. This has been an exceeding hot day, and I have been obliged to be upon the tramp all the forenoon, and am not a little fatigued. I will, if possible, get out of town a Fryday, though I can't as yet reduce it to a certainty. I don't remember how I expressed myself about Mrs Green's earrings, as to whom she intended them, but I take it for granted it was intended for her god daughter. I saw Mr Green a Sunday and think he looks pretty well and think to give him and his son an invitation as usual. Sure Sir Charles Eversfield's behaviour about the cricket players was very odd, and he certainly is very obstinately possitive in his conduct in everything. I told Jemmy to goe today and see Mr Chelsum and his wife from whence he is not as yet returned.

278 To Mary Collier, [Hastings] from Elizabeth Denham, 18 July 1740[1] [SAY 2182]

Madam, I recd your letter that you sent by London which encourages me to writ again it was some trouble to me to think I was deserted by one I allways had a love for. I am glad you have recovered the winter illness you sent me word off, you sent me word your little gierle was at holl, I wish it may be to your satiffaction, I believe shee will not be wanting in her carefull attendance over her. I believe you are sencable we are we are in a great many straits to live. I did think my cosin James would have been so kind as to have remembered me a little. I am sure I should were he in my case and I in his. The time is now coming that you will be happie in the enioyment of your relations which I cant say but I envey. Here is noise and hurry enough and more a coming which I perfectly hate but have no way to avoid it. I see very badly and begin to faile in all respects which is not to be wornder at. I thank God I goe somthing better then I did in the cold weather pray give my love and service to all that askes after me and tell Mrs Broadway I am very sorry for her loss which I have experienced in parting with a loving husband tho we were often in great dele of trouble that did not abate our affection to each other.[2] The nighbours continue very kind and I think Mr and Mrs Rideout happie togather. Here is great pulling down of houses and selling up others; mine and my daughter's service waits on you and all our cosins. Let me here how things goe in all our families for I never here but from you which is always aceptable to your loveing aunt, we expect Mr Apill however, give my service to my cosin Jame and tell him I hope he will be better natured somtime.

1 MS Sayer, in pencil, dates this letter 1737 or 1740.
2 Revd Thomas Broadway, clerk, rector, buried 17 May 1740, All Saints.

279 To Mary Collier, from Miss Mary Thorpe, Battle, 20 July [1740] [SAY 2203]

Dear Madam, I received your oblidging letter and as you are so kind to make the offer, which I should have been ashamed to ask just as you[1] are coming out of town, I would beg the favour of you to buy my sister and I each something to supply the place of a short cloak which we shall leave intirely to your fancy only please to remember it must not be the tip top, if 'twill be any inconviency to you pray omit it. Miss is very easey about the faire as you'll not be returned, I belive the disappointment will be greater to the ladies on the hill, they have one Mrs Sutherland from Bourne, the first night she fell down staires and lamed herselfe, they left her houskeeper to meet him at the Wells and came back a Sunday. I would have Miss stay for me which must be after the usal ceremony of washing and quilting, but she has not yet resovled for tho we have every day either coach, duke or lord, etc., and make it as pleasent as we possibly can, yesterday the coffe house a dozen strong, yet she wont allow it so agreeable as Hasting, yesterday all the relations to the weding dined at his vie Tilden's lodgings, she's retired to her father's to receve or avoid viseters and to stay till Christmas. I was drinking tea with Miss Carleton's, the docitor his son and grandson at cousin Geery's and think her the most rude ill behaved girle I ever saw and I hear every bodie else thought so. The reverse is Miss Collier, she by hers has not only charmed my brother but Sir Charles and his sister, pray Madam give my service to her and I shall expect to visit her at Grove. Please to present all our respects as due from your humble servant,

1 MS *r* erased.

280 To John Collier, Hastings, from James Nicholson, 13 September 1740 [SAY 362]

I take the liberty to inform you that Mr Chace is dangersly ill and is not expected to live long.[1] I beg the pawer youl give me live to purches his place at his disceace; I shal be vaery willing to give to the value of it. I have the money by me. I was an acquantance of the late Mr Shillets, and can be well recommended if you require it. Pray sir, be plased to faver me with an answar and inform me how I can treat with you about it and youl oblige your most humble sarvant to command. Please to direct for me at the Woolpack in Compton Street, near St Ann's Church, Soho.

1 Charles Chace, tipstaff and cryer, officer appointed to wait on the King's Bench in term.

281 To William Cranston, Hastings, from William Davison, clerk to Mr Assheton, Brooke Street, Holborn, 20 September 1740 [SAY 363]

Mr Assheton, my master, being very much indisposed, ordered me to write to you on behalf of a friend who has applyed to him this morning to know who had the disposal of the places of tipstaff of the court of King's Bench, the person hearing that Mr Chace, one of the tipstaffs, is now very ill and past all hopes of recovery. My master therefore beggs you'd be so kind to apply to Mr Collier, who has the disposal of those places, on behalf of this gentleman, and in case Chace should dye what Mr Collier will expect for that place. My master desires you'd be so kind to favour him with a line in answer, to acquaint him whether Mr Collier will (in case Chace dyes), treat with this gentleman on this affair, or whether Mr Collier has already determined who shall succeed Chace.

282 To William Cranston, Hastings, from Thomas Hardcastle, Wakefield, 20 September 1740 [SAY 364]

Mr Perkins writes that Chaese, the cryer of BR[1] is dangerously ill and that Mr Beardmore is not only willing to wave his pretensions to his place but wishes me success in obtaining it, and he desires me to remind you of your promise to assist him, which though a needless request I comply with.

1 King's Bench.

283 To Mr Scranstone,[1] at John Collier's, Hastings, from John Perkins, Seven Starrs, Pall Mall, 22 September 1740 [SAY 365]

Not haveing the pleasure of seing you at Mr Collier's, I beg leave to trubble you with a line to speak to Mr Collier in my behalf, to be cryer of the court of King's Bench in the roome of Mr Cheese who dyed this morning. The small profitt Mr Loyd can aford to give is not half bread for a man, and it was with hopes of the first vacancey that I was desierous of being in the court. I am willing to give as much as aney resonable man shall; should be glad of Mr Collier's promiss and to know his propocials. Mr Hardcastle is now in Yorkshire or he would have wrote for me. Mr Loyd gives his servis to you.

1 This is William Cranston.

284 To John Collier, Hastings, from John Perkins, London, 22 September 1740 [SAY 366]

By your commands I give you the trubble of this letter to acquaint you that your officer, Mr Charles Cheese, dyed this morning. Sir, I hope as I have the honour to be in the court you will lett me have your promiss, for it was with the[1] expectation I served Mr Loyd, and I am willing to continew in the court for the reasons I tould you and should be glad to know the purchase. I hope you have received the letter from Mr Bryon. Mr Walker expected you would receive it by Thursday's post. I hope I shall be favoured with your honour's answer.

1 MS damaged, could be 'this' or 'that'.

285 To John Collier, Hastings, from James Nicholson, London, 22 September 1740 [SAY 367]

I received yours, and take the liberty to send you this to acquaint you that Mr Chase departed this life on Monday last. I hope, sir, if the person you mentioned declines the purches youl let me treat with you for it. I will give to the worth, or as much as aney man in reason. I hope, sir, to have the fauer[1] of hearing from you, and you will vaery much oblige, sir.

1 'Fauer' is indicated, though v and u were interchangeable at this time.

286 To John Collier, Hastings, from Henry Pelham, Spring Gardens, 30 October 1740 [SAY 406]

I was not in town when your letter came here or I should have thanked you for it sooner. I am very glad you found our freinds at Hastings in so good homour and think myself much obliged to you for their being so. I entirely approve of the method you have taken to satisfie the absentees and shall very willingly comply with any further expence that may be necessary for that purpose. Mr Lamb has given me the same account of Rye and has proceeded in the same manner. I find Sir William Ashburnham is again alive and I think for his sake we should have annual Parliaments.[1] I hope we shall have him in as good health and spirits in town this session and, if so, I am not clear whether he should not take tother turn at Hastings, but this is only between you and I.

1 The 7th session of the Parliament summoned on 13 June 1734 lasted from 18 November 1740 to 25 April 1741; dissolved 27 April 1741 (*HBC*).

287 To Mary Collier, from James Collier, Johnson's Court, 6 November 1740[1] [SAY 2164]

Honoured Madam, I am just now retired out of the parlour from dinner to give you the history of our adventures at Battle. On our arrival there we found Mr Webster and Mr Johnson, the latter of whom some little time before we came had acquainted Mrs Worge of my sister Dely's and my being in the cabin of the Dutch ship on Sunday. Molly laid there all night and was exceedingly brisk and seemed to be very well; on mentioning what I was desired to my sister, her reply was to the following effect, that she was sorry you thought she was affronted, that she never expected to be sent to from us on that occasion, being before acquainted in what manner and by whom the company were invited and that on the Saturday preceding the Thursday Colonel Pelham met Mr Worge, and asked him if his wife ever frequented the Hasting ball on the king's birthday, and on his answering in the affirmative, no farther notice was taken, she denyed that she ever said at Mrs Marquick's what was spoken of at Hasting, and appealed to Molly who was then present for the truth of it. Mr Webster told us he had been informed by Mrs Tilden what grand doings there were. As I am now going to pay my respect to the Prince of Wales at Covent Garden theatre, hope you will excuse the shortness of this epistle, be pleased to give my love to my sisters, I am, honoured madam, your most dutifull son,

1 [*Reverse*] MS Sayer, in pencil, dates this letter '1742-45'. The Prince of Wales was present at Covent Garden Theatre, 6 November 1740 (Scouten Pt 3, vol. 2, 1736-1747, 861).

288 To Mary Collier, from James Collier, Johnson's Court, 10 November 1740

[SAY 2163]

Honoured Madam, our safe arrival here having been notified to you in a manner proper by my father, agreable to his directions, the following particulars in relation to our journey will I hope afford some little entertainment. Messrs Webster and Johnson together with my sister Molly were ready to receive us on our entrance into Mr Worge's parlour, the latter of which gentlemen had just before we came informed the company with whom he met with in the cabin of the Dutch ship the day preceding. The Place visitors left us about six, soon after which a game at cards being proposed we sit down to whisk, and I had the good fortune to encrease Molly's store, who entred into a partnership with me, by adding to it a shilling.

We were on horseback before eight the next morning, and reached Nutley before one, having the most favourable weather that could reasonably be expected. We dined there and set out for Godstone about two; at Grinstead we paid our respects to Mr Green, who acquainted us that his son at Bourne had lost a child eaten up with the itch, the infection of which distemper was received from the nurse.[1] On Wednesday between Croydon and London we met Mr Godfrey Webster on horseback attended at some distance by a servant with a led horse. A fine opportunity offered itself at Godstone of being conveyed to London in a coach, if we had been made sensible of it soon enough, and of sending our horses back from thence. Sir Robert Fagg's coach went up that morning quite empty to bring her ladyship down;[2] half a guinea rightly applyed making use of an irresistible torrent of rhetorick would have procured us places in the abovementioned vehicle. I did myself the pleasure of waiting on his royal highness the Prince of Wales, his consort on account of her mother's death not appearing in publick,[3] on Thursday evening at Covent Garden Theatre, and was obliged to go very early, the house being extraordinarily full by five o'clock; the prince not coming till near seven his entrance was accompanied with a hiss from the people ...[4] making them wait so long.

Rich's plays attract a crowded audience every night, chiefly occasioned by a new actress lately arrived from Dublin, and by the dancing of that famous Italian woman Signora Barbarini, who is allowed by everybody to exceed greatly any that ever were on these stages.[5] Monsieur Desnoyer is her partner which has been the reason of your old friend Mr Glover's retiring, been determined never to dance again unless some of the royal family are present. Drury Lane is quite desolate and forsaken, I was there last night, and extreamely cold during the whole continuance of the play, the house being so thin.

Mr Nichols letter to Dely excluding, I suppose, all formality, a copy of it would be very acceptable, in order to form a right judgement of a natural, easy, flowing style. Master Bossom was here this morning on purpose to acquaint my father of three fishermen belonging to Hasting being pressed by a tender. Many and considerable are the damages done about this place by the late high wind, my uncle is debtor to cash some of his windows being broke, particularly one in his office occasioned by a tiles blowing of the top of the house, which came thro the pane. My new suit of cloaths consists of a garter blue coat and breeches with brass metal buttons now worn by everybody, and a red scarlet waistcoat trimmed with a gold twist. The unfortunate fire at the Half Moon Inn in the Borough, as mentioned in the papers, had like to have demolished hops my uncle had received from Mr Roffe as part of payment, to the amount of sixty pounds. Mrs Roffe dined here this day who had just before received an account that the fine seat called Fairlawn near Sevenoak's in Kent, the property of the Lord Viscount Vane,[6] was on Saturday last almost entirely burnt down to the ground, how this accident happened is not as yet known.[7]

1 Scabies, contagious disease caused by the underskin scabies tick, results in skin gradually covered in pustules, may lead to bacterial infections (*OED*).
2 Sir Robert Fagg, 4th baronet, MP Steyning 1734; died 14 September 1740, left estate to his sister Elizabeth.
3 Magdalena Augusta, 13 October 1679 to 11 October 1740, daughter of Karl Wilhelm, prince of Anahlt-Zerbst; she was mother of Princess Augusta of Saxe Gotha (1719-1772) who married Frederick, Prince of Wales, 27 April 1736.
4 MS torn.
5 For details of theatre performances [**296**]
6 Hasted vol. 5, Wrotham, lists two fires at Fairlawn.
7 This is not the end of the letter, which is missing.

289 To Mary Collier, Hastings, from Elizabeth Denham, 12 November 1740

[SAY 1740]

I have been in expectation of hearing from madam I sent you a letter from the sessions and so did Beltie, but I can't omit this oppertunity because they seldom happen. I allways shall have a respect for my relations and wish it had been my fortune to have converst with them by a nearer conversation, but I think now I should not enjoy it long. The winter begins early; I hope it will not prove so hard as the last, but God knows who will live to see it. Mr Milburn's man has been here this week to prepare for his master coming, who comes with Mr Sergeson or before.[1] I hope they be all at quiet when they have done voting. I am not att all easie in the way we are in but I can't 0doe any otherwise. Pray let me know how it is with them at Hollington. I am affraid they are troubled to get a poor living as well as we; remember me to them. I hope you are there friend and I am sure she has reason to oblige you to continue so, and I believe will let me know if Jemy be gone to Cambridge again and where Dely is and how they all doe; and may you be all happy to gather many years is wisht you by your old aunt and humble servant. Mine and my daugters service waits on all our cosins. I did not know of Mr Michel's going till just now quetlike.

1 Thomas Sergison defeated in the 1734 Lewes election, and again on 2 May 1741; he considered standing in the Lewes by-election of 1743 though withdrew before the vote [**324**] (*HofP 1715-1754* vol. 1, 336). The Duke of Newcastle agreed to support Thomas Sergison for Lewes in the election of 1747 and Sergison continued as the town MP until his death in 1766 (Brent 1993).

290 To Mary Collier, Hastings, from John Collier, [Johnson's Court], 13 November 1740 [SAY 1741]

I am just returned home, Jemmy and I dining today at Colonel Pelham's with Lord Ashburnham, his tutor, Mr Thomas Pelham and Mr Longueville, and I found Dely's letter, so I have but just time to say I received it and am glad you and all are well and hope you'l receive and like your gown. I write this post to Mrs Hickes and presume she will send over to you a Munday morning for fifty pounds. If she does, desire you'l send it, and to enable you for that purpose, on the upper shelf of the bookcase in the tea room, at the right side of it, behind the books, there are rolled up in a paper 100 guineas, out of which you'l pay the 50 pounds and take what you otherwise want. We are all well, only I have a little cold and my left eye sore. I gave my sister a play last night, the Fair Quaker of Deal, and Orpheus and Euridice.[1] I am in the greatest hast; your nursery is hardly an excuse for not writing.

1 Covent Garden Theatre, *The Fair Quaker of Deal*, by Charles Shadwell, (Scouten Pt 3, vol. 2, 1736-47, 863).

291 To Mary Collier, Hastings, from John Collier, [Johnson's Court], 15 November 1740 [SAY 1742]

Before your letter came I ordered Jemmy to write a letter to Dely, which he accordingly had done and accompanys this. I am very sorry to hear the smallpox goes creeping on and am afraid it will not be extinguished without a flame.[1] I am glad to hear of Mr Godley's being at Hasting and hope he will take care to settle his post and other affairs and silence the just clamour raised on his conduct; and I have heard since I have been in town that the Widow Langford has publickly declared she don't design to marry him, and thereupon think the extraordinary familiarity talked of between them don't redound much to her honour or any of their reputations. As Jemmy tells me he mentioned Tommy Green's entertaining us last night, I only say it was very genteel and polite. I am glad your little girl is so very knowing and witty; to be sure something extra will attend her great abilitys, but am very glad she is so brisk and well. I have had a cold ever since Wednesday and an inflammation in my left eye not a little troublesom.

Sir William Ashburnham[2] was wrote for last post in a very pressing manner, and I sent to Richard Waters to send over the letters a Fryday night if no servant came for them. I now write to the mayor to have the Yarmouth freeholders, and other absentees at our last treat, regaled sometime this week coming.[3] Jemmy has not fixed any time for going to Yarmouth and I beleive will not till about the time of my leaving London. By a letter from Mrs Hickes it's not quite sure that she will send for the 50 pounds, but if she does, or for any part, pay it. Your letter don't mention what bullocks were bought or the price. When Dely makes for her Wicking visit let her tell Dr Thorpe. I have received £18 06s 0d for him of S. Wicking.

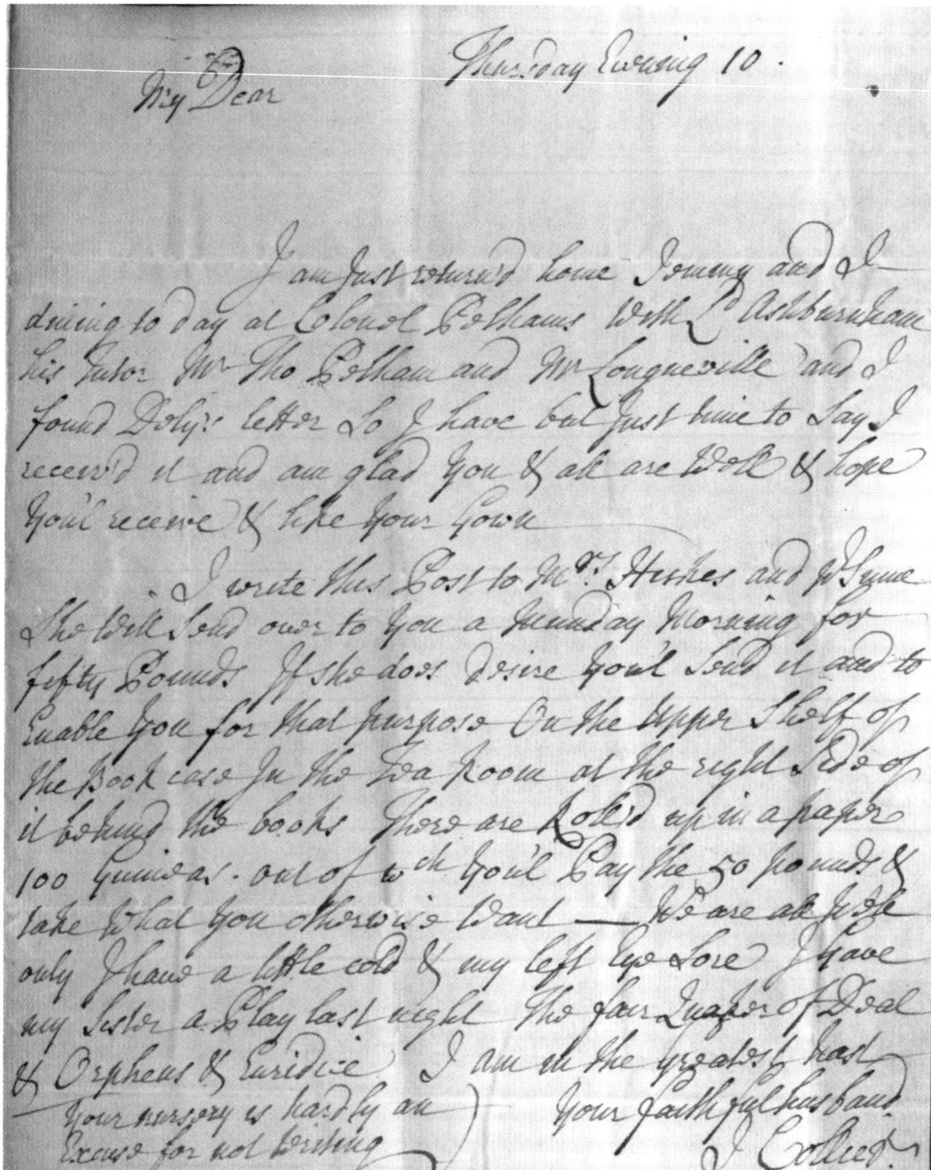

Thursday Evening 10.

My Dear

I am just return'd home Evening and I dining to day at Colonel Pelhams With Ld Ashburnham his Tutor Mr Tho Pelham and Mr Longueville and I found Dolly's letter So I have but just time to Say I receiv'd it and am glad You & all are Well & hope You'l receive & like Your Gown

I write this Post to Mrs Heskes and I Suppose She Will Send over to You a Munday Morning for fifty Pounds If she does Desire You'l Send it and to Enable You for that purpose On the Upper Shelf of the Book case In the Tea Room at the right Side of it behind the books There are Roll'd up in a paper 100 Guineas. out of wch You'l Pay the 50 pounds & take What You otherwise Want — We are all Well only I have a little cold & my left Eye Sore I gave my Sister a Play last night The fair Quaker of Deal & Orpheus & Euridice I am in the greatest hast

Your faithful husband
J Collier

Your nursery is hardly an Excuse for not Writing

Letter from John Collier to Mary Collier 13 November 1740, **[290]** SAY 1741, reproduced by permission of the County Archivist of East Sussex.

1 Within the bills of mortality deaths from smallpox totalled 1590 in 1738, 1690 in 1739, 2725 in 1740 and 1977 in 1741 (*Mortality*).

2 Sir William was required in the Commons to support the Government, then facing a tide of opposition over foreign affairs; especially over the threat from the Spanish and French fleets in the West Indies, which brought out critics in the City and among merchants, and concern over policy towards the warfare in the German and Austrian empires. The opposition tide ran on to February 1741 with an address to George II to dismiss Walpole; this motion defeated in the Commons 290 to 106, a severe defeat for William Pulteney (Owen 2-3).

3 This was the height of the herring fishery, and, with part of the Hastings fleet away in Yarmouth, Collier thought to remind the mayor and freemen of the worth of the Government connection, (Sayer 174 n).

292 To Mary Collier, Hastings, from John Collier, Johnson's Court, 18 November 1740 [SAY 1743]

I received your letter and am very much afraid of the smallpox getting the upper hand amongst us, which may be at this time wholly imputed to smugling.[1] Poor Jenny must have a dolorous time with the toothach and I am really concerned for her. I told my sister about your muslin and she will buy it. I have no manner of intimation but yours of Mr Medley, etc., being at Hasting,[2] and should have expected some account how they conducted, either from the mayor, Dr Thorpe or some one of the gentlemen. I am not able to fix anytime for my getting home and am afraid shall not send for the horses to come or meet me till Sunday's post. My cold has been very troublesom. I did not goe out of doors last Sunday and think it has made it better and hope it's going of. The Parliament met today and being at Westminster I heard the debates in the House of Commons on the king's speech, which I don't send, presuming it's of course transmitted with the newspapers.[3] I have not seen Jemmy since the morning, and it's now past 9.

1 A connection between the smuggling trades and smallpox was useful to authority and cited in seeking stiffer penalties for illegal importation. For the rise in smallpox in London see [**291** n 1]. John Hooker also mentioned the smallpox in his weather reports from Tonbridge (Hooker Mss).

2 Samuel Medley of Buxted, 1741 election, canvassed in the Tory interest, intent on standing in Sussex with Sir Cecil Bishop or John Peachey of West Dean (McCann 35, 40; [**306**]).

3 This, the 7th session of the 1734 Parliament, opened Tuesday 18 November 1740; the King's speech focused on war and the supply of troops for land fighting, the naval war with Spain, and noted the scarcity of corn across Europe (reported Rapin vol. 20, 472-3); accepted by the house with only minor amendment, though the opposition tried to extend the address of thanks to request an inquiry composed of MPs and Lords; this was defeated 226 to 159 (*CJ* 23 531-2; Egmont vol. 3, 165).

293 To Mary Collier, Hastings, from John Collier, [Johnson's Court], 20 November 1740 [SAY 1744]

I am to acknowledge the receipt of your letter by this post, and have likewise one from Mr Mayor with a particular account of the occurrences on last Saturday's visit from Mr Medley, etc.,[1] and I gave Jemmy his letter which mentioned something more particularly than the mayor's on that account. I now write to Patrick about business, more particularly of Morris's wive's mother's will. I think he has it, but if not have ordered him to apply to you to look for the same amongst the papers in the partitions before my desk or writing place. I cannot fix any time for my return but hope I shall be able to do it next post. I have bought candles, but give 7s 6d a dozen.

I think it very strange that Sir William Ashburnham has not resolution enough to come up; his behaviour is really scandalous in that respect, and I think he is under as great a necessity of attending as any one member in the House. The division a Tuesday was 226 and 159, Dodington and his party being 3 more voted against the ministry. The House of Lords were 60 odd and 30 odd.[2] I find you have destined little Sally for musick and as you don't mention Jenny's toothach hope she is better. Master Bossom intends to sail Saturday or Munday, on board of whom I have ordered several things.

1 Charles Stevens, elected mayor, 27 April 1740 (ESRO HAS CAA/5). From this date the mayor was allowed £10 a year for costs and the dignity of his office.
2 Division in the Commons [**292**] followed by two votes in the Lords, 62 for the government, 35 against, and 66 for 38 against (Rapin vol. 20, 472-3).

294 To Mary Collier, Hastings, from John Collier, [Johnson's Court], 25 November 1740 [SAY 1745]

I think your intentions as to Molly very just, and as in all probability I shall return through Battell I will then discourse her. I think the behaviour of Mr Worge and his wife to her, relating to the ball, just like him, and think in common civility and in good manners to us she should have been invited to it. I am afraid I shall not be able to get out of town a Fryday, and if so, not till the beginning of next week. We have very severe weather and last night a great deal of snow fell. I have had a creck in my neck these two days that I am obliged to keep my head very stately and I keep within as much as possibly I can.

I presume Master Bossom will be at Hasting before me. There is on board him currants and spices (there are no raisins this year, being the growth of Spain and therefore a prohibition), a cheshire cheese, candles, a flitch of bacon, a small box of china, a box of stationary, paper, etc., a table, little chest of drawers and a screen. I have told Jemmy to set out as next Munday, and goe this day and take a place for that purpose; he is gone out but I design to tell him to write to Dely. I begin to be very weary of this hurly burly[1] uncomfortable place, and wish myself at home with you.

This afternoon I had great itchings on my arms and neck, and opening my shirt found my arms and neck come out very full of broad blanes like a rash which I beleive the effects of a little fever I had last night. So I have not stirred out this evening but intend to have a little whey at going to bed.[2]

1 Hurley-burley, in this sense, adding to uncertainty and commotion in everyday life (*OED*).
2 Whey, simple milk product; wine whey, medicinal drink (Arbuthnot vol. 1, 252).

295 To Mary Collier, Hastings, from John Collier, [Johnson's Court], 22 or 28 November 1740 [SAY 1746]

I received your letter with pleasure, though I am concerned to hear such an account of the smallpox and much fear the consequences attending it. I am not able to fix on a certain time of leaving London, though I was in great hopes that I should next Thursday; however, desire you will, if not contradicted next post, send James out a Thursday morning with the horses and let him bring the portmanteau and come to the George Inn[1] where I set up on coming to town, and from thence to my brother's. I observe little Sally's mark, and as yesterday was a very dreadful day I presume she stays longer with you. Master Bossum intends to sayl the beginning of the week. I think I have executed all your commissions. I told Jemmy to write this post to Dely but he is just [*letter damaged*]

1 Most likely the George Inn, Sevenoaks or the George Inn, Southwark, although the George Inn, George Street, Croydon, was on a London south east route used by Cranston and Collier (P Walker *Croydon and its Pubs* (1999) 5 Table 1).

296 To Mary Collier, Hastings, from John Collier, London, 27 November 1740 [SAY 1747]

I am to acknowledge the receipt of your letter by this post, and to acquaint you that I am pretty well, but obliged to keep in all day yesterday and the greatest part of Tuesday; for the sort of a rash I had was out not only on my arms but my breast and leggs, but it began to dye away yesterday. I was necessitated to goe out today by ten but took a cloak and fortunately met with a coach which I kept above three hours and brought me home again. The afternoon was pretty free from the violent rain in the forenoon that I ventured out again, but it now rains extreamly hard and I am about half a mile from home waiting for a gentleman, and take the opportunity of writing this epistle. I now despair getting out till Munday, when I design Jemmy also goes for Cambridge; he is gone to the play tonight.[1] The king is to be there and the Countess of Yarmouth is also expected and that the house would be full by 4. I think Jemmy told me he mentioned our being to see the new actress and the fine dancer Signora Barberini; I think she dances exceeding fine. Tonight Glover and all the top dancers are to perform. An embargo for stopping all corn and provisions is hourly expected.[2] Tomorrow we dine in Sackville Street. I send nothing by the carrier.

1 Covent Garden Theatre, Thursday 27 November, *The Constant Couple*, by George Farquhar, dancing by Leach, dancer and actor; dancing also by Glover who organised a company of performers from 1732, last stage performance 1741, then dancing master for princesses Amelia and Caroline; also on stage, Mlle Michels, dancer, actress, singer, her brother Pierre Michels, her father Francois Michel, Covent Garden 1740-2, then to France; also Signora Barbarini Campanini, Italian dancer, 25 October 1740 to London, with Desnoyer to King's Theatre 1742-3, then to France. This performance included the ballet *'Mars and Venus'* and a comic dance *'the Italian Peasants'*, before the king, countess of Yarmouth, princesses Amelia, Caroline and Louisa (Highfill vol. 3, 25-8; vol. 10, 210-23; Scouten Pt 3, vol. 2, 1736-47, 868).

2 A serious shortfall in corn harvests over western and northern Europe followed the winter of 1739-40 and resulted in sharp price rises and widespread profiteering, this last noticed early autumn in Atlantic ports and in supplies to Paris. Widespread food riots in Britain and Ireland; speech from the throne 18 November 1740 suggested Parliament impose an embargo on exports; local restrictions already in place by several quarter sessions, and the king's remarks halted grain exports before the proclamation (Bibliotheca Lindesiana 52; Hoskins 23; Rapin vol. 20, 470, 473).

297 To Mary Collier, Hastings, from John Collier, [Johnson's Court], 29 November 1740 [SAY 1748]

I think at present that nothing shall prevent my getting out of town a Munday, but if it should happen otherwise I will not fayle writing next post. James came here yesterday noon, by whom I heard all the family was well but said the roads a Thursday were very bad. I intend Jemmy shall set out the same day for Cambridge, but I have not seen him since the morning and he is now, as I understand, gone to the play, there being new dancers come over to Drury Lane house.[1] I did not dine at home, having been hurried about on my intended journey.

1 Drury Lane Theatre, *A Fond Husband*, by Thomas D'Urfey; principal dancers were Signor and Signora Fausan, at Drury Lane from 29 November 1740 to 20 May 1741, also Michael Muilment, dancer, and Mlle Marie Chateauneuf, dancer, singer, manager. Anti-French riot halted performances during previous Drury Lane season 1739-40 (Highfill vol. 3, 181-2; Burney vol. 4, 447; Scouten Pt 3, vol. 2, 1736-47, 868-9).

298 To Mary Collier, Hastings, from Elizabeth Worge, January 1741[1]

[SAY 2161]

Honoured Madam, the gentlemen and ladys at the Place are to do me the faver of there companys next Thursday to dance. I should be very glad if you would be so good to lett my sister Dely make one among us, as to her haveing only a night gown that need be no objection to her comeing for we have not a soul has anything els. I should be glad to know by the bearer and you will very much oblige, honourable madam, your dutyfull daughter. Pray my compliments to all.

1 [*Reverse*] MS Sayer, in pencil, dates this letter 'about 1741'.

299 To Mary Collier, Hastings, from Cordelia Collier, Battle, 9 January 1741

[SAY 1749]

My sister[1] and I was at the abbey a Thursday, where there was a great deal of company, and we had a privite ball which lasted five hours and I had the honnor of opening it with Mr Webbster. Next Wednesday is fixt for Mrs Tilden's ball, so hope you will send my white cloths by Pallmer;[2] my purplel hankerchief is here and my sister is to lend me a short apron. This morning Mrs Tilden was here, who informs us that Mr Nickcoll is to have a ball but that there is too be no maried ladys and part of the company is too be Miss Webbster and the two young gentlemen, Miss Marquick and myself, so if it goes froward belive we must desire Miss Webbster to take us in the coach with her.[3]

This was the day fixt for my goeing to Catsfield, but the wheather is so bad that tis put off till Monday. Mr Jenkins informd me a Thuseday that you was all at a hang dog at Mrs Broadway's the day before. I have not done but very little of my hankerchief yet for have hardly been at home one day since I came. I should be very glad to have my muslin apron sent that I left behind me foul, for fine ones run short. Be pleased to give my duty to my papa and love to my sisters. My brother and sister desire there compliments. I should be very glad, madam, if you whould send me your Brussells hankerchief to goe to the assembly in for my best is quite foul. My sister Worge desire you would be so good as to send James down to Master Bossom and the serjiant to inquire if there is no sturgion nor sugar for they have had some come from London this six weeks and can't here anything of it.

1 Mary Collier, normally called Molly.
2 Dame Palmer, carrier on local roads, including Hastings to Battle.
3 If Mrs Tilden was correct, this ball may have been at Mountfield Court, the seat of John Nickcoll.

300 To John Collier, Hastings, from James Waller[1] agent, Duke of Newcastle, London, 15 January 1741

[SAY 100]

I do assure you if it was in my power, you should not have the trouble of asking twice for the money that remains due to you from my lord Duke of Newcastle. I was in hopes to have got some part of it at least for you out of this quarter's income, and when my lord duke, before he went into Sussex, was distributing the money to come in, I mentioned this debt to you. But so much was wanted for his journey, and my lady duchess' journey into Derbyshire, and for Lewes and other extraordinary occasions that the whole is quite exhausted, and nothing left hardly for housekeeping necessarys, which are greatly in arrear.[2] And at this rate it is impossible to fix times for any payments whatsoever, and I can only beg your patience in general by assuring you that nothing shall be omitted on my part for clearing this debt to you as soon as possible. At the meeting of the trustees a little before Christmas I mentioned again to them the notes you have on Mr Trumble's account,[3] and they sayed they would certainly put that matter upon such a foot as would be satisfactory to you as soon as the account is settled, which you know depends upon Mr Forbes.

1 This letter is reprinted in part by Kelch 116-7.
2 See [**221**] for note on the Newcastle finances.
3 Anthony Trumble, lawyer, Hastings rape coroner, agent for the Duke of Newcastle, died 1 September 1733.

301 To Mary Collier, Hastings, from Cordelia Collier, Battle Abbey, [1741]
[SAY 1750]

It is by Miss Webster's desire that I tell you she cannot let me come yet awhile and hopes you wont think of it, so must beg to have my cap to weare a Thursday for my other is durty, but Mrs Reuch will dress that up for me; when my shaw was sent the neck was forgot which I am in great want off. We had no company at all yesterday but Mr Loftus who I think looks sadly. Hary Fuller has taken orders,[1] so we have lost him for ever now which is a misfortune as times goe, for here is none to spare, and we often wish for Gore and Maull again to make up a dance.[2] Mr Webster is gone to London but does not stay long. The dinner bell has just rang so must conclude with my duty to my papa, and love to my sisters. Wednesday morning I should be very glad of a pocket handkerchief.

1 Henry Fuller, known as Harry, son of John Fuller and Elizabeth Rose, Brightling Park, MA Trinity, Cambridge, educated for the church. John Fuller's efforts to secure for him a position finally succeeded in 1749 when Henry was ordained priest and appointed rector of North Stoneham (Crossley & Saville 474, 475).
2 Army officers quartered at Hastings; Sayer surmised the posting was to support the Customs officers (Sayer vol. 1, 177).

302 To Jenny Collier, Hastings, from Cordelia Collier, Battle, January 1741[1]
[SAY 2166]

Dear Jenny, I have only just time to let you know that yesterday I dine and supt at the Abby, and am ingaged there next Thursday to a reail ball of the Fullers and Miss Eversfield and sister, if my brother holds prety well, this was a suden thing, ocasoned by the Tunbridge musick coming there yesterday, for they are to stay and play, and to prevent any form or ceremony we are to draw for partners and it is an agreed thing who Miss Webster and I are to have but that is a profound secret. Tomorrow I shall write to Molly to thank here for my hankerchief, my brother brought away a little stone yesterday so is in much better heart now, and next Thursday being there weding day all the Place family are to sup here. Pray give my duty to my papa and mama and am, dear sister, your affectionate,

1 MS Sayer, in pencil, dates this letter 'before 1747, probably 1746'; the handwriting is similar to Cordelia's letter of 9 January 1741, **[299]** SAY 1749.

303 To Mary Collier, Hastings, from Cordelia Collier, Battle, January 1741[1]
[SAY 2168]

Honoured Madam, I whent to Catsfield a Monday with Miss Webster and did not return till Thursday when Miss Eversfield was so oblidgeing as to bring me home in the chariot to the assembly but did not stay themselves we had a very agreable ball and I danced all the time and had one of the Fullers for my partner. Miss Nokes was there in blue and silver and very prety, yesterday we was at the Abby and tonight sup at Mrs Markwick's and next week here, and Mrs Tilden's, so hope you will give me leave to stay till the week following. I have this day began net a purse for Mr Webster who sent to London for tew sets of silver neting needles, one for his sister for muftas and the others for me, the asses milk agres very well, I have pinned my best stays up and layn them away safe, Miss Worge whent home a Thursday, be pleased to give my duty to my papa and love to my sisters, from, honoured madam, your obedient and dutyfull daughter,

1 The handwriting is similar to **[302]** SAY 2166.

304 To Mary Collier, from Cordelia Collier, [Battle Abbey] January 1741
[SAY 2170]

Honoured Madam, I had not your letter till eight a clock last night and as you must think me very heedless not to answer it have sent a man on purpose with it and at the same must let you know that I have not been at all out of order nor had the least pain in my side since I have been here ...[1] for about half an hour before we left off danceing the other night and I am very shure got no hurt by it for I have been perfectly well ever since and never eat better in my life than I do now, and indeed have no one complaint at all for I should not care myself at this time to run any hazard of laying myself up for then kno very well I should not see London this year, I dont wonder you thought I lookt thin when I dine at Hasting for I had my sister Worge's cap on which to be shure is the most frightfull one I ever saw and to big by half for me, but belive you wont think so when you see me in my own dress. I hope my sisters will be hear a Thursday for it will be a great disapointment if they are not, for my sister was here last night and depends upon them and I shall be ready to return home with them Friday or Satterday whichever is most convenient, for the horses, Miss Webster is greatly concerne at your this, for thought herself quite happy that she should send me home well but hopes when you see me you will think so as indeed I am shure you will. I beg my duty to to my papa and love to my sisters, we are just goeing to Catsfield, your most dutyfull daughter,

1 MS torn.

305 To Mary Collier, Hastings, from Cordelia Collier [Battle Abbey] February 1741[1]
[SAY 2171]

Honoured Madam, I am afraid you will think me very negligent not to write in so long a time and indeed I began a letter a Monday, but our hurrys are so great that I could not finish it, and for the futer must not defer it for morning's work but at night, for chanting and billiards take up all our time so that it is with great dificulty we get drest by dinner, Battle is not very gay at preasent, but however we am very merry amongst ourselves, and play blind mans buff often, which I beg you will tell my sisters is all the mode now, and we had a game last night of three hours without resting, till we all was quite undrest, and some broken shins, but I got off with only black arms which was great luck at that game.

Miss Webster and I went to Catsfield this afternoon in the coach, and should have spent the evening but indeed the truth is they did not ask us tho we are all very great. Miss Nolly is come but very lame with a strained foot, and quite full of Miss Russell's match which is off, for she does not like his way of life nor is age and everybody seems to commend her for it. We went yesterday morning to my sister Worge's, and she comes often here, but it is so cold we have not rode out much yet. I like my cross and eerrings very well and they sute the brown exctly, when my papa was here he gave me a guine, but I have been fortunate as yet and a Thursday night won ten and 20 shillings and I tene shillings which one whould think disposable. I sent the thin hankerchief home with my cap as it required carefull washing, my waiting maid is as fine as myself but I like her mightily tho I lie alone and a much better room than the other, my lady is very civill, and carefull of our geting cold but I have been quite well ever since I have been here. I think here is no news to send you so must conclude with my duty to my papa, your obedient and dutifull daughter,

1 MS Sayer, in pencil, dates this letter '1741'.

306 To John Collier, Hastings, from Henry Pelham, 11 April, 1741 [SAY 407]

I received your letter of the 29th of last month with the abstract inclosed. As I saw nothing that required an immediate answer and had a good deal of other busieness, I desisted acknowledging it till now that I have more leisure. I am of your opinion that it is absolutely necessary to think of another tennant for Sandhill farm[1] and am afraid we shall be losers by Deval; let us do our best. I desire therefore you would without loss of time give him warning, receive the rent as well as you can and get another tennant as soon as you can. I don't doubt but in executing these orders you will do it in the mildest manner you can and as little to the poor man's disadvantage as is possible. By the returns I am afraid it does not go much better with the Ellis's; but there I would be more willing to wait for better times if they mean to deal honestly, as I beleive they do.

The widow Thomas I am much concerned for, and for her own sake would have her spoke to not to go on much longer for as she is already so much in arrear. I am afraid her idle sons will draw her into greater difficultys if she continues a farmer her being behindhand can proceed from nothing but the negligence of her children and therefore the sooner she gets rid of em the better. I must recommend to you to speak to her in a freindly manner, for what I would have done there is more for her sake than my own. I am sorry for Mr Chambers' discontent and could wish Mr Acton were persuaded to comply with what he desires, but I doubt if he does not find it much for his own interest, he will not, and it will be hard for me to be put to still a greater charge in fencing the Lulhams, where formerly without any partition the rent was higher than it is now.[2] I conclude that affair will be suspended till I come into the country.

You have given very right orders upon the damage done to the Rushlake coppice; and if anything can be done to check the abominable behaviour of the poor people att Waldron, I should think the reasonable part of mankind would not blame it; but I must leave that to your discretion, att least for the present. We hear Mr Medley is very ill of the smallpox att Lewes.[3] Some say his life is dispaired of, tho I hope it is not so bad as that for I can't help being moved att so sudden a stroke to a young man just come to an affluent fortune; though perhaps brought upon him by an ill judged step that has given me some trouble, though as yet not much.

Whatever happens to him I can't think the opposition will go on, and if it does not, sure they will have so much behaviour of gentlemen left in em as to let us know it, that we may not unnecessarily spend our money, trouble our freinds and frighten the country now the smallpox is in almost all the great towns. When Collonel Pelham comes down to you he will propose something to you in relation to your town election. I will forestall nothing, only in general say to you, my opinion is the town can't do better for themselves.[4] I am sure they cannot serve their friends and country so well, as I could convince you if I saw you. The Parliament will probably rise in about a fortnight, and soon after that we shall know for certain where the election will be.[5] I desire my compliments to all friends and beleive me.

1 The rents due from widow Thomas, William and Nicholas Devall, and William and John Ellis are listed on the rentals for the Pelham estate (Appendix 4 **[606]** SAY 373).

2 For the rents due from James Chambers, the tenant at Great Lulhams, see Appendix 4: Pelham Estate **[606]** SAY 373, **[607]** SAY 374.

3 Samuel Medley died of smallpox, buried 16 April 1741. He worked for the Tory interest, (McCann 35, 40 [**292**]).

4 Henry Pelham and the Duke of Newcastle decided that Colonel James Pelham, known for his devotion to the family and the Whig cause, should represent Hastings, to replace Sir William Ashburnham whose undoubted support for the Hanoverian succession did not always translate to attending the Commons. Colonel Pelham was returned for Hastings, along with Andrew Stone, secretary to the Duke of Newcastle, 5th May 1741.

5 7th session of 1734 Parliament, 18 November 1740 to 25 April 1741; dissolved 27 April 1741; Parliament re-assembled 25 June 1741, 1st session 1 December 1741 to 15 July 1742 (*HBC* 578; Owen 2-7).

307 To Mary Collier, Hastings, from John Collier, [Tonbridge], 1741. [SAY 1751]

I beleive in a hurry putting up my papers a Saturday I forgot one that I shall have occasion for in town, and if not put up is in my study window looking out to the garden. It's three or four sheets of paper annexed togeather, and as I best remember endorsed on the back Mr Tarry and other to Mr Smith, draft of a lease or something to that effect; there is also besides it, or in that window, a letter from Tarry directed to John Collier, gent. I desire you will give Patrick the draft of lease and letter and let him inclose it and send to me by this post directed to the Custom house as usual, which will save the postage.

We got safe to Tunbridge about 6, but found the roads exceeding dirty and slippery from about a mile beyond Hurstgreen towards Stonecrouch and so increased fuller of water all the way hither, and to be sure they have had twenty times the rain we have. We stopped [1] where till Stonecrouch, and had for dinner mutton chaps and eggs and bacon and I don't know that ever I saw Molly eat so hearty. She held her journey very well, but the roads being so bad we were above 3 hours coming from Stonecrouch but luckily missed a prodigious shower that wet through and through a woman that I think they say is one of Mr Ashburnham's servants to go up in the coach, but I have not seen her; she was in about an hour before us. About a mile and a half before we came to Tunbridge we met Dr Carleton and his son and Miss Peggy in a chaise and pair intended to get to Lamberhurst or Stonecrouch. I a little thought we should meet them at Tunbridge and should then have spent the evening togeather.

1 MS damaged.

308 To Mary Collier, Hastings, from John Collier, Johnson's Court, 9 June 1741 [SAY 1752]

We got safe to Johnston's Court at six, found my brother and little Jemmy well, before I came from the inn I mentioned to Molly about going to her uncle's not as to lye but into the parlour, and she declared she had no manner of dread or objection; and being satisfyed myself there could be no danger, we came there but she has been only in the parlour where I opened her things in the portmanteau, and Mrs Nouns is to come here in about half an hour to eat some pease and she is to lye with her and the cloaths carried with her. I am really fatigued with the coach, etc., but Molly is very brisk, only thinks herself jumbling in the coach. I intend she shall goe to Hampstead a Thursday. Jemmy look strong and brisk. [1]

1 MS torn.

309 To Mary Collier, Hastings, from John Collier, [Johnson's Court], 11 June 1741 [SAY 1753]

I am to acquaint you that this afternoon I set out with Molly for Hampsted and left her there very brisk and well.[1] I hired a hackney coach, as thinking it much the properest way as carrying her cloaths with her, and shall buy and send a bureau tomorrow. She went yesterday to Mrs Isted's in the afternoon, and from thence I gave her and Jemmy the waxwork, and in the evening walked in the Temple gardens. In the morning she with Jenny went to Mrs Mariot's for her cap, etc; and as this was a holy day and she had a great desire to see St Paul's, she went thither and Jenny along with her and Jemmy, and my Lord Mayor came in his coach of state, and she is much delighted with the cathedral, organ, chaunting and Lord Mayor, etc. Madox has had the smallpox, taken ill in the country with it; a favourable sort, but has much affected his eyes. On my return from Hampsted found him returned home and my brother much surprized at it for he has had the distemper but a little time. However, I am glad Molly is gone from hence. Mrs Russell and her sister desired their humble service to you and Dely, and she said when she had examined Molly's cloaths would write to you. I paid 5 guineas entrance to her and a guinea entrance for musick, half a guinea for dancing and a guinea besides for all other things, though I thought all except musick was included in the five guineas. Whenever Morris thinks the hay proper to be cut let him have it done, though I imagine it is as yet hardly fitting.

1 Molly was entered for Elizabeth Russell's girls' school Hampstead.

310 To Mary Collier, Hastings, from Miss Russell, Hampstead, 12 June 1741 [SAY 1754]

I defered answering your oblidgeing letter till I had the pleasure of seeing your agreable daughter, who came last night. I am certain Miss will be an improving young lady and comes with an exceeding good will, which goes a great way, we being oblidged to Miss Collier, who has prepossest her sister in our favour. I wish Miss may like school as well as Miss Collier did, though I told her there was nothing to be learnt without pains, musick and French requires studdy. She answered she was certain of it and would do her endeavour to please. I don't find, madam, that Miss wants anything but a night gown to wear in a morning to get out of bed in and something done to her pullerane.[1] I beleive mock ermine will look pretty round it. Be pleased, madam, to make my compliments to Miss Collier and am, madam, your most obedient, humble servant. Miss designs writing tomorrow. Miss tells me you desire she may begin a pair of lappets; I think it a very pretty peice of work and will get it as soon as possible. Poor Mrs Cranston; I think Miss Collier very fortunate. I hope, Madam, you will be very easy on Misses account. I shall take care to indulge her as much as possible. I am certain her temper will both require and merrit it.

1 Pullerane, a fleece or jacket, one of several woollen-silk stuffs which included brilliants, pulerays, antherines and bombazines (*OED*).

311 To Mary Collier, Hastings, from John Collier, [Johnson's Court], 13 June 1741 [SAY 1755]

I find by your letter received this post your having been much indisposed in the manner therein described, but hope the same is entirely over. I did not return from Westminster till past 3 this afternoon, too late to write to Molly as I intended. I yesterday sent her chest of drawers by the Hampsted cart, and shall goe thither, I believe, more than once before my return home, which is so uncertain that I cannot by this post, as I intended, send for the horses to come up. Mr Worge came yesterday, but he said nothing of Dely's being at Battell market till I told him of it just now. I think it's right to have Mrs Thorpe with you, and perhaps her time may be prolonged when she is at Hasting beyond the supposed month. I shall remember to buy the things you propose and shall leave London as soon as possibly I can intending my survey soon,[1] but at present can fixe or propose no certain time. I have not been at any publick place, or seen any manner or sort of gayety or fine dressed people. I am, with the firmest attachment and value.

1 John Collier undertook his annual survey of the riding officers of Kent earlier than usual, from 26 June to 20 July 1741; the weather was miserable, cold and wet, the cost of bread high, and fodder and hay in short supply.

312 To Mary Collier, Hastings, from John Collier, [Johnson's Court], 16 June 1741 [SAY 1756]

I was glad to hear by Dely's letter that you was pretty well again; and find by it that you are much surprized about Mr Maddox; but I think there can be no manner of danger by infection from him for he has all fresh cloaths and had the smallpox down in Kent. Though I think he should have stayed longer, I have spoke to Mrs Nouns about Sally's coat and top of frock and told her of Mrs Acre. I herewith send you Dely's papers of her layings out in London. I have had them in my custody ever since I came up. I find she had fifty guineas of her uncle. The account doth not make it out but I observe Mrs Mariot's bill is not reckoned.

I sent a porter with a letter and Molly's cap to Hampsted a Sunday morning and design going thither tomorrow or next day. I would have James set out with the horses a Thursday, the same as I had to Tunbridge, but I am as yet uncertain when I shall come out of town. Jemmy Cranston went out yesterday in the stage coach to school very brisk and well. Opening the drawers of the dressing table to put my cloaths in there was a peece of blank paper folded up and taking it out found there was writing stitched like a book of which I send you inclosed a copy. I think it was more like a man's hand writing than a woman's but I know nothing of the hand nor never saw it before,

Dely had besides the 50 guineas, one guinea when she bought her uncle's china and Mrs Green paid 5s for her for necklaces, and earnest of coach 3s 6d and there was £1 7s 8d paid Mrs Nouns for her and Jemmy; but my brother can't tell what it was for in particular, save that Jemmy had some handkerchiefs. Mrs Selby's bill is £8 18s 0d.

313 To Mary Collier, Hastings, from John Collier, [Johnson's Court], 18 June 1741 [SAY 1757]

This day at eleven I set out for Hampsted, accompanyed with my brother, Mr Worge, and young Mr Green, where we arrived whilst they were at dinner at Mrs Russell's. Molly came to us presently, and eat no more, and Mrs Russell in a little time. We went to dine at the long room, and took Molly with us, and as the company went at my request, I gave the complement of the reckoning, and we walked up Hampstead Heath, and drank some tea at Mrs Russell's, and are just returned home (8 a clock), so weary that I can hardly set my feet to the ground.

Mrs Russell talked something of a morning, or bed gown, and a quilted petticoat, and I think said she had mentioned it to you. I am to send Molly some tea and sugar, and she told me she had wrote for the tea chest to be sent up. She looks and is very well, and I shall write to Mrs Russell what you desire about her walking. I had a letter yesterday from Jemmy, who is very well and will speak to Mrs Nouns about Sally's coat if tis not too late, as I suppose it will not. I am sorry you are disappointed of Mrs Blackman but hope her place will be supplyed to your satisfaction. I am really quite weary with my walk and conclude with assuring you that I am with all respect and faithfulness. I think Molly very easy and satisfyed and behaves very well. I have been fortunate to Captain Steevens in getting him a protection which no money could obtain.[1]

1 The Admiralty were anxious about the outcome of the expedition to the Spanish West Indies led by Admiral Edward Vernon and General Thomas Wentworth, and worried lest the French home fleet, anchored at Brest, might sail to support an invasion of the south coast, thus the urgent need to press mariners for the Channel fleet. Protections were issued to captains of essential cargo and fishing boats; on 9 May 1741 a proclamation pardoned persons guilty of clandestine importation who joined the navy, although not all smuggling cases were included (Bibliotheca Lindesiana vol. 8, 60; Williams 1945 223-5; Richmond vol. 1, 101-37). Richmond explains the campaign in the West Indies, and cites the reports from late 1739 and thereafter of the Spanish army in Galicia assembled for an invasion of Scotland or Ireland (*ibid*., 25, 30, 75, 80, 135).

314 To Mary Collier, Hastings, from John Collier, [Johnson's Court], 20 June 1741 [SAY 1758]

I was in some expectation of a letter by this post, but failing therein presume all things are well. James came hither yesterday morning, and I sent him today to Molly with tea, sugar, etc., and he brought back her quilted coat and Mrs Nouns buys one for her a Munday. We are all dolorous upon the account of Carthagena.[1] Everybody yesterday morning in high spirits that an express was come of its being taken, but it proved the contrary and the seige obliged to be raised. We have had rain every day and am afraid it reaches Hasting and gets amongst my hay. I fully intend to get out of town sometime a Munday, perhaps to Tunbridge. Mr Worge comes with me, so hope to dine at Battell a

Tuesday. I write to Jemmy this post and wrote to Molly this morning; as we had yesterday a great deal of thunder and lightening I imagine she was much terrifyed but I had given Mrs Russell a caution, etc., on that affair. I am glad Dely is free from her ague.[2]

1 Advice from the West Indies on the disaster afflicting General Wentworth's forces was received at Portsmouth on 18 June 1741 (McCann 64, Stone to Richmond, 20 June 1741).

2 Fevers, with symptoms similar to malaria, were prevalent in the marshes and river localities in Essex, Kent, and Sussex, although at times more widely spread. The ague concerned was vivax malaria, which took a serious toll of the population during regular seasonal outbreaks. It is clear from parish records that life expectancy varied sharply between the low lying parishes, compared with those on the Weald and the south and north Downs (Dobson 110-7, 139-42).

315 To Mary Collier, Hastings, from John Collier, Dover, 4 July 1741

[SAY 1759]

I hope this will find you pretty well and in good spirits, and heartily wish for a happy continuance of it, and assure you I have no little concern that I am necessitated to be so long absent from you at any time, but much more so in your present situation, from which I heartily pray for an agreeable deliverance.[1] It's very warm today but the two or three days before the wind being pretty fresh it has not been sultry hot riding, though for want of rain very dusty. I observe there is fine corn and a prospect of a plentiful harvest, especially of wheat, but the grass is much burnt up for want of rain. I propose finishing my business here this evening and proceed to Deal tomorrow and so on as fast as I possibly can to the places I am obliged to make my survey at. I am told poor Halsted is in a poor starving condition. If I can get any time, I will goe and see him, if not, send him something. I think it's barbarous in Mr Lamb to keep him in gaol, though I don't know what would become of him if he was out.[2] I am my dear life with the warmest affection and esteem.

1 Henrietta, bap. 4 September 1741, commonly Harriot, later Mrs Jackson.

2 Richard Halsted, innholder of the Swan, Hastings, also owner of land in Pett, a commission of bankruptcy was issued against him (*LG* 10 March 1740); Edwin Wardroper, attorney, Rye appointed by the Commission to collect Halsted's effects for the settlement with creditors, held meetings in Rye 25 April 1740; record of intended sale of Halsted's estate at Pett, containing several pieces of land and a barn, copyhold, let at yearly rent of £16 (*LG* 17 August 1742).

316 To John Collier, Hastings, from Molly Collier, Hampstead, 24 July 1741

[SAY 1760]

I received your letter with a great deal of pleasure and am glad to hear you are all well and that the assembly goes forward, which must make it a great deal better if it does. I have been at the long room once since, with Miss Russell, and am to go again next Monday or the week after. I suppose my uncle will soon be in the country. I have not seen him this fortnight, but expect him every day. I begin to be in expectation of seeing my brother, for I think it is near his time of coming. Pray tell my sister Dely Miss Russell expects a letter from her very soon. Be pleased, Sir, to give my duty to my mama, and love to my sisters, wishing them a merry fair, and to accept of my duty yourself. Our fair begins on Monday sevennight.[1]

1 Hampstead fair, a four day summer fair, at this time associated with the lower Flask taverns (*VCH Middlesex* vol. 9, 123).

317 To John Collier, Hastings, from John Coppinger, Hampstead, 5 September 1741 [SAY 673]

Inclosed is your bill which is scarce worth troubling you with, but as long vacation usually produces the smallest fruits of this sort you receive it. As to master Thayer and his brief in court, they pressed me much last terme to have the report signed. And I was alwayes ready, and the accounts being adjusted in every respect, save that of your bill about the will, etc., we went to the Master upon it and he setled it between us at £15, nothing then remained but to cast up and draw ballances; which, when we had done, and Thayer found a much smaller sume to be in our clyents' hands than he expected, he flew into a passion and would play no more; fell upon his brief in court and found fault with all that had been done; upon which, I being still ready to take the report when agreed to, marcht off with bagg and papers and left em to settle the merritts of the dispute together, after which I heard no more of ours, and so the poor report continues still in embrio. Your daughter is very well and a good neighbour my girl and she are to be very intimate and take their morning and evening walks together I give you joy of the increase of your family and hope the good lady in the straw and the young one are both well my wife joynes in our complements to you and her upon the occasion, and she sayes, not I, that Mrs Collier is now well entitled to a quietus. My service to William Cranston. [*Reverse*, *incidental expenses*] Michaelmas term 1739, stamp for petition against Mr Richards to have his bill taxed and to deliver up your mortgage 1s, paid answering the petition 5s 6d, paid for the order and entering 12s 6d; Hillary terme 1739, Morphet and Boykett, paid master's Chancery for copy 17s, copy per post 5s 8d, sold half fee 3s 4d; Hillary term 1740, spent 3 hours with pleaders Chancery and in amending and altering report in order to settle the same 6s 8d; Trinity term 1741, fair copy thereof as altered and amended 8s 4d, for attend Master on warrant thereon to approve the same when the difference settled by him 3s 4d, but afterwards disagreed to Mr Thayer and his Chancery in court not agreeing together thereon, paid expence at the tavern adjourning thither upon the dispute 1s 2d, [*sum*] £3 04s 06.

318 To Mary Collier, Hastings, from Molly Collier, Hampstead, 6 October 1741 [SAY 1761]

I should have wrote before but that my governess had not wrote the bill who, with it, sends her compliments. Pray tell my sister Jenny I received her letter and with a great deal of pleasure to see her write so well, and shall be very glad to hear from her often. I am in hopes it won't be long before I shall have the pleasure of seeing my brother and uncle which will be a great one to me, not having seen anybody so long, but hope I shall hear from you before that time. I should be very glad if you would be pleased to send me something for underpetticoats, for I have only my dimmity[1] ones here and that is not so proper for the winter; as also a night gown for I can't possibly do without one now. Miss Russell sends her service to my sister Dely and is very much obliged to her for answering her letter so soon. Be pleased to give my duty to my papa and love to my brother and sisters, from, honoured madam, your most obedient and dutifull daughter.

1 Dimity, stout cotton fabric, woven with raised stripes or figures, usually undyed, for bedspreads and hangings, also clothes, waistcoats, ladies morning dress (*OED*).

319 To John Collier, Hastings, from William Cranston, [Johnson's Court], 24 October 1741 [SAY 758]

Lord Chief Baron Lant died this day at 2 in the Temple. Sorsbie's tickett I sent him to Crowhurst last post. Hall paid Mrs Selby's bill last August and which you have inclosed as well as a bill to find out the staymaker by. I send you Latitat v Rogers[1] which if you can serve by the return, next Fryday, you may then get judgement this term. Upon inquiry I find no tidings of Winifred Bray's surrender. I've been much out of order these 3 days past but am, thank God, pretty well today. Did propose seeing Molly as tomorrow but beleive must not venture and of which I this morning advised her by letter with an invitation to town against Thursday next.

1 MS written as Late v Rogers.

320 To John Collier, [Hastings], from William Cranston, [Johnson's Court], 27 October 1741 [SAY 759]

I inclosed send you a copy of the account between us, out of the ballance of which if you could permitt me to make use of £150 I should be extreamly obliged to you, and I must be very much disappointed if I don't replace it again between this and Lady Day next. I have charged the whole 10 ticketts to you, which if you don't approve of will alter.[1] I have put the tea and chocolate bought by Hall whilst I was in Sussex and that sent the other day into one item, and 2s 6d of the portrage and carriage relates to Jemmy's box from Cambridge. I have the originall record of instructions still by me of Jemmy's hand, but not a word therein of pomatum or teeth powder, nor do I remember to have ever heard one word mentioned of either whilst I was at Sussex. Am satisfyed twas not menconed when the instructions were wrote which was in my roome, present my sister, Jemmy and self.

1 5th Westminster bridge lottery, 14 Geo II c.40, designed to raise £275,000 by £5 tickets, of which 15% went for the bridge; latest day for purchase of tickets 25 September 1741, to be drawn on or before 23 November 1741 (Ewen 147). John Collier's reply authorised the spending of £150.

321 To John Collier, [Hastings], from William Cranston, [Johnson's Court], 7 November 1741[1] [SAY 760]

I've entered the judgement v Cruttenden, but before I can compleat the judgement must have the date of the bond, which the lawyer has omitted to mention in the warrant attorney. Am glad have got Frewen's letter about Wittersham, and as all information is now got that can be, we must even strike out a way for ourselves. Am sorry for your account of Dely but hope all will come to rights again; as to Jemmy he is very well and hope will continue so, but if he should catch any cold will take all imaginable care of him. As the town is much fuller than twas a fortnight since, and the weekly bills less, consequently the sickness abates. Lip salve, teeth powder, pomatum, lavender water, and empty bottles for my brother were put on board Bossum yesterday.

1 Handwriting changes within this letter suggest that William Cranston made use of an assistant.

322 To John Collier, Custom house, London, from George Adams, Yalding, 7 December 1741 [SAY 408]

Received your first dated October the 24th. The reason not answered before received your last as followeth. First, after the court I was determind upon view of alterations to make a new rentall of both mannors, as is hinted in yours, before I made demand of lord's rents in arrear and had begun before I received yours and have since compleated. And since I have been with several of the tenants to demand, and have received between four and five pounds, the most part being obstinate and refuse to pay till the mannor pound is built; all whose names I have made a list of, and when I have been with the rest will give you the account that distress may be made, for in the holy days I design to viset the rest.

I have made a diligent enquiry after the horse seized on the death of Richard Stevens, and am well informed the same is in the hands of Ambrose Coveny of Brenchley, the executor, whom the parson says is under his care; the collour of the horse being a dark brown with a clig tail with some grizel hairs in his main and between 14 and 15 hands high. This is the true disscription of the beast, and beg you and the lady will persist in the recovery that persons in common conversation may not fleer at me and say there is no law to recover lords rents nor heriots, for if there was, they say, the lady woud not have lost it after fairly seized because the parson declared there was none due.

As to the list of all lord's rents in arrear to Michaelmas last, I am at a loss, for at the court I gave you the number of my receipts received to 1736 and in the hurry you took my rough draught of the whole number of receipts I wrote to that time, which I desire you'd would send inclosed to me the first opportunity, I having no account what I received from 1734 to 1736. I desire you'd forthwith consult the recovery of the quit rent due from Ambrose Gibbons for Marlplace and give me account of what part belongs to this mannor that I may proceed right, for he declares he will pay none. Likewise desire you'd not forgit what was presented the last court as to Mr Beeston taking and fencing in the waste land. He declares he will take a considerable quantity more that layeth next to his land; he saith Mr Plumer, his landlord, tells him the right belongs to him and not to the lady of the mannor; in short, if the lady do not exert herself in such cases farwell all.

Mr Edward Beeston, tenant, Paul Beston, declares to pay no quit rent and hath been with several of the tenants and perswaided them to pay none till the pound is built. Hatch Underwood, Thomas Chowinny, both tenants, have fenced part of the waste and digged the mould up to manware their own land and several others are upon the same designe. I have been with Love, tenant for a cottage for his quitrent; he hath given orders to John Featherstone, one of the tenants to this mannor, who hath pulled the house downe and carryed it uppon his own premisses, also hath dug the mould up belonging to the plot and carryed it to manware his own land.

I could ennumerate more of these instanses but let these suffice for the present, but desire you'd consider the ill consequence of such practice that may accrew to the lady. I desire you'd give me answer between this and the holy days of the lady's resolution of a mannor pound and also whether the lady will allow of such usuage as above presented or not. I could wish that time would admit of three or four hours' converse relating mannor affairs, which would be more satisfactory to both than pen can express. Sir, I desire you'd give me direction to proceed right, in felling timber upon the waste for the pound, of what distance it ought to stand from any person's fence for fear of mistake.

323 To John Collier, [Hastings], from William Cranston, [Johnson's Court], 12 December 1741 [SAY 761]

Your account of Mr Worge's amendment was very agreable and hope there will be a continuance of it. Maddox is much mended. No neice either yesterday or today though have been in full expectation. You herewith receive your warrant v Meadow.[1] I'll remember Gyles and also think of the brawn as well as tea and coffee next carrier to Battle; and to finish the parsonage affair upon its present footing, which I think well enough though my friend George has had 10,000 doubts. [*Postscript on lottery tickets*][2] No. 61 a £10; 3 B, poor neices; 4 & 5 undrawn, Mr Cruttenden's both, of which I write him word and about his Georgia bills; Sorsbie's B - ; Brother Jemmy's £81 10s; 82 undrawn. Since writing the above have received a letter from Molly that she does not break up till next Fryday and that I shall that morning see her here.

1 [**595**] Meadow v Collier (TNA ASSI 34/5). Sussex Assizes, Horsham, Monday 12 August 1734, 8 Geo. II damages 5/-, paperwork completed 28 October 1734.

2 This was the 5th Westminster Bridge Lottery, 14 Geo II c. 40; the 3B refers to 3 blank tickets, and in this lottery the blanks received no return, likewise the other four Bridge lotteries (*PGA* vol. 14, Geo II 703; Ewen 147).

324 To John Collier, [Hastings], from William Cranston, [Johnson's Court], 26 December 1741 [SAY 762]

I take it for granted that you by last, or at least by this post, will have authentic accounts of Mr Sergison's declining our county election, which I first heard of yesterday and have fully confirmed today, to my great pleasure, as I dare say also to yours *cum multis aliis.*[1] Masters v Austen, I had a letter sometime since from plaintiff as unintelligable as any to you can be. All I could pick up was that he would be with you as the holiday week, which I suppose is the next, and then you will have particulars. Though I think yours of today will do, only should know what the pewter was, whether dishes or plates or both sorts and how many of each, as also whether twas a copper or brass tea kettle and what species those 8 peices of brass are which you say were taken away. I send you our account beginning from the foot of that last sent.

The Westminster election both before as well as since its determination engrossed all discourse, and numbers of wagers were laid upon the event.[2] It seemed to be fought to the utmost by each party, nobody on either side stiring out of the house without his opposite, and the numbers on each question I am told was as enclosed. Molly will write per next; did intend it today but has been otherwise disposed of. Our wishing of a merry Xmas and many happy new years attend you and all at the port.

1 For Thomas Sergison [**289**].

2 Westminster election, 8 May 1741, won for the Government by Sir Charles Wager, 3686 votes, and William Clayton, 3533, defeating Admiral Edward Vernon, 3290 votes and Charles Edwin, 3161. The bailiff of Westminster, supported by soldiers, closed the election early when Vernon and Edwin looked to be gaining the lead, returning Wager and Clayton. A citizens' petition to the Commons chimed with the general distaste at the use of soldiers to support government candidates, and the Commons declared such practice a 'a high infringement of the liberties of the subject, a manifest violation of the freedom of elections, and an open defiance of the law and constitution of the kingdom'. The House voted for the arrest of the bailiff, unseated Wager and Clayton, calling a new election. The mood of the citizens was obvious, and although the court party asked eight to stand for their interest, all refused. John Lord Percival and Charles Edwin were elected unopposed, witnessed by a crowd of over 5000. Lord Egmont, delighted at the humiliation of the court, decided this forbode 'no good to Sir Robert Walpole' (Egmont vol. 3, 233-4).

325 To Mary Collier, Hastings, from Molly Collier, at William Cranston's, Johnson's Court, 5 January 1742 [SAY 1762]

I am very glad to hear by your letter that you begin to talk of coming to London, which I hope will be pretty early in the spring before the hot weather comes, and that I may have something of cloaths for I begin to be a little bare; I don't yet know whether I shall bespeak the stays so long before hand for they wont be long about …[1] Here is a great deal of feasting about this Christmas. Last Wednsday we were at Mr Coppinger's who are all to be here tomorrow, and Thursday Mr Cole's family were here, where we are to dine a Friday. And last Friday I was at the accademy, where the new year's ode was performed and a very fine piece of musick. The hogspuddings and sausages are very good, and we are all very fond of them and think they taste a little morish. My uncle sends his compliments and thanks for all the things, for he forgot it when he wrote. I should be very glad to have a letter from my sister Jenny to hear how she keeps her Christmas. With duty to my papa and love to my sisters. I must beg leave to conclude myself, honoured madam, your obedient and dutiful daughter. I beg you'l make my compliments to all my acquaintance.

1 MS obscured.

326 To Mary Collier, Hastings, from Mrs Markwick, 12 January 1742 [SAY 1763]

I understand Miss Collier is at Battle, but as I think I may subject myself to a second affront by sending there, shall beg the favour of you to let her know by the post that Miss Webster and other company will sup with me a Monday night next; and I purpose to have a fiddle and shall take it as a perticular favour if you will let her come. I am very sure Miss Webster will bring her, otherwise will send my chariot. My sisters tell me she is out of order, but saw her a Friday and thought she did not look the worse for dancing. If you will give her leave to stay any time with me and will send her, ass I'll take as much care of her as if she was my own child, and it is possible change of air may be of service to her, which I sincerely wish. Mr Markwick, my sisters and self joyn in compliments to you and Mr Collier.

327 To Mary Collier, Hastings, from Cordelia Collier [Battle] January 1742 [SAY 2172]

Honoured Madam, I have just now wrote to Mrs Markwick and sent a man to let her know I will wait on her to stay all the week, and belive I must have my other stays, for these are very foull and I cannot hide the crap with my cloaths and immagane I shall have a bead fellow. My brother Worge has been very ill this week and whould be very glad if you could get him arach for he has no stomatch and thinks he could eat a bit of that, tonight we are to sup at the Dean's where we shall meet Miss Webster, and shall let her know that I am one of the company but belive she is no stranger to it for she gave me a hint of it a Thursday. Be pleased to give my duty to my papa and love to my sisters, from, honoured madam, your dutyfull daughter, Jenny's cap will be sent a Satterday I have sent a pair of Sally's shoose which was brought at the market.

328 To Mary Collier, Hastings, from Molly Collier, Johnson's Court, 16 January 1742 [SAY 1764]

In my last I mentioned our being going to the play that evening, which we did and were very well entertained, and on Wednsday Mr Green treated Jemmy and I at the same house with the *Provoked Husband*, and *Orpheus and Euridice*, which I was the most charmed with of any I have seen, and a prodigious full house.[1] Next day I waited upon Mrs Carleton, got there by noon, but had not the pleasure of seeing Mr and Mrs Cullen till dinner time at 3, when they favoured us with their company till about half an hour afterwards when they retired to their musick, which at a distance I heard them at, then, as well as before dinner. About an hour afterwards Mrs Carleton shewed me the house, and in that walk found Mr and Mrs Cullen had just drank coffee by themselves. About 5 we drank tea, when Mrs Cullen came and drank one dish and staid a quarter of an hour during my singing a song, which at hers as well as the subdean's request I was prevailed upon to do, tho much against my will before such judges, but could not obtain the like favour from Mrs Cullen.

I got home about 8, very well pleasd with my reception from Mr and Mrs Carleton, but don't think Mrs Cullen behaved quite so genteel, tho did not expect more of there company by what I had heard of them. Last night I was at the accademy where there was a great deal of company. Jemmy went away this day for Wormley and I, having been here a month yesterday, go sometime next week but can't yet tell the day for there's nobody gone yet, be pleased to give my duty to my papa and love to my sisters.

1 Covent Garden Theatre, Wednesday 13 January 1742, *The Provoked Husband* by Colley Cibber, with *Orpheus and Eurydia*, (Scouten Pt 3, vol. 2, 1736-47, 956-8).

329 To Mary Collier, [Hastings], from James Collier, Clare Hall, Cambridge, 21 January 1742 [SAY 1765]

I received my father's letter on Tuesday, giving me a particular account of the proceedings at the late election in Sussex, the contents of which I communicated to Lord Ashburnham, who expressed great satisfaction therewith. I intended to have wrote yesterday, but had that day my infrequent distemper attended me, viz, a violent headach, which obliged me to defer it till this. The university, both in combinations and private rooms, affords no other topick of conversation but politicks. And as the opposition in the House of Commons is at present very strong, on those days in which the votes are expected down the coffee houses are crowded, and happy is the man who can seize on them first. Tho sometimes he is forced to read out to a gaping, attentive, audience, to prevent their being snatched out of his hands before he has compleatly finished. The only question asked now is, "had you a letter from London lately"? if answered in the affirmative, then, "what were the numbers in the last division"?

After a stay of almost four years without a junior, I shall soon have the pleasure of seeing two persons set below me at the fellows' table; for Mr Walner, a gentleman of the age of thirty-six, a master of arts at Aberdeen in Scotland, has this week admitted himself a fellow commoner of this college, in order to take a degree at this university, a qualification now esteemed necessary for the holding of any living. And Sir Richard Mill, member in the present parliament for Horsham, has entered two sons here, the eldest of whom imediately upon his coming to reside, which will be in a fortnight, is to turn fellow commoner.[1] Mr Walter by his examination in the theatre for his bachelor's degree has obtained great deal of honour. Be pleased to acquaint my father, that, since I begun to write this letter, I received his with an account of my bill for the last quarter, and as it is dated 12 January, and on the back is wrote "from Clare", imagine it's owing to some neglect that it came to my hands not sooner. Be pleased to give my duty to papa and love to my sisters.

1 Sir Richard Mill's sons Charles and Henry were admitted to Clare College 18 November 1741.

330 To John Collier, Hastings, from William Cranston, Johnson's Court, 23 January 1742 [SAY 763]

You herewith receive your warrant on Fieri Facias v Avane. The instructions in your last relateing to Mr Pelham's affair shall be observed. Now for the politicall news of the week.[1] Monday nothing was done; Tuesday the Berwickshire election, which though it lasted till near ten with much battling on both sides, yet there was no division upon the question. Wednesday, no division neither; Thursday there was a grand one about a secret committee, but Sir Robert carried it by a majority of 3 only, the numbers being 251, 248.[2] The fatigue of the night before made them put of the Westminster justices yesterday till Monday, so little was done. Today may possibly, they say, determine the fate of the minister, for the Milborn Port election is on.[3] If that question is carried against him he will consequently have 2 less and his opponents two more, and if he carries it he will but be just were he now is people are bigg with expectation, but no news as yet. I am just going to the Ship, to Copp Hayward, etc., possibly before we break up may hear, if so you shan't fail. Molly went to school yesterday. Irwin, exceeding bad with the gout, was carried in a litter through the City to Westminster Thursday evening at 10 to vote.

1 From the outset of the session, 1 December 1741, much time was occupied by challenges to election returns, of which the successful challenge to the Westminster election [**324**] was the cue for further contests. The king, the Duke of Cumberland and the court party took several weeks to realise that insistence on keeping Walpole was unsustainable (Egmont 235, 1/9 January 1742).

2 The absence of several members was widely noticed, and the government majority of only three in the defeat of William Pulteney's motion for a select committee to examine into the conduct of the war, 21 January 1742, was interpreted as a rebuff for Walpole (Egmont 239-40, 14 January 1742); see also for further discussion of this question, Taylor & Jones 55, 21, 174-5, 27/28 January 1742; H W V Temperley, 'The Age of Walpole and the Pelhams' in Acton 71-3; Sayer vol. 1, 185-6.

3 Milbourne Port, Somerset, election 12 May 1741, saw Thomas Medlycott junior and Jeffrey French win with 57 votes apiece, against Michael Harvey and William Thompson, but Harvey's petition for a new poll passed the Commons. Upon this Medlycott resigned his seat, and Harvey was returned unopposed, avoiding a new poll: Medlycott was rewarded with an Excise Commissioner's place.

331 To John Collier, [Hastings], from William Cranston, [Johnson's Court], 26 January 1742 [SAY 764]

I was again with Mr Mounsey yesterday when I found Merchant's dividend fixt at 9s 6d in the pound. So no allowance to the bankrupt, but as before, may have what debts he can gett in, for which, it seems, he has an authority from the assignees. Upon looking over my books I don't find that I have ever charged anything to Marchant in your bills upon this account. I had severall attendances on Mounsey about the certificate, etc., as well as upon the present occasion, attending the Commissioners, etc., and hope 13s 4d won't be thought too much. Mrs Townsett's dividend amounting to £17 18s 6d I have received, and about which I attended the Commissioners upon proving debt, attended em again upon the dividend, and attended Mounsey twice for his draft upon the assignee, and attended the assignee, Otway, at his house in the Borough for the money. For all which I think also that I deserve the like summe of 13s 4d and 1sh I paid the usuall fee to the clerk of the commission for his draft on Otway.

I have bespoke for a copy of the bill v Jenkin. Watson's behaviour gives both Mr Coles and self no small uneasiness, who ought to have paid the money without a word considering by what meanes he came by the goods. I now understand that last Thursday James was with him and settled the affair and took a note for the ballance payable at Easter, even that is but scrubb usage but don't know how to help it. However, tis both the first and last time that either of us will trouble ourselves about him. I've paid Coles £15 11s 10d and Day £5 9s 11d and yesterday received of Master Clarke £46 15s 0d.

The affair of Milborn port it seems is compromised; Medlycott is to be a Commissioner of Excise in the room of Sir Thomas Robinson, made governor of Barbadoes, which vacates his seat, and Harvey is to come in in his room without opposition. I wonder I hear nothing from Nathaniell Cruttenden about his brother Georgia Cole, having a fortnight ago wrote him word that I had received it.

332 To Mary Collier, Hastings, from James Collier, Clare Hall, Cambridge, 28 January 1742 [SAY 1766]

My father's letter arrived on Friday, and on Sunday I was agreably surprized with the receipt of one from my sister Molly, the contents of which were very acceptable in relation to so good an evidence, as I imagine it to be, being capable to be produced against Hollyday at the next assizes; her letter I will answer next post. The late sharp frost being imediately succeeded by warm weather occasioned many sore throats, etc., though attended with no bad effects, except in the case of Mr Goddard's brother, the consequence of whose contracting a great cold was a violent fever and he lies now so dangerously ill that it is judged almost impossible for him to recover.

The recruiting serjeant having met with good success here in enlisting men, will be of great service to this town by draining it of a set of people who, through the excessive dearness of provisions and scarcity of work, would necessarily have pilfered for their maintenance, which trade many of the now gentlemen soldiers had begun to exercise. Young Mr Eagles at the Sussex club held on Thursday last made us all stare by positively asserting, I suppose upon his father's authority, that Mr Medley's being to be chosen one of the knights of the shire was a matter now beyond all manner of doubt and offered to lay any bet whatever that Mr Butler would be turned out.

As the affair which happened in the House of Peers between the Lords of Wilmington and Halifax concerning the king's answer to an address would, I imagine, be no news, shall take no farther notice of it, and mention it only with a view of letting you know it had reached Cambridge. I had an account from my uncle last week that poor 27941 was drawn a blank about a month before and that he wou'd not acquaint me with it sooner for fear of disturbing my jollity during the Christmas holydays in the combination. I must confess my expectations were greatly raised, and the four last days of drawing wou'd not have taken £20 for my chance.[1] Be pleased to give my duty to papa and love to my sister.

1 5th Westminster Bridge lottery [**320**] [**323**].

333 To John Collier, [Hastings], from William Cranston, [Johnson's Court], 30 January 1742 [SAY 765]

I've no more to say in respect to Mr Watson; if you' ll send me an affidavit will send the bailiffs after him. In our corporation affair you had an account per last night's post, and as to Moore and Rogers I told Rochester your last resolution, who imediately wrote to Gilbert about it, who directly had an answer that the defendant was just then down with the smallpox and impossible to go to her. This seemed a reasonable foundation to a cessation till she gott up again which I suppose she may be by this time. Shall see Rochester tomorrow when I will rubb up his memory. The merchants' affair has taken up Wednesday and yesterday, and adjourned to Monday. Thursday evening at 12 there was a grand division about the Chippenham election when Sir Robert lost his point by one, the numbers being 236 - 235,[1] many young chaps going out before by couples to the masquerade.[2]

1 Chippenham election, before the Commons, 28 January 1742; Sir Robert Walpole lost 236 to 235; and when on the 2nd February the issue came back to the house, the Government again lost, this time by 241 to 225. On this Sir Robert Walpole departed the Commons. After discussions with the court, on 11th February the king elevated Sir Robert to be Viscount Walpole, Earl of Orford, and baron of Houghton, upon which Sir Robert resigned his government positions (Rapin vol. 20, 530; Egmont vol. 3, 247). For an overview of this event and it's broader implications, see Owen 33.

2 The views of Edward Gibson, bishop of London, epitomise the considerable clerical opposition to masquerades (Sykes 187-8).

334 To John Collier, Hastings, from William Cranston, Johnson's Court, 4 February 1742 [SAY 766]

Philcox v Jenkin; you herewith receive a copy of this bill. I shall observe the contents of yours of today. Now for more politicks. Monday not remarkable happened. Tuesday the Chippenham affair came on, in which, they say, Sir Robert still hoped for success, but that soon vanished; for a question was soon put in which he lost it by sixteen, and he knew also that 5 other of his opponents were accidentally shut out of the house upon the division, so that he looked upon himself to be beat by 21. Upon which, unwilling to stand another question, he gave the point up, went out of the house directly, and came not in again neither that day nor yesterday, and has entirely quitted the field, upon which both houses were adjourned yesterday till the 18th instant, that in the interim, successors to him, as well as many others, may be appointed, and publick business be put in a way to go forward.

Various and divers are the reports of who goes out and who comes in.[1] Lord Wilmington is generally talked of for Chancellor of the Exchequer; Lord Carteret, Secretary of State; Duke of Newcastle to go to Ireland; Lord Chesterfield instantly to go ambassador to Holland; all the lords of the Treasury, Admiralty, Trade and Plantation, Commissioners of Customs, Excise, Navy, etc., etc., etc., to be out, and a reconciliation to take place between the king and the prince, and which the latter would upon no terms come into without first discarding Sir Robert, to whom he had taken an utter aversion. People are pretty much divided whether Mr Pelham will stand or not, the only wager that I have laid about the whole affair is one bottle that he will.

1 For the new ministers and their offices see Coxe 1829 vol. 1, 30.

335 To Mary Collier, [Hastings], from Mrs Markwick, Catsfield. 5 February 1742
[SAY 1767]

The misrepresentation of things offter makes people odious to their best friends without the least foundation. Therefore, think it incumbent on me to relate an affair to you which happened between Miss Collier and myself, which I aver to be true in every circumstance. About a forthnight since she did me the favour of a visit and behaved, as usual, with a great deal of good humour and good sence. I, in a jocular way, told her she could not make me amends for not coming to Catesfield before but by staying 3 or 4 days with me before she left Mrs Worgge. She promised she would, upon which I was very earnest with her to let it be as the latter end of last weeke or the begining of this, designing in my own mind a dance next Friday for Miss Webster, which I imagined would be more divertion than Catesfield could afford at any other time, but did not mention my design to her lest Mrs Worgge should be offended, at who's house she was. She agreed to come and I was to send horses in case it was not walking weather.

Mrs Worgge has not used me with much good manners lately; therefore I thought to act with caution, and desired my sister Molly to go to Battle church last Sunday and tell Miss Collier I would send horsses for her the next morning if she would come. She immediately said she would wait on me and I accordingly sent two servants, the one to bring her, the other to ride by, but they returned with this answer, that she was obliged to be at home on Wednesday and would wait on me a Friday morning, as the servant told me. I could look on this no other ...[1] designed affront; therefore sent her word I was engaged …[1] a Friday.

I would not have you infer from this that I take …[1] from Miss Collier. No madam, without flattery she has too good sense to affront a woman that cannot be accused of ever doing a rude thing by her, but young minds are easily perswaded, especially where they have a diffidence of themselves, which, though a commendable quality most times, may lead them into errors when they submit to a judgment inferior to their own. As soon as the roads will permit, and have weaned my little boy, design myself the pleasure of waiting on you. Mr Markwick and my sisters joyn with me in compliments to you and all the good family.

1 MS damaged.

336 To Mary Collier, Hastings, from Cordelia Collier, Battle, 6 February 1742
[SAY 1768]

I caried your gown to Mrs Iiskip, who will do it as soon as possable, and I likewise bought me an apron at five and ninepence a yard which stood me in thirteen shillings and six pence, for somehow by misstake Miss Thorpe cut off two nail more than I wanted. Tomorrow I am to drink tea there, being engaged all next week in walks, etc., with Miss Webbster. I hope you will be so good as to let me stay till the Place family is gone, which will be some time the week after next, and then I shall be ready to see Hasting. We had the pleasure of all there company at supper here a Wednesday and we was very merry, Mrs Nearn haveing declared herself in her old condition again, and as bespoke Mr Godfrey Webbster and I for two of the gossops.

Here has been a very odd afair between Mrs Markwick and I. A Sunday at church Miss Nolly, as she went out by me, told me her sister whould send the horses in the morning early and that I must bring a gown and pettecoat, which was all that past. I, imaganig the ball to be that day, set drest up in my dubble ruffles, and when the servant came he told me it was not to be till Friday, when I sent my compliments that I was very sorry I had given her so much trouble but that I could not posable come to stay so long as Friday, but that then my brother whould send me over, and in the afternoon the servant came with is Mrs Service, and that she was engaged. The next day, meeting Miss Sopi at the Abby, I went to her and told her I was very sorry Mrs Markwick took it so amiss my not coming, to which she said they was not at all angry with me for they knew whose fault it was, and there it ended.

When we came from our walk a Satterday we supt at the Abby where my lady made me sing a song quite by myself, and it was, "Vainly now ye strive to charm me", and I was all in shuch a friat that I thought I should not have gone through with it, but have sung it since without any trembling.[1] If you please to tell Molly that a Sunday Miss Webbster is to wheare my new fan to church in order to set a fashon. Be pleased to give my duty to my papa and love to my sisters.

1 *The Ark: being a select collection of the most celebrated and newest songs, Scots and English* (Edinburgh: 1765). (Glen collection of printed songs, National Library of Scotland 56).

337 To John Collier, [Hastings], from William Cranston, [Johnson's Court], 6 February 1742 [SAY 767]

Walley v Waters. This debt and cost was setled between Mr Boughey and self at £48 7s 10d, which I accordingly this morning paid him and he paid me your £2 1s 8d, and for my own fees, etc., there being 3 causes, I demand 13s 4d. Mr Worge's Bristoll water went yesterday morn. The Spa[1] v Sir Charles is so uncouth an affair that I could not but send it by itself. Nothing new stirring, no more than notwithstanding the papers say Sir Robert resigned all employ last Wednesday, yet he is certainly to this hour in possession of em.

[Postscript][2]
£48 7s 10d, + 13s 4d = £49 1s 2d; £31 10 0d + £8 0s 0d + £44 10s 0d = £ 5 0s 0d

1 Subpoena.
2 In John Collier's handwriting.

338 To John Collier, Hastings, from William Cranston, Johnson's Court, 11 February 1742 [SAY 768]

Having a present made me last week of a pott of charr[1] which is esteemed a great rarity in this part of the world, it being the produce of Westmorland only, I yesterday sent it by the carrier to the port, having never seen or tasted any of it before myself. I opened it and sett before it Squire Howard, his bride, Counceller Jeake and Miss Bird last Fryday who did me the honour to spend the evening with me. What they left you receive, which is by much the greatest part of it. Tis at last agreed on all hands that Sir Robert resigns this day and that Lord Wilmington comes in pro tempore his being called to the peerage does not seem to disgust anybody, but he is universally condemned in the affair of Lady Maria.[2] They say his friends strongly perswaded him against it but he was determined, and it could serve no other end but to shew that he may still do what he thought proper with his master.

1 Char, small freshwater fish, common in lakes in the north of England and Wales, red and white char in Windermere; a similar fish existed in Swiss lakes (*OED*).

2 Named after Queen Maria Theresa; Lady Maria was Walpole's daughter by Miss Skerret, whom Sir Robert married when his wife died in 1737; Maria was granted the rank and precedence accorded the daughter of an Earl.

339 To Mary Collier, Hastings, from Molly Collier, Hampstead, 11 February 1742 [SAY 1769]

I received your letter with a great deal of pleasure to hear you are all well, for I was afraid, not having heard a pretty while, least somebody was ill. I hope soon to hear the time fixed for your coming to London, as I immagine it not to be a great way off. I believe my frocks may be of some service to my sister Jenny, for I have three that are very good and that is all; but I'm afraid if she is so tall she has outgrown me. I am very glad to hear my sister Dely spends her time so agreably at Battell and hope it will be of service to her. I am in expectation of a letter from her which I shall be very glad to receive. Be pleased to give my duty to my papa and love to my sisters, my governess and Miss Russel send their compliments.

340 To Mr Slaghtholm, from John Collier, judge of the vice admiralty court of Sussex, Hastings, 16 February 1742[1] [SAY 12]

Mr John Sargent of this town communicated to me your letter of the 2nd December last relating to the anchor, cable, sails and rigging which we was informed belonged to your vessel that foundered near Dengeness point; and information being given that a French fishing vessel belonging to Dieppe had taken them up and designed to carry the same to France, but lying in our road, a boat sufficiently manned with men and a proper power went of and took the goods and brought on shore, and the master of the fishing vessell came on shore to whom 2 guineas was paid, and likewise the informer gratifyed. The goods have been taken care of by Mr Sargent at a pretty deal of expense and are secured, but much wonder we have not heard from you.

The French master has made a sad complaint and sent a remonstrance over to some merchants at Rye and demands and insists on a full third part of the value and Mr Sargent is threatened if he parts with the goods he shall be obliged to pay them [2] and talks very bigg. It will be proper that some resolution should be come to either for sale of the goods or taking them away, for on paying of the disbursements and trouble and giving proper security to Mr Sargent, etc., they shall be delivered, but it cannot be expected without I desire an immediate answer [3]. This draft is not exact but to the effect: an anchor and about 90 fathom of the cable, 2 topsails, a peice of a sail and a small stay sail, about [4] £30 or £40. About 12 guineas clear of all charges. Cable half wore.

1 Laws on wreck and salvage updated by 12 Anne s. 2 c.18, made perpetual by 4 Geo I c. 12 and confirmed the Admiralty Court of the Cinque Ports in their jurisdiction on wrecks and salvage (*SL* vol. 5, 176).

2 MS *and seems to threaten much* struck through.

3 MS *either to Mr Sargent or myself* struck through.

4 MS *£40 or £50* struck through.

341 To John Collier, Hastings, from William Cranston, Johnson's Court, 11 March 1742 [SAY 769]

Am sorry to hear your account of our friend Godley, though I think he has nothing else for it but to drink and drive care away. I shall take care to pay your £200 draft, and squire Prosser yesterday sent you 6lbs chocolate. Moore[1] v Rogers, having now setled this affair I find you can have nothing at present but a Fieri Facias for £60 de bonis testoris for the cost de bonis proparijs, but upon the return of this writt the sherriffe will, of course, return nulla bona testatoris which amounts to a devastavit and then you may have Fieri Facia de bonis proporijs for the whole.

I find I must take a tripp to Maidstone next Sunday in order to prove a deed, if the fine weather continues, I won't be disagreable and this also makes me think of your and my sister's journey hither, which I hope will be in a little time, but if it tis thought of till the terme shall most likely make an excursion for a week or ten days in the hollidays somewhere or another, though should be glad to be disappointed with your early attendance. The late Sir Robert carried his point Tuesday evening, a secret comittee or not, by two voices.[2] There's great convulsions at the helm, and can't at all agree who are to be the outs and the inns, and in all which the late minister is generally allowed to have a great hand, being at present more in personall favour with his master than ever.

1 MS obscured by seal.
2 9 March 1742, opposition motion from Lord Limerick before the Commons for a committee of enquiry to examine into the conduct of affairs at home and abroad for the previous twenty years, defeated 244 to 242; 23 March, a second motion for enquiry, covering just ten years, also from Lord Limerick was carried 252 to 245, but the work of the committee was not well supported and interest waned as Lord Wilmington's government settled into office (Egmont vol. 3, 260 263-4; Mahon vol. 3, 121-3).

342 To Mary Collier, Hastings from Molly Collier, Hampstead, 23 March 1742 [SAY 1770]

I just now received your obliging letter and have the pleasure to acquaint you that I am now perfectly well as ever I was in my life, and am obliged to my governess for it who has taken a great deal of care of me. I have taken physick three times which has entirely cured my cough. I was not under any great surprize for I hardly knew I had anything out till it was almost gone. I am very glad to hear that both my sisters are better and hope they will continue so and that I shall soon have the pleasure of seeing you in town. My uncle came to see me on Sunday who says he is in expectation of you very soon, and pray tell my sister Jenny I think the first of April is very near at hand; I should be very glad to have a letter from her if she can spare time. Be pleased to give my duty to my papa and love to my sisters, from your most obedient and dutifull daughter.

343 To Mary Collier, at William Cranston's, Johnson's Court, from John Collier, Hastings, 24 April 1742 [SAY 1771]

I hope you got safe to London Saturday afternoon and found all friends well. I got a horse back in five minnets after the coach drove out of the yard, and came to Mr Worge's exactly at one, and dined, and came home at five, when Dely was down at her aunt's, but came home in about half an hour. She has a letter last night from Molly Smith[1] that she will be here a Tuesday and Mrs Worge has altered her design of being here one night next week by puting the same of till Munday sen'night, when she will come and stay till Fryday or Saturday.

I met Mr T. Pelham[2] at Hurstgreen returning to London, he really looks very thin, and I think is a little hoarser, though I told him I was glad to see him look so well. Dely twas a little sickish today after dinner, but Sarah says eat pretty well and I think she is pretty brisk withall. Though we looked about carefully to see whether anything was omitted being put up, I find your whip was left, and I write this post to our landlord to take care of it. I have nothing particularly to write so conclude with affection and respects. Tell my brother I received his letter last post that he need not hurry so very much about Jenkins answer, though I shall be glad to have it as soon as conveniently it may be, but am afraid I shall not get to London so soon as I wrote him. He must supply you with what money you want. Betty Wicking stayed with Dely all day a Fryday. She heard today by dame Dulvey that little Hariot is brisk and well.[3]

1 Molly Smith, neice of John Collier, lived in East Grinstead.
2 Thomas Pelham of Stanmer. For the details of his rentals see Appendix 4: Pelham estate **[607]** SAY 372.
3 Sayer supposes Henrietta was staying with the Denham family in Hollington (Sayer vol. 1, 198).

344 To Mary Collier, at William Cranston's, Johnson's Court, from Cordelia Collier, Hastings, 29 April 1742 [SAY 1772]

We received yours last night, with a great deal of pleasure to here you got safe to town, but am very sorry to here poor Mercy behaved herself so badly, for think she made great discoverys, that she had not been used to a coach. I have been ingaged every day since you went. A Monday I went drest out in my blue to visit Mrs Bowman, and yesterday she and Mrs Cruttenden, Mrs Sweetlove was here, and I, being willing to show away as much as possable, brought forth the kettle and lamp; but it soon took fire, and was forced to be removed, though not without first flowing the table, which had like to have spoilt the whole ceremony; for we did not speak above once in half an hour, and that by sentances only. Sir William was here about an hour but did not come into us. He drank tea with Mrs Medhurst who has been very bad with her fits but is now better, they are very much afraid her brother dyed without a will and then she wont have anything considarable.

I am very glad to here chipt hats are worn, and beg that you will buy me one, for belive I shall like it better than my bonnet, for everyboddy is goeing to have one. I am just now returnd from the triall of my dame Joy, where my cousin Molly and I have been all the morning and set with the gentlemen.[1] Poor Sarach was one of the chief witnesses, and frithten out of her witts. She was found guillty, and is to be wipt at the cart's tail round the town a Satturday, so desire Jenny whould think of it just at one a'clock, for that is to be the time. Mrs Cant is come to make us a vissit this afternoon, and find Poll wants to stay; but Mrs Cant says she shall not, though I belive she will, for she wont belive that she runs after the fellows now, here is a great many fine ladys come from Battell today, a chaise and tow single horses, but I have not seen them.

As to housekeeping, we have performed very well as yet, but now have quite a cleare house, only a piegion pie, which we must keep till next week that my sister Worge comes, so must fast till then. Tom Denham was here yesterday, and Henny is very well. Sally is very brisk, and everybody says grows fat. The wheather has been so cold, that I have not rode out, but have left off dockters and am better. I have moved my lodgeings into the blue room to my cousin Molly, and when my sister Worge is gone, then we shall goe into that, so take a course round the house. I was very glad to here Molly looks so well, and hope I shall here from her soon. Here is no news at all so will conclude with my duty to my uncle and love to my sisters. My papa will write next post but hopes to here from my uncle.

1 Hastings general quarter sessions, 29 April 1742, John Collier presided over the session, at which Elizabeth Arthur, widow, was indicted for receiving three fowls stolen from John P—ey, and selling the same; she was found guilty and ordered to be publicly whipped around Hastings the next market day (ESRO HAS CAA/5). For details of her punishment see [**345**].

345 To Mary Collier, [Johnson's Court], from John Collier, Hastings, 1 May 1742 [SAY 1773]

I received your letter by last post according to custom without a date, and am sorry to hear my brother is so sadly of about servants. I had last Thursday a present of a large pot of pickled oysters, which is sent by Guy, though opened, and I think pritty good but I forgot to tell Patrick to put carriage and porteredge paid, but that you'l supply. Dely rode out this morning about 10 and in the meantime Mark Sanford came. I was busy and sent him to walk half an hour in the garden, he dined and I paid him four pound for the chints,[1] he pressed to make a present but I absolutely refused. I think he is a very civil person and one of his station well behaved. Dame Arthur was about one a clock whipped at the cart's tayl round the town and had some strokes at every lane's end, but I find it's thought she had not half enough, but I inclined to mercy and compassion, and considered the long time of her confinement in the cold weather.

Tom Smith came this afternoon about 3 and brought some live pigeons, 2 dozen and 9 to eat. I am a little afraid our project will not take but will endeavour to make it. Sir W. A and Mr Frewen came to town about 12, dined at Thorpe's and I was sent for from the Swan about 4 and found them strongly engaged in the low, obscene, discourse and nothing diverted it during my stay about an hour. I came home at 6 and found Betty Wicking here. They had drunk tea but I had a little made. Mrs Gladwish had a son about 12 last night. I don't find but the child at Hollington is pretty well. My sister Cruttenden and Sal dined here yesterday. The dragoons went away that morning at 10 to joyn their corps and embark for the Spanish Netherlands. Dely is in high expectation of her hat. James Bossum's reckoning is to be next Tuesday at his brothers, so we are invited to dinner in form, and if my daughter Worge comes she makes one of the company. Multitudes of garlands according to custom and Sally came with great earnestness for money for the children. She has not forgot you when talked of but wants to see you sadly.

1 Chints, chintz, printed and plain white cottons, often with flower patterns of several colours; originally from India, and copied in England; used as ornamental covering for chairs and bedcovers.

346 To Mary Collier, Johnson's Court, from James Collier, Clare Hall, Cambridge, 7 May 1742 [SAY 1774]

By last Fryday's post I received a letter from my father, by which I was informed of your and my sister Jenny's arrival in Johnson's Court. Three Italians, after a stay at this place of ten days, set out on Tuesday morning for London with an intention of offering themselves at the opera house where in all probability they will meet with great encouragement.[1] Signor Piantinida is esteemed by the judges to play exceedingly well on the violin and the women Signora Posterla and Signora Chiari Posterla to have agreable voices joined to great judgement, but particularly the former is looked upon to sing not in the least inferior to Signora Visconti. They had here three crowded concerts of vocal and instrumental musick.

We have here a prevailing report in relation to a great disturbance at the theatre in the Haymarket lately, occasioned by a quarrel between Lord Lincoln and Colonel Ogle, the particulars of which story I presume you are sufficiently acquainted with.[2] Vauxhall Gardens I see by the publick papers are already opened, but if the trees there make no better appearance than those about Cambridge the gardens afford but a melancholy prospect, for the great trees have scarce any leaves upon them. The university affords no other news but political, which sort I think you don't delight in, so that I am obliged to conclude with presenting my duty to my uncle and love to my sisters.

1 Signora Giovanni Piantinida, fl. 1735-68, dancer, singer; (Highfill vol. 3, 203, vol. 11, 301).
2 W S Lewis, 29 April 1742, Lord Lincoln v Colonel Ogle.

347 To Mary Collier, [Johnson's Court], from John Collier, [Hastings], 8 May 1742 [SAY 1775]

Dely continues much as she was. Sally is alert and rude and I think, though she looks thin, is very well, and no ill news from Hollington. Dely writes to Molly and I presume sends all occurrences. I have sent a box with some shirts and a few books and papers, but I am not fully determined nor will my business permit me to fix the day for beginning my London journey. As you are in town I think you should not hurry home, but I can give no advice about it. I beleive Mr Coppard will be our mayor.[1] I think at present we are in an odd situation by the distance between us, and therefore something out of the way, but hope all that will center happily to our mutual pleasure. Mr Worge came here today at 12. I am afraid they depart a Munday, for my daughter Worge is, as I verily beleive, agreeable to Dely and of a very chearful temper, and the whole continue in a brisk way.

1 William Coppard, appointed mayor, 9 May 1742 (ESRO HAS CAA/5).

348 To Mary Collier, at William Cranston's, Johnson's Court, from John Collier, [Hastings], 11 or 13 May 1742[1] [SAY 1776]

I received your letter last Saturday's date which brought me an account of your having ordered places to be taken in the stage coach for next Fryday on your return home. The same was by me unexpected, and has determined an alteration in my intentions, for I designed to set out for London, as tomorrow or a Thursday. But on your letter shall postpone the same till next week, but meet you at Tunbridge Friday afternoon, in order I hope to bring you safe home, and Nabbs horse is to come. Mrs Worge went away yesterday afternoon, and Dely with her on this horse by Hollington to see the child, and I went on foot to meet her return, and she thinks the horse goes exceedingly well and easy.

Mr Coppard was elected mayor without opposition, and this morning, pursuant to what I find talked of, a voyage to the Tent[2] was performed, and Sal Cruttenden came up about 9 for that purpose. I thought it too cold, but I found Dely very desirous to goe, so would not put it by, and went myself on horseback 2 or 3 hours after. Rain came on and very cold weather in the afternoon, and I insisted on horses to be sent for. There were the mayor, Thorpe, and S. Cruttenden, Dely, M. Smith, Sal Cruttenden and Betty Wicking, but Mrs Cruttenden came after dinner in a smart shower of rain. We came home between 7 and 8.

I observed the mayor and doctor gay amongst the women, and the mayor mighty complaisant in his awkward way. Sir W. Ashburnham and Mr Frewen and my brother Cranston dined yesterday at the Swan. My brother went home, and between 4 and 5 I drank tea with Sir William and Mrs Geery's, and went to meet Dely. I defer all other occurrences till the pleasure of personally communicating the same. Sally is well, brisk and wanton, and I really think very good company. She comes in often every day for her fine baby I told her of. I find by Dely that Henny's issue is almost dryed up which I told Thorpe of.

1 Sayer vol. 1, 200 suggests the 11th May, William Coppard was elected mayor on the 9th May.
2 'Voyage to the Tent': the Tent was the white house on the cliff at Bo Peep, St Leonards, owned by the Pelhams, connected to Crowhurst Park by a private road.

349 To Mary Collier, Hastings, from John Collier, [Johnson's Court], 20 May 1742

[SAY 1777]

I send this to let you know of my arrival in town this day at 12, coming to Sennock last night; I was fortunate in my journey as to rain, but there was a great deal fell last night and this afternoon which will take away from the lustre of your company tomorrow, if you have had the same. I found my brother with his new maid or widow; and Thomas gone to Putney and little Jacky with him, being relapsed the day after you went from London, and I think there is but little probability of his being able to continue his service. It has been but a very dolorous afternoon, and I have heard little or no news, only my brother told me that Tom Green's archdeacon dyed yesterday, so it will be now known how their expectations are answered.[1] I design to write to the girls tomorrow and hope to send you more news by next post.

1 Revd Christopher Clarke, archdeacon of Norwich, 1722-42; prebendary of Ely Cathedral, 1732-42; Canon Ely Cathedral 1732-42, d. 19 May 1742 (Cedb; *Gentleman's Magazine* xii 275).

350 To Mary Collier, Hastings, from Molly Collier, Hampstead, 22 May 1742

[SAY 1778]

I received your letter and we are very glad to hear that you got home safe and that we shall soon have the pleasure of seeing my papa who we begin to be in expectation of everyday. My sister Jenny began upon the spinnet last Saturday, but the entrance was not given till we see my papa, at which Mr Sheeles was a little affronted and promised to be very punctuall. I am very glad to hear our gowns are new fashioned, for I think it the only thing to recommend it, and wish my sister Dely had had her choice but can hardly believe her. I am sorry to hear of poor Mercy's missfortune on being sick again and would advise her never to keep her coach. Hampstead affords no news at present worth your hearing so must beg leave to conclude. My sister Jenny joyns with me in duty to yourself and love to my sisters, from, honoured madam, your obedient and dutifull daughter.

351 To Mary Collier, Hastings, from John Collier, [Johnson's Court], 24 May 1742 [SAY 1779]

I am sorry to hear by your letter that you are joyned with us in complaints of depression of spirits, and that you imagine Dely is not so well as your last letter gave you reason to think. The report of Mr Thomas Pelham's death at Bristoll is certainly without foundation, for I have heard by several hands that the apprehension of immediate danger is over, but that the symptoms of a consumption remain very strong upon him, such as a hoarsness, violent spittings and some fever, which I thank God don't appear in Dely's case.

Mrs Broadway called here in the morning about 10 and I paid her Mr Child's money and she gave me the song accompanying this, to be sent to Dely. She stayed half an hour whilst I eat watergruell, but offered her tea which she refused having breakfasted. Mr Green senior came here before dinner, with rings for my brother, self and Jemmy on the archdeacon's death, and stayed dinner and we dine there tomorrow. There was a ridotto last night at Ranelaugh Gardens, but I have heard there was but indifferent company there, and great numbers at Vauxhall. I have bought Molly's ear rings, which I think very handsom, 8 guineas the price, and have chocolate and coffee and bespoke your fish kettle, etc., James Bossom called here this morning designing to sail tomorrow. I think there's nothing aboard him but bacon, hams and some chairs for the garden room.

I have got a promise of an ensign's commission for young Tom Smith, at his earnest desire, and I beleive the commission will be signed by the king the next time the Secretary at War has audience. It's an established regiment, but where at present I can't tell, but beleive at Gibralter or Port Mahon. I think there can be no dissappointment, but that it's prudent not to mension it till compleated, but this puts a stop to any application from me for Harry. I write to my brother Smith this post. The two Miss Green's dined here yesterday and go out of town a Munday. I heartily wish I could leave London, but am afraid it will be at least Thursday or Fryday first. I desire you will give Patrick this letter and if he delivers it to Robert Thomas of Westfield next Wednesday he will take care to send it.

352 To Mary Collier, Hastings, from John Collier, [Johnson's Court],[1] 1 June 1742 [SAY 1780]

Yesterday being the last term day, I went to Westminster Hall, but as I expected the girls about 12, did not set out till their arrival, which was in a quarter of an hour after, very brisk and well; and I went for Westminster at 1, and Jemmy Cranston came in 5 minnets after, but I did not see him till this morning. He is very much grown and looks well, but his hair, till regulated today by Pigeon, looked like the wild boy in the wood. We dined yesterday at Le Becks head, Chandois Street, from whence T. Green and I went to the play to see Mr Garrick.[2] It was debated whether to fetch Molly and Jenny, but the company, considering the warm weather, were against it, and if had been done, it was impossible to have got them in, for I never saw more crowded audience of good company.

The duke, Amelia and Carolina[3] there, and we in the little gallery over the stage box on the opposite side, though that was taken up, and footmen in possession; but by good words and promise to resign when the ladys came, we kept possession of the front seat the first act, and then only 2 ladys, that we had the second the whole play, and Mr Webster came in, in the second act, and thus we had a good deal of discourse between the acts. The play was *Richard the Third*, King Richard by Garrick. The justest, finest actor I ever saw, the house extreamly hot, I was at home before half an hour after 9.

I was this morning to wait on Lord Wilmington, and before I saw him Mr Carleton came in, I presume after Doctor Alured Clark's prebendary,[4] in which I wish him heartily success. But his lordship came into the room in 2 minutes that we had no time for discourse, and I had the first audience, though other gentlemen were waiting. So I marched of, I think the subdean looked very well but hear everyday of his unfortunate situation as to circumstances. Molly and Jenny have been with Mrs Nouns this morning about your fan, and tippets, or something they are to have at their governesses request to wear about their necks. They had Mrs Nouns to drink tea with them yesterday afternoon. Mrs Selby has not as yet sent for the chints and lining and I told Molly what you wrote about the white gown.

I am resolved to come out of town sometime next Fryday, and to get that night to Tonbridge. So would have James to come thither with horses that day to be there in the evening; for I don't propose getting there before 7 or 8 and lye there that night, and beleive come in a chaise thither. But if I should happen not to be there then he is to come forward Saturday morning with the horses. Mr Webster very handsomly asked after Miss Collier's health and whether the warmer weather had not contributed towards a recovery. Since writing the letter as it will be the same thing as to the journey for the horses I desire James may set out early a Fryday morning and get to Tunbridge by 2 or 3, that, if it happens, I come thither in the afternoon, and have an inclination of coming part of the way, I may have it in my power to make any option, adieu.

1 Easter term ran from the 5 May to 31 May 1742 and Trinity term 18 June to 7 July 1742.

2 Drury Lane Theatre, 31 May 1742, *Richard III*, adapted from Shakespeare by Colley Cibber, David Garrick as Richard, by command of their royal highnesses, the duke, princesses Amelia, Caroline and Louisa (Scouten Pt 3, vol. 2, 1736-47 997).

3 The MS reads as Carolina.

4 Dr Alured Clarke, rector Chilbolton 1723-36; Canon of Winchester, d. 31 May 1742, succeeded by John Hume, see Miege June 1742, 321 (Cedb).

353 To John Collier, Hastings, from William Cranston, [Johnson's Court], 5 June 1742 [SAY 770]

I hope this will find you safe arrived at the port and that you found all friends well there. Captain Bossum just paid me this morning upon your account £379 15s 0d. To make out the week, Fuller, Masterman, Coppinger and self rose from yesterday's dinner at the Mitre just before 1 this morning and dined upon a peice of park pale of Fuller's today at the Row, but broke up by 4, so that having finished the week as I began am determined to be upon the penitentiall all the next.

354 To John Collier, Hastings, from William Cranston, [Johnson's Court], 8 June 1742 [SAY 771]

Hasting v Eversfield;[1] you'll let me know the days of the chusing the mayors in each of the six years, the mayor's name, the jurats' names, the chamberlains' names, the sessors' names. I've heard nothing from Lyme,[2] write tonight, though unless I should hear by tomorrow's post don't see but that we must loose the benefitt of the next terme. We were at Keston yesterday, bunged rather too much; the two Green's sett out for Marlingford toomorrow.

1 Hastings v Eversfield (TNA C12/1178/84). Also see Hastings chamberlain's accounts, ESRO HAS DA 9 May 1742 to 24 April 1743, Sir Charles Eversfield's common fines upon outdwellers: for St Leonard's Clenfield and Bulverhythe, 9/-; Magdalen lands and Pope lands in William Farncomb's occupation 15/-; Newgate's, late in Hill's occupation, 4/-; Eversfield's arrears owed to the corporation for 6 years £8 8s. Also, John Collier held money from the corporation, for which he paid 3% interest, at the audit to 6 October 1742, this amounted to £200, plus one year's interest due 6th October 1743, £6, total £206; less, towards the expense of the corporation's suit with Sir Charles Eversfield £68 12s 0d; so: remaining with John Collier and owing to the corporation £137 8s 0d.

2 Payment to John Collier for the charges of a suit in the name of Henry Sargent against two persons at Lyme, being commenced by the agreement of the corporation at a public assembly, £13 11s 4d (ESRO HAS DA/4/1).

355 To John Collier, Hastings, from William Cranston, [Johnson's Court], 15 June 1742 [SAY 772]

Philcox v Jenkin; upon inquiry I find this answer was 56 sheets.[1] I rec'd per Monday's post your £28 draft, since which, I've sent twice to the person on whom it is drawn to know whether he'll pay it as it as present stands, but have not had the good fortune to meet with him, but shall send that way again tomorrow. I've at last got an answer that the Lyme writt is served but so late, Q. if not a juggle on purpose below that I can do no more than leave a declaration in the office and give defendants notice this terme, for they've not appeared but have done it for em. I've much obliged to you for your thoughts about the wine am in no hurry about it, whenever it comes twill be welcome and its being fine will fully make amends for staying.

Molly mentions Vauxhall, to which I have only to add, that I believe there were near or quite, 3000 people there, and at least fourteen starrs and garters. We remembred 4 years agoe, and wished for all the then company to be added to us, twas extremely pleasant, the water as still as a pond, and it vastly exceeds Ranelagh.

Everybody here are in high spirits, upon the peace between the queen of Hungary and king of Prussia, and looked upon as a master peice of politicks in its being done through our mediation.[2] The terrible scituation of the French also in Germany is also no small matter of joy, for tis generally thought that not a man of em will ever see his own country again, for those that are not demolished by prince Charles, etc., will certainly be knocked at head by the peasants. In short, it is agreed that France has not been so capotted this century last past in every one of her schemes. They talk of the house sitting till August.[3]

1 Philcox v Jenkin (TNA C11/2716/6 bill and answer).

2 After subterfuge and secrecy Frederick of Prussia invaded Silesia, part of the Austrian empire, in December 1740. Recognising the military reality Empress Maria Theresa signed a secret agreement with Frederick, by which Austria ceded lower Silesia with Breslau and Neisce, and the Prussian army would halt their advance. On this, the Austrian forces left Silesia, the Duke of Lorraine reconquered most of Bohemia from the French, and the Austrians defeated the French at Linz, and overran Bavaria, and on 12 March 1742 marched into Munich. At this point Frederick broke his agreement and attacked Austria. England's interest was to isolate France, and after pressure, Maria Theresa agreed to the peace of Breslau, preliminary signing 11 June 1742, final text 28 July. For Maria Theresa's defence of her position as Empress, guaranteed under the Pragmatic Sanction see Lecky 1892 vol. 1, 455-62.

3 Parliament sat from 1 December 1741 to 15 July 1742, and did not sit in August; the next session ran from 16 November 1742 to 21 April 1743 (*HBC* 578-9).

356 To Mary Collier, Hastings, from Molly Collier, Johnson's Court, London, 17 June 1742 [SAY 1781]

I write with a great deal of pleasure to let you know that we with Mr Coles, family, etc., eleven in number, were last night at Vauxhall where we were most agreably entertained and supped very elegantly. I beleive there are more lamps since you saw it and the pavillions, one of which is exceeding grand, and alltogether I think it far preferable to Ranelagh especially in hot weather. I went in my pink gown, but really it was hardly good enough for it is now allmost a white, as I have been forced to wear it constant, for I can't yet get the white one, though Mrs Selby has had it ever since I have been here. We were there on Sunday and staid supper and took one turn in the Mall. We are getting our things ready to sit of tomorrow for Hampstead and should be glad if you would please to send us a little bohea tea for our use there.[1]

Miss Russell called here on Tuesday and was paid my quarter's bill, and that afternoon we made her a visit, at Miss Agutter's in Bloomsbury, who I beleive my sister Dely knows, and there had the pleasure of seeing Miss Cotterell, and think I never saw such a figure in my life for she is as big as Mrs Medhurst. I don't find but that Miss Russell's spark is very dull, and am afraid it wont do. I beg you'll give my duty to my papa and love to my sisters and all freinds from, honoured madam, you most obedient and dutifull daughter. I hope I shall have the pleasure of a letter from my sister soon,

1 Bohea tea, at this time one of the finest of China's black teas, from the Wu-I hills north of Fuhkien (*OED*).

357 To John Collier, Hastings, from William Cranston, [Johnson's Court], 24 June 1742 [SAY 1782]

The inclosed from Molly came to me about Tuesday noon, which a little supprized me, because when they left me on Fryday, Jenny was exceeding well, and only had a slight bleeding in the nose just before they sett out; which I attributed to the heatt of the weather and fullness of blood, but in consequence must be a symptom of her disorder. I could not possibly go to Hampsted on Tuesday but went yesterday noon, when I found her in bed, without any sort of feaver and very little cough, and the measles just going off, but that she had had em exceeding full. I asked after her apothecary but found she had had none. Her physick having been only kitchen but as in distempers of this sort the consequence after it are often worst than the thing itself.

And as she had had em so much I thought, as Mrs Russell did likewise, that good care should be taken of her as to purging, etc., and thought it the best way, though perhaps some small additionall expence may attend it, to send up Mr Stacy who accordingly went last night, and this morning told me that he found her in very good order and that he would take all possible care of her during the remainder of it. And gave her one dose this morning and purposed going up again this evening to see how it agreed with her that he might be a judge how to deal with her hereafter, but bid me assure you that he looked upon her to be quite out of all danger, and that with proper care in her physick he was not under the least apprehension of any ill consequence. Jemmy, thank God, is got to be very well but is as yet under his courses.

The Austrians having taken Prague[1] is out of doubt as I think I may add to, that Bootle's was this day appointed chief baron.[2] Molly is very well, tell my sister her pink night gown suffered very much whilst in town and in good earnest wants mending with a new something of that sort, for twill never last out, with any decency, half the summer.

1 Winter 1741/2 one of the worst of the century, following the wet weather and deficient harvests of 1741; the French army under Marshall Belleisle was surrounded by the Austrians in Prague, part fought their way out, but many died of frostbite and hypothermia in a twelve day retreat to the frontier. The remnants of the French army was allowed to leave Prague on condition they left the city intact. England's policy was organised around defending Maria Theresa; as Carteret observed, the naval conflict between Spain and England blended into an European land and sea war, with France as the main opponent of England.

2 Thomas Bootle, 1685-1753, barrister, MP Liverpool 1724-34, Midhurst 1734-53; when Walpole demitted office Thomas Bootle turned down offer of the office of chief baron of the Exchequer, though proved solid for Wilmington, Newcastle and Pelham, and as result of active support in 1745 was knighted. 23 November.

358 To Mary Collier, Hastings, from Elizabeth Russell, Hampstead, 9 June 1742

[SAY 1783]

Miss Collier has just received your letter. I have the pleasure of telling you Miss Jenny is perfectly well after the most violent measels I ever saw. She was taken with a bleeding at the nose, which is common in this illness. As soon as she came in from town I observed she cough't and sneezed, and said "Miss you have a bad cold," and when I saluted her saw her neck very full out under her throat and the sides of her neck was very uneasie. The weather very hot, and I afraid of frighting them, I realy thought it was the smallpox. Till Sunday she cough't so much from her forehead to her toes one could not set a pin's head between and no scarlet cloth redder and would not let Miss see her sister till Monday evening. 3 days she eat nothing but one bit of toast and butter to clean her tongue, sweat very much and drank as much, has taken physick twice and am in great hopes it will cure her face at which, no doubt, she is much delighted.

And now, madam, as to gowns, London and Vauxhall and all these fine things have quite spoilt them both, I mean thier night gowns, and think it will quite cast down poor Miss Jenny if she has not one. Miss Collier seems to like a pale brown lutestring[1] and Miss Jenny says she will take great care of a pink. Madam, I shall take it as a favour if you will let Miss Jenny have one; indeed, she deserves it for her oblidgeing temper in doing everything that was desired in her illness and her great patience. My sister sat up with her one and said she never saw any like her but her sister. Miss Collier has wrott to Mr Belson to send her some patterns and the lowest price which we think will be the cheapest way, but shall do nothing till we hear from you and weather you have anything by you that will line them. My sister joyns with me in compliments to Mr Collier and self and Miss Dely, and am exceeding glad to hear she is better.

1 Lutestring, a glossy silk fabric, dress or ribbon, colours, included brown, pink, white and silver (*OED*).

359 To Mary Collier, Hastings, from Jane Collier, Hampstead, 8 July 1742 [SAY 1784]

I write with a great deal of pleasure to let you know that I am quite recovered and to thank you for my new gown. Miss Russell was so obliging as to go to town on Monday and bought me a striped with a shade of blue and my sister a pale blues, and ordered the bill to be carried to my uncle, and went with them to Mrs Sellby who promised to let us have them both next Saturday without fail. My brother Worge called to see us a Monday, and we whent and looked at the long room where there was a great deal of company, and Hampstead is now very full and very pleaseant. Pray tell my sister Dely I will write to her very soon, and am very sorry to here her bird is dead but hope by this time she has a little recovered the loss of it. My sister joyns with me in duty to my papa and you and love to my sisters from, honoured madam, your dutifull daughter. My governess and Miss Russell desire their compliments. Dear Madam, I have not missed learning upon the spinnet once in my illness for Mr Sheeles has been very dilligent, but my governess has not given entrance till you think proper.

360 To John Collier, from Dr Richard Russell, 30 July 1742 [SAY 1785]

The two last times I saw Miss Delia, viz at Battel and Hastings, I found she had a cough, and then thought her case not mieerly greensickness but that her lungs were concerned in it;[1] and I remembered that was my reason why I lay'd aside the thoughts of sheet,[2] but if those reasons are now removed and that she hath now no cough nor fever, the chalybeat water may be likely to do good in her other complaints, but must be entered upon under the care of the physitian on the place who, if he finds the least new symptom arise that concerns her weake lungs, should bleed, give some cooling physick and lay the use of them aside. But if she goes I will give her a letter to Dr Johnson and desire his care as for one who is my particular friend. We are all here, glad to hear she hath a design to favour us with her company when Mr Collier comes to you, where they will both be extreamly welcome and as much care shall be taken of her as is in our power to do. My wife and daughter join with me in most humble service to the good family.

1 Greensickness, pale or green tinge to complexion, an anaemic disease causing general weakness, the young were thought especially prone. Chalybeate waters, containing minerals including iron, were widely recommended (E S Turner *Taking the Cure* (1967) 88-91).
2 Enveloping patient in a sheet, to protect from cold (*OED*).

361 To John Collier, from William Cranston, Scarborough, 27 August 1742 [SAY 1786]

My epistle to Jemmy gave you an account of our travells to Mansfield and this will continue em hither for which place we left the former on Tuesday morning and for that morning's visit we took Kiveton (the Duke of Leeds) in our way which place having before seen I beleive you have heard me speak much in praise of. From thence we put to Rotherham to dinner which is but an indifferent place though the River Dun is navigable thither and cutts a good figure, about two miles, from thence and but little out of the road stands Wentworth Woodhouse, a seat of the Earl of Malton, 'tis now building and just all cased in but very few rooms finished and not above 2 well furnished. The aspect of it is prodigious grand being 600 foot in length and all the orders displayed in it to their utmost perfection. The scituation is very agreable and when all is finished (if ever), 'twill be very superbe. Taking leave of this this we got to Pontrefact, a large populous, well built town. The Castle which stood out so long in the Civil warrs is now quite demolished. From hence we reach Ferry Bridge which [1] the river Are is a large handsome navigable river to this place, setting out next morning we went through Tadcaster, a very neat small town at the end of which runs the river Wharfe, a very broad and navigable one, though the water was then as it seems it always is, of very dark black colour.

From this place we compass'd York about 11. This as farr as I could judge is about as bigg again as Canterbury, for the most part narrow and ill built though there are many good modern houses intermixt. It has much the face of London, hackney coaches and chairs plying in the streets and the generality of the people well dress'd. The town hall well built, an exceeding good mansion house for their lord mayor whom we saw distributing justice, it was a sort of Dover court. Their grand assembly roome is 140 by 40 in which is 42 large pillars, 'tis an expensive building and admired by many though I can't reckon myself amongst that number, 'twas a sad mortification to my fellow traveller that it was not assembly night nor none within a reasonable stay. The cathedrall is a very fine one though in my opinion it must give place to Canterbury. They have both of em their distinct beautys but the latter has the advantage. The castle (which is their county goal), is a wonderfull good building of stone, stands high, and in it are their courts of nisi prius and crown side; both very comodious and handsome.

Upon the whole York pleased me greatly. The county about it is but disagreable being a perfect flatt for at least 10 miles around it, that to the south very fertile and great quantity of corn feilds lyeing open, but this towards this place little else but boggs. We left York yesterday at the tipp and met with nothing worth observation till we came about 12 miles when we reached Castle Howard (which stands about a mile out of the road). The park avenues to the house, fine temples, mausoleums, obelisks, grand gateways and other buildings scattered about the park, are by much the most costly that ever I saw. The house is new, of stone, and in the south and north aspect of it, no cost spared in carve work or statuary to make it look like the outside of a cabinett, as the inside of it really is, being most elegantly finished and furnished and in such a particular taste in each way that I never met with anything like it in either. The [2] all inferior and the house being adorned with many valuable statues. Fine water works and of great extant, variegated with wood and lawns and all in the most exact order. Upon the whole, take the place all together it exceeds all I ever mett with not excepting Chattsworth.

From this place we reached Malton at dinner, a clean neat town well build with three churches and in a fine country. From thence hither we mett with little worth observation. The county but indifferent and the nigher this place the worse. The town itself seems to be well built and stands in a half moon form, with the castle at one point, which the aspect of which very much resembles Dover from that town) and some good buildings on the other. As to the company in it or the diversions, etc., I know very little of either as yet but a description of these I shall leave to Green (who purposes writing to Jemmy in a post or two) who intends entring fully into the spiritt of the place, as he expresses it. We are in private lodgings, but are to be heard of at the New Inn. Greene with Daheyne joins with me in compliments.

[*separate sheet, enclosed with above letter*]

Upon one of the obelisks which is 92 feet high is the following inscription.

If to perfection these plantations rise
If they agreably my heires surprize
This faithfull pillar will their age [3] declare
As long as time these characters shall spare
Here then with kind remembrance read his name
Who for posterity performed the same

Charles the III Earle of Carlisle
Of the family of the Howards
Erected a castle when the old castle of
Henderskelf stood and call'd it Castle Howard
He likewise made the plantations in this park
And all the outworks, monuments and other
plantations belonging to this seat
He began these works
In the year MDCCII
And set up this inscitpion
Anno MDCCXX-I

1 MS damaged.
2 MS damaged.
3 MS *display* struck through.

362 To John Collier, from William Cranston, Mansfield, 18 September 1742.
[SAY 1787]

I received the favour of yours last Tuesday and am obliged to you for the news thereby communicated. We left Scarbro Wednesday about 11 with but a malancholy prospect, as to weather, before us. But however, that soon cleared up and well it did for from that place to Driffield, sixteen miles, there is scarce a house and not one hedge or tree being all upon the hills resembling our south downs, though more in tillage from Driffield to Beverley, 10 miles, is a villanous, flatt country full of boggs, wild, dreary vasts and in short everything that is shocking.

Beverly is a large town well built but seems to be thin of inhabitants and very little shew of business in their phiz's. There are a pretty many gentlemen in it, a good assembly once a week, a playhouse generally in use and plenty of hackney coaches, the market house a modern genteel building, two churches or rather but one of that name and a minster and which last tops all of the kind I ever mett with. Tis not more than two thirds as big as Canterbury, tis in most excellent repair, clean as a dineing room, divine service is performed in the nave gallery, being erected on each side between the pillars, all oak and so ornamental with carving in white wood that the beauty of it can only be guessed at not expressed. The screen betweene the nave and choir in stone as white as marble with all manner of imbellishments cut upon it. The choir is small with stalls as in others with carve work over em as usuall and of most exquisite workmanship. The altar peice is modern, something like Canterbury but infinitely more grand. The spaces between the pillars being open, and these as high again with a magnificent eagle placed out of the top guilt with gold.

The communion table is marble of a most extra size. The floor of the choir and all the steps to the altar are black and white marble and the rails of the altar are iron of most exquisite workmanship and all guilt. I was assured that within these ten years above £15,000 has been laid out in beautifying and repairing the inside only. There are but few peices of antiquity in it and I shall only mention two, one is a painting, representing a king with his crown, etc., and a preist in discourse together, under in an old character is this inscription 'Als free make I the, as hert may think, or egh may see,' which is said to be King Althestan granting to St John of Beverley, the freedom of that corporation or I should rather have said making the town free upon his account. The other is an old inscription on lead, which was dug up about six years ago upon the new paving the nave and is as follows:

Anno ab incarnatione domini 1188 combusta fuit haec ecclesia in mense Septembris in sequenti nocte post festum Sanctum Matthaei apostoli et in anno 1197 in secto idium Martis facta fuit inquisitio reliquiarum beati Johannis in hoc loco et inventa sunt hae ossa ejuus in orientali parte sepulchri et hic recondita et pulvis cemento mixtus ibidem inventus est et reconditus.

There is also a fine monument of that Peircy Earl of Northumberland who was at the Battle of Bosworth field and his countess.

The river Hull is navigable hither and some miles farther. We left Beverly Thursday morn for Hull six miles all a flat but the soil much mended. Hull is a large town full of people of good trade and everybody appearing important. The Hull upon which it chiefly stands is not twice as broad as the Rother though very deep, but the Humber close by it also makes amends this being above 3 miles over. The town is walled round with double fosses very large without so that it appears capable of being made, as I suppose it once was, a place of great strength, though tis so large that it would require a numerous garrison to defend it. We were showed the gate at which King Charles demanded its surrender which has not been since opened. The town is pretty well built, streets narrow. The church a very ancient and good one with our saviour and the apostles receiving the eucharist excellently painted by a famous Italian whose name I have now forgott. The markett place is but small and that filled up with an equestrian statue of King William whose horse is very lame of all four, and his Majesty at least 6 feet high from his seat, and not raised above 8 foot from the ground.

We took shipping about 3 and crossed the Humber to Barton in Lincolnshire which we were an hour and 20 minutes in doing, though we had a fair wind it being computed 6 miles and for which 18d an horse is paid. From thence we reached Brigg, 8 miles, Thursday evening, but a scrub place, the road to it being over a pretty good country. From thence yesterday morn we reached Gainsbro being 16 miles the greatest part of which is over sandy desarts as black as your hatt and an impossibility of a blade of grass growing on it. Gainsbro is but a small town and but indifferently built. The Trent runs close by it and being very deep, vessels of 200 tuns get up hither which makes it a place of great trade. We crossed this river at the town's end which brought us into Nottshire and to Rhetford last night which lyeing in the north clay, the roads about it vie with the worst in our county. The town is a shabby place not unlike East Grinstead and their hops having failed em this year, there not being half an hundred on an acre one with another, makes abundance of dolorous countenances.

We left Rhetford this morning at 11, for Gamston, the villa of the Reverend John Henry Ott whom we met on the road just from his own house for Rhetford markett but he turned back with us, and we took a dinner with him and his lady with 2 other old ones being as I apprehended his wife's mother and aunt.[1] He looks as usuall, very thin, though well and brisk, we talked over Bexhill, etc., was extreamly glad to see me and pressed hard for my staying all night. His is a pretty good house and stands in a tolerable good country but complains much of his neighbourhood being every way closely pent up with dukes and lords. He laments his exchange and more especially just now when he has not 20 pounds of hops per acre in his parish.[2] We parted about four and reached this place between 7 and 8 where I purpose staying till about next Fryday and then for setting forth southward intending yet before tres Mich to pay my respects to the port to all friends at which place you'll make my compliments.

1 Revd John Henry Ott, vicar Bexhill 1722-39 (see SAY 3821; Cedb).
2 The prolonged winter of 1741-2 adversely affected the harvests in the summer of 1742 (Hoskins).

363 To John Collier, [Hastings], from Henry Pelham, 23 September 1742

[SAY 409]

I send you back the deputation, I hope duly executed. I have appointed this person gamekeeper in hopes of having some game sent me to London, which many years has either gone to Newcastle House or none been killed. I desire you will give him particular directions to send up to me every week what he can get, and, by taking care to detect pochers, I can't but think from all my mannors I may have sufficient for my own family at least.[1] You say nothing of my cousin Pelham; I hope he continues in the mending way he was when you wrote last. My service to him when you go to Crowhurst's farm.

1 By 22 & 23 Chas. II c.25, authority to hunt game including duck, rabbits, deer, boar, required holding the relevant manor, or office and instruction from the lord or landowner, such as the steward or bailiff; ownership of the woodland, chase, parklands wherein the hunting took place; or, to hold leasehold land for 99 years of £150 worth, or £100 for freehold. Further statutes and clauses widened the powers of the landowners, of which 9 Geo I, c.22, 1722, known as the Black Act, increased penalties for poachers carrying arms, etc., and going in disguise (Thompson 1967).

364 To Mary Collier, from Elizabeth Denham, Lewes, 10 October ?1742[1]

[SAY 2188]

Dear Cosen, in a letter to my mother you said you be glad to hear from me, it's what I have often thought of, but indeed I have had so bad a state of health that I have but littell heart for anything, all last winter I was ill that nobody thought I should ever go abroad again. I had a sad time of it it's certain and a great deal I went threw, but it pleased God to rais me up friends to help support me or I must have suffered much more for illness is very expencive and a great fatigue to them that are with one. I have been prettey well this summer, but now my old complaints begin to come on, and everybody must have soomthing to bring them to a end, for my part I am not much surprised at anything that shall befall me in this world, we took it very kind of my cosen Jame Collier that he called on us at the race, he was allways a favourit of mine. I should be glad to see you at Lewes that I might have the pleasur of your company once more, the man stays so I must conclud with my servic to all your family and pray except the same from, your humble servant

1 MS Sayer, in pencil, dates this letter '1742'; the letter is in a different hand from SAY 2181-2184 **[271]**, **[278]**, **[39]**, **[90]**.

365 To John Collier, from James Collier, Johnson's Court, 23 October 1742

[SAY 1788]

I went yesterday to Hampstead and saw Jenny who is very well and brisk and whose face in the opinion of Mrs Russell is greatly altered for the better. At that place I was informed that the favourite song at Hasting, *At the brow of a hill*, etc., was now entirely neglected, and had for its successor one on Vauxhall.[1] As Mr Greene is not yet arrived from Norfolk, whose judgment I was to follow in relation to the black chipt hats, I postponed the buying of them till next week, Mr Greene expecting him in town before Wednesday. Mr Gyles brought home my cloaths last night, the coat and breeches of a brown colour with a brass button, and a red cloath waistcoat with a lace somewhat broader than those which are termed chain ones.[2] I have not as yet had an opportunity of seeing Mr Garrick yet, but I find the town mightily divided in their sentiments concerning him and Mr Quin.[3] Be pleased to give my duty to mama and love to my sisters.

1 Thomas d'Urfey and Henry Purcell composed *On the brow of Richmond Hill* c. 1692.

2 Chain waistcoats, longitudinal threads often resembling chain mail, in a woven fabric; the warp for ornamental waistcoats, chain work for woven cloth (*OED*).

3 David Garrick, as Richard III, Monday 19 October 1741, Covent Garden Theatre, James Quin, seasons 1741 to 1743 (Scouten Pt 3, vol. 2, 1736-1747 923-926 935; Burney vol. 4, 447).

366 To John Collier, from James Collier, Johnson's Court, 26 October 1742

[SAY 1789]

I went yesterday morning accompanyed by my uncle to visit two setts of chambers, the only rooms now remaining empty in either of the Inns except some which let at an extravagant price; one in the King's Bench walks no 6, up two pairs of stairs, the other in Fig Tree Court, on the first floor with chambers under them; the rent of the former is 30 guineas, of the latter 36 pound. Those in the King's Bench walks are very ill contrived, an exceeding old, uneven floor in the dining room, and every chamber wants painting, which if done at the expense of the landlord I must take them for three years; otherwise must paint them myself and then be obliged to take them for a year certain, with a quarter's warning. Those in Fig Tree Court are very neat chambers, pleasantly situated and lately built, belonging to Mr Selby Amhurst, and have what I think one of the greatest conveniences, a fire place in the study; and the way leading to them from the street as warm as any in the Temple. This sett I must confess pleases me extreamly, and if its agreable to you will take them and enter imediately. My sister Jenny comes to town tomorrow in order to give her attendance at my lord mayor's show. Mr Steevens has waited on me to make an offer of his service in fitting up my rooms, when I promised as soon as fixed to send for him.

367 To John Collier, from William Cranston, [Johnson's Court], 26 October 1742

[SAY 773]

I paid Mr Forbes his £91 Saturday morning. By letter from Francis Green yesterday, I am desired to pay you £7 14s 0d for Mrs Platt, which I have accordingly given you credit for.

Mr Smith of Richmond sent today to inquire after you. Am in a sad fright about the gout being very lame in my left great toe and much worse since the morning.

Jemmy's letter which accompanys this, I've perused and confirm the truth thereof and as I don't find there is a possibility of getting chambers fitt to put a head in under £30 so I must confess the £36 chambers are better by more than double the difference of the 30 guineas ones; and am satisfyed he would think himself extreamly happy with your consent to his choice, though they are £4 10s dearer, which he purposes saving in some other article. We undertook to give a finall answer by this day sennight which I dare say you'll be so good as to enable us to do. I did think of going tomorrow myself to see after my neice's Joseph but doubt whether I shall be able.

368 To John Collier, Hastings, from William Cranston, Johnson's Court, 30 October 1742 [SAY 774]

As I feared so it turned out, having been confined to my chamber from Wednesday with the gout in both feet, but I think it going off and hope to get downstairs a Monday. Jenny arrived Thursday about 3, imediately after which Jemmy took to Drury Lane where was his Majesty and all the family.[1] Yesterday was spent at the lord mayor's show, and Mr Green squired her again to the old place where was the Prince and Princess of Wales, but, oh cruell fate, they could not get in, so that the remainder of the evening I had the favour of her company.

The journey proposed to Mrs Selby today by yours was prevented by her sending for the cole a Wednesday, which came to £3 19s 0d for the two capuchins and porter to the inn, a tolerable summe for such traps.[2] By yesterday's post I received a bill from Mr Goddard for £32 3s 0d; am obliged to you for paying Mr Cruttenden Mr Thorne's money, which I will give you creditt for as soon as I can get to my books. I received the bill and answer Roberts v Hood which I have just perused and think it hell and not to be got through, but as soon as ever I get out will consult the learned. Jemmy's in great spiritts with yours of today, we need only in generall at present answer that we'll have them; other preliminarys may be setled afterward.

1 Drury Lane Theatre, *Richard III* adapted from Shakespeare by Colley Cibber, Thursday 28 October, Richard played by David Garrick, his first appearance before George II (Scouten Pt 3 vol. 2, 1736-47, 1009).
2 Capuchins, cloak with hood, female dress in imitation of cloaks worn by Capuchin friars.

369 To John Collier, Hastings, from James Collier, Johnson's Court, 2 November 1742 [SAY 1790]

Yesterday being your birthday, my uncle treated the two Mr Greene's with a bottle of wine, and in the evening Mr Greene junior carried my sister Jenny to Covent Garden theatre to see *Venice Preserved*, with dancing by the celebrated comick dancer Signor Grimaldi.[1] This morning Mrs Nouns, attended by my sister, went to Paulin's wharehouse in order to purchase a Joseph for Dely; but he requiring a particular measure, an express was dispatched for Mr Holmes to desire him to send the last one for the stays. But, having for answer that he had lost it, as is now too late to send it by the carrier this week, we must beg the favour of a description of the true measure by a letter. I commenced tenant to Mr Selby Amhurst yesterday and sent for Mr Stevens this day; and nothing certain is yet agreed on for the furniture but a green haretine bed. Be pleased to give my duty to mama and love to my sisters. Jenny sets out for Hampstead tomorrow.

1 Covent Garden Theatre, Monday 1 November 1742, *Venice Preserved, or a Plot discovered* by Thomas Otway; John Baptist Grimaldi alias Nicolini, fl. 1740-2, dancer Covent Garden (Highfill vol. 3, 387-402). For the Grimaldi connections see Scouten Pt 3 vol. 2, 1736-47, 1010.

370 To John Collier, Hastings, from William Cranston, [Johnson's Court], 6 November 1742 [SAY 775]

Having settled accounts with Mr Cole, I inclosed send you a copy thereof. There is not at present any more talk of paying off any India bonds,[1] and as other stocks are exceeding high, I would, was it my own case, even let it stand and therefore shan't part with one to buy in tother without your farther orders for that purpose. Your Custom house receipts as well as draft on Jasper came safe per last post. The cash on all which I shall take the first oppurtunity to receive.

Tassell v Rootes.[2] I had an affidavit in this today from T. Frewen and shall per next send him a notice to serve on defendant; tis a queer agreement. George Worge seems to have halloo'd before he was quite out of the wood, for by Thursday's post his London letter came to hand, having been first amongst my namesakes in St John that before it got to Johnson's Court.

The Josephs arriveing today with you I suppose did not a little surprize the ladys.[3] The history of which stands thus: Tuesday morn Mrs Nouns and Jenny were dispatched express to Paulins; upon their return, we were told that all preliminaries were setled, that it was to be here the next day by 5, in case we could in 2 hours send an account of the shape by the measure in Mr Holmes's hands. Upon which he was imediately sent to and came, but informed us that he could not find it, and then the letter which you received was wrote and nothing more expected till an answer, but the next day, when least thought of, the chap brought it home ready cutt and dried as you read it, and the fellow insisting that he was to do it by that time whether he heard again, or not, and Jenny being that morning gone to Hampstead, and Mrs Nouns not to be mett with, upon a great consultation between Jemmy and myself we even took it in, paid £2 15s 0d for it and dispatched it away forthwith.

My old chap Thomas is got to town again and in good health. My nephew and he have agreed in case there is no objection on your side. I am fully persuaded of his honesty and sobriety. I gott out a little Wednesday, Thursday and yesterday and though withal pain yet walked dolorously, rather overdid it yesterday and therefore have have staid within all this day which I purpose also toomorrow and hope by Monday to be much recruited.

1 East India bonds paid 3% on face value, March 1737 to March 1746. They represented a good security for money and were easy to convert to cash. There were severe penalties for theft of these bonds and for forged indorsements when offered for sale (Dickson 409-10).

2 Tassell v Rootes [**373**] .

3 Joseph, long dark cloak worn by women, clasped at shoulder height with buttons or a broach.

371 To John Collier, from James Collier, Johnson's Court, 15 November 1742 [SAY 1791]

I called at Mrs Selby's on Thursday morning to speak to her in relation to the Joseph, who has undertaken to get it altered agreable to the directions in your letter by the appointed time. The two boxes of books came here together with the casks of brandy on Munday in the afternoon. My boxes were imediately conveyed into the Temple by the cart which brought them hither and placed in my chambers. I bought the other day the play of King Richard the third, as revised with alterations by Mr Cibber, and as I remember you expressed a desire of seeing it, will send it down by Wednesday's carrier. Admiral Vernon's birthday is now quite forgot, no manner of notice being taken of it last night in the publick streets.[1] I have dined three times in the Middle Temple hall and been so unfortunate as to meet with every time exceeding bad commons. I have some thoughts of having another suit of cloaths, appearing always in the same looking a little shabby. Be pleased to give my duty to mama and love to my sisters, I am, honoured sir, your most dutifull son.

1 Admiral Edward Vernon's birthday 12 November; his triumph at Porto Bello 22 November 1739 was received at St James' 13 March 1740 and celebrated in London and port towns for several years (Rapin vol. 20, 442-4, 455-6).

372 To John Collier, Hastings, from William Cranston, [Johnson's Court], 18 November 1742 [SAY 776]

You herewith receive your dedimus. I last Monday received Mrs Stevens's money of Jasper. Have not been able to see the Custom house. Amongst my papers I this day poped upon your receipt to Waller for Mr Pelham's rent, which is only to shew you that I havn't yet heard anything from him. I mentioned the affair of the locks to Jemmy of which in his next you will have some account, as well also as in respect to my neice's chipt hat for Beau Green has been miserably tardy in it. Roberts and Hood,[1] I shall push this as desired and will abreviate as soon as ever I can. The gout has thrown me pretty much behind hand with business, so that from rising till between 8 and 9 I am generally employed and later business will not go down. I'll see after your wine tomorrow.

Either my Saturday's letter about my neice's writing is interpreted wrong by you or expressed otherwise than I intended, for my meaning was that though at all times I should be glad of the favour of a line from her ladyship, yet that the subject upon which an epistle was intended was not worth the giving herself the trouble of it, and more especially as in her present scituation it was more than ordinarily tedious to her. But, however, am extreamly obliged to her for this day's favour and pity all your cases in respect to the smallpox.[2] The two Chambers's came to me today in order for innoculation and after all the trouble I have had in seeing Dr Jurin and taking lodgings for em in his neighbourhood no 4 has just now thought that will be too expensive; and therefore a common apothecary is to go through the whole, and if either of em are just upon poping off and no hopes of recovery then a phisician is to be called in.[3] In short, I've turned em over to Stacy and there my care shall end, but all this inter nos. They seem to have a deal of saving knowledge inculcated into em upon this occasion and beleive to save charges they'll pigg together during the whole operation. I think their journey hither might have been saved and Dr Frewen and Dr Young have done the business.

1 [**379**].
2 Commonplace entries at the front of the Fuller family letter book (ESRO RF 15/25) detail preparations for patients about to undergo innoculation using the Roger Sutton method (Crossley & Saville ix-x 23). The innoculation of the daughter of Lady Mary Wortley Montagu, in 1721 is commonly given as start of regular use in England. For two decades practice restricted to the wealthy and their connections (Razzell; Crook 18-33).
3 Dr James Jurin (1684-1750) physician, follower of Newton, FRS, FRCP.

373 To John Collier, Hastings, from William Cranston, [Johnson's Court], 27 November 1742 [SAY 777]

I last Tuesday received your Custom house salary. I've been just running through our cash account and you need be under no apprehensions of out running the constable. As Jemmy's chambers will be fitt for him to go into in a few days and as consequently bills will be then due, I shall soon afterwards discharge em and then you may expect a continuance of the account between us from my leaving town the long bow to the day I shall send it. I doubt by your silence, dame Sharpe has not been properly with you.

Tassell v Rootes. Defendant has pleaded the general issue; twill be impossible to go on upon it and think the best way would be to discontinue this and bring a new action against the son for the assault. Hasting v Eversfield; I've just now got this declaration from Hardcastle and a few days since got the amended bill in Wittersham from Mr Biddulph, which I am now copying of, and Mrs Hall shall have it as soon as done.

The gout still hangs in my toes and has confined me today, by which I find the difference of cold and warm weather after a fitt in regard to gathering strength. I don't know whether tis in today's papers, but have certain intelligence that Mr Murray was this day appointed Solicitor General and that Strange though as yet has a patent to take place next after the Attorney Generall.[1] There has been a strong talk all this week of several grandees resigning who but lately came into favour, and that an impeachment against the Earl of Orford would still take place.[2] All these things are confidently spoke off, but how true, time will discover, tho for my own part I remain an infidell.

1 William Murray, appointed Solicitor General, November 1742, in part to augment the government side in debates, a sure way of reinforcing the vote in this difficult session; Sir Dudley Ryder, Attorney General, 1737-1754 [**375**].
2 By June 1742 the government regularly lost by-elections, and eight petitions in disputed elections went to the opposition. For the session 16 November 1742 to 21 April 1743 when the adherents of Walpole and the old administration, plus the new Whigs elected in 1741, all attended the house, the new government held a majority. The address passed 259 to 150, and the opposition effort to re-convene the secret committee to look at Walpole's administration, agreed the previous session, was defeated 253 to 186 (McCann 150; Taylor & Jones 63; Owen 101, 150; Cobbett 12, 416-27).

374 To Mary Collier, Hastings, from Mary [Molly] Collier, [Battle] 1 December 1742[1] [SAY 2175]

Honoured Madam, we were very glad to hear by your letter that you are well and I have the pleasure to accquaint you that I think my sister is greatly altered for the better and believe if you was to see her you would think her quite well, and she eats 3 times as much as she did when at home. We drink tea at Mrs Thorpe's on Sunday and think Miss Thorpe looks sadly; we dined at the Abby yesterday but came away in good time and Miss Webster breakfasted here this morning, which I think is all the news I have to entertain you with. My sister would have wrote herself but I desired her to let it alone but she intends to write the next letter. I design to write to Jenny very soon for I want to hear from her. I should be glad if you would send me the scarlet muff when you have an oppurtunity, to keep my fingers warm, as also my girdle which is in the top of my bureau, all here joyn in duty to my papa and you and beg you'll accept the same from, honourable madam, your most dutifull daughter, we have a fire in our room every night.

1 MS Sayer, in pencil, dates this letter 'about 1743'; the handwriting is similar to **[397]** SAY 2174.

375 To John Collier, Hastings, from James Collier, Johnson's Court, 4 December 1742 [SAY 1792]

The publick business of the present sessions in the House of Commons is almost over already; at least what remains now to be done will meet with little opposition, for some unsuccesfull attempts having been made, several great patriot members are preparing to retire into the country. In the debates on Wednesday in relation to the revival of the secret committee two members whose names I have not yet been able to learn were severely reprimanded by Mr Speaker for making use of indecent expressions; the numbers on the division were, for the motion 186, against 253.

Yesterday the old affair was brought on the carpet for leave to bring in a bill to limit the number of officers, etc., which passed in the negative, 221 and 196.[1] Sir Watkins Williams Wynne made a point on Tuesday of getting Mr Trevor's petition, complaining of an undue return for Denbigh, to be heard at the bar of the House, but lost it by a majority of 45: 235 against 190.[2] Mr Littleton is already, or will in a few days, be turned out of his place as secretary to the Prince of Wales, he having made some vehement speeches and joined with the opposition in everything.[3] Mr Pitt has distinguished himself in so remarkable a manner as to have universally obtained the character of being the best speaker in the House of Commons. The ministry have called Mr Murray in to their assistance, who has undertaken always to give an answer to Mr Pitt. Young Mr Greene and I walked up to Hampstead on Wednesday to see Jenny who is very brisk and well. The two Mr Chambers are to be inoculated this afternoon. I am sorry my mama is displeased at my losing the directions about some false locks, but if she will favour me with farther orders I will execute them as soon as received. Be pleased, sir, to give my duty to mama and love to my sisters.

1 Lord Barrington moved a pension bill 'for the better securing the freedom of Parliaments by limiting the number of officers in the House of Commons', defeated 221 to 196, 3 December 1742 (Cobbett XII 874-906; Owen 150; Egmont vol. 3, 268).

2 Sir Watkin Williams Wynne, won Denbighshire county in the election of 1741, 1352 to 933, although his opponent, J. Middleton was returned by the sheriff, a relative of Middleton, on the grounds that near 600 of Sir Watkin's vote was falsely created. After Walpole's resignation the Commons accepted Sir Watkin's petition, and a similar one from the county freeholders, and removed Middleton, with the sheriff despatched to Newgate. When the cause went to the King's Bench, the jury awarded Sir Watkin £2800 plus £414 costs; judgement upheld in the Exchequer chamber (*ER* vol. 95, 530-1, Hilary term 19 Geo II 1745; *HofP 1715-54* vol. 2, 542-5).

3 George Lyttleton and William Pitt, regarded as opponents of the government for this session, thus a wide belief that Lyttleton would be dismissed from service to the Prince of Wales (Owen 150, 157).

376 To John Collier, Hastings, from James Collier, Fig Tree Court, Temple, 18 December [SAY 1793]

I lay in chambers last night for the first time and am extreamly well satisfied as to the bed, and when I am entirely setled will give you a particular account of the measure and furniture of my rooms. I saw at the Sussex coffee house this morning Mr Nicolls, who informed me that the match between Mr Randall and Miss Roberts was entirely broke of and that Mr Darrel Short's eldest son would be appointed by His Majesty, high sheriff of the county of Sussex for the ensueing year.[1] The House of Commons having now finished the publick business of the session, very few members give their attendance, for on Thursday last a debate arising whether any more money should be granted to the dean and chapter of Westminster toward repairing the collegiate church the numbers on the division were for complying with the petition 44 against 11, and imediately after this division they adjourned themselves to Thursday.

Mr Murray and Mr Pitt the other day, on the affair of taking the Hannoverian troops into British pay, made two of the finest speeches that ever were heard in the House of Commons, but Mr Pitt is generally allowed to have got the better of his antagonist.[2] To the great joy of everybody, this day there is a very great thaw, but the streets are almost unpassable, occasioned by a prodigious quantity of dirt being thrown by the scavengers within the posts.[3] Jenny came this morning to Johnston's Court and is very well. Be pleased sir, to give my duty to mama and love to my sisters. I intend in a post or two to write to my sister Dely.

1 John Denett of Bolney, high sheriff of Sussex, regnal year 15 Geo. 2, 1741-42; succeeded by John Edwards, 1742-3 (McCann 90). .

2 Commons debate, 10 December 1742, vote in favour of financial support for the Hanoverian troops 260 against 193; on the hostility to Hanover, Lord Chesterfield, 'suggested that the one effectual method of destroying Jacobitism would be to bestow Hanover on the Pretender, as the English people would never again tolerate a ruler from that country' (Lecky vol. 2, 12). The discussions in Parliament showed the strength of anti-Hanoverian feelings in the British army (Cobbett 12 cols. 940-1058; Taylor & Jones 63). .

3 By 22 & 23 Car II c. 17 'An Act for the better paving and cleansing the streets and sewers in and about the City of London' posts should be so fixed as to separate pavement from road; by 10 Geo. II c.22, this power was extended; by 9 Geo.II c. 18 the powers under 1 Geo I c. 52 for repairing highways altered to allow JPs in general, and quarter sessions, to appoint scavengers to clean streets of market towns and for the parish to levy 6d in the £ on property, lands, etc., to fund this (*SL* vols 2,5,6).

377 To Mary Collier, Hastings, from Cordelia Collier, Battle, c. 19 December 1742 [SAY 2167]

Honoured Madam, I must beg the favour of you to be so good as to let me have my best cloaths for belive we are to have a ball at Christmas and as I realy am much better and my papa thought I lookt so when he was here, hope that you will consent to it, and will promise not to dance if I find it fateauges me, but there is a law made that nobody is to dance after super they all thinking it long enought and then we shall break up in good time, which I hope will be another inducement to your consenting to it. Molly desires to have her Paris cap, but I shall not want mine for think my dormer full is genteel, Miss Thorpe was here a Satterday and told us of Ned Grayling's[1] being killed but no particulars how, she seems to think that Mrs Coper's haveing the smallpox whould be laid to her brother notwithstanding she went about all the time, my brother and sister supt at the Abby Sunday night but being wet wheather Molly and I kept house, and now Mary has a great wash about, against Xmas, I should have sent for some work before but Mary has been helping quilt a coat for my sister which is now done, and she has nothing to do, Miss Webster likt our workt ruffles prodigiously and desired to know how we did it upon which we promised to do her a pair but cant get shuch a thing as book muslin so must wait till we can. I have seen Miss Eversfield once since I came but they are very much confined now for Mrs Markquick has been ill some time and looks every day. My capachin fits very well but don't think it so hansome as yours, my sister and me are to walk to Crohurst the first frosty wheather that comes. I cannot think of any news to send you so must conclude with my duty to my papa and love to Sally, from, honoured madam, your obedient and dutifull daughter, I should be very glad if you will, when you send my cloths, put in a pint of penniroill water for I wanted some last week but however had cordial in the room of it.[2]

1 Edward Grayling, buried 19 December 1742, St Clements.
2 Pennyroyal water, distilled from leaves of the plant, antidote to spasmodic, nervous and hysterical afflictions.

378 To John Collier, Hastings, from William Cranston, [Johnsons's Court], 23 December 1742 [SAY 778]

[1]I return you your 2 bank post bills again, for if you'll observe they are both made payable to John Mead or order and the counceller has cunningly indorsed em to himself, which one would have thought a man of his sagacity could never have done; and even this indorsement is not signed, though I suppose the words John Mead in the body of it is of his own handy worke. It ought to be, pay to John Collier or myself, if you please, for the sake of saving indorsements, or order, and signed John Mead, for though these are delivered out by the bank yet they are exactly of the same form, and are passed from one to another in the same manner as all other notes are, as well from private persons as from companys, and because they are not so indorsed, the bank have refused to accept em, and to prevent his making farther mistakes I have indorsed them and let him only sign em. I shall take care not to disappoint Mrs Constable of her cole at the time appointed.

Before the post came in today Jenny set out from Sackville Street to dinner and from thence to the play, so that if the letter to her requires any answer it can't be had til next post. I yesterday sent by the carrier your tea, coffee, chocolate, sturgeon, brawn, for a share of which I return thanks, and a lamb, all which I hope will arrive safe.

1 MS Mr Fagge.

379 To John Collier, Hastings, from William Cranston, [Johnson's Court], 25 December 1742 [SAY 779]

Roberts v Hood. Naming yesterday the 4 Commissioners on each side and we naming first, I took em as they stood in your list and by naming Darell Short as my first, they named Thomas Frewen for their first, so that we are distanced as to him; and whether you'll let him stand against us, you'll consider of; being thus distrest, for want of another Commissioner to name in his stead, and being like to be drove hard in point of time as to execution the commission this term, our opponents being bent upon delay, and the writing for your answer would take up too much time, I could think of nobody so proper to supply Frewen's place as Eastchurch, who I well know, and had him for a commissioner at

Westram, October twelvemonth, and take him to be a sensible man and if he stands I make no doubt but he will attend. You'll by the return of the post let me know which of their two you would have me strike out and think by this day sennight's post to be able to send you the commission which will just give you time enough to have 4 or 5 days time to execute it in before terme.[1]

Darell Shorte	Thomas Frewen
Samuel Eastchurch (at Maidstone)	John Thawyer
William Cuckow	Francis Brooks
Henry Dodson	Edward Finch

You have also herewith a copy of the account between us, in which you'll find the fixing Jemmy in his chambers, etc., comes to a pretty deal of money; but I think everything is paid, and can't recollect that there is a penny now oweing on his account. As when we were at Hastyng there was some talk of a yearly allowance for him, so he and I have lately had some farther chatt upon the same occasion, by which I find him very desirous of being upon that footing; and as you seemed to have no dislike to it, the quantum is the only and principle matter to be setled. As he has been hitherto bred up in all respects as a gentleman, and has kept company always as such, so I dare say it is still your desire he should continue, and that an allowance as such should be made him, having regard to other circumstances of your family.

I have been dipping through our account from the time of his going to Cambridge, and by the money I have paid for and to him, and what you must have paid his taylor, with other expenses imediately from you, I calculate that he hath stood you in considerably more than £200 per annum. And though the expenses here and there may be pretty different, yet with the addition of chamber rent and servant, etc., I don't suppose you can imagine he can be less expensive for the time to come, than he has been for the time past, and that you would not be against allowing him accordingly. And therefore in my talking to him upon this occasion I have dropt it as my thoughts that if you was to allow him £200 per annum and pay his chamber rent, give him the run of the kitchen at the port for himself and servant, when there, where the more he is, I tell him, the more agreable to you, that this would enable him to live and appear always as he has hitherto done, and under such an allowance I can find he would think himself exceedingly happy, and dare say he would so well manage as to be always within compass, and yet at the same time to keep up his present acquaintance, which seems to me to be of the best sort. And if this meets with your approbation, I beleive you must also agree to advance one quarter in hand, which will keep him always before hand, and will also enable him to lay out something in law books, of which he really wants severall to begin his studies with. You'll excuse my giving my sentiments so freely on this occasion, but I am induced so to do from a throught[2] conviction that he would make no other use of a generous allowance than to do you and himself creditt, and to prepare himself by degrees to make a figure in life agreable to the share he may hereafter have in it.

We begun our brawn today and remembered the donor, Mrs Nouns dined here as also Jenny and Jemmy who has promised me to do so often, we all join in respect and wishes of a merry Xmas, etc.

1 The list led by Darell Shorte chosen by William Cranston for the Roberts side of this Chancery case; those in the list headed by Thomas Frewen, chosen for Hood (ESRO DUN 43/4/2-12).

2 Word damaged for last two letters.

380 To John Collier, Hastings, from William Cranston, [Johnson's Court], 30 December 1742 [SAY 780]

Roberts v Hood.[1] If I am not able to send you this commission by Saturday's post I shall take care to gett an order that you may continue your examination into the terme if necessary. I by yesterday's carrier sent you a briefe of the bill and answer, and also the interrogatories ingrossed, doubting whether you might have a proper stamp for that purpose. The necessary forms made use of in striking Commissioners in the Six Clerks' office has drove us this late, for I can assure you that nothing has been wanting on my part, nor I believe on Mr Cheveley's, to put us as forward as possible.

Hasting v Eversfield.[2] I have got this declaration from Sir John Strange with his approbation with little or no alteration and have this day made out a latitat and sent to Rochester to appear and on the first day of terme shall deliver the narration. The two post bills found their ways hither last Munday as did the turkeys, etc., yesterday for which you have the thanks of the house and for the hogspuddings, more especially of my boys. I've not had an oppertunity of shewing yours of today to Jemmy as yet though purpose doing it after our musick tonight. I heard him mention something of his sending you by yesterday's carrier a pott of charr.

1 Roberts v Hood [**379**] (ESRO DUN 43/4/2-12).
2 Hastings v Eversfield [**354**] [**373**] [**452**].

381 To Mary Collier, Hastings, from Molly Collier, [Battle], 1 January 1743
[SAY 1794]

I suppose my papa told you of the great pleasure we proposed in our ball on Monday and other things that were to have been next week, which are all prevented by a shocking accident which I immagine you may by this time have heard something of, tho an imperfect account, viz Mr Godfrey Webster got up yesterday morning with an intent to go a shooting and put half a pound of powder over a chaffing dish of coals to dry while he wrote two pretty long letters to go by the post, which when he had done went to stir the powder. At the instant the plate melted and immediately it blew up, threw him senceless on the floor, burst open the door and went out of another room window. He is miserably burnt in face, neck and hands, so that his cloaths was obliged to be cut of by bits, but the greatest danger is his eyes which they are very much afraid he will lose, tho Dr Young gives great hopes of them when the inflamation is over, but at present they are intirely gone. This mellancholly accident has put us all in a great consternation that we hardly know what we do, though all very well in health. My brother was down all day yesterday and is gone again today, for ther's a distracted house and I think I shall never bear the sight of powder or a gun again. All here joyn in duty to my papa and you from, honoured madam, your most obedient and dutifull daughter.

382 To John Collier, Hastings, from James Collier, Fig Tree Court, 1 January 1743
[SAY 1795]

Being with my uncle Thursday evening, I had an opportunity of seeing your letter by that days post. Wherein it gave me great concern to observe that my seeming not to have regarded your advice formerly given as to dancing, French and writing still harboured in your breast to my disadvantage. As to the first, you must be sensible that, during my residence at Cambridge, if I had had ever so great an inclination to learn, it was impracticable for me to do it at that place, there being no master in that way of any sort whatever for teaching gentlemen. As to French, I remember when you wrote to me about learning it at Cambridge. I gave you an answer which I always understood you looked on as satisfactory, viz, that there was no person of any note, or who could even speak French correctly, taught that language.

But to convince you that I was determined to follow your advice in this particular, imediately on young Mr Greene's return from Norfolk, soon after my arrival in town, I applied to know the character of the person who attended him. And, finding he bore a good one, I spoke to the master himself and agreed to employ him when I was setled in chambers, which not happening so soon as I expected, and the holydays imediately following, is the only reason why I have not yet begun. As to the last, though I know the strokes in writing pretty well, and think I do not stand in much need of a master's assistance, yet, not having the art of writing with my wrist, as my hand is none of the steadiest, the trouble to me in making fine strokes is so great, and the time it takes up so long, that was you but sensible of these, I am persuaded you would not consider my manner of writing to you in the light hitherto done. But you may be assured for the future that I will do all that lyes in my power to make my handwriting better.

It was in a letter to my uncle, that you recommended to me the making of a visit to Colonel Pelham and Mr Stone. But as both these gentlemen would probably be in town the greatest of the winter, I did not apprehend an imediate performance was required, but always intended it soon after my getting myself fully setled; and in respect to the other gentlemen of the county, I shall with pleasure embrace every opportunity of cultivating an acquaintance with them. I am sorry to find the proposed allowance does not meet with your approbation, and was in hopes that, as it did not exceed what I have hitherto expended, you would have been so good as to have agreed to it. For upon reflexion I can't see but that I must be at as much expence here as at Cambridge, for though there are some items there which are not here, yet I shall find an overbalance of them by the great difference in the rent of chambers, and the expence of a servant. And many other articles of the same nature as at Cambridge here much dearer, not forgetting the additional expence in my cloathing, and the purchasing of linnen, and the study which I am engaged in will unavoidably oblige me to buy many books, and those of the law are none of the cheapest. But upon the whole I submit myself entirely to your goodness and generosity, which has hitherto supported me like a gentleman and am perswaded you will still enable me to appear in the same character. I always proposed to visit Hasting in the manner prescribed in your letter.

Finding by my uncle and sister Jenny that you and my mama were extreamly fond of potted char, I desired Thomas to procure me a pot if possible, which he did accordingly; it went by this week's carrier and if it is already opened I hope it pleases you both. Be pleased, sir, to give my duty to mama, the complements of the season wait on you, mama and all friends.

383 To John Collier, Hastings, from William Cranston, [Johnson's Court], 4 January 1743 [SAY 781]

Your letter about Jemmy I gave to him and which he yesterday returned, telling me that by the last post he had wrote to you about the contents. To be sure you are to do in this case as you think proper, and I hope and doubt not but he will submitt to what you shall determine. But as twas myself that happened to propose the summe objected to, you must excuse me if I a little enter into the affair, and more particularly your epistle upon this occasion, promising you hereafter to give you no farther trouble upon this head. And in the first place I won't enter into the amount of the money already laid out, that being done, not to be recalled, only observe from it the necessity of coming to some certainty, the quantum of which is the present question.

That you have brought him up hitherto as a gentleman is apparent to all the world, and that the expense of it has been paid with cheerfulness that I am witness to, and that it is very proper he should cultivate an acquaintance and friendship with gentlemen of his own country, not entirely neglecting his others, is without doubt highly proper, and for that reason I make no doubt but he will. He is already in intimacy and friendship with Lord Ashburnham, Shadwell, Randoll, who may now be called one, Steele, others as they offer will be taken in. But this is naturally a work of time and persons cannot be acquainted at first sight; and he has not till now lived where he had a possibility of doing it, but even when this is done, to come to the matter in hand, how does it or can it appear that these sort of acquaintance will cost him less to keep company with than those he is already engaged with? That many of the present people he now keeps company, as well Sussex, (Lord Ashburnham, Randoll, Steele), as others as Sir Francis Drake, Tilson, Tourton, Wright, etc., etc., etc., have their estates in their own hands, as well as others who are only children, and have very large allowances as well as great farther expectances, is certainly true.

But [1] is it asked that he shall have such an annuall stipend as to be able to keep company with em at all times, and go even pace with them in spending? No - if he has but £200 per annum to spend, and keeps within that compass, as I dare say he would if he had it, he can but barely see em often enough just to keep up his acquaintance. For though some of em have ten times such a sume to spend, yet they will take it for granted whenever he is with them that he his enabled to pay his quota, and will scarcely do it for him. - For my part I must confess, when the stipend asked fell short of what he stood you in at the University, I did beleive twould have been come into, for I beleive that an instance cannot be named where a gentleman has come forth into the world with a less allowance than when at school, as the University may without much impropriety of diction be called one. His having been bred up there in the same station with the best commoner in the kingdom, must naturally, and unavoidably, have given him, from the company which he, of course, kept there, some sort of taste for the gaietys of life, and his years have not yet so much run upon him as to have rendred those things already insipid.

Young people are young people still, and nothing but time can make them see the folly of their present pursuits. And as you have hitherto for these four years past allowed him as much or more than he now wants, it will be a difficult thing to convince him that you are not able in circumstances still to continue it, or that you then expended upon him more than you could afford. If he had been admitted a pensioner, his acquaintance would naturally have been of another mould, and his notions consequently of another cast, but that they now be as they be, and for which I can see no reason for repentance, are entirely oweing to his manner of education. If he had not, yet I have an equall regard for his sisters as himself, and therefore in the proposall I thought it such a one as might square with their interest. Also, for though I cannot pretend to know your circumstances to the least degree of exactness, yet I have great reason to beleive em very considerable, and from my conception of em I thought this allowance might very well be agreed to without doing any other part of the family injustice; but if I had had no general notion at all of your affairs, yet from the personall intimacy with which I have been so many years favoured with by you, I always took it for granted that you would not nor could bring up any part of your family in a higher sphere than you would afterwards enable them to move in, and it was my opinion, and still is, that even the summe asked will not be more than sufficient for this purpose.

As to the instances of best allowances to some gentry in our own country, I shall only observe, that whatever was Jack Fuller's, whether £80 as you mention, or £150 as I have heard, yet I have heard the justice universally condemned in this point; though the expence of a pack of hounds must, as I best remember, be added to that of his education. In respect to Markwick, I know nothing, nor when he was in town never saw him nor ever heard of anybody than did, he may be, and beleive is, a very honest gentleman, but I dare say much less money than was spent on him might have made at least as good, if not a better grazier. As to Ashburnham, he was upon charity, a pensioner at colledge and therefore in this respect not to be named and as to Sir Thomas Dyke, his allowance at the university only is mentioned, and not what he had afterwards. As to such parts of yours which relates to and finds fault with him for some omissions, that I leave him to answer, as I suppose he may have done, and I hope to your satisfaction.

The qualification which you there recommend him farther to pursue will still be some additionall expense, and I cannot see but that his expenses now must be as considerable as they will be at any time in his life whilst he lives without keeping house and unmarried. And that whatsoever keeps him for the year to come may do it for twenty year after, and, as farr as I can judge of things, there will be need of good management to rubb handsomely round in the method I propose, and to conclude, I am fully convinced by numberless examples, that more young people have been ruined by too narrow, than a too liberall allowance, and that if in the present case a wrong use was to be made of [2] is proposed, it might be reduced.

Roberts v Hood. I've been in expectation all this evening of hearing from Cheveneley in this but no news of him; have been after him but not to be found. His honour of the Rolls may be out of town or some other unavoidable accident have happened, but then I should have known of it to have informed you, but as it is I can say nothing to the purpose.

1 MS *it* struck through.
2 MS *it* struck through.

384 To John Collier, Hastings, from William Cranston, [Johnson's Court], 6 January 1743 [SAY 782]

The being no seal on Monday or Tuesday, and not till yesterday, was the reason why you did not receive the inclosed per last post. I send you the order barely to satisfye the Commissioners when they meet for it has already been served where only tis necessary it should be. Your two banke notes came safe. I've not since seen Jemmy pursuant to a new regulation below and orders thereupon to be observed above, I send you for my sister an account which in yours I shall put down in one with an etc. By letter today I find myself in a fair way of either letting or selling Mr Roffe's, etc., credit at Sennocke, for which purpose have appointed a meeting there next Tuesday and shall set out, with T Greene senior, in my hand next Sunday. I shall leave my neice, etc., in the care of Jemmy, Mrs Nouns, etc., and make no doubt but all will be well. I shall most likely make the week out but am determined to return them the Saturday following.

385 To Mary Collier, Hastings, from Jane Collier, Johnson's Court, 11 January 1743 [SAY 1796]

I received your letter, and as my uncle is gone out for a week I must defer tiing the border for the apron till he comes home, for I have not monny enough at present, so will get it the begining of the week. They look very hansom, mine has been most prodigiously admired since I have been in town. I have sent James this morning, with the hair and Anderson's plis to Master Bossum, and likewise a fan for my sister Molly I should be very glad if you would be pleased to send me a little boehea tea for I go to Hampstead next week after spending my time very agreeable in town.[1]

We were at Mr Coles' last week and at Mr Coppingre's, and I was at the consort a Wednesday night, and Miss Coles went with me and their was a great dell of good company and all full drest, and the ladies was all with their hairs done up strait behind. Our school is much better this winter then it was last, for their was fornteene when I come away and their are to come a great many more after Christmas, and I hope my sister Molly will come then, I hope it wount be long before I shall have the pleasure of seeing you and my papa for I shall long now till the time comes. I was last night at the play and today we go to Mrs Belson's to diner. I am sorry to hear that Sally Cruttenden is in her old way again. Pray be pleased to give my duty to my papa and love to my sisters, from, honoured madam, your most dutifull daughter. S.p. as my uncle is gone out, I beleive I shall one day go to see Mrs Calton.

1 Patrick Anderson, physician in Edinburgh, made up a 'mild aloetic purgative' during the reign of Charles I: later taken up by James VII & II. During Anne's reign copied and sold by a former servant of his daughter in London; known as Anderson's pills, often referred to as the Scots pills, purgatives of this type with varied ingredients widely available (E L Furdell *Publishing and Medicine in early Modern England* (2002) 140).

386 To John Collier, Hastings, from William Cranston, [Johnson's Court], 19 January 1743 [SAY 783]

I got to town from Sennocke Sunday by dinner; my journey might have been spared for it came to nothing. By my day book I find the time when Mrs Hickes's Tunbridge Wells house was advertized, vizt in January 1737,[1] and take it for granted that I must have from you some particular account of it so as to draw up a form, but nothwithstanding I have looked over your letters of that year I can find nothing of it, and therefore am at a loss what it consist of and whether any land to it, and without some assistance of this sort I don't see how I can incert it in the papers. In one of your letters you have mentioned that the land, etc., besides goods has been appraised at £1640 without the furniture. Jemmy made me a present of his turkey and tongue and he with young Greene dined upon it here, when we remembred the founder. You inclosed receive Jenny's additionall account, which as before I shall set down in an article under tea, etc.

1 On leaving London 15 December 1737 John Collier visited Sevenoaks, Tonbridge, and then Tunbridge Wells and Elizabeth Hickes's house; his day book has a gap from this date to 1 May 1738 (SAY 1418 f 56).

387 To Mary Collier, Hastings, from Cordelia Collier, Battle, 21 January 1743 [SAY 1797]

I am afraid, indeed that you have thought us very neglignt in not hereing from us so long. But realy the only reason was the expectation of seeing you here, which we was in great hopes of yesterday and Wednesday, and as the fine wheather is like to continue hope it will not be long first. We have had but a dull Xmas this year, and have not supt out at one house since we have been here but at the Abby, and that I dont reakoned anything; but I had forgot, one night at Mrs Thorpe's we playd carads. I think that quarell is quite over, and everything as used to be in former days again. A Monday I spent all day at the Abby, and my sisters, and Miss Markwick, walkt to Ashburnham to see the house, and Molly was not at all fatiuged, which I was surprise at. The family goe all away next week but Mr Godfry, who must stay till he has got some eyebrows and lashes, which come as fast as posable. I had a letter from my brother a Sunday night by which I find Jenny was to goe to Hampsted the beginning of the week. We are going to Mrs Tildens today to meet the

Place family and one night here which is the last I am afraid, but that we must not say, if you please to give my duty to my papa, and love to Sally who I quite long to see.

388 To Mary Collier, Hastings, from James Collier, Fig Tree Court, ?22 January 1743[1] [SAY 1798]

Conversing with Mr Greene junior lately, I accidentally mentioned the desire you had of having some Scarborough water sent down to Hasting. Imediately upon the hearing of which he said he hoped he might have leave to make you a present of a dozen bottles, which offer I readily accepted as being absolutely certain the water was genuine, for he bought it at the spring last summer, and had it brought up here by sea from thence.[2] Finding upon enquiry that none of the Bossoms were in town or expected soon, the water was sent packed up in an hamper by the carrier of this week, in which was also put a little pot of Dr Johnson's yellow ointment. I return you hearty thanks for the present of a turkey and tongue, both of which soon after their arrival I sent to my uncle's who dressed them both the next day, and agreable to an invitation Mr Greene junior and I dined there.

Meeting with Mr Stephen Fuller the other day, and understanding he had not been made acquainted of the unhappy accident which had happened to Mr Godfry Webster, and seeing this week Mr Webster in town, I hope Mr Godfry's case is not so bad as it was first thought to be. Jemmy Cranston set out at one this afternoon for Wormly, and my sister, who is very well goes at four to Hampstead. I hope by the punctual observance for the future of your commands I shall make amends for my negligence in losing the paper of directions in relation to the curls. Be pleased to give my duty to my father. I wrote by last Saturday's post to Dely.

1 MS Sayer put 'about 1744', then overwrote in ink.
2 Scarborough's springs known for chalybeate water from the south well, and purging water from the north well: analysis in 1798 yielded 237 grains per gallon for purging water, comprising 128 grains sulphate of magnesia, 16 grains muriate of magnesia, 28 grains carbonate of lime, 2.6 grains carbonate of iron, 58.4 grains sulphate of lime, 4 grains muriate of natron; the 1798 analysis for the chalybeate water yielded 98 grains per gallon for sulphate of magnesia, 14 grains muriate of magnesia, 61.5 carbonate of lime, 3 grains carbonate of iron, 54.4 grains sulphate of lime, 2.1 muriate of natron; composition varied with rainfall (Hinderwell 168).

389 To John Collier, Hastings, from William Cranston, [Johnson's Court], 25 January 1743 [SAY 784]

I intend too morrow to look after 1737 London Evening and St James's for it was in both them, by my day book, that the Tunbridge Wells house was advertised, so that I would not have you give yourself any farther trouble in this affair unless you should hear of my ill success in my search. Tassell v Rootes: about ten days ago I sent Dodson a bill of cost in this affair, who then told me defendants should pay that, and the debt so that I hope you will soon hear from him.[1]

By the two Chambers's, who I saw for the first time today since their innoculation, I find they set out for Battle next Thursday. Jemmy left me at one, and Jenny at two last Saturday, the first for Wormley and the latter for Hampstead, so that am now alone, and miss them both much, though in their roome have got the gout returned in my elbow, and tis with no little pain that I write.

1 Henry Dodson, apprentice attorney to John Collier.

390 To Mary Collier, Hastings, from Molly Collier, [Battle], 28 January 1743
[SAY 1799]

We were in hopes we should have had the pleasure of seeing you before this, but as the weather has been bad hope that is the reason and that you will come soon. We have been pretty much taken up for this week past with Sir Thomas's family, to make up a little of the lost Christmas before they went away and have supped at Mr Tillden's, Mrs Markwick's, and the Dean's, and this morning they are all sett out for London and left us all dolorous. Mr Godfrey has not gone yet, but stays in the country till his eyelashes begin to grow, though I think he looks just the same as he did before the accident. My sister Delia is pretty well, but has this week had a little of the pain in her side, and as we shall live pretty much retired now and the spring coming on, we have perswaded her, if you approve on't, to take some draughts which she once took before and I think is tincture of hellebor, which may prevent it's coming bad for at present it is but very little. My sisters joyn with me in duty to my papa and yourself and love to little Sally who we often wish to see, I am, honoured madam, your most obedient and dutiful daughter.

391 To John Collier, Hastings, from William Cranston, [Johnson's Court], 1 February 1743
[SAY 785]

Your £150 draft on Crawley came safe to hand yesterday, as also your ejectment which I shall take care to move. I this day bought your spaw water, and by Bossom's calling had an oppurtunity of giving him my sister's pomatum which Jenny bought and left with me when she moved off. Tom Frewen is just arrived in town and tells me the roads are exceeding good, and if so, why in the present dolorous scituation of the port can't you, my sister, etc., take a tripp hither? The smallpox is extreamly low and favourable with us, and am sure my neices would not run more, nor perhaps so much hazard here, as at present they do at Battle.[1]

Besides, I am throughly perswaded, this is the proper season in respect to my eldest neice; for the sun is now high enough to make us clear days and nights, free from those foggs which generally attend November and December; the weather moderate as to heat and cold, and not near so damp and raw as the country. Their usuall time of coming has often some very hot days in it, which is to be spent either at a playhouse or at Vauxhall; the first creates surfeit as well as the latter colds. At this season all diversions without doors are at a stand, and within so temperate that seldom any inconvenience attends the being there, besides, the town is now full and very brilliant and gay. In short I could heartily wish all these things were duely considered and then I think they could not help being put in practice and that I should have the pleasure of seeing you all here in a fortnight's time which would be a most agreeable sight. Since writeing the above Mr Dawson has sent and paid me the £127 9s 6d on your account which you mention in yours.

1 Smallpox deaths within the bills of mortality fell to 1429 in 1742, though rose to 2029 in 1743 (*Mortality*). For the outbreak in Cambridge [**393**]. .

392 To John Collier, Hastings, from William Cranston, [Johnson's Court], 5 February 1743 [SAY 786]

I've appeared for Furner and as soon as I can get the bill, will send you a copy. Hastynge v Eversfield, doubts ariseing after I had this declaration from Strange was obliged to go to him again, and they being cleaned up, I delivered a copy last Thursday to Rochester. We are, strictly speaking, intituled to a plea this terme but as in a cause of this sort I dare say a judge would give them till next, so if they ask it of me, beleive shall complement em with time. I saw Willis yesterday, he has promised to procure madam one morning next week at his chambers, in order to talk affairs over. Not one frank left. A division last night in dom com, 58 majority for the court.[1] The hare and turkey came safe, the first we attacked Thursday, the other yesterday both exceeding good and sweet. Parham of Burwash here Thursday,[2] young Green, yesterday, Jemmy both. The founders were not forgott at either.

1 House of Commons, domus communium, 4 February 1743, motion from the opposition for an order to lay before the house official correspondence and papers to and from Maria Theresa, 1 September 1741 to 16 November 1742. The opposition position was understood as undermining the royal prerogative, which, together with the views that no foreign government would feel safe corresponding with George II, led to rejection 212 to 154; similar motions for Prussia and Sweden also rejected (Rapin vol. 20, 611-2; [**393**]).

2 Thomas Parham of Burwash, attorney.

393 To John Collier, Hastings, from James Collier, Fig Tree Court, 5 February 1743 [SAY 1800]

On Saturday last, on the motion of Mr Lawson, a rule was made by the court of King's Bench for Mr Sergeson to shew cause why an information should not go against him for a misdemeanor in his office as a justice of the peace. The case on the complainant's affidavit is as follows. In November last, meeting with an hired cart drawn by four horses contrary to an Act of Parliament, he seized the fourth horse, and agreable to the directions of the statute carryed the forfeiture and left it in the custody of the nearest constable;[1] and imediately went to Mr Sergeson, the next neighbouring justice, in order to make an affidavit of the legality of the seizure, which affidavit the justice is required to take, and then to issue a precept to the constable in whose hands the horse is lodged, to deliver the same with the harness, etc., to the distrainer. Mr Sergeson absolutely refusing to give the person the oath, the plaintiff after having shewn him the words of the Act left him and returned the next day imagining Mr Sergeson would, on consideration, find himself obliged to comply with his request. But he not only continued in the same resolution, by which means the informer was deprived of the benefit of the seizure, but on pretence of having a complaint lodged against him confined him for three hours.

What answer Mr Sergeson has to give I have not been able to learn, but he attended Westminster Hall this morning, expecting Sir John Strange would shew cause for him; but between twelve and one, a long, tedious affair being entred into relating to a conspiracy of the company of coopers in raising workmen's wages a penny a day,[2] he went out of court, which place I left soon after, finding that the affair above mentioned would take up the remaining part of the day and no one point of law to be argued, but only long affidavits to be read. Mr Goddard came to town on Munday last and called on me Tuesday morning, with whom I spent that evening and the following; the reason of his coming hither is to wait on Lord Palmerston, whose eldest son is shortly going to Clare Hall. Mr Goddard informed me that the smallpox rages violently at Cambridge and that when he came from thence Lord Ashburnham was determined to quit the place and is now I hear in town. The motion made yesterday for the papers that have passed between the courts of Vienna and London to be laid before the House, was carryed in the negative, 212 against 154.

1 Statutes aimed at protecting road surfaces from damage by overladen wagons and narrow wheels were difficult to enforce, thus by 1 Geo I stat. 2 c. 11, whilst wagons were not to be drawn by more than 5 horses in general, exceptions made for carting associated with husbandry, including carriage of manure, hay, straw, corn and chalk, also timber for ships, building materials, ammunition and for government service. The Act referred to here, 5 Geo. I c. 12, s. 1. & 2, 1718, 'An Act for making more effectual the several Acts past for repairing and amending the highways of this kingdom', laid down that wagons for hire should be drawn by no more than 6 horses, no cart by more than 3 horses; all wheels on hired wagons bound by streaks under 2½ in. in breadth and set with rose headed nails were to be forfeit along with bridles, halters, etc. The person who seized and delivered the horse, etc., to custody of the constable or other parish officer, was required to swear before a J.P, and, to receive the benefit of the Act, the J.P had to issue a precept (*SL* vols 4, 5). Seizures frequently led to court actions; for examples see TNA KB 1/5/4 Hilary term, bundle 2, 11 Geo II, 1738, 26 January 1738, seizure of horses from wagons with narrow wheels, contrary to statute; KB 1/4/4, Easter, 8 Geo. II, no 1, 12 May 1735; KB 1/4/4, Trinity, 8 Geo II, on damage to roads.

2 For tradition of wage regulation see W Cunningham D.D. *The Growth of English Industry and Commerce in Modern Times* 6th edn *The Mercantile System* (1919) 508-510. For reference to wage rates laid down by quarter sessions for this time see Lipson 1947 vol. 3, 263-4 and for the wage rates laid down at Lewes quarter sessions see ESRO QRE E/416.

394 To John Collier, Hastings, from James Collier, Fig Tree Court, 19 February 1743 [SAY 1801]

The inclosed letter in your last was sent by the post last Saturday as desired, enquiring of my uncle, and of the persons who frequent the Sussex coffee house, in relation to Mr William White; I find he is not in town. The rule for Mr Sergeson to shew cause as mentioned in my former was discharged last week; it appearing to the court on Mr Sergeson's affidavit, that the foundation of the complaint against him was his having a doubt about the meaning of some words in the statute of 5th of George the first, which he desired time to consider of. It is there said the distrainer 'shall make proof on oath', which words were capable of having a double construction put on them, either of proof to be made of the legality of the seizure by the informer's affidavit, or by other witnesses. Mr Justice Wright was clearly of the latter opinion; as by the practise of that court an informer was no credible witness, whereby such testimony he is entituled to a penalty. And farther Mr Sergeson swore as there are some exceptions in the latter part of the Act, in which cases a cart may be drawn by more than three horses, he thought it his duty before he proceeded one step to send for the owner, because it might possibly happen that at the time of the seizure he was allowed by the Act to draw his cart with four horses.[1]

And as to that part of the complaint about his being detained in custody, the case was this; the distrained horse was in the night time stolen out of the constable's stable, about which the informer with another man were seen lurking in the dusk of the evening. The next day the constable went to Mr Sergeson to acquaint him with what had happened, during whose stay the informer came a second time to have the oath given him, when Mr Sergeson insisted he should stay there till the return of a messenger, whom he had sent to a house in a neighbouring village to enquire what time he came to his lodgings, and what he did with himself the night before. This person is a Buckinghamshire man, and a common informer riding about the country with the Act above mentioned in hopes of making seizures. About three years since he moved the court of King's against a Surrey gentleman, lodging the same complaint as now, and then, as this was, the rule was discharged with costs; and at the last sessions at the Old Bailey his wife was tryed for felony, and he offered himself to be a witness for her, assuming another name, but being discovered to be her husband had liked to have been taken into custody.

A very nice affair is depending before all the judges in Serjeants' Inn hall, the determination of which will in all probability be attended with the laying down some certain rules in regard to the doctrine of evidence, for at present there is hardly one observation in relation to the admitting, or refusing evidence, but what can be contradicted by some cases in books of authority. In the latter end of Michaelmas term Sir John Strange moved the court of King's Bench for a new tryal between the East India Company and Captain Gosling alledging that verdict was given in favour of the plaintiffs with damages of 30,500, without any defence made by the defendant, whose witnesses, which ought to have been, were not allowed to be examined. The objection raised against the competency of the defendant's witnesses was founded on a custom, which all sailors comply with who are hired to go on board East India ships here in town; they give a bond to the captain in the penalty of an hundred pounds not to desert the ship without an absolute necessity, and as an inducement to give this bond they have two months advance.

When the sailors who were on board the *Sussex* Indiaman came to be examined in behalf of the defendant, the council for the prosecutors insisted they ought not to be admitted as witnesses, because they were materially interested in the question, being obliged to say there was an absolute necessity of leaving the ship, or else acknowledging their bonds to be forfeited. This affair the court did not care to determine, but left it to be argued before all the judges. The first meeting was on Wednesday sevenight, the second on Thursday last, and the third is to be on Monday next. The case is argued in favour of the East India Company by Mr Bootle, and Mr Floydd, on the behalf of the defendant by Sir John Strange, and Mr Serjeant Prime.[2] Mr Greene and I walked to Hampstead yesterday to see Jenny, who has been lately ill of a cold, and has not got rid of it yet. She proposed to write to Hasting by this post.

1 By 12 Geo I c. 28, 1725, the power to prosecute on information of smuggled goods was no longer permitted freely to anyone, including informers; this power was henceforth restricted to cases brought by the Attorney General, and the responsible Customs and Excise officers (*SL* vol. 5, 584-90).

2 East India Co. v Captain Francis Gosling of the *Sussex* (lost with most of the cargo off Madagascar); trial 1 November 1742; jury found against Gosling and awarded £30,202 to the East India Co. On 13 May 1743 King's Bench set aside the verdict and granted a new trial, and 12 July 1743 a verdict and award was given against Gosling for £25,000. The key evidence came from sailors who remained on board the *Sussex* after Gosling ordered the crew to abandon ship (Hinderwell 235-7).

395 To John Collier, Hastings, from James Collier, Fig Tree Court, 26 February 1743 [SAY 1802]

As the hearing of the affair mentioned in my last to be depending before the judges at Serjeants Inn Hall was of the utmost importance to students in the law, and as it was very uncertain when this matter would be finished, when I wrote my last letter, I did not fix any time for leaving this place. The council made an end of their pleadings on Tuesday night; and a day was fixed for the judges to meet at Lord Chief Justice Lee's chambers in order to give their opinions about this point. If there should be a dissension amongst the judges who are to stay in town these assizes, as is expected between Lee and Willes, from some words which dropped from them at the close of the arguings of the council, and if their reasons for granting a new trial, or rejecting the motion, should coincide with the reasons given by the judges who are obliged to go the circuit, for assenting or refusing, the foundations of the diversity of opinions will be delivered by the judges who remain here publickly next week. If they all should be of the same sentiment Lord Chief Justice Lee will give the reasons in general the first day of next term.

As I must confess I am not very fond of travelling in a stage coach, I should be glad if the horses could come up to London to be in readiness for me to set out on Munday sevenight in the morning, but if this scheme will be attended with any inconvenience I will meet the horses that evening at Tunbridge. A day is fixed in Easter term for a tryal at bar between Mr Annesly and Lord Anglesea, upon an ejectment brought by the former, when it will be seen what foundations there are to think that the plaintiff is the lawfull son of the late Lord Altham.[1] John Waite at his tryal on Thursday was greatly indebted to a nice distinction in law, viz that if at the time of secreting the bonds, they were in his possession, his sureties were only answerable for the act of secretion, but if the bonds were in his custody, then the secretion was a felonious act. And it appearing on the examination of the witnesses for the Bank, that the secreted bonds were in Waite's own desk, and not put into the strong box which by his duty he ought to have done, the court were of an opinion, that it was a possession.[2]

1 Annesley v Lord Anglesea; 13 February 1743 (*ER* vol. 21, 202, vol. 93, 969-972).

2 The case against John Waite was heard 23 February 1743. The Bank of England pursued Waite for two years, accusing him of stealing six East India bonds, the property of the Bank, a felony. After lengthy discussion the Court directed the jury to find Waite not guilty of felony as he had only the possession of the bonds; after further discussion the court granted leave for the Bank to prosecute Waite by a civil action, for £13,300 (*Old Bailey* 23 February 1743).

396 To John Collier, Hastings, from James Collier, Fig Tree Court, 5 March 1743 [SAY 1803]

I have this day taken a place for Fryday next in the Tunbridge stage coach and hope I shall be able to reach Battle the next day by dinner. Inclosed is the Lords' protest against the gin bill, in opposition to which the bishops of Salisbury and Oxford made two very long but, by all accounts, indifferent speeches.[1] The 28th of this month is fixed by his Majesty for putting an end to this session of Parliament and on the 12th of April he sets out to head the forces in Germany.[2]

1 Hervey complained that 'the whole of London, and many towns in the country, swarmed with drunken people of both sexes from morning till night' (Hervey vol. 2, 139). Sales of cheap brandy and geneva were noticed from the Commonwealth as impervious to rising levels of excise; such rises continued by demands of war. The bishops led the opposition and all their number present voted against the bill, including Canterbury, Rochester, Salisbury, Exeter, Hereford, Gloucester, Oxford, St Asaph, Norwich, Bristol and Chichester. Lord Hervey moved that doctors give evidence on the effects of gin, defeated 33 to 17, and on the final vote the Bishops lost 82 to 55; the Lords voting for a regime in line with manufacturers' needs (Rapin vol. 20, 602-4; Cobbett vol. 12 cols 1191 ff., 1206-10, 1237-9, 1299, 1439). For the resulting Act repealing certain duties on spirits etc., see *SL* vol. 6, 16 Geo. II c. 8 480-2.

2 Parliament prorogued, 21 April 1743. George II sailed to Holland 27 April, en route for Hanover (Taylor & Jones 65).

397 To Mary Collier, Hastings, from Mary [Molly] Collier, 6 March 1743[1] [SAY 2174]

Honoured Madam, I should have wrote to you before but as my brother has been so often at Hasting thought you would excuse it, my sister Delia is at present very well and I hope now she will continue so as the warm comes on, especialy when she comes to ride out which Dr Russell seemed to think would quite establish her health. I have done one breadth of the apron and we should be glad if you would send an exact measure of the length of your aprons, that the sides may be done alike, we intend to have a corner flower thinking it will look better than sett full, my brother mentioned poor Phillis's haveing got the smallpox and am afraid she wont have it very light. Philly Clarke was buried at Hailsham on Friday,[2] here is no news stiring and my time is short at present, so must beg leave to conclude myself, your most obedient and dutiful daughter, my sister joyn with me in duty to my papa and yourself,

1 MS Sayer dates this letter in pencil as '1741'; the handwriting of the letter is similar to **[374]** SAY 2175 and **[579]** SAY 2173.

2 Fill Clarke, daughter of William and Elizabeth Clarke, buried 4 March 1743.

398 To Mary Collier, Hastings, from Miss Elizabeth Russell, Hampstead, 10 March 1743 [SAY 1804]

Miss Jenny has just sent away her letter and forgot to inclose it in mine and is perfectly recovered of her cough that has held her almost 3 months; and verily beleive if she had continued another six weeks in town she would have gone into a deep consumption. The last medicine I gave her was oyl and honey and spermacity made into an electuary, which quite cured her.[1] I hope she will neither see town nor Mr Garrick till she sees him with you.

I am sorry, madam, you should think miss the more neglected because she lies in the English teacher's room, where there is 4 young ladies older than her and is laced every morning by her, and all the little ones in Henny's, who allways sees to the dressing of her. If she was the king's daughter she could not have more care taken of her, and hope you did not take it amiss I beged the favour of you to mention her carriage to her, I heartily wish you would in your letters. I know no fault in Miss Jenny but being careless of herself; for sweetness of temper there never was her fellow. I often tell her she would make an excellent martyr, and never would complain. I have, madam, sent inclosed missis bill and a receipt which I thought was least trouble to you; have likewise sent the bill of her peice of work which is paid, but did not know weather you might not think it dear for as they have raised the price of everything else, and see they have of worsteads and silks. My sister joyns with me in compliments to yourself and the young ladies.

1 In this case spermaeti, a fat substance found in the sperm whale; mixed with oil and honey to form a cough mixture (*OED*).

399 To John Collier, Hastings, from William Cranston, [Johnson's Court], 12 April 1743 [SAY 787]

Finding Mr Carleton is retired to the port without any thoughts of returning again and as he went out of town without taking the least notice of me, though I take it for granted he was alike complaisant to all in my scituation with him; and as the account between us is too considerable for me quietly to give up and sit down contented with the loss, without trying whether I can't by some means or other put myself in some way of payment and as two terms are now comenceing in which much can, if anything is to be done and as twill be the d ... ll take the hindmost; so upon all these considerations and duly and seriously consulting my old friend the pillow for this week past in this affair, I am come to a determined resolution to get a judgment upon my bond forthwith, and after that breath and look where to go next. And for this purpose I trouble you with the inclosed a copy of which I beg you will let Patrick serve upon him and then to favour me with an affidavit thereof.

Whether I have a judgement by this method of proceeding or he will give a warrant of attorney for one, the expence to me, though not to him, will be pretty much the same, and not much difference in point of time. But as the giving one will less expose him then my getting it otherwise so I think it proper to tell you that my bond is dated the 13 July 1739[1] and in the penalty of £300. You need not mention it to him but my view at present, if they are not already in limbo, is to attach his two Shropshire livings and which I cannot do till I have judgment and which if I can do, and he lives, I shall by that means get my money and doubtless the sooner tis done the better so that you here see the necessity of a judgement as soon as possible, for I would have the benefitt of the next harvest, and after I have judgement there will be some time taken up in proceedings in the ecclesiasticall court below.

I am very sorry to trouble you in this affair, but in lyeing still I am convinced that I have have no chance whatever I may have otherwise have. A judgement cannot make me worse, it may mend me. I this afternoon sent to Bossum, the remainder of the Irish shiff and the blue silk cleaned. T. Green called on me this morn and told me that his honour Ashburnham died yesterday. A blessed change of weather, pray God it may continue. The town has been terribly sickly, though now much abated, and abundance carried off. Am in hopes I shall be intituled to dine with Dr Mead the first of May, who is then to treat all the familys in the bills of mortality who have not have one down with the epidemicall disorder,[2] for thank God no one under my roof has as yet had anything of it. Hope it has been so with yours. I this morn let the sun into Jemmy's chambers when I found all things as, I beleive, he left them.

1 MS margin, £200.

2 Within the bills of mortality deaths from fevers fell from 5108 in 1742, to 3837 in 1743 and an average of 2680 for the following two years; only 17 cases of measles recorded in 1743, (*Mortality*). Sayer suggests the fever was influenza (Sayer vol. 1, 226). Horace Walpole describes symptoms of cold and fever (Lewis 1937 25 March 1743).

400 To John Collier, Hastings, from James Collier, Fig Tree Court, 21 April 1743 [SAY 1805]

I reached this place yesterday between eleven and twelve, having been so fortunate as to meet with warm weather and very good roads. I lay at Sevenoake on Monday night and Mr Coppard who came to enquire after his father supped with me, by whom I was informed numbers of people had been carried of there by the epidemick fever, which abates now so considerably here, that in another week the bills of mortality will be reduced to the same standard as before this illness began.

The king went about one o'clock this afternoon and put an end to the present session, to whom the speaker of the House of Commons addressed himself in a speech which lasted upwards of half an hour, putting him in mind of the great supplies raised this year, and concluded with not doubting but, in consideration of the present heavy taxes, his Majesty would apply the money in the most frugal manner.[1] The king goes abroad the latter end of next week, but as yet the Council have determined nothing certain in relation to the representation in his absence.[2] Lord Bath is at the head of a party who are for having the prince left sole regent, and Lord Carteret of another who recommend the Cabinet Council. Lord Gower is to be turned out tomorrow, the Duke of Devonshire is to be made Lord Privy Seal and Lord Cholmondely Lord Lieutenant of Ireland.

Mrs Roberts sent all my mother's things by Bossom who sailed yesterday, and is now getting the others done, all which together with the lycences, etc., shall be sent by the carrier of next week. Mr Goddard called on me this morning by whom I find Lord Ashburnham is in town again. I dined with my uncle yesterday and gave him your letter, as likewise Dr Thorpe's note about Mr Cole.

1 The speaker's address, 21 April 1743, confirmed opinion that the administration gained strength as the session progressed.

2 In the absence of George II, 11 May to 15 November 1743, the Lords Justices acted as regent; neither the Prince of Wales nor his supporters were trusted sufficiently to be left in charge. 3rd Duke of Devonshire was Lord Lieutenant of Ireland, September 1737 to January 1745; Lord Gower was the Lord Privy Seal, July 1742 to December 1743, then replaced by the Earl of Cholmondeley.

401 To John Collier, Hastings, from Thomas Smith, Gibraltar, 25 April 1743

[SAY 1806]

I received the favour of your letter dated February the 12th 1743 and am very sorry to hear you are troubled with so bad a distemper as the smallpox, but am hartily glad to hear my cousen Delea and Molly are got clean of from the Place.[1] According to your order I delivered your humble service to Lieutenant Waters and Gorden, and told the latter of the family haveing the Place. He desired I would return the favour to you in the most humblest manner I could, and that he was very sorry for it on Mr and Miss Worgs account, unto who he desires his humble service, and also I gave my aunt's service to Mr Waters lady, and told her of Miss Colliers being gone from the place on the account of the distemper. Lieutenant Waters and his lady are very much obliged to you both for remembering of them, and they desire their service to Madam Collier and you not forgetting Miss Collier and the rest of your family.

On the seventeenth February last, about three a clock in the morning, we had a great shock of an earthquake, which gave such a shock to the garrison that the houses shuk with it, and some of the gentlemen say there tables were overset with it, but there is not a great deal of credit given to that, we had one in January last, but did not give so great a shock as the latter.

The *Romney* man of war, Captain Granville, commander, on the 12 of February took one of the Spanish galloons of Cales, laden with money and cocheneal. I would have given you a more particular account of it, but haveing no opportunity before the ship was sent to England, I thought you would have it from people that was better judges of the thing then I am. Sir, this day Colonel Houghton lost his son, who was captain lieutenant in his regiment; he was taken with a flux, occasioned by eating seven oysters, and dyed in three days time. We have an ensign taken at the same time and in the same manner, and is given over by all the doctors. I am got into a quarter next door to the judg advocate's, and he invites me often to his house, and he is a very sober man and letts me drink as I please, which makes it as agreable to me as it can be. We have no farther news at presant; if we had I should look upon it as my duty to acquaint you with it and should do it with a great deal of pleasure in the best manner I could. Pray give my duty to my aunt and love to my cousens; sir, the plague continues in Tangear and Tetuan that our communication is not like to be upon this summer.

1 Battle Abbey.

402 To Mary Collier, Hastings, from John Collier, Johnson's Court, London, 7 May 1743 [SAY 1807]

I got into the Burrough today at 12 and arrived at Johnson's Court at one not a little fatigued with my journey, both days being the warmest of this year. I found my brother very well, Jacky very brisk and tendable about me, but can hardly see out of his eyes and his lips swelled with that terrible unfortunate humour. I find he took physick a Wednesday and frequently does. I ordered Sam to return home about 4 so as to reach Sennock tonight, and hope he will be at Hasting before this comes. The hot weather made it more dissagreable and anxious, and my right arm was much more troublesom than my hip.

I have been at Jemmy's chambers, which I think very good, and extreamly pleasant and well situated. The entrance, in my opinion, not so well as the rooms. I find he has bought a hole peice of Holland for shirts at 6s 6d an ell. I don't think I shall be able to goe to Hampsted tomorrow, for a London journey is quite different from what it used to be. I find Mr Green of Westerham is quite recovered, though given over by the physicians. I just now saw Mr Jeake and hear the old Lewes aunt has given to each of Mrs Winter's children a hundred pounds and to Mr Tucker and his sister the same, but by the death of the residuary legatees before her, Tucker will come in for about £600 which was intended for the Curteis's. I have just been at the coffee house and intend on finishing this letter to be there again. I design a Munday to think about your commissions. News I have heard none but find Hammond declared a member of Parliament for Southwark, is a practising apothecary surgeon and man midwife, and don't live in the most reputable part of the place.[1]

I would have all the horses turned to grass, I think I told Sam so, but perhaps he might not fully mind it. I sweat prodigiously a Fryday all day, but had fires and hope I did not take cold. I have seen none of the Pelham family but hear by Mr Legas that Mr Pelham of Crowhurst is extreamly ill, and that it was thought he could not bear the fatigue of going to Bristoll. This warm weather will be bad for the girls to be confined. I should think the gardens and Tarrfield, with a good lookout, might be safe. Mr Worge told me that Mr Williams was appointed by the Chancellor to officiate as surrogate.

1 Southwark returned 2 MPs, 6 May 1741, Thomas Inwen 829, Ralph Thrale 904; Inwen died 19 April 1743 and in the by-election Alexander Hume, Whig, received 792, William Hammond, Tory, 863; the result was overturned after scrutiny 30 June 1743 with Hume 732, Hammond 691 (*HofP 1715-54* vol. 1, 331).

403 To Mary Collier, Hastings, from John Collier, Johnson's Court, 12 May 1743
[SAY 1808]

I have the pleasure of your letter of the 10th with the letters that came since I left Hasting, by which I find little Harriott is come home and that you think Dely is better. Little Jacky has been ill with a little sort of a fever, two or three days and was yesterday let blood . I had not a little apprehension of the smallpox and therefore was uneasy on Jenny's account. This morning two or three pimples came out in his face but none on any other parts, and he is brisk, though some fever continues. As Jenny was by appointment to come hither today at noon, my son's man was directed to wait at Holborn at 12 to come with her to Johnson's Court, but she came hither by eleven having a porter from Holborn. Mr Markland has been here. This afternoon determines nothing certain, but as the child is very brisk and well and no further eruptions, we hope the fright is over. If not Jenny must go to Mrs Nouns or Mr Coles.

I assure you that Dely's birthday has not been forgot. I invited the two Mr Greens and Mrs Nouns. Mr Rowe came just after dinner, a very good turbet with lobster sauce, a chine of mutton and sallad, and a marrow pudding, sweet meats, etc. And my brother Cranston to shew honour to the occasion, for the first time used his silver handle knives and forks, etc.,[1] and we drank to the day, yours and all the children's healths, and were very cheerfully merry. I spoke to Mrs Nouns about your affairs, and promises assistance to Jenny, and tomorrow they are to set out. The hatts went yesterday by the carrier. They are the tip top of the mode, and I find Tom Greene was the buyer.

Poor Mr Pelham of Crowhurst, I hear by Mr Stone, is declining every day and I have not seen Colonel Pelham, he keeping with the melancholly family at Putney. The Dutchess of Kendall dyed 2 or 3 days agoe, and it's reported has left near one hundred thousand pounds to the Earl of Chesterfield's lady; money he much wants, so whatever sum it is will be agreeable. I find Mr Stone by mistake sent the protection for the fishery to me at Hasting. I make no doubt but you gave it Patrick, or sent it to the mayor, and if you have not already let the mayor know the letter about Chadderton; let it be signifyed by Patrick.

Though I absolutely denyed to be any way concerned about the widow Steeven's allowance, yet I have looked into it, and hope something may be done, but am not certain, though by the by, I am not pleased with her brother's conduct about Old Bayley's place, and think he carried it too far, and indeed in a silly way, without he had a greater command than I beleive he is in reason entituled unto. Jenny is at Mrs Nouns whither she went at 5 to drink tea. The weather has been excessive hot, though the easterly wind prevayle. I have bespoke the candlesticks as a present, etc., and forgot whether I mentioned it last post. The Bishops of Durham and Worcester are dead so translations are expected.[2] At dinner: Mrs Nouns, Jenny, Greene senior and junior, Brother Cranston, I and Jemmy besides Maddox; Jacky had some sent up.

Past 9: I find Jacky Cranston's ilness stands on an uncertainty, Mr Markland and Mr Stacey have been here, the former is apprehensive of the smallpox, the latter don't think it so, but thinks it's what they call the hog pox and that several children have had it, particularly Mr Sergison's children and a great many more, however, by tomorrow morning it will as they imagine be reduced to a certainty. So Jenny lyes with Mrs Nouns tonight.

1 Use of knives and forks was still rare in 1675, listed in only 8% of inventories in the Orphans Court, rising to 20% 1685, and 64% by 1725; for the rest of England still unusual in 1725, only 10% recorded knives and forks (Weatherill T.2.1, T.2.2).

2 John Hough, Bishop of Worcester, confirmed 28 September 1717, died 8 May 1743. The information about Edward Chandler, Bishop of Durham, confirmed 21 November 1730, was mistaken as he remained in office until his death in 1750.

404 To Mary Collier, Hastings, from John Collier, Johnson's Court, 14 May 1743 [SAY 1809]

I received your letter with one to Jenny which I have given her. Mrs Selby was to have been here last night at 6 to go to Mr Belson's about her gown along with her but she sent word she was engaged. My brother's man went this morning to her to come but she could not tell till Munday morning so it's again put of. Jacky Cranston is pretty full of this swine or hog pox and tis not gone yet but it's intirely agreed not to be the small pox. I have charged Jenny not to goe into his room. I this day bought a little flitch of bacon and ordered the sugar down by Bossom. Jenny much desired a pair of bobs[1] and Mrs Nouns went with her to Mrs Markham's and bought them, cost 25s. They are blew to suit her necklace, which Mrs Markham has promised to make some little alteration in, into the bargain. She was invited yesterday afternoon to Mrs Coles and stayed till ten a clock.

The news of the battell in Bavaria that is in the papers has given great joy to everybody.[2] I hear Mr Stone is going to be married to a lady worth 12 or 14,000 pounds. I was told yesterday that Mr Pelham is set out for Bristoll, but don't know the certainty of it. A prodigious number of people are gone this morning to Finchley common, about 7 miles distance, to see the review of the highlanders; but I did not choose any such journey, nor do I know of any of my acquaintance that are gone. As term ends a Munday Jemmy will have more time to attend on his sister. Jenny is to write next post. Since writing the above Jenny is sent for to Mrs Coles to drink tea and go to Ranelaugh, I am going into the city by appointment and if I get back in time and nothing interferes perhaps may go between 4 and 5.

1 Bobs, ornament designed to hang from necklace, or as an earring.

2 Marshall Broglie left Prague 27 October 1742 to command French forces in Bavaria for winter 1742/3. With the Austrians pressing towards Ratisbonne and Straubing on the Danube, Lord Stair was keen to march to the Danube with the British-Hanover army and fall on the French, whilst the Austrians attacked from the east. Plan blocked by George II who ordered Stair to a position which 'had no military object whatever'. In June 1743 Broglie marched back to the Rhine; the battle referred to may be the surrender of 6000 Bavarians at Simbach, or the earlier withdrawal by Broglie (Fortescue 89-93; Acton 237-8).

405 To Mary Collier, Hastings, from John Collier, [Johnson's Court], 17 May 1743 [SAY 1810]

I have your letter by last post and have great pleasure and satisfaction in hearing all continues well. I have been under a very great uneasiness since my last, when I sent you an account that Markland and Stacey both possitively affirmed little Jacky Cranston's was not the smallpox. We went a Saturday evening to Ranelaugh, and were very merry. Jenny went directly to Mrs Nouns but came the next morning and dressed herself in her uncle's chamber, and where her cloaths lay, and went to church with him.

I was obliged to goe out early but returned by eleven. Upon enquiry I found the child's eruptions stood up and increased and talked to my brother, and Stacey and Markland sent for both togeather, and they began to change their sentiments and beleive it might be the smallpox, but was not certain. I told them of Jenny's danger, and that their assurances to the contrary had brought her into an ugly situation. She has not been in the chamber since Fryday and then not long, so hope there could be no manner of infection, and they verily beleive could not; however, I determined she should not come to the house again. Mrs Nouns consulted, and in the afternoon all her clothes carried thither. We dined and supped at Mr Green's and no coach could be got, so she came home in a chair and James with a flambeau[1] before her, and went directly to Mrs Nouns, and when she saw her cloathes presently said she was sure little Jackey's was the smallpox, and at first talked much about it.

I went the next morning and found her very brisk and well and Mrs Nouns and she went out in the forenoon and she dined there. Mrs Selby again failed her and did not come till 6. I was of opinion with you, that Mrs Nouns's was too near, and just in her sight. Mr Green offered for her to be with Miss Page, but I thought that would be poor humdrum worke, so went to Mrs Coles and told her the situation, and they immediately gave a very strong and I beleive hearty invitation for her to be there, and I accordingly resolved on it. As I had told her in the morning that we would spend the evening in her brother's chambers I went in the afternoon, having seen Jemmy and bid him invite Mrs Coles and daughters. And I went with them before she returned from Mrs Belson's, but she soon came with Thomas, and we played 2 or 3 games at whist, and supped elegantly cold lamb, pickled salmon, lobsters, tarts, custards, etc. She went to Mr Coles where she continues and is very brisk there, supped Mrs Coles, 3 daughters, Jenny, my brother, young Green, Mr Coles and myself and Mr Rowe came in.

Today the young ones walked out and went to Lincoln's Inn chappell and I find tonight Mr Green and Jemmy are to carry them to the play at Covent Garden. *Othello, or the Moor of Venice* being expected the last.[2] There is not any danger in the child, as they say, has not above 60 or 80. Jemmy comes to London tomorrow. My brother first said he should go to Mrs Nouns till Fryday morning and then go to Sennock, and I told him I would take him thither in a chaise that day, but I beleive the same is now altered, and that he will stay in London and I fancy at Mr Coles. It quite takes of the design of being here much togeather, but I doubt not but Jenny will like it, and find them all exceeding civil and we see her very often.

I have told Jemmy to pay Mrs Roberts, and beleive he has done it today. Mr Pelham and his uncle with him set out for Bristoll a Saturday morning, and as I find in a very delining way, so that it's a question whether he can bear the fatigue of the journey. I design to come out of town Fryday morning early, so let Sam set out early that morning with my old mare led, and be at the King's Head at Tunbridge by 2 a clock that in case I come out time enough in the morning and have an inclination may go forward some part of the way.

Jenny is to write to you this post, so presume she will mention about her cloaths, etc., but I think she said last night she had not bought Dely's gown. I have bought no cloaths but a banjan. I think what you said about the candlesticks is the best way. Mr Markland really all along seemed more apprehensive than Stacey of the smallpox; what he says is that abundance of children have had the other which is often attended with the same symptoms, and at first appearing not to be distinguished.

1 Torch made with several thick wicks dipped in wax (*OED*).
2 Covent Garden Theatre, Tuesday 17 May 1743, *Othello, the Moor of Venice*; also *Perseus and Andromeda, or the cheats of Harlequin* (Scouten Pt 3 vol. 2, 1736-47, 1057).

406 To John Collier, Hastings, from James Collier, Fig Tree Court, 9 June 1743

[SAY 1811]

I received yesterday the Statutes at Large and beg leave to thank you for them; on looking into the first volume I found an account of all the Sussex persons who were subscribers to the work in a paper of your handwriting. Yesterday being the day appointed for Bread's execution I suppose he suffered.[1] I heard on Munday he was to be hanged on a gibbet erected on the Strand, on which afterwards he was to be hanged in chains. Mr Moneypenny informed me before the tryal that Mr Gybbon had made use of his utmost endeavours to perswade Mr Lamb to send the prisoner to the county goal, and have him tryed at the assizes; and that the Lord Chancellour had told young Lamb that considering the circumstances he would not have his father try this affair at Rye. Mr Burrel since his return has often declared that any unprejudiced jury in England woud have found the prisoner guilty of the indictment.

I hope the fashion of the cans sent down by the carrier of last week is agreable, and as Bossom is now in town if you would have me purchase some wine glasses and an additional number of cans; I will buy them imediately on the receipt of a letter and send them to the wharf. I saw Mr Rowe yesterday who acquainted me that an express arrived that morning at the Duke of Newcastle's office with a confirmation of a decisive battle's being fought between Prince Charles and Marshall Broglio wherein the latter was entirely defeated.

Tuesday was the day fixed for the judges to chose their circuits, but it is certain they are all determined not to go any of the circuits till all their arrears are paid and there are now five quarters due. Mr Brown, clerk to Lord Chief Baron Parker, who says he is acquainted with you, proposes treating Jenny, Miss Coles, and Miss Greene, at Vauxhall tomorrow evening. Be pleased, sir, to give my duty to Mama and love to my sisters.

1 Allen Grebell was murdered by John Breads, a Rye butcher, on 16 March 1743: Breads admitted intending to kill James Lamb. Although advice was given to move the case to the assizes, Rye insisted on the town's right to try such murder cases; the case was heard on 25 May with James Lamb, Mayor, presiding. Breads was hanged on Rye Strand 8 June 1743 and his body hung in chains for many years; (L A Vidler 'The Murder of Allen Grebell' *SNQ* xi 1946-7 49-51; P Monod *The Murder of Mr Grebell* (1999)).

407 To John Collier, Hastings, from James Collier, Fig Tree court, 21 June 1743

[SAY 1812]

Last night my uncle, Messrs Mitchel, Humphreys, Rowe, young Mr Greene, and I went in one boat from the Temple between eight and nine to Cuper's Gardens, being enticed thither by a pompous advertisement in the Daily Advertiser of yesterday, intimating that some new fire-works were to be exhibited there that evening. The company was very numerous, but we were all greatly disappointed, except my uncle who had never been there before. Having only the ordinary fireworks performed with this alteration only, that what used to be done on the top of the orchestra, was shewn on a scaffold erected for that purpose at the head of the canal.

I intend to send down Dr Pocock's observations on Ægypt in the box with my cloaths,[1] but as Dr Perry's voyage to the Levant is generally esteemed a very indifferent performance, and excessively dear, I shall not purchase it for myself, but if you would have it bought, tis easily obtained. I propose if the horses can be spared to set out tomorrow sevenight for Hasting. Jenny went from Mr Coles to Hampstead on Wednesday morning last, at which place Mr Greene and I design to pay her a visit the latter end of [2] this week.

There is a poem lately published entituled the Causidicade,[3] which has been universally read, and afforded a great deal of diversion, as it particularly enters into the characters of the most eminent in the profession of the law. We are in daily expectation of hearing an account of a battle between the allies and the army under Noailles, for tis generally agreed that the king is determined to pass the Main, notwithstanding the French army is imediately opposite. Mr Worge I hear comes to town tomorrow.

1 Dr Richard Pococke *A Description of the East and some other countries* 2 vols 1743-45, reprinted in John Pinkerton *A general collection of the best and most interesting voyages and travels in all parts of the world* 17 vols (1808-14). At this time Pococke kept the minute book of the Egyptian society, known as the Egypt Exploration Society.

2 MS *next* struck through

3 Porcupine Pelagius, *Causidicade, a Panegyri-Satiria-Serio-Comic-Dramatical Poem on the Strange resignation and Stranger Promotion* (London, 1743), a satirical commentary on the appointment of Sir William Murray to the office of Solicitor-General, replacing Sir John Strange.

408 To John Collier, Hastings, from James Collier, Sussex coffee house, 23 June 1743 [SAY 1813]

On account of the receipt of this letter inclosed the guns in the park and tower were fired about three o'clock this afternoon and preparations are now making for bonefires, etc. We all wait with great impatience for an authentick account of the particulars of this action.[1] Mr Worge arrived here this afternoon and is now writing at this place to Bourne to acquaint his father that only the horse were present at this attack as his brother is in a regiment of foot commanded by the Earl of Rothes.

1 Battle of Dettingen 16/27 June 1743 (McCann 161-3; Williams 1945 230-1; Horn & Ransome 853-5; [**416**]).

409 To John Collier, Hastings, from James Collier, [Fig Tree Court], 30 July 1743 [SAY 1814]

My sister and I reached Mr Luxford's on Thursday morning soon after ten, and about an hundred yards from the house we saw Mr Luxford mounting his horse in order to dine at Hailsham with Mr Johnson. But on my riding up to him he turned back; yet on our insisting, after he had waited on us to his house that he should put in execution his intended scheme, he set forward a second time, but returned in about an hour having been informed on the way, that Mr Johnson with the Herringly people was to dine at the seahouses on that day.[1]

We set out from thence about two and were obliged to stop for half an hour at a little alehouse in Ringmore on account of a very heavy rain which fell between five and six. We arrived at Dr Russell's a little before seven and on a consultation held at Mr Luxford's, judging it impossible if I lay there to set out early the next morning it was agreed I should proceed to Maresfield that night, which I accordingly did. And after dining at Croydon got here at five o'clock, and supped with my uncle Mr Worge, etc., on a neck of venison at the Bull Head. Mrs Whitby who was mentioned lately in the publick papers to be dead, is Mr Greene's lady on which account he appears in mourning. My uncle received this day the bill drawn by Captain Scot on Mr Furye, and intends writing you a letter by the next post, on account of some business which has fallen out since the appointing of Tuesday for our setting out on our journey; my uncle has been obliged to postpone it till Thursday.

1 George Luxford, family estate at Windmill Hill, Wartling. Davey lists 38 windows for Luxford's house, paying £2 (Davey, 2006). The seahouses were close by Eastbourne.

410 To Mary Collier, Hastings, from John Collier, Dover,[1] 20 August 1743

[SAY 1815]

I write this from Dover where I arrived last night and design setting out tomorrow morning for Deal. Wednesday night and most part of Thursday and till one in the morning there was a prodigious rain accompanyed with thunder and lightening and very hot sultry weather, and had a very indifferent ride from Romney to Hythe. People here have hopes and fears about warr or peace and seem very anxious, for a French warr must certainly be prejudicial to the trade of this town in a high degree. I hope I shall meet with nothing extraordinary in the course of my survey to retard my finishing it in the usual time for these journeys begin to be not a little irksome.

1 John Collier's survey of the riding officers of Kent, 8 August to 2 September 1743 (TNA CUST 148/11).

411 To Mary Collier, Hastings, from John Collier, Canterbury, 25 August 1743

[SAY 1816]

I did not intend to write any more but from Sandwich, which I hope you received last night, but could not neglect to acknowledge the receipt of your kind letter directed to this place with the agreeable account of your being all pretty well, and that the smallpox has not broke out afresh. The venison coming at the time you mention was a little unfortunate and wish it had happened to be postponed, but I think you could not better dispose of it than sending a haunch to Mr Markwick. Poor Sam Avan's death has nothing surprizing in it considering how he lived for so long a time. They are just now beginning to pick hops and have a much greater crop than was expected. Here are four companys of foot soldiers of Colonel Powlet's regiment, which are marines, I beleive more properly expressed than foot. The officers about ten days since made a ball for the ladys and a very handsom elegant entertainment. I design to set out tomorrow for Feversham and manage so as to get home a Munday or Tuesday, though all this is uncertain. I imagine that by this time you have received another letter from the travellers.

412 To John Collier, Hastings, from Colonel James Pelham, St James's, 17 October 1743 [SAY 410]

The wind being contrary for the Princess Louisa, who was to have sailed today, prevents my being at Crowhurst the 20th as I proposed. Mr Hay will I beleive be there to meet you. I send J. Gower to provide a diner for the tenants, and wish twas possible for me to be there. You will be so good as to distinguish my brother's, my late nephew's and my estate seperate. I suppose Mr Hay may be glad to have some little abstact of my brother's to carry to Lewes; the rest you'l make out against I see you, which must be at the county election. J. Gower brings you a book by which you will be able to settle the Mayfield account with Merchant the receiver. As to my brother's brook lands in Crowhurst which I propose to lay to my farm at Crowhurst, Bene, my tenant upon Breadhill Green, will take the parcels as they fall in and I will account to my brother for the rent, after the respective tenants have cleared to their time.

I am glad you have appointed courts for Wilting and Holington. I think twou'd be proper to hold one at Crowhurst as soon as is convenient and another for Pepsham. I shall discourse our counsellor about Mayfield when I see him next in town. Everything here must remain as they are till the king comes home. My neice Pelham has mended a little these two last days which is so very surprising that I begin to think she may possibly recover. I have ordered J. Grove to pay into your hands the money he received for the stock, etc., sold at Crowhurst and shall order all sums that come in upon account of my late nephew's administratrix to be lodged with you.

413 To Mary Collier, Hastings, from Miss Elizabeth Russell, 18 October 1743 [SAY 1817]

I hope this will find Miss Jenny safe at home and not much fateauged with her journey, but she has promised to write. Hope you will think Miss improved; should have been glad to have known sooner of missis going that she might have grounded her chair. I am sorry to set down with the grounding, worsted more floss silk which through carelessness, but will say no more. I beleive, madam, you had a mind to divert yourself, I am sure you did me though it is much the fashion in Hampstead for old maids to allmost run away with young fellows. But you may remember I once told you I was made for an old maid and a school mistress. I have here inclosed the bill and a receipt with it and am, dear madam, with wishes for health and prosperity to yourself and agreable family.

414 To Mary Collier, Hastings, from Miss Elizabeth Russell, Hampstead, received 13 November 1743[1] [SAY 1818]

To Miss Collier 1743

A quarters board, due November the 13	£1 10s 0d
2 pair of gloves	04s 0d
Ribin 3sh & 6d tape and thread 6d a lace,	£0 04s 6d
Brown worrstead 5sh, floss silk 3 sh	£0 08s 0d
A coppy book, pens and ink	£0 02s 0d
Starching 1sh, a pair of shoes 3s and 6d	£0 04s 6d
[Total]	£8 13s 0d

1 [*Reverse*] 'school bill 1743', written by Sayer; the bill is in Elizabeth Russell's handwriting.

415 To John Collier, [Hastings], from Henry Pelham, 18 October 1743

[SAY 411]

I received yesterday your letter of the 15th with the inclosed abstract of the audit. I hope you will be able to settle the account with Legas in relation to the furnace to our mutual satisfactions.[1] I observe but very little money comes in from the half year's audit in proportion to what used to do; taxes, repairs, etc., and the small quantity of wood cut this year I suppose is the occasion of it. You have done right in endeavouring to find the roguery about stealing the fish and cutting the pond.[2] I hope the country know it is felony, at least I take it to be so but you know better. I hope the estate is in pretty good repair. If not, I should be glad you would att your leisure visit the several farms in the spring, see what is wanting to be done to put everything upon a substantial foot, so as in time to come we may have less deductions. I am sorry for poor Chatfeild; see what his complaints are, and if the farm is to high rented we must fall, but I dont like that much. I hope to see you in town before the election, if not, I conclude I shall see you then.

1 Westfield forge, owned by Henry Pelham, operated by the partnership of Harrison and John Legas; the Waldron furnace was operated solely by John Legas (Cleere & Crossley 193, 200, 204-6).

2 For the legal position see Hay 192.

416 To John Collier, Hastings, from James Collier, Fig Tree Court, 27 October 1743.

[SAY 1819]

On Tuesday last, by the assistance of Mr Greene senior, I obtained a sight in the sutling room at the horse guards, of Thomas Browne, a Yorkshireman, who retook the standard at the battle of Dettingen. He has so many cuts, and those so very deep, that his face is indeed an extraordinary sight, but the worst wound he received is on the back part of his neck, occasioned by a French soldier's endeavouring to cut off his head. He has two bullets now remaining in his body, just above the hips, which the surgeons have despaired of ever being able to extricate. The tops of three fingers on his left hand are entirely chopped off in a slanting manner by an hanger.[1]

On the day above mentioned I dined at Mr Greene's, in company with Major Mackartee of the first troop of horse guards,[2] who said he had lately received a letter from the Lord Delawar, his colonel, with orders, agreable to the king's express command, to incorporate this Browne into the regiment, that his Majesty had sent for him three times since the action, and promised at Browne's departure for this place that he would provide for him in a better manner when he arrived in England. Mr Pelham took the oaths this day in the court of Chancery to qualifye himself for the place of first Lord Commissioner of the Treasury; as did also Mr Carpenter, but for what preferment I could not learn.

The conversation of the town is entirely engossed on the behaviour of the Duke of Marlborough in the army who publickly declared there that the Hannoverians were 'cowardly mercenaries'.[3] Tis not absolutely known whether he has resigned, or not, but this is certain, that he went out of London without seeing any of his officers, which being an uncustomary thing, the military gentlemen think he has quitted the regiment. Imediately before the Lord Stair's resignation, the duke, Lord Stair, and Lord Albermarle joined in presenting a memorial to the king, complaining of councills of war being held, to which the Hannoverian officers were only invited. This memorial the king refused to read, which so disgusted the duke, as to draw from him the expression before mentioned. I saw

Mr Steele yesterday, who is just returned from Germany after attending the combined army this summer, and by him I was informed, that there was no intercourse whatever between the English and Hannoverians, and indeed the English officers are so bent against them, that I beleive it will be very difficult for the ministry to get them put into British pay for another year.

The business of the court of King's Bench is at present remarkably trifling, for on Tuesday and this day the court were obliged to rise after setting, but three quarters of an hour.

1 Thomas Browne, 3rd dragoons regiment. After their third charge the regiment 'were well-nigh annihilated' and the French captured the regimental standard; although wounded, Thomas Browne recaptured the standard behind French lines and fought his way back single-handed, with seven wounds to his face and body (Fortescue vol. 2, 98-9). With success in the battle George II revived the ancient knights banneret, to which Browne was appointed.

2 John, Lord Delawar, took over the 1st troop on 30 August 1737 and led a brigade at Dettingen; the troop comprised 181 gentlemen, the officers included 2 lieutenants, a captain, cornet, guidon, 4 brigadiers 4 sub-brigadiers, and 156 privates (G Arthur *The Story of the Household Cavalry* 3 vols (1909) vol. 2, 407-8).

3 Dettingen offered another chance to inflict serious damage on French forces, yet George II and his Hanoverian advisors preferred diplomacy to settle affairs in Germany. With the summer months clear of serious fighting, French forces focused on the Austrian Netherlands, with renewed efforts to organise a Jacobite uprising in Britain. On resigning command Lord Stair, 4 September 1743, specifically condemned the torpor of the summer as giving the French hope they might emerge victorious, also among the reasons given by the 3rd Duke of Marlborough on resigning his command in November 1743. Widespread hostility was felt in English regiments towards George II's preference for his Hanoverian officers as well as annoyance that he failed to recognise the prowess of the English (Lecky vol. 2, 13-16; McCann 184, 188-9; Owen 184-5). The question of pay and supplies was raised when Parliament convened 1 December 1743 to 12 May 1744.

417 To John Collier, Hastings, from James Collier, Fig Tree Court, 10 November 1743 [SAY 1820]

On Munday morning, as I was setting out for Westminster Hall, I was surprized at the appearance of an unknown visitor, and on my asking what occasioned her coming to me, she said her name was Phipps, that she lived with the late Mrs Pelham, and was now a servant to Mr Nesbitt in Coleman Street. And at the same time produced a letter from you to her, relating to a sum offered for the purchase of her estate and desired me to acquaint you, that if she could dispose of it for an hundred pounds, clear of all charges, she would willingly part with it; she mentioned also her inclination of having the writings, but begged the favour of a letter from you. Mr O'Keith and I always exchange compliments when we meet, which is very often, and this day he called to me in the hall, and desired I would go home and dine with him on a Sussex hare, which request I should willingly have complyed with, had not a prior engagement at the Crown and Rolls prevented me.

The business of the court of King's Bench is less now by far than ever in the memory of any of the present attenders, and indeed it is so trifling, that the council within the bar begin to despair of having anything to do. I attended the tryal at bar, between Sir Watkins Williams Wynne and Mr Middleton from ten on Fryday till five on Saturday morning, and think there was sufficient foundation for a verdict for the plaintiff, but not for the excessive damages.[1] Lord Ashburnham, I see, is in town, and hear lodges at a millener's in Pall Mall, on whom I intend to wait shortly. Mr Wickens has been very dangerously indisposed, but is now past all danger though not so well today as yesterday.

1 [**375**].

418 To John Collier, [Hastings], from Colonel J. Pelham, St James, 15 November 1743 [SAY 412]

His Majesty and the duke arrived this afternoon in perfect health, loud huzzas all thro' the city and nothing but bonfires all over the town.[1] I trouble you now to desire you will remitt the money you had of J. Grove to Mr Albert Nesbitt in Coleman Street, the death of my neice Pelham had made another jumble in our administratorship. I have not time in this hurry to be particular. You know the Parliament won't meet till the begining of next month, before that time our ministry will be a little settled.

[*at end*] Albert Nesbitt Esq.

1 George II arrived in London from Hanover on Tuesday evening 15 November and passed through Pall Mall en route to St James house; 'the whole street was speedily lighted up to escape the mob's breaking the windows, as they did those of the Earl of Stair, Lady Hamilton's and some others who were not quick enough in giving that demonstration of their joy' (Egmont vol. 3, 276, 15 November 1743). For reference to the political standing of the king after Dettingen see Taylor & Jones 188-9, 1 December 1743.

419 To John Collier, Hastings, from James Collier, Fig Tree Court, 24 November 1743 [SAY 1821]

Being informed on Munday morning that Mr Stone was gone with the Duke of Newcastle to Claremount,[1] and thinking Tuesday an improper day as it was celebrated as the king's birthday, I went dressed yesterday morning to pay my respects to Mr Stone in relation to the franks. But he not being at the office, by the advice of Mr Rowe, who said it was usual, I inclosed the intended franks in a cover directed to Andrew Stone esq., and placed at the bottom this inscription 'franks for Mr Collier'; and this day returning from Westminster Hall about one o'clock I called at the office but could neither meet with Mr Stone, Mr Rowe or the clerk with whom I left the letter. I intend to call at the office tomorrow morning and will give you a farther account by Saturday's post.

The reports at present with regard to the Duke of Marlborough's resignation are totally different, but this is certain, that the Earl of Bath was not at court on Tuesday. All parties unite in thinking the measure right of the ministry in taking up of the publishers of *Old England's Te Deum*, and indeed it well deserves the character given of it in the Duke of Newcastle's warrant, vizt a blasphemous, impious seditious libel.[2] The town is very impatient to hear the determination of the great cause depending now in Ireland between the Earl of Anglesea and Mr Annesley.

1 Claremont, Esher, Surrey.
2 Sir Charles Hanbury Williams, *Old England*'s *Te Deum* (London, 1743).

420 To John Collier, Hastings, from James Collier, Fig Tree Court, 1 December 1743[1] [SAY 1822]

I called on Mr Rowe last Saturday, but finding the antichamber of the Treasury to be shut, I sent my man in the afternoon to Mr Rowe's lodgings to beg the favour of him to ask the clerk with whom I left the covers, if they were delivered to Mr Stone. He went to the office but could not find the clerk. Staying too late on Munday in Westminster Hall, I did not call again till Tuesday, when I was informed by Mr Rowe that the clerk with whom I left the covers had been ill ever since the delivery, and that he had made an enquiry of the other clerks in that office relating to this affair, but could gain no intelligence, but acquainted me at the same time, that he had frequent opportunities of seeing Mr Stone's gentleman, for I find he keeps one out of livery, and would ask him if the covers were received.

I was at the Treasury yesterday, but found Mr Rowe had neither seen the clerk or gentleman, though indeed I am much obliged to him, Mr Rowe, for his trouble in this affair, though not attended with the desired success. I called again [2] this morning, and receiving the like answer, I took some covers and went to Mr Stone's house, and had delivered to me the covers francked, which I had left with the clerk, and indeed, till I had good reasons for my conduct, I judged it improper to call there, not being able to gain certain intelligence whether the covers were received. I have only two dozen francked now, but if insufficient will wait on Colonel Pelham with the like number. Six I shall give to my uncle, two keep for myself, three send now and the remaining the first opportunity.

1 [*Front cover*] Free, Andrew Stone.
2 MS *yesterday* struck through.

421 To Elizabeth Worge, Battle, from Mrs E. Goddard, Norwich, 5 December 1743 [SAY 1823]

I beg the favour of you to interceed with your father in behalf of my poor brother, John Waller. As Mr Collier was so good to promise he would get him a place, dont dout but he will, if you'd be so good as to ask him which I shall take as the greatest favour. Dear madam, I ask pardon for giveing you this trouble but as my brother's nesesities force me to it, hope you will excuse it. His case is very hard as never being brought up to any trade so is distitude of geting his bread and twas as hard with him in the Excise for if everyone was to be dismissed for such trifles as he was nobody could stand in it, for he never commited any fraud in it. I am not so far mistress of my house as to give him his board otherwise he should not want bread. I hope you will use your good intersestion and excuse this freedom and shall think myself every oblidged to you and your good father, and am with the greatest respect to yourself and spouse Mr Collier and his lady and all the good family. Dear madam, I should be very proud of a line from you if you would pleas to give yourself the trouble.

422 To John Collier, Hastings, from James Collier, Fig Tree court, 20 December 1743 [SAY 1824]

Had I not been assured of your determined resolution to go to Chichester on Mr Pelham's re-election,[1] I should have wrote to you last week; but on Saturday night was prevented by a violent cold, attended by an headach. I wrote to my sister Dely at Battle by the post of Saturday sevenight, agreable to your directions of sending a letter, within a week from the reception of yours. As I find sir, you would be glad to have the most early intelligence of the divisions in the houses of Parliament, I shall endeavour to get them as soon as possible, and send you them imediately for the future; and least you should not have seen the lists, on the several political divisions this year in both houses. I will here subjoin a particular account, viz on the first day of the sessions, December 1st: an objection was made to the address of the Commons to the king, in relation to the treaty of Worms, which was carried in the negative 278 against 143.[2] On the 7th of December a motion was made in the Commons to address his Majesty, not to continue the Hanoverian forces in the pay of Great Britain after the 25th of this instant. This motion passed in the negative 231 against 181.[3] On the 9th the like motion was made by the Lord Sandwich in the House of Lords; but there met with a more severe repulse, the numbers being, for 36 against 71.

On Thursday a motion was made in the Commons for to desire the king, not to prosecute the war without the concurrence of the states general. This passed in the negative, 209 against 132.[4] Mr Parker has been dead these four years, and I have not been able to meet with any common prayer books printed by him.[5] J. Beecroft who succeeded Parker, viz at the sign of the Bible and Crown in Lombard Street, has desired me to send down one book, which specimen he doubts not will meet with approbation. Indeed, the singing psalms are annexed, which he says is usual, but to oblige me, if this book is approved of, he will take from the remaining two, which if this is liked I shall send the before mentioned psalms, and abate in the price. This common prayer book, with the windows blind, and the things mentioned in your letter of yesterday shall be sent tomorrow. I understand by my uncle, that Mr Greene, junior, has given orders to Rent to send you one Ragg of sturgeon so that I apprehend another will be sufficient. Mr Greene set out for Norfolk early on Munday morning, and agreable to a promise made a month ago, I beleive I shall in a short time pay him a visit for a week. The remaining part of the franks I sent by Mr Worge, only reserving three to myself, including one sent to my sister, as also a parcell from Mr Cole.

1 On the occasion of the Sussex by-election after death of the Earl of Wilmington 2 July 1743 and appointment of Henry Pelham as 1st Lord of the Treasury, 27 August 1743, Pelham required a vote from electors and was re-elected 15 December 1743; the result was declared at Chichester (*HofP 1715-54* vol. 1, 331-2).

2 Address to the king, 1 December 1743 (Taylor & Jones 188-9). The Treaty of Worms formalised an alliance between Sardinia, Hungary and Britain 13 September 1743, ratified by Britain 20 September, and the British government engaged to support Sardinia for the length of the war (Parry vol. 37 13 September 1743). For details of the subsidy and purchase of Wealden cannon see [**429**].

3 Second challenge from the opposition, 6 December 1743, requesting the king to end the service of Hanoverian soldiers paid for by Britain, defeated 231 to 181; although less sympathy for the government, the logic of keeping 16,000 regulars told on the house; a like motion lost in the Lords 71 to 36 (Cobbett vol. 13, App. 135-46; Taylor & Jones 66).

4 Opposition motion for an address to the king, 15 December 1743, 'in consideration of the exhausted and impoverished state of the kingdom' to ask the States General and other allies to agree to a plan of spending for the proposed fighting. As the motion offered a diplomatic minefield, it was rejected 209 to 132 (*CJ* vol. 24, 492; Egmont 279 vote of 209 to 130; Owen 205).

5 Edmund Parker, bookseller, Bible and Crown, Lombard Street died 16 Dec. 1739, succeeded by Mr Mellor, who died 13 Dec.1740 (H R Plomer, G H Bushnell, E R McC.Dix *A Dictionary of the Printers and Booksellers who were at work in England, Scotland and Ireland 1726 to 1775* (1932) 190-1).

423 To John Collier, Hastings, from William Cranston, [Johnson's Court], 27 December 1743 [SAY 788]

You herewith receive a copy of our transactions in money matters from my leaving town in August to this time.[1] The family of the Coles with T. Greene, Rowe and Jemmy dined here yesterday and held it till 2. Very dolorous today. We remembred the port with compliments of the season to all there. A strong rumour about town that Willes is to be chancellor, the other voteing against the treaty of Worms and refuses, as he said, to put the great seal to it, but this I much doubt nor shan't beleive till I see it.[2] Young George Carleton when in town did not see Lord Northampton, and the interest he had in Mr

Gibbon amounted to no more than that if his lordship asked him, Gibbon, whom to recommend for Rye liveing that it should be Mr Carleton.[3] As monstrous as this is, yet if George's own word is to be taken it is true.

1 SAY 788 includes the account, which covers the same period as SAY 702 and MIL 7/24.

2 Sir John Willes, appointed Lord Chief Justice of the Common Pleas, occupied the office for 24 years

3. James Compton, 5th Earl of Northampton (1687-1754), nephew of Spencer Compton, Earl of Wilmington, of Compton Place, Eastbourne, Prime Minister 1742-3; the patronage of Rye vicarage and Westham vicarage was held by the Spencer Compton family (Ford 100-1, 185).

424 To John Collier, Hastings, from James Collier, Fig Tree Court, 31 December 1743 [SAY 1825]

I have not been able as yet to meet with any common prayer books in the smaller size that are either handsome in the print or paper. The report prevails still of the present Lord Chancellor's being to be succeeded by the Lord Chief Justice Willes; the reason I find was communicated to you in a letter from my uncle by Tuesday's post. If Mr Willes succeeds in his election at Worcester tis generally apprehended that circumstance will greatly contribute to his father's advancement[1] Great interest is making on both sides to engage members to give their votes in the affair of the election for the town of Denbigh, the merits of which are to entred into at the bar of the House in February, Mr Trevor, a near relation of Sir Watkin Williams Wynne having presented a petition against the sitting member, Mr Wynne.

The late Mr Pelham's brother, is, I hear, appointed collector of the Customs at the port of Chester, a place executed by a deputy and in value almost £700 per annum. There were great disputes, and consequently different parties at court, whether the Lord Sandys or the Lord Herbert should have the precedency, but the king himself determined in favour of the former. I called on my Lord Ashburnham this morning and afterwards walked in the park upon the canal in which great numbers were scating, but chiefly of the meaner sort. The frost this evening begins to give. By the first opportunity I shall send you Wentworth's answer to Vernon's pamphlet, published at the close of the last session.[2] I think in most things tis a clear satisfactory one.

1 Worcester election, 23 May 1741, Thomas Winnington 1462, Samuel Sandys 1217; on the 9 March 1742 Sandys was re-elected after appointment as Chancellor of the Exchequer; on the 27 December 1743 Winnington was re-elected on succeeding Henry Pelham as Paymaster General. When Sandys was created a peer, his nominee for the seat, John Willis, was defeated by Sir Henry Harpur, a Tory, 10 January 1744 (*HofP 1715-54* vol. 1, 356).

2 Sir Charles Knowles, *An Account of the expedition to Carthagena with explanatory notes and observations* (London, 1743).

425 To John Collier, Hastings, from James Collier, Fig Tree Court, 7 January 1744[1] [SAY 1826]

I have at last found some copies of the Book of Common Prayer, at Mr Ware's in Paternoster Row, which I beleive will be satisfactory in paper and print; and as to the bindings, those indeed have been directed by my own taste, and I hope will be liked. These together with some pamphlets shall be sent by the carrier of next week. I saw Mr Carleton this morning, who acquainted me that the Lord Northampton had signed his presentation to the vicarage of Rye, and that he was by order to wait on the bishop this evening to receive institution.[2] The Lord Bath is certainly to be made President of the Council, in the room of the Lord Harrington[3] who is to have the regiment of foot guards, vacated by the resignation of the Duke of Marlborough, and to attend his Majesty abroad. The managers of the lottery, are universally blamed for not pulling the case from the wheel in Guildhall on Thursday last, which they did after the wheels were conveyed to the lottery office in Duke Street, Westminster, and then found a number sticking in the wheel.[4] The common people, though without any foundation, talk very freely on the subject.

1 [*Cover*] Free, Andrew Stone.
2 Rye patrons: Earl of Northampton, Earl of Wilmington, Lord George Cavendish (Ford 100).
3 William Stanhope, (c. 1683-1756) 1st Earl of Harrington, 9th February 1742, Lord President of the Council, 13 February 1742, succeeded by Lionel Cranfield Sackville, Duke of Dorset, 3 January 1745.
4 16 Geo II c.13, 1743, 'An Act for raising by Annuities and a lottery £1.8 million at 3 per cent per annum' of which sum £800,000 was raised for the lottery, with tickets at £10; the draw started on 23 November 1743, the minimum return for a ticket owner with a blank was £7 plus 3% per annum until redeemed (*PGA* 16 Geo II 299, Ewen 147-8).

426 To Mary Collier, from Cordelia Collier, Battle Abbey, January 1744 [SAY 1827]

As Miss Webster wrote in shuch a hurry makes me do it again lest you should not be able to read it, for I receivd yours just at dinner and she did not stay till it was over because the man waited for it. But it is the request of my lady and all that you wont send for me, and if you have no objection to my staying longer but that of my health, do ashure you I am better now than I have been since I came, and have not had the stomach ake since Satterday which make me quite happy for it was very bad at all the balls but belive I have cured it by takeing a little vomit, but if it returns again will come home directly. We are to ride down as soon as the roads will let us which I hope will be soon. I beg my duty to my papa, and love to my sisters.

427 To Mary Collier, from Mary Collier, Battle Abbey, January 1744 [SAY 1828]

My sister Worge begs the favour of you to send three or four pickled herrings tomorrow by Palmer to make sollomun-gundy[1] for the ball, which is next Monday; and the captain talks of having his ball some time next week, and if he does, believe it will be a Friday. So hope you will be so good as to let us stay till Saturday, but we hope to see my papa at the market when we can settle that. Our ball at the abbey was very agreable. We broke up between five and six in the morning and I staid and lay with my sister Delia which was much more comfortable than mounting the hill after danceing. This evening we are all invited to spend at Miss Smith's, but the gentlemen are gone to Mr Nicholl's to dinner so believe we sha'nt have their company. I carnt say my sister Delia looks so well as she did when she came, but she has lost the pain in her stomach again and is, she says, very well now. We staid the evening a Tuesday at the abbey and my lady is prodigious civil to us. I have no time for anything farther now, being just going to Miss Smith's. Jenny joyns with me in duty to my papa and yourself.

1 Solomon-gundy; derivation of Salmagundi, a savoury dish composed of chopped meat, anchovies, eggs and onions with oil and flavourings (*OED*).

428 To John Collier, Hastings, from James Collier, Fig Tree Court, 19 January 1744 [SAY 1829]

The question yesterday in the House of Commons in relation to the continuing of the 16,000 Hanoverians in British pay for the current year passing in the affirmative by a majority of 45 has, I beleive, entirely put an end to any farther opposition this session.[1] Both parties in the House were equally certain of success, which occasioned an inconceivable impatience without doors for their rising. The House did not divide till between eleven and twelve in the evening, and then the numbers stood thus, for the motion 271, against 226, exclusive of the tellers on each side by which it appears that there were present 501 members. The debates on both sides were carried on with great warmth, and Mr Hans Stanley, member for St Albans, reflecting personally on the king by name, was called upon by Mr Winnington to repeat his words and would certainly have been sent to the Tower had not the Speaker interposed.[2] The opposition made yesterday sevenight to the maintaining of English troops in Flanders this year is universally blamed by the friends to the minority. The numbers then were, for 227, against 165.

I saw my uncle on Tuesday night, who acquainted me that he had received a letter from Mr Patrick the day before, mentioning your having a fit of the gout, the excessive pain attending which I hope is now entirely ceased. I had this morning sent me the second number of Mr Annesly's trial, etc., which shall be sent the first opportunity and some of the numbers of the *Collection of Voyages and Travels* shall accompany it.[3] Be pleased to give my duty to mama, and love to my sisters if returned from Battle.

1 Opposition split on the supply vote, 11 January 1744, in effect a motion to withdraw British troops from Flanders; court victory 227 to 165. Subsequent clash, 18 January 1744 on call to withdraw British funds from Hanoverian troops resulted in defeat for the opposition 271 to 226; this underlined the view that good oratory could alter the mood of the house (Owen 207-8; Egmont vol. 3, 283).

2 Sir Hans Sloane, MP for St Albans claimed, contrary to a rule of Parliament, that George II 'had a partiality for his electoral troops', for which the Speaker called him to order (Egmont vol. 3, 283 18 January 1744).

3 *A Collection of Voyages and Travels now first printed from original manuscripts*, 6 vols (London, 1732); *A New Collection of Voyages and Travels*, 19 parts (London, 1743-44). For James Annesley's case see Howell vols xvi, xvii.

429 To John Collier, Hastings, from James Collier, Fig Tree Court, 28 January 1744 [SAY 1830]

I mentioned in my last of the apprehensions I entertained of an entire stop being put to any farther opposition to the ministerial measures; but I find since my mistake, for when the report was made to the House of Commons, from the committee of the whole House, in relation to the Hanover troops, the numbers on the division in which committee I then gave you an account of, it was debated over again. And at the conclusion a motion [1] was made by Mr Pitt, that the debate should be adjourned till a farther day, which passed in the negative 266 against 178, and then the resolution of the committee was agreed to.[2] On Wednesday the treaty of Worms was taken into consideration by both Lords and Commons, and an address being proposed to his Majesty in both houses for him to lay before them the several instructions, memorials, etc., both before and after the conclusion of the treaty; it passed in the negative in both places,[3] the numbers in the Lords I have not been able to learn. But in the Commons the division was 207 against 149.

An estimate of the charges of the Hanoverian forces being laid before the House of Lords yesterday, a motion was made by the Lord Sandwich and seconded by the Lord Hervey, to address the king to discharge the aforesaid troops out of British pay. And after several lords speaking, the Lord Chancellor observed to the House that this motion was the same as was made on the 9th of December last, and consequently disagreable to the rules established by usage, viz that the same motion cannot be made if rejected the same sessions. After long debate on this subject, it being proposed by the Lord Gower to defer the consideration of it till next Fryday, and seconded by the Duke of Newcastle, only with an alteration of the day, viz next Tuesday, it was unanimously agreed to.[4] My uncle was yesterday morning seized with a fit of the gout, I went to see him this day, but I found him just out of bed after one o'clock, and afraid to stir out of his great armchair. I hope the potted char will prove as agreable as that of last year.

1 MS *being* struck through.

2 Opposition call for enquiry into George II's favouritism towards the Hanoverian troops, defeated 226 to 178 (Taylor & Jones 191).

3 Treaty of Worms, negotiated summer 1743, signed 2 September 1743; primary focus on the Italian states and Sardinia; by the 7th article Britain to maintain a fleet in the Mediterranean, and to act in concert with Sardinia and Maria Theresa; by the 8th article, Britain to pay subsidies to the king of Sardinia of £280,000 a year, every three months, in advance, starting 1 February 1742/3. Subsidies agreed by the Commons 167 to 125 (Williams 1966, 144; Rapin vol. 20, 641-5). John Fuller cast cannon for Maria Theresa and Sardinia (Crossley & Saville xxii, 769n, 777-80, 782-3, 792, 801-2).

4 House of Lords, 27 January 1744, motion against continuing pay for Hanoverian soldiers, moved by Lord Sandwich and the Duke of Marlborough, 'who has been at Dettingen and saw the scandalous behaviour of the Hanoverians'; motion defeated 86 to 41 (Taylor & Jones 67).

430 To John Collier, Hastings, from Henry Pelham, Arlington Street, 4th February 1744 [SAY 413]

I received your letter of the 31st of last month and am obliged to you for the trouble you have taken about Mr Payne's land. I am very willing to be a purchaser att any reasonable rate, but whatever may be thought I am not in circumstances to throw money away. A thousand pounds for twenty five pounds a year in land is a great deal to give and I cannot think of having a better rent than what is given att present, att least whilst old Chatfeild lives. 96[1] years' purchase att the present rent is a great price; that I am willing to give more I should think extravagant. I don't beleive Mr Fagg will come up to that; I must leave this affair to your conduct, I cannot think of going beyond £800. These times don't encourage a reasonable man to buy land, nor would I give near so much were it not for the proximity of the ground. I am sorry to hear you have the gout. I don't doubt of your care and judgement as to what is to be done at Herringales.

1 A thousand pounds for twenty five pounds rental is forty years purchase, which would be a high price for land in the early 1740s. The figure of 96 years purchase is probably a mistake and could be read as 36; £800 or 32 years purchase is closer to contemporary transactions.

431 To John Collier, Hastings, from James Collier, Fig Tree Court, 4 February 1744 [SAY 1831]

I mentioned in my last that an objection was made to the regularity of the motion, in relation to the Hanover troops, in the House of Lords yesterday sevenight, and that the consideration of it was adjourned till Tuesday; on which day the motion was altered and couched in the following words, viz 'that tis the resolution of this house, that the continuance of the 16,000 Hanoverians in British pay, is prejudicial to the true interest of his Majesty, useless to the common cause, and dangerous to the welfare and tranquillity of this nation'. This motion as the former was made by the Lord Sandwich, but then seconded by the Duke of Marlborough. After long debate it passed in the negative 86 against 41. In the House of Commons on Wednesday there was a division on the motion for adjourning the order of the day, viz for the House to resolve itself into a committee, to consider of ways and means for raising the supply granted to the king, yeas 146 noes 214, and on Thursday the House divided in relation to the giving of the King of Sardinia £20,000 in consequence of the treaty of Worms, 167 against 125.[1]

But as great a contest as hath hitherto been this sessions will be in a short time with regard to the laying an additional duty on sugar.[2] The sailing of the Brest squadron has at present entirely put a stop to the mentioning of the Hanoverians; persons of all parties are extreamly anxious to know whither they are bound, and indeed the ministry are put into some hurry, frequent consultations having been held since the advice.[3] For my part I expect to hear shortly the heralds proclaiming war against France, and what confirms me in it is the declaration of the Lord Carteret to the Lords on Tuesday last, who assured the House then that the French king's declaration of war against England was printing at the royal press in Paris. I shewed your letter to my uncle this afternoon, who told me he had wrote to you by the same post about receiving the money, etc. I will take care to get the things mentioned in your letter.

1 See [**429**] for subsidy to Sardinia.
2 Henry Pelham, 13 February 1744, moved in the Commons for 2/6d extra per cwt on imports of sugar, to raise £80,000 in the next financial year, sufficient to fund borrowing of £1.8 million at 3%. The Treasury and Customs thought the rise in consumption provided a reliable basis for borrowing. In the vote, Scottish MPs and the opposition combined to defeat Pelham, 176 to 88. As the government alternative was an impost on linen imports, which would damage relations with Russia and Maria Theresa, the Commons eventually settled on raising taxes on spirits (Dowell vol. 2, 113; Sheridan table 2.1, colonial sugar, imports, re-exports and retained imports).
3 The first reliable news of the sailing of the Brest fleet of 21 warships arrived in Whitehall on the evening of the 1st February, and was placed before the Privy Council the next day (Richmond vol. 2, 61-7).

432 To John Collier, Hastings, from James Collier, Fig Tree Court, 11 February 1744 [SAY 1832]

The petition of Mr Trevor complaining of an undue return for the borough of Denbigh, takes up at present almost the whole time of the House of Commons. Both sides are equally certain of success; the two divisions hitherto have been in favour of the sitting member, but the numbers as follows, viz on the first 177 against 174, on the second 175 against 174. This day Mr Chetwynd, who unfortunately killed his schoolfellow Mr Rickets, was had up to the King's bar, and pleading his Majesty's pardon prayed to be discharged.[1] The council against him were no less than six, viz Sir John Strange, Serjeant Wynne, Mr Lacy, Mr Morton, Mr Areskine, Mr Purcas, who all insisted upon it, that the prisoner agreable to the 3d of Henry VII cap 1st, should either be remanded back to prison, or to give bail for his appearance in case of an appeal; and by virtue of the 5th of William & Mary cap 13th to give security for his good behaviour for any term, not exceeding seven years. The whole court entirely agreed with his three councill, viz Mr Lloyd, Mr Legg, Mr Hume; that this case was not within the first mentioned Act of Parliament; and as to the finding of sureties as it lay in the discretion of the court, who were of an opinion that in this case none were wanting, he was imediately discharged. The Lord Chief Justice made a very handsome speech to Chetwynd, importing, that he hoped this would be a warning to him for the future not to give way to his passion. The term ends on Monday,[2] but as I shall attend the sittings after it, as I did those of the last, the horses need not come up till Tuesday or Wednesday sevenight. Be pleased to give my duty to mama and love to my sisters. The whig could not possibly be made by last Wednesday.

1 Crown v Chetwynd (*ER* vol. 21, 101-103).
2 Hilary law term, 23 January to 13 February 1744; Easter law term 11 April to 7 May.

433 To John Collier, Hastings, from James Collier, Fig Tree Court, 16 February 1744 [SAY 1833]

A message from the king was yesterday delivered to the House of Lords, signifying that the pretender's eldest son was now in France and that an invasion was intended, supported by the French fleet cruizing on the British coast, and desiring their imediate advice and assistance.[1] When the Lord Chancellor had read this message, the Duke of Marlborough rose up, and declared that he would spend the last drop of his blood in support of the present royal family and moved for an address to his Majesty to assure him that the Lords would stand by and support him and his family with their lives and fortunes. This motion was seconded by the Duke of Newcastle, and then the Lord Chesterfield proposed an amendment to the address importing that the entrance of the Brest squadron into the Channel was owing to the negligence and indolence of the Admiralty; but the Lord Londsdale getting up and addressing himself to the last mentioned Lord and telling him that now was a time for action and not for enquiry, and declaring that he entirely approved of the motion, the same was imediately unanimously agreed to by the House.

The Lords sent directly to the Commons, and in a manner somewhat particular, viz ordering the judges to go, acquainting them with their resolution on the message and desiring their concurrence. The same amendment as the Lord Chesterfield made was offered by Mr Waller in the Commons, and after a short debate, the question being put, the numbers were as follows, viz for 123 against 287, and then the address was unanimously agreed to. The king was extreamly pleased at the Duke of Marlborough's declaration, but more so at a letter he received from the Lord Stair on Tuesday night purporting that he had heard an invasion was intended by the French and offering his life and fortune in support of him if they were of any significancy. His Majesty imediately sent for him, and he, General Wade, Lord Cadogan, Lord Delawar are appointed generals to command the English army now at home in case of an invasion.[2]

The king certainly does not go abroad, and now tis universally agreed that the Lord Stair will have the command of the allied army in Flanders. The lord mayor, court of Aldermen and Common Council have this day, nem con, agreed to address his Majesty to make a tender of their lives and fortunes in support of him. Sir John Norris has absolutely orders to attack the French fleet, so that the news of an engagement is expected by tomorrow noon. Be pleased sir, to give my duty to mama and love to my sisters. The guards at St James's are doubled, as also at the Tower, and most of the troops at home arrived near London.

1 On 15th February 1744, the king informed both houses that the French king intended to invade England, with support from the Jacobite exiles, to place the pretender on the throne. An amendment to the loyal address, to examine the Admiralty, defeated 287 to 123 (Owen 213; *CJ* vol. 24, 568). The urgency of the situation is conveyed in McCann 194-8; and by Egmont vol. 3, 283 ff.

2 For the weakness of the garrison troops in England see Fortescue vol. 2, 103 ff.

434 To Mary Collier, Hastings, from Jane Collier, Hampstead, 22 February 1744 [SAY 1834]

I should have done myself the pleasure of writeing to you before this, but have been ill with a cold ever since I came from London, but am now much better for my governess has taken a great deall of care of me. My brother and Mr Green came to see me last Friday and they will come again this week. I hope you will come up to town soon. I have had my green gown turned and it looks very well. I had a letter from my sister Molly last week, wherein she gave me an account of Mr Hammond's going away with Whitfield and that Sir Thommas Webster's family are gone from Battell and that they were all very dolororous. Pray be pleased to give my duty to my papa and love to my sisters from your most dutyfull daughter. My governess and Miss Russell desire their compliments. I have began my chairs.

435 To John Collier, Hastings, from Sackville Bale, Whitehall, 25 February 1744 [SAY 104]

My lord duke sends his compliments to you and as he intends to fill up the vacant commissions in the cinque ports[1] he desires you will give him by the first opportunity the names of three gentlemen that are fit and willing to serve as captain, lieutenant and ensign in the company belonging to your port; and his grace likewise desires your recommendation of three proper persons for Winchelsea and three for Pevensey. In the year 1725 commissions were sent for Lewis Gilbert to be captain, Edward Hall lieutenant and Thomas Giles ensign at Hasting; and John Walsh, John Parnell and Thomas Jenkins at Winchelsea; and Edward Milward, William Richardson and John Kine for Pevensey. We don't know if any of the gentlemen above mentioned are now living. His grace will be glad to be informed if there are any arms, drums or colours belonging to the companies of those three places. We expect every minute to hear from Sir John Norris who passed by Dover at 10 o'clock yesterday morning; 15 sail of French ships lay off of Dimchurch at that time.

1 Cinque Ports militia consisted of captain, lieutenants, ensigns and serjeants and as many volunteers as each port could muster; they were stationed in the home port. Watch and ward were levied on Hastings townsfolk during this war (general quarter sessions, 17 July 1746). John Davey was arraigned for refusing to do duty of watch and ward in time of war, though discharged by proclamation, paying the court fees

(ESRO HAS CAA/5 fol.89r). For reference to the social and military aspects of the county militia see J R Western *The English Militia in the Eighteenth Century, the story of a political issue 1660-1802* (1965)).

436 To John Collier, Hastings, from Andrew Stone, Whitehall, 25 February 1744

[SAY 103]

My Lord Duke of Newcastle having received an account that the French squadron is gone westward and that Sir John Norris has followed them, his grace desires that you will employ some proper persons to keep a good look out upon the coast, and when they shall see either of those squadrons, or any part of them, that you will send immediate notice of it by express to my lord duke.

[*Endorsed*] Mr Stone's letter, and the express I sent to the Duke of Newcastle thereon the 26th at 10 in the evening.

437 To Duke of Newcastle, from John Collier, Hastings, 26 February 1744[1]

[SAY105]

15 sail of French men of war went by this [2] place about 4 or 5 leagues from the shore, the 22th instant, about 5 in the afternoon to the eastward, and the next day we heard they cast anchor in Romney Bay to the east of Dengeness Point, and continued there till Fryday afternoon, when a French ship that lay off [3] Dover, observing Sir John Norris coming out of the Downs beating up to the west, the French [4] ship beat up also that way, and as soon as she came in sight of the squadron under the Ness Point made signalls, and immediately the French admiral fired a gun and made several signalls, and they all got under sail before the evening and made westward, and Sir John Norris was seen coming that way at about 7 miles distant from them before night came on. There was a violent rain that evening and the wind changed [5] about 8 and blew very hard all night at about north east.

We neither saw or heard anything further till this afternoon about 4, [6] Sir John Norris [7] came off the sea to the westward of the town, and in about an hour and a half a gun was fired, and the fleet tacked about 5 leagues from the shore, and seemed to stand of, and his flag on the main top mast head was very plainly seen. There was 7 very large shipps, and in the whole about 20 sail, one large ship went by to the eastward, having lost her topmasts, and a ship about 50 guns with her, but before out of our sight. The last, with all the sail she could make, stood out to sea. One of the king's messengers arrived here this forenoon from Deal with dispatches for the admiral and, as we could give him no intelligence [8], proceeded [9] forthwith to Borne, etc. A good look out shall be kept, and if any of the [10] fleets are seen an imediate account shall be given by express. Just as I was making up this letter to send to your grace the king's messenger returned from the westward, and we thought it best to stay here this night, and a boat or vessell shall be got ready to carry him off if possible to the admiral very early in the morning, if anything can be seen of the squadron.

1 Penned at 10 p.m., and handwriting suggests in haste.
2 MS *town* struck through.
3 MS *Dunkirk* struck through.
4 MS *forthwith came away* struck through.
5 MS *in the evening* struck through.
6 MS *we saw* struck through.
7 MS *coming out* struck through.

8 MS *of the fleet here* struck through.
9 MS *towards* struck through.
10 MS *squadron* struck through.

438 To John Collier, Hastings, from William Cranston, [Johnson's Court], 27 March 1744 [SAY 789]

Yesterday's post brought me the £157 10s 0d bill from Lamb as you mentioned in yours. The same post also brought me a letter of attorney from Mr Holmes[1] impowering me to take a surrender of a copyhold estate in the mannor of Slindon[2] from Mary Phipps, widow, to the use of John Reynolds and his heires. As to the forme of the surrender, that I must have from you for I know no more of the matter than the man in the moon. I heartily wish the ladys a good journey. I could have wished that they had been here as today, for we have it just now very hott that we in our turn shall proclaim warr against France on Thursday, which cavalcade is well worth the seeing. I'm very glad to see in our papers of today from Dover that the famous Mr Pike & Co is at last borrowed. Your scituation as to soldiers is truly miserable but there's no help for it, better them than Frenchmen.

1 The Holmes family of Arundel were the family solicitors and manorial stewards for the Duke of Norfolk's estate at this time.
2 Slindon manor, West Sussex (Dunkin 1914-1915 vol. 2).

439 To John Collier, Hastings, from Henry Pelham, 29 March 1744 [SAY 417]

I received yours of the 19 instant, and am sorry to find the country in so bad a way, possibly the farmers may get by this declaration of war,[1] but the landlords I am afraid will suffer. The great assembling of troops at present has been on account of the late threatened invasion, a little time must clear up these affairs, and when the government is safe, you may be assured the people will be eased; in the meantime we must face it as well as we can. I entirely approve of every thing you have done in relation to the estate, it is pity that we are under a necessity of dunning the Duke of Newcastle's agents for the rent which was promised to be regularly paid. However, as it is, I think you should write Mr Waller word, that in case some orders are not given forthwith for the payment of what is due, I shall be necessitated to complain to my brother. I am glad you have ordered the remittance of £700 to Mr Hoare, for strange as it may seem to you, I can assure you I want money.

I received a letter from Mr Payne a few posts agoe, upon the affair of the purchase of his land in Laughton; I think I offered enough, but if it is your opinion it is worth what he asks, I would not lose it, tho I shall have difficulty in raising the money.[2] I desire you would get some meeting with him, and fix this price, on or off, I am not very sollicitous about it. Pray make my excuse for not writing to him and tell him, as I have the whole to you, I thought it was but troubling him for me to write. I desired Colonel Pelham to write to you, about your son's being a Commissioner in the present lottery, I wish it were in my power to serve him now but I am afraid I cannot. H.P.[3]

1 France declared war on England, 20 March 1744, and George II declared war 29 March 1744, with the king's speeech to Parliament on Tuesday 3 April 1744 (Egmont vol. 3, 293, 295; Bibliotheca Lindesiana vol. 8, 60).
2 Thomas Payne of Brighton, and his wife Hannah, conveyed to Henry Pelham in June 1744, Cooks farm in Laughton, 33 acres, for £950 (ESRO CHR 3/17/1-3).

3 This is probably 17 Geo II c. 18 1744 designed to raise £1.8 million by annuities and a lottery, the latter to raise £600,000; the draw started on 26 November 1744 (PGA 1744 379, Ewen 148-9).

440 To Mary Collier, at William Cranston's, Johnson's Court, from John Collier, Hastings, written 31 March, postmark 2 April 1744 [SAY 1835]

I received Jemmy's letter dated from Stonecrouch last night by the post, and by Morris a confirmation of geting there safe, through bad ways, and happily continuing so to Tunbridge. I am surprized Master Hayward did not meet you at the end of Swiftsden to carry you through the land. My brother Cruttenden did not come home with Morris and Coleman, stoping at Battell, but Jenny tells me he is just returned; she and Sally having been there this afternoon. I told Jenny to invite him and my sister and their daughter to dinner tomorrow, when we are to have the rump of beef, a pudding and two yellow fowles bought today at the door ready dressed.

The box and also Jemmy's are sent by the carrier, who promises they shall be delivered early Wednesday afternoon. I put your watch into yours in a little box, and there are, in a peice of paper, Sally's buckles to be changed away, the holding part must be of steel to make them of any service.[1] The watch wants cleaning and a fitter key. You'l consider whither necessary to wear to the play or out late in the evenings. I hope you'l think of the swelling in your neck and having the same taken out. Dr Russell, going up to the cave, told me there was not any the least danger, hazard or so much pain as cuting an issue.

Yesterday was quite dolorous, a long forenoon, and as I knew the roads must be bad, though said little about them and afraid of accidents. I went to the seaside after 5, met Lord Fitzwilliams and walked about an hour. Seems quite a sober, good natured man. Munday there is to be a draft of ten men of a company out of this regiment, so 100 in all, and the same out of every regiment in England, to go directly for Flanders. This is very far from being dissagreeable to the soldiers, or occasion any desertion, for there's more than 30 in each company have given in their names to be of the number, and some threaten to desert if they don't go, and I hear the like is at Rye in Lord Harry Beauclerk's regiment quartered there and in Romney Marsh, etc.

I hope, my dearest, you'l have good health and spirits in London and have pleasure in your journey, as also the girls, but think it necessary they are in some bounds about plays, etc., and not give too great a loose to them kind of pleasures, for that may in some measure determine me in any little matter of decorations, etc. I hope for an agreeable letter of your safe arrival in town from your brother or Jemmy for I don't expect any from you by this post. My service to my brother and all friends and respects to my daughters and Jemmy.

1 Tin, brass, copper, iron and steel household articles, including buckles of every description, were widely made by this time (P Mantoux *The Industrial Revolution in the Eighteenth Century* (rev. edn 1961) 274-5, 326-7).

441 To John Collier, Hastings, from James Collier, Fig Tree Court, 5 April 1744 [SAY 1836]

Being necessitated by reason of the fullness of the portmanteau to bring from Hasting a pair of baggs, I sent them down yesterday by the carrier, in one of which is inclosed no 5, which compleats the tryal between Mr Annesly and the Earl of Anglesey. My uncle, by standing two hours in Mr Isted's balcony on Saturday last to see the procession at the declaration of war, has got the gout and been confined within doors ever since our arrival; and indeed, the ladies have hardly stirred out, but Dely by an invitation yesterday from Miss Webster by letter dined this day in St James's Street.

The Earl of Barrymore was released on Saturday on giving bail for his appearance, himself being bound in £4000 and four other gentlemen in £1500 each, viz, Lord Granard, Lord Doneraile, Mr Crew, Mr Shuttleworth.[1] My Lord Ashburnham set out last week from Harwich in a common packet boat for Holland, from whence he intends to proceed through Switzerland to Turin. Sir Charles Goring, Mr Sergeson, Mr John Fuller, etc., dined yesterday with the Duke of Richmond and this day with the Duke of Newcastle. Sir Charles Hardy certainly carries instructions to Admiral Mathews to try Lestock by a court martial, whose conduct is universally blamed here.[2]

I find by Thomas that the mayor's horse has been stolen out of the stable and that he and Mr Wickins are to go tomorrow to Smithfield to see if they can find him there. My mother will write next post and desires with her bedgown Molly's straw coloured gown may be sent. My uncle will send tomorrow morning to Colonel Pelham about the payment of the money for the six lottery tickets. Be pleased to give my love to Jenny.

1 James Barry, 4th Earl of Barrymore, Tory and Jacobite plotter, at this time MP for Wigan, his efforts to support a French invasion led to house arrest 27 February 1744, released on bail at the end of March, whereon he continued his correspondence with the French and the pretender (*HofP 1715-54* vol. 2, 440-2).

2 As a result of the battle of Toulon, 10-13 February 1744, eleven captains and Vice-Admiral Richard Lestock were court martialled, Lestock was acquitted; Admiral Thomas Matthews, as the overall commander, was condemned by his court martial, 22 October 1746 (Richmond vol. 2, chs. 1, 2).

442 To Mary Collier, at William Cranston's, Johnson's Court, from John Collier, Hastings, 5 April 1744 [SAY 1837]

I have great satisfaction in receiving your letter, though am sorry the weather is so very bad and prevents your geting out. It has been the worst I can recollect at this season of the year. It has been so uncomfortable and lying hours awake. I have had the old repeating clock cleaned and fitted up yesterday for the first time. I beleive you have a loss in Tom Greene, but the weather has been so very dissagreeable that I think it's couragious to venture out. I hope your brother's confinement will not prove the gout. I have told Jenny about the child's stays, bedgown and handkerchief, so will be sent a Saturday, and to prevent mistakes, I have rehearsed it to Sarah.

I fully design to come to town and beleive about the 18th or 19th, but there's continual plague, etc., about the soldiers, and consulting about the trained bands. I live as merrily as I can with the little girls, though I think it sometimes very dolorous. The mayor has had his mare stoln which he had from me and sent out advertisements, and I have wrote for him about her to the Custom officers in Kent who well know the mare, and Mr Carswell lost a saddle and bridle the same night. I had Gower and his architect Farless dined with me yesterday, seeing them the night before as I came up town.

Henry Sargent came to me today about his son Captain Jack being taken up for piracy and robbery on the high seas and it was beleived he would be sent to Newgate. His intelligence is from a second or third hand, for no letter from him. It looks to me to be only a contrivance of his merchant and others, and don't beleive there's any real foundation. I told him if he wanted any assistance and twas by letter signifyed this post to Captain Jack, I would write to my brother Cranston that if he sent to him and desired assistance he would go and give me a state of the case, and that was all I could say. My sister Sally and Miss Cruttenden came up this afternoon and are now here. I have been in the parlour to drink tea and find my sisters not here.

443 To Mary Collier, at William Cranston's, Johnson's Court, from John Collier, Hastings, 7 April 1744 [SAY 1838]

Sally's stays, your bedgown, handkerchief and Molly's gown is send this day by the carrier, and to fill up the box, my wastcoat and some shirts, etc., and two books are put in; I am in hopes to be in town about Wednesday sennight. I was yesterday morning about half an hour after ten alarmed by Sally's coming into me, and saying her sister was not well; I went out and found Hariot in Sarah's arms and had been taken with a cold fit, telling Sarah her head acked and she was very cold. She had set with me in the parlour just before above half an hour and was very brisk and I was gone into my study; in less than half an hour, she begun to be hot, a great colour and very heavy eyed, and complained of a great pain in her right foot. She continued bad till about two, and when I asked her how she did always answered, pitt is bad Sir. It gradually went of, and in the evening was brisk and so went to bed, and the same this morning. Sally came in just before dinner yesterday and told me Hariot was going to have the tantrums again, Saint Anthony's fire, but no sign appeared. I beleive it was an ague and much expected a return today, and about the same hour she complained of a pain in her foot, that I expected a return but nothing has happened and she went to bed very well.

Jenny has wrote a letter to her sister Molly, but I know nothing of the contents, but presume the child's ilness is mentioned. I heard this afternoon that war was proclaimed today at Rye about 11; I think it's premature, for no order is come in the proper manner from the Lord Warden. I'le assure you when it's done here, we design it in a pompous manner. I saw one of the late Miss Dyne's tenants at Westfield today, who told me Mr Briscoe is to be down next Tuesday but did not know anything about her coming, only that she was in London. I know no particular occurrences; I presume, if any, Jenny has communicated.

This day the inclosed letter[1] was sent me from Borne. I should be glad to be in town when anything is done to your neck, but as Dr Russell assured me there was no danger and very little or no pain you'l consider whether it may not for sometime put a little confinement. I have asked Captain Hide to dine with me tomorrow and intend Mr Williams.

1 [no longer attached]

444 To John Collier, Hastings, from James Collier, Fig Tree Court, 10 April 1744 [SAY 1839]

This evening a very great meeting of the members of the House of Commons in the court interest is to be held at the Crown tavern in King Street; but why is not as yet known to the publick and consequently our attentions greatly raised.[1] Prosser last week bought for

Mr Worge and you an hogshead of cyder each and ordered them on board old Bossom, who I find is in hopes of being convoyed safe home. The price of the cyder is £8 7s per hogshead. Young Hargrave, who was supported by the Duke of Newcastle at Oxford, has lately left that place and is now in town, the duke being determined to get him a commission in the army. Mr Rochester told me yesterday that the Duke of Richmond informed him that, by some papers found on board Holman's ship when taken, several persons of Chichester not in the least suspected of smugling appeared to be the freighters of the vessel.

My mother was prevented from writing his morning by visiting Covent Garden and Ludgate Hill in order to buy a gown for Mrs Worge. This afternoon we are going to Covent Garden Theatre to see the play of the *Provoked Hushband*, in which Mr Sheridan is to perform the part of Lord Townly, who is lately come from Ireland and cried up by some as Mr Garrick's rival.[2] I am just now told that Captain Purvis of the Princessa has been acquitted by a court martial and that Mathews was determined to send Lestock home in irons. My mother and sisters desire to be remembred to you and Jenny.

1 Questions were raised in the Commons on this date as to whether the king should visit Europe or remain in England, and a supply to Maria Theresa of £40,000 was agreed should this be required in the recess.

2 Covent Garden Theatre, Tuesday 10 April, *The Provoked Husband*, by Colley Cibber, with Sir John Vanbrugh (Scouten Pt 3, vol. 2, 1736-47 1100).

445 To Mary Collier, at William Cranston's, Johnson's Court, from John Collier, Hastings, written 10-11 April, postmark 12 April 1744 [SAY 1840]

I am sorry to find by your letter of last post the situation you are in as to your brother's maid, etc., and I am really concerned at the dolorous weather that has attended you; but as my brother is again got on his feet and young Mr Greene in town to assist Jemmy, I presume they'l make it as agreeable as they can. I had a little conflict with myself whether to mention little Hariot's ague, but really thought, though I knew it would create an uneasiness to you, I should in faithfulness do it. Sunday morning by 8 she was again attacked and the paroxism and all the stages went through regularly and went of with a sweat about 4. I sent for Mr Thorpe who prepared tincture of the bark and it was given. I thought at first it would be impracticable for her to be prevayled on to take it, shewing the utmost aversion, but came on to be a little reconciled, and that night and the next day took the whole quantity so that we did not expect any more of it. But this morning before 8 it came on again and has been severe but went on regularly and went of at 4 with a sweat, and she has since taken the tincture again and very brisk and good company and make no doubt but she will be prevayled on to take it tomorrow to effect.

Sally was out of order last night going to bed and was restless and a little feverish all night and vomited once, flegm and yellow stuff, and has today twice brought up a pretty deal of flegm, but tonight is in better temper and chearful. I told Jenny last night at supper to invite her aunt and daughter to dinner this morning, but as the children were ill we sent down, and they came up in the forenoon, and stayed till between 7 and 8. Cozen Denham came hither yesterday about noon accidentally when the children were very brisk and well. If they or any one is out of order tomorrow, I'll send for her to come. It's settled that Sarah and Anne are to be in the room all night with them, and I think Sarah determines to set up and give little Hariot the bark. I did not go to Battell market, neither will a Fryday to Tenterden, where business is appointed, unless I find them perfectly well.

Thus I have wrote you from the bottom of my heart and really think no manner of danger. Molly Wimble supped with us.

Tuesday night, ten; I must write something about our declaration of war. I much approve of your taking advice about your neck and hope it has been done and the operation. Sunday afternoon, the king's order for declaring war against the French king, signifyed by the Lord Warden of the Cinque Ports, came hither by the proper officer. They proclaimed it at Rye a Saturday before their order arrived and we hear fired guns. This we thought not proper. At our club Sunday night resolved to do it yesterday at 2 in the afternoon, if a fine day, the soldiers to be under arms. Having setled preliminarys, met at 2; the captain and other officers had their corps, about 110 men, drawn up in the fish market, all clean and powdered, when we assembled sent down to the captain, and the march was to begin there to the old market. Mr Maule, 3 serjeants and 12 men, with the drums, came up with the ceremony of carrying the colours down then we had notice they were ready to attend us. We went down and saluted the officers, and after a little exercise proceeded; first the six dragoons mounted with their swords drawn rode before to clear the way. Then the mayor and jurats, followed by Captain Scot and the whole body, 2 drums in the front after one rank. The colours in the middle, carried by Maul, and ensign Thomas as senior ensign brought up the rear. Marched as slow as possible, and the soldiers drawn up at the old market, Patrick read the declaration with the usual previous proclamation, then 3 loud huzzas. Then proceeded in like manner to the fish market, read again, and ordered the soldiers drink, and adjourned to the Swan. A very fine afternoon, though foul weather and rain came on at 9. A prodigious number of people present.

Wednesday morning, 6. Hariot has taken the bark two or three times in the night and is very well and in good temper. Sally has sweat pretty much, has some candle two or three times and has layn very still from before 4 and they are now both asleep. I hope and beleive we shall have no return. Abundance of people have colds and agues by this inclement weather.

446 To Mary Collier, at William Cranston's, Johnson's Court, from John Collier, Hastings, postmark 14 April 1744 [SAY 1841]

I have much greater pleasure and satisfaction to write to you than I had last post, though I then thought the worst was over with the two children, but about two hours after my letter gone, Sally waked in a great agony, crying out for Sarah, who then stood by her, but it was some time before she was pacifyed and knew her; she was very feverish and restless and though she had sweat did not carry it of. I sent for Mr Thorpe again and we could hardly prevayl with her to take some cordial with powders; I suppose she sweat again but did not perceive any releif till between 4 and 5, when she waked and smiled and begin to talk and her eyes quicker; and I thank God has been better ever since, had a pretty good night, but has at times cryed out prodigiously with a pain in her right ear, and once about noon today for some time; it has been bathed with rum and easier tonight, and she has sung all her songs, and went to bed easy, and they are both comfortably asleep.

As soon as poor Sally awak'd yesterday morning in so melancholly a way I sent Coleman for my cosen Denham who forthwith came. Hariot took the bark, though made much stronger in a surprizing manner, and went to bed a little after 6 quite spent, having talked the whole day. She had then a little shivering and cold, and as soon as layn down was very hot, but it went of in about 3 hours and she was not at all restless afterwards, and rose this morning very brisk and so has continued, and has taken more bark four times in the day. Sally not having had a stool for some time took some manna about ten a clock, but it has not worked with her.[1] She was brought down to me in my study at 3 for two minutes. Thus I write you very minute particulars which will appear to anybody but ourselves very triffling, but I solemnly assure you I have not for a long, long time passed such a dismal day as yesterday. Preaching fore and afternoon and to a very crowded audience, but none from hence, but Patrick and Tom in the forenoon. About 1 Mrs Wicking came declaring she knew nothing of it before my sister Cruttenden, and after church Mrs Mead, Mrs Cant, etc.

As you did not write last post I was dissappointed, and told Jenny I would not write now but she should. She has expected every post a letter from Molly, who she says promised to write and joyned to that, as Jenny wrote to her a Saturday night, it's more than unhandsome and she was really like to cry. I much blame the girls, but as they are in a full swing of plays, etc., think nothing of her. Sarah and my cosen Denham lye in the room with the children tonight. The route came last night for all the soldiers except the old corps of Captain Scot, etc., to return to Canterbury, and they set out a Saturday morning. It's very inclinable to rain which brings on grass, etc., but dismal roads. I don't design to go to Tenterden tomorrow. I am glad to find my brother's gout is departed. Tell Jemmy I thank him for his politicks, but am not a little surprized at the price of cyder.

1 Manna juice, a gentle laxative, from the bark of the manna ash, and similar plants; grown for export in Sicily and Calabria (*OED*).

447 To Mary Collier, at William Cranston's, Johnson's Court, from John Collier, Hastings, 14 April 1744 [SAY 1842]

I have your letter by last post without date, as usual, and am much satisfyed that you have been with Mr Shipton, and with the opinion he gave you about your neck swelling, and assure you I shall be much easier on that account; and must confess it was the principal reason of my sort of silence about the London journey, though I hope all will end well. The little girles continue both well, Sally is very thin, and as deaf almost as a post, and won't bear Sarah a moment out of the room. Hariot, though she looks a little wan, is exceeding brisk and a comical girl, keeps on taking a little bark. Mr Williams dined with us yesterday, and in the afternoon the subdean wife and daughters drank tea and coffee. Mr Worge dined here today and has promised Jenny a visit from him and his wife. I hope and design to set out a Tuesday for London. The roads I hear are by the continual rains made much worse.

The soldiers marched this morning towards Canterbury but 3 companys of Lord Harry Beauclerk's, who have been at Portsmouth, supplyed their places from Bourne, and I suppose we shall have the pleasure of their company till Munday. They seem a parcel of dirty ill cloathed creatures to Flemings. Ours went to Battell this morning, those before at Borne likewise, and with their two companys before, they are in a fine condition. All these marches have been made without a due consideration to this country, as to quarters, lodgings, etc. The poor creatures, especially the women have a terrible time of it, not beds for a quarter. Mr Steevens told me today he sets out for London tomorrow, it's much he did not go before, Hide and Horn are much talked of, very seldom apart. Jenny is now come in from Mrs Carleton's and her aunt's and don't write this post. My cozen Denham is still here and unless she says something of going home, I shan't. We have her at breakfast, dinner and supper, but she and Sarah keep upstairs with the children. Saturday night past 9. I was up with the children when they went to bed, poor Sally, very fretfull. Mrs Wicking here this afternoon drinking tea.

448 To Mary Collier, from Margaret Ashburnham, Crowhurst, April 1744 [SAY 1843]

What there was left of the Irish poplin,[1] more then I had occasion for, I have realy disposed of to my Lady Poole which I am sorry for now I find you would have liked to have had it yourself. I am very glad to hear Miss Collier is better, but am sorry your two little ones are out of order; mine are all very well and have been so ever since we came hither. I am obliged to you for inquiring after them. Mr Ashburnham joyns with me in compliments to Mr Collier and Miss.

1 Silk or cotton warp, worsted weft, giving a cord like texture.

449 To John Collier, Hastings, from William Cranston, Johnson's Court, 17 May 1744 [SAY 790]

Upon rumaging into the Hastyng box and compareing books, etc., with former extracts, I find a great many chamberlains' books missing. When I looked into em at the port I found em compleat from 1609 to this time except 1634, 59, 75, 79 and 91, but I have not now but 24 in the whole. I well remember tyeing them up in bundles and placeing em to follow each other in point of time. I suppose Thayer may have misplaced em but hope none are missing and must beg to have em up by Wednesday's carrier together with the court books to this time; for I'm gott very deep into the affair[1] and am determined to have briefs ready to deliver to councill by the end of next week, in order in a few days after to have a consultation of what will be necessary to be farther done, especially in respect to living evidence.

All that I can at present think necessary will be to prove the lands to lye within the corporation and the payment of the taxes by the present defendant as well as by his father. There will, of course, be 20 other things to prove but these may be likely to be all within the knowledge of a person or two. I think, besides Mr Mead, you should pick out one or two of the oldest and most sensible of your people who have been chamberlains, always remembring that if any of your witnesses are freemen that they must be disfranchised. You may assure yourself that I won't lose sight of this affair but push on for tryall if upon consult it shall be thought practicable with success.

1 Hastings corporation v Sir Charles Eversfield of Grove, over non-payment by Eversfield of local taxes; original statement of Hastings' case heard before Lord Hardwicke 5 February 1741 (TNA C/1178/84). The debt owed by Sir Charles is recorded in the Hastings chamberlains' books [**452**].

450 To John Collier, Hastings, from James Collier, Fig Tree Court, 17 May 1744 [SAY 1844]

The mare that Thomas brought to town with him is sold this day for four guineas and an half. The buyer at first bid four and my man asked five, but my uncle proposing to split the difference, after two days' refusal, he has now complyed with it.

The generality of people are inclined to think, that the king will not go abroad this campain, and the prevailing report is that the differences between the Pelhams and Lord Carteret, etc., are through the king's means entirely adjusted.[1] Tar water at present engrosses almost the whole conversation of the town and is sold at all the polite coffee houses for 3 pence a glass.[2] Mr Pope, who is at present with Mr Sollicitor General in Lincoln's Inn Fields, is so dangerously ill, that the physicians have adjudged it impossible for him to recover.[3] The Lord Marchmont, one of his most intimate acquaintance, went the other day to visit him, but on seeing of him in such a condition, he burst out into tears and left the room immediately without speaking a word.[4] I suppose you are acquainted with the circumstances attending the marriage between Mr Fox and Lady Caroline Lenox, absolutely against the consent of the duke and duchess, and therefore all that I shall mention of it is that the Duke of Marlborough gave her away, for which he is universally blamed.[5] The ladies were extreamly unfortunate in their setting out, for the day after the Prince and Princess of Wales with their children were at Covent Garden theatre to see the play of Henry the eighth.[6] I hope they are all extreamly well after their journey.

1 George II returned on 15 November 1743, and the parliamentary session opened on 1 December 1743 and ran to 12 May 1744. Henry Pelham took the view that sound foreign affairs required each ally to provide for their own forces, and rely less on cash and supplies from England. Subsidies to Austria and Sardinia alone amounted to more than 1/- in the £ land tax. George II, with Hanover in mind, took a softer approach to chime with the sentiments of continental allies, and thus try to minimise the risk of defections to the neutral camp (Owen 223-5; Williams 1966 27-9).

2 Tar water, an infusion of tar and turpentine from fir trees in cold water, of wide repute as a medicine at this time. George Berkeley, Bishop of Cloyne, claimed in *Philosophical Reflections and Inquiries concerning the virtues of tar water*, that the infusion of tar water in the colonies and Ireland was a preservative against smallpox, and pointed out its use in problems of the blood, cutaneous eruptions, ulcers, ulceration of the bowels, consumptive cough, pleurisy, indigestion and asthma; by comparison with salivations and wood drinks the tar water was more effective.

3 Alexander Pope, the poet and author, 21 May 1688-30 May 1744, died of tuberculosis.

4 Hugh Hume Campbell, 3rd Earl of Marchmont (1708-1794).

5 Lady Caroline Lennox married Henry Fox MP, Windsor, 1741-46 and Secretary at War 1746-55, on 2 May 1744, against the wishes of her father, the Duke of Richmond (McCann 136-8).

6 Covent Garden Theatre, Thursday 10 May 1744, Henry VIII by Shakespeare; attended by Prince and Princess of Wales, Princes George and Edward and Lady Augusta. Wednesday 9 May 1744, *The Double Gallant*, by Colley Cibber, also *An old man taught wisdom, or the virgin unmasked* by Henry Fielding (Scouten Pt 3, vol. 2, 1736-47 1109).

451 To John Collier, Hastings, from James Collier, Fig Tree Court, 31 May 1744

[SAY 1845]

I am just come from the Apollo at the Devil tavern, and shall return as soon as this letter is finished, where a commission is held to enquire whether the son of the late Mr Barnesly is a lunatick or not. The father, whom possibly you may have heard of, was near 50 years bencher of the Inner Temple, and left behind him £1500 a year in land, and £50,000 in money.[1] The Lord Chief Justice Lee being a little indisposed, with a slight touch of the gout, for these three days we have had scarce any business done in the court of King's Bench. James Dougan who was to have been tryed on Monday last for high treason, will I beleive, be soon discharged out of Newgate, upwards of an hundred affidavits having been laid before the Attorney General from persons of great credit in Ireland who all positively swear that, at the time the witnesses against him alledge he was in Spain, they saw him at his native place in Ireland.[2]

The last express from General Wade has made it a little doubtfull, whether the king will not go abroad; for in his letter he mentioned that it was agreed in a council of war to march to the plain of Oudenard and give the French battle there; which, putting his Majesty in mind of the action in that place the last wars, it so fired him that he swore by God he would go and head the troops. The merchants are extreamly alert at the number and richness of the prizes lately taken, and highly applaud the conduct of the Lords of the Admiralty. On Saturday next the two Mr Greene's, my uncle, I, and the family of the Coles, together with Miss Green, are to go to Vauxhall; at present Ranelagh is the politest place, all the great people going there, and since the late robbery near Newington turnpike, nobody has ventured in a coach to the former place.

1 William Barnesley of Eardisley, Hertfordshire, who died April 1737.

2 James Dougan, alias O'Daniel, held in Chester gaol charged with being an officer of the king of Spain and for enlisting men in Spanish military service (*Calendar of Treasury Books and Papers 1742-5*, 13 Sept. 19 Oct. 1743, citing Treasury Board papers 312 no 14, and Letter Book vol. xx, p. 115).

452 To John Collier, Hastings, from William Cranston, Johnson's Court, 7 June 1744 [SAY 791]

Hastynge against Sir Charles Eversfield.[1] I am just now returned from a two hours consultation and by which my 3 gentry seemed to have read their breifs and fully to understand the point in question. It was generally agreed on that the custom insisted on was not repugnant to law but that, however, many difficultys arose from our own books against our recovery, but concluded that their was about an equall chance that we might as that we might not.

So farr we went on very well for I never expected more hopes than they gave me by this, many things were naturally spoke off and after considering the written evidence, that of viva voce came into question. And one point upon this head started me, vizt that as this annuall scott or fine was assessed, as well on inhabitants as forreigners, consequently no inhabitants could be evidence, at least as to many particulars which were necessary to be proved, though, as to some others they might, and distinctions were accordingly made, and in cases were they could not be witnesses, facts must be proved by persons not inhabitants and the reasons why inhabitants cannot be evidence is that in consequence of Sir Charles being charged or not, they will be more or less so.

This being the case and imagineing it must be with great difficulty if not impossible to gett proper evidence and at the least it could not be done by any means in proper time and as Saturday is the last day of countermanding without payment of cost, and laying all these difficultys before Sir John, etc., they thought it by all means the most advisable to give over thoughts of tryall it this next sittings, but advised a countermand and to take the long bow in getting proper evidence and so shall accordingly take their advice and counermand tomorrow or next day. I gave Sir John, Grayling's case and am promised it per next post. I am now just come to the Devill with Jemmy and Greene who join in compliments with.

1 The suit between Hastings corporation and Sir Charles Eversfield of Grove cost the corporation £68 12s 0d in 1742-3, and £59 12s 6d in 1743-4 [**457**].

453 To John Collier, Hastings, from James Collier, Fig Tree Court, 16 June 1744 [SAY 1846]

The term is at length ended without having any material business done, the greatest part of it occasioned by the absence of the Lord Chief Justice, who is now so perfectly recovered from his indispotion that he proposes attending the sittings in Westminster Hall on Munday. There are no less than three trials at bar granted in the subsequent term, the first obtained after long debate, is to be on Saturday 27 October, between the king and Roberts, to see if the defendant is capable of managing his affairs. He is at present in possession of an estate of £600 a year in Barbadoes, and of £200 per annum in Kent, and has another in reversion of £1000 per annum in Essex. The next trial is that of Dougan's on Saturday November 3rd, prayed for in behalf of his Majesty by the Attorney General to the surprize of most of the counsel, as imagining all proceedings against him were stayed. The counsel assigned by the court for the prisoner are, Serjeant Haywood and Mr Smith, who married a daughter of the late Sir Charles Farnaby. The third and last is between East and West of Bristol. The plaintiff as heir at law endeavouring to set aside a will under which the defendant claims.

Commodore Anson is certainly arrived at Spithead, and has brought in with him a very rich aquapulca ship. He narrowly missed the Brest squadron, and had it in his power to have taken two French Indiamen; but not knowing of the war, he permitted them to proceed quietly on their voyage. Our men of war still lying at Spithead, we look upon it as a thing certain here, that the reason of their not sailing to the westward is in order to be in readiness to convey his Majesty to Flanders.

Master Bossum called on me yesterday morning and seems to be in very high spirits, that his son has got a ship, which will be taken into the government's service.[1] On Wednesday I treated Jemmy and Jacky at Cuper's Gardens, who were both extreamly well pleased at the fireworks, and indeed the taste in which they are done is so curious and uncommon, that the gravest man in the Temple need not be ashamed to cross the water and see them. I have not been lately at Ranelagh, but am informed that the amphitheatre is crouded every night with the best of company. Mr Greene presses me very hard to go down with him for ten days, but I beleive I shall soon after the sittings are over come directly into Sussex.

1 James Bossom, master of the *James and Mary*, a tender on naval service; request for stores, 23 June 1744 (TNA ADM 106/987 fol. 288; ADM 106/1005 fol. 142).

454 To John Collier, Hastings, from Henry Pelham, 26 June 1744 [SAY 414]

I could not answer your letter the last post but hope it is not too late now, since we have agreed with Mr Payne I would have that affair finished as soon as can be conveniently and, upon notice from Mr Cranston, I will take care to have the money ready. I conclude you have looked into the title and are satisfyed with it; otherwise I am not over fond of purchasing; that little piece of land that John Vine mentions does lye convenient, and therefore that I agree to also; but would by no means have him engage me in things of this kind for the future. I have the pleasure to tell you the king has laid aside all thoughts of going abroad this year, which I doubt not will be a great satisfaction to his people.[1] The French are running post through Flanders; what our friends the Dutch mean by being so dilutory? I conclude Shoosmith will take this small parcel of land and add it to his farm. If so were, it would be right to pull down the house.

1 With the military situation facing Austria, the Dutch and Britain deteriorating, Henry Pelham persuaded the king to lay aside his usual idea of travelling to Hanover for a lengthy summer and autumn break.

455 To John Collier, Hastings, from William Cranston, [Johnson's Court], 26 June 1744

[SAY 792]

Your lottery tickett affair was taken care of and but just in time for I forgott it till the very last day but have taken care for the future. I was with Grayling[1] this morning and told him as from you that all should be done for him in your power, and that you took amiss his making use of your name and insisted on his mentioning it no more, which he has promised. I called this evening on Mr Simon for your cole, found him at home, but having mislaid his keys could not pay me, but promises to send it me tomorrow morning; and Tom Salmon was their with him and Grayling told me that he had before I came been with him which I now understand was by Simon's order.

I find that he must be tryed in Sussex, as the conviction and his being seen at large was both in that county. He tells me that he hears strong interest is making for him, and which, if true, he thinks had better be applyed to prevent a tryall than to gett a pardon after conviction, which to be sure he is in the right of. I by this post send a copy of Mrs Hicke's will and also a copy of the abstract of the title,[2] which I made yesterday, to Mr Bishop. I doubt there will be some demurr in the difference of describing the estate between the writings, and will the former calling it Craig Farm in the parish of Kerry and the latter near Newtown.[2] In other respects there is not fault to be found in the title.

1 The background to this smuggling episode is discussed in the Introduction and [**456 457**].
2 Elizabeth Hickes's will (TNA PROB 11/732/324 28 March 1744).
3 Newtown, Montgomeryshire.

456 To John Collier, Hastings, from Colonel James Pelham, St James's, 28 June 1744

[SAY 106]

I am favoured with yours and the enclosed petition which I have shewed to the Duke of Newcastle. Tis a great concern to me that I am obliged to acquaint you nothing can be done to releive the unhappy men, their returning from transportation is so notorious, and one being already in Newgate, tis impossible to attempt bringing them within the Act that pardons such as list for seamen; it never meant any that were transported.

John Hyde's warrant was signed today. Here is flying news of some good success in Italy and that Prince Charles had passed the Rhine but neither confirmed; the Dutch are certainly marching their troops to joyn ours in Flanders; tis hoped we shall then be strong enough to stop the French from taking any more towns. Part of the Dutch fleet will soon be at Spithead, so tis most likely our coast will be well guarded; there is no thoughts of suffering the French to fish upon our coast. His Majesty has declared he will not go abroad this sumer, which is very much approved of by all his best freinds. I am to make his grace's compliments to the mayor and gentlemen who signed the petition. He is very sory twas not in his power to be of any service to the persons they recommended.

457 To John Collier, [Hastings], from Francis Harbin, London, 30 June 1744
[SAY 107]

I was favoured with yours of the 26 instant and if not very much mistaken have had the honour of your acquaintance some years past, in company with the late unhappy Captain Saxby of the Grange, near Maidstone, I mean Town Malling in Kent, which made me presume to write in that frank manner I did. Mr Stone acknowledges the receipt of your letter in behalfe of Grayling and the other five unhappy persons, and Colonel Pelham hath read their petition and the recommendation under it to his grace of Newcastle, and told me that the petition had undone them, for that therein they had acknowledged to have been at large long before the proclamation of the 9th of May. And therefore it was his grace's opinion that they deserved no mercy and that he, Colonel Pelham, had writ so to Hastings by the last Thursday's post. I carried the petition from the Colonel to Mr Stone, who was at that time going to Clermont with his grace and had only time to say that Grayling must be tried, but that he should always have a great regard to Mr Collier, and the other gentlemen's recommendation.[1]

He returns to town on Munday next, and then shall know his sentiments on their case. I presume Monsieur Callio will be with you tomorrow and acquaint you with the steps taken here which I hope will prove effectual. There is a petition drawn up which was designed to be sent to Mr Callio this post which would have given reasons for their return, but as there is great reason to beleive that Grayling may be admitted to baile, it will be postponed untill next post. I observe your prudential hint and shall not mention you on any account. Please to present my service to Mr Callio and acquaint him that by the advice of counsel the above mentioned petition will not come to your hands till next post. The motion for bayling came on since the above written, which I did not expect, the court would not consent to it and therefore have sent a rough draft of the petition in his favour to Mr Callio and hope, sir, you'l excuse this trouble and give your generous assistance in Grayling's favour.

1 Andrew Stone MP for Hastings 1741-61, private secretary to the Duke of Newcastle 1732-4 and remained his grace's devoted servant throughout the years of these letters and beyond. Stone always went with his grace to Claremont at weekends and drafted many of the letters now in the Newcastle papers in the BL (*HofP 1715-54* 449-51).

458 To John Collier, Hastings, from James Collier, Fig Tree Court, 30 June 1744
[SAY 1847]

Inclosed is a paper published by authority this day at noon, which has occasioned great joy here as you will easily imagine by perusing the contents. I had determined to accompany Mr Green into Norfolk, but as you propose shortly going your survey, will wait on the ladies at Hasting and meet the horses at Tunbridge on Munday sevenight. The treasure on board the *Centurion*[1] is to be carried to the Bank in five and thirty carts in a triumphal manner through the principal streets on Wednesday next, and for that purpose orders are gone down to Portsmouth for the carriages to come over Fulham Bridge. The dispute between Admiral Anson and the Lords of the Admiralty is not finally adjusted, the former insisting that Captain Brett should have captain's pay from the time of his making him one, which their lordships at present refuse. Everybody seems extreamly well satisfied at the king's not being to go abroad this campain, for fear of any jealousies arising between the English and Hannoverians, who at present agree very well.

1 *Centurion* left for voyage to plunder Spanish possessions across the world, 18 September 1740; arrived Spithead, 15 June 1744; the £500,000 sterling, mostly silver, was deposited in government war stock (Anderson vol. 3, 229).

459 To Mary Collier, Hastings, from James Collier, Fig Tree Court, 7 July 1744

[SAY 1848]

As the Lord Chancellor on Tuesday next is to make a decree by which it will be determined how far the express words of a will can counteract the custom of the City of London with regard to the disposal of the personal estate,[1] I shall beg leave to stay and hear it and will be at Tunbridge on Wednesday evening but if any inconvenience will attend the sending of the horses that day, will hire horses at Tunbridge to proceed to Hasting. As to bridles and sadles, there is no occasion of sending any. We expect every day the news of a battle between Count Saxe and the allied army.

1 The Custom of the City of London for the distribution of the personal estate of the deceased is discussed in Richard Burn *The Ecclesiastical Law* 9th edition (1842) vol. 4, 570 ff.

460 To John Collier, Hastings, from H. Smith, Spithead, 25 July 1744

[SAY 1849]

I make buould by this to inform you the particarlors of the last cruice betwin the *Dreadnought* and us. On Thursday the 12th of July last, about 10 in the morning, we gave chase to 4 sail of ships, and at 4 decoverd 11 sail which afterwards we made to be the French fleet; att 5 the headmost of their fleet bore down upon us and engaged us about three quarters of an hour, but finding us too hott a ship for her she sheerd off from us and engaged the *Dreadnought*, as didd another off their fleet all thatt day, though as itt happened att too great a distance to doe her much damage. The next morning we pereived the French men att work on stages over their sides, which made us believe they had recevd some damgee from us; on Fryday, having a fine breeze of wind, we run the French fleet all out of sight; we had no men neither killd nor wounded on board us, nor aney of their shott struck us. The *Dreadnought* had one man had his ribb broke by a splinter, and several shott through her sails, butt didd not anyways disable any off her masts or riggin, otherways she must have been taken, their being their whole fleet consisting of 11 sail. After this, itt was a great happines we both saild well, otherways we must have fallen into their hands; we have taken this cruice 2 French bankers[1] which we burnt, and one ship which we sent in from the coast of Guinea, but don't know what value she may amount too. We are all in good health and spiret; I have no more news worth to inform you; so I shall conclude with my duty to yourself and my aunt and love to my couzens who I hope is well.

1 French bankers trawled the Newfoundland cod grounds, disrupted in the Anglo-French wars by British privateers and warships.

461 To John Collier, Hastings, from Mercy Grove, Burwash, 1 September 1744

[SAY 415]

When you was att Burwash I was a mentioning to you about my plate, but I not haveing the acount, my cousin John Weston had itt, and he hath sent itt me; their is one pairer of silver salts, one silver peper boox, one salver, one sauspan, six large spoons, one pap spone. I have wrote to my aunt about it but have had no answer from her about it, but shall be glad to hear what she said about it, but I hope she will part without farder trouble so hope she will deliver it to you and if you please to not part with to anybody but my cousin John Weston or me.

462 To John Collier, Hastings, from Edward Caryll,[1] Winchester, 13 September 1744 [SAY 619]

I should be glad if I could sell the advowsons of Ore and Winchelsea; my nephew has given me his leave; you know the value of them both per annum and I think that they are both rectorys. I do not remember any deed, nor Mr Eversfield does not remember any such thing; to be sure they will sell better jointly together; in case they could not be sold together, could not I sell Ore's advowsons? Sometimes it falls out so. I should be very much obliged to you to know from you what, how and what manner I can sell it and I will be intierely governd by you in this affair. As you are the only person I can rely on in these affaires, so I make bold to trouble you with them hoping that by your help and assistance I shall meet with my desire and long wished for effect.

I hear that Doctor Carleton is dead. Is there no fine there coming, and how many years quitrents is there due, and who is to pay his quitrent for the future? They are more quitrents due from the manner, I may presume. Please to get them all, and I will let you know, that perhaps you may hear of somebody coming this way. Winchester fair is very soon. I do assure you faithfully that the old woeman has a mind, I think, to live eternally.

1 For the Caryll family see T J McCann 'West Grinstead: A Centre of Catholicism in Sussex' 1671-1814 *SAC* 124, Caffyn 263-4, Ford Appendix 5 'Returns of Catholic Recusants' 1727.

463 To Mary Collier, [Hastings] from John Collier, Dartford c. 4 October 1744 [SAY 2156]

My Dearest, I got here last night and am now setting out for Rochester, I found the roads exceeding bad, for I made it almost dark, a Thursday to Stonecrouch, though I made no stay but just 3 minnetts at Mrs Hickes's. My Fryday's journey to Tunbridge Wells, which is almost a desart, and from thence to Tunbridge town was for the badness of the ways worse than to Stonecrouch. Yesterday I came to Se'nnock from whence will be sent my thick boots and great coat by the carrier. I hope this will find you and all the family very well and cannot help wishing myself with you. As I dined at Sen'nock Mr Roffe came to me by accident and we drank to all friends at Hasting.

I forgot to give my brother the sessions book, but it lyes behind the door in Patrick's room, the sessions is the 4th of October[1], I know of no business, but he will be so kind as to attend and at the court day. As there is no cause in court, it's only to take an account of the jurats' names that be in the Court hall. I have not heard one word of news worth communicating and really was not able to get any at the Wells. Of the few remaining company, three coaches went through Tunbridge yesterday before I set out from thence. I hope and expect a letter to Rochester from you or Jemmy, to hear from you is what is the greatest satisfaction I can possibly receive in my absence from you. My service to my brother and sister and Mr Green and love to all the remainder concludes this epistle, I am my Dear, most faithfully yours.

1 Hastings General Hundred court and Quarter Sessions, 4 October 1744, (ESRO HAS CAA/5).

464 To John Collier, Hastings, from William Cranston, [Johnson's Court], 18 October 1744 [SAY 793]

We compassed no 4 soon after 3 after a pleasant morning's ride, but cannot say so much of yesterday's for so much dirt and bad roads I never mett with before. I called Morlands, and was freighted from thence with compliments from the toast and Miss Frewen to the young ladys at the port. Having time, I made out and send you your 2 writts. Row called here this minute and tells me that the old Dutchess of Marlborough and Countess of Granvill both died this morning, and that there is all the circumstances imaginable to believe that the *Victory* and every soul in her, about 1500, are gone to the bottom.[1] A 1000 thanks for your past favours. Looking over some of my letters I found your inclosed one and if it does not concern you I know not who it does. As to the hare mentioned in it, it came on Monday and my virgin feasted on it today for it seems twould keep no longer.

1 Sir John Balchem, admiral in charge of blockade of Cadiz, sailed from thence for Spithead with his Dutch-English squadron; overnight 4 October the *Victory* sank. It was for long thought she struck Casquets reef off Guernsey but the wreck has now been probably located 50 miles south east of Plymouth; none of the 1100 aboard were found alive (Richmond vol. 2, 113).

465 To John Collier, Hastings, from Samuel Burt, Newcastle House, 23 October 1744 [SAY 108]

My lord duke ordered me to desire you to be so good as to act as usual on the king's birthday at Hasting. I heartily wish you joy of the wedding we have lately had; the new married couple are now at dinner here with my lord duke. I return you my most humble thanks for your civilitys to us when we were last at Hasting and should have been very happy if our affairs would have permitted us to have staid longer with you.

Memorandum [by John Collier]: December the 7th, wrote to Mr Burt and sent account of money due to me as in pocket book, which vide, ballance £60 6s 6d. I also mentioned the money due to me about the Admiralty, being £203 13s 4d.

466 To John Collier, Hastings, from James Collier, Fig Tree Court, 6 November 1744 [SAY 1850]

Last Saturday being the customary day for nominating persons qualified to be pricked for sheriffs, I went into the court of Exchequer, on purpose to see Mr Pelham in his robes, who attended as Chancellor for the first time, and had the honour of a bow from him when on the bench. On looking over Mr Chambers's paper, I find that if any objection had been made to any of the gentlemen proposed for the county of Sussex, Mr Sivier of Bodiham would have been in the list.

The weather on Fryday morning being extreamly disagreable, I did not attend Mr Greene as I had determined and returning from seeing him take horse, I accidentally met with Mr Coppard on Ludgate Hill, whom I took with me here and gave him two dishes of chocolate with which he seemed very well pleased. The ministers have frequent consultations about raising the supplies for the ensueing year but hitherto have been very secret in what manner they are to levied, though most people think that the additional duty on sugar, proposed last year and afterwards dropped, must be laid this.[1]

Tis generally reckoned this will be warmest sessions ever known, people talking very freely in all publick places about the present state of affairs;[2] and if the 16,000 Hanoverians should be under a necessity, which appears unavoidable, of marching out of Flanders into Westphalia in order to protect the Electorate, it will be absolutely impossible ever to have those troops in British pay again. One motion already agreed on is to address the king to know why the Duke of Aremberg was appointed commander in chief of the allied army.[3] The officers returned from abroad speaking very disrespectfully of the duke and almost accusing him of holding a correspondence with Count Saxe in order to preserve his estate in the Low Countries from being plundered; and also declaring that if Wade's councills had prevailed many signal advantages would have been gained over the French this last campaign. The Lord Granville's only son, now Lord Carteret, is now confined, having lately betrayed great symptoms of lunacy.

I have sent this evening the abstract and warrants together with some things from my uncle to Mr Gyles, and this evening I saw a letter from Mr Dunster by which I find the pots sent me in the summer had moor game in them, killed by himself near Rochdale in Lancashire.

1 Sugar, specified in the Navigation Acts as an enumerated plantation commodity, was required to be landed first in Britain from the colonies in order to pay duty, only then might the sugar be exported. The French and Portuguese were more efficient at producing sugar, and their merchants could export anywhere, so their prices undercut British sugar. By 12 Geo. II c.1739, British-owned ships, built and crewed according to the Navigation Acts, could henceforth ship enumerated commodities direct to foreign ports south of Cape Finisterre (Anderson vol. 3, 223).

2 For Newcastle, Richmond, Henry Pelham and senior members of the government, three significant questions required settlement: (i) the removal of Lord Carteret, who resigned 24 November 1744; (ii) after the caution of the summer campaign, the Dutch and Austrians needed to be convinced of a concerted effort in Flanders; (iii) settling the costs of the war for each ally, including the contribution from Hanover and in support thereof from the government. This last was settled by raising the British subvention to Maria Theresa, who took over payment of the Hanoverian troops on the understanding these regiments remained in Flanders; agreed by Parliament 18 February 1745 (McCann 236-8; Owen 252-4). Lord Hardwicke's *Reflections upon the Changes made in 1744*, considers the strengths of government policy.

3 Leopold Philippe d'Arenberg, 4th Duke of Arenberg (1690-1754), Austrian general and diplomat whose efforts were crucial to holding together the alliance of Austria, Britain, Hanover and the Netherlands during the war of the Austrian succession.

467 To John Collier, Hastings, from William Cranston, Johnson's Court, 10 November 1744 [SAY 794]

Wednesday's post brought me a letter from Mr Payne informing me of his having your note for £465 and that he had drawn on me 5 bills amounting in the whole to £165 and that as for the remaining £300 he desired to be paid in the country as soon as possible, so that as to his drafts I shall now pay as they come and the other you'll take care of. Besides the 2 drafts of £50 and £36 15s 1½d to Mr Worge which you mention in yours of today, I yesterday paid a note of £100 dated the 27 October and which I don't recollect you have in any of yours taken notice of. Though I have not at present any cole of the subdean's in my hands yet have it in my power whenever I get abroad, but in the interim a little advance would be very acceptable; therefore if to the £4 you would add £16 or £20 more, as he pleases, you would very much oblige us both and when I know the sume will give you creditt for it in the account between us.

I've been severely handled since my last, having the gout in both toes, both knees and one ancle, and thank God, much better and hope to gett into the dining room tomorrow and downstairs on Monday. These frequent and more sensible attacks make me determined to alter my diet for the future, and to leave off all salt provision, meat nor wine intirely I won't pretend to attempt, but should think of abstaining from all salt and high seasoned victualls may be of service.

468 To John Collier, Hastings, from James Collier, Fig Tree Court, 20 November 1744 [SAY 1851]

Last Wednesday morning I was extreamly surprized at an unexpected visit from Captain Murray,[1] who came to town the day before. He breakfasted here, and as we were afterwards walking in the park we accidentally met with Mr Cowssmaker, who having before invited Mr Randoll, Mr Shadwell, and some other gentlemen to spend that evening with him, asked us also; whither we repaired about seven, played at cards till ten, at which time we sat down to an elegant supper, and parted about twelve. I have seen the captain since and find that at present he has thoughts of going into Scotland. Lord Granville's party being the minority on Sunday last in the Cabinet Council on a division after a long and warm debate, his lordship at last finds himself obliged to resign shortly; and as neither he or his countess were at the Prince of Wales's court yesterday, some people are induced to think he has done it already.

The two persons of distinction mentioned in the Daily Advertiser of this day to have fought a duel in Hyde Park last week were General Oglethorpe and Colonel Van der Dussen, on account of the latter's ridiculing his conduct at the siege of St Augustine.[2] They had fought a considerable time before they were parted and Oglethorpe narrowly escaped being killed, receiving his antagonist's sword along his breast and under his left arm. The Lord Chancellor has not been able to give his attendance in Westminster Hall these two days occasioned by a violent cold, and of consequence but little business done in that court, and in ours indeed but little this term. I have got some francks from Colonel Pelham and given my uncle a dozen, and will send down some tomorrow along with my sister's earings, etc., a set of which would have been sent last week, had not Captain Murray, on my shewing them to him, declared my sister chose blue preferable to any other. The earings and cross cost £1 6s 0d, half of which I paid and the remainder is charged in Mrs Nouns' inclosed bill, which my uncle gave me to to send down. Mr Hill is now in town and looks very hearty. He complains of Wade's being outvoted in the councils of war.

1 Captain, later General, James Murray.

2 For a discussion of duelling amongst the European armed forces see V Kiernan *The Duel in European History* (1988).

469 To John Collier, Hastings, from Elizabeth Pelham, Lewes[1] 24 November 1744 [SAY 416]

I hope by this time Mr Pelham's tennants may have paid some rent to you or that it will not be long now before they do. When you have any money for us I desire you will return it to Messrs Hoare's in Fleet Street or send it to me as shall be most convenient for you to do. I desire you will please to consider what gratuity you would have for the trouble you are at for us. I am sencible that our affairs being under your direction may be of great service to us.

1 Elizabeth, wife of Thomas Pelham of Lewes (*HofP 1715-54* vol. 2, 333).

470 To John Collier, Hastings, from James Collier, Fig Tree Court, 8 December 1744 [SAY 1852]

The many different changes and alterations publickly talked of, have had such an effect on the members of the House of Commons, that few of them, though by far the greatest part in town, have attended, as you'll easily perceive by the subsequent numbers in a division last night. A motion was made by Mr Archer, and seconded by Mr Viner, that all persons who had places or pensions should pay 8s in the pound land tax, which passed in the negative, 95 against 53. The report that prevails at present is, that the Duke of Bedford is to have a blue ribbon, and to be made first Commissioner of the Admiralty, Lord Gower, Lord Privy Seal, the Earl of Aylesbury to be made a duke, Sir Watkins Williams Wynne to be created a peer, Mr Pit to succeed Sir William Yonge as Secretary at War, Mr Waller to be made cofferer, Vernon, Anson and some of the Granvilles to be in the Admiralty.[1]

Colonel Pelham sent here yesterday for an impression of your crest to be put on a four wheel chaise, which I accordingly sent by his servant. I imagine by this time you are no stranger to a verdict's being given against Mr Whitfield in the court of Exchequer I attended the greatest part of the trial, and was exceedingly sorry to find that the defendant had no great occasion to go to Ireland for witnesses. I was also present at Pigram's affair on Saturday, and the shuffling of Baily and Taught had such an imediate effect on the jury, that they gave no credit in the least to their testimony.[2] In Whitfield's affair one point was reserved which will be of no service to him, as the Lord Chief Baron was so clear in his opinion against him, and that was, as it was confessed on the part of the crown that the wines seized had been regularly entred and paid the duty; the onus probandi did lye on the Attorney General to satisfye the jury that the wines were Spanish, whereas in this case the defendant at first setting out was called on to prove the negative, id est, by giving an account from whence they came. Mr Wicker was I beleive married to Miss Hooker this week. Mrs Isted dyed this afternoon about half an hour after one. I sent down by my uncle Cruttenden three pound of chocolate.

1 The new administration was stronger in Parliament, and closely attuned to the needs of war and the organisation of administration and finance. Bedford was now 1st Lord of the Admiralty, Gower returned as Lord Privy Seal; George II blocked elevation of William Pitt to be Secretary at War, and so Sir William Yonge remained in place (Owen 244-9).

2 For reference to this case, Pigram v Betts and other smugglers, conducted by the Attorney General, see TNA CUST 148/12; SP 36/63 and **[489]** [**517**].

471 To Henry Simon, Solicitor for Bonds and Criminal Prosecutions, Board of Customs from John Collier, Hastings, 11 December 1744[1]

The smuglers are got to an amazing height on the Kentish and Sussex coasts that it has for some time become a very serious thing and highly worthy the consideration of the senate, in regard to the vast quantitys of goods clandestinely imported, and in a triumphant manner, and the insults, menaces and abuses given not only to the officers of the revenue but to any other persons that offer to speak against their detestable practices. The civil magistrates fully decline putting the laws in execution against them. In September last I had a great deal of discourse with the Chancellor of the Exchequer on the situation thereof. As to Macdonald's affair, I would not for double the money his being apprehended has cost the government ... be so much concerned in such another affair.[2]

As the duty required by the post I have the honour to serve the government in is in Kent, I shall perform the same to the utmost of my power, but as I advance in years and often attacked by the gout and other disorders, and having for some years quitted Westminster Hall and the assizes and sessions, except attending crown business at assizes, etc., and joyned thereto the audacious insolence of the smuglers, I do not think of being concerned for the future in any prosecutions, and herein I have the advice and approbation, inter nos, of my great friends. I shall never cease to acknowledge my obligations to you and give the utmost intelligence I can to the Board and to the secretarys and all my assistance for the service of the revenue.

1 The text of this letter is from Sayer vol. 1, 262-4; C Winslow in Hay (et al.) refers to this letter.
2 The case of Macdonald the smuggler is referred to in TNA CUST 148/12 f. 659-661.

472 To John Collier, Hastings, from William Cranston, [Johnson's Court], 18 December 1744 [SAY 795]

I thank my starrs I've once more gott the use of my sword arm, though tis but very so so, insomuch that the inclosed was too much for my own act and deed. Being obliged to get out yesterday evening I searched your ticketts and found 11 and 13 blanks, the other 4 in the wheel. I also at that same time took your King's Bench money. Cossum v Sutton, I have delivered a declaration. If you think proper to proceed, defendant will find himself mistaken as to his not being to be taken again per plaintiff. The jayl fees I know nothing about. The brawn is arrived and after the usuall tribute I shall dispatch the remainder by toomorrow's carrier.

473 To John Collier, Hastings, from William Cranston, [Johnson's Court], 22 December 1744 [SAY 796]

The next morning after I sent you the account I looked to see for the ballance and I made it to be due to you £411 15s 0d which is one farthing more than yours and which I suppose, to make even money, I might throw into the bargain. I've just now compared what you sent me today with my books and every item exactly agrees. I can assure you the affair of the shoemaker is strictly honest, for I would have gott that bill as well as my own before I set out for Sussex but could gett neither till since my return.

When I sent the brawn to the carrier on Wednesday I bid James ask Guy whether he came up again on that day sennight. He at first said not till Thursday, but upon his asking James the reason of the inquiry and James telling him twas because I should send a lamb by him to you as usuall, he then said he would be up on Wednesday and I shall accordingly be ready with it for that day; but yours of today makes me doubt least James should be mistaken, but upon calling him this instant he perseveres that Guy promised to be up on Wednesday. Numberless changes amongst the grandees yesterday, an account of all which I suppose you'll have per this night's Gazett. Howell is the stable keeper and to debit £2 2s 0d for housekeeping and credit £4 for horseflesh.

474 To John Collier, Hastings, from William Cranston, [Johnson's Court], 27 December 1744 [SAY 797]

Your load of provender came safe yesterday for which you have the hearty thanks both of young and old. We shall strongly attack too morrow. When I saw the Gazett Sunday morning, and no changes in it, was very sorry that I did not write an account of em, but then the colonel came into my head, and took it for granted that he would be with the club that night and of course have a full account and consequently communicate, but his having no intelligence is very marvellous. I don't find but that everybody is extreamly well pleased with the alteration, and our grace with his brother seem to be in high esteem with the people as they are looked upon to be the chief instruments of it and Englishmen to all intents and purposes, for there it is apprehended has been the main struggle. I imagine this will find you at some of your meetings, if so and you should thereopen this, my respects to present with the compliments of the season from your and their most humble servant W.C. I beleive it may be depended upon that Lord Chesterfield goes to Holland next week, and that great discoverys are made from the papers found with Belleisle's brother, the former of whom tis said is on his journey hither.

475 To John Collier, Hastings, from James Collier, Fig Tree Court, 3 January 1745 [SAY 1853]

The storm raised by the Lord Granville's measures is at length appeased by the alterations, so often publickly talked of, having been ascertained by the Gazettes; and yet the coffee house politicians, since the changes in the ministry, have almost, nay altogether, distrusted the present set, by hoping that every member of the House of Commons will attend for the remaining part of the sessions for fear of the new placemen imposing on the nation. The news of the day is that Lord Baltimore has resigned, because he was not named in the commission before Lord Vere Beauclerc, and that Mr Philipson is to succeed him. The Prince of Wales has turned out Lord Halifax without admitting him to an audience on account of his accepting of the place of master of the king's buckhounds without acquainting his highness beforehand, and has appointed the Earl of Inchiquin in his room. He is also very angry with Mr Littleton and has given the secretrary's place to Mr Drax, father of the Countess of Berkeley.[1]

Last Saturday I had such a violent tooth-ack attended with a prodigious swelled face that in the evening I went to Mr Rutter's, who not being at home, Mr Greene, his cooper, at once drew out the tooth in my upper jaw which gave me such uneasiness at Hastings; the tooth having three fangs was so riveted in the socket and the gums that I was obliged to have Mr Greene attend me three times on Sunday. The swelling in the cheek began to abate on Tuesday and is now entirely gone.

The lottery ended this day and attended with the like circumstance at the conclusion as last year; only with this difference, that, as then a blank was found in one wheel without a number to answer it (though found afterwards at Whitehall), now a twenty pound was found in box B without any number in box A. Upon searching out of your six tickets, four are blanks and two twenty pounds. Lestock is ordered to prepare for his tryal which will be in three weeks time; Matthews has been busily employed in making interest to succeed Lord Mansel in Glamorganshire, and in the opinion of the town he will carry it against Sir Charles Tynte.[2] The admiral sets up in the court interest, the other in the country. When the publick begin to talk more fully of the transactions of the new ministry I shall not fail to communicate their observations.

1 Lord Lyttleton, private secretary to the Prince of Wales, removed after taking a place as junior Treasury Lord; replaced by Henry Drax of Charborough in Dorset, whose daughter married Augustus 4th Earl of Berkeley. Lord Halifax removed as Lord of the Bedchamber to the Prince, a Colonel during the rebellion, and Lieutenant General, 1759. For reference to the re-organisation of the government see Owen 250-1.

2 Sir Charles Kemeys Tynte, Tory, defeated by Admiral Mathews in the Glamorgan county by-election, January 1746.

476 To John Collier, Hastings, from William Cranston, [Johnson's Court], 15 January 174 [SAY 798]

Your £47 10s 0d bank note came safe to hand. I can't help wishing in opposition to yours about the affair of your coming to town. My uncle Francis has desired me to advance him Mrs Platt's £7 14s 0d, which I have accordingly done and given you creditt for it. I am sorry to have such an account as you give of my eldest neice hope home and a quiet life free from the hurry and fatigue of balls, etc., may be of service to her. The inclosed which should have gone per last but forgott, you'll please to give and forward as directed.

477 To John Collier, Hastings, from James Collier, Fig Tree Court, 17 January 1745 [SAY 1854]

Since my last, the conversation on the late changes has been dropped. Entirely dropped, I cannot say, since some shallow politicians have asserted in all the publick coffee houses that the differences between the new comers in, and the Pelhams, are so great, that the former will surrender their posts very soon. The paper intituled *Old England, or, Constitutional Journal*, gave us to understand last Saturday, that he would lay down his paper, as having got a ministry that would act agreable to his principles, the meaning of which is, that the Duke of Bedford has procured a pension for Mr Guthrie and Mr Ralph, the two principal persons concerned in the journal.[1]

The Parliament met on Thursday, agreable to their adjourment, and were hardly able to make an house till Tuesday, the day of the call, when but few, considering the circumstances of that day, made their appearance, as conscious that the call would be put of. Sir John Philips one of the new Commissioners for Trade, made a motion just at the rising of the house, that the 27th day of February should be appointed for the hearing of the merits of Mr Lloyd's petition, against Mr Pryse the sitting member for the town of Cardigan; which being opposed by Mr Pelham, after some debate it passed in the negative 160 against 125.[2] Yesterday more members attended, and when the house resolved itself into a committee, about the number of troops that were to be employed in Flanders for the current year, a motion was made that Mr Fane should leave the chair, which passed in the negative 238 against 113,[3] and then the house came to several resolutions, the particulars of which I have not been able to learn.

As the change of men in the ministry always produces some verses on the occasion, I inclosed send you two pamphlets on the alterations, the only ones hitherto published, and though the performances are not extraordinary in their kind, yet imagine you would be glad to see everything that is wrote on this occasion. If Dr Thorpe's malicious sneers and envious insinuations have not been prevented by the just chastisement from Captain Murray, I hope it will be in my power to make him hold his tongue. Be pleased, sir, to give my duty to mama and love to my sisters.

1 William Guthrie and James Ralph, joint editors of *Old England, or, the Constitutional Journal* first issue in 1743, supported and part funded by the Earl of Chesterfield.

2 Cardigan borough election 29 May 1741, Thomas Pryse, Tory, 1034, Richard Lloyd 697; the motion to remove Thomas Pryse was defeated 160 to 125. On 20 March 1746, John Symmons, Tory, returned, defeating Walter Lloyd (*HofP 1715-54* vol. 1, 374, vol. 2, 221-2).

3 On 16 January with criticism of the Ordnance estimates in the House, the procedure for the estimates was put to a vote, and defeated 238 to 113 (Owen 251-2).

478 To Mary Collier, Hastings, from John Collier, Johnson's Court, 22 January 1745 [SAY 1855]

I thank God I got safe to town today between one and two, had yesterday exceeding bad roads, and hardly patience to ride them, however, I got to Sennock, and from thence came a horseback to Bromley, and there took a post chaize, returning Peter back with the horses, and hope he will be with you before this letter. When I came to Johnson's Court was surprized to find my brother was again attacked with the gout and confined, though able to hobble about house. It's really a melancholly thing, though he is very cheary. His maid is confined to her bed, so James is cook and everything, but I find there is to be another come this evening, during the maid's ilness. The two boys went to school last Thursday. It's now past six and I have not seen my son I stayed till now in expectation of seeing him and having some intelligence but must write without.

I find old Mr Green is in town, but far from being well; the son is in Norfolk, and has not been up this winter and I fancy settles there. I saw Mr Rowe who looks very thin but is got about again. I found by my brother at dinner that Jemmy acquainted him of Mr Cummings being in town, and had called at his chambers but not seen him. We had a great deal of rain at Sennock last night, but it turned to a frost, made it a little slippery, but nothing comparable to what was yesterday, for I really had hardly resolution to keep on.

I was surprized at Stonecrouch to find that Mr Langton and his wife lay there a Saturday night in their way to Battell, with a sick child, carried in a little cradle by Mr Langton himself on a male pilion before him. It was a prodigious undertaking, and I think the greatest hazard, and more safety must have been for two persons to have taken turns to carry it on foot, or else by poles have fastned the cradle to be carried between them, but as I heard nothing of them on the road, presume they met with no disaster, which I look upon to be providential. I am with respects to all friends, my love to all the girls, my dear creature. Jemmy is just come in before I seal my letter is very well and sends duty and love.

479 To Mary Collier, Hastings, from John Collier, [Johnson's Court], 24 January 1745[1] [SAY 1856]

As I have no letter from you, satisfactorily conclude you and yours are all well, and that nothing has happened at Hasting worth communicating. Your brother is much better of the gout than when I came to town. The Apollo is tonight, the *Charms of Florimel*. I don't see any way I can be an auditor, for we can't contrive to manage a ticket, and before the next assembly I hope to be with you, infinitely more to my satisfaction. Jemmy told me last night he had seen Mr Cumming's and that he intended to be this way this evening.

I was passing the King's Bench walks yesterday and saw Mr Wicking, so went in about five a clock, saw his wife, drank 2 dishes of tea. I think the woman appears to be very well, born at Epsom, talked of Sir Thomas Webster's family, her ...[2] other serving them, I suppose, with candles. Godley's present of a watch to spousee is come out not paid for, and the man swears he'l sue him having wrote several letters for the money, but this is a secret. Jemmy told me of, as I am to be in the Temple for an ...[2] evening and as it's far from being ... by candle I chuse to send you this before I have heard but very little politicks not having seen any people for that purpose.

1 MS *damaged*; Sayer suggested 24 or 25 January 1744 (Sayer vol. 1, 268); postmark 24 January.
2 MS *damaged*.

480 To Mary Collier, Hastings, from John Collier, [Johnson's Court], 29 January 1745 [SAY 1857]

I find by your letter received yesterday that you have had Dely with Miss Webster and her brother, and presume as nothing is mentioned of Mr Worge or his wife, none of them were with you, but that's a misfortune must be borne as well as it can. I am sorry to hear

Dely is soe pale and thin, and am fearful she has more fatigue than her constitution will well bear, though I presume, as she is treated with so much civility, it makes it much more agreeable to her to be at Battell than otherwise it would naturally be. The conduct and behaviour of her brother and sister there is not a little surprizing and I resent it as much as if to myself.

Jemmy is very well, I don't find that he will be down till the latter end of February till the sittings are over, which is really a very just reason, and I beleive he is very regular and constant in his attendance at Westminster Hall. There has been a prodigious snow this morning, I designed to go to Colonel Pelham's but have kept close within. I will get the netts you mention for Molly's and Jenny's hair. If you have anything to buy, I expect to hear by this post. I must buy the little dear girles something, but I know not what. You'l think me very gay when I tell you that I have been at two plays. There's a mock opera set to musick by Mr Lamp, taken out of Shakespear's *Pyramus and Thisbe*, that has at present a run at Covent Garden.[1] I was there last night to see the *Maid's Tragedy* and that performed, and it was a very good house. It's a whimsical thing, reflecting on the Italian operas, and seemed much to please the audience. There are one or two of the tunes with French horns, trumpets, etc., very pretty, but the greatest part seems common musick.

I hope you go out in the chaize in fine weather, or order William to take out the horses every day for exercise, but I desire you'l never attempt to go out but with a horseman before. I presume by this time the harness may be come, and the horses tryed, just to keep them in good health and order, and a little gentle drawing, if every day, will be better for them. I find your brother and son strong for a coach. I pray God to keep you all under his protection, and am with the truest regard and affection. The Apollo musick has been prodigiously admired, and is much talked of about town, and there has been very brilliant company. I don't find by my brother that Mr Cullen has been there this winter.

1 Covent Garden Theatre, *The Maid's Tragedy*, by Francis Beaumont and John Fletcher; also *Pyramus and Thisbe*, a mock opera, after Shakespeare, music by J F Lampe (Scouten Pt 3 vol. 2, 1736-1747 1148).

481 To Mary Collier, Hastings, from John Collier, [Johnson's Court], 30 January postmark 31 January 1745 [SAY 1858]

I am this moment come home from a whole day of business, very fatiguing and really too much for me. I have received and read your letter and would not omit acknowledging the receipt of it. I am sorry poor Sally is out of order and hope she'l mend. I dined at home yesterday, and presently after Mrs Nouns and then Mrs Selby came in. The latter has promised to buy for me the two silk netts for the girls' hair, though both of them seemed to know nothing of such affairs. I found by Mrs Selby she sends down this week cloathes for Mrs Carleton and one of her daughters and beleives it the favour of your recommendation. I have seen no person today nor heard no news. I am entirely weary of being here and have got a little cold.

482 To Mary Collier, Hastings, from John Collier, Johnson's Court, 2 February 1745 [SAY 1859]

I waited with great impatience for the posts coming today, being 2 hours later than usual, I presume occasioned by the frost, but had the pleasure of your letter with the account of

Sally's being better. I gave my cozen Denham's certificate to my brother. I have no objection to your visit from my sister Cruttenden and her daughter, and think after this distance of time it's not amiss. I am heartily weary of this place and much long for my return, but cannot fix a time. I beleive Mrs Nouns will dine here tomorrow and I will desire her to buy Sally's, and likewise Hariot's, diamond affairs.[1] I am glad to hear that Dely thinks herself well and you'l send for her whenever you please. Tom Greene came to town last night on a letter from his father, who apprehends and I beleive is in a very declining way. I find by his discourse he will fully settle in the country, very handsomly obliging, and gives his humble service to you, Dely and all the family. All day yesterday we were alarmed with the death of the Queen of Hungary after being 36 hours in labour,[2] but as there is not the least mention of it in any of the papers today hope it's only a Change Alley report.[3] I hope to be at home by the time the inquisition of the smugler is adjourned; if not, will give some directions. It's impossible for you to know how much I longe to see and be with you, but during absence as I have the pleasure to hear of the welfare of you and our children I have great satisfaction.

1 G.Yogev *Diamonds and Coral: Anglo-Dutch Jews and Eighteenth Century Trade* (1978) ch. 5. For reference to the import of Brazilian diamonds in the 1730s see Yogev ch. 7 and L Neal *I am not the master of events: the speculations of John Law and Lord Londonderry* (2012) ch. 3.

2 The report was mistaken, Maria Theresa survived her son's birth.

3 Change Alley, the common term for Exchange Alley, comprising two alleyways connecting Birchin Lane, Lombard Street and Cornhill.

483 To Mary Collier, Hastings, from John Collier, [Johnson's Court], 5 February 1745 [SAY 1860]

I received your letter yesterday and am much concerned at your being out of order but hope the cold, ugly weather has been much the occasion of it. I have been much troubled with my head and stomach and can hardly refrain from having an apothecary, though I have hitherto stood it out; this has been an exceeding dolorous day, raw, cold, snow and dark weather. I beleive we shall spend this evening at my son's chambers, though am not certain; we talked of it last night. I am exceeding sorry to be kept in town and cannot as yet fix any time for proposing to set out which gives me great uneasiness. I must beg you will continue writing every post you can't imagine how comfortable and agreeable it is to me.

The unmannerly rudeness you met with at Mr Loftus's from a certain person does not at all surprize me, not being the first time by a thousand, though I can't help being provoked at it. I should not at all be concerned at an open breach and really I don't well know how it can be avoided. I solemnly assure you that any such behaviour to you fires me with resentment much more than to myself. I have no news to impart to you worth writing. I have bought, by Mrs Nouns' recommendation, 6 blew and white china dishes being a whole set, only there is but one dozen of plates which makes it awkward; suppose I get her to endeavour to match them. Mrs Selby has not sent the silk nets but I'le send after them in a day or two.

I heard yesterday that Mr Wardroper,[1] who has been in town almost as long as I, brought up with him Holt's wife of Peasmarsh and took lodgings in Hatton Garden. It seems it's an old intrigue. I see him every day at the coffee house and he has dined here 2 or 3 times but nothing has been hinted. Mr Dodson[1] is in town and full of the affair, but he has a mortal hatred to the other of whom your brother has a good opinion, though in this he must be condemned by all.

1 Edwin Wardroper, mayor, Winchelsea, 1747, 1749, 1751, 1754 and town clerk 1735 to 1740, in which year he was joined by Henry Dodson (Pratt Appendix 1, mayors of Winchelsea; Appendix 2, town clerks).

484 To Mary Collier, Hastings, from John Collier, [Johnson's Court], 7 February 1745 [SAY 1861]

I am still in a state of uncertainty about my coming out of town, which makes me very uneasy and impatient, but I have truly comfort in hearing you are all well at home and I hope in God Dely is the same and that she'l get safe home to you. Our going to Jemmy's chambers was postponed till last night, when there were my brother, T. Green, Cole, Dakeyne, Dodson, Wardroper and myself. We had a dish of Scotch collops, three roasted fowles and tarts. I came away and was abed by 12, but the rest stayed till 2. I am glad to hear you goe out sometimes. I beleive I have forgot to mention anything to you about the beds for the stable. There is but one objection, and that is fear of candles and giving them a sort of a lawless liberty of keeping bad hours if so inclined, but that we can't help. I have not bespoke the beds nor will not till I come home and can then send for them for as it's agreeable to you I'le readily come into it. We have cold weather and had more snow last night I presume you have pretty hard frost in the country.

485 To John Collier, Hastings, from James Collier, Fig Tree Court, 28 February 1745 [SAY 1862]

Though twould almost be needless to communicate by letter the news of the town since I shall see you soon in person, yet I cannot help acquainting you with an extraordinary division in the House of Commons on Monday in relation to the giving 57,000 to the Hannoverians for eight weeks pay in order to defray their expences in returning home.[1] This motion was opposed by Sir John Philipps, and Sir Francis Dashwood who insisted on dividing the House, and the numbers were, for the motion 244, against 40. Sir John is very much chagrined and determined to print the names of the minority. If it is convenient this day seve'night, the horses may come up to town. I saw Captain Pigram yesterday, who gave me a particular account of one of our smugling boats being taken, after some resistance, by the Custom house sloop at Shoreham, laden with seven ton of tea.[2]

1 Commons motion, 22 February 1745, on proposed payment for the Hanoverian soldiers; the Secretary at War asked for £57,965 9s 2½d eight weeks pay, known as two short months, the usual end of service payment to foreign troops in British pay: agreed 244 to 40 (Owen 256; *CJ* Vol. 24, 771).
2 Captain Nathaniel Pigram (TNA CUST 148/12).

486 To John Collier, Hastings, from William Cranston, [Johnson's Court], 12 March 1745 [SAY 799]

I received the favour of yours and, as you observe, our Hasting chaps are gott to be very unfortunate. Morphett and his crew were yesterday shoped in Newgate; I've got a copy of their committment and am to endeavour at bailing em, but doubt. I shall make out the best story I can for my Ryers[1] but twill be but a lame peice of business. There are abundance of anvills in the fire and Eastgrinsted will overun with smugglers. In order to endeavour at a little present support, I by last post wrote to Dr Thorpe acquainting him that I had an account the day before that my couzin David Denham was bad of the smallpox in the King's Bench and pennyless, etc., and the next morning I had an account that he died that night and of which I now also write the doctor.[2] I shall gett to East Grinstead on Sunday and shall be in expectation of seeing you there the next day.

1 Folk born within the walls of Rye were known as Ryers, a term still in use in the twenty-first century. I am indebted to the staff of Rye Castle Museum for their knowledge of local language and folk lore.

2 David Denham, who died in the King's Bench prison.

487 To John Collier, Hastings, from William Cranston, [Johnson's Court], 14 March 1745 [SAY 800]

You inclosed receive your Latitat v King. Your 3 bills for £220 came safe to hand and which shall be received as they become due. I yesterday sold the lottery ticketts.[1] The £20 prizes for £17 13s 0d each neat and £5 5s 0d neat for the blank so that your two prizes come to £35 6s 0d and the blanks to £21 total £56 6s 0d and which I have accordingly given you creditt for as well as for £25 15s 0d received a few days since of Mr Dawson. The third seal was this day, the next not till the 26th instant, till when you can't have your dedimus. I think the alienation fine can't exceed £1 6s 8d but will fall little short of it. Mr Baron Carter sett out for his grand and last assize this morning.[2] I'm now pretty well satisfyed Morphett and his chaps may be bailed but when to gett em is the question. I shall give notice of a couple of which you'll hear more, I presume, by some other hand.

1 This is 17 Geo II c. 18 1744 designed to collect £1.8 million by annuities and a lottery, the latter to raise £600,000; the draw started on 26 November 1744 (*PGA* 17 Geo II 379, Ewen 148-50).

2 Sir Lawrence Carter, Baron of the Exchequer Court.

488 To John Collier, Hastings, from James Collier, Fig Tree Court, 16 March 1745 [SAY 1863]

I beleive you have been not a little surprized in not seeing me at Hasting this week, which was occasioned by my great curiosity to see the procession at the publick entry of the Venetian ambassador which was fixed for this day. I should have wrote this week, but waited for a message from Mr Rowe whom I had desired to enquire whether the minister would make his entry as on this day, but received no information from him till Fryday. I now only wait to try my cloaths, and as I am informed the Grinstead road is the best, shall dine with my uncle at the above mentioned place on Tuesday. The keeping of the horses in town I hope has been attended with no inconvenience.

Admiral Lestock will certainly get the better of Mathews; the latter has had some warm words in the House with Mr Greenville, one of the new Lords of the Admiralty. Hitherto this enquiry has been carried on without the intervention of party and both sides pretend to wish it may be an impartial one. Two men of war were certainly lost in the late hurricane at Jamaica and the merchants expect a most terrible account of the loss their ships sustained.[1] The House of Lords is to be moved on Tuesday next by the Duke of Bedford to have the minutes laid before them of the court martial lately held at Spithead in relation to Captain Mostyn's not engaging the French men of war; this motion will be made at the instigation of Admiral Vernon.[2]

1 Jamaica hurricane, Saturday 20 October 1744. Reports reached London five weeks later referring to the huge damage to the sugar canes, the buildings and works, the destruction of stores, the destruction of Savannah-la-Mar and severe damage to Kingston and Port Royal; eight warships and ninety-six merchant vessels sunk or wrecked. (TNA ADM 1/233/ box 1 Pt 2 f. 132, 154; Pt 4 f. 148).

2 Savage Mostyn, Captain of the *Hampton Court*, charged at his own request with failing to engage and seize a French warship 7/8 January 1745, exonerated and returned to command by unanimous decision of the court martial.

489 To John Collier, Hastings, from William Cranston, [Johnson's Court], 16 March 1745 [SAY 801]

The Attorney Generall against Betts *et alios*.[1] within two hours after I had given briefs in this affair to Wynn and Lacy I received a countermand of this notice of tryall so that now the culpritts may take the advantage of endeavouring to make this matter up before the next assizes. I understand tis put off by the express direction of the Board this morning.

1 For this case see [**470**] [**517**].

490 To John Collier, Hastings, from William Cranston, [Johnson's Court], 2 April 1745 [SAY 802]

Yesterday's post brought me a bill from Mr Lamb for £300 dated 30 March and payable 21 days afterwards, and which when due I shall take care to receive and place to your account. If my little Chossam journey is to take place, by way of an airing, you'll be so good as to furnish me with a proper authority and a state of the account as farr as you know of the matter. In my own mind I am for setting out the Sunday after Easter and return the Tuesday following.

About 4 or 5 year ago I troubled you with a petition on behalf of Henry Roffe which you was so kind as to comply with and thereby he was made a midshipman on board the *Sutherland* man of warr, but the poor young fellow died on board in the river without ever seeing the sea. Upon my hopefull Christopher Roffe's and my parting last summer, and his determineing for the sea also, I did give him to understand that if it was in my power I would do by him as by his brother; and he accordingly went on board the *Ludlow Castle*, man of warr, where he still continues a common sailor.[1]

Soon after his entrance, which was in September last, complaints of hardships soon reached me, and so have from time to time continued, but was determined to take no notice of em presently, for two reasons. First, that he might have sufficient time to repent of his misbehaviour to me, and next that his removall out of em might have the better effect upon him. But upon a letter from him yesterday I am satisfyed he has been sufficiently humbled and, therefore, if a letter in his favour to the captain from the Lords of the Admiralty, as was done in the case of his brother, can be obtained without much difficulty, I must beg to be a humble petitioner for him. How affairs stand now among the great ones I know not, but a line from you to Mr Stone would soon sett you right as to that particular as well as to the main point. The man of warr is at present at Plimouth.

1 Henry and Christopher Roffe of Sevenoaks.

491 To John Collier, [Hastings], from Henry Pelham, Esher Place, 12 April 1745 [SAY 418]

Since the receipt of your letter I have been so taken up with busieness att London that I have not had time to answer it till now that I have got a little quiet in this place. Considering the times, which I hear from all parts are very hard with tennants, I think mine under your collection have performed pretty well. These you mention as in great arrear I am afraid will never recover, and I think you have taken very right methods with em. I would have em used gently, though too much forbearance can do them no good, and may do me hurt.

I wish Chatfeild would be satisfied to let his farm go to such of his sons as are willing and able to carry it on; it was always looked upon as a pretty farm, till of late he has neglected his busieness by age and drunkenesse. I see the widow Thomas still continues in arrear. I wish she be able to go on with the farming busieness to advantage. I observe there is nothing come in this [1] half year by proffits of courts, nor receipt of quit rents. I should be glad to know whether there is any timber that would not be the better for standing if so, I am willing to have it viewd and a price sett upon it, for I can assure you, tho I believe it is not thought so, a little ready money would be very convenient for me att this time.

As to the two little purchases you mention of Barham and Alchorne, I am not against hearkening to them if you realy think they are worth the money, but att this distance I must depend upon you, and I think I can. As to Mr Fagg's farm, I should like to have that very much, but am afraid it will cost more than I can raise, however, you will be ready to hear what Mr Rideout says, and when he speaks more particularly to you about it I shall be glad to hear from you again. I was very sorry that I could not have the pleasure to see you for any time when you were in town; I hope in the summer, when our Parliamentary affairs are over and other troubles subside, I shall have your company for a day or two in this place, where we can, at leisure, settle our affairs and talk over what is proper to be done for the future. I must desire my service to all friends in your part of the country.

1 MS *affair* struck through.

492 To John Collier, Hastings, from William Cranston, [Johnson's Court], 16 April 1745 [SAY 803]

This lowring cold weather does not seem to promise well for my Chessam expedition but I suppose if it's deferred till the Whitsun hollydays when the weather will be warmer and more setled and myself perhaps more at leisure, there will no great inconvenience attend it. Upon perusal of yours in respect to the coach, it is doubtless the constant practice to quarter the wive's arms thereon with the husband's and thereupon I this morning sent an epistle for that purpose to Mr Gower, but James brought it me back again, acquainting me that he was now at Crowhurst, but, however, I shall return it again too morrow morning to be left for him against his return from thence and as soon as I know where it stands, will go and view it. That you may see your news from Hasting is in print, I send you the inclosed but whether any of the evenings post have it, I know not, not having as yet seen any of em. You'll be so good as to help my cousin Denham to her £3 for which I have given you creditt.

493 To John Collier, Hastings, from William Cranston, [Johnson's Court], 18 April 1745 [SAY 804]

The Chessam parcell came yesterday safe to hand, but exclusive of the very indifferent weather I doubt it will be impossible for me to stirr on Sunday as I proposed and to be absent Monday and Tuesdays. Your fine also came safe and the place wherein the caption is not necessary to be incerted. I've given Swain's name in today to Mr Simon but as to Gurr's he was given in at first so no occasion for the doing it again.[1] There will be no occasion for each person to have 2 separate bail for supposing 2 bail for each are required for £500, there can be no question but that a man worth £1000 may be bail for two. Upon searching I find a fine passed in Trinity term last from John Sargent and Elizabeth his wife to John Balding, Thomas Steward, Robert Turlington and Edward Backhouse of 5 messuages, 5 gardens and the 3rd part of 80 acres of land in All Saints and castle in the town of Hasting.[2]

I think Pascall's behaviour very insolent. Before your consultation begun this morning I was at Dr Lee's, when I was not a little surprized to find that he declined being concerned in the affair for us and therefore returned his retainer but kept his reasons to himself. But, however, this did not hinder our attendance upon Edmonds and Jennour with whom we were near 2 hours and the whole matter fully discoursed over. And they were both of opinion that she could not fairly and by law be made a prize, but that they were doubtfull whether the judge would not condemn her from the character of her and her crew as to smuggling, though they were both clear that that point in strictness of law ought not to have any consideration but doubted it might; but, however, thought so much might be said in favour of her as to make the condemning her an act by no means clearly to be justifyed, and therefore by all means advised a vigorous defence.

And to this purpose directed in the first place that all the owners should made an affidavit of their property as well those who claim the vessell as those to whom the money belonged, to shew that neither is French property; to shew, by indifferent people and nobody better than one of the officers, that when she came in the road the 15th January that they were on board her to search for but found no prohibited goods, that she continued in the road from that time to her being taken; to clearly and possitively to deny any resistance made; to prove the falsity of their deposition of money[3] as well as oil skin baggs, etc., being carryed on shore and put upon horses and[4] into carts and carried away; to prove if possible a threats used to the French prisoners which Gurr talked something about, not to have anybody examined as to any of those facts except the property, who sailed or is anyways concerned in the cutter; to have some persons who stood on the shore and saw the whole transaction to prove there being no horses or carts made use of as above, and if such bear any other tithe than marriners it will not be the worse and lett em also add that during the transaction all the officers of the Customs, with their number, and the soldiers were present and saw the whole, and that if anything contraband had been attempted to be run it must have fallen into their hands.

These are the facts to be examined to; therefore Gurr and his company should collect together proper persons and as it will be necessary that you should see so much of their deposition as relates to the transaction before any answer can be drawn to em; and as they are pretty long and now past 8 it is impossible to send em now but will per next post and at the same time a sketch of one affidavit which may serve as some guidance towards the rest and as these affidavits must be returned me by the end of next week. Upon second thought I fancy Gurr can't well be spared to go to Shoreham so think Grayling or some others might do that jobb but it must be so ordered that these 2 affairs don't so clash as to neglect the cutter, for that may be beyond redress.

1 John Swain, mate of the Customs sloop *Amelia*; Thomas Gurr, boatowner and smuggler.
2 These lands are in the Hastings Chamberlains' reports under John Sargent.
3 MS *being brought* struck through.
4 MS *carried* struck through.

494 To John Collier, Hastings, from William Cranston, [Johnson's Court], 20 April 1745 [SAY 805]

This part of the packett will shew you how the privateer gentry swear and will help you into the meaning of the remainder of the packetts, which are sketches of affidavits, and may possibly save you some trouble in the fixing the proper ones.[1] I don't find that there was anybody on board from the first to the last, except either the crew or owners, but Michael Wright and as he is in Newgate I have sett out the whole matter fully in an affidavit I intend he shall swear to and which I shewed him yesterday and that is the reason why the other affidavits are not filled with more of that affair whilst at sea. Grayling, indeed, was also on board the whole time, and though he says he is no owner or partly concerned, yet I think it better not to meddle with him; but I have made some of em say what I think is material and is also agreable to truth, that he never sailed in her. Tis from Wright that I have settled the number of people that went on board and in what clans and in how many boats and how often each boat was backwards and forwards. Therefore, you'll be so good as to attend to that particular affair in each affidavit, for as I shall put the whole of it in his affidavit, the others confirming each particular as to this point will add strength to Wright's affidavit in the whole.

If more boatmen than one can be gott as to their previous search, etc., twill be better, and I don't see what objection they can make to it, or any harm can proceed from it to them, as it is only speaking to a matter of fact and in which their diligence also will appear. As to any horses and carts, if there were any nigh, it would be necessary, if it can be done, to have the persons' affidavit who belonged to them and to give an account how and for what reason they were there and to deny their carrying anything off or their intention so to do. I remember you mentioned it to me as your opinion of the people that the cutter might easily have outsailed and gott away from the privateer. If Bossom or any of the rest of the chaps saw the coming up of the privateer and the position of the cutter I think twould be materiall to give their judgement of it in case they should be of that opinion.

Mr Carswell, who I suppose bears the title of gentleman, with some others may, if they can be procured, make an affidavit generally of their seeing the skirmish and that they saw no baggs of money, oil baggs, horses or carts, etc., etc. In short you'll have a good deal of trouble in this matter and should be glad if with a wish I could be at the port to assist. They must be sworn before the mayor and I hope to have em by some contrivance or another by Thursday night, otherwise twill be impossible to be ready against the day they may be wanted. Benjamin Wright died whilst I was yesterday at Newgate. You'll be so good as to return me the draft with the originalls for they'll be of use to me possibly. I by this post send my brother about his curacy. I beleive he much wants to hear from me. Therefore if my nephew's man has leisure on Monday morn my brother would be much obliged if he would carry my epistle to him.

1 This is the Grayling, Morphet smuggling case (Introduction; TNA CUST 148/12).

495 To John Collier, Hastings, from William Cranston, [Johnson's Court], 23 April 1745 [SAY 806]

Gower and the coachmaker called here on Fryday whilst I was at Newgate, and the latter was here again the next day when we setled my sister's arms; and also furnished him, from a letter, with your crest, about which there was some little doubt. I found Gower was to set out as today or toomorrow for the Bath with the colonel, who attends the Duke of Grafton thither; and after about 10 days will be back again, till which time I suppose the horses won't be bought, and in the interim you may depend upon my taking a survey. I compute that passing Bristy's fine at £4 12s 0d, besides the post fine 10s if the praefine is 6s 8d, which I think it can't exceed and over and besides the 10s which you intend to charge about the carriage and execution.

As you observe, the smuggs have a busy week of it. Morphett was with me with a full affidavit by 8 this morning. I hope to have em all sometime toomorrow, having given notice for Thursday 12 at the Old Bailey, setling the time today with Simon who I found in good temper and complaisant, after a strong tiff together at our last meeting upon this occasion when I thought he used me ill and not like a gentleman, of which I told him, in Masterman's presence, who thought me clearly in the right to resent it. I write tonight to Wales.

496 To John Collier, Hastings, from William Cranston, [Johnson's Court], 2 May 1745 [SAY 807]

Evenden v King:[1] If I do not in a day or two hear of defendant's appearing, will send you a notice of a declaration to serve on him. Wood v Wells ex dimissione Bossom. I've heard nothing of this affair as yet, though tis early in the terme. I shall observe the paying all your drafts, etc., and May and Willis shall not escape this terme.

Being sent for to attend, I was yesterday morning at Mr Pelham's when his commands were to tell me that he wanted to settle at Hoare's, and for that purpose wanted such receipts of theirs for money which you may have paid in upon his account; that upon having em delivered he will give you a receipt to the amount of the whole; that he should be glad to settle with you that, the Parliament being over, he should have time and would be glad to have it done either here or Esher or Greenwich either this or in the next month at your own conveniency. This was the whole of the conference, so you'll enable me to give an answer which I shall very readily do, though between you and I yesterday's business might have been done without a personall interview, though the remnant may make such a visit necessary.

As to Hasting and Eversfield,[2] Mr Dodson and I never have had an oppurtunity of much discourse together upon it, and which I in great measure lett alone the last time he was here, expecting his return again ere now. But I never did and, upon looking into the papers today, do not now think that there is anything done at the mayor's election which is, or can be, necessary to prove by *viva voce* evidence. As you are a court of record and as the whole transaction of that day is entred of record, the producing the book will prove it effectually. The acts subsequent and consequentiall to this court, being done in a …[3] private manner, must be proved by liveing evidence, such as the assessors actually making and signing their assessment, the demand of it by the chamberlains and the refusall, Sir

Chas liveing out of the corporation and the lands lyeing within it, as the custom of granting the assessment and the like in respect to the constitution of the place. If Dodson should happen to be with you on Sunday he may attend to at all your movements but am satisfyed tis not absolutely necessary.

I was yesterday morning with your equipage which in the main I like very well; tis strong and will be heavy, but Sussex roads might shake a lighter too much; I can't think it dear at the price you mention. Mr Gower was expected in town as yesterday. I don't find any horses are yet bought, but I told the chap to tell Mr Gower that, as the summer was advancing apace, no time should be lost in getting both the horses and coach ready for the country.

1 Evenden v King, summer assizes, Lewes, Saturday 10 August 1745, before Sir William Lee, Chief Justice, Thomas Burnett; cause 2, for plaintiff, damages £5 19s 8d, costs 40/-; Henry Penfold, clerk to William Cranston, received this record, 31 October, [**506**].

2 Hastings v Eversfield [**354**] [**373**] [**380**] [**392**][**449**] [**452**].

3 MS torn.

497 To John Collier, Hastings, from William Cranston, [Johnson's Court], 4 May 1745 [SAY 808]

Mr Gower called upon me yesterday morning, and told me that in his way to town he bought a pair of horses at Reading, for which I paid him £31. He informed me also that the Colonel and he had setled it that the coach should go down as next Wednesday; and in it some of his females, that he would hire 4 horses, 2 of which you was to pay for, and 2 himself, and if they used your 2 new beasts, which was not then determined, they should be six strong. He concluded that your paying for the hire of 2 horses would come as cheap to you as the sending the present 2 to town, etc. I've just been able to finish your bill which I inclose you, as also that upon account of the Newgate chaps, which Gurr said should be paid to you as soon as I could send it and which I promised before but was disappointed by Masterman till this morning. I send a receipt at the bottom of it as well as a loose one, either of which you may deliver as you please. I've sorry it comes to so much money but fees, etc., run high.

That there is an account come of an action from Flanders is certain,[1] and to the disadvantage of the allies, which is likewise as certain, but to how great a degree is variously reported, some to the amount of 20,000, others of 8000 and others but of 2000, but that they retreated, and are under the cannon of Aeth, seems agreed upon. As the numbers lost are uncertain, so is their quality also, some affirming that Lord Albermarle and his elder son and Lord Ancram are dead, Campbell, Cope with one leg each, the Duke and Lord Crowford wounded,[2] the former looseing 2 horses from under him; and Legonier missing, but whether among the slain or prisoners not known. But I don't doubt but you'll have all this or more in some of the evening post. I beg you would be so kind as to pay Mr Carleton £10 upon my account.

1 Fontenoy, Tuesday 30 April OS, 11 May 1745 NS, a serious defeat for the British and Dutch; following the battle Marshall Saxe captured Tournay, Ghent, Bruges, Oudenarde, Dendermonde, Ostend, Nieuport and Aeth (Williams 1945 238; Fortescue vol. 2, 109-121; W Adams *England at War* (1886) 176-81).

2 Crawford's conduct at Fontenoy led to promotion to major-general (R Rolt, *Memoirs of the Life of the late Rt Hon John Lindesay 20thEarl of Crawfurd* (1753) 415-6).

498 To John Collier, Hastings, from Captain James Murray, Saturday 4 May 1745 [SAY 1864]

I am favoured with both yours, for which and the trouble you have often had with my affairs, you'll please accept of my hearty and sincere thanks. I think Mr Lemon has been more generous than could have been expected and, all things considered, the sailers and soldiers have great reason to be thankfull.

Everybody here is greatly alarmed by the express that arrived this morning from the army in Flanders, which attacked the French entrenched the 30th April OS. The first and second attacks were successfull, but the third proved as bloody as fruitless; for the ennemy, annimated by the presence of the dauphne at the head of 5000 of the housold troops, made so vigerous a stand, that we were obliged to retreat with a very great loss, though in the outmost order. The affair lasted seven hours, and it is universally agreed that the Dutch behaved with unexpected resolution and zeal, their numbers lost are a proof of this, as it far exceeds that of any of the powers in the alliance.

These particulars I have from a letter of the duke's to Mr Poyntz, who writes with great spirit, and says that, as the troops behaved with uncommon bravary, and the ennemy's loss is no less than ours, he only regreats the many brave heros now dead who that day distinguished themselves. However, you'll agree with me in concluding we have done little good, since the French still vigorously prosecute the seige, and must in a few days be masters of the place. As the express came away before returns were made from each regiment, few particulars are known, though most immagine that our loss can't be less than 10,000. Sir James Campbell is mortally wounded, Ponsonby killed, and all the guards cut to pieces, as is the hiland regiment to a man. As every opportunity I have of shewing my gratitude for the uncommon civillitys I have met with from you and family, will give me infinite joy, I hope you'll lay your commands allways upon me, and in the meantime make my compliments acceptible to Mrs Collier, Miss Delia, and the other young ladys.

499 To John Collier, Hastings, from William Cranston, [Johnson's Court], 7 May 1745 [SAY 809]

Bristy and his wife were with me this morning, for yesterday did not suit me and which I altered by a private hand to Sennocke on Saturday, and executed the mortgage and bond and passed the fine, upon which I paid em £33 11s 4d as directed, and after shewing them Westminster Abbey and the park, etc., I put em on shipboard at Whitehall and went from thence to your coach which I found quite finished and the setting out tomorrow morning still remaining fixed. Your first letter upon this occasion mentioned £45, but Gower told me on Fryday that severall additionall articles having been since thought of, etc., etc., that the money must be £50 neat. I forgott to mention it per last post and, concludeing that you would make no difficulty in submitting, as I should not in the like case, I even paid the cole and think the whole well worth the money, and I heartily wish you may long live to have the benefitt of it. I shall take as an oppurtunity …[1] few days of waiting upon Mr Pelham. Your indorsement about the receipts had very nigh escaped me. I just send you a printed letter about our unfortunate battle.[2]

1 MS words covered by seal.
2 [*no longer attached*].

500 To John Collier, Hastings, from William Cranston, [Johnson's Court], 9 May 1745 [SAY 810]

This is my last frank. Messrs Worge and Collier arrived in town today about 1 and I saw em at 5. I find they mett your coach today at Bromley, so could not sett out yesterday as proposed. I this morning sent for and perused the indempnity Act for smugglers,[1] and to my great surprize and really concern, find it will do no good to any of the country smugglers, for as it pardons only the clandestine running, loading, unshipping, concealing or receiveing prohibited goods, and goods liable to customs or excise, and as it does not pardon offences for obstructing officers in the execution of their office, nor the being armed within 5 miles, etc., with an intent to run, and as I beleive there is none of them either by land or by water but have been guilty of one or t'other, so consequently none of em, and more especially the more desperate, are pardoned; but it sufficiently excuses all our London gentry who deserve as much censure as the country. I always understood it was to be generall and the same as 1736, and what reason there was for the contrary is past my comprehension and think twould have been much better to have had none than so partial a one. So that at last our Hasting gentry, etc., must go upon their travells. I can't say that anything has more vexed me many a day, and tis evident to me that they that made it knew nothing of the scituation of the country in general and how many people are, and will be, made desperate by it, and of necessity by obliged to follow their old trade or upon the highway.

1 18 Geo II c. 28 (*SL* vol. 6, 628-9).

501 To John Collier, Hastings, from James Collier, Fig Tree Court, 11 May 1745 [SAY 1865]

I take the liberty to send you inclosed an account of the late action near Tournay, as published by authority this day at noon, least the persons who are intrusted to supply you with the Gazette, might forget to send it. My uncle informed you last post of our arrivall here, and to his account I shall only add that Mr Worge and I were heartily tired occasioned by the excessive heat; and that we passed by the coach about a mile on the other side of Bromly without taking any particular notice of it, but soon after met Mr Gower who acquainted us for whom the coach was.

You'll easily perceive by the account above mentioned that Fleming's regiment was not engaged in the action, so that in all probability Gore and Maul were safe at either Brussells or Ghant. Mr Worge was very uneasy about his brother and is glad to find he is only wounded. It's generally agreed that if the Dutch horse had behaved as they ought to have done that we should certainly have succeeded in our attempt. The Duke of Cumberland's behaviour was such that he is now the general toast of all companies, and the event appears not half so fatal as was first apprehended. Sir John Strange moved the court this morning to bring on the affair of Serjeant and Read,[1] on the behalf of the latter, but Serjeant Belfild who is employed by the [2] former, being engaged in a trial at barr in the Common Pleas, the hearing of it was put of till a further day. The news that I hear I shall think myself bound to give you the earliest account.

1 Serjeant v Read, Easter term 18 Geo II, 1745, King's Bench, decision that the general toll of three bushels of barley upon every ship's cargo brought to a quay to be exported is good, as put to the repair of said quay by the manor of Penzeance (*ER* vol. 95, 509-10).

2 MS *latter* struck through.

502 To John Collier, Hastings, from William Cranston, [Johnson's Court], 21 May 1745 [SAY 811]

Sargent v Read: I shall observe your orders to a tittle in this matter. Yesterday and this afternoon I've been at least 20[1] times after Mr Tomlins but without success and though I am and will gett an answer directly from him, which Johnson desires I would, yet this letter tells me that he is pretty sure Bett's vessell will be tryed the sittings after next terme and if this should be fact then there seems to be an end of the present scheme, which Johnson thinks might be put in execution in case a tryall was not intended. As to Morphett's vessel, he beleives that is condemned and if so nothing to be done. Being willing to know what construction the Custom house people put upon the smugglers Act,[2] I went to Mr Symon who told me that he apprehended it would not pardon our culpritts but that some of his brethren were of a contrary opinion and apprehended they might be hooked in, but, however, that he should lay the case before the Attorney Generall and should follow his advice, which he has promised me to lett me know and which I hope to have by Saturday's post so as to send some account. As to the Royall ...[3] know not when it will come on, there are a many before ...[3] the judge most slow as well in motion as comprehension.

1 Either 10 or 20 times.
2 See [**500**]
3 MS word obscured by seal.

503 To John Collier, Hastings, from William Cranston, Johnson's Court, 25 May 1745 [SAY 812]

Mr Symon forestalled me, and called upon me this evening and said that he had not been able to gett sight of the Attorney Generall as yet, and that he might have more time for that purpose made a proposall which I came into, and from which no possible inconvenience can happen to Morphett and his companions nor their bail; vizt to put this matter of till July sessions, which are the 10th of that month, and for which purpose, he signed a note consenting to the respiteing the recognizances till that time. And I undertooke to gett it moved to the court who will order it of course, having since been with the clerk of the arraigns for Middlesex who assured me thereof and that he will speak about it. For my own part I think it of equall convenience to defendants as to the crown to have time to know what explanation can be put upon the Act of Parliament in their case, for it is a very unintelligible affair, it certainly means something and yet is most darkly expressed. As I am distressed for him, I hope you'll excuse the trouble if I begg that you would inform Gurr of what I now write and prevent their coming up. I have this evening gott the Chief Justice's warrant against Bazely, etc. Rochester is concerned for King to whom I have this afternoon spoke for a plea, which I'm promised in a day or two.

504 To John Collier, Hastings, from James Collier, Fig Tree Court, 28 May 1745 [SAY 1866]

Since my last I have attended Mr Bowlby, who is one of my intimate friends, and is gone to travell for two years, down to Harwich. As it was a road I had never been, I was extreamly glad to embrace this opportunity. The most remarkable towns that we passed through were Chelmsford, Witham and Colchester. The former is but an indifferent place, but has a delightfull walk for the ladies in the churchyard. Whitham is a good handsome town, and has many good houses; but in particular two, one a very ancient and excessive pile of building which belongs to Sir Edward Southcote; the other a modern house in which the Earl of Abercorn resides. The names of this place is universally known on account of the spaw, which has two very agreeable walks about it.[1] Colchester is a very large place, consisting of many streets and churches, but the houses in general not very extraordinary; on the last survey it contained 26,000 inhabitants, but as the manafacture of bays has not been lately in a flourishing condition, the number is very much reduced.[2] We visited the ruins of the old castle, and in the yard were shewn the particular spot on which Sir George Lisle and Sir Charles Lucas knelt when they were shot.

Expecting to find something very considerable at Harwich, I was not a little disappointed on my arrival, in finding only a dirty mean place, with nothing to recommend it but the broadness of the streets; the house in which Mrs Philipson, the mother of the member, lives, and that in which Marshal Belleisle lodged, together with our Inn, The Three Cups, are the only tolerable buildings in town. The king's yard here is tolerably decent, and there are now two ships building in it, vizt the *Centurion* of 60 guns, and the *Litchfield* of 50. We set out from London on Sunday sevenight, and got to Harwich the next evening, but were obliged to stay there till Thursday noon, on account of the packet boats waiting for a wind, and a messenger from the Duke of Newcastle's office. Mr Alt the Hessian minister was there, and very impatient to be gone. On the Tuesday we hired a boat and went over to Landguard fort on the Suffolk shore, distant about three miles. This fort commands the entrance into Harwich, and has mounted at present 20 18 pounders, with a garrison of 50 men, but there are now at work above an 100 labourers, in order to raise new works, and make it four times larger.

Mr Justice Wright is very much out of order by reason of an inflammation in his eyes, which has occasioned the court not to go into any of the paper causes. Sir Michael Foster, our new judge, having been long absent from London, and not very well acquainted with the practice of the court, has contented himself hitherto with only saying that he was of the same opinion. I was in hopes that the papers of this day would have mentioned something relating to the engagement in the postscript of my sister's letter of yesterday, but find no notice in the least taken. Mr Rowe has just left me, who sets out for Sussex on Fryday morning. Captain Murray I find by my uncle is gone for Hasting, and got there I suppose by this time.

1 Witham, Essex, medieval wool town, known for medicinal springs and spa, endorsed by Dr James Taverner, College of Physicians 1731-2, who published *An Essay on the Witham spa, or a brief enquiry into the nature, virtues and uses of a mineral chalybeate water at Witham, Essex* (1737)

2 Colchester bays, advanced, fine and light woollen cloths, so named because of the Dutch Bay Hall regulations in their production. The town and environs famed from 16th century for these new draperies, comprising wool textures in a wide range of colours; originally made by Dutch and Huguenot immigrants; by 17th century production was widespread in East Anglia; later this industry migrated to the West and North Ridings (Lipson 1921 230-1, 248-9).

505 To John Collier, Hastings, from William Cranston, [Johnson's Court], 1 June 1745 [SAY 813]

I have with much difficulty, and with an assurance that I veryly beleft it would be then paid, though no undertaking, gott the quietus affair put off to Michaelmas terme as you desired it should. Sargent v Read, the bill brought in by defendant came to £114 02s 6d and which was yesterday taxed at £67 10s 0d of which I by this post acquaint the plaintiff and tell him also that in a few posts hence he shall have his own bill. Dicker v Dicker, this judgement is entred up and as soon as I can gett the number roll you shall have a copy. I yesterday petitioned in Bett's affair which was referred to Medcalfe, so that soon after the holydays shall know whether our proposall is come into, to which I should think must be almost of course, as the Sollicitor will report for us. I had before the arrivall of yours hinted to Tomlyn that his assistance should not go unrewarded.

I've been this morning consulting Chossam papers, before being determined, God willing, for tomorrow sennight and of which I this post advertise Wade to gett his account, etc., ready. Though you have sent me more than one account, yet I presume I must take up the present one from the footing of that which seems to have been setled by you the 25 November 1740[1] and £21 19s 5d, the ballance then paid to you also, if I misapprehend not, if I do then you'll be so good as to sett me right in time.

1 William Cranston's copy of John Collier's account for 25 November 1740 (ESRO MIL 7/24).

506 To John Collier, Hastings, from William Cranston, [Johnson's Court], 4 June 1745 [SAY 814]

I remember when at Chessam I took an exact rentall of that estate and really thought I had had a copy of it by me but upon search can find nothing of it. I think it might be of service, therefore, if you have anything of it and can remitt it me per the return of the post, shall be obliged to you for it. Sunday morning is fixed, Jemmy Collier and self in a chaise and pair and old Tom Greene on his own horse.

Evenden v King.[1] Defendant has pleaded the generall issue. In your ejectment on the demise of Bossom, Taught the tenant in possession has appeared, you call the premises one third part or share of one messuage, etc., I think this description too uncertain. I spoke to Charles Rochester about it who has consented to the altering it if I think proper and I really am of that opinion unless any material which you may offer may otherwise determine me for I shall do nothing in it till I hear again from you.

1 See [**496**]

507 To John Collier, Hastings, from William Cranston, [Johnson's Court], 13 June 1745 [SAY 815]

My nephew, self and Thomas sett out Sunday morning about 9, reached Uxbridge about one, dined, set forward and gott to Chesham between 8 and 9, but an indifferent day though little rain. I sent my compliments to Mr Wade that I was arrived and should be glad to see him that evening, but that if it was inconvenient or disagreeable, the next morning would be the same, upon which I had his approbation of the latter. Accordingly Monday morn about 10, a gentleman called on me on horseback who turned out to be our steward, pretended extra business but that he would be back again by one or 2 o'clock. I told him I did not send him word a week beforehand and come on purpose to be so served, and therefore insisted upon his alighting, which with difficulty and almost force I gott him to do.

This kind of behaviour did not presage anything to my chaps advantage or indeed our own, for upon calling for the accounts, etc., etc., etc., they with the vouchers and ballance, it seems were all at London and nothing therefore could be then done. I expostulated with him upon his monstrous behaviour in suffering me to go thither for so shriefless an errand, rogued him off, threatened, abused and tryed all ways I could do, but to no effect; so came away as wise as I went, excepting that I made him go with me to take a survey of the houses, etc., and faithfull promises of being in town either next Monday or that day sennight and then all should be put to right but of this I think there is great reason to doubt.

Having thus done all my business by noon, we sett forth again, gott to Beconsfield to dinner, afterwards saw Mr Waller's fine gardens and grand roome at that place, then set forwards to Windsor which we reached about 8; saw the palace next morning, sallyed about in hopes of a peep at the Mars hall but disappointed.[1] Left that place about one, gott to the Starr and Garter at Richmond Hill about 4, dined there and gott to Johnston Court about 10. Mett with most villainous weather as to wett and cold, dismall roads and upon the whole a most unpleasant uncomfortable journey and I might add also unprofittable.

I've no sooner received your account of your having paid the subdean the £10 but that I must begg you would add to it £5 more, or £10, if he has no objection as I suppose he will not for then we shall be pretty near even. I thank you for your account of my brother who I am glad to hear has gott the better of his dissorder though, as you mention, he seems to have behaved very imprudently under it. Your mackrell make my mouth water. On my return I found the following letter 'Yours I received and observe what you wright, I desier you'll pay the agent the £67 10s 0d and I will send you a bill to pay you again in a post or two. I desier you will furthwith pay it, and let me know when you have down it, for I would not have it known here that I pay it: is the needfull from, etc., Robert Sargent' [2] Marazion 6 June 1745.[3] I shall deferr doing anything in it till I have your orders. 39 toomorrow.

1 The King's Guard Chamber, Windsor Castle: Mars is the centrepiece of the ceiling (*The Visitant's Guide to Windsor Castle and its Vicinity* (2nd edn 1828) 40).
2 [In margin] from
3 Marazion is in Cornwall near St Michael's Mount. Robert Sargent was sorting out debts owed to him.

508 To John Collier, Hastings, from James Collier, Fig Tree Court, 18 June 1745

[SAY 1867]

My uncle by his letter of Thursday's post gave you so particular an account of our expedition into Buckinghamshire, that considering the badness of the weather, it was almost impossible to subjoin any more observations. I take it for granted you observed the paragraph in the Daily Advertiser of Fryday, in relation to the ringing of bells on yesterday sevenight; indeed the bells did ring which gave me an opportunity of seeing the church gratis, but considering the nature and disposition of the inhabitants of Chesham, the design must be invented, as well on account of the principles of the major part, and the stupidity of the remaining who seem scarce capable of knowing one day from another. I met Sir William Ashburnham in a chair coming from the Alienation office, and asked him if he would give me leave to wait on him, but his answer was, that he was glad to see me, but should not tell me where he lodged, for he came up in a private manner, and should stay but a few days in town. I saw Mr Courtail, fellow of our college, lately who I find has got Mr Pelham of Stanmore under his care.

The court of King's Bench was wholly taken up this day on a very important point, the determination of which will be of the greatest consequence.[1] The case is this: a butcher at Northampton erected a stall in the market without paying an acknowledgement to the corporation, who are seized in fee of the soil, upon which the mayor, etc., brought an action of trespass. Two points were before the court today, 1st, whether the receiving a satisfaction for the erecting of a stall is of common right, as incident to the soil, and secondly, if so, whether an action of trespass would lye for not paying it. It was argued on behalf of the corporation by Sir John Strange, and on the other side by Mr Gundry, to both of whom the Chief Justice paid great complements, but the court deferred giving their opinion till a farther day.

I suppose my uncle acquainted you of our expedition to Ranelagh on Saturday night with the family of the Coles and Miss Green, where we met with our usual luck, to have but very few persons there. Mr Greene looks something better, but cannot hold out long; the young gentleman comes to town on Fryday evening. The town is grown so very barren of news lately that I have not been able to pick up anything. Be pleased to give my duty to my mother, and love to my sisters.

1 Mayor and corporation of Northampton, an ancient town v Ward, a complicated case with many legal and historical precedents; Sir John Strange, for the town, argued that a market might be compared with a parish church, whither the parishioners have a right to divine service, but no liberty to furnish themselves with pews without the appointment of the ordinary, adding that no case showed a man had a right to erect a stall without licence from the owner of the soil, otherwise it is a trespass, and damages accordingly. Nathaniel Gundry, KC 14 July 1742, chief justice Court of Common Pleas, 23 June 1750, died 1754 (*ER* vol. 95, 518-23 19 Geo. II 1745).

509 To John Collier, Hastings, from William Cranston, [Johnson's Court], 20 June 1745 [SAY 816]

I was yesterday morning with Mr Symon about our Hasting culpritts when he shewed me the Attorney Generall's opinion which he had obtained upon the late Act, and which is clear and positive that they are not included in it nor pardoned by it, just as I apprehended it, though tis shocking. So that they must appear at the next sessions, will be tryed and doubtless convicted, though I shall advise em to be strong in councill and insist upon the Act, and, if a special verdict can be gott, they may perhaps afterwards be somehow got off; though if anything can be done to that purpose before tryall it would be much better, and Symon thinks a petition properly recommended would find no great difficulty in going down with the Commissioners whose wrath upon this head, he says, seems to be much abated. I write to Gurr about it by this post who I suppose will soon be with you. If anything can be done no time should be lost; they would not deserve half the commiseration if no Act at all had passed, but such a one as did is the D ... ill.[1]

I was also last night with Tomlins about Bett's vessell in which they are at a stand for want of an answer from young Captain Pigram who they imagine must be on a cruize, if not, it would be of service to contrive to gett at him to hasten him, for the terme will soon slip over. These people also are in the same scituation with Morphett, etc., but as there's is an old story and not so clear a case I am apt to think that a petition with an offer to pay all the cost, etc., might be of service and stop farther proceedings at the next assizes.

Since I wrote the other side I've heard that one Gilbert, being in custody for being armed, etc., applyed yesterday to Banco Rogin to be bailed, insisting that his crime is pardoned by the late Act; that the court doubted, the chief said between this and Tuesday or Wednesday next he would consult the whole bench upon it and then declare his and their opinion, so that this case will try Morphett's and you shall know the event the next post after.

1 William Cranston uses this notation (viz for the Devill tavern) on several occasions in his letters.

510 To John Collier, Hastings, from James Collier, Fig Tree Court, 30 June 1745 [SAY 1868]

On Thursday last after some debate, a trial at bar was granted on the motion, Mr Lloyd, in behalf of Sir John Shelley, who has been served with an ejectment for some lands in Wiltshire to the value of about £270 a year, by Mr Hilton, a member in the present Parliament for Carlisle. Sir John himself made the affidavit couched in the necessary terms for the attainment of the motion, and is I beleive the only instance, where on the like occasion, it was not done by the Sollicitor. The day fixed on by the court is the 31st October.

Mr Rowe was so kind as to make up four dozen of covers to be franked by Mr Stone, and has delivered them to a clerk at his office, but as it was only yesterday morning, I have not thought it decent to call for them yet. Colonel Pelham I hear is in town, whom I will call upon in a day or two. You may have observed in the papers that a French ship of eighty guns was taken, but it is certainly true that one of 64 fell in with with Brett,[1] who with two ships more was going to join Warren at Cape Breton, and surrendred in a short time. I shall not stay till the sittings in London are over, but must beg leave to attend those in Westminster Hall, and more especially as a weeks difference is not of any great moment, for I intend to set out on Tuesday or Wednesday sevenight. Mr Greene jun, came to London but lately, in order I beleive to settle some points with his father, and sets out on Monday for Norfolk, whom I beleive I shall attend for the first days journay.

1 Captain Percy Brett of the *Lion* 58 guns, intercepted the Pretender's ship on the 7th July 1745.

511 To John Collier, Hastings, from William Cranston, Johnson's Court, 2 July 1745 [SAY 817]

I am sorry for your gout and wish you well through it. I find by Jemmy today that he wrote you per last post about his journey homewards. I this day fugged upon a petition for Morphett, etc., to the Customs. Symon extreamly civil and promised his interposition but don't see what can be done. Still wet weather. No news from Chesham, a sad scoundrell.

512 To John Collier, Hastings, from William Cranston, [Johnson's Court], 4 July 1745 [SAY 818]

Yours with the papers inclosed came safe to hand today and all things are sett to rights in respect to Bett's vessell; and as the sittings in the Exchequer begin next Thursday, I am then to move to have the recognizances vacated upon our former terms, which Tomlins will consent to by councill, so that as the terms will be in the order there will be no occasion for farther releases to Pigram. I would willingly have this over before I petition in the other matter. As to Morphett, etc., they must stand tryall. The Commissioners are relentless. Symon shewed me his report which was really favourable but all to no purpose. I send Gurr word of it tonight. I hope you continue mending.

513 To John Collier, Hastings, from James Collier, Fig Tree Court, 6 July 1745 [SAY 1869]

As stage coaches in general are very tiresome and disagreable, and more particularly the Tunbridge and especially at this time of the year, I had much rather ride down on horseback, and shall expect the horses by the carrier and will set out Wednesday afternoon. We were terribly downcast on Wednesday last on the current report of the army under the command of his royal highness the Duke of Cumberland being routed and entirely dispersed, but are now recovered from that fright by positive advices that there had been no general engagement, and are now in high spirits on account of 13,000 French who were out a foraging being cut off by Count Traun.[1]

1 After Fontenoy it became clear that the Dutch, the Austrians and the British were unable to cope effectively with the Prussians and the French. Saxe overran Flanders, Frederick of Prussia worsted the Austrians in Silesia, and the French were now preparing a second front with an invasion of the south coast of England. Further, on the 7th July Prince Charles Edward sailed for Scotland on the *Doutelle* escorted by the *Elizabeth*, 64 guns. Newcastle took full note of these threats in his correspondence with Richmond (McCann 250-5, 18th July to 10th August 1745). For the naval situation see Richmond vol. 2, 160-1.

514 To John Collier, Hastings, from William Cranston, [Johnson's Court], 9 July 1745 [SAY 819]

I am to acknowledge the receipt of your 2 last and, in answer to your first, inclosed send you Messrs Hoare's receipt for £69 upon Mr Pelham's account and will take the first oppurtunity of recieving your Custom house salary. I also send you Master Clark's account of Easter terme in which he had by mistake wrote 1274 bails instead of 1257, as he convinced me by a sight of his generall account, and on the back of this you will find a particular of Hillary terme.

Gurr and Morphett have been just now with me and hope the others with the whole cropp of bail will be here by Thursday noon, for there's but a scanty number of prisoners and a probability of the sessions ending Thursday evening. As I am fully perswaded we have a right to traverse[1] and as time is everything, and more especially at this critical juncture, and as we shall not otherwise have an oppurtunity of seeing what effect yours to Mr Stone must have, which I can't think but must be a good one, I am determined to take the advantage of it and thereby gett over to September sessions and accordingly have told my chaps thereof, who seem highly pleased. Have just now been with Mr Symon also to acquaint him therewith and which he also thinks is to be done and that twill be clearly the best method and that he will make no opposition to it. The expence with so many runs plaguy high but I've apprized them of it and they submitt. When I gett all the freemen together I shall discourse em over and really think their going to Stone may be of service. I paid Mr Hyatt's draft today but twas by his deputy.

1 Traverse, a formal denial in the pleading over a matter of fact stated by the other side, in this case the prosecution.

515 To John Collier, Hastings, from James Collier, Fig Tree Court, 9 July 1745 [SAY 1870]

In my last I promised to set out as tomorrow in the afternoon, but as the conversation of the town turns entirely upon the great match at cricket between Kent and all England, to be plaid at Bromley common next Fryday. I hope you will not be angry if I don't set out from London till that morning.[1] The Prince of Wales and all the nobility in town will be present. Mr Rowe has promised to accompany me so far, and I am in hopes of entertaining the club with the particulars of the game, as it will certainly produce another poeem, because I know a gentleman who is in fact ordered to attend on purpose. I have been at several china shops, but hitherto unsuccesfull, but have encouragement given me by a man in the Strand that he will be able to furnish me with a set tomorrow. I have enquired lately once at Mr Stone's house, twice at the office, but find he has been engaged so much lately in the business of the regency, that not one franck was been delivered out. The French are certainly in possession of the citadel of Ghent and we wait with the greatest impatience for news from the camp of the Duke of Cumberland. At all events I shall certainly be with you by Saturday evening.

1 Kent v All England, at Bromley common; played for a wager of 1000 guineas, Friday 12 July 1745. Kent won (D Underdown *Start of Play Cricket and Culture in Eighteenth Century England* (2000) 63-5). For reference to cricket at Bromley and more widely in Kent, Surrey, Middlesex and Hampshire see T J McCann *Sussex Cricket in the Eighteenth Century* (2004).

516 To John Collier, at Mr Luxford's, Boreham Street, Wartling, from James Collier, Hastings, 1745[1] [SAY 1871]

When I came home yesterday I was determined to take a vomit, but Mr Soresby, who was here with the colonel and all the family in order to dine with Mr Gower, disswaded me from trying that violent remedy first, but desired I would try what effect 20 grains of rhubarb would have. I accordingly took his advice and drank the potion at going to bed, the consequence of which was a violent sweating in the night and three stools this morning. The pain in my breast is very much alleviated, but as my stomach continues but bad, I am determined to take a vomit this evening and am in hopes of waiting on you tomorrow early. I thought proper to acquaint you with this least my not coming might occasion any uneasiness.

Mr Williams favoured me with his company last night and dined here today and is now in the parlour. A privateer belonging to Dover, commanded by Mr Owen, came into the road this day at noon, and when opposite to the eastern fort saluted it with 11 guns, with drums beating, colours flying and three huzzas from all the men.[2] This was the ship that fired the guns which were heard here on Sunday between five and six, being in chase of a French privateer, whom she, after a pursuit of nine [3] hours, ran ashore at St Maloes.

1 MS no postmark; JC's note, 'My son's letter to Mr Luxford at Boreham'.
2 Captain Owen *Carlisle* 10 cannon and 20 swivel guns; Hastings east fort was 200 ft. to the east side of the Bourne close by the east cliff, and facing directly onto the beach (TNA WO 78/1560).
3 MS *five* struck through.

517 To John Collier, Hastings, from William Cranston, [Johnson's Court], 23 July 1745 [SAY 820]

Pigram against Betts:[1] the order in this affair has been drawn up and entred ever since Fryday last, but the sending it to you is not to any great purpose, nor indeed can it be done till everything above is finished, for one of the terms of having the reconnizances vacated is upon payment of the cost, and therefore till I have got the bill and actually paid the cost, and produce to the proper officer the receipt for it, he cannot enter up the vacatur; nor can he then do it neither unless I also then produce to him the order for that purpose. You'll perhaps think it strange that I can't gett a bill from Tomlins, but strange as tis, tis also true, for notwithstanding I have been in person at the office ten times since yesterday noon, I've not been able to see either Tomlins, Johnston or the other chap, and though I have my name and business with the old chap, who in the intervals has seen em all, yet I can hear nothing from em nor is the any answer left to my messages. So that as affairs at present stand I know not what to make of it and can undertake nothing certain, but sure I shall be able to send something certain by next post.

As to the Crown Office affair, I was with Simon this morning who tells me that the Commissioners with much difficulty came yesterday into our proposall of putting a stop to farther prosecutions upon payment of cost and which I was afraid would run high and, accordingly, since I've been writing this he has sent me his bill amounting to £78 12s 6d a copy of which, it being long and now neer ten, I must put off sending till next post. He mentions that as the assizes draw nigh he shall expect a speedy determination as to payment. I send the sessions paper, etc., directed to the collonel as usuall.

1 Pigram v Betts (TNA SP 36/63; CUST 148/12; [**470**] [**489**]).

518 To John Collier, Hastings, from Henry Pelham, Esher Place, 15 September 1745 [SAY 419]

Saxby is now here, and tells me he has agreed for a small parcel of land att Laughton with Mr Alchorne of Chilly;[1] the purchase money is £400, the rent he proposes to give fifteen pounds a year. It is copyhold and pays a quit rent of ten shillings a year. I think the tennant should pay the quit rent but that I leave to you. If you think the land worth the money, I am willing you should agree for it; the title I must also leave to you. I conclude you can easily procure the money and either place it to account the next audit or draw upon me, which is most convenient. I am sorry I could not comply with the request of the Hasting men.[2] I never heard of it in a regular way till the day of tryal, it seemed to me a bad case, and you know I have always been a great enemy to smuglers, and should be sorry to be upbraided for giving them protection in my publick capacity, who have always been their enemy in my private one.

As I had no opportunity of seeing you this summer in the country, I should be glad to know when you come to town, that I may have notice sufficient to prepare myself for settling our account. It is now a pretty while since that was adjusted, and for both our sakes, I am of opinion it should not be deferred much longer, my service to all freinds. If you should have any proposals of more purchases on my account, I desire you will give the very true answer, that I have no money to make purchases with.

1 Chilley in Pevensey parish (Mawer & Stenton vol. 2, 444). For Laughton see [**519**].

2 This refers to recruitment of smugglers for the navy, and smugglers were also considered for the Army and the volunteer regiments; Sir John Miller, a neighbour of the Duke of Richmond in Lavant, made efforts to recruit smugglers for his regiment of volunteers. Such recruitment by landlords required care to avoid offence to the Army nor annoy the Treasury over the costs involved (McCann 266; Owen 287-8).

519 To [Henry] Pelham, from John Collier, 26 September 1745 [SAY 420]

I have the honour of your letter of the 15th instant in regard to the purchase of a parcel of land in Laughton from Mr Alehouse of Chilley. I beg leave to [1] mention that I took notice of it [2] in my letter to you of the 25th of October [3] last, and in my letter of the 28th of March [4] I wrote [5] that Mr Saxby informed me [6] he was very much for your buying it, lying so well to the Laughton estate. That there were no buildings the rent £15 a year assart hold of Laughton mannor, and 10s a year Lord's rent, that nothing would be abated of £400 for the estate which is a little over 26 years purchase.

And in my letter of the 25th of May [7] that as to Alchouse's land lying in Laughton, Mr Saxby has taken the same and says that your honour shall have it if you please, otherwise will keep it as he did not seem pressing for the result. You'l signify your pleasure when you see him. I think as the estate is copyhold tis dear, tho considering where it lies I am of opinion you should take it and I will endeavour for the tenant to pay the lord's rent. In my letter of the 18th of June last I mentioned to your honour that the purchase of the barn and 45 acres of land, [8] lying contiguous to John Vine's farm was compleated, and the money paid the whole amounting to £392 7s 0d. I will forthwith compleat Alchorne's [9] and incert an account of both in that of your next audit which I have fixed for the 17th of October. As to Mr Fagge or any more proposals [10] further purchases I shall obey your commands. [11] I shall be very glad to wait on your honour whenever it is agreeable [12] and receive your commands [13] to have my accounts examined and setled, having for about a year past been followed pretty strong by the gout and the increase of my paralitick dissorders, etc., that I have quitted great part of business as being too fatiguing for my state of health, and increase in years.

As to the case of the Hasting smuglers, as I well know the abhorrence you have to the villaneous practices of those people, I fully declined any sort of application to your honour [14] and heartily detest [15] their behaviour, but as Parliament thought proper to pass another Act of indemnity in regard to smugling, and twas given out, and generally thought [16] to be, on the like footing of that in the 9th of the king, and those [17] fellows having smarted pretty sufficiently by loosing their vessell and about 5,000 pounds worth of goods, two of them shot on board the vessel, two more dyed in Newgate, and the others lay a great while in that gaol before bailed, and being friends and relations to a [18] many of our freemen, and making promises of never being again concerned in smugling, and being teazed with daily applications, I did, on their not being cleared by the indemnity Act [19] I thought I might take the liberty [20] write to Mr Stone a state of their case, and [21] recommend it to him, that he might have a little trouble therein as well as myself, and by an answer [22] I had some reason to beleive they might be thought objects of compassion.

I never was otherwise concerned [23] or recommended their employing William Cranston, and beleive [24] they applyed to him as a townsman, and having some knowledge of him; and I did not in the least know when he went to London, about ten days since, that he would make any personal application to your honour, and find what he did therein was by the [25] directions of Mr Stone, and I solemnly declare it was no job of mine, and what I did was on the above motives.

I humbly take the liberty to mention, that the late indempnity Act was but of very little service to any persons in this county, but on the contrary has made the great lawless gangs more desperate; swearing that, as they are lyable to be gaoled and transported for past offences, they must and will keep on. It has pardoned those that are thought in the country to deserve as great punishment at least, the merchants and [26] tradesmen in London that employed them and received their smugled goods. I humbly hope you'l please to pardon my long writing on this subject, but I am prompted to it by a desire that your honour should know [27] the whole affair, and that no further imputation might be made than my [28] conduct deserves [29].

1 MS *incert gave you* struck through.
2 MS *by* struck through.
3 MS *1744* struck through.
4 MS *signifyed* struck through.
5 MS *last* struck through.
6 MS *it was then to be sold and in my letter of the* struck through.
7 MS *last I wrote you as followeth the following paragraph struck through.*
8 MS *that belonged to Mr Nathaniel Barham* struck through.
9 MS *unless I hear from you to the contrary* struck through.
10 MS *that shall made of* struck through.
11 MS *I have for about a year past had the gout follow me [very much] pretty strong and increase of my paralitick disorder and other illness attending an advancement in years, that I have quitted great part of my business, not being capable to go through the fatigue with the same agreeableness as formerly, but hoped to continue in yours as long as it was your pleasure to permit me, but if I have not a better share of health which I cannot now reasonably expect shall resign it whenever your honour pleases and fixed on a successor* struck through.
12 MS *to you* struck through.
13 MS *for the setling adjusting* struck through.
14 MS *on that account* struck through.
15 MS *that abominable practice* struck through.
16 MS *would have been upon* struck through.
17 MS *persons* struck through.
18 MS *great* struck through.
19 MS *not clearing them* struck through.
20 MS *of sending* struck through.
21 MS *desire his assistance to them* struck through.
22 MS *a letter from him* struck through.
23 MS *for them* struck through.
24 MS *it was on the motive of knowing him and being their townsman* struck through.
25 MS *advice and* struck through.
26 MS *persons* struck through.
27 MS *a true state* struck through.
28 MS *behaviour therein* struck through.
29 MS *prompted me to do it* struck through.

520 To John Collier, Hastings, from William Cranston, [Johnson's Court], 15 October 1745 [SAY 821]

Staying dinner at Dr Russell's of course flung us till within a quarter of four before we mounted, so that by that time I gott to Maresfield could scarce see the church, but however, being well acquainted with the road, I ventured over the forest, upon which I found a great fogg and bitter dark, but surmounted all difficulty, and reached

Eastgrinstead before 8, and which place I left yesterday morning, and came up, like myself, in Lord Delawarr's landau, and arrived at no 4 soon after 6, following from St Paul's a large number of militia marching in solemn pomp with drums beating and colours flying, but wither bound I know not. The news of this day I know not, not having been out nor seen one mortall, that of last night was, that upon the late success of the rebells,[1] their neighbours in the highlands who were before esteemed well affected, had imprisoned their chiefs, and were marching in great numbers to join the pretender.

As I don't suppose anything passed between Mr Pelham and you relating to Morphett, or at least to any purpose, I am preparing for their defence, and shall expect em all toomorrow, and if they have told me the whole of the affair, which I much doubt, and Nic. Bossoms proves what he told me he could, I really think they have a chance. A few days before I left the port, was in chatt with the ladys and among other subjects, London was one, which naturally brought Johnson's Court into my head, when I told em how much I should be obliged to one of them for their company for the winter, I found no objection from that quarter, I intimated and accordingly fully intended to have mentioned it to you but it was sometimes forgott and when in mind, not a proper oppurtunity, but I perswaded myself this method will be the same as if in person. It would be extreamly agreable to me and not, I believe, the contrary to either of them and should be highly pleased should it meet with your approbation. As they have each of em every good qualification, so have consequently no choice left, either of them being equally acceptable, I would say more if necessary. The mayor, I suppose comes up soon after the birthday. My compliments and 10,000 thanks for the last favours.

1 Battle of Prestonpans, near Edinburgh, shortly after dawn 1 September 1745. For the travels of the Pretender see Blaikie.

521 To John Collier, Hastings, from William Cranston, Johnson's Court, 22 October 1745 [SAY 822]

Yours with the bills inclosed for £363 came safe to hand. You'll have your *dedimus* per next, and also the lottery ticketts according to my present opinion.[1] I sent to Bossom today 6 gallons of madeira which I think very good, a feather for my neice's hatt and 2 fire skreens. The rest per tomorrow's carrier with 18 franks, retaining 17 myself, which with 11 used since I had em is the account of the 4 dozen from Mr Stone.

As to news, we have hourly something fresh starting up and of that kind as seems plainly to be made by the enemies of the government in order to intimidate and dishearten; idle, ridiculous storys, though what is in the papers of 6 ships being taken with arms, etc., for Scotland and carried into Ireland is generally beleft to be true. They talk also of an adjournment of the Parliament for a month now the *habeas corpus* Act is suspended and a vote of creditt to pass, for that the nobility, etc., are wanted in their respective countrys, which seems reasonable.[2] The effect this rebellion has already had upon creditt is almost past beleief, and could not have guested at it but by being amongst it.[3] I was in company last night with 2 topp Lancashire and Cheshire agents, who assured me neither of em had made out a writt in either county for near 6 weeks past, so but a gloomy prospect for the law. No new birthday cloaths for the ladys, the looms being all at a stand. Our 6 companys of city militia, now compleat, amount to near 12,000 men, as many more than I imagined.

1 By 18 Geo II c. 9 £2 million for war purposes, of which £½ million from the lottery and £1½ million from annuities; blanks at £6 each to pay £3 per cent per annum (*SL* vol. 6, 588-98).

2 5th session of Parliament, 17 October 1745 to 12 August 1746; on 21 October habeas corpus was suspended for six months; by mid-November the majority of members were in their constituencies, although numbers fluctuated. No formal adjournment, and serious efforts by the opposition (Owen 290-2).

3 The sharpest decline in London credit occurred in the autumn of 1745 as the fear of invasion affected sentiment; Bank of England stock fell to 143½ on 7 September 1745, 136¼ 12 November, 125 from 19 December to 22 January 1746; for the invasion scare of 12 December 1745 see [**535**]; Government borrowing against taxes was not taken up fully, difficulties were experienced with the circulation of Exchequer bills, and the price of 3% government stock fell to 74 by the end of January 1746. The Bank of England discount department dealt only in one month bills and promissory notes, and only for Bank of England customers. During pressure the Bank paid cash in small silver, notably sixpences, and held on to the gold reserves in case rebels tried to discount bills and cash bank notes for gold coin; late in 1745, to support confidence, over 1100 City bankers and merchants announced they would take Bank of England notes at all times: in January 1746 the Bank made a 10 per cent call on capital, yielding £980,000. Uncertainty continued until Culloden and spring brought revival. In Scotland the Bank of Scotland closed its doors on 22 August 1744, and the directors moved the bank's books, papers and cash to Edinburgh castle, and destroyed £82,775 of bank notes lest the castle fall. The Royal Bank of Scotland took similar action. When Prince Charles Edward left Edinburgh for the invasion of England Bank of Scotland directors resumed modest lending on 16 November, and later advanced £10,000 to General Husk (R Saville *Bank of Scotland: A History* (1996) 123-4; J Clapham *The Bank of England: A History* (1970) 2 vols vol. 1, 1694-1797 233-5; Dickson 223).

522 To John Collier, Hastings, from William Cranston, Johnson's Court, 31 October 1745 [SAY 823]

Our chap Sisley made his appearance again yesterday and this evening came with his bail justifyed and that part of the affair is thereby at an end. Igglesden v Illenden and Watts: having now finished this answer I shall lay it before councill learned toomorrow but as Watts appears to be a trustee in the conveyance, son in law to Illenden, I should think that he is able to give some more account of this matter than a common tenant. And his answer must be accordingly therefore it certainly must be contrived to see him and have instructions for his answer from his own mouth. They begin to call upon us on the other side. I find the writt of summons in Meadow's *dedimus* is returned *octabis martini* as I imagined it was. My nephew may sign the deed when he arrives which I suppose won't be long first. I sent pass to the devill last night where the day and founder was remembred. Dr Russell's son dined with me today in his way to Oxford. Universally agreed that the pretender's son is missing from his army and gone to France, but the reason impenetrable. Since a £4 draft of Henry Smith's in long …[1] I paid a £6 one yesterday.

1 MS indecipherable.

523 To John Collier, Hastings, from William Cranston, [Johnson's Court], 5 November 1745 [SAY 824]

I by this post send your warrant against Alce to Mr Worge. Upon sight of this name I recollected that you had asked me whether or not that he had been paid his debt due to him from the late Mr Wellard; and from my information from Gibbs, Rochester's clerk, I told you that he had; but upon seeing the affidavit today and concludeing that your relyed upon that information as authentic and therefore as he had received that money and not paid you, you for that reason attached him. I thought it proper before affairs were carryed so farr, for fear of a mistake in Gibbs, to have Rochester's account *in propria persona*, which I accordingly gott this afternoon, who assures me that Mrs Willard swears in her affidavit to have paid Alce upwards of £600 and that, when last at Bourne, Alce admitted to him that twas true. He beleives there is rather better than £100 more due to him, and for the comfort of the other bond creditors he told me that he beleft there would not be 5s in the pound.

You don't say a word of any body accompanying my nephew which I was in expectation and hopes of. By a line from Captain Murray about his horses I find he is ere now on shipboard with his regiment for Plymouth. Affairs drawing to a crisis we are all in great uneasiness for the event, though in a matter of less consequence we should not doubt of success. I conclude we now resemble a garrison town, for, not to say a word of the other parts of it, we have 200 men every night at 6 regularly mount guard at St Dunstan's vestry room, with detachments at the Barr and Fetter Lane end, and no coach after 10 admitted to pass without stopping it, opening a door and examining into it with a link. I last night saw a train of at least 40 from the playhouse looked into in that manner. I don't hear a word of our Sussex soldiery, etc. I saw the Deptford procession of the pope and the pretender, etc., repeated today in Cornhill.

524 To John Collier, Hastings, from James Collier, Fig Tree Court, 7 November 1745 [SAY 1872]

I got here yesterday about three o'clock in the afternoon after passing through intolerable bad roads, nay, in some places between Battle and Stonecrouch they were so excessively bad as to be almost beyond conception; and indeed I am surprized Winter reached Hasting so soon on Sunday night, considering what time he set out. Mr Webster came into Tunbridge 5 minutes after me we were in different rooms about a quarter of an hour, and then joined company and supped together. The debate in the House of Commons on Munday was managed with great warmth on the side of the address in relation to the ranking of the officers in the regiments raised by the Duke of Bedford, Lord Gower, etc., and the officers in general are greatly affronted at it. The two Houses had a conference this day about the pretender's declaration, but the result is not yet known.[1] Stocks fell very much yesterday in the afternoon on a rumour that 6000 French were landed in Scotland.

The City militia are constantly exercised and part do duty every night in several places; at six o'clock 100 march with beat of drum and fix their headquarters in St Dunstan's vestry room, from whence at ten a party of them are detached to take post at Temple Bar and releived every two hours. They stand on each side of the way with their bayonets fixed, challenge every foot passenger, and stop every coach and open the doors to see that no arms are concealed. I have not delivered Captain Murray's horses to the servant who came for them, his actions being a little inconsistent with his account; for he told my uncle and me that he was now with Mr Johnson in Suffolk Street and had orders to stay there till he was ready to go to Plymouth, for Mr Johnson was to ride one of the horses and he was to take down the other two. But immediately on coming to the inn he offered two to sale and said the black horse would carry him down. I shall send to Mr Johnson tomorrow and that will clear up the affair.

1 Commons discussion, 1, 4 November 1745; while the king granted permission for regiments to be raised by the nobility and landowners, the regular army officers complained about the suitability of such recruits for fighting and the diversion of money to these temporary forces (Owen 287-9).

525 To John Collier, Hastings, from William Cranston, [Johnson's Court], 9 November 1745 [SAY 825]

Igglesden v Illenden and Watts: I shall per Wednesday carrier send you these 2 answers with the *dedimus*. Pope must have altered his mind since you wrote, for he is now a Commissioner and 6 days notice to him. Upon getting a month's time from the 29th ultimo I promised to ask for no more, so you'll take em with that time. I thank you for your intelligence, but the chief of which I had picked up by peice meals before. Lieutenant Worge is what I should not have expected. My nephew informed me of the intended journey of the ladys soon after Xmas. I could have wished it had been before but better late than never. I must beg you will splice out the subdean with £30 if not inconvenient. Ten thousand different reports amongst the rest one last night was that Guise from Berwick had marched with a good body and recovered Edingburgh, but in generall the news seems rather to blacken matters than to clear up. Evernden v King: damages in the whole £21 10s 0d.[1]

1 Evenden v King [**504**].

526 To John Collier, Hastings, from Colonel J. Pelham, St James's, 12 November 1745 [SAY 421]

I hope my letter to you last post explained what John Gower hinted about auditing young Mr Pelham. Tis matter of curiosity for there is not the lest suspicion of Mr Streeke, or any design of removing him from the collection; so that if the tenant bring any of their arrears when you meet, let Streeke receive and remitt them to me as he did to Mr Longuevill. As to Josias Smith's affair he certainly lent money upon the cottage, in hopes of making a peny of me, for he would venture to ask a question of the Duke of Newcastle's steward or any one belonging to me, and after a thing had gone through so many hands tis not likely he would venture his money so privately. I have quite forgot the offer I made him but shal be ready to discourse him when I am in the countrey.

I forgot to acquaint last post that his grace and we all think there should be an address to his Majesty from our corporation, since they are so general. We are time enough, and no reason to fear our loyalty and zeal for the government can be suspected. I wil be sure to present it in the usual form as soon as it comes to my hands. I am very much obliged to Mrs Collier for her obliging offer of some honey and shall very readily accept. I hope she won't send me too much for I hope to eat some with her at Hastings at Christmas. We hear the rebels are got near Carlisle.[1] I cant yet think they will venture to proceed in England and let Wade get behind them. Ligonier is going with a body of eleven thousand to meet them the Duke of Richmond is to comand the horse.

1 11-16 November 1745, Prince Charles Edward was due east of Carlisle waiting for Marshall Wade to attack; Wade reached Hexham, 17 November, but heavy snow blocked his advance west; Sir John Ligonier was ill, and the Duke of Cumberland was promoted to commanding officer. For correspondence between the Dukes of Richmond and Newcastle on this military crisis see McCann 172-212.

527 To John Collier, Hastings, from James Collier, Fig Tree Court, 12 November 1745 [SAY 1873]

This morning I applyed to Mr Coles in relation to the unhappy affair of Mary Cousens,[1] whom my uncle and I thought a proper person. He has been twice today to wait on Mr Joseph Taylor of Bridewell who is the chief clerk, but has not yet been able to see him, but has instructions from his deputy, to whom he told the business, to be at Mr Taylor's at nine tomorrow morning. I shall be able I beleive to have some respite in regard to her removal, and when the committee are known shall endeavour to get her minuted down for the ward of the incurables which depends principally on the report of Dr Monro, and am glad to find that our case, viz a raving madness, is a circumstance that particularly induces the committee to send such poor people there. However, by next post I shall be able to acquaint you with certainty what will be done. As to Guy's hospital they never suffer anybody to enter there who has once been in Bedlam, and I am afraid private madhouses will be attended with great expence.

No news stirring at present but what is included in the publick papers. I shall send you down some pamplets tomorrow, but as to Eachard's *History*,[2] I never saw a continuation; the third volume, I beleive, is in Patrick's study; and in relation to Burnet, I can't conceive where they are for I never carried them out of the tearoom. A book of 4 shillings price appeared about fourteen months ago regarding the four last years of Queen Ann which I shall send. At the Union coffee house in Cornhill I saw the ceremony of burning the pretender's declaration, etc.[3] There was the greatest concourse of people I ever saw on any occasion, and when the papers were put into the fire three universal huzzas given.

1 Mary Cousens was born in Hastings and dealing with her illness was the responsibility of the parish [**530**].
2 Laurence Eachard, *The History of England from the first entrance of Julius Ceasar* (London, 1707) 3 vols, vol. 3 published 1718, large folio size. The history closed with the Convention Parliament of 1689.
3 The first declaration from the Pretender was published in Paris, 16 May 1745, the second declaration was printed in Edinburgh, 10 October 1745; Philip Carteret Webb, barrister and political theorist, published *Remarks on the pretender's declaration and commission*, 12 October 1745, a criticism of the theology and history behind the Stuart claim to the throne, and his subsequent *Remarks on the Pretender's eldest son's second declaration,* 6 November 1745. The burning of the Pretender's declarations by the common hangman at the Royal Exchange on 12 November 1745 was unanimously authorised by both houses of Parliament.

528 To John Collier, Hastings, from William Cranston, Johnson's Court, 16 November 1745 [SAY 826]

I am to thank you for your list. The squire of Glinley's generosity is without precedent, the English of which I suppose to be that he will generously give 10s to save the payment of £20.[1] I am glad to hear of your good account of my brother. His worship has spent the greatest part of this day in quest of Dr Munro but without success, so that that affair must be in suspence till next week. He knows nothing of Dr Burnett. I fancy it must have been long missing for I don't recollect so much as ever to have em at your house. We seem to have a certain account this evening of the rebells being returned to the attack of Carlise with a determined resolution to have it, so that there's likely to be warm work.[2]

1 John Meres Fagge of Glinley in Westham, on the disputed copyhold (WSRO Add Ms 20,488). N.B. the sum could be read as 20s.

2 Carlisle town and castle surrendered to the Pretender on 15 November 1745. Prince Charles Edward and his army entered 17 November, stayed to the 18-20 November, and marched south to Penrith 21/22 November, reaching Kendal on 23 November (Blaikie 26-7).

529 To John Collier, Hastings, from John Streeke,[1] Lewes, 18 November 1745 [SAY 371]

I am favoured with yours of 12th; what his grace the Duke of Newcastle, the honourable Mr Pelham and Colonel Pelham require I have no objection to, but approve very well of it, and shall summons the tenants to be at the White Hart on Tewsday the 3d day of December, next by eleven of the clock in the forenoon with their accounts and arrears. I beleeve if I order a shilling ordinary it would be better and cheaper than to order perticularly what they should provide, but if you think otherwise please to let me know.

I herewith send you a rentall of the landed estate of Thomas Pelham esqr., of Stanmer [2] and what arrears were due at Ladyday and Michaelmas last and what I have received since. Is very few of the farms on lease; I have just mentioned them against the respective names of the tenants. There were several leases intended if my late master had lived. I hope you will be here the day or evening before the audit, and that you will please to take a bed and such accomodation as my house will afford with a hearty welcome and I will give you all the light I can to answer what is required.

1 John Streeke, steward to Thomas Pelham of Stanmer.
2 Appendix 4: Pelham Estate [**607**]. For the transcript of the rental of the Sussex estate of Thomas Pelham of Stanmer see SAY 372; SAY 370 was also enclosed with the above letter, and is similar to SAY 372.

530 To John Collier, Hastings, from James Collier, Fig Tree Court, 21 November 1745 [SAY 1874]

I received yesterday by the carrier the Hasting address and carried it myself to Colonel Pelham's this morning, and though he was not at home I left it with his servant, and shall call there tomorrow, as I know it can't be presented till Saturday, to find out what his sentiments on the affair are. The town in general has been very much disappointed with regard to the behaviour of the Carlisle men, inasmuch as Marshall Wade offered to garrison the city with regular troops, which proposal was waved with thanks, and declaring that the townsmen were determined to hold out to the last extremity; but immediately on the rebels investing the city, the inhabitants rose and fired on the militia who guarded the place, which obliged the town to surrender; and Colonel Durand with 200 invalids, with most of the militia, retired into the castle with a determined resolution to hold out ten days; but on Fryday evening the militia basely deserted the governour by jumping down the walls and obliged him to capitulate on the same terms with the town, viz to pay a sum of money and not to serve against the pretender for a year and a day.

Marshall Wade was within ten miles of Carlisle on Tuesday, but, however, the rebels seem determined to push on southward, for the same day, in the morning, an officer of theirs came to Penrith, sixteen miles of this side, to order the inhabitants to furnish provisions for 8000 foot and 500 horse, half of which came in there that evening; but when the messenger came away, who arrived this morning, it was not known whether the remaining body had left Carlisle. However, out of precaution Warrington bridge in Lancashire, which lately cost 8000 pounds, is broken down and people are ready to demolish Preston bridge, which cost more, in half an hour's time in order to give time for Ligonier to collect his forces, and if they do march this way inevitable destruction will fall upon them for they will be put between two fires without any possibility of escaping.

Captain Worge, who has been recruiting here, sets out for his regiment, which is already in Lancashire, next week. He is in high spirits, but misses his finger very much. I called on Mr Rowe this morning, who told me they had received certain intelligence of the French man of war from Dunkirk being lost near Boston in Lincolnshire, having on board 300 soldiers with arms and ammunition for the use of the rebels. Most of the soldiers and sailors got on shore and had some skirmishes with the country people who assembled in order to take them, but finding some of their comrades to fall, they surrendred themselves and were sent as prisoners to the several gaols of the county. And it is likewise as certain that the brave Captain Beavour of the *Fox* man of war, with all his gallant crew, perished in the storm some few days since near Dunbar; and more northward at the same time the Tryal sloop foundered at sea, and all the men were drowned.[1]

Mary Cousens is not as yet removed out of Bethlem hospitall, but it is impossible to get her continued there.[2] Mr Alwright of Lambeth marsh will take her for one month upon tryal for 8sh per week, but if her distemper is such as to require a more than ordinary attendance he will have more. I don't despair at present of getting her minuted down in the list of persons who are to supply the vacancys in the ward of incurables.

1 *Fox* 6th rate, 24 guns, whilst patrolling the southern shore of the Firth of Forth with orders to intercept enemy ships was driven onto rocks off Dunbar during a gale, 14 November 1745; few sailors survived.

2 Mary Cousens is not recorded in the admission books of Bethlem Hospital; the Bethlem archives department have noted that she may have been admitted for a short time, although the long-term nature of her illness would have precluded an agreed admission with a parish authority.

531 To John Collier, Hastings, from William Cranston, [Johnson's Court], 26 November 1745 [SAY 827]

Our townsmen Morphett, etc., were with me yesterday by 10 according to appointment was with em today at 12 at the Custom house when they were entered on board the *Prince George* man of warr now at Portsmouth.[1] It was agreed that Morphett should stay on shore a day or two to look after their cloaths, but upon their being examined by the surgeon, Ridley was found to have a rupture, and therefore unfitt for service, so he was left on shore. The rest went imediately on board a tender and go toomorrow for the Nore, and back again Thursday sennight to appear at the Old Baily to be acquitted and thereby their bail discharged afterwards to the Nore again, or the board the *Royall Soveraign*, and by the first tender to Portsmouth. They were entered as volunteers, good usage, handsomely recommended by Symon and promised by a leiutenant of the *Prince George*, one Young, then present.

After all over and Symon under a difficulty what to do with Ridley, I told him of his being something of kin to me and that if he could be gott off should be obliged to him, which he fairly promised that he must represent it to the board, but would do it in such manner as he did not doubt but would be come into. Ridley knows nothing of it as yet, nor shall till after the appearance at the Old Baily, nor do either of the others know of anything of the matter nor of the objection made to him. The affair of a privateer takeing a French ship with about 60 Irish and Scotch officers on board off Scotland is doubtless true, but who in particular they are is various; Lord Derwentwater, Lord John Drumond, Kelly and even the pretender's 2nd son talked of. [2] I had per last post a notification in form of Leiutenant George Worge's military preferrment with orders to buy buff in abundance.

1 *Prince George*, 90 guns, unsuited to holding the Channel between Ostend and Dover in winter weather; her 100 marines were despatched for the defence of London, 3 December (Richmond vol. 2, 177-8).

2 Cruisers seized two transports of Lord John Drummond 12 October 1745; lists of those aboard (*LG* 7 December 1745, 10 December 1745).

532 To John Collier, Hastings, from William Cranston, [Johnson's Court], 30 November 1745 [SAY 828]

The inclosed will give you some small insight into the Chesham affairs. I doubt not but that it will be the best to come into Potter's proposall of clearing all to Michaelmas last, upon payment of one year's neat rent, and then he may go on regularly for the future, but this I did not care to do, to give him authority, till I had your thoughts upon the matter and which after I receive I will transmitt to him. Imagineing that it had slipt your memory, and it not coming into mine time enough to have your authority for it, I ventured to pay your quitt rents as usuall on Thursday to Hickman as I will those to Tempest in a day or two. Mr Collier told me tonight that Mary Cousins is out of Bedlam and in a private madhouse at 8s per week. Your mentioning in a letter to Jemmy your intending to send me some red herrings and seeing Master Bossom on Thursday, I asked him after em but found none, and I now only mention it least by some mischance they should be gott into wrong hands.

What I hinted at in generall in my last about the pretender's second son being on board the French privateer taken by the *Sheerness* man of war, turns out to be matter of fact beyond doubt.[1] Affidavits of the identity of the person having been transmitted to the Admiralty, he and his companions are expected in town this evening. The Duke de Richeleiu and count Clermont, who commanded at the siege of Aeth, being amongst em.

The late Lord Provost of Edingburg, Stewart,[2] was also seized this morning at 7, and in custody of Ward the messenger, under a warrant of detainer for high treason. This also is fact, as is likewise another fatall overthrow to Prince Charles of Lorrain and his army by the Prussians, with their king at their head, and that the prince of Annalt Dessau with his army is ravaging and laying waste Saxony almost to the gates of Dresden. Perhaps you may have all this news in the Gazett, but if you have, don't think me the worst politician for that, for that or that what I write is out of the publick newspapers; for I can assure you, that I've not see the Gazett till next morning since I've been out of Sussex; for tis very rarely published till 12 o'clock, and very often not till the morning. Marshall Wade left not Newcastle till Wednesday morning, could not gett his horses shoed before. I hope my brother continues mending.

I made an end of Beal's affair at the wine licence office on Thursday, the whole of which with some small matter for my trouble and of a lycence to lady day next came to £9 01s 10d so that I have 18s 2d to return him of his £10 of all which I wrote him per last post. The Commissioners did not forgett to tell me that it was the regard they had to Mr Pelham's intercession that lett him off upon so easy terms.

1 Officers captured included the Earl of Derwentwater and his son (*LG* 26 November 1745).

2 Archibald Stewart, Lord Provost, Edinburgh, arrested 30 November 1745 and charged with treason.

533 To John Collier, Hastings, from William Cranston, [Johnson's Court], 7 December 1745 [SAY 829]

Your long silence gave me roome to doubt something extra had happened to occasion it, and the cause of which am very sorry to hear but hope the doctor's prescriptions, closely followed, will have the desired effect. Morphett, etc., were discharged yesterday together with his bail, in which I was unexpectedly out of pockett and must beg your advice and assistance to Mr Gurr to gett me reimbursed. I've wrote him the particulars of the affair which I've desired him to show to you.

Evernden v King: the old practice used to be to allow half the poundage, never more, but that seems to be now entirely disused and have not given nor taken it these 10 years. As I take the defendant to be a responsible person and if Thayer has or should so shuffle as that you have a fair oppurtunity to gett off, with honour, from any promise that may have been made him, don't allow him one penny; bring an action of debt upon the judgment, which is your own way to bring such gentry to reason. I've had from Bossum ½ a hundred of herrings since my last for which you've my hearty thanks. I think no excuse but sickness should have prevented our collectors from appearing. Wicker is in town.

We are in a good deal of consternation in town, more from an assurance of a large embarkation from Dunkirk than from the rebells, who now may be said to be flying from the duke's army, and who must in the end come up with em and will then in all humane probability defeat em. But the apprehension of a landing in Suffolk, Norfolk or Lincolnshire and of the rebells' getting thither to join em, and towards which countrys they are supposed to be pointing, greatly alarms us.[1] Insomuch that you may be assured that the king has this evening sent to the body of the law to tell them of his intention of heading a third army and that he shall depend upon them, the law, for their protection to his own royal family; and the principell of the severall houses are now setting takeing the names of the gentlemen of the barr who will attend this service, and Chief Justice Willes is agreed upon to be their collonell and approved on as such by his Majesty. Pray God send us out of these difficultys speedily. Guy was here on Wednesday with the answers. Not a bad circumstance of the inclination of the populace that they broke the glasses of [2] the coaches yesterday in which the prisoners came to the tower, and but for the guards would have pulled em to pieces.

1 For reference to the panic in the coastal regions of these counties see Pyle 56, 113.
2 MS *the windows of* struck through.

534 To John Collier, Hastings, from William Cranston, [Johnson's Court], 10 December 1745 [SAY 830]

Fryday afternoon and Saturday morning we were terribly alarmed here from the rumour and belief that the rebells were south of the duke and posting with all imaginable hast to usward. This brought the message I mentioned in my last from the king to the law on Saturday and a determined resolution of his and the Prince of Wales's going forth as yesterday morning for Finchley with a third army and there setting up his standard, but Saturday afternoon brought some hopes that what was reported in respect to the rebells was not true, and the next day the contrary was out of doubt.

Yesterday brought us still better and today yet better, it being confidently reported that the horse, with the duke at their head, have so hemmed in the rebells that he is able to keep em at bay till his foot can come up, which will oblige em to a battle the success of which does not seem to be doubted. Whether this is precisely true I know, but there is doubtless some good news, since the king sent this evening to the law to thank em for their loyalty, etc., and to tell them that he hoped he should have no occasion for their service in the manner proposed. I hope we shall be able yet to keep a merry Xmas. The club have engaged to meet and bung it away upon the news of good luck in the duke's battle. Amongst too many in trade, etc., who will feel the bad effects of these times upon creditt, Knight and Hanson in Exchange Alley seem to be the first,have this day shutt up. Mitford, our receiver generall, is £3000 deep; besides, I fear some of our Sussex subscription. Legas, I know, used to keep cash there and doubt is as much in the mire as Mitford. The latter was to have been married as toomorrow morning to Miss Wicker, and how will it be now know not.

535 To John Collier, Hastings, from William Cranston, [Johnson's Court], 12 December 1745 [SAY 831]

I am to acknowledge the favour of yours of today with the £50 bank bill inclosed, and am also to thank you for your intelligence which I this evening shewed to Jemmy, who desired me to tell you that he was determined to sett out for the port next Wednesday morning; that he neither had as yet nor should have a man to carry down with him but intended the letting that alone till his return again, and therefore desired you would send up somebody from the port with his horse and to squire him down and to be in town either Monday or Tuesday as you thought proper.

The alarm the town was in this morning, and especially the great ones, is not to be expressed, occasioned by a messenger from Mr Harrison of Seaford, the whole of which is this. Sir Thomas Webster sends a letter to Mr Medley to Friston that there were a number of French ships actually in Pemsey Bay, and the soldiers landing. Medley sends this account to Harrison; Harrison sends an express of it imediately away to the Custom house. It gott there about 1 this morning, to the Duke of Newcastle's office by 2, he called up and gott to St James's by 3, Lord Chancellor, Lord Harrington, etc., etc., etc., all assembled in councill by 4. The guards of all kinds instantly called up and imediately to assemble in the park. These transactions took up some time and the duke etc., surprized no farther accounts came in from Sussex, staid together till 8, then seperated and adjourned to 11. Before 10 another express came to the Custom house from Harrison telling that he was misinformed, that the ships seen were only severall cutters, etc., sent out by Vernon, so all is hush again; but between 8 and 12 all this news flew like wild fire through the streets into the City. The 2 chief justices then actually sitting at Guildhall rose from their benches in the middle of their causes, and posted to St James's, but as I said before, now all is quiet, and as our enemies are still on the other side, we hope, and almost conclude that when they hear of the scituation of the rebells that they will not attempt an invasion. By yesterday's post I had a letter from Hadley,[1] who lives at Ashburn, Derbyshire, a copy of which you receive underneath.

[*Captain Hadley*] The rebells came here on Tuesday. The damage they have done me is at present seemingly irreparable, but you shall have better information per next. This day sennight was the Excise day. Tuesday as above they demanded the Excise again, in obedience to which commands they received a third part. Wednesday they went to Derby and there ransomed the town for £3000, and then to Ashburne again on Fryday, and have in short destroyed us and plundered and eat us up, and so all along the road to Leek where they have done the like, and shott severall that would not comply with their diabolicall demands. Oh, terrible people! To what place they have steered their course from Leek we know not, but messengers are out for information. In short, I am so frightened I don't know well what I do, but will write to you again by Wednesday's post; don't regard the papers much.

1 The Jacobite army camped in Ashbourne overnight 3/4 December 1745, leaving for Derby the next day, and returned to Ashbourne on the 6/7 December on their retreat.

536 To John Collier, Hastings, from Duke of Newcastle, Whitehall, 13 December 1745 [SAY 109]

His Majesty having received certain intelligence that preparations are made at Dunkirk, and other ports in France, for making an immediate descent upon some part of the coast, I am commanded to signify to you his Majesty's pleasure, that you should direct the several Custom house officers along the coast to keep a good look-out, and upon the first appearance of any vessels off the coast to send an immediate account of it by express to me, and also to Admiral Vernon in the Downs; and I must also desire you would keep a constant correspondence with me during the present alarm.

537 To Duke of Newcastle, Whitehall, from John Collier, Hastings, 14 December 1745 [SAY 110]

I had the honour of your grace's letter of yesterday's date by express this morning at three in regard to the immediate descent intended by the French king on some part of the coast, and in humble obedience to your commands [1] immediately dispatched directions to all the Custom officers on the coast of this county and Kent, to keep a good look out and constantly patroll [2] day and night and on the first appearance of any vessels off the coast to send your grace an immediate account by express, and likewise to Admiral Vernon in the Downs. We have a constant double watch patrolling the coast at this place and proper persons at Farleight church and the summit of all the hills near the town to observe and give intelligence which are releived every two hours. I shall not fayle from time to time to transmit your grace an immediate account [3] of anything material that shall happen.[4]

1 MS *the same* struck through.
2 MS *the coast* struck through.
3 MS *on any emergence* struck through.
4 MS *on this coast* struck through.

538 To Admiral Edward Vernon, from John Collier, Hastings, 15 December 1745 [SAY 111]

[1] The 9th instant I had intelligence that [2] there were fitting out with the utmost expedition at Boulogne all their privateers, trading ships, fishing boats and all the prizes in that harbour taken from us in this war, and cleansing the slub out of their harbour or bason that

they might ride a float; and that it was publickly talked of that they were designed to bring over soldiers to be landed on the coast of Kent or Sussex and were to be got ready in ten days. [3] I forthwith transmitted an account thereof to my lord Duke of Newcastle.

The 14th instant, at 3 in the morning, I [4] had a letter by express from his grace that his Majesty had received certain intelligence [5] preparations are making at Dunkirk and other ports in France, for making an immediate descent upon some part of the coast; and have thereon directions from his grace for a good look out to be kept [6], and upon the first appearance of any vessels off the coast to send his grace an immediate account of it, and likewise the same to you in the Downs. I mention this, though I am [7] satisfyed you have much better and certain intelligence of [8] the designs of the French king against us. But at this critical juncture think it the duty of every Englishman to give the government any intelligence he meets with, though much better accounts may have been before in all probability given.

The bearers hereof, George Harrison and [9] W. Phillips, are natives of this town, and bread to the sea from their infancy, and esteemed, particularly Harrison, to be good sailors and perfectly well acquainted with the French coast on this part of the Channel. They have been reputed, and I beleive with truth, to have followed the detestable practice of smugling, but both faithfully promise never to be again concerned thereon, and Harrison's cutter was one of them taken the 8th out of this road by the *Badger* sloop. The lieutenant came on shore to know the character of the masters, not finding any goods on board.

Upon enquiry I found who were masters and told him they were reputed smuglers, upon which he carried the two boats away. Harrison came yesterday to me and desired I would give him a letter to you, that if you'd please to let him and Phillips go in his own or any other cutter, and put a lieutenant and seamen on board him, he is confident he can be of service in making discoverys of what is doing at Boulogne or elsewhere on the French coast. The man's character is not impeached but only in the infamous practice of smugling. At his request, and at the desire of several gentlemen here, I presume to give you this epistle, [10] and it's left to your pleasure and consideration; but if nothing is done, hope you'l pardon it.[11]

1 MS *having received* struck through.
2 MS *they* struck through.
3 MS *the 9th instant* struck through.
4 MS *received* struck through.
5 MS *that* struck through.
6 MS *on the coast* struck through.
7 MS *well* struck through
8 MS *what is ...* struck through.
9 MS *James* struck through.
10 MS *and hope* struck through.
11 This incident is discussed in Admiral Vernon's correspondence with the Admiralty, part reprinted in *Some Seasonable Advice from an Honest Sailor* (London, 1746) and in B McL. Ranft (ed) *The Vernon Papers NRS* vol. 99 (1958).

539 To John Collier, Hastings, from Samuel Burt, Newcastle House, 17 December 1745 [SAY 112]

I was last week favoured with yours with the account of the expence of the two last birthdays[1] and also money paid for newspapers, which I will be sure to lay before my lord duke the first oppurtunity; but at present he is so very buissy that there is no speaking to him about his own affairs. Here is no news in London of any sort, but we are hourly in expectation of having a good account of the rebells from the Duke of Cumberland.

1 Payment for the king's birthday celebrations at Hastings.

540 To John Collier, Hastings, from William Cranston, [Johnson's Court], 17 December 1745 [SAY 832]

My old enemy attacked me Fryday last since which have not been down stairs. My left foot first, then my right and now my knee, but abated in all, though write this in bed not being able to gett out of it. If we have no insurrections from within ourselves, then I apprehend this place the safest from the enemy, for if they arrive in your neighbourhood, Crowhurst can be no abideing place.[1] What with my own and one of Mrs Nouns', I can harbour my sister, the 5 girls and 1 maid they need not be told of a hearty welcome though I could wish it was not upon so unhappy an occasion.

The fast day[2] not being thought of when I wrote for horses, Jemmy will not sett out till Thursday morning. We have no kind of news in town either from the duke or rebells which puzzles us much; nor from my visitors today, Jemmy, T. Green and Rowe can I pick up any other kind of publick or private intelligence. The brawn arrived last Fryday and after taking the accustomed toll shall send the remainder by toomorrow's carrier. Since 8, Mr Collier called upon me with the inclosed, having just then received it.

1 Crowhurst, three miles north-west of Hastings.
2 The king appointed 18 December 1745 as a fast day.

541 To John Collier, Hastings, from James Collier, Fig Tree Court, 21 December 1745 [SAY 1875]

Mr Humphreys and I have expected to set out every hour since my last; he was obliged to stay for an answer from a gentleman and has this evening got it. We set out tomorrow morning. I mentioned in Thursday's letter that the House of Commons would not divide, but Mr Pitt insisted on it and the numbers were, for the Hessians 190, against 44, which great majority very much chagrined him.[1] Great encomiums are bestowed here on the behaviour of the Dover privateers and Captain Owen will soon have the command of one of his Majesty's ships.[2] The two 10,000 pounds were drawn this morning, the numbers as follows, viz 18,542 and 48,070.[3] The last I heard drawn and, what is more remarkable, the former was advertized about ten days ago as a lost or mislaid ticket. Tis generally beleived here that the invasion will not take place in the south part of Great Britain, but that they will attempt to land their forces at Montrose. I am in great hopes that tomorrow will prove a more favourable day than this which has been the most disagreable this season. My uncle is very much out of order, be pleased to give my duty to my mother and love to my sisters.

1 Opposition to government policy continued for the session. On 10 December 1745 Pitt moved for papers on the recall of British cavalry from Europe, defeated 138 to 41 on assurances that departure was hindered by cold east winds across the North Sea. The opposition was defeated again 20 December over the cost of deployment of Hessian soldiers in Scotland (Owen 290-1).
2 Three Dover privateers were involved in an attack on French transports outside Dunkirk: *Carlisle* Captain Owen, *Eagle* Captain Barclay, *York* Captain Gravener (Richmond vol. 2, 179-80).
3 For details of this lottery see, 18 Geo. II c. 9 (*SL* vol. 6, 588-98 [**521**]).

542 To John Collier, Hastings, from Andrew Stone, Whitehall, 24 December 1745
[SAY 113]

Colonel Ellison,[1] who acts as adjutant general of his Majesty's forces, being ordered to take a survey of the coast of Sussex and of the country about it, I am ordered by my Lord Duke of Newcastle to desire you would give him all the information and assistance in your power.

1 Colonel Cuthbert Ellison, Deputy Adjutant General to Earl of Stair, 1744, Colonel 1745, MP Shaftesbury 1747-54.

543 To John Collier, Hastings, from William Cranston, Johnson's Court, 24 December 1745
[SAY 833]

This my last letter for this evening must be short having quite wasted my spiritts and therefore can only just tell you that I am much mended, that I wish you all a merry Xmas, that I've received 3 guineas of Cole's from Mrs Presade, and that I shall toomorrow send you a lamb which I hope will come safe to hand.

544 To John Collier, Hastings, from William Cranston, [Johnson's Court], 4 January 1746 [SAY 834]

I am to acknowledge, and thank you for yours of Monday last and today, not forgetting his worship's of Thursday. On Wednesday I had Captain Gourlay with me, with a letter from Patrick about a debt due to Rice, which he promissed to bring me as soon as he had received his freight, which he expected would be in 10 days time, etc.

I setled with Master Clarke the day before I was laid up but had quite forgott it till upon my getting down stairs again I mett with the inclosed, and looking also yesterday amongst some old letters I accendentally poped upon that of yours, wherein you tell me that when I had received Lamb's bill I should pay £200 into Messrs Hoare for Mr Lewes Pelham, and which I really took to be but £100 which I accordingly then paid in, but upon discovery my mistake yesterday, I instantly sent over and made that one, two.

You mention in yours of today the sending me your two blank ticketts inclosed, but I could find none in it so hope you will find that you forgott to put em up. You shan't fail of your vouchers, and rheubarb by the next carrier, and if possible Meadow's recovery. I observe by Mr Rideout's letter that the revertionary estate intended to be assigned, is to be for the benefitt of all Read's creditors which remain unpaid, and yours seems to apply it only to your client Smith's demand. So that how this matter stands is not quite clear to me as to this particular. Smith's debt you doubtless know, but dare say not the others. Therefore if all are to be included we should have a list of their names, additions and sumes due, mine is £22 on judgement.

Both publick and private intelligence seems to confirm Admirall Vernon haveing struck his flagg and arriving in town last night.[1] If so, one would imagine the apprehension of an invasion is over, at least for the present, and that you may yet have some joyous hours upon the coast before Xmas is over, which upon this occasion may fairly be lengthened out till candlemas. This severe weather but ill agrees with my gout, as I fear it also does with yours. I've as yet been out but once, and that was Thursday, but both out and in, in a chair.

The duke is expected in town tonight or too-morrow, but tis generally said his stay will be but short, for that he will soon sett out for Edingburgh. Hume Campbell you see is turned out.[2] The Marquis of Tweedale goes next, who will be succeeded by the Duke of Buccleugh, but who will take the former's place is not said.

It may be depended upon that upon Miss Camerons, etc., coming into Derby, they were in high spirits, and fully satisfied of keeping 12th night at St James's. That when they went away they wept like church spouts, that the pretender's son also, just before he left his quarters there, drank all his friends in England in a bumper; said he was now even with them, had done as much for them as they for him. That he lay at councellor Starky's house both going to and coming from the north; that in his way upwards he was cheery, and eat like a traveller, and looked well. That on his return, he was so much altered in his countenance, that he was not known again for some time by the servants. That he continued 22 hours in the house and eat only a little mutton broth and a wing of fowl, and drank not a drop. They expressed great concern that they had not time in their retreat to pay a visit to Sir Thomas Booth's, and levy the £500 he had subscribed to the raiseing the Liverpool troops.[3]

1 Admiral Vernon was superseded in command of the Downs due to disagreements with the Admiralty, 26 December 1745. He left the fleet for London, 2 January 1746 (Richmond vol. 2, 181-6).

2 Hume Campbell, 3rd Earl of Marchmont.

3 The Corporation of Liverpool together with a town subscription raised £4859 to pay for the 648 volunteers of the Liverpool Blues regiment during the 1745 rising, in pay from 7 October to 15 January 1746.

545 To John Collier, Hastings, from Colonel James Pelham, St James's, 16 January 1746 [SAY 422]

Mr Streeke has informed me, as you'l see by the enclosed, that Mr Pelham's tenant Weeden of the Hoathdown is at a stand. Streeke has done right to enter upon his effects; I don't think by the inventory there appears so great an overplus as he represents. However, I have not the lest objection to letting Weeden go on with the farm, in one shape or other, if you think it may be done with safety till next Michaelmas; guardians are not at liberty to make concessions, nor ought they to run any risque in regard to themselves, but I am for lenity in these bad times, and we shal be entirely governed by you, fearing you can't venture to go over this cold weather. I have ordered Streeke to send Weeden to you that no time may be lost for your farther information.

J. Gower not coming to town last week, I opened your letter to him imagining there was some comission, and I have sent by the carryer this week a pot of his deputy's poison for ratts. Storey has lately been very ill of a goutish humour flying about him and a good deal in his stomach. He is got about again and ordered by the physicians to go to the Bath in the spring. He proposes being there the begining of March and we have agreed it would be the best thing for you that's possible, and I should be glad you would think of it. You can't have a better companion, there are very few instances where the Bath has failed being of great service to persons in your circumstances.

We have now begun upon busieness and set out with a declaration to assist the Dutch, which is carrying on the war in Flanders.[1] I think everybody thinks it a necessary measure; there were but 53 against it in our house. We expect in a few days to hear of an action in Scotland General Hawley marched towards them last Sunday. I desire my compliments to the ladys and thanks to Mrs Collier for the honey.

1 Declaration to assist the Dutch passed the Commons, along with the subsidy (Owen 293-4). On 31 January 1746 Henry Pelham was successful in extending the life of the new volunteer regiments by eight months, and their officers in full pay, beyond the four months agreed on 1 November 1745 (Mahon vol. 3, 191).

546 To John Collier, Hastings, from William Cranston, [Johnson's Court], 21 January 1746 [SAY 835]

Captain John Gourlay was with me this afternoon and paid me £24 09s 0d upon George Tree's account, and for which I gave a receipt accordingly. I've paid your severall small dribbletts as, the tenths, day, Potts, Elphick, Walker, Lambert for wine £2 19s 6d and Jemmy's chamber rent, all since my last. I hope to be able to gett abroad for good by Thursday, being much mended since the warm weather.

Our chief talk is at present of General Oglethorpe,[1] who it seems behaved greatly amiss with his detachment of 1200 horse from Wade; was up with the rear guard with the rebells, never touched em, went 7 miles to the west, and, from being the avaunt guard of the duke, was at the brush of Clifton moor, 10 miles behind him. The duke at the seeing him afterwards told him that he was either a coward or a traitor, but did not beleive the former. His being foster brother to the pretender is now called to remembrance, is charged with giving the rebells notice of every step of Wade and, in short, from publick talk is a most villainous chap, but time, as the newsmongers say, will discover how much of is true, how much false. Tis the generall opinion here that the rebells won't stand a brush with Hawley. R-we tells me that they are sadly put to it in his office for ways and means. A scheme of Sir John Barnard's upon the carpett for calling in all plate and to melt and coin it, and to give 3 per cent interest till principall paid, for that we have not specie enough amongst us to go on. A dismall wett afternoon.

1 Lord Egmont reported that Oglethorpe was accused by the Duke of Cumberland of allowing the Jacobite forces to escape; the story spread as Oglethorpe was disliked among army officers (Egmont vol. 3, 312-3).

547 To John Collier, Hastings, from Mrs Henrietta Ashburnham, 24 January 1746 [SAY 600]

You may remember I some time ago spoke to you upon an affair of poor Mrs Puckles, and the reason of my giving you this trouble now, is to let you know Clark was with her yesterday to demand the money which she has most certainly paid. He told her when he went away he should come no more about it himself, but as he does not give it up, I suppose he intends to be further troublesome to her. And in case he should be so, I beg you will be so good to her, as to let me know in what maner you would advise her to act. You were so kind as to tell her and me that you would be her friend in the affair, and advised her not to pay the money, which makes her wholly relye on you. She told Clark she was advised not to pay the money, but did not tell him who gave the advice, if you have forgott any part of the affair, she shall wait on you, whenever you will apoint a day, to give you an account of every circumstance of it and her oath that she paid it at so many payments. It will be so great a piece of charity in you to help a poor distressed person in so just a cause, that I make no doubt of your doing all you can for her; my brother and she desire their complyments to you and joyn in mine to all your good family. If you have time I should be obliged to you if you could write to me two or three words which will be a great comfort to her.

548 To John Collier, Hastings, from Sir Thomas Webster, Battle Abbey, 27 January 1746 [SAY 115]

This morning I had a message from an honest and very unfortunate man, Mark Taught, to let me know one of your boatmen at Hastings dyed last night, and begging me to recommend him to your favour to succeed in the place; if it is in your power and no præingagement, it would be a generous act of charity in you, and a pleasing one to me. Our unaccountable miscarriage in Scotland causes great consternation;[1] these repeated pannicks, and ill behaviour of so many of our troops, becomes serious and big with just apprehensions of bad consequences. I am with my compliments to your family.

1 Defeat of General Hawley, then C-in-C Scotland, 17 January 1746, Falkirk. Hawley's army of 9000 was based in Edinburgh, and left the capital towards Falkirk intending to attack Prince Charles Edward then besieging Stirling castle; on learning of this the rebels, in similar numbers to Hawley's army, marched to Falkirk and attacked first, across a broad front. Hawley's right flank held, but the dragoons and much of the centre and left flank infantry fled; not a defeat suggested Fortescue, but a disgrace. Hawley was clear, 'such scandalous cowardice I never saw before. The whole second line of foot ran away without firing a shot.' (Fortescue 138-41). Lord Egmont, citing Hawley, noted 'three-quarters of the army ran away, some examples must be made'; and subsequently Hawley informed the Duke of Newcastle of 14 deserters to be hanged, '31 of Hamilton's dragoons likewise for desertion to the rebels, and 32 of the foot shot for cowardice' (McCann 300, 29 January 1746).

549 To Duke of Newcastle, from John Collier, Hastings, [29] January 1746 [SAY 88]

Last night, about 9, I had information that there were three men at Hooe who had made great application for a boat to be procured to carry them over to France. Hooe is about 9 miles from the town, a very smugling place upon which I presumed they grounded their hopes. I found they were [1] secured and I sent a party to take care of and bring them hither, which they did about 10 this morning. I examined [2] several persons who swear possitively as to their desiring a boat to carry some of them to France and if possible to be landed last night. Upon which I have examined the 3 persons seperately and kept them apart, but they all decline signing any examination. One of them calls himself James Bishop, brother to Sir Cecil Bishop of this county, aged about 30.[3] Another, his servant named James Cravellion, about 35, says he was born at Walhen near Gemblon in Brabant. The third one, [4] Abraham Ibbotson, a farmer at Tortington near Arundel, in this county, about 60 years of age.[5]

They all declined answering several questions or submitting to a regular examiantion, but on asking Mr Bisshop and Ibbotson whether they had ever taken the oaths to the government, they acknowledged themselves Roman Catholicks. They manifestly contradicted one another and though they refused regular examinations it appears[6] evident that Bisshop and his servant intended for France. I have kept them under a guard of the countrymen that brought them in till this evening, and as we have a company of Highlanders, Captain Campbell commander, at present quartered here, I have applyed to him and put them under his care as to a guard, centinells, etc., till the pleasure of the government is known, and dismissed the other guard. As they refuse a regular examination it is my humble opinion they should be sent for and examined as above, and may be escorted by a detachment of Captain Campbell's company. If it's thought proper to send a messenger for them, or such other way as shall be thought proper, I have defrayed the present expense and shall continue the future till I know my lord Duke of Newcastle's pleasure.

1 MS *had been* struck through.

2 MS *them this day* struck through.

3 James Bishop, younger brother of Sir Cecil Bishop. Papers on this episode were despatched by the Duke of Richmond to Sir Cecil Bishop at Parham (McCann 306, 5 February 1746). In addition to the letter here and the statement relating to James Bishop [**550**], a further four statements made by John Collier on this case are SAY 84, 85, 86, 87.

4 MS *one* struck through.

5 Abraham Ibbotson, gentleman of Arundel, a past steward to the Duke of Norfolk to whom the duke rented several farms, appointed woodward to the Duke of Norfolk 1710.

6 MS *very plain* struck through.

550 To the Duke of Newcastle, from John Collier, Hastings, [early] February 1746: statement concerning James Bishop,[1] [SAY 89]

Tuesday, the 21st of January, Mr Bishop and his servant, two of the persons under confinement here, came on shore at Eastborne, about 17 miles west of this place, in a very small boat with only one sailor, being drove in by stress of weather, and it was 50 to 1 they got safe on shore being very stormy and tempestuous. The sailor was a stranger and the little boat being damaged was sold for 2 guineas. Bishop and his servant went into an alehouse near the seaside and he forthwith took to a chamber and stayed till the Fryday following but never come downstairs or seen by anybody but one Keys, master of the alehouse. That during that time, by Keys and his own servant, application was made to the fishermen there for a boat to go to Boulogne; [2] none was procured, so Fryday he hired horses and a guide for himself and servant and went to the Star at Lewes and the horses sent back.

What became of him from thence till the 27th I have not intelligence. But Monday the 27th in the evening he and servant and the other person now here, Abraham Ibbotson, a farmer at Tortington near Arundell, about 8 or 9 in the evening came togeather to Pevensey and lay at a little alehouse there where was one Francis Poleard, a reputed smugler. That they enquired after a boat there and this Poleard asked one William Wenham, a farmer that was accidentally drinking there, if he would go with some gentlemen to shew the way to Hooe, about 5 miles distant, to the house of one Blackman, the alehouse keeper and reputed smugler, and he told them he would and there Poleard intimated that they wanted to go over to France.

Wenham went home for his horse and Bishop servant, and Ibbotson met him on horseback at Pemsey bridge, but instead of going the direct way to Hooe they struck of directly to the seaside, being a great way about, and seeing a cutter under sail, Bishop asked Wenham if he thought it was a smugling vessell; and he answering he beleived it was, Bishop wished he could get on board of her, and they called [3] and went into the sluce house, being an alehouse much frequented by the smuglers, and got of their horses and there they went in and stayed, and stayed about an hour, and there enquiry was made of the alehouse keeper for a boat but none could be got.

That then they went to Hooe to Blackman's house and got there about 3 or 4 of the clock, desired to have a private room and was shewn upstairs and in a little time Wenham told Blackman's wife that these persons wanted to be carried over to France which she inimated to James Blackman, her husband's brother then being in the house; and on his giving encouragement he believed that a boat might be had for that purpose. The woman came down to see him herself to desire he would goe up to the gentleman but before he did he went to one John Dunk that lived near and told him the affair and they [4] 2 went upstairs togeather and Mr Bishop told him his intentions and begged, if possible, he might go over that night and asked what they must have for a boat. They answered that they would leave it to his generosity, upon which he said he would give them ten guineas for their trouble in geting the boat or to that effect, but the servant followed Blackman and told him that though his master said ten guineas he would give anything they'd[5] ask for a boat, upon which Blackman and Dunk went downstairs and talked with Wenham, and also with one Joseph Bartholomew who accidentally came by, and they concluded that it was with no good design he was so pressing to go over, and resolved to secure them; and then

Bartholomew, personating a seaman, went and told them there was no boat to be had on the coast or at Hasting or Rye for everybody was afraid to go over to France.

On which they seemed to be in great confusion and hurry to be gone and got out their horses as fast as they could, but a great many people being about the door Bishop mounted first and rode of, on which they stoped the other two; and one John Edwards, having a horse in the stable, ran and got him out and pursued and brought Bishop back. Then they carried all 3 upstairs and confined them in a room and sent for a constable. James Blackman and John Dunk came [6] forthwith to Hasting and informed me of the affair; I despatched them back with a reinforcement and strict orders to secure and bring them hither this morning (here I refer to my two letters of the 29 and 30 of January).

My son has several times been in company with Mr Bishop,[7] who often seemed very uneasy and pensive [8] and displeased with the account that he must be carried to London. Talks sometimes a little unguarded, full of praises of the French officers and that they are the best troops in the world. That he was bred up with the Duke of Perth and Lord John Drummond; that he might have been aid du camp to the Duke of D'Aremberg; that he don't know that the Duke of Newcastle has any power to ask him his motives for his going to France. That he supposes the suspension of the *habeas corpus* act which takes away the rights of an Englishman will be made use of; that he supposes he shall be used the harder on account of his religion. There has been a strict guard over him and the rest. Old Ibbotson desired to send a messenger with a letter to his wife for some clothes, etc., [9] was told if he would write and shew his letter a messenger should be sent with it but he not see him. It was accordingly done but no cloaths, no letter nor no person came back by or with the messenger.

All that was in the letter besides cloaths was of his being deteyned here happening to be in company with one Mr Bishop. Bishop says he has known and well acquainted with Ibbotson ever since he was a child of 5 or 6 years old. Ibbotson declared he never saw Bishop till about a fortnight since at Mr Kemp's at Slindon and that was accidentally as he came from Chichester market, and that he asked Mr Kemp and his daughters who the gentleman was and was told it was Sir Cecil Bishop's brother. Ibbotson, that he accidentally met Mr Bishop at Slindon as he was coming to Pemsey on business and so came with him. That he thought Mr Bishop was a merchant in London, but did not know where he lived but that he intended to lay out £7000 in buying land in Sussex and would employ him to buy it for him and 7000 in buying of corn. Mr Bishop says as he is a younger brother his fortune very small and has no estate in lands and but little money. Denys he saw Ibbotson at Mr Kemp's but says he saw him at Mr Biddulph's at Burton. Bishop and Ibbotson that they came togeather from Findon. The servant that he never saw Ibbotson till they fell in accidentally with him between Lewes and Pemsey. Findon is 20 or 30 miles west of Lewes, Pemsey east.

Hooe is certainly a [10] place of rendezvous of the smuglers. I cannot take upon me to [11] to determine to say whether the motives of stoping and confining those persons were from a true regard to the service of their country or a diffidence of one another, but I have applauded their zeal and indeed they were hearty and honest in their assistance. Several of them and other reputed smuglers have been since here and seemed desirous of seeing them, but I told them they were delivered over to Captain Campbell and his soldiers so avoided it, and more especially as I had heard some smuglers, though not these, had talked a little favourable about their confinement.

1 [*Pencil*] principal statement re suspected Jacobite.
2 MS *but not* struck through.
3 MS *at the* struck through.
4 MS *and Wenham concluded it was with an ill design that they wanted* struck through.
5 MS words obscured
6 MS *away* struck through.
7 MS *Mr Bishop has at times* struck through.
8 MS *don't at all like the news of* struck through.
9 MS *which was consented to if I* struck through.
10 MS *great* struck through.
11 MS *say the motives* struck through.

551 To Andrew Stone, Whitehall, from John Collier, Hastings [early February 1746] [SAY 90]

I had the pleasure and happiness to receive by express your letter of yesterday, accompanyed with a great many of the London Gazette's extraordinary of the same date, with the agreeable news from the duke out of Scotland. I had the same instantly proclaimed and the joy of the inhabitants [1] was testifyed in all possible [2] demonstrations.[3]

I hope Mr Lambe by the time this comes to hand will be arrived safe with his culprits. The last moments of Mr Bishop at this place did not so fully come up to the character of a gentleman; he was used as such, though made the greatest suspicion of being a traytor and villain to his country. He and his associates were permitted to remain in an inn under a proper guard and he directed his provision, wine etc., and intimated discharging the same, but at his departure he refused paying a shilling; said he was a state prisoner he could contract no debts nor would pay a shilling, and indeed went off in a surly abrupt manner.[4] The three persons being deteyned here a week and the first securing them [5] at Hooe, watch guard, etc., from thence till the constable and his posse discharged and put into safe custody of the highland company amounts to £18 14s 8d which I have paid tho I think and am afraid it will be esteemed highly extravagant [6] to discover all that was possible in regard to this affair and getting the best intelligence, I have used my utmost care and diligence not only in going myselfe but imploying other persons that I could put confidence in. This I know and esteem to be the duty of every Englishman at this critical conjuncture and have the greatest pleasure in performing it and [7] desire no compensation but, as I can have the liberty of writing to you as a friend, if these things are usually allowed and [8] you think I should mention it; I will not otherwise.

I [9] hope the [10] happy event [11] on the duke's first entring Scotland is the prelude of his puting an entire end to the rebellion in that part of the kingdom and setling us in futurily on a more better and secure foundation; and will convince all Britons that have a regard to the happiness of their country that lenity and indulgence to a set of people brought up in a religion and principles destructive to our libertys and constition are not to [12] be trusted with [13] power, or their faith and honour to be depended upon.

1 MS *expressed by bells ringing* struck through.
2 MS *manner* struck through.
3 MS *of joy* struck through.
4 MS *forfeiting the character of a gentleman* struck through.

5 MS *in the country* struck through
6 MS *I have* struck through
7 MS *don't in the least* struck through.
8 MS *without it is so* struck through.
9 MS *make not doubt but* struck through.
10 MS *dawnings* struck through.
11 MS *progress of* struck through.
12 MS *have any the least confide* struck through.
13 MS *any the least* struck through.

552 To John Collier, Hastings, from Andrew Stone, Whitehall, 1 February 1746 [SAY 116]

I have been favoured with your two letters relating to the persons who were lately apprehended in your neighbourhood and are now under confinement. My lord Duke of Newcastle orders me to acquaint you that he shall very soon, and probably tomorrow, send a messenger to bring them to town in custody. In the meantime, his grace recommends it to you to take care that they may be safely kept and so as to prevent any possibility of an escape. His grace doubts not but you will continue to employ your usual care and vigilance upon this occasion and desires, that you would transmit a particular account of every circumstance that may have come to your knowledge relating to these persons, and of what may have been observed in their behaviour since their confinement. His royal highness the duke, we conclude, arrived at Edenburgh on Wednesday last.[1] He will have found the army in good condition and ready to march, so that we hope in God a few days will bring us good news.

1 The *London Gazette* carried bulletins on the progress of the Duke of Cumberland; that of 28 January 1745/6 stated the Duke was expected in Edinburgh; the issue of 1 February reported his arrival in the capital and ready to march after the Pretender. The 8 February the *Gazette* announced the Duke and the army had reached Crieff. In addition the government published a *London Gazette extraordinary*, and the issue of 5 February reprinted a letter from the Duke, then at Falkirk, reporting that the Pretender had abandoned the siege of Stirling; the 6 February issue published letters about the relief of Stirling. These *London Gazettes* were reprinted in newspapers and journals, including the *Gentleman's Magazine*.

553 To John Collier, Hastings, from Duke of Newcastle, Whitehall, 3 February 1746 [SAY 117]

Mr Stone having laid before me your letter, in which you give an account that James Bisshopp, esqr. James Cavellion and Abraham Ibbotson had been apprehended at Hooe endeavouring to get a vessel to carry them to France, and that they are now under confinement at Hasting. His Majesty has commanded me to send Mr Lambe, one of his Majesty's messengers, by whom you will receive this letter, with a warrant to bring the said persons in custody to London in order to their being examined. He has also an order to the commanding officer of the troops quartered at Hasting to appoint a sufficient number of soldiers, to guard them on the road. You will therefore take care that Mr Bisshopp and the two other persons may be delivered to the messenger by the person or persons in whose custody they now are, pursuant to the warrant directed to them for that purpose, and that they may set out for London as soon as may be. And you will transmit to me a particular account of all the circumstances, and relating to the siezing and detaining these persons, and any examinations that may have been taken, relating thereto, and send up any papers that may have been taken with them. His Majesty very much approves the zeal and attention you have shewed for his service on this occasion. You will send me an account of any expence you have been or shall be at for the subsistence of the prisoners, or otherwise; and I will take care that it shall be repaid you.

554 To an unidentified recipient from John Collier, Hastings, 6 February 1746
[SAY 91]

Last Tuesday about 4 in the afternoon Mr Lambe one of the king's messengers brought me a letter from the Duke of Newcastle signifying his being sent to conduct to [1] London the three persons here in custody and a warrant for the delivering them to him. Also an order from my Lord Stair to the commanding officer [2] of the detachment sent into Sussex after the smuglers to escort them with a sufficient number of soldiers to London.

The detachment sent to Lewes were ordered by Lord Stair and directed to -,[3] in his absence to the commanding officer, and Lord Stair's warrant for escorting these persons being so directed to Major Kendall and the [4] highland companys here and at Rye being ordered down by the duke, made a confusion, for [5] the commanding officer said he could not justify going with them on that order. But at last he was satisfyed with the D of N letter to me intimating that the commanding officer of the forces at Hasting were ordered to escort them. Accordingly they set out yesterday escorted by a serjeant and 12 men and hope they will be safe in town by the time this reaches you.

Mr Bishop in his last moments at this place did not keep up the character of a gentleman, he was used as such though under suspicion of being a traytor to his country, permitted to remain under guard in an inn, directed his own provisions, wine, etc., and during the whole time intimated discharging the same, but at his departure refused paying a shilling said he was a state prisoner and therefore could contract no debt nor none would pay and indeed went off in a surly, abrupt manner.

During his stay here he was often unguarded in his conversation my son frequently at his earnest request visiting him. Full of praises of the French officers. The French the best troops in the world. That he was bred up with the Duke of Perth and Lord John Drummond; that he might have been aid de camp to the Duke d'Aremberg; that he did not know the Duke of Newcastle had any power to ask him his motives for going to France. That he supposed the suspension of the *habeas corpus* act which took away the rights of an English man would be made use of. That he supposed he should [6] fare the harder on account of his religion. He was uneasy and pensive on the thoughts of going to London. Hooe is certainly a place of rendezvous of the smuglers *inter nos*, I cannot take upon me to determine whether, etc.

I thought of securing Hemmings als Emmens of Rye yesterday in Pemsey Bay but failed, he is a sad dog and has certainly brought and carried over persons from Boulogne I have good intelligence that Staffield of Rye, another notorious smugler went yesterday to Boulogne, I still hope to secure him. It is beleived that Hemmings is paid by the governour or intendant there. What I mention of Rye smuglers I beg may not be thought of or mentioned in any respect as any reflextion or neglect of duty on Major Battine. [7] This happens only as I am near the place and he at 60 miles distance. [8] I know who I write to and have the greatest respect for the major and know his vigilance. This day at 2 I had by express a letter from Mr Stone, with several of the extraordinary gazettes of yesterday upon which there has been this afternoon the greatest rejoycings that are in our power to make. Though [9] Hastings is often in the newspapers as smuglers apprehended here goods seized, etc., I assure it's without foundation. I can take upon me to affirm that none one smugling boat has been out this 6 weeks nor noe smugling practises here.

1 MS *carry to L* struck through.
2 MS *for a sufficient number* struck through.
3 MS left blank
4 MS *two* struck through.
5 MS *they said* struck through.
6 MS *fear the worst* struck through.
7 MS *whose conduct you'l consider* struck through.
8 MS *therefore beg* struck through.
9 MS *I observe* struck through.

555 To Mary Collier, from Revd James Cranston, Bexhill, 10 February 1746

[SAY 1876]

Dear sister, I am infinitely oblidged to you for your care in providing a reception for me and our girl at Mr Cruttenden's which I like extreamly well. I shall think of getting to town in a short time after I have settled things here and propose to lay hold on a fine day, if I am not worse than I am at present being much as when you left me, and ride directly to your house, which perhaps may be with more ease to me than a better convenience. If you chuse in the meantime to take an airyng to this place I should be very glad to see you. My best respects to Mr Collier and my other relations with many thanks for the civilities offered, but as yet I have not spirits enough to engage in anything relating to housekeeping by myself. I have no more at present than to add that a Saturday night I had a short note from Dr Thorpe wherein he told me Mr Lintott required a few days to consider of it, and the doctor himself made me an offer of his house, but I have sent him word by Mr Cruttenden that I am provided, which I assure you is much to the satisfaction of.

556 To John Collier, Hastings, from James Collier, Fig Tree Court, 18 February 1746

[SAY 1877]

Peter, I imagine, has acquainted you with the particulars of my journey as far as Bromley and the motives that induced me to reach Lamberhurst on Sunday night, though it rained excessive hard when I passed by Stonecrouch. The person who keeps the posthouse at Bromley told me at first that it was impossible for him to supply me with a post chaise as both his were out, but that if I would ride on a horse to London he would get me one. Upon which, with an air of authority, I told him that I was obliged to be at the Secretary of State's office within two hours, and that my portmanteau contained letters of the greatest importance; immediately he went out of doors, hired horses and a lad of the town to ride as postboy, and a chaise was ready in a very little time.

I found by my landlord Mr Bishop hired a post chaise of him about two o'clock in the afternoon of Fryday sevenight, and that only a serjeant and one man accompanied him on horseback; the messenger went with him in the chaise. Ibbotson and Cavillion followed about an hour afterwards, attended by three highlanders. Baldwin of the George Inn told me that he never saw Mr Bishop, for that immediately on their coming into the borough the messenger and he alighted and took a hackney coach which drove directly to Pall

Mall, so that he went through the streets without any notice being taken of him. My uncle, I, Mr Rowe and Cole were at the Devil tavern last night and I find by them that everybody, almost, is extreamly pleased at the restoration. No news today except a report of the surrender of Brussells.[1]

1 The French onslaught in Flanders led by Marshall Saxe, taking advantage of the departure of British troops and lack of Austrian support, took Brussels on the 16 February, followed by Antwerp; so future operations by the British would be via Dutch ports. The summer campaign of 1746 was largely to Saxe's benefit.

557 To John Collier, Hastings, from William Cranston, [Johnson's Court], 20 February 1746 [SAY 836]

Watts ads Ward. I staved off the paying this money to this afternoon till after the comeing in of the post but could deferr it no longer. I've been very footsore all this week and not able to go again either after Willis or May but hope to do it in a day or two. Within an hour after yours came in on Monday, Jemmy followed, just arrived safe and sound and so continues, dineing with me today and are just parted from the Appollo. As I have for this 2 months past expected a brace of my neices, whenever his worship arrived, I was not a little surprized to hear no account of their setting forward with him, when I had notice of his motion. I hope, though, notwithstanding that I shall see them and that soon otherwise I shall be grievously disappointed, for I always have looked upon it as having it under your hand that I should see em and better late than never. Publick news seems to be quite at a stand, that of the affair of Brussells seems to give much concern. I have received my cousin Denham's £3 which I have given you credit for and beg you will be so good as to pay it to her.

558 To John Collier, Hastings, from William Cranston, [Johnson's Court], 25 February 1746 [SAY 837]

Not knowing but you might possibly want the inclosed bill of sale I therefore send it you. I am glad to hear my brother is on the mending hand, and doubt not but a little company will sett him up again. I find by the Mayor that your late prisoners Mr Bishop, etc., are out on bail, Lord Gage and Earl Berkley for him, two tradesmen for Ibbotson and the servant discharged. I wish the gentry in Scotland don't once more gett a head. It seems the duke writes word that he looks upon himself entirely in an enemy's country, not being able to gett the least intelligence of the rebells' motions. Lord Loudon's men at Inverness seem to be in jeopardy. A strange rumour about that the king of Prussia, etc., insist on the Dutch making the Prince of Orange stadtholder, if not that he'll make em choose himself, either of em seem to be very well relished, for by the present behaviour I believe their hogan moganships have very few friends this side of the water. Just come from a dish of coffee at Prosser, where squire Butler is feloniously drunk and excessive wise and noisy.

559 To Mary Collier, Hastings, from William Cranston, [Johnson's Court], 25 February 1746 [SAY 1878]

Dear sister, I received the favour of yours of the 11th instant, and as Mr Holmes has been your old operator, and not having heard of his death and unwilling that by any mistake or accident he should loose your custom, I sent James to inquire after him who found him at his old habitation, still alive and acknowledging the receipt of yours, but that an excessive fitt of illness had made him unable to do any business, was then but little better. However, promised at all events you should have Sally's stays as by last carrier. But in the meantime, hearing by Mrs Nouns that his disorder proceeded from bunging the eye, and which he was not likely to leave off, and for fear of farther disappointments, I sent again on Fryday morning to know whether he had sent em on the Wednesday before, and that if he had not then to forbid him troubling his head farther about em. And James returning again with an account that they were not sent, and that he had plainly and distinctly delivered the other part of my message, I thereupon applyed to Mrs Cole in the evening who the next morning sent me an operator who most faithfully promised that a stay should be sent on toomorrows carrier when also you shall have your 12s pound of tea, and so much for the history of the two staymakers.

I extreamly applaud and approve of my brother Jemmy's resolution of leaving Bexhill and his actuall putting it in execution and like also the house where he is fixed as both our friend Samuel and Mrs Cruttenden, as chearfull people and very proper persons to assist in diverting the vapours. I thank God I know not as yet what the spleen is and hope never shall though am satisfyed by seeing it in others that is is a very bad disorder. I have thought the being alone many of the late winter evenings, has rather been more irksome than usual but have and still do attribute it chiefly to my having been in almost daily expectation of having a couple of your lilly brights for my companions. And the thoughts of how much more comfortable I was to have been this winter, than for some few before, and the disappointment, naturally contributed to make it the more uneasy. But, however, though the winter is now almost worn out without em, yet I should nevertleless still be glad to see their ladyships make their appearance, but shall not now expect em till I see em, I am with proper respects to all sorts and sizes, your most affectionate brother and very humble servant.

560 To John Collier, Hastings, from James Collier, Fig Tree Court, 25 February 1746 [SAY 1879]

I called on Mr Lamb this morning and found that Mr Bishop, after an examination of about half an hour by the Duke of Newcastle on Thursday last, was admitted to bail. His sureties were Earl Berkely and Lord Gage in two thousand pound each and himself in five to appear the first and last days of term in Westminster Hall. His man was discharged immediately, and Ibbotson got bail last night, himself in a thousand, and two tradesmen in 500 pound each.[1]

The rebels who were thought to be dispersed have again united and formed a body of 6000 men and intend to attack Lord Loudon at Inverness, which is the place appointed for the French transports to disembark their troops at. Three have actually landed their men near that place who will be greatly distressed for want of pay, for the whole military chest consisting of 17,000 pound, designed for the use of the French and the whole rebel army, was taken by Commodore Knowles on board the ship that Count Fitz-James was in.[2] Admiral Vernon has been very hot in the house since his return to London, and last Fryday, reflecting on the Lords of the Admiralty for the orders they sent him whilst he commanded in the Downs, Mr Greenville and Mr Legge got up and acquainted the House with all the instructions they had sent the admiral, and the motives inducing thereto, which quite confounded him.[3] And the latter in allusion to the title of his late pamphlet, concluding that what he affirmed was "the naked truth", occasioned a great laughter. I have seen Mr Staples and have conversed with him about our sessions affairs. I am to call upon him some evening this week and then will communicate to you our results.

1 The Duke of Richmond decided that James Bishop's 'designs must have been treasonable because my Lord Gage assured me they were not,' (McCann 310).

2 On the 21 February three French ships bound for north east Scotland from Ostend were intercepted by Commodore Knowles on the *Devonshire*, two of which were seized, the *Bourbon* and *Charite* with Count Fitzjames, his personal staff and over 500 soldiers; only the 3rd vessel with a company of soldiers escaped to Scotland (Richmond vol. 2, 188-9).

561 To John Collier, Hastings, from William Cranston, [Johnson's Court], 4 March 1746 [SAY 838]

I received yours yesterday with the £60 draft inclosed, the money due on which I will receive when due. I received of Master Clarke yesterday £29 13s 0d neat but have not a frank to inclose his note of particulars. I shall observe your orders about the coat and stockings and have taken upon me the care of spaw water for my brother, which shan't fail going by Bossom at his next return. I've signed a judgement long since against Dr Gladwish. Am glad to hear my brother holds out so well; the late cold weather so much affected my right knee and left foot that Wednesday, Thursday and Fryday last could but just crawl out, laid up quite Saturday and Sunday but out again yesterday and today. I had the Pipe Office chap with me last week, was very hard, threatened for the arrears for the Cinque Ports there;[1] with great difficulty gott him once more to postpone process to the end of Trinity terme, but if not cleared in the interim can gett no farther time, nor indeed can't with any modesty desire it. An intire dearth of news.

1 The ex-annual rolls for debts of the Cinque Ports residents kept in the pipe office of the Exchequer which include some lists from 12 Geo II onwards (TNA E 363/15).

562 To John Collier, Hastings, from William Cranston, 6 March 1746 [SAY 839]

Ward and Pope against Watts. I have an issue in this cause delivered me with notice of tryall for the next assizes in Kent.[1] I'll call tomorrow on Tomlins and sound him about the 2 cutters, but it seems to me at present to be Admiralty business and if so then I shall want the captain of the *Badger's* name.

[*Reverse*] To Admiral Vernon from John Collier.

I hope you'll forgive [2] this repeated application on the behalf of George Harrison who I sent on board you in the Downs with some intelligence [3] in regard to the late intended invasion from Boulogne, etc., who, after his examination, you was pleased to order on board the *Badge*r sloop of war, Captain Scot commander, where he still remains. Harrison has a wife and several children and his whole fishing craft lyes neglected. As I sent him with a sincere intention for the service of our king and country and gave him assuranses of not being impressed or deteyned, I humbly hope your honour will please to let me have a letter or order to Captain Scot for his discharge, on which the captain says he will instantly set him on shore; the captain gives him a good character as to his behaviour on board.

1 Kent assizes Maidstone, 6 March, (TNA ASSI 34/11).

2 MS *my presuming my putting you in mind of* struck through.
3 MS *relateing* struck through.

563 To John Collier, Hastings, from James Collier, Fig Tree Court, 8 March [SAY 1880]

Agreable to your desire I saw Mr Staples last night, and had some discourse with him about the points mentioned in his letter, which indeed were the same that we had debated before. I communicated to him the contents of your letter, but had prior to that told him the order would stand clear of his objections, and acquainted him that I had applyed to my uncle who had undertaken to write a letter to the clerk of the peace for a copy of it, which when received I would send down to him. If the parish of Guestling should attempt to appeal in relation to the removal of the widow Bannister, there is a case directly in point determined in our favour about 14 years ago in the court of King's Bench.

Since the last accounts from Scotland stocks have risen, and everybody waits with great impatience for the news of a battle, which in all human probability must end on the side of the king's forces, if the rebels do not make a stand at Inverness they must certainly disperse; to return is impossible, all the passes into the Lowlands being guarded by the Hessians. The print lately published under the title of "the noble game of bobcherry", and which my uncle proposes sending down by the post tonight, is greatly admired here for the excellent conceit of it. Mr Lord Bath is certainly retired into the country, and does not propose coming to town again very soon, and my Lord Granville publickly declares that the alterations made in the ministry, were done solely under the influence of Lord Bath. I have just received the repeating watch from Delander, which with some other things I shall send down next week. This last night it has snowed incessantly and the weather reckoned extremly unwholesome at this time of the year, as a thaw succeeds so soon. Be pleased to give my duty to my mother, and my uncle, and love to my sisters.

564 To John Collier, Hastings, from William Cranston, [Johnson's Court], 13 March 1746 [SAY 840]

Your box went yesterday freighted with Sally's coat, lavender, spiritts, my sister's watch and neice's ear rings, one part of the session papers and 2 chirograph indenture of fines, all which I hope will arrive safe. I was yesterday at the Admiralty Office and nothing is to be done there about the cutters without first entring a claim, giveing security for cost, then a monition in each will go out against the captain of the *Badger*, and, if he does not proceed to condemn her, they will be ordered to be restored. If all this should be done and the captain go into an examination for that purpose, and give any kind of evidence by which the judge has the least room to guess they are smugglers, they'll stand but a poor chance, for in all probability they'll be condemned a la mode the royall ranger. But I really know of, nor can think of, no other way of getting at them unless the chaps themselves can by fair or foul words cajole or intimidate the collector so as to deliver em up; they are in a queer scituation but nothing otherwise I verily beleive can be done.

The noble captains may have helped to make your box of Cole, but if not and £40 can be conveniently spared, I must begg you to splice the subdean out with that summe, you'll never have but one more of that bulk, for all our stocks are now gone except one solitary £50 which I suppose won't be long behind, and then must buy a pig with a shorter tail or will soon be in as bad a pickle as ever, nay worse, for I never heard that they have the least expectancy of any other windfall. A glorious day.

565 To John Collier, Hastings, from William Cranston, Johnson's Court, 25 March 1746 [SAY 841]

Messrs Lamb's and Odiarne's 2 drafts came safe to hand yesterday, which with the former £300 draft you may be assured of my making up and paying to Messrs Hoare £933 upon Mr Pelham's account, before they become payable. I've this day paid your tenths as well as master subdean's but don't recollect your mentioning them before. Your order from Coles, with mustard and chocolate and also some cotton which you never mentioned till last Thursday, shall go toomorrow, but as to spectacles, if I take you right, there will be none as I don't expect the frame till toomorrow sennight. I know nothing about your news paragraph; to be sure twas to have been done at that instant or not at all and gave my opinion accordingly, but have not heard one word of it since but will contradict it the first time I see his worship. No kind of news; you must be in a sad condition as to roads and waters.

566 To John Collier, Hastings, from William Cranston, Johnson's Court, 3 April 1746[1] [SAY 842]

The account of which the inclosed is a copy, comeing in my way this morning it imediately occurred to me that I had never given you any notice of my having setled it with Mr Potter and received of him the ballance, which I did so long ago as it appears to bear date, and at the same time gave you creditt for it in your account. Everything is paid to Michaelmas and dare say you will have from henceforth a just and good account of this estate and some money will now always be comeing from it. We setled the salary at 2 guineas per annum, which though it exceeds 1s per pound yet as the whole is but triffling and in many hands, I can't think tis too much.

Being a very exact man, he made some little scruple at paying me, but I undertook that if I was continued in my office of auditor, that I would again the next time, gett an order from you and Mr Davis that he should pay all future rent to me and that my receipt should be his sufficient discharge. Your account of young Rowe greatly surprized me, his brother dined and supped with me on Monday last and I asked him in generall of news from Sussex and how is brother did, but he took no sort of notice nor did I. Q: my salary in my new office, is half a peice too much? Past 7 Jemmy has just now been with me and shewed me yours of to him this day, and says you shall hear from him without fail per Saturday's post, your parcell by yesterday's carrier is also just now arrived. No franks. Stone was called upon for em today by his worship.

1 William Cranston gives the date as 3 April 1745; John Collier has 3 April 1746.

567 To John Collier, Hastings, from James Collier, Fig Tree Court, 5 April 1746 [SAY 1881]

I have been considering our two cases and make no doubt but that a cinque port has within itself a jurisdiction, exclusive of the foreign one, in regards to appeals within the liberty; and as to the levying of the five pounds on Lingham for not receiving Edwards, is a very plain case that it should be so. He by appealing supposes we have a right to make an order on him, and then complains of an imaginary grievance since the family have been no burthen in the least to his parish, and though the recital in the Act of Parliament is not extensive enough, which has been often determined to be of no force at all, yet the enacting clause is much in our favour. Mr Carew is determined this year to increase the penalty of overseers refusing to receive persons removed in a regular manner. Mr Staples is sufficiently prepared for the widow Bannister's case and I find it is a determined point with us.

As to the case of Beville, I find I am mistaken, Mr Hay proposed the scheme, twas read twice and then thrown out; if it does not appear that she was hired for a year I am afraid we are wrong. The resolutions of the court of King's Bench go so far, viz, A hires B for five months only, at the expiration of which A contracts with B for a whole year, and yet if B serves only seven months, that with the five before has been determined to be a good hiring and service for a year. We are at the eve of some great alterations in the ministry. Mr Pelham is confidently reported to be made a lord but to keep his post. The Lord Granville to be Secretary of State, Lord Chancellor to resign, Sir Dudley Ryder, Attorney General, to have the seals, Lord Chief Justice Willes to be made a lord and appointed Speaker to the House and Winnington, who was proposed by the Lord Granville in the former scheme to have the management in the House of Commons, is now to be that man.[1]

Affairs in Italy go extreamly well; I wish I could say so of the transactions in Scotland. Last night I supped with the Captains Murray, Smith, Campbell and Lieutenant Colonel Monroe, who was a near relation to Sir Robert, who told us he had just received intelligence that his house and all his estate had been destroyed by the rebells. I find by Mr Randoll, who had his intelligence from Mr Collins, that Sir Thomas Webster and his whole family are coming to town. I have called on Dr Monroe thrice without success, and last Thursday I went into the borough and saw Mr Webb, who told me that she was much altered for the better. I have intelligence where the doctor will be on Monday, and will follow him there. I called at Mr Stone's on Thursday but no franks either there or at the office; my name I left at his house. The Carlisle rebels are to be tryed next Wednesday. If the horses are in town by Thursday I shall be ready for them, but have not as yet a servant.

1 Lord Granville tried and failed to form a ministry 10-12 February 1746, though he returned to the government in June 1751 as Lord President of the Council. Lord Egmont pointed to the sudden about turn in the king's failed efforts to appoint Granville as 1st Lord of the Treasury instead of Henry Pelham (Egmont vol. 3, 315).

568 To John Collier, Hastings, from James Collier, Fig Tree Court, 10 April 1746

[SAY 1882]

Master Ellams came to me this morning about eleven o clock. I wait indeed for a wig and a great coat and cannot set out till Saturday. I have called upon Mr Rowe twice this week who has not taken the least notice of his brother's affair, but I find your account confirmed by Mr Rochester who is just come to town. I was at Mr Stone's house this morning, but neither he was at home or any franks left out.

Mr Randoll told me this day that the highland regiment, and Harrison's with four others were under orders to go to Cape Breton in order to conquer Canada and to be all on board by the first of May. I was at the Old Baily this evening in hopes of seeing the rebel prisoners; they were ordered to be brought to the bar, but the keeper of Newgate would not take upon him to bring them down as it was dark and tomorrow morning they are to appear. Twelve thousand Hanoverians are certainly to be taken into British pay this year.[1] As I almost promised Crouch to make him free, if you like it, Mr Patrick may write the usual form as I think I have signed my name as often as there are jurats.

1 Strength of the Pelham administration illustrated by the two votes on 11 and 14 April 1746 with majorities of 133 and 116 for a grant of £300,000 for 18,000 Hanoverian troops (Owen 306; Egmont vol. 3, 315).

569 To John Collier, Hastings, from William Cranston, [Johnson's Court], 12 April 1746 [SAY 843]

I yesterday morning sent to my nephew your spectacles, tea and the indentures stamp together with the dyeing speeches. I understand he setts out at the tip toomorrow. Sisley ads Humphrey: we are now too late to give a rule, either to inforce a declaration or non pros it cannot be done in the Common Pleas after 4 days after the end of the terme in which the declaration ought to have been delivered, which in this case, as the writt was returned in Michaelmas terme, should have been before the end of Hillary and consequently the rule been given within 4 days afterwards. In the King's Bench there is no occasion for any rule to be given at all nor no time confined to the signing such a non pros.

I put up also a receipt for 2 pair of stays, and seeing from under her own hand that one of em was for my neice Cordelia, I now give over all thoughts of seeing her here, though till then I had not the least notion of such a disappointment. We have had a flying report today of a party of the Hessians having demolished a party of the rebells and handled them very roughly and which seems to be credited. Mrs Wellman called a day or two again for her fine, which she desires you will take the first oppurtunity of sending up either to her or me.

570 To John Collier, Hastings, from William Cranston, [Johnson's Court], 16 April 1746 [SAY 844]

I received yours yesterday with the £45 draft inclosed. I am much obliged to you for the receiveing my rent of Gower. As I was not able to gett the folios from the Chancery office this morning, so could not comply your bill so as to send it by my nephew. Whilst Coles was at Leicester assizes, his man told me that Mrs Presade[1] had sent there 2 guineas he would have it me then, but I deferred it till his master's arrival but from that instant till this morning when I happened to pop upon her name in your account where I was going to charge you with the above rent, it never entered into my head to ask him for it, nor I suppose him to give it me, but I then directly sent for it, and had it so that if you write to her about it, you'll make some excuse about the delay.

If twas the mayor's intention to make Dick Crouch a freeman, I am sorry he did not look into it before he came to town or that he had not gone down a week or 10 days sooner, for Dick's really an honest, industrious fellow and I should give my vote for no man in town to be promoted sooner than for him. I am pleased with the account you give of my brother and methinks I much want to see him in his new scituation. You'll perceive I've taken your direction as to my chargeing in my new office of auditor. Don't hear of any sort of news stirring. Was at Deptford a Fryday, Mr Russell would have fain have had me put my Jemmy on board the *Kent* a 70 gun ship just ready to be launched there, under Captain Wyndham, his particular acquaintance, but he's too young and cannot consent to it yet.

Since writeing the within we have a strong rumour of a bloody battle in Italy wherein the Spaniards had 12,000 killed and wounded and the Austrians 3000 and amongst the rest old General Nadashi, but that is a total demolition of the French and Spanish scheme in that part of the world.

1 Presade or Presode.

571 To John Collier, Hastings, from William Cranston, [Johnson's Court], 22 April 1746 [SAY 845]

Staples says he is sure that he gave Patrick the order wanted, so you'll give tother search and if not found we must gett one more from Midhurst. I'll speak to Michell about Wilks when he comes to town. I intend my chaps shall accept of the invitation to the port and which I know they depend upon. Q: whether the waggon, if it goes, will not be a better method than the coach; in either way you must have the trouble, as tis not in my power, of getting em from one or tother to Hasting. I think Jemmy may be trusted upon a small gentle horse alone, and Jacky with a mail pillion and ropes for stirups, behind a man; the particular time I know not as yet but shall in a day or two, having per last post wrote to Jemmy for that purpose.

We were a good deal alarmed today, with an account of the rebells having forced the duke over the Spey again; it had a considerable effect on the stocks and tis believed was raised for that purpose but it seems to have now lost creditt. I had just now 48 franks brought me. This same Lady Dalrimple turns out to be Collonel Hamilton's daughter of Kent, married to Stede, soon afterwards run away with Captain Dalrymple to Jaimaica and since Stede's death supposed to be married to him but doubted a pickle good one.

572 To John Collier, from William Cranston, [Johnson's Court], 24 April 1746 [SAY 846]

I think an happy occasion is at last arrived when we may fairly congratulate one another. The victory seems to be compleat and the rebells totally demolished. We have had nothing but bells, guns ere since ten this morning. Those of the Tower and in the park led the van, and, whilst I was on the water the standard was put up at the Tower. I don't beleive there will be a horse in the town that won't have lights. The joy seems to be universall. The usuall sett having been summoned, am just setting out to meet them at the Devill.

APPENDICES 1-8

ADDITIONAL PAPERS AND DEPOSITIONS COLLECTED BY JOHN COLLIER AND HIS FAMILY.

Appendix 1: Undated Letters

573 To Mary Collier, from [Lady] Henrietta Ashburnham [1740][1] [SAY 2193]

Dear Madam, I should in no degree deserve the favour of your kind invitation to Hastings if I did not take the first opportunity of thanking you for it, and at the same time assure you, I want no other indusment to bring me to Hastings then to wait on you, which would be a much greater pleasure to me then the seeing Mr Perry's performancys but must defer it till the roads are better, or my courage greater, and in the meantime please myself with the hopes of our being very good neighbours when we can meet with safty, my brother joyns with me in service to all your family and the complyments of he season, I am, dear madam, your very affectionate humble servant, Mrs Puckle begs her respects, pray tell Miss Collier if I were as young as she, I should venture on horseback to spend some time with her.

1 MS Sayer,dates this letter, 'about 1740'; this is Lady Henrietta, daughter of the 3rd baronet Ashburnham (Steer xiv).

574 To Mary Collier, from [Lady] Henrietta Ashburnham, autumn 1740 or later [SAY 2194]

Dear Madam, any day that is most convenient for you to come to Broomham will be very agreeable to my brother and I, for all days are alike to us, if we can but have the pleasure of yours and your family's company, which I hope to have on Friday. I was sadly mortifed when I heard your coach went through the park one day last week and did not stop here and cant help taking it unkindly, for as the days are growing short, and our roads I fear will soon be bad, I think we should looss no opportunity of meeting as often as we can, I beg my service to all your family and that you will belive how much I am, dear madam yours very affectionatly, my brother and Mrs Puckle desire their complyments.

575 To Mary Collier, from [Lady] Henrietta Ashburnham, autumn 1740 or later year [SAY 2195]

Dear Madam, Mr Puckle came to me today to desire me to recomend his daughter to you for a servant to wait on yours, hearing you want one in that place, she is a very sober, good sort of a young woman, workes and irons well, has had the smallpox, and I belive you will find her very handy and willing in every respect, and for wages I belive wont differ with you, she is near twenty four, and quite setate. I was very sorry to hear Miss Colliers were disapointed in going to London, but hope they will yet go for I know it must be a sad affliction to young folks, I have felt the same uneasiness myself, and tho tis long ago, I still remember the smart, I beg an answer to this because Mr Puckle stays for it, that he may send his daughter to wait on you soon, if you are not provided, my brother and

Mrs Puckle joyn with me in service to all your family, I hope this fine weather will enable us to meet here soon that I may in person repeat how much, I am, dear madam, your very affectionatly.

576 To Mary Collier, Hastings, from [Lady] Henrietta Ashburnham [SAY 2196]

Dear Madam, Mrs Gardener and I will certainly give our selves the pleasure of dyning with you next Thursday, my brother gives his service to you and Mr Collier and will be of the party if he thinks himself well enough at that time. I thank God he is much better then he was, when you were here, which gives me some hopes of his waiting on you, we all beg our complyments to your family and in that you will believe how much, I am, madam, your most obliged humble servant.

577 To Mary Collier, from John Collier, autumn 1741 or 1742 [SAY 2157]

My Dear, Though I wrote by the postboy sending down last night for mackrell, and six coming up this morning, I designed sending them but they dressed them before I knew it, and geting four more line ones, I send them and two of the other, and hope they'll come time enough for dinner. I also send two rabbets which are young but almost full grown, sent me yesterday morning, so don't know when taken. Colonel Pelham sent this morning for me to drive there today or tomorrow, so I design going today. I hear there is Lord Ashburnham, one of the Pelhams, and Stone,[1] I am in hast, going almost 10.

1 MS unclear: could be Store or Storie.

578 To Mary Collier, from Elizabeth Worge 1740 or 1741 [SAY 2162]

Honoured Madam, I should be very much obliged to you if you culd be so good to send me the receipt to make Daccass eale such as Mr Cranston drank. Mr Worge being very much troubled with the gravell has a great fansy to try it. I beg you will tell my sister Dely I should be very glad of her company at Battell I being all alone and hope you want deny me that faver, for at present we are very gay with the players who performe very well and have a very good house every night. I beg you'll make my complements to the young ladys and Miss Thrope, and am, honoured madam, your dutyfull daughter.

579 To Mary Collier, Hastings, from Mary [Molly] Collier, Battle c1740 – c1741[1] [SAY 2173]

Honoured Madam, My pappa told me at the fair that you desired I would write to you which I would have done before but the Place family being down I have been so took up with assemblys and publick days that I have had no time to do any work or anything. I hope my sister Jenny liked the buckles I sent her but indeed I was almost ashamed to send such a small present in return for her handsome one, but it was as good as I could get in the fair for there was nothing extrodinary. I like Battle better and better every day and there is nothing wanting to make it completely agreable but the roads being a little better that we might have the pleasure of seeing you often we have had nothing new since the fair so have no news to send you, but am honoured madam, your dutiful daughter, my sister joins with me in duty to you and love and service to all friends.

1 MS Sayer, in pencil, dates this letter 'about 1740'. The handwriting here is a younger hand compared with SAY 2174 **[397]** 6 March 1743.

580 To Mary Collier, from Charles Webster, [Battle Abbey] c1740 - c1742 [SAY 2204]

Hearing you desire sending for Miss Colier home tomorrow makes me give you this trouble to beg the favour of her company a fortnight or 3 weeks longer. I hope it will not be diagreeable to her, my mother joins with me in this request which if granted will very much oblige. Miss Colier's duty attends you and Mr Colier.

581 To Mary Collier, [Hastings], from Mary Markwick, [Catsfield] [SAY 2199]

Madam, I am informed your servant Alec Wichen and her sister who lives with Mrs Crittenden both leave their places, I want a cook and housemaid but the latter must take care of my dairy, which I design for the future shall consist of 3 cows, now if you and Mrs Crittenden can any ways recommend then I shall be greatly obliged if you would order them to come over to Catesfield to talk to me, Miss Colier is very well and desires her duty to you and her pape. She already talks of making but a short stay here, but I hope you will have more compassion for us than to send for her, or upon your man, for I shall send him back without her, Mr Markwick and my sisters joyn with me in service to you and Mrs Colier and the rest of the good family and I am madam your most obliged humble servant.

582 To Mary Collier, from John Collier [SAY 2158]

My Dearest, I am this moment returned from Mr Pelham's, dined at 4 and afterwards had above 4 hours business with him. I am to acknowledge Dely's obliging letter and will not forget the contents. Lady Katherine and Lady Frances Arundel dined, and behaved with handsom freedom and chearfulness, and the last lady owe me a recipe for the gout and I never saw anybody behave with more civility, I am, my dear creature, in the utmost hast, yours for ever.

Appendix 2: Hastings Town Business

583 Writ concerning John Sargent,[1] 23 January 1734 [SAY 82]

Writ to the mayor, jurats and commonalty of the town and port of Hastings George the second by the grace of God of Great Britain, France and Ireland, king, defender of the faith, to the mayor, jurats and commonalty of the town and port of Hastinge in our county of Sussex, greeting. Whereas the said town and port is an ancient town and port and one of the five ancient ports of this kingdom; and whereas there is and, for time out of mind, hath been, a certain antient and laudable custom used and approved within the said town and port that every person of the age of one and twenty yeares and upwards and being the son of any freeman of the said town and port and born after the admission of his father into the place and office of one of the freemen of the said town and port, hath a right in respect thereof to be admitted and sworn into the place and office of one of the freemen of the said town and port and ought by you to be admitted and sworn into the place and office of one of the freemen of the said town and port according to the custom of the said town and port.[2]

And whereas one John Sargent is of the age of one and twenty yeares and upwards, and is the son of John Sargent deceased, late one of the freemen of the said town and port, and was born after the admission and swearing of his said father into the place and office of one of the freemen of the said town and port. And whereas the said John Sargent by virtue thereof, and according to the said custom ought by you to be admitted and sworn into the said place and office of one of the freemen of the said town and port; yet you well knowing the premisses, but not regarding your duty in this behalf, have not as yet admitted the said John Sargent into the place and office of one of the freemen of the said town and port, nor have you administred the oaths to the said John Sargent which are in that case usually administred and taken although you have been often requested so to do by the said John Sargent, but have refused and yet do refuse, to admit and swear the said John Sargent into the said place and office of one of the freemen of the said town and port, in contempt of us, and to the no small damage and grievance of him, the said John Sargent, and the manifest injury of his estate, as we have been informed from his complaint to us.

We therefore willing that due and speedy justice be done to the said John Sargent in this behalf, as it is reasonable, do command you by firmly injoyning that immediately after the receipt of this writ, you do without delay, admit, or cause to be admitted, the said John Sargent into the said place and office of one of the freemen of the said town and port, together with all the libertys, priviledges, franchises, emoluments and commoditys to a freeman of the said town and port belonging and appertaining, and that you administer or cause to be administred to the said John Sargent the oaths which are in that case usually administered and taken according to the said custom, or shew to us cause to the contrary thereof, that the same complaint may not by your default be repeated to us, and how you shall have executed this our writ, make it appear to us at Westminster upon Wednesday next after the morrow of the purification of the blessed Mary virgin, then returning to us this our writ, and this you are not to omit upon peril that may fall theron.

Witness of Philip, Lord Hardwicke, at Westminster the twenty third day of January in the seventh year of our reign. By the court, Burrow.[3]

1 This John Sargent, christened 18 November 1712, son of John and Anne Sargeant.
2 John Collier was among the subscribers listed in Samuel Jeake *A Collection of the Statutes for the Cinque Ports* (London, 1728)
3 James Burrow, law reporter and attorney in the King's Bench.

584 Writ concerning John Shorter, 23 January 1734 [SAY 83]

Writ to the mayor, jurats and commonalty of the town and port of Hastings.

Whereas the said town and port is an ancient town and port and one of the five ancient ports of this kingdom; and whereas there is and, for time out of mind, hath been, a certain antient and laudable custom used and approved within the said town and port that every person of the age of one and twenty yeares and upwards who marryed the daughter of any freeman of the said town and port who said daughter was born after the admission of her father into the place and office of one of her freemen of the said town and port hath a right in respect thereof to be admitted and sworn into the place and office of one of the said freemen of the said town and port according to the custom of the said town and port. And whereas one John Shorter is of the age of one and twenty yeares and upwards, and marryed Mary Meadow, daughter of Benjamin Meadow, one of the freemen of the said town and port which said Mary was born within the said town and port after the admission and swearing of her said father into the said place and office of the one of the freemen of the said town and port.

And whereas one John Shorter is of the age of one and twenty yeares and upwards, and marryed Mary Meadow, daughter of Benjamin Meadow, one of the freemen of the said town and port which said Mary was born within the said town and port after the admission and swearing of her said father into the said place and office of the one of the freemen of the said town and port. And whereas the said John Shorter by virtue thereof, and according to the said custom ought by you to be admitted and sworn into the said place and office of one of the freemen of the said town and port; yet you well knowing the premisses, but not regarding your duty in this behalf, have not as yet admitted the said John Shorter into the place and office of one of the freemen of the said town and port, nor have you administered the oaths to the said John Shorter which are in that case usually administred and taken although you have been often requested so to do by the said John Shorter, but have refused and yet do refuse, to admit and swear the said John Shorter into the said place and office of one of the freemen of the said town and port, in contempt of us, and to the no small damage and grievance of him, the said John Shorter, and the manifest injury of his estate, as we have been informed from his complaint to us.

We therefore willing that due and speedy justice be done to the said John Shorter in this behalf, as it is reasonable, do command you by firmly injoyning that immediately after the receipt of this writ, you do without delay, admit, or cause to be admitted, the said John Shorter into the said place and office of one of the freemen of the said town and port, together with all the libertys, priviledges, franchises, emoluments and commoditys to a freeman of the said town and port belonging and appertaining, and that you administer or cause to be administred to the said John Shorter the oaths which are in that case usually administered and taken according to the said custom, or shew to us cause to the contrary thereof, that the same complaint may not by your default be repeated to us, and how you shall have executed this our writ, make it appear to us at Westminster upon Wednesday next after the morrow of the purification of the blessed Mary virgin, then returning to us this our writ, and this you are not to omit upon peril that may fall theron.

Witness of Philip, Lord Hardwicke, at Westminster.

585 Order in Council, 20 February 1742[1] [SAY 11]

Wheras there hath been presented to his Majesty at this board a petition in the names of the majors, jurats and commonalty of the town and port of Hasting in the county of Sussex, praying, in regard to the defenceless state and condition of the said town and port of Hasting, that the guns now there may be searched and mounted on carriages, and that powder, shott and other warlike stores may be delivered to the petitioners for the defence and safety of the said town and of the merchant vessels trading up and down the Channel.

His Majesty in Council this day took the same into consideration and received the opinions of the master general and principal officers of the board of ordnance' as also of a committee of the lords of the Privy Council thereupon, and is hereby pleased to order that the twenty-three guns now there, which are become unserviceable, be brought away and that the portion of ordnance and stores contained in the paper hereunto annexed, estimated by the said board of ordnance at £807 0s 7d, be sent to the said town and port of Hasting in lieu thereof and delivered into the custody of the mayor for the time being who is to indent for the same; provided the petitioners do supply themselves with powder from time to time, as occasion may require, and put their forts or batterys into good order, and do provide a proper place for the preservation of the carriages and stores at their own charge; and that the same be surveyed and certified to the said board of ordnance by one of his Majesty's engineers or other proper person to be appointed for that purpose before this supply be sent thither; and his grace the Duke of Argyll, master general of the ordnance is to cause the necessary directions to be given herein accordingly.

[*Enclosed*] A proportion of ordnance and stores proposed for the security and defence of the town and port of Hasting in the county of Sussex prepared in consequence of an order of a committee of the lords of his Majesty's most honourable Privy Council dated the 26 November 1741.

Iron ordnance, 9 pounders 18; standing carriages of oak with 1 bed, 1 coin, and 2 pdr iron trucks each 9 pounders, 18 [*sub total*] £718 4s 0d;

ladles and sponges; round shot 900, tampeons for guns 36, formers for cartridges 2, paper cartridges 450, copper powder measure 1, wadhooks for rammers 5, spare staves for ladles, etc., 6, aprons of lead 18 [*sub total*] £4 15s 0d;

corn powder barrels nil, match cwt 1, primary irons 18, powder horns 9, handspikes 36, crows of iron 4, linstocks without cocks 9, budge barrels 3, handscrew 1 [*sub total*] £10 7s 9d;

sheepskins to coat spunges 4, spunge tacks 200, copper nails for ladles 20, small hammer 1, tarred marlin skains 5, funnel of plate 1, [*sub total*] 13s 10d;

package, cartage, freight and incidents on the above, stones and freight on 23 guns to be brought from thence [*sub* total] £114;

[*total*] £848 0s 7d.

1 [*Signed*] W. Sharpe. SAY 13 includes this list, see [**586**]. The original decision by the Privy Council to supply this equipment is recorded in similar wording to the above (TNA PC2 92-5, 20 October 1742).

586 To the Corporation of Hastings, from John Croome, Board of Ordnance, 2 August 1742 [SAY 13]

Laden on board the Cordelia sloop, James Bossom, master, the iron ordnance and hereafter mentioned to be by him transported to Hasting in the county of Sussex, the danger of the seas excepted, and there delivered into the custody of the worshipful the mayor of that place for the time being, for the security and defence of the town and port there pursuant to His Majesty's warrant bearing date the 20 February 1741/2, and by order of the Board dated the 29 April 1742.[1]

1 For the warrant with the details of the iron ordnance and associated supplies see SAY 11 [**585**]

587 To the King's most exalted Majesty, the humble address of the Mayor, Jurats and Freemen of the corporation of Hastings, [October] 1745[1] [SAY 6]

We beg leave with others of your Majesty's loyall subjects to offer our most humble acknowledgements for the happiness we enjoy under your Majesty's auspicious reign, and more particularly for the effectual measures, which your Majesty has at this time taken, for preventing the ill consequences of the late engagements entered into by some foreign powers in order to disturb your Majesty's government, by endeavouring to place a popish pretender upon your throne and deprive your faithful subjects of their rights and privileges in trade which were secured to them at the expence of so much blood and treasure, and by the most solemn treaties, and this design carried on by princes who are under the greatest obligations to your Majesty and the British nation, which cannot but raise in us our highest resentment and indignation.

We therefore with the greatest sincerity do assure your Majesty that we are determined to hazard our lives and fortunes, and all that is dear to us, in defence of your sacred person and government and to support the succession of your royal family against any attempts of your Majesty's ennemies.

We are sensible that under God the preservation of our happy constitution in church and state is entirely oweing to your Majesty, and that the same good providence which has hitherto crowned with success all your Majesty's endeavours for the welfare of your people, may still assist and support you in the maintaining the interests of your subjects in their trade and commerce, upon which the prosperity of this country does so much depend, and in securing those possessions which are of infinite advantage for that purpose is the hearty prayer of.

1 This address was acknowledged in the *London Gazette* 12 November 1745. The address of the constables and inhabitants of Lewes, signed 8 October 1745, was noted in the issue for 2 November 1745.

588 To the church wardens of the parish of Hastings, from Admiral Edward Vernon, *Monmouth*, Downs, 25 December 1745 [SAY 114]

As it would be for his Majesty's service to have a speedy communication of intelligence, either by night or by day, of the enemy's appearance, with any embarcations for attempting to invade his Majesty's dominions, I desire you would write letters to the respective church wardens of the parishes, etc., here undermentioned to hoist a flagg upon their church steeple, as a signal for it by day, and keep a fire alight in an iron pott as a signal by night, at the same place, to be repeated from the respective churches for communicating the intelligence from Beachy Head to the South Foreland.[1]

List of the churches and castles from the South Foreland to Beachy Head: Dover castle, Folkstone church, Sandgate castle, Dymin church, Rye church, Fair Lee church, Hasting church, Pemsey church, the Ness.

To the church wardens of the parish of Hastings, from Lancelott Burton, naval officer at Deal, 25 December 1745. The above is a copy of an order I have received this afternoon from the honourable Edward Vernon, esqr., admiral of the white squadron of his Majesty's fleet, which I send you and am to desire you will strictly comply with his directions, as it is of the utmost consequence to his Majesty's service, and beg you will own the receipt of this by the bearer.

[*Cover*] On his Majesty's service to the church wardens of the parish at Hastings by express.

1 For instructions on beacons and the watch see *SNQ* vol. 1, 116-8.

Appendix 3: Hastings Water Supply

589 Heads of an agreement between Henry Carleton and John Collier of the one part, and Robert Rosam[1] of Herstmonceux of the other part, 3 February 1733

[SAY 20]

Whereas the said Henry Carleton and John Collier have for some time intended to attempt supplying the inhabitants of the town of Hasting with fresh water, by laying of elm pipes for that purpose from a spring or rivulet of water called the Bourne.[2] And whereas an assembly hath been held of the mayor, juratts and commonalty of the said town and port to make them acquainted with the intended project, and consent was given to the same. And whereas the said Robert Rosam hath proposed to doe, perform and accomplish the said work, in manner and for the price hereafter menconed. It is thereupon concluded and agreed upon between the parties in manner following:

Imprimis: between the parties in manner following: the said Robert Rosam doth covenant and agree to make a good and substantiall bay for stopping and damming up a sufficient quantity of water, in a peece of ground belonging to the said John Collier called the hanger, which has been mearked and staked out for that purpose. And that he will well, sufficiently and in good workmanlike and substantiall manner, make the said bay crosse the said ground of the said John Collier, and of Anne Gyles,[3] widdow, ten foot at least from the bottom of the Borne or rivulet, and lay a gut with a proper penstock or shut, and also a wast pipe for conveying of the surplusage of the water.

Item: the said Robert Rosam for the purposes afd, is to[4] find, provide and in a good substantiall and workmanlike manner, lay good strong and sound elm pipes of 4 inches bore from the said bay to, or as near as shall be thought convenient to, the flood gates of the Bourne at the upper end of the town, and from thence down the High Street, at such places as shall be thought convenient, to the sign of the Royall Oak, of three inches bore, and the said Robert Rosam is to find, provide, allow and be at the expences and charges of all workmanship, in placeing and laying the said pipes and in digging of trenches for that purpose and stopping the same up again.

Item: the said Robert Rosam is to bee at the charge and expence of placeing at such distances as shall be thought proper four stop[5] cocks for the better accomodateing the inhabitants with water and better answering the intentions of the said Henry Carleton and John Collier.

Item: the said Henry Carleton and John Collier are to procure liberty for the said Robert Rosam, his workmen, agents and assignes, to digg up the ground and streets where the said pypes are to be laid without his paying any consideraton therefore.

Item: the said Robert Rosam doth promise, and agree, to finish, or cause to be finished the said work in all manner of respects by the 24th of June next and the said Henry Carleton and John Collier doe contract and promise to pay to the said Robert Rosam on his completion of the same according to the true intent and meaning of these presents the sume of two hundred pound of good and lawfull money of Great Britain.

Item: the said Robert Rosam for the construction afd doth undertake to warrant the standing of the said bay and the gut to be therein laid and also a gut for the wast water for the space of three years from the placeing down the same.

[signed] Henry Carleton, John Collier, Robert Rosam. [witness] Richard Halsted, the mark of Richard Hall.

1 Robert Rosam, engineer, builder, landholder, Hurstmonceaux, listed in *A poll taken by Henry Montague, sheriff of the county of Sussex, at the city of Chichester, Thursday and Friday, 9 and 10 May 1734*, printed by John Coles.
2 See Introduction.
3 Anne Gyles, widow of Thomas Gyles who died 4 December 1732, continued support for the waterworks, re-married Thomas Carswell, Customs officer, 3 July 1734, St Clement's; he was murdered by smugglers, 26 December 1740 (Hunnisett 416, 417).
4 MS *make* struck through.
5 MS *pipes* struck through.

590 To John Collier and Henry Carleton, from Robert Rosam, 18 August 1733 [SAY 25]

Received the 18th of August 1733, of Mr Carleton and Mr Collier, the sume of one hundred pound, which, with one hundred pound they paid me the eleaventh day of May last, makes two hundred pound, on account of my laying the pipes for supplying the town of Hasting with water, I say received by me.

591 Robert Rosam, waterworks accounts [before 23 October 1733] [SAY 24]

	£	s	d
The pipe from Mr Ridley's to Mr Hall's	18	17	02
From the wooden pipe to Ridley's	14	01	06
A large brasse cock, 68 pd at 1s 2d a pound	3	19	04
Laying the wood pipes below the oake	2	05	00
[Total]	39	03	00
From Ridley's to Hall's 93 yds and 1 foot at 3s 6d	16	06	08
17 joynts at 3s 6d per joynt	2	02	06
Digging the ditch and paving it down again and work	0	08	00
[Total]	18	17	02
From wooden pipes to Ridley's 43 yds and 2 foot at 4s 6d a yard	9	16	06
7yds of inch and qr pipe at 3s 6d a yard	1	04	06
9 joynts at 4s 6d, £2 0s 6d, 1 large cock and fusil	3	00	06
[Total]	14	01	06
Mr Collier			
53 yards of pipe at 2s 6d a yard	6	12	06

2 cocks, 2 bosses, 1 fusil 10s; 8 joynts £1	1 10 00
Mr Harrison, 25 yds at 2s 6d	3 02 06
2 cocks, 2 bosses, 1 fusil and 5 joynts	1 02 06
Mr Hall, 30 yds and 1 foot at 2s 6d	3 15 10
3 cocks, 3 boses, 1 fusill and 8 joynts	1 14 00
Mr Ridley, 12 yds large pipe at 3s 6d per yd	2 02 00
4 yds of small pipe at 2s 6d per yd	0 10 00
2 cocks, 2 bosses 8s; 5 joynts 12s 6d	1 00 00
Memo: a stopt cock and 2 joynts to my house	0 11 00
[Total]	22 00 10

Memorandum: received the 23th of October 1733 of John Collier two and twenty pound in full of this account for laying in the pipes to his own house, Roger Harrison, Mr John Hall's, John Crouch and John Ridley and a stop cock at his own house. [Signed] Robert Rosam.
[*Reverse*] Account about the pipes and waterworks and Mr Rosam's receipt October 1733. Memorandum, the 9th of September 1738, for the pipes, etc., laid in Tarrfield for £43 17s 0d is on my fyle. The within account of £39 3s 0d the pipes etc., belong to Dr Carleton and I jointly. The rest at my house, Roger Harrison's, Mr Hall's and Mrs Ridley's are my own.

592 Payments to Robert Rosam for waterworks, May to October 1733. [SAY 26]

May 11 1733 paid Robert Rosam £50 0s 0d; August 18 1733 paid ditto £50 0s 0d; August 23 1733 paid ditto in partnership £19 10s 0d.

Paid Robert Rosam, for my own pipes of lead; at home £8 13s 6d; Roger Harrison's £4 05s 0d; John Hall's £5 09s 10d; John Ridley's £3 12s 6d.

[Reverse: sums without attribution]

593 Henry Sargent, plaintiff,[1] John Collier and Henry Carleton, defendants: papers for the defendants, trespass upon the case [SAY 21]

Sussex to wit: the plaintiff declares that whereas on the 25th of June in the 7th year of his present majesty, and long before, he was and continually from thenceforth hitherto hath been, and still is, seized in his demesn as of fee of and in a certain ancient messuage with the appurtences scituat in the town of Hasting in the said county. And whereas the plaintiff and all those whose estate he hath of and in the said messuage with the appurtences, from the time whereof the memory of man is not to the contrary, were used every year and at all times in the year to have and take water from and out of a certain rivulet or stream called the Bourne, which during all the time aforesaid used to run through the said town of Hasting near unto the plaintiff's said messuage for his and their necessary use, convenience and accomodation without any contradiction, hindrance or molestation of or by any person or persons whatsoever and of right ought so to doe.

Nevertheless, the defendants, not being ignorant of the premises, but contriving and malitiously intending to deprive the plaintiff of the convenience, advantage and benefit of taking water from and out of the said rivulet or stream, the said 25th of June in the 7th year aforesaid at the parish of All Saints in Hasting aforesaid, in the county aforesaid did make and cause to bee made a dam crosse the said rivulet or stream called the Bourne above the plaintiff's said messuage, and thereby stopped the current of the of the said rivulet or stream and did then and there also digg, and make cause to be digged, and made a large bason or receptacle for receiving the water of the said rivulet or stream; and did then and there in the said dam fix and place and cause to be fixed and placed certain pipes, made of elm or other wood, for conveying the water from and out of the said bason to other places remote from the same by reason whereof great part of the water of the said rivulet or stream was carried away and diverted from itts antient and usuall course or channell, soe that the plaintiff could not take water from and out of the said rivulet or stream to supply his occasions in so ample, convenient and beneficiall manner as before that time he used, and of right ought to doe, wherefore he is prejudiced. Damage 20 pounds. Not guilty pleaded.

The Case. About half a mile distant from the town and corporation of Hasting there arises severall small springs of water which all unite [2] just above the town and from thence run through a channell called the Bourne between the two principall streets thereof. And the greatest part of the inhabitants supply themselves with water out of the said stream and though there are [3] near 2000 inhabitants they don't use a hundredth part thereof, and the surplusage runs off into the sea.

By the scituation of the town much the greatest number of the inhabitants live at a distance from this watercourse to whom it was very inconvenient and expensive to supply themselves with water, and in rainy weather the slub and filth of the great high roads leading to the town runs off into [4] this rivulet, just at the entrance of the water into the Bourne or channell, which renders it soe exceeding thick and muddy that itt's useless, sometimes for a week or ten dayes togeather. At the entrance of the water into [5] this channell or Bourn the corporation of Hasting have immemorially maintained floodgates, and an officer [6] on purpose to take care of them, and every Tuesday and Friday afternoon throughout the year these floodgates are shut up close for at least 24 hours each time to let the water off at once, to cleanse off the filth and nastiness thrown into the Bourne by the poor people that live by the sides of it; during which 24 hours, twice a week, the inhabitants can have thereby no supply of water.

Some [7] of the springs uniteing in the defendant Collier's ground, which lying higher than the town, the defendants to remedy the great inconveniencys that themselves and the other inhabitants lay under by not having constantly good water had thoughts of conveying a supply by pipes from the defendant's ground which would be clear from the filth and slubb of the high roads and from all the common drains of the town which discharge themselves into the Bourn and from the careless nastiness of the poor inhabitants living neer it, and for being supplyed with water those days that the floodgates are shut down.

Though the proposall met with a universall approbation, the defendants, being desireous to leave noe room for complaint, desired the mayor would hold a common hall of the town to have the opinion of the corporation thereon. And accordingly one was held the 9th day of November 1732, at which there were present the whole body of mayor, juratts and freemen, except 5 or 6 freemen that were absent from the town or hindred by sickness, and in particular the plaintiff was present.[8] The defendants then proposed remedying the great inconvenience the inhabitants laboured under about water by conveying it by pipes to be laid through the streets for the inhabitants' use and the same met with a generall approbation, not one dissenting, so as the remainder of the water run into the Bourne as usuall for supplying those inhabitants that would [9] not be at the expence of haveing it by pipes, and the same was accordingly entred as an Act of the common hall.

The defendants thereupon the next summer proceeded to put the same into execution and finished it through one of the principall streets, though at the expence of a great many hundred pounds. And the same had the desired effect to the satisfaction of all the principall inhabitants, who are thereby constantly supplyed with water that is good, at [10] an easy expence, and those that do not come into the project have the use of [11] the water not conveyed by the pipes and which is enough to supply twenty such towns, and those that have the water by pipes [12] the plaintiff [13] admits have a right to the water [14] but [15] they must fetch it by buckets or barrells and not convey it by pipes. The defendants have also at their own expence for the advantage of the town (the buildings being generally timber and old), at convenient distances, placed [16] fire pluggs through the street for a supply [17] there being before noe [18] conveniency of water if a fire [19] should happen.

The plaintiff himselfe, whilst the pipes were laying, and afterwards, much approved of the project and often declared the same and that he intended to take it in of the pipes. But setting up for a manager of the town at the late elections, and finding he should be disappointed therein, he and two or three more hot headed fellows stirred up the common people against it; and raised a clamour and went about the town with a paper and with falshoods and threats prevailed with a great many of the mean inhabitants to sign a paper to goe to law in order for the pipes to be removed and accordingly have brought this action and 3 more for the same purpose.

Note, these actions were brought last Michalmas term, and issue joyned in Hillary term, and notice of tryall given for the last assizes. But there being alwayes in the winter such a great quantity of water the plaintiff and his associates were afraid and ashamed to go forward to tryall then and lay by for this dead part of the year when the springs are generally low. But as there had been a view by the jury, who well know the great want of water at severall places in the country, and see that there is a good supply now for the inhabitants, apprehend this stratagem will not turn out to his advantage.

Mr John Reynolds.[20] About a fortnight since, this witness, who is an engineer, took a survey of the springs and made an experiment with a vessell how much water run in those above the bason, and those that unite in the Bourne, and found that those in the bason were 5 minutes running off 29 gallons and those into the Borne but one minute and halfe running the same quantity. Besides, at trying the experiment all the springs above the bason were stopped from running; at other times the surplusage of these springs, which is at least two thirds of that water, runs off into the Bourne and makes an addition to it. Please to examine him as to the scituation of the town and quantity of water and how the high roads and common drains of the town run into it and the great use of the pipes for conveying good water and that there is water enough to supply ten such towns.

Samuel Lawrence, William Gawen.[21] These witnesses assisted Mr Reynolds in making the experiment, have lived all their time in the town and will prove that in rainy weather, sometimes for a week or ten dayes together, there is not any water in the Borne fit for use by the slub and filth of the high roads and common drains of all the streets and gutters being discharged into it; and that they have in dry summers known much less water in the Borne before the pipes were laid than since and that the water in the Borne, by the careless nastiness of the inhabitants, in the summertime often stinks and breeds maggots, and will speak as to the shutting down the floodgates twice a week, during which time the inhabitants cannot have water.

Richard Halsted, William Gawen.[22] To prove that the plaintiff who is a free man of the town was present the 9th day of November 1732 at the Common Hall when the approbation of the whole corporation was given to the project, and Mr Halsted has heard the plaintiff since declare that the pipes did noe hurt to the Bourne. Note: Halsted will also prove what distress the inhabitants were in for water before the pipes were laid and how difficult it was to get any good water and how farr he has been obliged to goe severall times for water and how all the common drains run into the Bourne etc.

The plaintiff hath subpeona'd a great number of witnesses, most of them mean inhabitants, and we hear they will pretend to prove that part of the springs running into the Bourne below the bason are minerall and that the water will not wash so well as it did before. The truth is that a bank in Bakers field, marked in the mapp, is morasse ground, a little tinged with minerall or red marlewater. But part of that also runs into the bason, as well as below it, which makes it all alike and there is no manner of difference as to itts not washing soe well, abundance of experiments having been made of it. Just at the bank the ground is a little matter tinged with red but it is not discernable by the tast.

Samuel Lawrence, William Gawen, Thomas Adams, Anne Barry, Elizabeth Honey.[23] These witnesses have made the experiment of the water about washing and cannot perceive any manner of difference. The plaintiff has subpena'd Robert Rosam, the person that laid the pipes for the defendants, we suppose to prove the work done. Please to crosse examine him and he will speak as to the scituation of the town, the usefulness of the project and that there is water enough for 20 such towns and that it is the best thing that ever was done for the town.

Please to examine all the plaintiff's witnesses about the high roads and common draines running into the Borne and the carelessness of the inhabitants living near it and whether the defendants and the other persons that have water by the pipes have not a right to the Borne water. Note: the plaintiff himselfe, who seems so very carefull relating to water for the inhabitants, about 12 or 14 years since turned from a seaman to a sort of common brewer, and his house being scituated just by the side of the Borne, placed down 2 stumpps with grooves in them, and when he wants water putts in it a plank of about 18 inches breadth and stopps it close with clay, that noe water can passe for the inhabitants below it, which are a great number, till the water runs over that plank which is a considerable time in riseing that height and the nature of it was seen by the jury on the view.

Upon the whole this and the other actions are brought purely by malice against the defendants and carried on by a joynt purse; and now the defendants have been at soe very great expence in effecting the work, nothing will serve the plaintiff and his adherents but that all the pipes must be taken up again and rendred useless. And though it is heartily applauded by all the cheife inhabitants who are by this means supplyed with good water, they must not enjoy the benefit of it for the caprice of 3 or 4 malitious, hot headed fellows and as there has been a view by ten of the jury they will be thereby judges of what is given in evidence on the tryall.

Nathaniel Crutenden, Thomas Carswell, William Coppard, Thomas Godley.[24] Since finishing the breife these witnesses, who are gentlemen of the town of Hasting, were very free to appear and give evidence that they look upon the laying of the pipes as a very great service to the inhabitants, that there is a very full supply of water in the Bourne for the other inhabitants, that all the high roads and common drains run into the Bourne, that in rainy times there is not any water fit for use etc. Note: Mr Godley was mayor of the town when the common hall was held in November 1732 about the project and he, Mr Carswell and Mr Coppard will prove that the plaintiff was present and that it was unanimously agreed to. [*end sheet*] for the defendants, Collier and Carleton, at the suite of Meadow, briefe J. Marsh.

1 MS *Benjamin Meadow* struck through and Henry Sargent written above Benjamin Meadow.
2 MS *about … rodd* struck through MS damaged.
3 MS *about* struck through.
4 MS*the said* struck through.
5 MS *the said* struck through.
6 *Baines* ch. 21 the Bourne stream, discusses the work of the water bailiff.
7 MS *few* struck through.
8 ESRO HAS CAA/2 9 November 1732.
9 MS *joyn in* struck through.
10 MS *a very* struck through.
11 MS *all* struck through.
12 MS *have by* struck through.
13 MS *even consent* struck through
14 MS *in the Bourne* struck through.
15 MS *foolishly pretend that though they have* struck through.
16 MS *down* struck through
17 MS *of water* struck through.
18 MS *manner of* struck through.
19 MS *if such an accident* struck through.
20 In the margin.
21 In the margin.
22 In the margin.
23 In the margin.
24 In the margin, *Nathaniell Cruttenden* struck through.

594 Opinion of John Darnell for John Collier and Henry Carleton, in the case of John Sargent, 12 February 1734 [SAY 22]

Some distance from the town and corporation of Hasting there arise severall small springs which unite about a quarter of a mile above the town, and from thence run through a channell between the two principall streets thereof into the sea, which is called the Bourne. And all the inhabitants and householders of the town have supplyed themselves with what water they have occasion for out of the said stream and though there are about two thousand inhabitants they don't use a hundredth part of the water and the surplusages run into the sea.

The greatest part of the inhabitants live at a distance from this water course to whom it was very inconvenient and expensive to supply themselves with water; especially those that used large quantitys. And, besides, the scituation of the town is such that in rainy weather the slub and filth of severall high roads runs off into the said rivulett just at the entrance into the town which rendered it very thick and muddy and so useless, sometimes for a week or ten days together.

The springs riseing and uniteing on higher ground than the town, the defendants for the advantage of themselves and the other inhabitants, for sometime had the thoughts of conveying the water by pipes quite clear of the filth and slubb of the high road, and also free from all the common drains of the town. And at a publick assembly or meeting of the mayor, juratts and freemen of the town and corporation convened for that purpose in November 1732 made a proposall of their intentions which were unanimously agreed to, and so entered in their town records, plaintiff being then present. And thereupon the defendants at the expence of severall hundreds of pounds have compleated the said works and most of the substantiall inhabitants are thereby supplyed with water, always perfectly good, on paying a small annuall summe not a tenth part of what the charge and trouble was before of having their water fetched from the Bourne. And those that do not come into the project take their water out of the said Bourne as before; for the remainder not conveyed by the pipes, and which at no time is a tenth part, runs as formerly and when the pipes are full the surplusage of that which should run into em, were they not so, runs with the other in its old channell and there is not the one hundredth part of it used by the inhabitants.

N.B. By the above tis to be observed that this water is a common water and every person in the town has a right to it. And consequently that no person has the water conveyed to em by these pipes but what is intitled to fetch it from the Bourne and that no part of the water by means of these pipes is wasted. As this manifestly appears to be a most malicious action and of great consequence to defendants all lawfull means are to be used to defeat it. Therefore,

Q. Whether defendants upon pleading not guilty will not be let in to give this whole matter in evidence and whether any damage or not to be left to a jury? A. I think we will be intitled to give the whole matter in evidence on not guilty.

Q. Whether, if any, this will not be deemed a publick nuisance for which no action will lye, but the partyes must have recourse to indictment? A. Any private person injured may maintain an action for that injury.

The plaintiff has prescribed in his declaration for water generally without saying that he is intitled to use it in and about his house as belonging to his house. Q. Whether advantage may not be taken of this at a tryall? A. I think the prescription is well enough.

Q. Whether the word 'same' in the declaration will not be taken to have reference to bason made immediately preceding [1] may run remote from the bason yet go by plaintiff's house since the bason and house are at least half a mile from each other? A. I think the word 'same' will referr to the water and not to the bason.

Q. Upon the whole whether either by the merits of the cause or the seeming slip of the declaration the defendants have not a probable cause to expect success upon a triall?

A. I think there is very good grounds for the defendant to dispute with the plaintiff this question and not to give it up, and especially if there is not a want of water, I think the plaintiff cannot maintain this action, J. Darnell, 12 Feb 1734.

1 MS damaged

595 To John Collier, Hastings, from William Cranston, Johnson's Court, 8 August 1734, with copy of proceedings in King's Bench [SAY 23]

Hillary Term, 7 King George the second. Roll Ventris

Sussex to wit - Be it remembred that in the term of St Michael last past before our lord the king at Westminster came Benjamin Meadow by John Thayer, his attorney, and brought in the court of our said lord the king, then there his bill against John Collier and Henry Carlton, being in the custody of the marshall of the king's marshalsea before the king himself, of a plea of trespass upon the case and there are pledges of prosecuting, to wit John Doe and Richard Roe, which said bill follows in these words.

Sussex to wit - Benjamin Meadow complains of John Collier and Henry Carlton, in the custody of the marshall of the king's marshalsea, before the king himself, for that whereas the said Benjamin on the twenty fifth day of June, in the seventh year of the reign of our sovereign lord George the second, now king of Great Britain and so forth, and long before was and continually from thenceforth hitherto hath been, and still is, possessed of and in a certain ancient messuage and brewhouse, with the appurtences, scituate in the town of Hasting in the county of Sussex. And whereas there is and from the time whereof the memory of man is not to the contrary there hath been a certain ancient rivulett or stream called the Bourne which all the time aforesaid did and used to run through the said town of Hasting, by and near to the said messuage and brewhouse of the said Benjamin, from and out of which said rivulet or stream the said Benjamin and all other possessors and occupiers of the said ancient messuage and brewhouse, with the appurtences, during all the time aforesaid used and were accustomed every year, at all times of the year, to have and take water to and for his and their necessary use, convenience and accomodation without any contradiction, hinderance or molestation of or by any person or persons whatsoever, and of right ought so to do.

Nevertheless the said John Collier and Henry Carlton, not being ignorant of the premises, but contriving and maliciously intending to deprive the said Benjamin of the convenience, advantage and benefit of taking water from and out of the said rivulett or stream, afterwards, to wit on the same 25th day of June in the seventh year aforesaid, at the parish of All Saints in Hasting aforesaid in the county aforesaid, did make and cause to be made a dam cross the said rivulett or stream called the Bourne above the said messuage and brewhouse of the said Benjamin, and thereby stopped the current of the said rivulett or stream and did then and there also dig and make and caused to be digged and made a large bason or receptacle for receiving the water of the said rivulett or stream and did then and there in the said dam fix and place, and cause to be fixed and placed, certain pipes made of elm or other wood for conveying the water from and out of the said bason to other places remote from the same. By reason whereof great part of the water of the said rivulett or stream was carryed away and diverted from its ancient and usuall course or channell, so that the said Benjamin could not take water from and out of the said rivulett or stream to supply his occasions in so ample, convenient and beneficiall manner as before that time he used, and of right ought to do, wherefore he sayth that he is prejudiced and hath damage to the value of twenty pounds and thereupon he bringeth his suit, and so forth.

And now at this day, to wit - Wednesday next after the octave of St Hillary in this same term, untill which day the said John and Henry had licence to imparle to the bill aforesaid and then to answer the same before our lord the king at Westminster, came as well the said Benjamin by his attorney aforesaid as the said John and Henry by William Cranston, their attorney, and the said John and Henry defend the wrong and injury when and etc., and say that they are not guilty of this premises in manner and form as the said Benjamin hath above complained against them. And hereupon they put themselves upon the country and the said Benjamin does the like. Therefore let a jury come before our lord the king at Westminster on Tuesday next after the octave of the purification of the blessed virgin Mary, who are in no ways of kin either to the said Benjamin or to the said John Collier and Henry, to take cognizance upon their oath of the whole truth of the premises. Because as well the said John Collier and Henry as the said Benjamin have put themselves upon that jury, the same day is given to the partyes aforesaid at the same place.

Above [1] is a copy of the issue in Meadow's cause which I thought you had had before, in those of Guy and Serjeant. I had this day a countermand to that; Meadow and Taught only remain to be tryed.[2] Eadnell at present is upon the Midland circuit where he's associate but as soon as that ends he'll be in town, which I'll pay him and let you know. I paid Bayley's bill yesterday; we have had a dispute about it subsisting ere since Saturday. They would take none of Master Page's Portugall money in part; I insisted they should, so accordingly today the gentry submitted. I sent my sister's bit of silk yesterday. Bobby Page's journey seems to be at an end, so shall take a place tomorrow for Jemmy only for Monday sennight. Sparrow goes at the same time for Mr Boy's at Hawkhurst; he goes to Tunbridge in the coach the horses meet him so I fancy had better do the same. We christened our little one last night by the name of Thomas.

1 Additional notes by William Cranston.
2 Case referred from King's Bench to Sussex assizes, Horsham, Monday 12 August 1734, 8 Geo II, Benjamin Meadow v John Collier and Henry Carleton, 5/- damages awarded against Collier and Carleton, for which case see [**108**]. This case is listed in SAY 1418 f. 24v.

596 Draft account for waterworks, 1735. [SAY 27]

Jun the 20 1735, an accompt taken of leaden pipp; layd for Mr John Collier, by Mr Robert Rosam, of inches ¼ pipp, 223 foot 9 inch, 74 yards 1f-9in; joyntes in that lenght ten of ¾ of an inch pippe, 628 foot 6 inch, 209 yard 1f-6in; joynts in that lenght, twenty five.

Jun the 20 1735, an accompt of labrours' work about the same,[1] 1735; for 2 day to Stephen Morriss £0 3s 0d; for 2 day John Foord; £0 03s 0d; for 2 day Richard Scott £0 03s 0d; for 2 days Master Huneychurch £0 03s 0d; for 2 days Thomas Carman £0 03s 0d; this my wife paid £0 12s 0d; for 3 day ½ myself £0 07s 0d; for putting in of cocks, £0 02s 0d; paid Samuel Lawrence, July 15th 1735, £0 09s 0d.

[*Reverse: sums without attribution*]

1 The general quarter sessions laid down wage rates: the quarter sessions Lewes, Thursday 5 April 1733, determined servants and labourers wages from Annunciation to Michaelmas. For the best of a group of

skilled trades, not above 10d day with meat and drink, nor without meat and drink 16d; second sort of artificers, over 21, served 2 years, 6d with meat and drink, without 12d. Labourers who worked by the great for ditches, 1 rod of new ditch 3 ft on the top and 1 ft deep, not above 1d (ESRO QRE/416 f.24).

597 To John Collier, bill from Robert Rosam, plumber, 20 June 1735 [SAY 28]

June the 20 1735;

For 74 yards and 1 foot 9 inches of large pipe at 3:6 per yard,	£13 1s 0 ½d
10 joynts	£1 15s 0d
for 209 yards and 1 foot and a half of small pipe at 2:6 per yard	£26 03s 09d
25 joynts	£2 10s 0d
one large stop cocks	£0 07s 06d
[Total]	£43 17s 03½d

[*Reverse*] received the 9th of September 1738 of John Collier twenty three pounds seventeen shillings, which with twenty pounds before received of him makes forty three pounds, seventeen shillings, in full of the within bill and all demands, witness my hand, Robert Rosam.

598 To John Collier, Account for waterworks, 18 July 1740 [SAY 29]

Mr James Bossom to Robert Still is debited,
1740 July 11th for 16 yards of 5 inch pipe at 3s 6d per yard. £2 16s 00d
Received att the same time the above contents for Robert Still
per mee, George Thomas.

[*Reverse*] Account of elm pipes, paid James Bossom the 18th July 1740 for Dr Carleton and self; carriage from London 7 0 up to the bay, drawing afterwards 0 04s 00d paid workmen.

599 Account for waterworks, 31 December 1742 [SAY 30]

Dec the 30th and 31st 1742 Mamaranam[1]

	Hund:	qr:	lb
The leading pipes Mr Harrison maid	2	0	13
Mr John Chrouch maid	2	1	27
	4	2	12

3 cocks from Mr John Chrouch
2 cocks from Mr Harrison

by me John Reed

1 Presumably *memorandum*.

600 Account for waterworks, 22 December 1742 [SAY 31]

Memranam[1] of the waight of leading

	hunds:	Qr:	L
Pipes: the waight of the great pipes	6	2	24
the waight of the small pipes	9	0	9
	15	3	5
The waight of a peece of pipe that went into the George		0	15

by me, John Reed

[*Reverse*] Account of weight of pipes: J Reed taking up 0 13 4; more to him 0 8 8; more to weighing pipes; more carriage up.

[*Note by John Collier*] East Farley, John Cousins and Margaret his wife.

1 Presumably *memorandum.*

Appendix 4: Pelham Estate

601 To John Collier, from Henry Pelham,[1] 13 September 1733 [SAY 369]

These presents testify that the right honourable Henry Pelham esq., hath made, constituted and appointed, and by these presents doth make, constitute and appoint John Collier of Hasting in the county of Sussex, gentleman, his steward to all his mannors and lordships within the said county of Sussex, giveing and by these presents granting unto the said John Collier and to his sufficient deputy or deputys in that behalfe made and to every or either of them full power and authority to keep and hold all his court leets, views of frankpledge, court barons and other courts within the said mannors and lordships, and to doe and execute all things belonging to the office of a steward during the will and pleasure of him the said Henry Pelham. In witnesse whereof, he hath hereunto set his hand and seal this thirteenth day of September in the seaventh year of the reign of our soverign Lord King George the Second over Great Britain and so forth and in the year of our lord God one thousand, seaven hundred and thirty-three. Sealed and delivered in the presence, Peter Dubourg, John Heath.

1 For explanation of courts leet and courts baron and duties of all parties see J Ritson *The Jurisdiction of the Court Leet* 2nd edn (London, 1809).

602 Audit expenses for Henry Pelham,[1] 12 March 1735 [SAY 375]

To Joseph Fuller, butcher £1 2s 6d; Samuel Vergoe, butcher £1 1s 0d; Francis Weller, shopkeeper £2 13s 7d; to brandy £1 18s 0d; to lemons £0 15s 9d; to candles £0 11s 0d; to butter, 15 lb; £0 7s 6d; to bacon, £0 5s 3d; to wheat £0 8s 0d; to expenses of Mr Collier's horses £0 3s 0d; to hay for the tenants' horses £0 4s 0d; to milk and cream £0 3s 6d; use of linen etc., £1 11s 6d; servants, £1 1s 0d.

1 It was common practice for landlords to provide food and drink for tenants collected together to settle rents.

603 Henry Pelham, estate audit, expenses, 18 October 1738 [SAY 376]

Two bushels of wheat, £0 8s 0d; a shopkeeper's bill to Mr Francis Weller, £2 8s 3 ½d; a butcher's bill to Mr Vergoe, £0 18s 2d; ditto Joseph Fuller, £1 06s 0d; two halk ankers of brandy, £2 06s 0d; one hundred and fifty lemons, carriage, £1 7s 0d; ten pound of butter at 6d lb, £0 05s 0d; a goose, £0 02s 6d; eggs and milk, £0 02s 0d; wine, £0 16s 0d; ware and tare, £1 11s 6d; horses'corn, £0 11s 0d; hay, £0 06s 0d; two dozen candles, £0 10s 0d; servants, £1 01s 0d;
[*sum*] £13 18s 5½d.

604 Expenses of audit 23 March 1739, for the use of the Rt Hon Mr Pelham [SAY 377]

Lemons, £0 14s 0d; brandy, £2 04s 0d; 2 galons of wine, £0 16s 0d; 13 lb butter; £0 06s 6d; eggs and milk, £0 01s 6d; leg of pork, £0 06s 8d; 2 bushels of wheat, £0 08s 0d; 2 dusn candles, £0 10s 0d; tenants' hay, £0 06s 0d; Samuel Virgo, £1 15s 0d; Joseph Fuller, £0 15s 2d; for beer, £1 10s 0d; corn for horses, £0 05s 0d; Mr Weller's bill, £2 02s 9d; linen ware, £1 01s 0d; servants, £1 01s 0d; a bell, £0 05s 0d; [*sum*] £14 07s 7d.

605 Expenses of the audit for Henry Pelham's estate, held the 18th October 1739 [SAY 378]

M. Weller's bill, £2 04s 3d; Joseph Fuller's bill; £1 02s 10d; lemons and carriage, £1 00s 06d; Samuel Virgoe's bill, £0 15s 5 ½d; brandy, £2 04s 0d; a goose, £0 02s 6d; 2 bushells of wheat, £0 08s 0d; 6 pound of bacon and 14 pound of butter, £0 10s 0d; eggs and cream, £0 01s 6d; beer, £2 00s 0d; horses' hay and corn, £0 07s 0d; tenants horses' hay, £0 05s 0d; wear and tare, £1 10s 0d; servants £1 01s 0d;
[*sum*] £13 12s 0d; candles £0 11s 4d; [*sum*] £14 03s 4d.

606 An Abstract of the Audit held for Henry Pelham 14 October 1741 for receipt of rents at Lady Day last[1] [SAY 373]

	Tenants names	Half yearly rents	Rents in Arrear	Land Taxes	Lords rents	Water-scotts	Repairs	Clear Money	
1	The Duke of Newcastle	£76.1.3							
2	Robert Saxby	£121.0.0					in part	£17.0.0	
3	Edward Shoosmith	£54.5.0		£10.16.0				£43.9.0	
4	James Shoosmith	£10.0.0		£2.0.0				£8.0.0	
5	William Shoosmith	£74.0.0		£14.16.0		£2.7.3	£10.0.5 ½	£46.16.3 ½	
6	Robert Turner son of John	£10.10.0		£2.0.0				£8.8.0	
7	Thomas Jones	£19.5.0		£3.16.0				£15.9.0	
8	William Peckham	£18.15.0		£3.14.0			£2.11.2	£12.9.10	
9	William Durrant	£18.10.0		£3.14.0				£14.16.0	
10	James Chambers	£37.10.0							
11	ditto: Great Lulhams	£35.0.0							
12	John Earle	£43.15.0		£8.14.10			£44.14.3 ½	£2.5.10 ½	
	more the Weeklands	£12.0.0							
13	Samuel Gower	£2.10.0		£0.10.0				£2.0.0	
14	Josias Smith	£46.1.3	£11.1.3	£17.17.4	£1.1.3 ½		£10.1.8 ½	£28.2.2 ½	
15	Widow Thomas	£35.0.0	£35.0.0	£6.6.0	half yr in part		£8.13.10	£20.0.2	
16	Mr Francis Weller	£2.10.0							
17	Widow Tomkin	£30.0.0		£5.12.0				£24.8.0	
18	William Burwash	£4.10.0		£0.14.0			£3.9.4	£0.6.8	
19	J Lavender & John Gilbert	£20.0.0		£3.16.0			£0.10.7	£15.13.5	
20	William Devall	£37.10.0		£8.16.0	£0.11.10			£28.2.2	
21	John Manser	£2.5.0						£2.5.0	
22	Thomas Slater	£1.0.0							
23	William Ellis	£20.0.0	£40.0.0						
24	John Collins	£4.0.0		£1.12.0				£2.8.0	
25	John Newington	£7.10.0							

	Tenants names	Half yearly rents	Rents in Arrear	Land Taxes	Lords rents	Water-scotts	Repairs	Clear Money	
26	Mr John Legas & Co	£25.0.0	Mr Legas also paid the half year due Mich. 1741					£50.0.0	
27	John Young	£6.0.0		£1.4.0			£0.5.6	£4.10.6	
28	David Collins	£5.15.0		£2.3.3				£3.11.9	
29	Tobias Cox	£1.5.0						£1.5.0	
30	Mr Robert Burnet	£10.15.0							
31	Thomas Chatfield	£36.10.0	£36.10.0	£7.4.0	£1.3.3	one half years rent paid		£28.2.9	
32	Nicholas Devall	£17.5.10 ½	£55.1.11 ½	£3.8.0	£0.10.2		£5.6.8	£25.6.11	On account
33	Thomas Venner	£2.10.0	£7.10.0					£10.0.0	
34	Mr John Goldham	£10.0.0	£20.0.0						
35	Henry Walker	£40.0.0		£9.8.0			£4.18.10	£25.13.2	
36	Robert Turner	£45.0.0		£9.0.0			£10.18.5	£25.1.7	
37	Widow Lidlow	£21.0.0		£4.0.0			£2.1.11	£14.18.1	
38	John Ellis	£15.0.0							
39	William Avery	£2.10.0	£3.15.0						
40	Mr Francis Hickes	£35.0.0		£6.12.0	£0.18.2		£6.6.6 ½	£21.3.3 ½	
41	Widow Blackman	£8.0.0		£1.8.0				£6.12.0	
42	John Cuthbert	£8.18.4	£26.15.0						
43	Samuel French	£0.10.0							
44	John Vine	£12.10.0		£1.16.0			£4.3.5	£6.10.7	
	Totals							£514.15.3	
							Wood	£134.14.0	
								£649.9.3	

1. An abstract of the audit for Henry Pelham for rents held 10 March 1741 for receipt of rents due at Michaelmas last similar in form and with tenants as above is SAY 374.

607 Rental of the estate of Thomas Pelham of Stanmer to Michaelmas 1745 [SAY 372]

No	Tenant	Farm	Parish	Yearly Rent	Arrears Mich 1745	Money rec'd from Mich 1745	
1	William Ridge	Stanmer farm	Stanmer	£390	£510.00		lease agreement not executed
2	Edward Weeden	Deans farm & Heath Down	Piddinghoe	£350	£926 19s 7½d	£240	ditto
3	John Bean	Sluce farm	Bexhill & Hooe	£300	£375.00	£162	no lease
4	Joseph Rickman	Park Farm, Spiggetts marsh & Chilley	Hellingly, Pevensey	£150	£240 5s 6d	£90 5s	lease expired 1737
5	Thomas Burgess	Highland & Cold Harbour, Foote marsh	Chiddingly & Hoadly	£103	£399 4s 9d	£40 10s	never had a lease
6	Stephen Gower	Blackstock & Bingleys, Storseye & Bees marsh	Hellingly, Pevensey, Hailsham	£100	£83 15s		ditto
7	Thomas Lulham	Lies & Barnets	Hellingly	£70	£70.00	£35	no lease
8	Richard Comber	Godmans Land	Bexhill	£45	£56 5s		no lease
9	Joseph Newington	Moors	Mayfield	£8	£12.00	£8	no lease
10	Thomas Moon	Moat Mill farm	Mayfield	£33 10s	£33 10s		no lease agreement in writing
11	John Ashby	Moat Hill	Mayfield	£16			
12	John Wood	Wooton	Chillington	£100	£65.00	£15	agreement only
13	Michael Martin	Plumpton & Whales	Plumpton	£180	£180.00		20 year lease from 1733
14	William Poole	Plumpton Place land	Plumpton	£20	£70.00		no lease
15	Francis Holmwood	Pages Croft	Plumpton	£3	£1 10s		ditto
16	William Tuttee	Copyhold lands	Colworth	£20	£60.00		no lease
17	Thomas Butler	Park farm	Burwash	£75	£75.00	£37 10s	lease expires LD 1748

No	Tenant	Farm	Parish	Yearly Rent	Arrears Mich 1745	Money rec'd from Mich 1745	
18	Richard Trill	Hendall	Buxsted	£50	£25.00		lease expired
19	John Wood	Ewhurst	Shermanbury	£115	£115.00	£57 9s 11¾d	lease expires 1746
19	John Wood	Ewhurst	Shermanbury	£115	£115.00	£57 9s 11¾d	lease expires 1746
20	James Cripps	James's Land	Nuthurst,	£18	£28 16s	£10 16s	no lease
21	Stephen Martin	Kenwards, Naldred, Cripps & Virgoes	Linfield, Ardingly, Cockfield	£127	£190 10s		by agreement
22	Samuel Andrews	Cootham	Storrington	£47	£47.00	£47	by agreement
23	Thomas Coats	Mill farm	Storrington	£23	£23.00	£ 23	ditto
24	William Lamb	a parcel of land	Milton Street	£8	£8.00	£ 8	no lease
25	Thomas Wolvin	part of Bines	Westgrinsted	£55	£110.00		lease expired 1737
26	James Wotton	home lands	Westgrinsted	£20	£30.00	£ 20	no lease
27	John Burgess	Lamphams marsh	Westgrinsted	£46	£11 10s		no lease
			yearly rents	£2472 10s			
Cottages							
No	Tenant	farm name	parish	yearly rent	Arrears due Mich 1745		
1	Richard Richardson	a cottage	Stanmer	£2	£1.00		
2	John Groves	a cottage	Stanmer	£2 10s	£1 17s 6d		
3	Richard Banks	a cottage	Stanmer	£2 10s	£2 10s		
4	Robert Cooper	a cottage	Stanmer	£1 10s	£0 15s		
5	Widow Lawson	a cottage	Plumpton	£2	£2.00		

Manors							
1	Wooten	Lords rent per annum	£6 13s 7 ½d				
2	Plumpton	ditto	£14 13s 7d				
3,4,5	Linfield, South Malling, Walstead	ditto	£14 6s 5¼d				
6	Ewhurst	This Lords rent is incl' in farm rent					
		Yearly Lords rents	£35 13s 7¾d				
Francis Warden is steward of these mannors, the casual profits exclusive of the Lords rents by Heriots, reliefs, fines on the death or alienation of copyholds, tenements, I presume he particularly accounts for.							
Woodlands preserved from the tenants							
1	Hendall Woods		Buxsted	£50			
2	Hellingly Park		Hellingly	£40			
3	Blackstock Wood		Hellingly	£8			
4	Lies and Barnet		Hellingly	£7			
5	Tilehurst Wood		Hailsham	£30			
6	Oldland Wood		East Hoadley	£15			
7	Kenwards		Linfield				
Computed yearly rents for these woods				£165			
Houses in Lewes		yearly rent	rents in arrears for Mich 1745	Money received since Mich' 1745			
1	William Mitchell	£12	£96				
2	John Streeke	£10	query arrears				
3	John Stonestreet	£18	query arrears				
4	John Durrant	£2	£2				
5	Richard Thomas	£14	£4 14s 6d				
6	Widow Grisbrook	£3.00	£24				

7	Richard Palmer	£12	£9				
8	Robert Chester	£13	£6 10s				
9	John Harland	£7	£10 10s	£8			
10	Henry Pierce	£4	£4	£4			
11	Gabriel Ayres	£5 10s	£11				
Yearly rents of houses in Lewes			£88 15s				
Yearly rents of farms			£2472 10s				
Yearly rents of cottages			£10 10s				
Yearly Lords rents of manors			£35 13s 7¾d				
Computed yearly rents for woodgrounds			£165				
In arrears from former tenants							
Daniel Skinner	£274 12s 4d						
John Ridge	£286 8s 11d Quere £50, of this insisted to be abated but no foundation for it but Mr Ridge's word.						
Daniel Stephens supposed to be bad but quere the amount.							

1 Another rental of houses in Lewes belonging to Thomas Pelham of Stanmer, with arrears, and a rental of woodlands and manors, dated 29 September 1745, [SAY 370] is included with John Streeke's letter of 18 November 1745 to John Collier, for which see [**529**]; this rental is similar to the rental transcribed above [**607**]

Appendix 5: 1734 Election

608 Election list of the freeholders of the county of Sussex resident in Hastings and libertys thereof, May 1734[1] [SAY 10]

1. Richard Bridger *
2. Mr Collier * PB
3. Dr Carleton
4. Thomas Barry [*crossed out*] PB
5. William Pierce * PB
6. George Gallop * PB
7. Samuel Cruttenden PB*
8. James Winter * BiF
9. John Hussey PB
10. Mark Ridley *PB
11. Robert Lucas *
12. John Hussey * PB
13. Henry Palmer * PB
14. Thomas Page * PB
15. Joseph Dupelock *
16. Hugh Evans * PB
17. Michael Wright *
18. John Taught PB
19. Richard Bayley PB
20. Edward White * PB
21. William Markwick * PB
22. Thomas Coleman *
23. Edward Lintott *
24. William Geery * PB
25. Thomas Sweetlove * PB
26. Mr Nathaniel Cruttenden *
27. Thomas Bourn * PB
28. Mr Bayley * PB
29. Nicholas Watters PB
30. Richard Hall * PB
31. William Coppard * PB
32. Thomas Lulham *
33. John Manser *
34. Samuel Moore * BiF
35. Mr Thomas Carswell PB
36. Mr Thomas Moore * PB
37. John Cossum * BiF
38. Mr Coombridge *
39. Mr Edward Milward *
40. John Tyler *

41. Titus Lawrence * BiF
42. Richard Tutt *
43. William Richardson *
44. Thomas Whales * PB
45. Roger Harrison * BiF
46. Mr Godley
47. John Boyket sen * PB
48. John Boyket jun
49. Thomas West *
50. Robert Meadow*
51. Richard Geery * BiF
52. Edward Hill * BP
53. Mr Thorpe *
54. John Guy * BiF
55. Thomas Guy BP
56. John Read * P
57. James White * BP
58. Thomas Salmon * BP
59. Robert Hussey * BiF
60. Thomas Sargent BiF
61. James Bossum sen BP
62. James Bossum jun
63. Edward Taught PB
64. Robert Pollard * BP
65. Nicholas Page
66. John Ball * BP
67. Henry Sargent PF
68. John Arnold *
69. Stephen Sargent * BiF
70. John Adams BiF
71. Benjamin Meadow * BiF
72. John Meadow *
73. Jeremiah Thwaits *
74. Mark Bossum PB
75. Richard Chadderton * PB
76. Robert Henkley PB
77. James Essex * BiF
78. John Alisbury
79. James Grimes PB
80. Thomas Adams * BiF
81. John Chambers * BiF
82. John Shorter
83. Thomas Mitchell
84. William Wood * BiF
85. John Martin PB
86. William Lock PB
87. John Broadbridge * PB

88. William Bourne * PB
89. Thomas Bossum *
90. Andrew Dean * PB
91. John Coleman * PB
92. Robert Colbourne PB
93. William Willis *
94. Thomas Morffee PB
95. Edward Thatcher PB
96. Edward Sargent
97. Thomas Alisbury *
98. Stephen Taught * PB
99. Robert Phillip PB
100. Richard Page * PB
101. Thomas Chadderton PB
102. William Smith * PB
103. Drue Shingleton *
104. Joseph Turner *
105. William Stonehouse * PB
106. Thomas Morffee
107. Robert Evernden * BiF
108. James Hutcheson * PB
109. John Curtis PB
110. Edward Grayling * PB
111. Thomas Page *
112. Thomas Webb
113. John Bayley PB
114. John Thurgle *
115. Michael King
116. Thomas Ellams sen PB
117. Thomas Ellams jun * PB
118. William Pickerden PB
119. Thomas Horn PB
120. Henry Steevenson *
121. John Ball * PB
122. Thomas Hadden
123. Reuben Arthur
124. Benjamin Carswell * BiF
125. Francis Hugh
126. Henry Green BiF
127. William Phillip BiF
128. John Fautley PB
129. William Phillip PB
130. Thomas White PB
131. John White *PB
132. Richard White * BiF
133. William Shorter * BiF
134. Jacob Fautley * PB

135.Richard Fautley
136.John Henson * BiF
137.William Phillip * PB
138.Robert Sargent BiF
139.George Harrison * PB
140.Robert Taught * PB
141.Mark Taught BiF
142.John Lee *
143.John Bossum * PB
144.Benjamin Steevens
145.John Sargent * PB
146.Nicholas Bossum PB
147.Richard Davis
148.Robert Manser *
149.John Plane *
150.John Sargent
151.Philip Gawen BiF
152.John Thatcher PB
153.Robert Thatcher * BiF
154.Robert Thatcher jun *
155.Philip Steevenson *
156.William Bowen *
157.Thomas Thatcher * PB
158.William Thatcher *
159.John Sargent
160.John Barry * PB
161.John Hadden
162.John Hide * PB
163.Richard Wingfield PB
164.Richard Ball * BiF
165.Mark Meadow * BiF
166.John Steevens * BiF
167.Edward Morffee
168.Thomas Morffee
169.Zebediah Fantley
170.Thomas Daniell * PB
171.Paul Thurgle * PB
172.Thomas Hide * BiF
173.John Phillip * PB
174.John Mead *
175.George Page *
176.William Stedman PB
177.Mark Cosens *
178.Richard Honychurch * PB
179.Christopher Thorpe
180.Mr William King
181.Daniel Martin

182. Richard Hall * PB
183. John Taught *
184. John Gourlay

May 1734, Pelham 124, Butler 123, Byshoppe 43, Fuller 44.

1 Comparing this list, SAY 10, with the printed poll list for the Sussex country election 1734, *A poll taken by Henry Montague, Sheriff of the County of Sussex, at the City of Chichester, Thursday and Friday, 9 and 10 May 1734*, printed by John Coles, it will be seen that of the 167 noted on the printed list as voting, 110 match those on this document, SAY 10, although several may have been attributed mistakenly, or names misspelt, on the printed list. John Fuller complained that not taking a poll at Lewes as well as, or instead of, Chichester, ensured the number of voters who came off the Weald, where Fuller and Bishop enjoyed a majority, was reduced. SAY 10 was collated in 1734, and endorsed 1741 when John Collier used the list for the election of that year. For the 1734 election see Williams 1897; Crossley & Saville xiv-xv 76.

Appendix 6: Smuggling

609 Deposition concerning the attack by smugglers on 4th April 1733[1] [SAY 282]

On the 4th April 1733 out on duty with Mr Orton and Mr Coopper to Newbridge, saw a larg company of smuglers, then folowed them. Met Mr Hosfild and Mr Peadell[2] at Iden Streeat, agreed to send Mr Orton to Rye for to geet som farther asistance; folowed them to Peasmash, heard that they wear put oup ther by the consent of Mr Hosfild. I was to goe round the parish by the curch for to geet som further intiligence of the said smuglers; standing at a farmer's dor, ther coun the osler of the Sin of the Couck of the said parish, wich wee soopoasd that the smouglers had stopt ther. The said osler desired the farmer would bring in a load of hay and a quarter of oats dyrackly wich gave me a great ell of rom to thenck that they was stopt ther.

I returnd back to the pleace wear I left Mr Hosfild and the other offsers wich beefor I cam back Mr Orton cam with tow dragons and a fut soulder and had som fresh intiligence that the smuglers was gone, an soo they folowed after and I folowed them to Stoncrough wear they brook road and ther I mist them. I went on to Lambhost and found that neither smugler nor offser had ben ther, wich acashon me to cras the roads to Wodhost and Tighhost, but heard nothing of neigher party till I cam to back Flimwell. Ther I heard of some dragons been gust gone by ther [3] and over tuck them wich was the two dragons wich was with the offsers. I inquird of them wear the offsers wear they toud me that they was just beefor, wich in an veary litell time I over tuck them all but Mr Orton. They toud me that Mr Orton mad his escape from the smuglers but they wear all confind by them for about three ours and then released, soo wee returnd henc to Rye abought teen at night.

1 Deposition may have been penned by Thomas Sargent, riding officer stationed at Rye.
2 William Horsefield, Surveyor Rye, Moses Peadle, tidesman and boatman Rye, 1733 (TNA CUST 18/178; 1734 TNA CUST 18/182; 1735 TNA CUST 18/186).
3 MS two words unclear.

610 Draft of deposition taken by John Collier, Hastings, 22 July 1734, concerning incident 20 July 1734. [SAY 271]

Philip Gawen, the younger, of the town and port of Hasting in the county of Sussex, marriner, master of the sloop or cutter [1] called the Prince George, of the burthen of 20 tunns or thereabouts, voluntarily maketh oath that, on or about the 10th day of this instant July Thomas Darby, who is a notorious smuggler, came to this deponent at Hasting aforesaid and desired this deponent to goe a voyage to Flushing[2] for a cargoe of tea. And this deponent did agree to goe accordingly in his said sloop or vessell, and took in the said Thomas Darby, according to appointment, at a place called the Gobus about two miles east of Hasting, and proceeded from thence to the said port of Flushing; and did there the 14th day of this July, English style, take on board his said sloop or vessel 160 baggs of green tea and bohea tea, all in canvas and oyle skin baggs and marked and numbered, and which this deponent looked upon to be the property of the said Thomas Darby, for that he behaved as merchant and owner of the same.

And this deponent further saith that [3] he had a bill of ladeing delivered to him at the said port of Flushing, as if the said goods were consigned to Lisbon. But that was only a pretence, for that the said Thomas Darby informed this deponent that the said tea was to be run [4] at some place on the coast of Sussex between Rye and Pevensey, and directed this deponent to set him, the said Darby, on shore between Rye and Hasting, in order for him to get the smuggling gang ready to come down to the seaside to receive the said goods. And this deponent further saith that the said 14th day of July the said Thomas Darby, in the presence of Mr Samuel De Task of Flushing aforesaid, merchant, paid this deponent 30 guineas for the freight of the said tea soe to be landed as aforesaid.[5]

And this deponent further saith that he came out of Flushing with the said tea on board his said vessell, and the said Thomas Darby, the merchant, in order to come on the English coast. But on Saturday the 20th day of this instant July, about 4 a clock in the morning, about two or three leagues off of Rye, this deponent fell in with a sloop or cutter belonging to Captain Nathaniell Pigram, commander of the Custom sloop [6] of the port of Rye, upon which this deponent made all the sayle he possibly could off to sea to escape [7] the said sloop,[8] but about 7 a clock of the said morning the said [9] sloop, in which was John Swaine, the said Pigram's mate, and some of his men, came up [10] on side of this deponent and offered to board him; upon which this deponent and the said Thomas Darby and this deponent's men, made some resistance but at length the said John Swaine [11] and some of his men boarded this deponent and [12] finding the said tea on board carried the same and this deponent's vessel into Rye harbour.

[*Reverse*] Philip Gawen, jun., of Hasting, Prince George, sloop or cutter, was freighted by Thomas Darby; took him in at the Gobus about 4 dayes. Told him to goe to Flushing for a cargoe of tea; 14 July, I signed the bill of lading; received 30 guineas for freight at Flushing, to land it in Sussex beween Rye and Pevensey. Saturday morning, the 20th at 4 a clock, Capt Pilgram's cutter came up with them. Went sometimes one way and sometimes another, we saw the cutter which they knew made the best of their way, about 7 a clock came up alongside off of Rye. Swore Swaine should not come on board or have anything and Darby. Mr De Task paid the freight but had it from Darby. Took him to be merchant and entirely under his directions and to put him on shore about Winchelsea to get the gang down ready to receive the goods.

1 MS *of Hasting* struck through.
2 Flushing, Vlissingen, due east of Thames estuary.
3 MS *the said Thomas Darby* struck through.
4 MS *on* struck through.
5 MS *which money the said De Task received from the said Thomas Darby for that purpose, as the deponent verily beleived* struck through.
6 MS *belonging to* struck through.
7 MS *him* struck through.
8 MS*cutter* struck through.
9 MS *Pigram's cutter or boat* struck through.
10 MS *to* struck through.
11 MS *the said Captain Pigram's mate which was on board the said cutter* struck through.
12 MS *carried* struck through.

611 Depositions by John Swaine, James Rydeard, Thomas Gilbert, Thomas Young, mariners, *Amelia*, Customs sloop, written by Edwin Wardroper, Winchelsea, 22 July 1734[1] concerning incident 20 July 1734 [SAY 272]

John Swaine, one of the mates of his Majestie's Custom house sloop, the *Amelia*, Captain Nathaniel Pigram, [2] commander, James Rydeard and Thomas Gilbert, marriners on board the same, do severally make oath and say that Saturday last, about 4 o clock in the morning, being at sea in the *Nelly*, cutter, they mett with a cutter called the Prince George of Hasting, Philip Gawen, master, a noted smugler, hovering on the coast near Dungeness, and boarded the same about 7 o'clock the same morning, haveing chased her to the mid channell off Rye. But before they boarded the same the said John Swaine acquainted them they belonged to the Customs whereupon the said Phillip Gawen and his company, vizt Robert Gurr, Thomas Helsebury, John Tutt, Thomas Darby, Joseph Harman and William Marsh, threatened these deponents; they would murder them if they came on board, at the same time shewing these deponents handspikes, an axe and a broad axe.

And that upon these deponents boarding the said cutter, they were beat and abused by the said cutter's company, particularly by the said Phillip Gawen and Thomas Darby, who struck the said James Rydeard and Thomas Gilbert, and did also strike at the said John Swaine with a long clubb, but missed him. And the said Phillip Gawen and Thomas Darby struck Thomas Young, another of the marriners of the said sloop, with their clubbs which has wounded and bruised him very much, and these deponents do further make oath that they heard the said Phillip Gawen say severall times that he intended to disable the said *Nelly*, cutter, by cutting away part of her rigging. But the said John Swaine, knowing there was a large quantity of tea on board the said Prince George, cutter, brought her with her cargoe into Rye harbour, within the liberty and jurisdiction of the ancient town of Winchelsea. John Swaine, James Rydeard, Thomas Gilbert, his mark, sworne at Winchelsea above written the 22nd day of July 1734, before me, John Parnell, mayor.[3]

Thomas Young, one of the marriners belonging to his Majestie's Custom house sloop the *Amelia*, Captain Nathaniel Pigram, commander, maketh oath that on Saturday, the twentieth day of July instant, being in the *Nelly*, cutter, John Swaine master, sent by the said Nathaniel Pigram in search for smuglers, they mett with the *Prince George*, cutter, of Hasting, Phillip Gawen, master, a noted smugler, within six miles of the shore off Dungeness and chased her into the mid-channell off of Rye. And being within hearth, the said John Swaine told them he belonged to the Customs and demanded them to come on board, whereupon the said Phillip Gawen and his company threatened them, holding up handspikes, an ax and a broad ax, and swore they would murder them if they came on board, and said they, meaning the said Swaine and company, should have nothing that they had on board. And this deponent saith that they boarded the said *Prince George*, cutter, who had on board, besides the master, six men, vizt, Robert Gurr, Thomas Helsebury, John Tutt, Thomas Darby, Joseph Harman and William Marsh. And further this deponent saith that as soon as he went on board their said cutter, the said Thomas Darby struck his deponent with a large stick, and the said Phillip Gawen likewise struck the deponent with the tillow that stears vessell a blow on the jaw which beat him down and has very much hurt him, being now in great pain with the same, and the said Phillip Gawen and his men struck him, this deponent, severall blows on the head, after he was down till he was rescued by the said John Swaine and his company; and this deponent does verily believe that the said Philip Gawn, and his company, would have murdered him, the deponent, if he had not been rescued as aforesaid. And further the deponent saith that the said Phillip Gawen confessing they had a large quantity of tea on board, the said John Swaine brought the said *Prince George*, cutter, into Rye harbour, but within the jurisdiction of the the ancient town of Winchelsea. Thomas Young his mark, sworne at Winchelsea, above written the 22nd day of July 1734, before me John Parnell, mayor.

[4]Phillip Gawen of Hasting in the county of Sussex, marriner, in one hundred pounds, John Lawrence of the ancient town of Winchelsea in the said county, fellmonger, in fifty pounds, and Thomas Collins of Winchelsea aforesaid, miller in fifty pounds. To be levyed on their severall goods and chattells, lands and tenements for the use of our sovereign lord the king and so forth.

The condition of this recognizance is such that if the above bounden Phillip Gawen, shall and do personally appear in court, in the next general generall quarter sessions of the peace to be held in and for the said town of Winchelsea, to answer unto such matters and things as shall be then and there objected against him by John Swaine, James Rydeard, Thomas Young and Thomas Gilbert, marriners, for assaulting, beating, wounding and abuseing them; and shall and do receive what shall be then and there enjoyned by the said court, and in the meantime keep the peace of our sovereign lord the king, as well towards his Majesty as all his liege people, especially the said John Swaine, James Rydeard, Thomas Young and Thomas Gilbert, that then the above written recognizance to be void and of none effect, otherwise to remain in full force and virtue. Philip Gawen, John Lawrence, Thomas Collens. Taken and acknowledged at Winchelsea the two and twentieth day of July, in the year of our lord 1734, before me John Parnell, mayor.

[5]Thomas Darby of Wadhurst in the county of Sussex, marriner, in one hundred pounds, John Lawrence of the ancient town of Winchelsea in the said county, fellmonger, in fifty pounds and Thomas Collins of Winchelsea aforesaid, miller in fifty pounds. To be levyed on their several goods and chattells, lands and tenements for the use of our sovereign lord the king and so forth.

The condition of this recognizance is such that if the above bounden, Thomas Darby shall and do personally appear in court, at the next generall quarter sessions of the peace to be held in and for the said town of Winchelsea, to answer unto such matters and things as shall be then and there objected against him by John Swaine, James Rydeard, Thomas Young and Thomas Gilbert, for assaulting, wounding, beating and abuseing them and shall and do receive what shall be then and there enjoyned by the said court and in the meantime keep the peace of our sovereign lord the king, as well towards his Majesty as all his liege people especially the said John Swaine, James Rydeard, Thomas Young and Thomas Gilbert, that then the above written recognizance to be void and of none effect, otherwise to remain in full force and virtue. Thomas Darby, John Lawrence, Thomas Collens. Taken and acknowledged at Winchelsea the two and twentieth day of July, in the year of our lord 1734, before me, John Parnell, mayor.

1 Edwin Wardroper, town clerk, Winchelsea 1735-40 (Pratt; Appendix 2). John Collier noted two Customs cases in his London notebook in Trinity term 1734: Pigram and Hide, and Pigram against six persons at Rye (SAY 1418 f. 22v-23v).
2 Captain Nathaniel Pigram Amelia, Customs sloop, station from Dungeness to Beachy Head, one mate, eleven mariners and one boy (TNA CUST 18/182, 183).
3 John Parnell, mayor of Winchelsea, 19 occasions, 1710-1752 (Pratt; Appendix 1). Parnell was also supervisor of the Customs riding officers from East Guildeford to Hastings (TNA CUST 18/178, 182).
4 The recognizance entered into by Philip Gawen was a bond and obligation recorded by John Parnell, mayor of Winchelsea, to appear at the next Winchelsea quarter sessions to answer the charges as above, or failing so to appear to forfeit £100, his two guarantors answering for £50 each.
5 This recognizance entered into by Thomas Darby was also a bond for £100, with the same guarantors answering for £50 apiece, with the obligation to appear at the next Winchelsea quarter sessions.

612 To John Collier, Surveyor General of Kent, Hastings, from Henry Hall, Sir John Evelyn, Brian Fairfax, Customs Commissioners, London, 23 July 1734, concerning incident 19 July 1735. [SAY 337]

Mr Battine, Surveyor General of Sussex, having laid before us a letter he received from Mr Coppard, supervisor of the riding officers at Hastings, dated 20th instant,[1] signifying that John Hide, boatman there, lately met with a smugling vessell; and on endeavouring to board her, the smuglers fired into his boat and wounded him and one of the men in the boat with him, on which one of the officers fired at the smuglers and shot one of them who is supposed to be killed. Inclosed we send you copy of the said letter,[2] and you are to enquire whether the smugling vessell was in port when the officers first discovered her, as also whether she was in port at the time they fired at the officers, with all other circumstances, and take the examination of the officers who were in the king's boat and transmit the same with such further particulars upon oath as you can learn with your observations and opinion on the whole.

1 Major William Battine, Surveyor General of the officers appointed to guard the coast of Sussex (TNA CUST 17/178).
2 For the copy forwarded to John Collier see [**95**] SAY 338.

613 Note by John Collier of discussion of smuggling case [1] heard before John Parnell, mayor of Winchelsea, 8 October 1734 [SAY 273]

Humphrey Butler, town clerk,[2] read the affidavit twice over, and used all the arguments he could to prevayle with the mayor to continue the recognizance.
Mayor said the person that made the affidavit was a paltry fellow and his affidavit ought not to be regarded or to that effect.
The principal objection made to the affidavit was that it was not made in their court, nor before him or any justice of the peace of Winchelsea, and therefore was to be taken noe notice of.

The affidavit was drawn by Mr Butler, town clerk of Winchelsea, and sworn before Mr Waters,[3] one of the justices of Rye, the 8th day of October, the morning of the sessions. The mayor, Mr Gyles,[4] a riding officer and Mr Pavis ,[5] the justices of Winchelsea present. Darby has [6] resided near Winchelsea for several yeers and been always a reputed smuggler and belongs to the great gangs.
James Levereau made the affidavit before Mr Waters.
James Rhidard says that Dodson[7] told him he had taken care that [8] Darby should be cleered, that he had opened the eyes of the Winchelsea justices.
Swaine and Young both told Captain Pigram that Thomas Darby and Gawen were not committed to gaol.
Captain Pigram went to the town clerk of Winchelsea, the day before John Swaine and James Rhidard, Thomas Gilbert and Thomas Young, materiall evidence.

1 Perhaps relating to the incident 4 April 1733.
2 Winchelsea town clerks, Richard Butler 1710-1734, Humphrey Butler 1734, Edwin Wardroper 1735-1740 (Pratt; Appendix 2).
3 Walter Water, J.P., Rye.
4 William Gyles, Customs riding officer, Winchelsea (TNA CUST 18/178/182).
5 *Jenkin* struck through; this was Thomas Jenkins sen. Winchelsea riding officer, succeeded 1734 by John Pavis (TNA CUST 18/178/182).
6 MS *lived* struck through.
7 Henry Dodson, attorney, Rye; case referred to by John Collier, Michaelmas term 1734 (SAY 1418 f. 27v).
8 MS *the man* struck through.

614 Affidavit on the attack by smugglers on Rye officers, 4 April 1733, sworn 10 October 1735 [SAY 280]

G.W. of White Chappell in the county of Middlesex, joyner, voluntarily maketh oath that sometime the latter end of March or beginning of April 1733 this deponent togeather with Thomas Care or Old Toll, John Henning, Isaac Pope or Towzer, Thomas Brett or the Miller, John Bruce, Stephen Merchant, all of London, George Watson or Yorkshire George and Francis Kitson or Nasty Face, both of the Isle of Sheppey in the county of Kent, George Cole of Westram in Kent, shoomaker, Robert Moreton of Witheram in Sussex, a dealer in hard ware, John Russell of Silcomb in Sussex,[1] farmer, William Weston of Groombridge in Sussex, labourer, George Rawlinson who lives at the sign of the Cock and Bottle at Chepsted in Kent, John Barber of Staplecross in the parish of Ewhurst in Sussex, husbandman, William Cook of Selcomb afd, victualler, since dead, Richard Blueman of London, since dead, with severall others whose names this deponent doth not know went down to the seaside near Lydd in the said county of Kent where there was unshipped without payment of duty out of a vessell whereof Thomas Toms, since dead, was master and brought to the shoar in a boat belonging to the said vessell, upwards of 3000 pounds weight of tea, and all the beforenamed persons togeather with this deponent helped and assisted in taking all the said 3000 pounds of tea out of the said boat and loaded it on horses, and then proceeded with the same up into the country, and at a place near Stonecrouch in Kent, they, the said persons, and this deponent were overtaken by five officers of the Customs,[2] Sargent, Houghton and three officers whose names this deponent does not know, and two soldiers.

Whereupon the said persons and this deponent got out of the road into a field adjoyning and were followed by the said officers and soldiers, but upon the said persons facing about and flourishing their firearms and swearing they should not have any of the said tea, the officers and soldiers made off; but were soon pursued and stopped by the said persons, their arms taken from them, and their pistolls fired off, and compelled to goe with the said persons, and to lead some of their horses about five or six miles on their road towards Groombridge afd, and after having deteyned the officers and soldiers above four hours, they, the said persons, then restored them their arms and bid them go home about their business. And this deponent saith that he and the aforenamed persons proceeded with the said tea to Groombridge afd, where they stayed that night, and next morning some of the said persons went for London and other different ways into the country, but how the said tea was afterwards disposed or to whom the deponent cannot say. The time of the opposition about the 7th or 8th April 1733. The officers were --- Horton, deceased, Sargent, riding officer at Rye. [3]

1 Sedlescombe.
2 For the officers opposed by the smugglers at Stonecrouch, 4 April 1733 see [**136**].
3 Thomas Sargent, riding officer, Hastings. The three Lydd riding officers for 1733 were Henry Brackenbury, Lytcott Gill, listed under Dover Customs, plus John Hilditch, listed under Rye Customs.

615 Note by John Collier, 13 November 1735, concerning the affidavit from Rye officers, 10 October 1735, referring to the events of 4 April 1733 [SAY 283]

Thomas Sargent, out on duty, saw the gang at Newbridge about 6 or 7 in the morning. Cooper saw a large gang of smugglers about 4 in the morning, about 30 armed men and about fifty horses laden with oyl skin baggs. Gave Mr Sargent, Mr Horsfield and Mr Orton notice. Mr Orton, Mr Cooper and Sargent to Newbridge, but seeing the gang soe large did not attack them. Met Mr Horsfield and Peadle in Iden Street after they had seen them. Mr Orton went back for more assistance and brought two dragoons and a foot soldier, pursued them on.

When Horsfield, Cooper, Peadle, Orton and the two dragoons [1] Orton rode fastest saw the gang at Stonecrouch, came back and they pursued them as fast as they could down [2] a lane, and about a mile or two [3] from Stonecrouch came up with the gang, who seeing the officers, the gang came down with them all armed with firearms and clubbs and swore [4] at the officers; damned them what were they come to rob them, and came up with their pistoles cocked, and swore they would shoot them through the head and clapped their pistoles cocked close to their heads, and [5] Peadle says he was pretty much beat and abused and threatened to tye them back to back and leave them there, but afterwards seized their arms and obliged them to goe with them along the road for about 3 or 4 hours and during that time kept along with them to a green on the back of Lamberhurst [6] furnace, where they discharged these deponents armes, and knock their flints out of their pistoles and then released them being about 5 a clock. Not one of the officers know one of the persons, nor don't remember to have seen any of them, only Mr Cooper beleives he since saw one of them at Peasmarsh lock but knows not his name, nor where he belongs to. Told the officers that they see the gang was to hard for them and if they pursued after them they should fare worse.

1 MS *came up with* struck through.
2 MS *a place called* struck through.
3 MS *through* struck through.
4 MS *dam* struck through.
5 MS *beat* struck through.
6 MS *forge* struck through.

616 To Commissioners of Customs, from John Collier, 19 February 1736: revised draft of Thomas Pettit's affidavit relating to events in October 1735, sworn at Battle, 18 February 1736, before John Collier, one of the Commissioners of the court. [SAY 284]

Thomas Pettit of Battell in the county of Sussex, aged 30 years, voluntarily maketh oath that on Fryday the 24th day of October last, being at the house of William Jewhurst, [1] under the sign of the Black Horse, in the parish of Battell aforesaid, [2] an alehouse much frequented by smugglers and about four or five miles from the sea side, he saw a [3] great many persons there, and knowing several of them [4] were smugglers; he suspected [5] that there was a design [6] to run goods that night. And thereupon he [7] went to [8] Hollington [9] about two or three miles nearer the sea,[10] by which way he [11] imagined they [12] would come [13] from the seaside with their goods, if any was landed, and kept himself concealed to watch them.

And about eleaven a clock ,[14] it being [15] clear weather [16] and the moon shining [17] bright,[18] he saw two men ride up [19] in the highway leading from the sea [20] into the country, being two of the persons he had seen at [21] Jewhurst's that afternoon,[22] who had some small quantity of goods under them [23] and they called at [24] an alehouse kept by one Richard Maplesden, and drank something but made [25] very little stay, and presently [26] afterwards the [27] remainder of the smuggling gang came up the same way, being [28] above twenty horses, several of which were drove,[29] but all [30] loaded with dry goods [31] covered over with canvas baggs, and there were at least 12 or 15 men with them.

And soon after they were gone by this deponent, he heard two or three guns [32] discharged, and immediately afterwards the [33] gang came back in great dissorder and confusion whipping their horses, and broke [34] the road into the adjoyning grounds where some of them [35] unlade their goods and others broke [36] through all the fences into another [37] way, where they could goe of with their goods, and [38] this deponent [39] heard two of the smugglers [40] propose goeing to Whatlington and conceal [41] their goods up in Turner's Hole. And this deponent knowing that [42] John Turner, an alehousekeeper of Whatlington, [43] where the smugglers frequented and where [44] he had sometime lodged, had a private place in his barn, he [45] made the best of his way to [46] Turner's, and [47] about 5 of the clock [48] next morning five men, and a boy with seaven horse load of tea, [49] came thither and put all their tea into a hole in the said Turner's barn, except three baggs which the hole would not hold, and they they carried away.[50]

And further maketh oath that he know three of the said five persons, and they they were in the gang [51] the goods at Hollington [52] aforesaid ,[53] and further [54] saith that he sent an information of the said tea being soe [55] concealed in [56] Turner's [57] barn to Mr Sansum, a riding officer at the port of Hasting, who came thither on Sunday the 26th day of the said month of October, with severall other Customs officers and soldiers, and seized the same, [58] and carried it [59] the king's warehouse at Hasting aforesaid.

And this deponent further maketh oath that in the night of the 14th day of March 1733 Thorp Diamond of Montfield in the county of Sussex, farmer at the great groyne in the parish of Bexhill, assisted in landing about 2000 weight of tea out of a smuggling vessell, but cannot set forth to what place she belonged to or who [60] but cannot set forth to what place she belonged to or who,[61] which was carried up in the country. That there were about 9 more persons present and about 16 horses, but doth not know the names of any other of the men, but saith they belong to Hawkhurst in Kent and to a London gang.

And further maketh oath that early in the morning of the 16th day of October last William Wood of Mountfeild in the county of Sussex, farmer ...[62] Shawes of Seddlescomb in the said county, farmer, and another person residing at Seddlescomb aforesaid, who goes by the name of London Tom, and about eight or ten more persons whose names he doth not know assisted in unlading out of a smuggling vessel at the hutches near Hasting, upwards of a hundred half ankers of French brandy [63] which was carried brandy off into the country. And this deponent further saith that in the morning of the 14th day of December last Thomas Blackman of Bexhill aforesaid ,[64] farmer, and about seaven other persons belonging to a London gang, whose names this deponent doth not know, did unlade out of a smuggling vessell at the great groynes [65] aforesaid twenty four baggs of tea, each bag conteyning about 56 pounds weight, some of which was carried to the said Thomas Blackman's house and the remainder into the country, and there were about twelve or thirteen horses employed in carrying the same.

And this deponent further maketh oath that in the night of the 24th of December last William Weston of Rotherfield in the afd county of Sussex, farmer, with about 10 more persons, did assist in landing out of a smuggling vessell at the great groynes aforesaid, about 700 weight of tea covered with canvas baggs which was carrried of up into the country by the said persons.[66] This deponent doth not know any of their names except the said Weston, but saith that they belonged to a London gang of smugglers. And this deponent further maketh oath that in the night of the 2nd day of January last William Woodger of Battell, [67] aforesaid, Richard Vidler of [68] the same place, labourer, and a [69] person that lives with the said William Woodger, whose name this deponent doth not remember, togeather with three or four more persons, did land out of a smuggling vessell at the great groyne aforesaid, about 1200 weight of tea in oyl skin baggs, covered with canvas, which was carried of by the said persons to the county of Kent on about eight horses. And this deponent further saith that he [70] doth not know to what place the smuggling vessells go as aforesaid, landing the said goods or any or either of them belonged, but he beleives the greatest part belonged to Hasting aforesaid. Neither doth he know who was master of any of the said boats or vessells, and further maketh oath that he was aiding and assisting in landing all the aforesaid tea and brandy and in carrying of the same.[71]

1 MS *being* struck through.
2 MS *in Battell* struck through.
3 MS *pretty large company of men there which gave this deponent a suspicion* struck through.
4 MS *to be* struck through.
5 MS *gave him* struck through.
6 MS *of running some smuggling* struck through.
7 MS *this deponent* struck through.
8 MS *a place called* struck through.
9 MS *corn in the said county* struck through.
10 MS *who* struck through.
11 MS *believed* struck through.
12 MS *smugglers* struck through.
13 MS *up* struck through.
14 MS *in the night* struck through.
15 MS *a very* struck through.
16 MS *night evening* struck through.

17 MS *very* struck through.
18 MS *this deponent* struck through.
19 MS *on horseback* struck through.
20 MS *side* struck through.
21 MS *Bredsell* struck through.
22 MS *before and as they seemed to have* struck through.
23 MS *and in a very little time, which said two persons who* struck through.
24 MS *the corner house being* struck through.
25 MS *no* struck through.
26 MS *in a little time* struck through.
27 MS *whole company* struck through.
28 MS *upwards of* struck through.
29 MS *horses* struck through.
30 MS *of them* struck through.
31 MS *being in canvas and which this deponent, and oylskin baggs under it, and in a very little time* struck through.
32 MS *gone of* struck through.
33 MS *smugglers turned back* struck through.
34 MS *way into the* struck through.
35 MS *unloaded* struck through.
36 MS *down* struck through.
37 MS *road* struck through.
38 MS *it being near the place where* struck through.
39 MS *lay concealed* struck through.
40 MS *say to one another that they would make* struck through.
41 MS *lay* struck through.
42 MS *there was one* struck through.
43 MS *an alehousekeeper* struck through.
44 MS *this deponent* struck through.
45 MS *this deponent went* struck through.
46 MS *the said Whatlington* struck through.
47 MS *the next* struck through.
48 MS *the* struck through.
49 *MS and the said tea was put* struck through.
50 MS *which the whole would not conteyn, by the smugglers and saith that three of the said men were persons that he saw with* struck through.
51 MS *with* struck through.
52 MS *as* struck through.
53 MS *which this deponent knows their names* struck through.
54 MS *this deponent* struck through.
55 MS *as aforesaid* struck through.
56 MS *the said* struck through.
57 MS *hole* struck through.
58 MS *which they* struck through.
59 MS *to* struck through.
60 MS *and that this deponent assisted in unloading the same, and took some little part of the tea out of one of the bags, but this deponent cannot tell to what place the vessel belonged, out of which the said tea was landed, or who was master thereof and neither doth this deponent know any more of them persons names, but that they belonged to Hasting, London and Hawkhurst* struck through.
61 MS *was master* struck through.
62 MS blank.
63 MS *out of a smuggling boat which this deponent believes belonged to Hasting but doth not know the master's name, and that this was besides the said Wood, about ten other persons assisting therein and about 26 horses* struck through.
64 MS *county in Sussex* struck through.
65 MS *in Bexhill* struck through.
66 MS *being about ten persons in number but being a London gang* struck through.
67 MS *in the said county of Sussex and 5 or 6 more persons* struck through.
68 MS *Battell* struck through.

69 MS *man that is servant to* struck through.

70 MS *is the more certain of the before smuggled goods being landed as aforesaid, for that this deponent asssisted in running the same* struck through.

71 As a result of legal cases arising from prosecutions undertaken by informers, including frivolous and vexatious prosecutions, the Customs Commissioners agreed to a strict vetting procedure before bringing smuggling and related cases to court. By 12 Geo. I c.28 s. 28 the power to prosecute on information derived solely from informers was restricted to actions undertaken by the Attorney General and Customs and Excise officers in respect of smuggled goods, the use of horses and carts, and illegal practices such as the carrying of guns, although in practice this limitation proved complicated. For reference to seizures see Hoon ch. 8. For views on vexatious suits see *PS* vol. 42, July-December 1731. In the case of Thomas Pettit (also spelt Pettett) of Battle it appears from the correspondence that John Collier advised the informer for part of the time the information was before the Customs officers in London (TNA CUST 148/12).

Appendix 7: Elizabeth Hickes Estate

617 Dudley Ryder, Attorney General, opinion on the case of Mrs Martha Boys, daughter of Mrs Elizabeth Hickes, 29 Sept 1738 [SAY 1354]

Considering the nature of this agrement which is comprised in a deed which I am informed Mrs Hickes, the mother, was a party. It is I think probable that a court of equity will establish it as well with regard to the mother as the father's estate so that if she should give her daughter Martha any sum or estate over and above the sum mentioned in the deed I should settle the like sum or estate for the separate use of her daughter Boys instead of setling it according to the agreement, a court of equity would releive Mr Boys and decree it to be setled on him for life with remainders according to the agreement but this is a question that may admit of some doubt, 23 Sept 1738, D. Ryder.

I think what is proposed in this letter will not answer the purpose and is not proper to be pursued nor do I know any method by which if the mother divides the estate equally between the daughters, Mrs Boys share can be effectually clearly settled for her separate use. But if the mother thinks proper to give her more than the other daughter that overplus may be given to trustees for her seperate use, be secured against her husband, and made subject to her own absolute disposal without his controul or any ways intermedling, D. Ryder, 29 September 1738.

618 Elizabeth Hickes, general release to John Collier, 26 March 1741 [SAY 1355]

Know all men by these presents that I, Elizabeth Hickes of Salehurst in the county of Sussex, widow, sister and heir at law, and also administratrix of all and singular the goods, chattells, rights and credits of John Dunmoll, late of Tunbridge Wells in the county of Kent, gentleman, deceased, have remised, released and for ever quit claymed and do by these presents for myself, my heirs, executors and administrators remise, release and for ever quit claym unto John Collier of the town and port of Hasting in the said county of Sussex, esquire, all and all manner of action and actions, cause and causes of actions, suites, troubles, controversies, trespasses, damages and demands whatsoever, either in law or equity or otherwise howsoever which against the said John Collier, I ever had and which I, my heirs, executors, administrators or assignes shall or may have claym, challenge or demand for or by reason or means of any matter, cause or thing whatsoever from the beginning of the world to the day of the date of these presents. In witness whereof I, the said Elizabeth Hickes, have hereunto set my hand and seal this 26 March 1741 in the fourteenth year of the reign of our sovereign Lord George the second by the grace of God of Great Britain, France and Ireland, King defender of the faith and in the year of our Lord God one thousand, seven hundred and forty one. Dealed and delivered in the presence of Francis Hickes, Richard Patrick.

Appendix 8: Collier family affairs

619 John Collier, account for executors of the Earl of Ashburnham for the month of November 1736 [SAY 596]

[*debit*] JC received £46 12s 2d, lordship rents for the manors of
[*credit*] JC paid out for Ashburnham the following,
Mr Coppard, collector of the Customs at Hasting for two half ankers of brandy sent to his lordship at London, £2 10s 0; journey to Ashburnham and staying overnight, £1 11s 6; Thomas Salmon by his lordship's verbal order, £25 2s 6; searching the court rolls and ecclesiastical court relating to Widow Hook's estate as per his lordship's order, £1 4s 0; making a copy of the furnace articles, £0 5s 0; attending Mr Harrison, Mr Jukes, in London and Mr Legas in the country about the furnace lease and the repairs several times, £2 2s 0; allowed the bedells of the manors collecting lords' rent, seizing heriots, £3 10s 0; two years' allowance for my salary, £10 10s 0.

620 Surrender by Michael Reeve, Ore manor, 14 June 1740 [SAY 617]

Michael Reeve one of the customary tenants of the said mannor did surrender into the hands of the lord of the said mannor by the acceptance of John Collier, esquire, steward thereof, and by the rod according to the custom of the said mannor, all that customary messuage or tenement lands, and premises, conteyning by estimation eleven acres more or less, commonly called Hobbs, holden of the lord of this mannor by the yearly rent of vi s viii d, heriot releif, and other services, and also all other the customary and copyhold lands, tenements and hereditaments of him the said Michael Reeve, holden of the said mannor:

To the use and behoof of James Cranston of Bexhill in the county of Sussex, clerk, and his heirs and assignes for ever, provided nevertheless and upon this condition that if the said Michael Reeve, his heirs and executors, administrators or assignes shall and do well and truly pay, or cause to be paid, unto the said James Cranston, his executors, administrators or assignes the full and just sum of fifty one pounds and five shillings of good and lawful money of Great Britain on or upon the fourteenth day of December next ensuing the date hereof, then the said surrender shall be void, otherwise remain in full force, power and virtue. Taken and acknowledged the day and year above written before, John Collier, steward, Michael Reeve, his mark, Richard Patrick. [*On cover*]: I am paid this principal and interest, [*Signed*] John Collier. Mem, took this in my brother Cranston's name but it's my own money.

621 John Piddlesden of Rotherfield to John Collier, 28 March 1741 [SAY 1356]

Whereas my late brother in law Thomas Pack of the parish of Saint Clement in Hasting in the county of Sussex deceased dyed[1] but in mean circumstances leaving a son and daughter, the son about 9 or 10 years of age so not capable of maintaining himself and likely to come to the parish, and in consideration of my having some part of the houshold goods he left and in regard that John Collier of Hasting aforesaid hath out of compassion to the boy and to prevent his coming to the parish given out of charity four guineas to me on my undertaking to bring up the said boy and to maintain, provide and take care of him so as he shall not be chargeable to the said parish of St Clement or the parishoners of the same, now I do hereby acknowledge to have received of the said John Collier the said four guineas and do hereby engage and promise in case the said boy shall become at any time or upon any account chargeable to the said parish, I will repay the said John Collier the said four guineas upon demand. Witness my hand this 28th of March 1741. The Mark of John Piddlesden. Witness Robert James, messenger at the Swan, on a commission of bankrupt against Richard Halsted.

1 Thomas Pack, buried St Clements, 15 November 1740.

622 Elizabeth Crowly, widow and executor of Mark Crowthy, mariner, 24 February 1746 [SAY 1358]

To all people to whome these presents shall come I Elizabeth Crowthy widow and executor of Mark Crowthy, marriner, deceased, doe send greeting know yee that I the said Elizabeth Crowthy for and in consideration of the sum of forty two pounds of good and lawfull money of Great Britain to me in hand paid at and before the insealing and delivery hereof by John Collier of the town and port of Hasting in Sussex esquire, the receipt whereof I doe hereby ackcknowledge and myself to be therewith fully sattisfyed, have any by these presents doe fully and absolutely bargaine, sell, aliene and assigne unto to the said John Collier all the wages, pay, bounty money, short allowance money, prize money, tickets, and otherwise whatsoever belonging to me as executor of my said late deceased husband for the service in and abroad his Majesty's ships *Marlborough* and the *Mercury* fireship and either of them.

To have and to hold the said the said wages pay, service on all accounts, and the full money due for the same unto the aforesaid John Collier, his executors, administrators and assignes as his or their own proper use and uses for ever together with full power and authority to receive the same of the Rt honourable the Treasurer or Paymaster of his Majesties Navy or whome else it may concern and I the said Elizabeth Crowthy for myself, my executors and administrators, the said premises unto the said John Collier, his executors, administrators and assignes against all persons shall and will warrant and for ever defend and make good the aforesaid wages pay and service, against the claim or any person or persons, free and clear of and from all manner of former gifts and grants, forfeiture, claim or demands or to the same by any way or meanes whatsoever, wittness my hand and seal this twenty fourth day of February in the year of our Lord 1745 and in the nineteenth year of the reign of our soveraign Lord George the second by the grace of God of Great Brittain, France and Ireland, King defender of the faith etc. Sealed and delivered in the presence of the mark of Elizabeth Crowthy, the mark of William Lock, Richard Patrick.

COLLIER'S LOCAL AND FAMILY CONNECTIONS

This appendix lists persons in Hastings who held offices in the town corporation, the church and the law, with details from the manuscripts which may assist in offering a clearer picture of the person concerned, in addition to the material in the letters.

Appointments to Hastings corporation offices and local legal and church affairs were covered by four town courts, as well as in the vestries of St Clements parish, All Saints parish and Castle St Mary's: all had distinct jurisdictions.

(1) The town assembly, in order of precedence, consisted of the Mayor, who took the chair of the assembly and was appointed for a year at a time; the deputy Mayor appointed by the Mayor from among the jurats whose numbers fluctuated between eight and twelve in the years covered by this volume, 1731-46, and who sat for life. Whilst the freemen could nominate jurats, in practice appointment required the endorsement of the Mayor and jurats. The Assembly included all the town's freemen, also appointed for life, although they were occasionally removed through non-payment of taxes; several serious disputes over creation of new freemen are discussed in the letters. The powers exercised by the courts and the vestries encompassed all questions of civic life. The freemen also elected the town's two MPs. Apart from the powers of the Mayor for the appointment of the deputy Mayor and the jurats, these officials were key to filling the positions of town clerk and the town chamberlains. Manwaring Baines adds that the assembly was really the parliament of Hastings, as it dealt with the foreign affairs of the town including questions before the Cinque Ports, the Brotherhood and Guestling, the bailiffs who attended the mackerel fleet in the voyage to Yarmouth, the work of the Solicitors of the Cinque Ports, and it was here in the assembly that the yearly budget and Scot was fixed, and in wartime the freemen discussed the militia and the watch and ward, and the recruitment of Hastings mariners for the naval forces.

(2), The Hundred Court met on the Monday fortnight after the election of the Mayor, deputy Mayor and Jurats, and also swore the Grand Jury; followed by the election of many of the lesser town officials, including the Common Serjeant, the Guardians of the Pier, the Pierwardens, the Bailiff of the Bourne, the Common Measurer, the Leather Sealers, the Key keepers of the town, the Keepers of money and markets. The Hundred licensed the town alehouses setting the fines for the yearly licences of ale house keepers and their guarantors.

(3), The General Quarter Sessions: the bench of the Sessions comprised the Mayor, deputy Mayor and jurats, each endowed with the powers of a justice of the peace, and before whom the Grand Jury appeared. Oaths required to be sworn by holders of public office, as listed in statute law, were heard here. The Sessions appointed officials whose work was defined by statute: (i) Surveyor of the Highways, usually two surveyors per parish; (ii) holders of corn licences, from whom the sessions took recognizance of £20 per licensee as a bond not to forestall, regrate and ingross; (iii) the packer of fish, 'pursuant to the Act of Parliament'; (iv) the Quarter Sessions took bonds of £10 for each ale and spirit licence.

(4) The Court of Record held before the Mayor and jurats heard nominations for freemen and then took the oaths for new freemen; the Court also heard other oaths required by statute.

The information below is listed for: birth and death, marriage, freeman, Mayor, jurat, lesser town appointments, church office, trade, reference in Hastings Quarter Sessions, property, taxes, payments to the Hastings Annuity fund, whether eligible to vote in the 1734 Sussex county election, and voting record for this election recorded in the Hastings poll book, miscellaneous information collected by Charles Lane Sayer, Manwaring Baines, Hastings Corporation archives, East Sussex Record Office or otherwise available. Most residents with land, trade, shops etc., appear in the Chamberlain's accounts, and 74 paid into the Annuity fund. Where information is unclear, for example where another family member might be referred to, it is not included, and references to wills are usually omitted.

Abbreviations used:

alekg	ale house keeper and/or guarantor.
Annuity	Contribution to Hastings Annuity fund.
corn	Corn dealer's licence.
cm	Common Measurer.
cs	Common Serjeant.
cw	Churchwarden.
fh1734	Freeholder eligible to vote in Sussex county 1734, and voting outcome, if recorded in poll book.
gjury	Grand Jury.
gp	Guardian of the Pier.
GQrS	General Quarter Sessions.
kmfm	Keeper of money, fairs, markets, poundage.
key	Keykeeper of the town.
m	Married.
op	overseer of the poor.
pf	Packer of fish.
pw	Pierwarden.
rmv	Receipt for mackerel voyage.
rhv	Receipt for herring voyage.
sh	Surveyor of the Highways.
sm	Serjeant of the Mace, Mayor's Serjeant.

Biographies

Bartholomew, Robert, 1654-173F8, m. 1680, Margaret Meadow, she d. 1736; freeman 1692, jurat 1704-38, Mayor 1718, deputy Mayor 1728; Annuity 1715 and 1716 4/-; *State Trials* vol. 17, case 497; mariner, fisherman, inherited in 1699 his father's shop on Stonebeach, and one quarter ownership of the pink *Neptune*, registered at Hastings, of which he was master, two eighths of two barques, both of Hastings, for one Thomas Gawen, the elder, master, for the other James Moore, master; to his wife Elizabeth he left one eighth of a 'pinke now upon the stocks being in building under Castle cliffe', and to three granddaughters of Robert Sargent when 16, one quarter of a pink *Phoenix*, master Robert Sargent, one fifth of the *John*, master Thomas Sergeant, my son-in-law, and one eighth of a ketch, of Rye, master Thomas Bartholomew of Rye.

Bossom, James, the elder, 1688-1764; m. Mary Boniface, 1712, 9 children; freeman 1730, Jurat 1730, Town Chamberlain 1731, Auditor of the Scot, 1739, 1742, pw 1740, 1743, cw St Clements, 1726 and 1727; master of the *Cordelia* sloop, trading between Hastings and London; 1742 owned a deeze on Mercer's Bank near the Stonebeach, noted in his 1764 will as left to his son James (1716-); also owned two messuages on the hill near St Clements, left to his widow; Annuity 1742 2/-; contributed to pier repairs 1742-3.

Bossom, James, the younger, 1716-, son of James (1686-1764); freeman 1730, Town chamberlain 1730, pw 1743, Annuity, contributed to pier repairs 1742-1743, his vessel chartered by the Navy Board 1744.

Bossom, Nicholas, James' brother, 1698-177, m. Elizabeth Phillips 1720; freeman 1731, Town Chamberlain 1732, auditor of the Scot 1736, 1746, pw 1731, 1736, 1739, 1742, kmfm 1745, ; op All Saints 1735, cw All Saints 1740, 1741, 1746, boatman, owned shop and deeze; mackerel voyage 1742, 1743; herring voyage 1742, 1743; fh1734 voted for Pelham and Butler; in signing the All Saints vestry book he used a mark like a sail.

Bossom, Thomas, James' brother, 1686-1760; m. (1) Ann Lucket 1718, (2) Mary Shorter; 1731; freeman 1734, tax assessor, Castle Parish and outbounds, 1735, Town Chamberlain 1740, auditor of the Scot 1738, pf 1740, 1742, 1743, 1744; pw 1738, 1741, 1744, 1745, 20 April 1746; sidesman All Saints 1715, op All Saints 1743; master of ship trading between Hastings and London, mackerel voyage 1742, 1743; alekg, 1728, 1736-46, innholder 1760; fh1734, voted for Bishop and Fuller.

Boykett, 'Old', John, d. 1707; his widow Sarah d. 1718.

Boyket, John, the elder, d. 1752. on the General Quarter Sessions jury 1701; fh1734; gave evidence for Sir Thomas Webster in Kings Bench 1736, his testimony is in *State Trials* vol. 17, his evidence also related to discrimination against dissenters by the Corporation of Hastings in 1690s; at the GQrS 1731 a licence was granted to John Hande and Stephen Kember sen. 'for a meeting or assembly for religious worship of people called Quakers' in St Mary of the Castle parish.

Boyket, John m. Elizabeth, of Castle parish in 1728; she d. 1730; corn dealer, 1729, rippier 1715; op St Clements 1728, 1729; fh1734 voted for Pelham and Butler; window tax collector, St Clements, 19 July 1735; paid Hastings taxes for porch and house, 1742 and 1743.

Boykett, Robert, Quaker, d. 1692; his widow, Mary, d. 1681.

Bourne, Thomas, d. 1734; mariner; customs boatman, freeman 1701, fh1734 voted for Pelham and Butler; his son William Bourne was appointed boatman when Thomas was superannuated.

Bourne, William, the elder, 1678-1749, m. Margaret Broadbridge 1701; mariner; Auditor and assessor of the Common Scot, 1729; fh1734 voted for Pelham and Butler.

Bourne, William, junior, 1710-87, m. Ann Arter, 1751, seven female children.

Broadway, Revd Thomas, d. 1740; deacon 1718, priest 1720, rector 1729, All Saints Church, patron Sir Thomas Webster; 1731 rector, Ewhurst, patron Sir Thomas Webster; canvassed in Hastings for Webster interest with Mr Eversfield and Captain Milward in 1732, and again during the 1734 election; fh1734 voted for Fuller and Bishop; 1731 Broadway replaced Revd Richard Nairn, in part after a vote of All Saints vestry against Nairn for using the church land to graze his horse.

Cant, Samuel, d. 1759, schoolmaster Hastings grammar school 1738-59; originally from Leicestershire, persuaded by Edward Milward to remove to Hastings c.1731; op All Saints; 1740, 1741, signed vestry accounts; cw St Clements 1745; Annuity 1742 2/-; fh1734 voted for Pelham and Butler at Eastbourne; cartographer and drew maps of Hastings, including the estate of John Collier; collector of instruments, globes, and books bequeathed to his sister Sarah Cook.

Carleton, Revd George B.A., 1706 deacon, St Andrew, Holborn; rector and vicar, Ninfield 1709-30.

Carleton Revd George 'Georgy' B.A., 1742 deacon, Rye; 1743 priest, St Margaret's Westminster; 1744 vicar, Rye.

Carleton, Henry, Dr in physic, (1656-1744), St Clements; father was Thomas Carleton, Mayor 1677; Henry was Mayor in 1706, 1714, deputy Mayor 1733, 1728, 1729, 1732, 1736, when appointed deputy Mayor by John Collier in 1741 Henry was noted as 'the oldest jurat'; cw St Clements 1729, 1731; fh1734; on 28 June 1735 he was one of six jurats to relinquish office, re-admitted 12 July 1735, also one of five jurats to relinquish office 31 May 1736 and reinstated 31 August 1736; proponent of Hastings water supply scheme, 1723, and also the scheme led by John Collier from 1733, also advised on the Rye water works scheme of 1734. Eleven children, including his son Henry who was elected a Hastings freeman in 1736; Miss Nanny Carleton and Miss Betty Carleton, referred to in the letters, were grandchildren.

Carleton, Henry, (1693-1771), freeman of Rye 1726, also Rye jurat and chamberlain, Mayor of Rye 1734, 1743; fh1734 voted Pelham and Butler; out of 88 Rye freeholders only eight voted for Fuller and Bishop, one for Pelham and Bishop, the rest for Pelham and Butler.

Carswell, Thomas, Customs Riding officer, Hastings, killed 26 December 1740; m. Anne Gyles (nee Lovell) 1734; freeman, jurat 1728-40; Mayor 1734; cw St Clements 1724, 1732, 1733, 1735; fh1734 voted for Pelham and Butler; 28 June 1735, one of the six jurats to relinquish office and re-admitted 12 July 1735; 31 May 1736, one of five jurats to relinquish office, re-admitted 21 August 1736; 1736 auditor of town accounts and assessor of the Scot; 27 April 1740 elected auditor by freemen; witness in Hastings waterworks case; killed by smugglers on Silverhill to Hurst Green road.

Chadderton, Thomas, (1683-1743) All Saints; m Elizabeth Hope; fh1734 voted for Pelham and Butler; cw All Saints 1735; freeman 1740; pw 1741, shopkeeper 1742-3, shop kept on by widow 1743-4. GQrS 1737, bound over in respect of statute against smuggling, 'Act for indemnifying persons guilty of offences against the laws made for securing the revenues of customs and excise'.

Chadderton, Richard, d. 1746, m. 1711 Elizabeth Midmore, widow; fh1734 voted for Pelham and Butler; freeman 1740, pw 1741, Annuity 1742 and 1743 2/-; offered £20 recognizance for John Gourlay's corn seller's licence 1742.

Chambers, John, b. 1690, m. Frances Phipps, St Clements, 1731; freeman 13 May 1715; recorded as a saddler 1715; cw St Clements 1720; fh1734 voted for Fuller and Bishop; leather sealer 1739, 1740, 1741, 1742, 1743, 1744, 1745, bailiff of the Bourne and common cryer 1746.

Coppard, William, d. 1766, m. Martha Hicks of Salehurst, 1722, she d. 1739; freeman 1725, paid the fine of 13/4d; jurat 1725, Mayor 1727, 1735, 1742, 1746, 1751; fh1734 voted for Pelham and Butler; Auditor and assessor of the Scot, 1729, 1742, 1743, 1744, 1746; Commissioner of land and window taxes 1743; at the GQrS 1744 delivered certificate of receipt of sacrament; 6 children, 3 died in infancy; of whom Revd William Hicks Coppard, b. 1725 St Clements, freeman and jurat 1746.

Cousens, Mary (Cousins), placed in Bethlem hospital by St Clements vestry, 1747, bond granted by vestry for £100 to indemnify Thomas Webb and William Coffin of all charges incurred being sureties for receiving Mary Cousens out of Bethlem.

Cranston, Revd James, d. 1726 St Clements, m. Cordelia, daughter of Revd Thomas Delves, rector of Bexhill, she d. 1711, St Clements; deacon 1683, priest 1684, rector of All Saints, 1690-1722, and of St Clements 1722-26, rector of Pett, 1702-26, 7 children.

Cranston, Revd James, (1692-1770), M.A., Jesus College, Cambridge, eldest son of above, curate Bexhill 1724, rector of Stowting, Kent, lived at Kewhurst, Bexhill, his marble monument is in Bexhill church.

Cranston, William, (1706-62) third son of Revd James Cranston; solicitor, 4 Johnson's Court, m. 1732, Mary Swaysland,; fh1734 voted for Pelham and Butler, and was elected a freeman and jurat 1754 and Mayor in 1760; his elder sister Mary m. John Collier 13 August 1717; William's eldest son, James, was a Captain in the Royal Navy.

Cruttenden, Nathaniel, jurat, 1732; rented marshland at Pett from John Collier; fh1734; auditor 1737, 1738, 1739, 1742, 1746; Commissioner for Sussex land tax 1731; Commissioner land and window taxes in Hastings, Mayor 1743, 1744; brickmaker and landowner.

Cruttenden, Samuel, senior, of St Leonards next Hollington, 1723 m. Sarah Collier, John Collier's sister, known as 'aunt' Cruttenden in these letters; fh1734 voted for Pelham and Butler; jurat, 1744.

Denham, Revd Thomas (1683-1734) m. Cordelia Delves, sister of Mary Collier's mother, originally Delves; St John's Cambridge, curate Pett, 1731; vicar, Hollington 1707-10, 1712-34, church patron Charles Eversfield; for inventory see Hughes 105-6.

Dyne, Mary Fletcher (1714-81) Guestling, m. Musgrave Brisco of Wakefield; daughter of Edward Dyne who d. 1732, jurat 1708, Mayor 1720, 1724, 1728, canopy bearer 1727 at the coronation of George II and Queen Caroline

Ellams, John, (1653-1733), m. Mary Bossom, All Saints, 1680.

Ellams, Eleames, John, son of above, b. 1685; 1734 Surveyor of the Highways, Castle parish; op Castle parish, 1745; Alekg, 1736, 1739-44, guarantor for licence.

Eversfield, Sir Charles, of Denn Park, Horsham, (1682-1749) m. Mary, daughter of Henry Duncombe; Eversfield was MP Horsham 1705-10, Sussex 1710-13, Horsham 1713-16, 1721-41, Steyning 1741-47, originally Tory, by autumn of 1722 supported Walpole, and co-operated with the Duke of Newcastle in Sussex county elections; Eversfield was a landowner paying the common fines to Hastings corporation for outdwellers, 9/- for St Leonard's Clenfield and Rotherhythe, 15/- for Magdalen lands and Pope lands, 4/- for Newgate's, in arrears for six years by 1743, £8 8s; John Collier worked on the lengthy legal case brought by Hastings Corporation for payment of rents due from Eversfield for lands, tenements and shops, two parcels of Magdalen lands, and for Old Lane; Eversfield held the advowson of Hollington church, Ore rectory, and was one of three patrons for Winchelsea rectory.

Eversfield, Charles, son of above, Tory and independent, d. 1784; fh1734 voted for Fuller and Bishop.

Frewen, Charles, 1701-62, son of Revd. Thankful, m. Alice Severne of Claines, Worcestershire.

Frewen, Revd Thankful, (1669-1749) of Northiam, m. Sarah, nee Stevens, of Cranbrook in Kent.

Frewen, Thomas, 1704-91, son of Revd Thankful, doctor and apothecary, Rye, Lewes, author *The theory and practice of inoculation* (1749); Commissioner of Sewers, 1738, wide acquaintance including Ashburnham family.

Geery, John, d. 1733, St Clements; freeman and jurat, and postmaster Hastings.

Geery, William, son of above (1698-1755) m. Frances Meadow 1722; freeman 1725, fh1734 voted for Pelham and Butler; 1738 auditor of the Scot; cw St Clements 1740, jurat 1744.

Gyles, Thomas, d. 1732, m. Anne Lovell; cordwainer and shoemaker, freeman 1707, jurat 1713, Mayor 1723, 1725, 1729, 1731, gentleman of ability, St Clements, 1724, taxed at 5/-; auditor of the Scot 1729, his widow allowed the waterwork pipes to cross her land and she re-married in 1734 to Thomas Carswell the Mayor.

Godley, Thomas, d. 1765, m. Elizabeth Wicking 1744, All Saints; indentures for five years to John Collier, from 18 January 1717 for £105; Town Clerk 1719, 1722, jurat 1729, 1735, Mayor 1732; cw St Clements 1730; supporter of Hastings waterworks 1733, auditor of the Scot 1739; postmaster 1742; lapsed as jurat in 1743 for living outwith the Corporation in London for a year and a day, re-elected jurat and auditor of the Scot 1744, gentleman of ability St Clements taxed at 5/-.

Grayling, Edward, d. 1742; fh1734 voted for Pelham and Butler, op St Clements 1737, surveyor of highways St Clements 1741, cornseller 14 January 1742; blacksmith, owned a shop and a smithy 1742, after his death his widow continued the business.

Grayling, Thomas, of Westfield, d. 1739, m. Anne Sargent 1730; ironmonger, apprenticed to Peter Roberts, watchmaker in Rye, at seven years for £8, 1718; land tax collector St Clements 1735; cw St Clements 1736.

Grebell, Allen, killed 1741; Mayor of Rye, 1720, 1724, 1726, 1728, 1730, 1732, 1735, 1737, 1739, 1741; fh1734 voted for Pelham and Butler.

Holman, Thomas, cousin of Mary Collier, nee Cranston; convicted of assault on Customs officer 1737; later captain of the Hastings packet; gaoled for his part in killing Customs officer 1749, reprieved 1750 on condition of transportation to the colonies: at his trial twenty-three persons testified in his favour, and Sir Charles Eversfield supported his defence.

Markwicke, James, of Catsfield, d. 1715, clockmaker.

Markwicke, Captain William, second son of James, d. 1740, m. Elizabeth Baker of Wilmington, 1698; drainage engineer, Romney marsh, Pevensey sluice 1694, Folkestone pier 1709, sea defences Brighton 1724; resided in Bexhill after marriage and Catsfield after 1715; fh1734 voted for Fuller and Bishop.

Meadow, Benjamin, the elder, (1671-1745) St Clements, m. Anne Waters 1694, she d. 1712; he then married Susan Steevens 1715; freeman 1693; fh1734 voted for Fuller and Bishop.

Meadow, Benjamin, b. 1697, the son of Robert Meadow, brewer, freeman 1721. It is unclear which Benjamin held the offices listed in the Corporation records.

Mead, John, op 1728 St Clements, signed vestry book St Clements 1729; cw 1732 St Clements; op 1739 All Saints; cw 1742 All Saints; fh1734; Mead was refused freedom of Hastings in 1735 and he later abandoned a legal challenge to this decision in Kings Bench.

Milward, Edward (1682-1749) St Clements, m. 1721 Elizabeth Shirley of Chiddingly, widow, she d. 1742 St Clements; freeman, jurat 1720; fh1734; executor to his father's will, witnesses John Steevens, Thomas Lovell jun, John Collier.

Milward, Edward, (1723-1811), originally from Chiddingly, m. Mary Collier daughter of John Collier in 1754; freeman and jurat 1746, Annuity 1742, 1743, 4/-; emerged in the 1750s as the leading Treasury agent for Hastings for the Duke of Newcastle; Surveyor General of riding officers, Kent, 1756; 26 times Mayor of Hastings, canopy bearer for George III; in several of John Collier's letters this Milward is misnamed Miller.

Moore, Thomas, already a freeman by 1735; shipowner, this is the Captain Moore of the above letters who refused to support the Corporation's petition to the King's Bench against the application by Henry Moore for a grant of the freedom of Hastings; fh1734 voted for Pelham and Butler.

Patrick, Richard, d. 1763, m. Elizabeth Carswell, 1748; their daughter was Elizabeth (1749-1780); attorney and clerk to John Collier, Town Clerk 1741, 1750-62; cw St Clements 1746, 1747; apprenticed to John Collier 1747 for five years on payment of £10; read declaration of war at Hastings on 12 April 1744, used an office in Old Hastings house; owned land and houses in Hastings, Bexhill, Ninfield and Surrey.

Pigram, Captain Nathaniell, commander of *Aurelia* the Customs sloop based at Rye, 1731 and 1732, recorded as a jurat at Rye 1730; although resident at Rye also paid a Scot at Hastings; paid common fines as outdweller for a brewhouse and part of Godbeds; fh1734 recorded on the Rye poll list voting for Pelham and Butler.

Russell, Richard, physician (1687-1759). See below: National and Political Figures.

Salmon, Thomas, (1696-1769) St Clements, m. Anne Palmer 1720; ship's master Hastings to London coasting vessel, freeman 1731, fh1734; auditor of the common scot 1743.

Sargent, family: several members opposed the strength of the Mayor and jurats in Hastings corporation and the restrictions on the number of Hastings freemen; Quaker connections from the mid seventeenth century; family trading included corn dealing, shipowning, several shops, and cross Channel and the London coastal trade; there was one appointment to the Customs service; Four voted for Fuller and Bishop in 1734, one for Pelham and Butler, and there was one split vote.

Sargent, Henry, seaman 1720, then common brewer; pf 1728, corn licence 1729, 1741; fh1734 voted for Fuller and Pelham.

Sargent, John, 'the elder', d. 1762, commonly called Hinkley, mariner and customs officer; accepted as apprentice Richard Beale, son of John Beale, mariner, 1715 for £7 10s; auditor of the Scot 1729; fh1734 voted for Pelham and Butler; pw 1738; corn licence 1741.

Sargent, John, m. Elizabeth, licencee of alehouse, 1728, 1736 to 1745.

Sargent, John, junior, admitted to freedom via the mandamus to King's Bench, son of John Sargent deceased.

Sargent, Mark, senior, freeman 1700, rented house from John Collier in All Saints 1732 to 1735.

Sargent, Robert, m. Constance Gray 1740, All Saints; fh1734 voted Fuller and Bishop.

Sargent, Robert, mariner, parish assessor All Saints, land tax collector All Saints 1735; Customs officer 1733 involved in fighting against smugglers at Bexhill; fh1734 voted for Fuller and Bishop; supported mandamus in Kings Bench for admission of freemen 1735, 1736; his dissent was recorded by John Collier in the above letters.

Sargent, Steven, cordwainer and cooper, accepted an apprentice for 7 years at £12 in 1721; corn licence, 1738, 1741; fh1734 voted for Fuller and Bishop; supported the admission of Henry Moore at Hastings Assembly in 1736.

Sargent, Thomas, fh1734 voted for Fuller and Bishop, common measurer.

Shorter, John, son of William, b. 1701, m. Anne Meadow 6 May 1724; similar wording in the mandamus from Kings Bench over the freedom of Hastings to the wording of the mandamus in favour of John Sargent.

Shorter, William, d. 1738 m. Anne Coulstock 1689; fh1734 voted for Fuller and Bishop.

Shorter, William, son of William, (1689-1757) freedom 1722; fh1734 voted for Fuller and Bishop.

Taught, Totteigh, family, six members of this family were listed as county freeholders living in Hastings in 1734 with the right to vote; four voted at Hastings for Pelham and Butler, one for Fuller and Bishop.

Taught, Edward, fisherman, mariner, op St Clements 1724, 1725; freeman 1733; fh1734 voted for Pelham and Butler; cw St Clements 1735; land tax collector 1736; mackerel and herring voyages 1742-3; Annuity 2/- 1742 to 1745.

Taught, Henry, freeman 1731, pw 1737, op All Saints 1739, Auditor of the Scot 1741, mackerel and herring voyages 1742 and 1743.

Taught, Mark, sidesman All Saints 1722; cw All Saints 1726; fh1734 voted for Fuller and Bishop, recommended as a Customs boatman by Sir Thomas Webster; pw 1745.

Taught, Stephen, m. Martha; fh1734 voted for Pelham and Butler; freeman 1735; Town Chamberlain 1733, Auditor of the Scot 1737.

Wicking, Stephen, schoolmaster, Hastings, d. 1734, m. Elizabeth Cooper, she d. 1754; freeman 1730; Stephen Wicking, their son, b. 1706; also Mercy Wicking, daughter of above b. 1717 m. 19 July 1744 at St Clements to John Thorpe of Battle.

NATIONAL AND POLITICAL FIGURES APPEARING IN THE CORRESPONDENCE

The following short biographies cover persons in public life who appear in the Collier papers and who lived, mostly, outside the Hastings and Battle area. Sufficient information is given for the years 1731-46 to help clarify the identity of these individuals, and this may be especially useful where there are other entries of a similar name, and thus helping to avoid confusion. Whilst the details below are not exhaustive, confident connections may be made with the biographical sources listed in the Bibliography, including the *Oxford Dictionary of National Biography*, the *History of Parliament*, the Church of England database, publications on the Army and Navy, and works on the lawyers of the time.

Abbreviations used:

adc	aide de camp.
Brig.	brigadier.
c-in-c	Commander in Chief.
Col.	Colonel.
cr.	created.
DofN	Duke of Newcastle.
educ.	educated.
Gen.	General.
Gns	guineas.
knt	knight.
Lord	Lord.
Lt	Lieutenant.
PofW	Prince of Wales.
P.C.	Privy Council.
regt	regiment.
succ.	succeeded.

Biographies

Abney, Sir Thomas; of Inner Temple, knt 1735, cr. serjeant November 1740, third baron of Exchequer, 1740-43.

Albermarle, Lord William, 2nd Earl of Albermarle (1702-54) m. Lady Anne Lennox, (1705-89), 2nd daughter of Charles, 1st Duke of Richmond, 1723; Whig, educ. Netherlands, estates in Gelderland; adc George II, 1727; Col. 29th Regt Foot, 1731 to 1733, then Col. 3rd troop of Horse Guards; absentee governor of Virginia 1737 to 1754; Brig. Gen. 1739, Major Gen. 1742, Lt Gen. 1745; wounded Fontenoy 1745; by November 1745 with Gen. Wade at Newcastle; in command of the front line at Culloden 1746.

Ancrum, Lord William Henry Kerr, Earl of Ancrum (c.1710-75) m. Lady Caroline Darcy, daughter of the Earl of Holderness, 1735; Whig, MP Richmond 1747-63; Captain in 1st

Regt Foot guards 1741; Lt Col. 11th Dragoons, 1745, Col. 1745; adc Duke of Cumberland, wounded Fontenoy 1745; at Culloden 1746 command of cavalry on left wing; later command of army in the east of Scotland.

Anson, George, Admiral (1697-1762); Whig, MP Hedon 1744-47; naval Captain, sailed on forty-five month raid against Spanish possessions in Pacific and, on return, June 1744, with 1,313,843 pieces of eight and 35,682 ounces in silver bullion paraded through the City of London; Rear Admiral of the White, 1745.

Arbuthnot, John (1667-1735); Whig, physician, associate of 1st Duke of Argyll; arts degree Marishall College, Aberdeen; Royal College of Physicians 1710, writer on medicine and politics.

Archer, Henry (1700-68); Whig, MP Warwick 1735-68; Middle Temple 1718, Inner Temple 1723, called to the bar 1726; close to Sir Robert Walpole. In December 1744, with war costs rising, Archer advocated doubling taxes on pensions and places, rejected by the Commons.

Armstrong, John (1674-1742) civil and military engineer, FRS; Col. of 18th Foot 1735; Brig. Gen. 1735; Major Gen. 1739;

Armstrong, John (1706-58) civil and military engineer, cousin to above; Minorca 1738-42, published *History of the Island of Minorca* (1752).

Ashburnham, Hon. John (1687-1737) cr. Earl 1730; Whig, MP Hastings 1710, succ. to Barony and entered House of Lords 1710; succ. as MP by Sir William Ashburnham (qv); appointed Col. of horse, Duke of Ormond's Regt, 1713, deputy governor and deputy warden, Cinque Ports, 1714, Lord of Bedchamber to PofW, 1728-31; Captain Yeoman of the Guard, November 1731 to death in 1737. For the Ashburnham family estate ownership of manors and advowsons etc. see Dunkin 1914-15. John, 1st baron Ashburnham, d. 1710; for his daughters Elizabeth, Anne and Jane whose mother d. 1719 see *SAC* vol. 88 3-14 and Steer *Ashburnham Archives*.

Ashburnham, Sir William, 2nd baronet Ashburnham of Broomham (c.1677-1755) m. Margaret, daughter of Sir Nicholas Pelham of Catsfield, 1701; Whig, MP Hastings, 1710-13, 1727-34, and 1735-41 when re-elected by Hastings assembly after appointment to office; Seaford 1715- 1717; retired from Parliament 1741 due to ill-health. Chamberlain of the Tally Court 1710-55, Commissioner of the Alienation Office 1717-55; receiver of fines in the Alienation Office 1735-55.

Ashburnham, Revd Sir William (d. 1797); deacon 1733, priest 1734, vicar of St Peter, Bexhill 1739-42, Dean of Chichester 1742-54, Bishop of Chichester 1754, succ. as 4th baronet Ashburnham 1762; m. Margaret daughter of Thomas Pelham of Lewes.

Aylesbury, Earl of (1715-77); Tory independent, MP Leicestershire 1739-41, Maidstone 1741-47; opposed subsidy for Hanoverian troops.

Barnard, Sir John (c.1685-1764); Quaker, later Church of England, MP City of London 1722-61; financier, wine importer, shipping insurer. Frequent contributions in Parliament on monetary and tax affairs, as with Francis Hutcheson [qv] when opposed financial schemes which encouraged speculation; important role in financial stability during Jacobite rebellion and threat of French invasion 1744-46; statue in his honour erected outside Royal Exchange in 1747.

Barrymore, 4th Earl, Barry James, 1667-1748; Tory, MP Stockbridge 1710-13, 1714-15, Wigan 1715-27, 1734-47; Jacobite plotter who encouraged a French invasion in 1744-45, arrested though not brought to trial; parts of his correspondence were made available in trials after the defeat of the rebellion.

Beauclerk, Lord Harry (1701-61); Whig, MP Plymouth 1740-41, Thetford 1741-61; Captain and Lt Col. 1st Foot Guards, 1735; Col. 48th Foot 1743-5; Col. 31st Foot 1745-49; Thetford was a gift from his cousin the 2nd Duke of Grafton. Lord Harry was brother to Lord George Beauclerk (1704-68), also Whig, and MP New Windsor 1744-54.

Beaufort, 3rd Duke of, Henry Somerset-Scudamore (1707-45) succ. 1714, m. Frances daughter of Viscount Scudamore and took her surname in 1729.

Bedford, 4th Duke, John Russell (1710-71) succ. 1732; supported Walpole in opposing war with Spain, later opposed subsidy for 16,000 Hanoverian troops; first Lord of the Admiralty, 1744; argued for the right of landowners to raise volunteer regiments in 1745.

Belfield, John, (1669-1751); Tory, MP Exeter 1728-34; Inner Temple, serjeant 1716; as recorder of Exeter signed the loyal address in 1745.

Berkeley, Countess of, daughter of Henry Drax, Charborough, Dorset; Lady of the Bedchamber to Augusta Princess of Wales; wife of Augustus, 4th Earl of Berkeley (1716-55), Lord Lt Gloucestershire 1737, Order of the Thistle 1739; Lt Col. 2nd Regt Foot Guards 1737, Col. 1745.

Bishop (Bishopp), Sir Cecil, of Parham (1700-78); m. 1726, Anne dau. Hugh Boscawen, eight daus, four sons; Tory, MP Penryn 1727-34, Boroughbridge 1755-68; stood with John Fuller in 1734 Sussex county election; for the Bishop family ownership of manors and advowsons etc. see Dunkin 1914-15. His interest in the Pretender faded by 1746, and appointed by DofN as superintendent of the Ordnance foundries, 1751.

Brian, Thomas, Solicitor for Bonds and Criminal Prosecutions, Customs; Solicitor for the Port of London and the western ports of England and Wales 1737.

Buccleuch, 2nd Duke, Francis Scott (1695-1751), Scots representative peer, 1734-41.

Bundy, Dr Richard (1694-1739), Christ Church Oxford, BA 1713; Chaplain in Ordinary to George II 1732, Canon, Westminster 1732-39.

Burnett, Robert, Steward for the Newcastle household, 1715-41; also agent for Newcastle political affairs and estates in Sussex; succ. by Samuel Burt.

Bussiere, Huguenot doctor; in 1737 80 years old; favourite of the royal family.

Butler, James (c.1680-1741) of Warminghurst Park, Sussex; Whig, MP Arundel 1705-8, Sussex 1715-22, 1728-41; died from smallpox ten days after the 1741 election result.

Campbell, Alexander Hume (1708-60); lawyer, Whig, MP Berwickshire 1734-41, 1742-60; a part of the Squadrone Whig faction which opposed the more influential Argyll Campbells; Solicitor General to PofW 1741-46; after Culloden Pelham and DofN settled with the Squadrone, and thereby broadened the government's support in Scotland.

Campbell, Hugh Hume, Lord Polwarth, 3rd Earl of Marchmont (1708-94); lawyer, Whig, MP Berwick-on-Tweed 1734-40, succ. as 3rd Earl 1740; supplied arms for defence of Berwick in 1745; twin brother of Alexander Hume Campbell.

Campbell, Sir James of Lawers (c.1680-1743); Whig, Lt Col. 2nd Royal North British Dragoons, 1706, fought at Oudenarde and Malplaquet; Groom of Bedchamber 1726; Brig. Gen. 1735, Governor of Edinburgh castle 1738, Major Gen. 1739, General commanding cavalry 1742, killed at Fontenoy 1745.

Carkasse, Charles, Secretary to Customs Commissioners 1709-41, re-organised Customs rates and much of the legislation against tax evasion. John Collier dealt with Carkasse for almost three decades; succ. by William Wood 1742-46.

Carteret, John (1690-1763), 1st Earl Granville and 2nd Baron Carteret; Secretary of State 1721-24, Lord Lt Ireland 1724-30, Secretary of State Northern Dept 1742.

Caryll, Edward, for the Caryll family interests in Sussex manors, advowsons etc., including Ore, Higham alias Iham, Winchelsea alias New Winchelsea, see Dunkin 1914-15, also McCann *SAC* 124, Caplan *SAC* 116. John Collier was steward for several of the Caryll family manors.

Cavendish, William (1720-64); Whig, MP Derbyshire 1741-51; succ. as 4th Duke of Devonshire 1755.

Cathcart, 9th Lord (1721-76) adc to Cumberland at Fontenoy, seriously wounded; Captain 3rd Regt Foot June 1745, Col. and Adjutant Gen. to forces in Scotland 1750.

Chesterfield, Lord, Philip Stanhope (1694-1773) succ. as 4th Earl of Chesterfield 1726; m. Petronilla Melusina van der Schulenburg, daughter of George I and Duchess of Kendall, 1733; Whig, KG 1730, Gentleman of the Bedchamber PofW 1715-27, Lord of the Bedchamber 1727-30, ambassador to the Hague 1728-32 and 1745; Lord Lt Ireland 1744-46.

Cholmondeley, Hon. George (1703-70), m. daughter of Sir Robert Walpole; Whig, MP Eastbourne 1724-27, New Windsor 1727-33, then succ. as 3rd Earl of Cholmondeley, Lord Lt North Wales 1733-61, Chancellor Duchy of Lancaster 1736-43; Col. 1745, Lord Lt Ireland 1743.

Clarke, Dr Alured, d. 1742; Canon of Westminster 1731.

Compton, Hon. Spencer, (1674-1743) of Compton Place, Eastbourne; 1st Earl of Wilmington 1730, KG 1733; Whig, MP Eye 1698-1710, East Grinstead 1713-15, Sussex 1715-28; Speaker 1715-27, Lord President P.C., 1730-42, Prime Minister 1742-43.

Cope, Sir John (1690-1760); Whig, MP Queenborough 1722-27, Liskeard 1727-34, Orford 1738-41; Col. 39th Foot 1730-32, 5th Foot 1732-37; 9th dragoons 1737-41; 7th Dragoons 1741-60; Brig. Gen. 1735, Major Gen. 1739, Lt Gen. 1743, c-in-c Scotland 1745.

Cresset, Edward, d. 1755; Dean of Hereford, 1736-49, rector, Cound 1737-55.

Darnall, Sir John (1672-1735); Middle Temple, Serjeant 1715, knt. 1724, Judge in Court of Marshalsea 1733.

Dashwood, Sir Francis (1708-81); MP New Romney 1741-47, Weymouth and Melcombe Regis 1761-63; opposed Sir Robert Walpole and continued in opposition to government after 1742.

De la Warr, Lord, John West, 7th baron de la Warr (1693-1766); MP Grampound 1715-22, succ. to title 1723; clerk to the P.C. 1712-23; Lt Col. Horse Guards 1717, commanded brigade at Dettingen 1743, Major Gen. 1745, Lt Gen. 1747; Lord of the Bedchamber to George I 1725. Opposed international treaty for security of trade and navigation in wartime 1742.

Dorset, Duke of (1688-1765), Sackville, Lionel Cranfield; Whig, Lord High Steward of England at coronation of George II; re-appointed in 1728 as Constable of Dover castle and Lord Warden of Cinque Ports; Lord Lt of Ireland 1730-37, Lord President P.C. 1745. His elder son Charles Sackville, Earl of Middlesex (1711-69), MP East Grinstead 1734-42, 1761-65, Sussex 1742-47, Old Sarum 1747-54; his younger son Lord John Philip Sackville (1713-65) MP Tamworth 1734-47.

Fazakerly, Nicholas (1685-1767); lawyer, Tory, MP Preston, 1732-67, opposed to Walpole and Wilmington, though supported Pelham and Newcastle in 1745 and 1746, and introduced a bill to make correspondence with Jacobite court illegal.

Fuller, John (1680-1745); Tory, MP Sussex 1713-15, ironmaster, plantation owner, Sussex landowner.

Gage, Sir William of Firle, 7th baronet (1695-1744); Whig, MP Seaford 1722-44; on his death estate passed to Thomas Gage (d. 1754), MP Minehead 1717, Tewkesbury 1721-54, who was a baron of the peerage of Ireland.

Godolphin, Francis, 2nd Earl of Godolphin (1678-1766), m. Henrietta Churchill; MP Helston 1695-98, 1701-10, East Looe 1701, Oxfordshire 1708-10, Tregony 1710-12; Lord Lt Oxfordshire 1715-35, 1st Lord of Bedchamber 1727-35, Lord Privy Seal 1735-40, succ. as 2nd Earl 1712 on d. of Sidney Godolphin; his daughter Lady Mary Godolphin (1723-64) m. Thomas Osborne, 4th Duke of Leeds.

Goring, Sir Charles Mathew (1706-69), m. (1) Mary Blackburne (2) Elizabeth, elder sister of Sir Robert Fagge, 4th baronet of Wiston; Tory, voted for Bishop and Fuller 1734; succ. Sir Henry Goring MP, a Jacobite who fled to France in 1722.

Grafton, Duke of, Charles Fitzroy 2nd Duke (1683-1759); Lord Lt of Ireland 1720-24, Lord Chamberlain 1724-57; his son George Fitzroy, Lord Euston.

Grenville, George, (1712-70); MP Buckingham 1741-70, opposition at first and switched to support government in 1744, appointed Admiralty Lord 1744-47, Treasury Lord 1747-54.

Gundry, Nathaniel, (1701-54); lawyer, MP Dorchester 1741-50, KC 1742, Judge Court of Common Pleas 1750-54.

Hales, Sir Thomas 2nd baronet (1666-1748) of Bekesbourne, Canterbury; Whig, MP Canterbury 1715-34, 1735-41; supported the general excise, defeated at the 1734 election though re-seated after petition, defeated again 1741, returned at by-election 1746.

Hammond, William (d.1763); Southwark brewer, JP and surgeon; victor in Southwark by-election May 1743, his opponent Alexander Hume, director of the East India Company, succeeded in overturning the result.

Hardwicke, Earl of, Yorke, Sir Philip (1690-1764), knt. 1720, cr. Baron Hardwicke of Hardwicke 1733, cr. Viscount Royston and Earl of Hardwicke 1754; Whig, MP Lewes 1719-22, Seaford 1722-33; Attorney General 1724-33, Serjeant 1733, Chief Justice King's Bench 1733-37, Lord Chancellor 1737-56.

Hawley, Henry, General (1679-1759); father killed at Steenkirke 1692; Col. 1712, wounded Sheriffmuir 1715; Col. 13th Dragoons 1730, Major Gen. 1739, Lt Gen. 1743; at Dettingen and Flanders 1744, at Fontenoy took command of right wing on death of Sir James Campbell; c-in-c Scotland 1745; defeated at Falkirk 1746; after Culloden remained c-in-c Scotland; subsequent career included planning for war against Sussex and Kent smugglers.

Hutcheson, Archibald (c.1660-1740); lawyer, MP, Hastings 1713-27, Attorney General, Leeward Isles 1688-1704, Lord of Trade 1714-16, specialist in financial affairs, appointed advisor to the Duke of Ormond who nominated Hutcheson for Hastings 1713, re-elected 1715. Generally supported the Whig position, though agreed with the Hastings corporation to oppose the Septennial bill, 1716, and voted against the government; built up a following in Hastings, and with the support of John Collier was returned in 1722.

Jeake, Samuel (1623-1690); radical, merchant, author of the constitutional history of the Cinque Ports, 1678, published in 1728, subscribers included numerous Sussex connections of John Collier; Jeake's son, also Samuel (1652-1699) merchant and freeman of Rye; and his grandson Samuel Jeake, 'Counsellor' Jeake, b. 1697, Customs collector of Rye.

Knowles, Sir Charles (1704-77); Whig, MP Gatton 1749-52; engineer and demolition expert, Commodore of naval forces ordered to attack New Spain in the Caribbean, 1746; with fleet in the Downs as Captain of the *Canterbury* captured *Bourbon* and *La Charite* 21 February 1746; Governor of Louisberg 1746-48.

Lee, Sir William of Totteridge, Herts (1688-1754); MP Chipping Wycombe 1727-30, Latin secretary to George I and II 1718-30, KC 1728, serjeant 1730, attorney general to PofW 1728-30, Justice of the King's Bench 1730, Chief Justice 1737.

Legge, Hon. Henry (1706-64); MP East Looe, 1740-41, Orford 1741-59; Secretary to Walpole 1735-39, Secretary to Lord Lt of Ireland 1739-41, Secretary to Treasury 1741-42, Surveyor of Woods and Forests north and south of the Trent 1742-45; Admiralty Lord 1745-46; supported subsidy for Hanoverian troops 1744, argued in favour of Admiral Mathews 1745, and against Admiral Vernon.

Legonier, Jean-Louis (1680-1770) Huguenot, soldier and diplomat; Col. 7th dragoon guards 1720-49, adc George II 1729-43; Brig. Gen. 1735, Major Gen. 1739, Lt Gen. 1743, General 1746; highly regarded by George II and the Dutch during the fighting in Flanders after 1742 and at Fontenoy organised the retreat of the infantry.

Lestock, Captain Richard, later Admiral (1679-1746); exonerated by court martial for his conduct at the battle of Toulon.

Leveson-Gower, John, 1st Earl Gower (1694-1754); Tory, Lord Justice 1740, 1743, 1745 raised Regt of Foot 1745, cr. Viscount Trentham and Earl Gower 1746.

Lincoln, Henry Fiennes Clinton, 9th Earl of Lincoln (1720-94); the 7th Earl m. Lucy, daughter of Thomas Lord Pelham, and was succ. by George 8th Earl who d. 1730 aged 13, in turn succ. by the 9th Earl, who m. 1744 Catherine, dau. of Henry Pelham; the 9th Earl appointed Lord of the Bedchamber 1742, Lord Lt Cambridgeshire 1742; extensive ownership of Sussex manors etc., including many on the Weald.

Lloyd, Sir Richard of Hintlesham Hall, Suffolk (1696-1761); knt. 1745, lawyer, Whig, MP Mitchell 1745-47, Maldon 1747-54; KC 1738.

Lonsdale, Lord, Henry Lowther, 3rd Viscount Lonsdale (1694-1751); Whig, fought the Jacobites in 1715; Lord of the Bedchamber 1717, Constable of the Tower 1726, Lord Privy Seal 1733-35; Lord Lt Cumberland and Westmorland 1738-51 and organised their defence in 1745.

Lynch, John, Dean of Canterbury, installed 1734, d. 1760.

Marlborough, 3rd Duke, (1706-58); succ. 1722, supporter of PofW until 1738, Col. 38th Regt of Foot 1738, Lord of the Bedchamber 1738, Col. of 1st Royal Dragoons 1739, Col. 2nd troop of Horse Guards; Dettingen 1743, resigned commission over George II's partiality for officers from Hanover and opposed the subsidy to Hanoverian troops; supported declaration of war and active in 1745-46 against the Jacobites, Major Gen. 1745, Lt Gen. 1747.

Mathews, Thomas (1676-1751); MP Glamorgan 1745-47, Carmarthen 1747-51; Captain 1703, Commissioner Chatham dockyard 1736-42; c-in-c Mediterranean and minister to Sardinia and Italian states, March 1742 to August 1744; Vice Admiral 1742, Admiral 1743, rear-admiral 1744-47, court martialled over defeat at Toulon 22 October 1746, dismissed the service 1747.

Medley, Samuel, of Buxted Place; worked for Sussex Tories 1741, thought of standing with Sir Cecil Bishop or John Peachey, died of smallpox before poll.

Montagu, George, 2nd Earl of Halifax (1716-71); Whig, Col. 1745, succ. as Earl 1739, President of the Board of Trade 1748-61.

Mostyn, Captain Savage (1713-57); Whig, MP Weobley 1747-57; cousin of Lord Winchelsea, naval captain 1739, fought at Cartagena 1741, accused of failing to intercept two French ships in 1745, court martial at his own request 16 March 1745, and restored to command.

Murray, William (1705-93) lawyer; Whig, MP Boroughbridge 1742-56, appointed Solicitor General by Lord Wilmington 1742, cr. Lord Mansfield 1756.

Murray, James (1721-94), s. of Alexander Murray, 4th Lord Elibank, 3rd Scots Regt in Netherlands 1736, Captain 1742, Major 1745, Lt Col. 1751; sailed with General Wolfe to Quebec, and appointed Governor of Quebec 1760-68, Major Gen. 1762, Dep. Governor and Governor Minorca 1774-84; m. Cordelia Collier December 1748 and subsequently in Hollington bought lands which formed Beauport Park.

Newcastle, Thomas Pelham Holles, Duke of Newcastle, had extensive ownership of Sussex manors and advowsons etc.

Nicoll, John, Westminster school, undermaster 1714-33 headmaster 1733-53; opposed beating of pupils.

Norris, Sir John (1670-1749); Whig, MP Rye 1708-22, 1734-49, Portsmouth 1722-34; Admiralty Lord 1718-30, Admiral of the Fleet and c-in-c 1734, in command of the Channel fleet 1739-44; after Sir Robert Walpole's resignation, 1742, George II refused Norris's offer to resign; aged 74 on his last command in the Channel Norris played a key role in the failure of French efforts to invade Kent and Sussex.

Oglethorpe, James Edward (1696-1755); MP Haslemere 1722-54, founder of Georgia colony, Brig. Gen. 1741, Major Gen. 1745.

Orange, Prince of, William Charles Henry, m. Princess Royal 14 March 1734.

Parker, Sir Walter of Ratton (1694-1750); his family interests in manors included Willingdon, Jevington, Eastbourne, St John of Jerusalem and in Willingdon Park and tenements.

Pelham, Henry, of Esher Place (1695-54); Whig, Prime Minister, MP Seaford 1717-22, Sussex 1722-54, Paymaster General 1730-43, 1st Lord of Treasury 1743-54; extensive holdings of manors, lands etc., in Sussex; John Collier was appointed in 1734 as steward for the manors and lordships of the Pelham estate. For tables of the genealogy of the Pelham family see Coxe 1829.

Pelham, James, Colonel, of Crowhurst (1683-1761); Whig, MP Newark 1722-41, Hastings 1741-61, worked closely with Henry Pelham and the Duke of Newcastle.

Pelham, Sir Nicholas, of Catsfield and Crowhurst (c. 1650-1739); MP Seaford 1671-79, 1689-90, Sussex 1679-81, Lewes 1702-05, 1726-27.

Pelham, Thomas (1678-1760); Whig, MP Lewes 1705-41, Lord of Trade 1717-41.

Pelham, Thomas of Stanmer (1705-37); Whig, MP Lewes 1727-37, often referred to by contemporaries as 'Turk' Pelham.

Pelham, Thomas of Stanmer, jun. (1728-1805); Whig, MP Rye 1749-54, Sussex 1754-68.

Pelham, Thomas, jun. (1705-43); Whig, MP Hastings 1728-41, Lewes 1741-43.

Philips, Sir John, of Picton Castle, Pembrokeshire (1700-64); lawyer, Jacobite Tory, MP Carmarthen 1741-47, Petersfield 1754-61; Commissioner for Trade 1744-45.

Pitt, William of Hayes, Kent (1708-78); MP Old Sarum 1738-47, Seaford 1747-54; cornet of horse 1731-36, groom of bedchamber for PofW 1737-45, P.C. 1746, Paymaster General 1746-55, unequalled in oratory except by Lord Mansfield, settled differences with Henry Pelham and DofN in November 1744.

Ponsonby, Henry (1685-1745); Irish landowner, Lt Col. 27th Regt Foot, Ireland 1715, Col. 37th Foot 1735, Brig. Gen. 1742, killed Fontenoy 1745.

Potter, Dr John, (1674-1747); Archbishop of Canterbury 1737-47.

Pryse, Thomas (?1716-45); Tory, MP Cardigan boroughs 1741-45.

Pulteney John (1661-1726); Whig, MP Hastings, 1695-1710, defeated 1710; early correspondent of John Collier, Pulteney was defeated at Hastings by one vote in 1722;

several offices before appointed as Commissioner of Customs 1714-22; assisted in placing Thomas Holman in the Customs, a nephew of Mary and William Cranston.

Pulteney, William, Earl of Bath (1684-1764); Whig, MP Hedon 1705-34, Middlesex 1734-42; cr Earl of Bath 13 July 1742; worked with ministers after the South Sea Bubble, though excluded from office when Walpole was appointed 1st Lord of the Treasury. With Bolingbroke funded the *Craftsman* edited by Nicholas Amhurst; later joined with Sir William Wyndham and country party to oppose the general excise, to dispute the government's view of foreign affairs, and support petitions over election results which facilitated the change in government in 1742.

Robinson, Sir Thomas (1702-77); Whig, MP Morpeth 1727-34; ensign 1st Foot Guards 1727; Excise Commissioner 1735-42, Governor of Barbados 1742-47.

Rothes, John Leslie, 10th Earl of (c.1698-1767); Whig, Col. 25th 1732-45, Brig. Gen. 1739, Major Gen. 1743, Col. 2nd troop of Horse Grenadier Guards 1745, Col. 6th Dragoons 1745.

Rowe, Milward (1717-92) born in Pevensey, son of Thomas Rowe, m. Susan daughter of John Handley in the six clerks office, Court of Chancery, clerk in Andrew Stone's office; one of the two lives for whom John Collier held the office of Usher and Cryer of the King's Bench.

Royal family: George II (1683-1760) accession 11 June 1727, absences in Hanover May-Sept 1729, June-Sept 1732, May-Oct 1735, May 1736-Jan 1737, May-Oct 1740, May-Oct 1741, May-Nov 1743, May-Aug 1745 (and later absences); m. Caroline of Ansbach (1683-1737), who was regent in 1729, 1732, 1735, 1736-7, after her death Lords Justices acted when the king was in Hanover; Prince of Wales, Frederick Louis (1707-51); Duke of Cumberland, William Augustus (1721-65); Anne (1709-59) m. Prince of Orange 14 March 1734; Emily Sophia Eleanora (1711-86); Caroline Elizabeth (1713-57); Mary (1723-72) m. Frederick, later landgrave of Hesse Cassel 8 May 1740; Louisa (1724-51) m. Frederick, later Frederick V of Denmark 27 Oct 1743.

Russell, Dr Richard (1687-1759) son of Nathaniel and Mary Russell; educ. Free Grammar school, St Anne's Lewes, m. Mary Kempe, 1719; probably apprenticed in London, accepted as apprentice John Snashall of Lewes for seven years at £80; accepted Henry Manning as apprentice in 1716 for seven years at £100; studied medicine at Leyden, doctor of medicine 1724, living in Lewes by October 1725. Whig. Among other advice recommended sea water for glands and skin afflictions including eczema; consulted by John Collier over Mary Collier's and Cordelia Collier's conditions. Often confused with Dr Richard Russell, 1714-71, MD Rheims, son of a Sussex vicar.

Ryder, Sir Dudley, of Tooting, Surrey (1691-1756); lawyer, Whig, MP St Germans 1733-34, Tiverton 1734-54, Solicitor General, 1733 to 1737; Attorney General 1737, Chief Justice King's Bench 1754.

Sandwich, 4th Earl of, John Montagu (1718-92); Admiralty Commissioner 1744-51.

Sergison, Thomas (1701-66) of Cuckfield Place; Tory, stood for Lewes 1741, gained 117 votes, defeated by Thomas Pelham of Crowhurst on 156 and John Trevor on 154; in 1743 Sergison intended to stand again, but withdrew before the poll, held on 6 August 1743; later reached agreement with DofN and was elected unopposed in 1747, and sat for Lewes until d. 1766.

Simon, Henry, appointed 1744 as Solicitor for Bonds and criminal prosecutions in the Customs.

Stanhope, William, Earl of Harrington (c.1683-1756); MP Derby 1715-22, 1727-30, Steyning 1727; cr. Baron Harrington 1730, Earl 1742, Secretary of State northern dept 1730-42, 1744-46, Lord President P.C. 1742-45, Major Gen. 1735, Lt Gen. 1739, General 1747.

Stanley, Hans (1721-80); opposition Whig, MP St Albans 1743-47.

Stewart, Charles Edward (1720-88), the Young Pretender; landed on Eriskay 3 August 1745, sailed from Scotland 20 September 1746.

Stewart, James Francis Edward (1688-1766); James VIII of Scotland and III of England, the Old Pretender, son of James VII and II; after Jacobite defeat at Sheriffmuir 13 November 1715, landed 22 December 1715 at Peterhead, left from Montrose 4 February 1716.

Stone, Andrew (1703-73); Whig, MP Hastings 1741-61, son of Andrew Stone, goldsmith with family connection to Martin's Bank; private secretary to the DofN 1732-34, under secretary of state 1734-51, paid £200 a year by Newcastle, and offices raised this to over £4000, important to the organisation of politics for Henry Pelham and Newcastle.

Strange, Sir John (c.1696-1754); lawyer, Whig, MP West Looe 1737-41, Totnes 1742-54, Solicitor General 1737-42, Recorder of London 1739-42, KC 1736, Master of the Rolls 1750-54.

Talbot, Charles (1685-1737); Solicitor General 1726-33, P.C. 1733, Lord Chancellor 1733-37.

Vernon, Edward, Admiral (1684-1757); Whig, MP Penrhyn 1722-34, Portsmouth 1741, Ipswich 1741-57, in the election of 1741 elected at Portsmouth, Rochester, Ipswich and Penrhyn; Captain 1706, Admiral 1745, reputation for sympathy for ordinary sailors and soldiers; in 1731 spoke of the life service for soldiers as a form of slavery, opposed the general excise and the salt tax as taxes bearing especially hard on the poor; during Spanish war captured Porto Bello, and from 1744 was vocal in criticism of the Admiralty, and in turn was criticised for his lax attitude to the lower decks. At own request removed from command in the Channel, December 1745. His pamphlet *Seasonable Advice* (1746) included specific criticism of the work of John Collier in dealing with Kent smugglers.

Wade, George, General (1673-1748); Whig, MP Hindon 1715-22, Bath 1722-48; army career included c-in-c Scotland 1724-40, Lt Gen. Ordnance 1742-48; Field Marshal 1743.

Wager, Sir Charles (1666-1743); Whig, MP Portsmouth 1710-11, 1715-34, West Looe 1713-15, 1741-43, Westminster 1734-41, 1st Lord of the Admiralty, 1733-42, Treasurer of the Navy 1742-3; understood the tactical questions facing captains, as well as the strategic questions for the overall effectiveness of the fleet; pioneered effective treatment for scurvy, using vegetables, oranges and lemons, together with the circulation of air within vessels.

Wake, William (1657-1737) Archbishop of Canterbury; Christ Church Oxford, deacon 1681, priest 1682, lived in France 1682-85, opponent of James II; appointed Bishop of London 1705, Archbishop of Canterbury from 1716, argued for alliance of protestant nations.

Westmorland, Earl of, John Fane (1686-1762); Whig, Emmanuel College, Cambridge, Lincoln's Inn, Col. 1st troop Life Guards, 1733-7; MP Hythe 1708, Kent 1715-22, Buckingham 1727, failed to obtain Cinque port seat in 1735, despite support from Duke of Dorset. When succ. to title in 1737 Westmorland supported the Tory position on the PofW's position in the constitution, and was dismissed from the army for voting to increase the Prince's allowance; reinstated in 1742 with the ranks of Major Gen. and Lt Gen. allowed from 1735 and 1739.

Wiles, Sir John (1685-1761); Whig, MP Launceston 1724-26, Weymouth and Melcombe Regis 1726-27, West Looe 1727-37; knt 1737; KC 1719, attorney general 1734, Chief Justice Common Pleas, 1737-61.

Willis, Browne (1682-1760); Tory, MP Buckingham 1705-08; antiquary and historian, funded church restoration, collector of trade tokens, coins, books and church manuscripts, mostly left to the University of Oxford.

Yonge, Sir William of Colyton, Devon (c.1693-1755); Whig, MP Honiton 1715-54, Tiverton 1754-55; good with accounts, excellent memory for Parliamentary affairs and statutes.

GLOSSARY

Includes terms mainly relating to the law, health and medicine, and Hastings corporation.

Item	**Description**
Affidavit	statement in writing, supported by oath, for use in judicial process.
Anodyne necklace	for soothing teething pain; anodyne creams available for sores, mouth ulcers, fungal and scabies infections.
Attornment	an assignment, a transfer of homage and service to a new manorial lord.
Banian	a loose flannel jacket, or flannel shirt.
Bank post bill	Bank of England bill promising to pay to a named bearer or order a specified sum so many days after the date on the bill.
Bills of mortality	deaths in Church of England London parishes.
Blister	a patch to raise the skin and remove ill humours containing fluid.
Bloodletting	by leeches, for the alleviation of symptoms in ailments and in convalescence.
Bobs	ornament designed to hang from necklace, or as an earring.
Bohea tea	finest black tea used as nourishment during convalescence.
Bolus	purgative by mouth to clear stomach and intestines.
Brawn	flesh of pig or boar, boiled, pickled with salt or potted.
Bryonia	south of England climbing plant; juice extracted from the roots mixed with honey or oil a cure for deafness.
Brocade	silk or satin cloth with taffeta, on which is woven patterns standing proud of basic textile, often used as a wrap for shoulders and chairs.
Calamanco	woollen cloth, the silk in the warp imparting a gloss surface, resembling satin.
Candied eryngo	Colchester candy, a sweet syrup from the roots of Essex marsh holly, combined with sugar and water; medicine for agues.
Cantharides	Spanish flies, applied to skin to raise blister containing fluid.
Caption	certificate on document.
Capuchin	female cloak with hood in imitation of Capuchin friars.
Certiorari	writ from a higher court calling for the records of a case at a lower court upon the complaint of a party that the lower court has not dispensed justice.
Chalybeate	mineral water usually from springs.
Change Alley	exchange alley, two alleys connecting Lombard Street, Birchin Lane and Cornhill, a centre for bond and stock dealing.
Chanter	clergyman responsible for music in cathedral or collegiate church.
Char(r)	small freshwater fish.
Chariot	four wheeled carriage designed for speed with strong suspension.
Chessam, Chossam	Chesham, Buckinghamshire, north-west of London.

Chints, chintz,	printed and plain white cottons, often with flower patterns of several colours.
Chipt hats	palm leaves or woody fibre split and plaited for hats and bonnets.
Cole	money, usually cash.
Commission of sewers	local commission for managing ditches, fens and marshlands.
Common Pleas	Court of Common Pleas.
Dedimus potestatem	writ allowing legal process to be conducted outside the Westminster courts by a country attorney.
Deeze (deese)	three or four storey timber tower with internal rails from which herrings hung and dried out, and were often smoked by means of a charcoal fire; example remain on the Hastings beach.
Dimity	cotton fabric, woven with raised stripes or figures, usually undyed.
Ejectment	expulsion or dispossession by legal process.
Eligit/elegit	writ of execution by which a creditor takes over half the goods and lands of the debtor until the claim is settled.
Elixer proprietatis	recipes common in kitchen physic for recovery and convalescence.
Escritoire	writing desk, cabinet for storing papers and belongings.
Executions	confiscation of property of debtor for non-payment in bankruptcy proceedings, also for imprisonment of debtor.
Fellmonger	merchant or trader in hides, fleeces, hair.
Fieri Facias	writ to a sheriff for executing judgement.
Fine	legal document often used as part of conveyance.
Firkin	small cask for food products, including butter and brawn.
Flambeau	torch made with several thick wicks dipped in wax.
Franks	signature for letters and parcels sent on official and Parliament business.
Fusil	attachment for waterworks equipment.
Gargarism	cough mixture.
Glister	enema or liquid injection into anus to clear intestines.
Gravel	accumulation of urinary crystals, indicated by pain or partial blockage in passing urine.
Half anchor	wooden tubs able to hold about 3.5 to 4 gallons of spirits.
Hanger	a rope, chain or hook.
Hartshorn	solution of ammonia and hart's antlers in white wine or whey to expel cold from body, also diluted in smelling salts.
Heriot	payment to the lord of the manor in cash or by animal(s) on death of tenant by the successor.
Hogshead	cask for water, alcohol, etc., various sizes, commonly over 50 gallons.
Hog's pudding	stomach and entrails of a pig or boar, stuffed with oatmeal, suet, or flour and tripe, with raisins, currants, salt and spices.
Hoop	made from flexible material, such as whalebone or thin steel, worn under a petticoat, or, a wool tuft in the hat.
Incally	replacing the callow, the stratum of vegetable and humus soil lying above the subsoil or top bed of a quarry.

In propria persona	in his or her own person.
Jackboots	leather riding boots, square block toes, wide heels, with bucket tops to fit over knees.
Japanning	addition of paint to woodwork to give a hard glossy finish, used also for earthenware and ironwork.
Joseph	long dark cloak worn by women, clasped at shoulder height with buttons or brooch.
Jurat	elected corporation official.
Latitat/Late	Latitat, a writ from the King's Bench to a person assumed to be in hiding to appear before the court.
Lutestring	glossy silk fabric, dress or ribbon.
Mandamus	from the King's Bench to an inferior court, with the object of enforcing the performance of a public duty.
Manna juice	gentle laxative, from bark of the manna ash, and similar plants.
Manor	right of the lord of the manor to hold court and exact certain fines and dues from occupiers within the manorial bounds.
Mantua	loose gown or coat without stays designed for women.
Marshalsea	prison in Southwark.
Messuage	building with accompanying land.
Onus probandi	burden of proof.
Packet boat	fast sailing ship carrying mail and passengers including officials.
Padusway waistcoat	silk manufacture in Padua developed a corded or cross hatch silk fabric, of various colours, popular for waistcoats, coats, breeches.
Paregoric	medicine which quietens patient, reduces vomiting and diarrhoea, aids rest.
Pink(e)	sailing vessel, of small size used for coasting and fishing, described in the OED as flat bottomed and with bulging sides.
Plaintiff	party which brings a case in a legal process.
Pleura	membranes lining the thorax and lungs.
Pockets	separate purses attached to a dress or skirt by cords.
Pomatum, Pomade	skin and hair cream with a base of pig grease, lemon juice, apple pulp, rose water, dried ingredients used as a powder .
Poplin	silk or cotton warp, worsted weft, giving a cord like texture.
Prebendary	clergyman holder of post in a cathedral or collegiate church.
Pullerane	a woollen-silk stuff.
Pumps	light shoes, comprising textiles often of bright colours, kept on the foot by a close fit without fastening; slippers for indoor use; also, a low heel shoes for dancers.
Quadrille	four person card game, eventually replaced by whist.
Quarter sessions	county or borough quarterly criminal and civil court, consisting of Justices of the Peace; in Hastings comprising mayor and jurats.
Rand	a strip or slice, often with reference to fish, about an ell in length.
Ranelagh Gardens	pleasure gardens, south side of Thames.
Recognizance	legally binding bond, usually with surety, by which person agrees to keep a condition, such as date to appear in court, pay a debt, deliver documents etc.

Recovery	common recovery, a deed providing a legal process to ensure a clean freehold title.
Ridotto	entertainment at a social assembly consisting of food and drink, music and dancing.
Rippier	one who carries fish inland to sell, the fish usually carried on horseback in panniers. The OED citing a source from 1516 has 'repiers and other fisshers' with fish from Rye and Winchelsea'.
Roquelaure	after Duke of Roquelaure, 1656-1738, cloak reaching down to the knees, with collar fitting round the shoulders.
Saint Anthony's fire	skin disease caused by infected grain leading to scratching, lesions and eruptions, with a variety of symptoms including pain and nervous disorders .
Salivation	mercury compound to combat disease.
Serjeant at Law,	rank granted to the most knowledgeable and experienced lawyers in the Westminster courts; although they could plead in any Westminster court, the Common Pleas was reserved to Serjeants.
Shammy gloves	made of soft, pliable, leather.
Solomon-gundy	derivation of Salmagundi, a savoury dish comprising meat, anchovies, eggs, onions with oil and flavourings.
Shagreen	a white silk fabric, with a slight rough surface.
Short mob	ordinary morning headdress for ladies, cotton with lace edging widely copied by the lower ranks.
Skimington	punishment of the violent behaviour by a wife towards her husband and vice versa, by procession of neighbours.
Sloop	vessel with mainsail and jib, used as Customs interceptor, able to sail in shallow waters.
Spaw	water from a spa, also term for bottled mineral water.
Spinet	musical instrument with keys similar to the harpsichord.
Stadtholder	Netherlands military commander and chief magistrate in time of war; also governor of a province or town.
Stars and Garters	members of royal orders and courtiers.
Sussex coffee house	17-18 Bouverie Street, the lower end of Fleet Street.
Tar water	infusion of tar and turpentine from fir trees in cold water, prized as a medicine.
Traverse	a formal denial in the pleading over a matter of fact stated by the other side.
Vauxhall gardens	south side of the Thames, 12 acres, on site of the old Spring gardens, with boxes for entertaining (ridotto al fresco) with orchestra.
Virgins fever	hysterical disorders and state of intense, nervous, excitability; seldom required bleeding; purges to be used with caution.
Vitriol drops	composed of sulphates of metals and used as medicine.
Vomit	medicine designed to empty contents of stomach.
Westminster Hall	hall containing the King's Bench, court of Common Pleas and the court of Chancery.
Worsted	yarn, long staple wool, closely twisted together; weaving shades and colours, suitable for jackets, suits, waistcoats.

WESTMINSTER LAW TERMS, AND JOHN COLLIER'S TIMES ON CUSTOMS SURVEYS 1731 TO 1746

	Hilary term	Easter term	Trinity term	Michaelmas term	Customs Surveys [1]
1731	23 Jan to 12 Feb	5 May to 31 May	18 June to 17 July	23 Oct to 29 Nov	
1732	24 Jan to 12 Feb	26 Apr to 22 May	9 June to 28 June	23 Oct to 28 Nov	
1733	23 Jan to 12 Feb	11 Apr to 7 May	25 May to 13 June	23 Oct to 28 Nov	
1734	23 Jan to 12 Feb	1 May to 27 May	14 June to 3 July	23 Oct to 28 Nov	16 Sept to mid-Oct
1735	23 Jan to 12 Feb	23 Apr to 19 May	6 June to 25 June	23 Oct to 28 Nov	8 to 30 Sept
1736	23 Jan to 12 Feb	12 May to 7 June	25 June to 14 July	23 Oct to 29 Nov	6 to 30 Sept
1737	24 Jan to 12 Feb	27 Apr to 23 May	10 June to 29 June	24 Oct to 28 Nov	
1738	23 Jan to 13 Feb	19 Apr to 15 May	2 June to 21 June	23 Oct to 28 Nov	17 July to early Aug
1739	23 Jan to 12 Feb	9 May to 4 June	22 June to 11 July	23 Oct to 28 Nov	17 Sept to early Oct
1740	23 Jan to 12 Feb	23 Apr to 19 May	6 June to 25 June	23 Oct to 28 Nov	
1741	23 Jan to 12 Feb	15 Apr to 11 May	29 May to 17 June	23 Oct to 28 Nov	26 June to 20 July
1742	23 Jan to 12 Feb	5 May to 31 May	18 June to 7 July	23 Oct to 29 Nov	
1743	24 Jan to 12 Feb	20 Apr to 16 May	3 June to 22 June	24 Oct to 28 Nov	8 Aug to 2 Sept
1744	23 Jan to 13 Feb	11 Apr to 7 May	25 May to 13 June	23 Oct to 28 Nov	[*Oct*]
1745	23 Jan to 12 Feb	1 May to 27 May	14 June to 3 July	23 Oct to 28 Nov	
1746	23 Jan to 12 Feb	16 Apr to 12 May	30 May to 18 June	23 Oct to 28 Nov	

The Law Terms, when the Westminster courts were sitting, dictated the main periods for Collier's residence in London and of course the times when he was most likely to be writing home to Hastings.

Sources:
C.R. Cheney (ed.) *A Handbook of Dates* (2000), RHS Guides and Handbooks, no. 4.
TNA CUST 148/11, 13 Customs surveys of Kent.

[1] Where known.

SELECTIVE INDEX OF SUBJECTS

The index is created from the text of the letters, with the related entry notes, and the Introduction. It is aimed at pointing the reader to subjects where the Collier letters will provide unique or special insights. It focuses on the largest areas of John Collier's activities: business with Hastings Corporation; political and business relations with the Duke of Newcastle and the Pelham family; his London law practice; his work for the Customs Commissioners including the combating of smuggling, and of course his family life, his leisure activities in London and the reactions to public events

It is also selective in restricting the references to each specific subject: they are not intended to be exhaustive but are restricted to the most significant. They will however enable the reader to make a full exploration of the topics concerned. Minor references to Hastings and environs, Westminster courts, Johnson's Court and Fleet Street are generally omitted

As with the indexes of the persons and places, the arabic numbers refer to the entry numbers of letters and papers, the small Roman numerals refer to the pages of the introduction

INDEX OF PERSONS

This index includes all persons mentioned in the introduction and the text of the letters and appendices (i.e. items 1-622) and also includes all persons in the rental and voting lists. References to the introduction are indicated by roman rather than arabic numerals. As John and Mary Collier are listed in most letters, and their children and Mary's brother William Cranston in a large number, they are not referenced in the index. Some index numbers may refer to several occurrences of the same name in one letter and the attached endnotes. Persons who have an entry in the two separate series of biographical notes are identified by the symbols ‡ (local) and † (national). Titles (aristocrats, bishops etc) are normally given in the form they appear in the text, rather than by precise family name. Where information is available, different persons of the same name have been identified separately by occupation, title or other detail

INDEX OF PLACES

Although the index does not claim to include all references to places, the intention has been to include all those which are significant in the text

Modern spelling has been adopted for the index entries. Where a place lies in Sussex (obviously the majority of entries) it has not been felt necessary to indicate this. Places identified as 'London' lie in the City or the county of Middlesex; other places within the modern London area have been identified by their traditional (pre 1889) county. Well known place names within Britain and abroad have been given an identifier only where there might be uncertainty

As Hastings figures constantly throughout the correspondence, a multiplicity of entries would be more confusing than helpful; The references have therefore been reduced to a selective minimum; but they are reinforced by the Subject Index which provides a gateway to substantial Hastings material.